MK Hughes

® Jamie & Ian

MOTHERLAND IN DANGER

MOTHERLAND IN DANGER

SOVIET PROPAGANDA DURING WORLD WAR II

Karel C. Berkhoff

HARVARD UNIVERSITY PRESS
Cambridge, Massachusetts
London, England
2012

Copyright © 2012 by the President and Fellows of Harvard College

All rights reserved

Printed in the United States of America

Library of Congress Cataloging-in-Publication Data

Berkhoff, Karel C. (Karel Cornelis), 1965–
Motherland in danger : Soviet propaganda during World War II / Karel C. Berkhoff.
    p. cm.
Includes bibliographical references and index.
ISBN 978-0-674-04924-6 (alkaline paper)
1. World War, 1939–1945—Soviet Union—Propaganda. 2. World War, 1939–1945—Soviet Union—Mass media and the war. 3. Mass media and war—Soviet Union. 4. Propaganda, Soviet—History. I. Title.
D810.P7S6525 2012
940.54′88647—dc23   2011041322

To Simon and Abel

Contents

	Introduction	1
1.	Stalinist Propaganda as a System for Control	7
2.	Selfless Obedience and Heroism at the Front	35
3.	A Single Forced Labor Camp	68
4.	Material Privations	96
5.	Monstrous Atrocities	116
6.	A Bestial Plan for Physical Extermination	134
7.	Hatred with All the Might of the Soul	167
8.	The Motherland and Its People	202
9.	Immortal Avengers and Enemy Accomplices	223
10.	Allies Who Must Join the Action	244
	Conclusion	269
	Notes	281
	Sources	389
	Acknowledgments	393
	Index	397

Introduction

This book is about one of the least understood issues in modern European history: the victory of the Soviet Union over Nazi Germany. It was far from self-evident that Joseph Stalin's regime, unpopular especially among peasants, would survive the war and that the Soviet state could mobilize most of the citizens against the German-led invasion. Many Soviet-era taboos and myths about this period, including the name "Great Patriotic War," have proven to be resilient in and beyond Russia. Ten years after the Soviet Union fell apart, a book about the city of Rostov during the war managed to completely ignore the German occupation, and 67 percent of Russian respondents to an opinion poll believed Allied aid had not been needed.[1] In May 2009 the Commission of the President of the Russian Federation for Countering Attempts to Falsify History at the Expense of Russia's Interests was founded. A key target was the "falsifications" of Russia's record of its struggle against its former ally, Nazi Germany. One year later a website specifically for presenting "objective historical information about the Great Patriotic War" was created by the Russian Ministry of Communication and Mass Media.[2]

Historians in some other former Soviet republics do not face such a threat. But even they rarely dare to write unconcerned about the political implications of their findings about a war that began over seven decades ago. Historians in other countries, if they study the Nazi-Soviet war at all, tend to focus on events in the Soviet territories that temporarily slipped from Stalin's control; these often excellent studies usually do not employ Slavic sources.[3]

The underdeveloped state of research is also evident with regard to the wartime Soviet media. Despite valuable undertakings, such as the publication of documents and studies dealing with posters, documentaries, and films, and the censorship to which all were subjected, there is still no comprehensive survey of the Soviet propaganda effort during the war. The one English-language monograph about the Soviet press with a substantial discussion of the war is valuable but does not cite archival records. A Russian counterpart cites such records (and the press itself), but does so in a naïve manner.[4] This book offers a description and interpretation of the main features of the wartime Soviet propaganda directed at the population of the Soviet home front—the part of the Soviet Union that during the war never saw a regime change. What did Stalin's system choose to tell its subjects, and why? How did this compare to prewar Soviet propaganda and to the propaganda of other countries during the war? What if anything can be said about the results, intended or not? Although Soviet visual materials are not entirely neglected, these questions will be addressed through a close look at newspapers and radio broadcasts.[5] My broader aim is to contribute to the debate on the goals and effectiveness of Soviet propaganda in general.

In modern Western history, *propaganda* at first was a neutral term. It became pejorative once people began to realize that they would always disagree about the best way to organize society. The carnage of World War I played its part as well: relatives of the millions of people killed felt betrayed and demanded change. Since then only two groups have proudly admitted to producing propaganda: Roman Catholics and Communists. From the very beginning the Soviet media were overtly and proudly ideological in the selection and coverage of items. There never was a Bolshevik sense of *news*—an effort to quickly and objectively record events. It was symptomatic of the extremes reached under Stalin that from the early 1930s the country no longer had a single school of journalism.[6]

It is not easy to provide a precise definition of propaganda that covers all of it—not less and not more—and that is also valid across time and space. It is often considered simply biased information spread to shape public opinion and behavior. In this book it is more than a kind of information, namely a deliberate and systematic attempt to shape perceptions, mental states, and, above all, behavior, so as to achieve a response that furthers the propagandist's intent.[7] But the word also appears in this study as shorthand for the tools: the Soviet newspapers and radio broadcasts.

In the early Soviet years illiteracy hampered the penetration of the ideas of the Communist (Bolshevik) Party into popular consciousness, so much was made of *agitation*, as an activity allegedly distinct from propaganda.[8] Invented by the father of Russian Marxism, Georgii Plekhanov, the concept gained strong support from the founder of the world's first party-state, Vladimir Lenin. Whereas propagandists focused their attention on literate people and explained dogmas to them, *agitators*, basically demagogues, used posted pamphlets ("wall newspapers"), theater sketches, demonstrations, and meetings, and in them made no attempt to explain but exploited emotions. Eventually the Soviet population became more literate; on the eve of the war, officially at least, only 9 percent had received a secondary education, but 80 percent could read and write.[9] That is why the distinction between propaganda and agitation disappeared, except in the word *Agitprop* and in the name of the Central Committee body that it abbreviated, the Directorate on Propaganda and Agitation, led by the philosopher Georgii Aleksandrov (1908–1961).[10]

Despite his overriding concern with imposing his will on his subjects, Stalin always considered propaganda important. To him it was self-evident that the Bolshevik regime needed moral and other support from the workers. Therefore in principle he was interested in every propaganda detail. However busy he might be, he watched every single feature film before it was distributed. The prewar Soviet Union was truly a propaganda state—a political system that subjugated mass culture, education, and the media for the purposes of popular indoctrination.[11]

A historian noted once that there was no Bolshevik Goebbels, no Soviet theorist fascinated by propaganda techniques, and ascribed this to a key difference between Soviet and Nazi propaganda. Unlike the Nazis, the Bolsheviks "never looked for and did not find devilishly clever methods to influence people's minds, to brainwash them." They did not care about the techniques of propaganda because they saw it as part of something bigger: education. The observation is generally correct, even when referring to Stalin; he and the other Bolsheviks believed that their scientific worldview did not need trickery or fanciness. But beginning in the 1930s one section of the Soviet media, the press, largely—but unofficially—abandoned its aim to reeducate ("enlighten") or persuade and began focusing on the pragmatic and seemingly more modest goal of *mobilization*. In practice the media often no longer seemed to target the entire population but only insiders: officials and enthusiasts.[12]

During the war, as this book argues, the tasks of the press grew again. Even small papers were supposed to "teach and politically educate the masses" and to "organize them for the resolution of tasks." But in attempting to increase popular interest, Moscow reduced the editorial staffs of the regional papers; the idea was that worker and peasant "correspondents" would fill most of the pages. (It failed, as it had in the early 1920s.) In the battle against Nazi Germany, mobilization of the entire population, soldiers and workers in particular, became the Soviet media's paramount official goal. Mobilization was not defined well, but it was essentially getting people to do what they were told, while allowing them a small measure of initiative. Agitprop cited Lenin when it warned editors that the press had roles to play in propaganda and agitation, but also in *organization*, meaning mobilization, and that role might occasionally become paramount. That time was now, when the press "sets hundreds of thousands and millions of workers in motion."[13]

Chapter 1 describes the structure of the Soviet media apparatus: the new Soviet Information Bureau, the newspapers, and the radio. All newspaper editors faced highly unrealistic demands from the official propagandists; the voices of ordinary citizens were barely audible; and the press and the radio were poorly disseminated. Above all, reporting was centralized to an extreme without precedent in Soviet history. Propaganda thus became a means for tightly controlled mobilization for war. The attempt to control reappears in Chapter 2, in which I analyze the reports of the fight by the Soviet armed forces against Germany and its allies. Stalin imposed silence on virtually all military defeats, at the cost of countless military and civilian lives. He did not blink and imposed a surreal narrative: surrender was always treason and dying in battle was always normal and heroic. The ranks of the Red Army, their loved ones, and everyone else should accept death, and the military were even supposed to aim for it.

In the hinterland forced labor and famine were pervasive. How the wartime Soviet media portrayed these conditions, to the extent that they are known, is the subject of Chapters 3 and 4. Remarkable again is the pervasive secrecy, such as about the various laws and decrees on the militarization of labor. Propaganda presented a dual image of the workers and the peasants. On the one hand, they were severely warned to obey orders, to work overtime, and to combat labor "desertion." On the other hand, the media portrayed them as mostly patriotic and willingly selfless. Public campaigns for production and other records and collective and individual competitions supposedly showed this. The media also claimed that the state was successfully taking care of the most vulnerable social groups in the hinterland: refugees, families of servicemen, war invalids, and orphans. They revealed, indirectly, the threat and actuality of famine, but officially its scale was minor, and the only causes were and remained the laziness and greed of some citizens.

Soviet propaganda had to find a response to the mass killings committed by the invaders. As Chapter 5 shows, early on it was decided to publicize them extensively. The Germans themselves helped a great deal, with corpses left behind along with policy documents, personal letters, photographs, and testimonies, obtained from German corpses or war prisoners or simply found. There was no particular propaganda line on what today is known as the Holocaust, the subject of Chapter 6. The Soviet reader and radio listener who wanted to know could find references to that specifically anti-Jewish campaign. Chapter 7 shows that hate propaganda blurred and occasionally erased the distinction between fascists and Germans. Soviet citizens understood that Stalin, in order to mobilize them, licensed them to hate not simply the "occupiers," but indeed all Germans. Whether this hatred became pervasive remains unclear, although various sources suggest the opposite. The question remains whether Soviet propaganda achieved its unstated goal of creating, magnifying, and distributing hatred.

Chapters 8 and 9 deal with patriots and traitors. Despite Russocentric tendencies, the propaganda was more restrained than might have been expected. Stalin did not allow it to explicitly denigrate the non-Russians of the Soviet state. He did not even glorify "Russia," but the *motherland*, an affectionate term that meant many things and thus something different in each citizen's imagination. The partisans were heroes, but they acted amid "enemy accomplices," the worst of whom were traitors to the motherland. Here too restraint generally prevailed; for the purpose of mobilization, the propaganda did not state what Stalin really believed, namely that most inhabitants of the occupied territories had betrayed him.

Chapter 10 deals with the portrayal of the Soviet Union's foreign allies, in particular Poland, the United Kingdom, and the United States. That portrayal was stinting, because Stalin never wanted to give foreigners a share of the credit for the war's outcome. The victory of May 1945 showed the superiority of the Soviet state and its system, not of international collaboration.

I

Stalinist Propaganda as a System for Control

Friends and foes of the Bolsheviks have always agreed that one reason they won the Civil War was their superior skill in getting their message across.[1] Then and later, that message had specific traits. One stemmed from Lenin's personal style. The founder of the Soviet state often used military metaphors and pejorative neologisms, tautologies, and paraphrases, and his regime forced the media to adopt them. Such verbal and visual violence—against "class enemies," "wreckers," and others—paved the way to violence in real life and readied Soviet citizens' minds for warfare. Another peculiarity, strengthened by Stalin, was deliberate omission: perusal of the press for the most basic information was often in vain, and there was an eerie silence about the horrific fate of millions—those alleged enemies who were deported, imprisoned, starved, and shot.[2]

The propaganda success of the Civil War period did not last. Focused on materialism and anonymous social forces, Soviet propaganda in the 1920s was too arcane and abstract to resonate much in a society where class consciousness ran deep but whose people were poorly educated. The regime became aware of this failure through surveillance reports. Thus in the early 1930s Stalin mandated changes.³ One change brought about an ideologically heretical cult of contemporary heroes. Writers, journalists, artists, publishers, and filmmakers developed it, while most of the professional propagandists, what could be called the ideological establishment, remained hesitant. When in 1933 Soviet sailors became stranded on Arctic ice while the *Cheliuskin* sank, the pilots who rescued them were presented as and widely considered to be heroes worthy of emulation. Other heroes in the new line were fictionalized, such as in the popular Civil War film *Chapaev*. By 1936 Soviet mass culture was dominated by contemporary and ordinary heroes, role models, and iconic personalities. Everyone knew about the shock worker Aleksei Stakhanov and Marshal Mikhail Tukhachevskii, to mention just two.

An equally heretical innovation was a turn away from other countries and the rehabilitation of patriotism, heretofore derided as hostile to brotherhood and cooperation. In a telegram about the rescue of the *Cheliuskin* crew Stalin used the word *motherland* for the first time in years, and then prescribed its use in May Day slogans. A fiction film in 1936 about the response of a test pilot to a surprise Nazi German invasion was called *The Motherland Is Calling*.⁴

The populist hero cult and the new patriotism were widely distributed, while censorship barred alternative views. The result was a new, dynamic mass culture. Recent research shows that it provided a sense of belonging and a code of honor that appealed to many, particularly young people, who succumbed to its spell or at least attempted to "speak Bolshevik." One historian concludes that "it is impossible to overstate the contribution that this propaganda made to mobilizational efforts in the USSR during these years." Stalin was aware of this.⁵

But then, in the late summer of 1936, he and his entourage launched what would become the Great Terror: three years of arrests and executions. The unintended effect was that the party could no longer mobilize through appeals to a usable Soviet past. That countless popular heroes suddenly became villains and disappeared from sight undermined the confidence of large parts of Soviet society. Particularly inexplicable was the treason charge against the military high command. In 1939, after the terror had ended, articles, novels, films, and exhibitions began showing new heroes, but, unlike their predecessors, these were too self-assured and selfless to function as role models in everyday life.[6]

War and the Media

Whereas in the mid-1920s *Pravda,* the main newspaper, had devoted nearly two-thirds of its editorials to international relations and foreign countries, with the rise of Stalin a steady decline began that one decade later approached zero. Beginning in the 1930s Soviet propaganda about the outside world argued above all that foreign working people thought more of the Soviet Union and its security than about bettering their own lives. To a country now redefined as a motherland, actual foreign events were presented as nearly irrelevant. Almost all foreign news was consigned to the last or penultimate (fifth) pages of the newspaper, even in 1939 and 1940. The rise of fascism did not change this parochialism, as one historian writes: "While European and American intellectuals linked communism with antifascism and European Communists advocated a popular front against fascism, *Pravda* and other central newspapers promoted a Soviet identity in which the country's opposition to Hitler, Mussolini, and Franco was largely irrelevant." It was a "bipolar world, divided into the spheres of home and abroad." Hitler's appointment as chancellor in January 1933 merited a back-page item, not an editorial; the destruction of the German Communist Party was declared nothing new; and the Spanish Civil War rarely appeared on front pages.[7]

Well before the German invasion, Stalin was extremely cautious with media reports about diplomatic relations. On August 21, 1939, *Pravda* announced that a trade-credit agreement would be signed with Germany and, in a departure from the norm, omitted the standard term "fascist." A stated reason for the sudden desire to improve relations was fully absent. The curt announcement probably was intended to ready readers' minds for the big news, announced on August 24: a military nonaggression pact with Hitler's Germany.

Pravda declared merely that "political and ideological differences" were less important than "the development and flourishing of friendly relations" between the two countries.[8] The German invasion of Poland facilitated by the pact appeared in an item titled "Military Action between Germany and Poland" on *Pravda*'s fifth page on September 3; the British declaration of war on Germany went to page 4.[9]

On September 17 Foreign Commissar Viacheslav Molotov announced that the Red Army had invaded the Polish state from the east, to "protect the life and property of the population of western Ukraine and western Belorussia."[10] When he visited Berlin in November 1940, a photograph of him standing beside Hitler appeared in *Pravda*. Movie showings were preceded by a newsreel that presented Germany as an ally that could be relied upon. A Russian remembers the following details: "Hitler welcomes Molotov warmly like a long-lost brother, keeps shaking him by the hand; they are immediately immersed in conversation, and the photographers crowd around with their flash-guns busy."[11] By that time confidential materials supplied to high-ranking members of the propaganda structure already contained anti-German motifs, but Stalin, who wished to avoid alienating Germany, still barred major changes in international reporting.[12] Soviet censors did reportedly black out Hitler's face from photographs and scratch out the tiny swastika on German stamps.[13]

The real change came only much later, under pressure of a totally new situation. On June 22, 1941, at 12:15 P.M., Molotov—not Stalin—addressed the citizens of the USSR on the radio. At 4 o'clock last night, he said in a bland voice, Germany had attacked the Soviet Union. The cities of Zhytomyr, Kiev, Sevastopol, Kaunas, and "several" others had been bombed from planes. "Over two hundred people have been killed and wounded." There had also been attacks from "Romanian and Finnish territories." The history of the "civilized peoples" had never seen such betrayal. At 5:30 (over six hours earlier) a declaration of war had been received that blamed the concentration of Red Army troops at the "eastern German border," even though the USSR had always strictly adhered to the Soviet-

German pact. Hitler would be defeated just as Napoleon had been. "The government calls on you, citizens of the Soviet Union, to close still stronger the ranks around our famous Bolshevik party, around our Soviet government, around our great leader comrade Stalin. Our cause is just! The enemy will be beaten! Victory will be ours!"[14] Eyewitnesses report different reactions. In Leningrad, close to the border, there was "panic": people were "hastily exchanging words, filling the stores, buying up everything they could lay their hands on, aimlessly milling about the streets. Many rushed to the bank to withdraw their savings." In Rostov people dispersed in silence; in Kramatorsk, in Ukraine's Donbas region, they talked in groups and "many" said they did not believe Molotov.[15]

In the war that now began, the Soviet state had a huge propaganda machine at its disposal, and a captive audience. A Polish woman born in 1922 spent the war in Soviet Kazakhstan. From her perspective, propaganda was "omnipresent—it completely dominated social life."[16] Given the absence from almost the entire country of direct access to foreign media, this dominance was inevitable. Yet, as will be shown, there were important limitations. Newspapers were few in number, they appeared in small print runs, and distribution was slow and uneven. Radio, both central and local, was inaudible in many parts of the country.

Ever since the late 1920s, all the media, from *Pravda* down to the smallest paper, and indeed every single publication, had a tremendous responsibility, namely to mobilize. Thus early in 1942 Agitprop informed the editors of the raion (district) newspapers that in the current war, their "main task" was to "educate the workers in a fiery hatred of the German-fascist scoundrels, who are encroaching upon the life and freedom of our motherland; to inspire our people to a great patriotic war of liberation; and to mobilize the workers for the fulfillment of the concrete tasks in the matter of active support of the front standing before the raion." In general, "all the work of the newspaper editors must be subordinated to the interests of the front and the tasks to organize the crushing defeat of the German-fascist invaders. The papers are obliged to daily explain to the workers the danger that is threatening our country, to overcome carelessness and indifference, to develop Soviet patriotism, to cultivate hatred of the German occupiers and readiness to give up all one's strength for the crushing defeat of the enemy." In short, the workers had to be Soviet patriots, hateful, and willing to die in the war, and the media had to explain and sustain these notions and actions.[17]

In reality, however, as this book argues, Stalin, his entourage, and all who took his orders tended to sacrifice the goals of mobilization and education to keeping total control. Prioritizing control best explains the immediate formation of an "information bureau" with a near-complete monopoly; the unrealistic guidelines for local papers, unadjusted year by year despite an immediate awareness of the ineffectiveness of the papers; the meager presence on the air of voices other than journalists; the confiscation of radio receivers from all citizens, unique in wartime Europe; and the extremely harsh line of the censors.

TASS and the Soviet Information Bureau

During the war with Germany, Stalin and about sixty of his associates received firsthand knowledge of events by way of a top-secret bulletin prepared by TASS, the Telegraph Agency of the Soviet Union. Usually referred to in the inner circle as the agency's "office bulletin," it was a mimeographed digest of translated reports from foreign publications, radio programs, and agencies such as Reuters and the Associated Press. (Before the German invasion, part of the bulletin—less than 10 percent—had also included foreign information from TASS correspondents.) The June 22, 1941, issue of the bulletin contained a translation of Hitler's declaration on the occasion of the German attack on the Soviet Union (never published in the Soviet Union) in which, among other things, he said that Germany was proceeding against the "Jewish-Anglo-Saxon war mongers and their aides, as well as the Jews from the Muscovite Bolshevik center."[18] On at least some occasions TASS even compiled news for Stalin's eyes only. After an eyewitness account about the Eastern Front was serialized in a Turkish newspaper, the TASS leader Iakov Khavinson (1901–1989) supplied Stalin with a special bulletin on it. The Turkish author mentioned releases of Muslim and Ukrainian war prisoners and quoted Hitler's statement that no treaty or consideration could have prevented the war with the Soviet Union—provoking Stalin to write in the sideline, "Why? Scumbag!"[19]

For everyone else, on June 24, 1941, the Soviet Information Bureau was founded with the explicit aim of monopolizing all information about internal, international, and military affairs. No major event in these fields could be reported before the Bureau mentioned it, unless (although this was not made official) the reporter was Stalin himself or others from his inner circle. By 1944 the agency had a staff of 238, including its own front correspondents. Staff members of newspapers or of TASS also contributed material. The Bureau issued "morning" and "evening" reports, occasional "At the Last Moment" reports (November 1941 to March 1943), and, from early July 1943, "operational" reports. The leader of the entity was Aleksandr Shcherbakov (1901–1945), first secretary of the Moscow party and a recently appointed secretary of the union party's Central Committee. In June 1942 this workaholic also became director of the Red Army's main political administration, thus of the army commissars; deputy people's commissar of defense; and chairman of the Council on Military and Political Propaganda. Either he or Stalin or both wrote many of the reports. The deputy leader of the Bureau was the deputy people's commissar of foreign affairs, Solomon Lozovskii (1878–1952). He often met with foreign correspondents, which Shcherbakov did just once (early in 1943; he asked when they would open the "second front"). Other Bureau members included the TASS leader Khavinson and Dmitrii Polikarpov (1905–1965), the new chairman of the Radio Committee, formally called the Council of People's Commissars' All-Union Committee on Radio Installation and Radio Broadcasting.[20]

Thus TASS was not abolished, and neither were the Soviet republics' separate news agencies and radio committees. TASS remained the single channel through which media outlets (newspapers and radio committees) received the Bureau reports and international news. TASS transmitted via radio waves (the "radio telephone") or via telegraph. Before the German invasion it used to inform oblast (provincial), raion, and city newspapers over the radio, but this practice soon faced hurdles because long-wave broadcasting was discarded and few newspaper editors could pick up short waves. Moreover by late September 1941 the number of cities that Moscow could reach via telegraph had dropped from forty-seven to twenty, and transmission often took several attempts, if not failing entirely. As a result oblast newspapers often published TASS materials two or three days late, and raion papers carried them one week late.[21]

By the end of 1942 TASS was sending telegrams to Moscow papers (and the Central Committee) and radio transmissions (most of the time) to republic, oblast, and raion papers.[22] It could transmit to papers outside Moscow via radio only late at night, after the Radio Committee freed up the transmitters. Thus sometime between 3 and 7 P.M. it released the Bureau's morning report, *Pravda*'s editorial, and about fifty lines of other information. The agency's own daily reports arrived in the two hours around midnight, followed between 2 and 4 by the Bureau's evening report and the final bulletin. The inevitable result was the publication of old information.[23] TASS—or rather a group of artists and writers employed by it—was much better at producing colorful and often satirical wall posters with topical texts, a revived genre now called *TASS Windows*. More than 800,000 copies of 1,250 different such posters appeared.[24]

Newspapers

Before 1939 there had been about 45 "central" (or "all-Union") newspapers and 110 republican papers, besides about 120 autonomous republic and autonomous oblast papers and about 275 krai, oblast, and district (*okrug*) papers. The number of smaller newspapers was even larger: there were about 3,400 city and raion papers and some 4,600 "local" (*nizovye*) papers, usually factory newsletters and wall newspapers. In total there officially appeared 8,521 Soviet newspapers in 1937 and 8,550 in 1938. In 1939 the secret but imprecise count grew by 230, but it declined slightly the next year to 8,754. In 1941 an unknown number of titles was classified and excluded from counts, which reduced the official total to a mere 6,543.[25]

No one knew at the time—or can calculate today—exactly how many Soviet newspapers appeared during the war, in what print run, and how often. Virtually all publishers had to send copies of anything published for registration and safekeeping to the All-Union Book Chamber. Using those publications, lists supplied by Glavlit, and reports by republican book chambers, the chamber estimated the total number of newspapers. It often could not identify local papers because they had become (or still were) "of defense significance," thus classified, and thus unavailable. Classification befell, among others, the newspapers published by military districts, army and fleet units, military industry enterprises, and the periodicals of the militia and the NKVD.[26] The NKVD also published papers for its Gulag prisoners, also excluded from book chamber counts. In 1942 in many camps there was on average one newspaper issue per two to three thousand prisoners, and in some there was none whatsoever. Beginning in 1943 there were thirty-six newspaper titles for Gulag camps and work sites, mostly weeklies 11.7 by 16.5 inches (international standard paper size A3) and with a print run of 700 to 3,000.[27]

The war with Germany differed from the pre-1941 period in the greater number of occasional newspapers, appearing in small numbers and sizes. According to incomplete data, there were 260 titles in 1943 in the RSFSR (the Russian Soviet republic) alone; some lasted as long as ten months and appeared twelve to fifteen times each month.[28] Officially the "local" press also included brochures known as "fighting leaflets" or "express notices." Behind closed doors, Moscow regularly expressed unease about the very existence of such leaflets, finding them hard to supervise. In August 1942 therefore the censorship agency Glavlit warned noncentral papers that unless the Central Committee gave them a green light, they were forbidden to publish the leaflets, and the same rule applied to newspaper supplements. The editor of the Sverdlovsk paper *Uralskii rabochii* objected to no avail as late as 1944, telling Moscow that he had ample paper.²⁹ The only special leaflets that Moscow trusted and allowed were produced and printed by correspondents of central papers, in a revival of a ten-year-old practice. In the fall of 1942 in particular, *Pravda* correspondents and printers worked at twenty-four sites (plane, car, and metallurgical factories, mines, peat digging sites, and agricultural sites), sometimes for many months on end.³⁰

Disregarding *Krasnaia zvezda* and the classified or occasional titles, it can be estimated that by 1942 there were 4,561 Soviet newspapers, declining the next year to 3,725 and rising thereafter to 4,872. The approximate total circulation amounted to 13,777,000 issues in 1943 and 16,713,000 in 1944. (The year totals of copies were close to 2.4 billion in 1943 and 2.7 billion in 1944.) In 1937, when all newspapers were included in the counts, the total circulation was 36,197,000 issues (and the year total of copies was close to 7.1 billion).³¹ Given the immense size of the country, not to mention the media's alleged importance, the wartime numbers were on the low side.

The Central Committee's Politburo imposed new rules on the papers on August 20, 1941: every week, republic, oblast, and krai papers had to appear three times with four rows of text or images, but on the other three days they could print only two rows. Raion papers could no longer appear four or more days per week; three days became the new maximum, and only raion papers that reduced themselves to weeklies might have more than two rows.³² Beginning on October 19, 1941, *Izvestiia* (like *Pravda* already) had six instead of eight rows. All Komsomol and youth newspapers but two were suspended; their role was supposed to be adopted by new rubrics in the republic and regional papers, but the Komsomol often complained. The Central Committee warned specific papers to comply with the new rules, but real change came only after a convention of editors in the middle of 1944. The retaken republics received their own youth papers back in the fall of 1944, well before any Soviet region that had not been occupied.³³

Paper shortages were so severe that sometimes even the central press approached collapse. In 1942 6.5 tons of newsprint were needed each month, but on average only 4.1 tons were produced because a lack of electricity often idled the single large factory for such paper, in the Gorkii oblast.[34] In February 1943 Molotov and two candidate members of the Politburo, Shcherbakov and Georgii Malenkov, alarmed Stalin: without action, they said, "already in the second quarter of the current year there will be a real threat of massive stoppages in paper publishing." Each month, they wrote, 6.9 tons were needed, but the factories produced only 4.6 (a quarter of the prewar level). It was decided to print many fewer copies of the local papers and to do so less frequently; to print 100,000 fewer copies of *Izvestiia* and 300,000 fewer copies of *Pravda*; and to publish *Pravda* only six days a week. The other central newspapers also received much less paper.[35] Meanwhile all papers officially remained inexpensive; in 1943, when purchased at kiosks or via a subscription, most cost just 20 kopecks. A monthly subscription to *Pravda* cost six rubles, and to *Izvestiia* and *Trud*, which appeared six times per week, just five.[36]

There were twenty-two central papers in 1942 and twenty-three in early 1945. In the midst of the war, of all papers citizens were most likely to come across copies of *Pravda, Izvestiia, Komsomolskaia pravda, Sotsialisticheskoe zemledelie*, and *Trud*. These papers' year-long *total* print runs in 1943 were, respectively, 338, 124, 74, 21, and 15 million.[37] The print run of the Defense Commissariat paper *Krasnaia zvezda*, which before the war had been available only within the armed forces, is still classified—secrecy that is also relevant when evaluating the other calculations—but it probably rose significantly.[38] Another central paper that, like *Komsomolskaia Pravda, Trud*, and *Krasnaia zvezda*, appeared around 300 times per year was *Krasny flot*. The periodical of the Supreme Soviet, *Vedomosti Verkhovnogo Soveta SSSR*, was also large, mainly because it appeared not only in Russian but also in separate editions in ten other languages.

Stalin and his circle themselves seemingly used the wrong figures about the central press. In August 1941 the Politburo resolved to cut *Pravda*'s alleged circulation of "three million" to one million and to cut in half *Izvestiia*'s alleged circulation of "1.6 million." But the archival record shows that *Pravda*'s circulation had been *two* million. Its actual circulation decline—the first since 1932—was mild, to 1,905,000 by late 1941. It continued to slide but remained over one million.[39] The average circulation of the second-largest Soviet newspaper, *Izvestiia*, in the whole year of 1941 was 1,276,000. Here the shrinkage that began after August 1941 continued for years and was severe: in 1942 its print run was 573,000; in 1943 and 1944, 400,000; and in the first half of 1945, a mere 360,000. *Trud*'s average circulation in 1941 was 100,000; in 1942–1944, 50,000; and in the first half of 1945, 63,500.[40] These figures merit repetition of the conclusion that for such a large country, the papers had a small circulation. Assuming the presence in the hinterland of some 130 million people, the average copy of *Pravda* in 1942 had to serve 100 people; the average copy of *Izvestiia*, 227; and the average copy of *Trud*, 2,600.[41]

Well before the war Soviet newspapers often appeared in a language other than Russian. In 1937 seventy-one languages were used and there were 2,587 non-Russian papers, besides 5,934 Russian-language ones. In 1940 the respective totals were 2,261 and 6,493. Particularly numerous in 1940 were titles in Ukrainian (948), Belarusian (179), Kazakh (163), Uzbek (147), and Tatar (119). There were also papers in German (twenty-one in 1940), Yiddish (thirteen in 1937), and Polish (five in 1940).[42] It was an achievement that the German invasion did not put an end to the linguistic diversity. In 1943, 888 titles, or close to one in four (23.8 percent), were in a language other than Russian. The next year saw an increase to 1,575 titles, close to a third of all titles. In 1943 non-Russian titles constituted 16.7 percent of the total circulation of individual newspapers, and in 1944, 24.6 percent (2,305,000 and 4,110,000, respectively).[43] In early 1945 newspapers appeared in fifty languages.[44]

In 1940 there were 3,500 different raion newspapers, with a combined circulation of about 10 million—thus several times higher than that of the central papers.[45] During the war with Germany, most titles continued to be raion papers.[46] In 1943 several temporarily suspended publication, largely due to paper supply limitations; in the Azerbaijan SSR, for example, this happened to half of them. As for city newspapers (many of which doubled as raion papers), in 1944 there were 261.[47]

By the middle of 1942 almost all the editors at raion newspapers were new to the profession. Agitprop gave them booklets with practical information but remained dissatisfied: these local papers paid insufficient attention to Nazi crimes, failed to mobilize readers for tasks that assisted the front, neglected readers' letters, and often consisted almost entirely of long and vague articles or reprints from the oblast and central press. The directorate made known its like or dislike of specially selected papers through classified notices that served as warnings to all local papers. Thus in the spring of 1942, attempting to revive the failed prewar concept of letting locals and not editors write critical articles (the "movement" of "worker-peasant correspondents"), the directorate ordered the papers to do so in a resolution condemning one paper. Forty of *Tambovskaia pravda*'s fifty monthly items about agriculture had been written by the paper staff. Agitprop warned that at least 60 percent of honorariums for such reports had to go to non-staff members. At that stage it did not dare launch the same complaint against central papers such as *Pravda,* which carried articles by outsiders in name only; they were often written by staff members in exchange for much of the honorarium.[48]

Agitprop distributed six exemplary issues of the paper *Kommunist* from the Voskresenskii raion in the Moscow oblast. Most of the authors were local people and not journalists. But even this sample of best practices was reprimanded for devoting too little attention to Nazi crimes and Red Army heroism, for not publishing letters to and from the front, and for not reiterating constantly that at issue was both the threat of "enslavement" by Nazi Germany and the Soviet state's and its people's "life and death." Every issue of raion papers, Agitprop warned, had to have an original editorial and should tell readers exactly how they could assist the front. And it had to "wage a merciless war with any disorganizers of the hinterland, deserters, panic-mongers, disseminators of all kinds of rumors, while educating among the people confidence in our victory over the enemy." Every issue had to "cultivate hatred" of the occupiers. All this was apart from the prior and unmitigated obligation to mention in every issue military matters, a Soviet Information Bureau report, two to three TASS reports on international affairs, and two to three brief TASS reports on Soviet life.[49]

At first TASS sent out the same Bureau and other reports everywhere. But small papers lacked the space and thus had to edit the material or to fill up to a third of their pages with them. Very late, only in March 1943, did Moscow make some sensible decisions on this matter, at the same time as it reduced the frequency of papers. From then on, republican, oblast, and city newspapers came out less often, five times per week (Tuesday, Wednesday, and Friday through Sunday), and they no longer had to carry the penultimate Bureau reports that they now inevitably missed. They and the krai papers published in every issue that day's two Bureau reports, and on Tuesday and Friday only two Bureau reports. Now TASS began also sending them, twice a month, brief surveys of foreign affairs. Also beginning in March 1943, raion papers came out only on Thursdays and no longer needed to publish Bureau reports; instead they received TASS materials on the Soviet-German front (weekly surveys, biweekly surveys, and other compilations) and brief weekly surveys of international affairs. In general the rule became that noncentral papers should not spend more than 150 lines on foreign affairs.[50] But in the most crucial period, before the victory at Stalingrad, the political demands on the local press were extremely unrealistic.

Radio

Soviet radio used to have little prestige, and this would not change after June 1941. For instance, only in 1944 was a radio department created within Agitprop, and for virtually the entire war (until March 1945) there was just one channel of central radio. The one remaining live genre, the talk show (*pereklichka*), had been abolished in 1937. The Central Committee stated openly that the press was far more effective than "oral propaganda" because it reached all people at once, as if radio (or cinema) did not enter into the equation. Radio work also paid less than newspaper work.[51] Before 1941 there were officially about a million actual radio sets. (In the United States there were about 56 million wireless receivers, and also almost all British households had them.) More than any other country, the Soviet Union used wire-fed transmission, as its rulers rightly deemed it easier to bar outside voices from a wire than from the ether. Wire radio speakers were often cardboard cones, and although the volume could be turned down, the devices could not be switched off. On January 1, 1941, there were about thirty-five places for every thousand people to pick up the radio, such as loudspeakers in streets. Moscow had about 630,000 "radio points": wired speakers at apartments, factories, and clubs and also—loudly—on streets and squares.[52] By the fall of 1944 there were officially in the entire Soviet Union about five million radio receivers, "radio points," and loudspeakers.[53] Compared to other countries, these were low numbers.

Data on Ukraine further demonstrate the scarcity of wireless radio before 1941. Probably no more than 3 percent of Kievans, mostly high-ranking party members, had such a radio. They could receive Moscow, sometimes Kharkiv and Leningrad, and, in wintertime, Berlin or Sophia. (Radios in Soviet Ukraine's formerly Polish regions picked up the BBC.) The average large Ukrainian village (1,500 to 2,000 households) had just one or two wireless radios.[54]

As early as June 25, 1941, the Politburo confirmed a decision by the Council of People's Commissars obliging all people to hand in all radio sets or other radio transmission devices held by them within five days at the local office of the Commissariat of Communication, so as to preclude "hostile elements" from abusing them. Those who did not comply would be held "criminally responsible according to the laws of wartime." The resolution did allow public organizations to use wireless radio receivers, but "exclusively for collective listening of radio broadcasts at strictly defined hours." Thus began a nearly total radio blackout. The people involved ("owners" would be too strong a term in the Soviet context) received the order in the mail. In contravention of the resolution, receivers in the countryside often were confiscated from points where people had been listening collectively, such as clubs and reading rooms.[55]

Exempted in practice were foreign diplomats and a few Soviet officials and journalists, listed on an NKVD list of "responsible workers and institutions." After being moved by the government to Kuibyshev (today's Samara) on the Volga in October 1941, these people could receive on the radios they brought along German stations with evening broadcasts in Russian, Ukrainian, and Belarusian. Not everyone obliged to hand in the receiver did so. In Taganrog, for example, many civilians hid them—and thus, under the Germans, also were able to pick up Soviet broadcasts.[56] In March 1945 the government was to order the receivers returned or a reimbursement paid, though the largely empty gesture did not apply to some Soviet Asian regions and definitely not to the western regions annexed in 1939 and 1940.[57]

Unlike before the war, finding out in advance what would be broadcast and when was impossible unless one kept the radio on at all times. One could rely only on the *Latest News* (*Poslednie izvestiia*), a program that included commentaries. By the fall of 1944 central radio broadcast it twenty times (up from twelve before the invasion) every twenty-four hours. Also daily were music (about twenty pieces) and programs specifically for peasants, the armed forces, young people, and children. The daily total broadcast of central radio thus came to almost twenty-one hours. In addition, there were daily special broadcasts for the twenty-nine union and autonomous republics, the eighty-one oblasts and krais, and the 2,000 raions.[58]

The *Latest News* offered Bureau reports nine times: at 6, 7, and 7:45 in the morning; at noon; at 2 and 4 in the afternoon; and at 7 in the evening. The noon broadcast was repeated at 12:45, and there was also a *Latest News* issue at 10:30. Local wire radio provided only the 7 A.M., 7:45 A.M., and 7 P.M. broadcasts. (In addition, the program was broadcast at certain times to faraway Soviet regions only.) In July 1942 up to 18 million people were believed to be listening to these broadcasts. The *Latest News* also included *Pravda*'s editorial, from 8 to 8:14 in the morning, and again at 12:30 in the afternoon. "Materials from the Newspapers" other than *Pravda*'s editorial were read at 5 A.M., 9 A.M., and 1:40 P.M. Every day at 7 P.M. there were ten minutes of "reports from the Acting army," except on Wednesdays and Sundays, when the *Red Army Hour* was on, a program that also appeared every Friday evening. (In 1943 there was also a weekly *Red Fleet Radio Hour*.) Finally, on Tuesdays, Thursdays, and Sundays in 1942 at 8:20 P.M. there were also fifteen minutes of "Front Information from Leningrad," and on Sundays at 2:45 to 2:59 P.M. there was the program's one and only segment "from outside the studio," only rarely recorded for posterity.

Thus, excluding the program *Here Is the Western Front* or (beginning in the fall of 1942) the *Red Army Hour*, there were seventeen broadcasts of *Latest News* per twenty-four hours, totaling almost five hours. Early in 1943 *Latest News* went on the air less often, but later that year five editions were added and the total time came to 233 minutes. By then the Bureau reports were read nine times daily. But most people listened to the program only in the evening.[59]

Commentaries on the Bureau reports were provided by the program's own war correspondents, about fifteen people in 1942. There were also news flashes called *At the Last Moment*. Everything these programs could offer was outdated. Many correspondents supplied nothing whatsoever for months. Whereas there were around forty city correspondents and seven correspondents at Moscow-based people's commissariats and organizations, various oblasts of great economic importance either had no permanent *Latest News* correspondent or one who filed next to nothing. Therefore in 1942 most regional reports on central radio came from just eight cities: Baku, Gorkii, Kalinin, Kuibyshev, Molotov, Stalinabad, Tashkent, and Vologda.[60] The total number of *Latest News* correspondents rose to sixty-seven the next year, including one each per front or fleet.[61]

Central radio broadcast to Soviet citizens in Russian and six other languages, all from the western regions (Estonian, Latvian, Lithuanian, Belarusian, Ukrainian, and Romanian); early in 1943 Tatar was added.[62] Late in 1944 central and regional radio combined broadcast in thirty-seven languages "of the USSR" (the propaganda falsely spoke of over seventy), as well as in twenty-eight languages declared to be foreign.[63]

Announcers aimed for a confident and restrained manner of speaking, which produced permanent seriousness. Messages of utmost importance were read by Iurii Levitan, born in 1914 from a Jewish background and a candidate party member with an incomplete higher education but gifted with a distinctive voice. He and the others also reread live statements; for instance, several times on June 22, 1941, they read Molotov's statement, even though a recording of it was available.⁶⁴ Visitors to a studio always spoke from a text. On the rare occasions when they deviated, the announcer or the censor switched off the microphone. The dry texts usually were ghostwritten or edited, particularly when the speaker was an official.⁶⁵ One such "performance at the microphone," as it was called, popularized Aleksandr Tvardovskii's long poem *Vasilii Terkin*, about a regular Russian soldier; both the author and an actor read it in September 1942. Mikhail Kalinin, the chairman of the Supreme Soviet and thus the head of state, spoke live on the radio a few minutes after New Year's Eve.⁶⁶

There was a special program with heavily edited letters to and from the front, usually read by staff members, and there were "radio meetings." For instance, a gathering in Saratov of people declared to be "representatives" of the Polish people spoke on November 27, 1941, and a "meeting" of athletes went on the air on August 2, 1942. Overall, however, guest speakers were allowed only a tiny share of the broadcast time. (Many writers and others themselves were not interested in speaking.) At a very late stage, in early 1944, Georgii Aleksandrov proposed weekly radio speeches by party and government leaders, but his idea was ignored.⁶⁷

The absence of prominent guests mirrored the situation outside the media. All leaders shunned political speeches before mass audiences, deeming them undignified or risky lest someone might question them.⁶⁸ Stalin set the example of speaking in public as little as possible. During the entire war he spoke in public fewer than ten times, and radio listeners had only about a dozen opportunities to hear his voice: besides his radio speech of July 1941, his four speeches to meetings of the Moscow City Council marking the anniversary of the October Revolution (the first of which, on November 6, 1941, from a subway station); his brief address to the Red Army from the Lenin Mausoleum on November 7, 1941 (unusual in being rebroadcast several times);⁶⁹ and his emotionally barren radio speech marking victory on May 9, 1945. Strictly speaking, only the first and last of these were directed toward the entire population. He did also address everyone each year on May 1, but only in writing.

Late at night on July 1, 1941, for the first time since the invasion, the Politburo decided when and where Stalin was to speak on the radio. A Kremlin room was used on July 3, where Stalin spoke for over twenty-one minutes. It was his first public speech on the radio or anywhere else in over two years, and the first indication ordinary citizens received of his thoughts since the start of the war with Germany. But not many citizens actually heard him, for the timing was odd, 6 A.M., and the sound recording was not rebroadcast. Instead the text was reread by Levitan on the radio and by other speakers in meetings. The speech appeared in newspapers and as a separate brochure, of which 4,369,000 copies were printed within a year.[70]

Central Soviet radio broadcast a lot of music: an average of six hours per day in 1942, 7.5 hours in 1943, increasing in the second half of that year, when radio broadcasting was prolonged to 1 A.M., to nine hours and twenty minutes, and there was still more on Sundays. These averages excluded the music following the gun salutes in Moscow marking military achievements, which took over the rest of the broadcasting day, usually lasting four to five hours without interruption. Music also was used to replace cancelled programs. In contrast to the spoken word, much music went on the air live, about half on central radio in 1943. New recordings were rare; in all of 1942 and 1943 the Radio Committee recorded, respectively, only sixteen and forty-one hours of music.

The first wartime broadcast by central radio of a symphony concert of Russian music that was both live and in the presence of an audience was organized in Moscow on December 21, 1941. Most famous in this regard was Dmitrii Shostakovich's Seventh (Leningrad) Symphony. Debuting live in Leningrad on August 9, 1941, its countrywide radio premiere was on March 5, 1942, with a performance in Kuibyshev. Its first performance in Moscow was broadcast to the country (and also to the United Kingdom and the United States) twenty-four days later. The proportion on central radio of "native" music (including pre-Soviet compositions) to "western" music was about three to one. Western entertainment music was almost absent; in 1943 it constituted just 6 percent of all broadcast music.[71]

Local radio was in disarray almost constantly, in many ways. In October 1941 Shcherbakov was informed that due to bad work at the relay centers in many Russian oblasts, a "large part of the radio listeners is deprived of the possibility to pick up political information from Moscow over the radio." Of the 189 radio relay centers in the Voronezh oblast only ten were picking up short-wave transmissions, and more than thirty had been totally idle ever since the German invasion. Just five of the forty raions in the Penza oblast received Moscow radio. Only nine of the 136 relay centers in the Ivanovo oblast transmitted it, due to shortages (of short-wave receivers, electricity, and fuel). Similar disruptions were reported in the Sverdlovsk oblast.[72]

Moreover discipline fell at many relay centers. The radio technician on duty in the Ivanovo oblast showed a colleague how to turn on the microphone and forgot to turn it off. The two then "started to swear obscenities. All this hooligan language was transmitted during four minutes to over 250 radio points." Worse, as Polikarpov reported, "several" relay centers transmitted "hostile" broadcasts. The head of the relay center at the Agricultural Institute in Ivanovo forgot to turn off the equipment when leaving, and as a "result" for thirty minutes a Russian-language "anti-Soviet" broadcast, probably from Germany, went out. Such a broadcast also went on the air for several minutes in the Voronezh oblast while a technician was napping.[73]

In July 1942 the People's Commissariat of Communication and the Radio Committee ordered their representatives to install radios in those village soviets that had telephones. Less than a year later more than 4,200 village soviets regularly received radio. But it remained inaudible in ordinary villages and places outside the raion centers. Also in July 1942 Agitprop "proposed" a daily increase of local broadcasting to thirty minutes in the countryside and sixty in large industrial raions; by the next year most raion radio met this standard only by half. The local programs consisted of readings of old newspaper clippings and dated information; the news was almost always positive. Taking their cue from central radio, raion leaders and prominent industrial or agricultural figures (the so-called *peredoviki,* or "advanced people") hardly ever came to speak. Only in 1943, when raion newspapers were turned into weeklies, did Moscow begin to really value local radio. The Central Committee ordered local newspaper editors in June of that year to also edit the raion radio programs. But the impact was minor; overall local radio remained in poor shape. Agitprop accurately blamed not only shortages but also disinterest among local authorities.[74]

Scarcity

As before the war, Moscow rationed the press, which meant, for instance, that one could not subscribe to an oblast or raion paper if one did not reside in that region. Each region received a predetermined quota for each paper. For instance, the Altai krai in 1943 had to make do with 6,670 copies of *Pravda* and fewer than 4,000 of *Izvestiia;* until 1944 the region was not allotted a single copy of *Krasnaia zvezda*. The central papers were regionally distributed according to a "card system." Manipulation worsened the shortages; it was telling that some officials in Kazakhstan managed to obtain several additional copies, which they used presumably to get fires going, as wrapping and toilet paper, and for smoking.[75] Various foreigners noted with some hyperbole that newspapers were sold almost nowhere except at open markets, and were primarily purchased for toilet or smoking paper. It was true that railway newsstands usually had just one copy, available only for on-the-spot reading, because whenever a closed stand opened, lines of people appeared to buy up the papers.[76]

Rationing worked to place most of the print run of the central newspapers in state and party offices. It was typical that of the twenty-four copies of *Trud* allotted to the Ordzhonikizde factory in the Cheliabinsk oblast in early 1944, only three went to the twelve workers' hostels. Rural raions both officially and in practice received very few central papers. Those central and oblast papers that did make it to raion centers often stayed there and did not reach ordinary people, a problem eventually acknowledged in *Pravda* but not resolved. For instance, in September 1942 a certain raion in the Tatar SSR was allotted sixty-four copies of *Pravda* and *Izvestiia*, but thirty went no farther than the raion center and twenty-seven to the nearest seven post offices; no copy reached other offices delivering to forty-seven collective farms. Two years later villages of the Irkutsk oblast received only 115 copies of *Komsomolskaia pravda*, out of an oblast total of 2,300. The oblasts of Ivanovo, Gorkii, Riazan, and Iaroslavl were exceptional in that here almost all copies (around 80 percent in mid-1943) of the paper *Sotsialisticheskoe zemledelie* were sent to farms, but even then most did not leave the hands of the local dignitaries. In short, the system precluded ordinary farmers from subscribing to a central paper or even seeing one on a regular basis.[77]

War delayed the distribution and made it irregular, even though beginning in October 19, 1941, at the height of the battle for Moscow, *Pravda* and *Izvestiia* were printed not only in Moscow but also, using flown-in page images, in Kazan and Kuibyshev.[78] The Moscow papers received in besieged Leningrad during the winter of 1941–1942 were five to seven days old. *Pravda* and *Izvestiia* were distributed to Muscovites in the afternoon and copies for other destinations were sent out by train only the next day. In 1944 they traveled for nine or ten days to reach Chita, an oblast on the Chinese border; even as late as April 1945 to reach Vladivostok took fifteen to eighteen days. For central papers to then move from the oblast capitals to the raion centers also took a long time, a week or more in the Tula oblast in the fall of 1942, for instance. Distribution of raion papers also took time; distant villages were reached in two to three days.[79] Another phenomenon, widespread despite repeated government decrees opposing it, was theft of central papers from trains and post offices.[80] (It may be assumed that the thieves were not interested in reading them.)

In theory people could also read the papers in libraries and countryside "reading rooms" or in display windows, and, as before the war, they were read out during meal breaks at farms and on other occasions. Yet here too reality diverged greatly from theory. In seven RSFSR oblasts in September 1943, for example, there were not enough copies of *Pravda* and *Izvestiia* to place one in every reading room, and of display windows there were also few, and those poorly maintained; only sixteen percent of the windows in cities were in order in early 1943. Factory papers were a different matter; they simply were not allowed to be taken outside the gates.[81]

The distribution of radio propaganda faced other obstacles. As noted, radio generally failed to reach most villages. At the other end, there were also constant problems with the transmissions from the center (even though the equipment of the radio stations was moved from Moscow to the east and put to use again). Before the German invasion, central radio used to broadcast through long- and medium-wave stations such as the (long-wave) Komintern station, and oblasts picked up the waves from relay centers. But some months into the new war suspicion arose in the Kremlin that enemy planes might use Soviet radio waves to determine their positions. Therefore, beginning in October 1941, the long-wave and medium-wave stations were no longer used at night, at first only in and around Moscow, then in all cities west of the Volga River. The idea was to fully switch to transmission over phone lines, but it seems that the center also started using the prewar television center's ultra-short-wave transmitters, to be picked up by television equipment at radio relay centers.[82]

The signals were weak and the sound was poor, sometimes to the point of being inaudible due to crackling and other noises. In 1943 the Soviet Union's main radio broadcasting station, not in Moscow but in Kuibyshev, had a strength of 1,200 kW, allegedly the strongest radio signal in the world. But the government realized that this was not enough given the size of the country, and that the signal was actually ten times weaker than in "any other state."[83] The sound of airborne radio was also far less clear than in other countries. The station that was built in Kuibyshev during the war produced very poor sound because it received programs from Moscow by a telephone cable negatively influenced by poor maintenance and the atmosphere. Responsibilities for these technical matters were divided between the Commissariat, the Radio Committee, and these organizations' local representatives, in ways that varied from city to city.[84] And, at the receiving end, many loudspeakers inherently produced a muffled sound and easily broke down.[85]

On the evening of July 8, 1941, central Moscow radio fell silent in the entire Rostov oblast. No one explained it to the citizens, rumors ascribed it to the bombing of Moscow, and the result was what the local party reported as a "mass panic." Leningrad was not just encircled by Germans, but also isolated from airwaves. In early 1942, if not earlier, up to seventy-five percent of Moscow radio could not be heard in Leningrad; by the fall Leningrad decided to replace Moscow's time slot with local radio. (Conversely the local programs of large cities such as Leningrad could not be heard elsewhere in the country.) The phenomenon of radio silence affected a vast portion of the country. Even as late as early 1945, only the "central-European" parts of the USSR were receiving the center at all times. Moscow radio was often inaudible in Siberia, the Far East, Central Asia, the Caucasus, the north, and at the fronts. As a government official informed Stalin, the problem was mirrored locally: much of republican, krai, and oblast radio was also inaudible. (Even those oblasts with the technical capabilities tended to transmit local broadcasting only for brief stretches.) And the Central Committee resolution on central broadcasting had improved matters only in the country's central European cities, he wrote: "As used to be the case, the population of the rest of the Union, and also the village population of the European part of the Union, can [only] hear Moscow in separate time stretches."[86]

Censorship

Literally nothing was published or broadcast without prior permission from the party-state. Day in and day out, Agitprop's mostly young staff of 150 scrutinized published central newspapers, the plans for upcoming issues, and drafts of the main propaganda articles. The agency also often summoned editors. The directorate's Press Department also read the republican, oblast, and krai newspapers, but mostly left it up to regional ideologists to verify the raion press, although near the end of the war Aleksandrov concluded that this was insufficient because those ideologists hardly bothered to read them. *Pravda* began criticizing local papers in review articles.[87]

The center of professional censorship was the Main Directorate on Matters of Literature and Publishing Houses of the RSFSR, abbreviated as Glavlit. Strictly speaking a government body (and of the Russian Soviet republic only), it was actually controlled by Agitprop. (A prewar proposal to rename it the Main Directorate of Censorship at the Council of People's Commissars of the USSR was not adopted. Stalin still did not want any public word about the very existence of censorship.) Glavlit collaborated with various government bodies, such as newly created departments of military censorship at the commissariats of defense and the fleet. Since the Great Terror the body was led by N. G. Sadchikov, thirty-seven years old in 1941, who also held the position of plenipotentiary of the Council of People's Commissars of the USSR for the Protection of Military Secrets in the Press. Compared to most of his predecessors and subordinates, Sadchikov was almost an intellectual. Highly motivated, within months after his appointment he began warning against enemies, spies, and saboteurs in his office.[88]

One of censorship's aims was to verify letters and telegrams, but the main purpose was to verify the political and ideological content of the media and to bar state secrets from being published. Using the cover title of "literary editor" at publishing houses and periodicals, the censors called their work "control" and "*de visu* investigation" (*vizirovanie*). They also removed existing publications and initiated the prosecution of censorship transgressors. Unlike censors in some other countries, Soviet censors did not give positive advice on what to write or say; that task was reserved for Agitprop.

Although at the time of the Nazi-Soviet pact, in 1940, military "departments" that also censored materials had been introduced in many organizations, the position of main military censor at the Council of People's Commissars was created only on June 2, 1941.[89] Yet the Soviet Information Bureau also operated in this field; *Pravda*, for instance, sent draft articles to the Bureau's Military Department for confirmation, where they sometimes were reconciled with prior

Bureau reports or banned altogether.⁹⁰ As for censorship of foreign affairs, it had been carried out by Molotov's Press Department, but after the German attack the job went to the Bureau, which held it until December 1942.⁹¹

Almost 700 full-time and 2,250 part-time censors worked at Glavlit in the middle of the war. They were supposed to refer particular removals only to editors in chief or the chairman or first deputy chairman of the radio committee in question. They looked over the page proofs, watched for "ambiguous" juxtaposition of articles and illustrations, stamped *signalny eksempliar* on them, and signed each galley. The approved final page proofs went not only to the publishing house but also to Sadchikov, the Central Committee, and—unless the material was not in Russian—the NKVD headquarters and the commissariats of defense and of the fleet. Only raion papers did not have to be sent to Moscow. Beyond the RSFSR, the materials were not sent to Sadchikov's office but to its republican branches. In the absence of problems a new stamp allowed for "release." All publications printed the responsible censor's identification number. There was also "post hoc control," in part or in full. The only materials entirely excluded from this screening were inherently or explicitly secret anyhow, such as publications by military units, the military industry, and the Gulag.⁹²

Oblast and republican Glavlits prepared reports with details of their "strike-throughs" (*vycherki*), and, on a daily basis beginning in July 1942, so did the central Glavlit with regard to the central press published in Moscow. Glavlit in turn received analogous daily reports from the military censor and the radio censors. Sadchikov used all these compilations to report to Agitprop once or twice each month.⁹³ In May 1942 he complained about the work of the Glavlits of the Kazakh SSR, the Bashir ASSR, the Saratov, Novosibirsk, Riazan, and Penza oblasts, and the Krasnoiarsk krai. The next year he himself overstepped his authority, sending his subordinates a printed brochure with quotations from local papers' errors (with regard to Nazi speeches and inadvertent revelation of factory locations). He had not even shown the brochure, an expanded edition of a 1942 brochure, to the Central Committee. It was destroyed, and its arrogant author received a severe reprimand.[94] Censorship at the republic level also had its problems; some newspapers in Ukraine's Kharkiv and Voroshylovhrad oblasts appeared without official censorship for almost two years.[95] In general, however, publication censorship was highly effective.

There were no radio broadcasts whatsoever at the countless enterprises of "defense significance." Elsewhere radio censors read the program texts and also listened while the programs were on the air. In the case of the *Latest News* and other major broadcasts, the censor was the chairman of the Radio Committee himself. Rebroadcasting needed new permission. Very little was free from prebroadcasting censorship, including standard phrases such as "Attention, listen" and "With that we end the broadcast," printed matter, authorized music, and special broadcasts over office (*vedomstvennye*) relay centers. In everything else censors cut words or passages and made notes. Tape recordings that were cut were burned. Tapes and "sound films" produced outside a studio were checked on the basis of a stenographic report; here typescripts were supposed to suffice (although censors were authorized to listen in advance to broadcasts). For the live broadcasting of music and theater the presence of the censor at two rehearsals was required.

A vital issue was "protection of the microphones": censors ensured the absence of working microphones from radio relay centers where programs were not produced, and although the radio committees were responsible for barring outsider access to them elsewhere, the censor also checked and might intervene.[96] Transgressions did occur. In February 1942 a censor removed from the "microphone material" of the Novosibirsk radio committee for Red Army Day the announcement of the presence of Major General Moskvitin, commander of the Fourth Guards Division. But during the live broadcast the speaker ignored the cut.[97]

A striving for total control was why members of Stalin's closest entourage also themselves monitored and censored the central newspapers. For some time David Ortenberg of *Krasnaia zvezda* visited Lev Mekhlis, the main army commissar, to show him page proofs. A former *Pravda* editor, Mekhlis made only minor changes, but he could have made more.⁹⁸ Even Agitprop regularly sought out the inner circle's prior approval. And when Kalinin, the head of state, had revised a speech for publication, Aleksandrov felt compelled to obtain Shcherbakov's green light. He did the same with articles intended for several central newspapers marking the twentieth anniversary of the formation of the Soviet Union.⁹⁹

As later chapters will also show, Stalin personally joined the supervision. At his office he often glanced at the page proofs of the central papers and verbally instructed the editors on the spot. It was on his order that beginning in December 7, 1942, all Soviet papers pedantically began spelling the letter *io* not as *e* but as *ë*. For some time early in the next year he called the *Pravda* office over the phone to verify that the newest issue had been printed at the expected time. When one day the paper deigned to omit the text of a short foreign telegram, Stalin called in as well. And he told Shcherbakov to complain on his behalf about airbrushed photographs that he believed were showing tiny swastikas.¹⁰⁰

Because censors knew that Stalin and his inner circle would never complain about excessive control, they ignored virtually all complaints from the editors and became stricter than ever, not simply reporting "counterrevolutionary" printing errors but banning the slightest ambiguity or deviation from the guidelines and political line. After having Agitprop review Glavlit's activities, Aleksandrov concluded that there was "serious exaggeration," including perceiving political agendas behind simple errors. But this review came only in mid-1944, some months after a new censor's blacklist came into force but years after regional authorities had begun complaining.¹⁰¹

As the next chapters will show, the censorship, together with the other key features of the Soviet media landscape—extreme centralization, unrealistic demands, a tiny share of nonjournalistic voices, small print runs, and poor distribution—in some ways supported the ostensibly paramount goal of all-out mobilization, but also often obstructed it.

2

Selfless Obedience and Heroism at the Front

There were two cardinal rules for Soviet reporting about military affairs, stemming from Stalin's concern lest his media somehow "please Goebbels," that is, assist Nazi German propaganda. Rule 1 was that if the Soviet Information Bureau did not mention an event on the war's eastern European front, no one else could. Stalin kept a close watch, personally editing draft texts, and his army of censors checked for transgressions before and after publication or broadcast. (In addition, regional papers could not scoop central ones.) Rule 2 was about morale and ordered censors to ban "without exception all pieces of information that can call forth a panicky and depressed mood in the army or in the hinterland—exaggerated data on the results of enemy military actions and on its material and technical resources, overestimation of the enemy army's morale and military situation, and so on."[1]

The two rules were mostly followed, with grotesque and dangerous results, but, as will be shown, there were exceptions and paradoxes. Sometimes persistence by a leading newspaper editor paid off. With regard to the second rule, the leadership did not see a contradiction with the glorification of soldiers who, reports said, sacrificed their lives willingly to avoid German captivity.

A Time of Troubles

The extent of the cover-up of the early disasters at the front was enormous. Partly due to Stalin's willful disregard of warnings of an impending invasion, the defeats delegitimized much of the prewar propaganda. "For two decades we had been starved and tortured and driven in the name of military preparedness," recalled Victor Kravchenko, a high-ranking Soviet official who gained asylum in the United States during the war. "Our leaders had boasted of Soviet superiority in trained manpower and armament. Now the humiliating rout of our armies was being explained [in verbal propaganda] by lack of guns, planes, munitions."[2] That was why for many weeks Soviet reports of the "fierce," "stubborn," or "heavy" fighting hid far more than they told. References were not to locations but to "directions," often named after little-known places and used even when the front had moved on. And instead of identifying any Red Army front or unit, word was about the "army." Not a single loss of a city was reported for two months.[3]

Drafts of Bureau statements from the first weeks show Stalin and Shcherbakov working away to modify reports compiled by members of the General Staff. The two removed details of setbacks and exaggerated the few achievements. For example, "hundreds of Germans corpses" left on a battlefield in the draft report for the evening of July 3, 1941, became "thousands." A draft report for the morning of July 5 had a litany of bad news: enemy crossings of the Soviet Karelian border; German aerial bombings of airports, troops, and cities (Kamianets-Podilsky, Mohyliv-Podilsky, Pervomaisk, and Shepetivka in Ukraine; Chișinău/Kishinev in Moldavia; and Smolensk in Russia). It also spoke of Soviet aerial attacks in Volhynia in western Ukraine and of a Soviet attack on a German plane "near Kiev." Stalin or Shcherbakov deleted all of this.[4]

For weeks typical reports read, "During the night to July 11 nothing of significance happened" and "Our troops continued to engage the opponent in battle all along the front."[5] The media fully ignored the enormously embarrassing losses of Minsk on June 28 and of Chișinău and Smolensk on July 16, actually hiding the battle for Smolensk by referring only to some "Ostrov direction" and "Polotsk direction." Stalin or Shcherbakov replaced the word "counterattack" with "offensive"; a "significant number" of destroyed German tanks with an invented number, 140; and "knocked-out tanks" with "many knocked-out tanks." The new round of German bombings of Smolensk on July 9 and 10 was also omitted. (Only in some ways did Stalin adjust the draft texts toward reality: the "great defeat" supposedly inflicted on the Germans in two raions "in the Polotsk direction" on the morning of July 9 became "great losses.") The report for the morning of July 11 stated, "In the Ostrov-Polotsk direction, our troops have withdrawn to new positions where they are preparing for the defense against the enemy's mechanized units." Polatsk/Polotsk, a town in the Vitsebsk oblast, fell on July 15, the day of another bombing of Smolensk; the Bureau was silent about both events. When Smolensk fell the next day, literally nothing was said about it. The very first report of the Soviet loss of a city appeared only on August 26: "After stubborn fights our troops abandoned Novgorod." Three days later the same statement was made about Dnipropetrovsk.[6]

Memoirs and eyewitness accounts written beyond the Soviet zone of influence sometimes testify that few or even "no one" believed the Soviet front reports. "The war communiqués in the first weeks proved so misleading," Kravchenko wrote, "that few Russians believed them at any time thereafter." By October 1941 a Ukrainian physician practicing in the Siberian town of Timiriazev knew many people there, both locals and evacuees. Aware of his Galician provenance and therefore unafraid that he might denounce them, many were candid and some even expressed skepticism about the radio announcers' statement *This Is Moscow Speaking*: Moscow had already fallen, they believed, or, in the physician's view, *wanted* to believe.[7]

Despite the rule that all military events were to be reported by the Bureau first, a few times in 1941 the Soviet leadership gave the green light to reports about important events not—or barely—mentioned by the Bureau. These inconsistencies in the propaganda monitoring system were not numerous, but they show that Stalin and his entourage recognized that omitting facts commonly known to all was impossible—the media had to say *something*. Allowing others than the Bureau to do this made such statements both retractable and less official. Particularly remarkable cases concerned the Soviet scorched-earth policy, the fall of Kiev, and the German advance on Moscow.

Possibly in view of future claims against Germany for war damages, the general line was to be vague or silent about Soviet demolitions in abandoned terrain, even though Stalin had proclaimed this policy of scorched earth in his speech of July 1941. When, on August 17, 1941, Soviet engineers exploded the central part of the dam of the Dnieper Hydroelectric Station (or Dniprohes) and produced a large flood, deputy Bureau chief Solomon Lozovskii told foreign correspondents, but Soviet citizens were kept in the dark.[8] Having heard about the demolition from a witness, David Ortenberg, the editor in chief of *Krasnaia zvezda*, asked Shcherbakov in the last days of September 1941 to allow an article about the dam he had commissioned from the writer Aleksei Tolstoi. The manuscript quoted Stalin on the need to destroy unevacuated property and stated that in general, "in the Right Bank, we left the Germans an empty plain." It mentioned the blowing up and flooding of the mines in Kryvy Rih, the demolition of the wharfs in Mykolaïv, and that "we blew up the first born child of our Five-Year-Plan": the Dniprohes dam. Tolstoi added that Moscow would not be given up. (By that time the fate of the Soviet capital was in the balance and Stalin was secretly planning its demolition by mines in case of its loss.) No record of Shcherbakov's response, if any, has been found. When the revised version was held up and Ortenberg became impatient, he resubmitted it (or so he claims) under another title—and obtained permission for publication, even though the Bureau still had not mentioned the dam's demolition.[9]

The acknowledgment did not really make this case of Soviet demolition easier to handle, however. In April 1943 a censor removed much about it from *Komsomolskaia pravda* because providing "details on our explosion and destruction of our largest enterprises and buildings" was "politically inexpedient." When the Red Army recaptured the area, the Soviet Ukrainian press admitted that the Soviet authorities had "partly damaged" the dam, but subsequent reports tended to describe the demolition in the passive voice: the upper part of the dam "was blown up" during the Red Army's retreat. In the fall of 1944 the entire country was called on to assist in the reconstruction of Soviet power engineering's biggest site; the order focused on the real German attempts in 1943 to fully demolish the dam and the German demolition of the attached power station. Nor did the case of the Dniprohes set a precedent; the media never acknowledged the Soviet mining of Kiev, for instance. Many of those mines were set off after the German occupation, in large numbers on September 24, and produced casualties. The Soviet media could have presented this as a success, but kept silent.[10]

The Wehrmacht occupied Kiev on the morning of September 19, 1941. Just days before, Soviet propaganda had continued to operate within and from the city. Early that month a TASS correspondent typically reported that heroism abounded among able-bodied Kievans, just as among the Red Army and the People's Home Guard. A republican Communist Party official appeared in *Pravda* on September 11 with a lengthy article said to have been submitted over the phone from Kiev. In August alone, this secretary wrote, more than 30,000 "fascist" soldiers and officers had perished near Kiev, a city that would "never bow its head to the Hitlerite barbarians." Its defenders would fight "up to the last drop of blood. . . . Never shall the Hitlerite bandits rule over the free city of Kiev! Kiev is and shall be Soviet!"[11]

A radio broadcast from Kiev meant for the entire country the next day, also reported in the press, consisted of speeches and a new song about the city's Home Guard. The secretary of the city party committee said, "Already more than once, regiments and divisions of the fascist cutthroats actually approached Kiev itself. . . . For just a minute, the enemy could glance at mighty and stern Kiev from the Holosiïv Forest. But our batteries and machine-guns closed their evil eyes forever." Paradoxically everyday life in the city was ordinary, with workers overfulfilling their labor targets. "We vow to you, our comrades in arms, that we will carry out honorably the order of the People's Commissar of Defense, our wise leader and dear comrade Stalin. We shall not surrender Kiev to the enemy!" A brigade army commissar, a member of a Home Guard unit, and a railroad worker made the same vows.[12]

On September 14 a program on central radio, which also resounded from loudspeakers in Kiev, consisted of contributions read in three cities, Leningrad, Moscow, and Kiev, and was also duly reported in print the next day. From Kiev a secretary of the Kiev oblast party committee spoke, and a medical sister who had "displayed heroism on the battlefield." This Nadezhda Stachko said, "Together with their fathers and brothers, the girls of Kiev are fighting selflessly against the enemy. Many Komsomol girls have already become famous on the battlefield: the eighteen-year-old Tania Didenko, the female machine-gunner Olga Iakimova, the medical sister Nezamykina, the partisan Katia Abramova. They are everywhere, these bold girls of our city." Meanwhile posters called on Kievans to create a "second Tsaritsyn," a reference to the city, by then called Stalingrad, where during the Civil War the Red Army had stopped the Whites, supposedly thanks to Stalin. The public connection with Stalin's prestige informed all that he wanted and expected the city to hold. An article in *Krasnaia zvezda* with the dateline September 18 asserted that Kiev's main street was as crowded and noisy as always. All of Kiev was a "grim, industrious, fierce, and immortal Soviet city." The text actually had become available to the editors at least two days earlier.[13]

"Over the course of recent days there has been heavy fighting near Kiev. The fascist-German armies, disregarding the enormous losses in people and armaments, again and again throw new units into the fight. At one of the sectors of Kiev's defense, the opponent managed to breach our fortifications and to move out to the city outskirts. The heavy fighting is continuing." Thus reported *Pravda* on September 19, the day the Germans entered the city.[14] Two items then foretold the fall in a way the Bureau could not. Ortenberg wrote and published a report on the situation in Kiev to which he falsely added, "Kiev, September 18 (by telegraph from our special correspondent)." It was ominous: "Our units have taken up new lines, while preserving their human resources and military capability, while organizing the repulse of the enemy. And in Kiev the fascists won't succeed in realizing their schemes. Kiev's situation is grave. Its valiant defenders must be prepared for everything. Through their heroism they have covered themselves with ever-lasting glory." It was far from the only case during the war when an editor acted as ghostwriter for a correspondent who could not be reached. *Izvestiia* also gave a report supposedly from its correspondent in Kiev. Referring to German "numerical superiority" and Soviet "losses" of various kinds, it declared, "The situation of the defenders of the city has become more serious."[15]

September 20 was first day on which the press could have reported Kiev's fall. But *Pravda*'s front page contained only an irrelevant editorial on tank builders, the full texts of decrees creating new awards, and long lists of their recipients. Page 2 had the Bureau reports for the morning and evening of September 19; all they said about the matter was "Our troops fought with the opponent along the entire front and especially fiercely near Kiev." The next day's Bureau report, back on the front page, still reported nothing more specific than fierce fights "near Kiev."

Meanwhile, responding to questions from foreign correspondents, Lozovskii confirmed to them—not to his compatriots—that the Germans had occupied the city. Ilia Ehrenburg, the prominent Russian Jewish writer, sent a daring letter to Shcherbakov, Aleksandrov, and Lozovskii condemning the media silences about major events, mentioning specifically the Dniprohes dam and Kiev: "People talk about this: in factories, in army units, in the street.... Nobody understands why the military situation is reflected through the answers of comrade Lozovskii to foreign correspondents at a press conference. People say (in my view, justly so), 'So foreigners may ask questions, they get answers, but we are not told.'" Only on the evening of September 22 did the Bureau acknowledge, in a single sentence that falsified the date, "Over the course of September 21 our troops fought the enemy along the entire front. After many days of fierce fighting, our troops abandoned Kiev."[16]

The incessant earlier claims that Kiev "was, is, and shall remain Soviet" made the defeat all the more embarrassing, so Stalin ordered editors to say nothing specific. But when Ehrenburg and Ortenberg attempted to publish something more, Shcherbakov (surely with Stalin's permission) allowed a few words expressing sadness about the event: a column by Ehrenburg in *Krasnaia zvezda* on September 27 that declared, "We will liberate Kiev. The enemy's blood will wash the enemy's footprints. Like the ancient Phoenix, Kiev will rise from the ashes, young and beautiful. Sorrow feeds hatred. Hatred strengthens hope."[17]

The German army attacked Moscow in two waves, beginning on September 30 and again on November 17, 1941, and ultimately came as close as twenty-five kilometers from the city. Towns occupied along the way included Kaluga, Kalinin, Mozhaisk, and Volokolamsk. Early in October 1941 reading between the lines gave some sense of the situation. On the 8th *Krasnaia zvezda* warned that "the very existence of the Soviet state" was at stake; the next day's *Pravda* condemned "careless complacency" among some Muscovites. *Krasnaia zvezda*'s editorial on the 10th quoted the Bureau's statement that fully omitted Moscow and merely added, "The enemy is attempting to break through to our most important life centers of industry at any price." But when the Germans reached Borodino Field, where Napoleon's army had suffered its main setback, the paper quoted the classical writer Lermontov's "Isn't Moscow behind us?"[18]

At this stage Ehrenburg submitted for publication "Hold Out!," a column that stated plainly that the enemy "is threatening Moscow" and gave a rousing call to defend what he called Russia: "Our only thought must be to hold out. They are advancing because they want to plunder and ravage. We are defending ourselves because we want to live. We want to live like human beings and not like German cattle. Reinforcements are coming from the east. Ships with war material from England and America are being unloaded. Every day piles of corpses mark Hitler's route. We must hold out.... Hitler shall not destroy Russia! Russia was, is, and shall be." The text appeared in *Krasnaia zvezda* on October 12, when *Pravda* was still referring only to an indistinct "grave danger." It is not clear who allowed Ehrenburg's frankness. If Ortenberg's memoirs are to be believed, Shcherbakov reproached him afterward for reporting the reinforcements and for sowing panic. But no one was punished.[19]

Three days later, on October 15, Stalin secretly ordered foreign diplomats, the Presidium of the Supreme Soviet, and the Soviet government to leave Moscow that very day. He himself would leave "tomorrow or so." According to the Bureau, on the previous evening the Germans had breached the "Volokolamsk sector." Now, at last, *Pravda* said the "bloody Hitlerites" were "reaching toward Moscow." Panic and disorder erupted in the city streets on the 16th: officials who were leaving were beaten up, massive looting began, and there were anti-Semitic slogans. On the 17th Shcherbakov spoke on Moscow's wire radio (not elsewhere on the air or in print) to say that Stalin was in the city, that "panic" should not be allowed, and that reinforcements were being organized.[20] Three days later, when a state of siege was declared on the basis of a resolution dated October 19, the central press reported, "Those who violate the order shall be immediately called to account through delivery to a court of the Military Tribunal; and provocateurs, spies, and other enemy agents calling for disturbances shall be shot on the spot." The media were also suddenly candid in mentioning the German bombings of Moscow, now said to inflict casualties. Also on the 20th Stalin ordered central newspaper editors by phone to publish a portrait of General Georgii Zhukov, the commander of the Red Army's Western Front. Up to then only portraits of lower-ranking commanders, at best of armies, had appeared, so Zhukov himself concluded that Stalin's purpose now was not to mobilize but to have a scapegoat on hand if Moscow should fall.[21]

The month-long Soviet counteroffensive beginning on December 5 was successful, and on December 13 *Pravda* declared victory. Its front page showed Zhukov again, and eight other commanders, including Andrei Vlasov (a general who was to surrender to the

Germans the next year). But Stalin received most of the credit. Even Ehrenburg wrote that Stalin had wisely foreseen the outcome; already before the German invasion, the leader had never forgotten the "danger threatening the country" and had "said, 'We won't give up Moscow.' We did not give up Moscow. He said, 'We shall beat the Germans.' And we have started to beat the Germans."[22] On the last day of 1941 a picture in *Pravda* was captioned "The retreat of the fascist troops from Moscow (Picture obtained from the Mozhaisk direction)," which suggested it was a German photograph. The Germans were actually war prisoners in a snowy wind created by a Soviet airplane.[23]

Thus, as in the case of the scorched-earth policy and Kiev's fall, various statements appeared in connection with the German advance on Moscow that were more explicit than the Bureau's report or *Pravda*'s editorial. But it was remarkable that neither in Moscow's case nor later, with regard to other cities, did the stock slogan that the city "was, is, and shall remain Soviet" reappear. Stalin was likely unsure, and possibly also realized that many of his subjects tended to interpret such propaganda cynically.

Stalin's Announcement of the Year of Final Victory

On November 6, 1941, marking October Revolution Day in besieged Moscow, Stalin acknowledged recent "failures" by the Red Army. The next day, in his one and only wartime address to a military parade, he predicted, "Some more months, another half year, perhaps a year, and Hitlerite Germany will have to break under the weight of its crimes."[24] Many people must have believed or tried to believe him—to foresee years of war ahead is difficult. In accordance with this scenario, the citizens were told that defeat of Nazi Germany in 1942 was at the very least thinkable. In a speech marking the beginning of the year, Mikhail Kalinin said he hoped that the Soviet people would "fully defeat" the German invaders in 1942. A long collective open letter to Stalin, released on January 1 after public "discussion" in the Sverdlovsk oblast and "signed by 1,017,237 people," was unambiguously optimistic: "For Hitler the year 1942 is a fateful date, the year of shameful ruin, of dishonorable death. In this new year that is starting, Hitler's predatory empire shall fall apart under the weight of the crimes of fascism, crushed by the grave soil of the thousands of cemeteries in Europe and Africa."[25]

In his May 1, 1942, "order," Stalin explicitly demanded two specific goals before the end of the year: the "definitive defeat" of the German armed forces and the "liberation of Soviet soil." Had he not believed these were possible, the cautious dictator would have said something else. But such goals sounded unrealistic even at that time. Editorials and articles began saying daily, "The Red Army, the entire Soviet people have pledged to carry out this order. It will be carried out!" The vow was still in force on the first anniversary of the German invasion: "1942 shall be the year of the final defeat of the enemy, the year of our final victory." With the apparent exception of Ehrenburg, writers also stepped in line.[26]

On May 12 the Soviet command launched an immediately disastrous offensive that had the unstated aim of recapturing Kharkiv. (In anticipation, not only the staff of the Red Army's Southwestern Front but also the Soviet Ukrainian government, prominent writers, and Kharkiv oblast authorities all traveled to nearby Voronezh.) A Bureau report of May 18 spoke of a successful advance of "our troops"—Stalin omitted "of the Southwestern Front" from the draft—in the "Kharkiv direction." "About 12,000 German soldiers and officers have been destroyed," it said. "The offensive is continuing."[27] Yet on that day the Red Army actually lost Barvenkove, a town near Kharkiv, which it had recaptured in January.

The first public signs of deep trouble were reports that mentioned nothing but the enemy's "large losses" in the "Kharkiv direction" and its "enormous" losses in the "Izium-Barvenkove direction." In an item on May 29 with the previous day's dateline, *Izvestiia* commented, "The fights in the Izium-Barvenkove direction shall go in the history of the patriotic war as a new testimony to the staunchness and fearlessness of the Soviet warriors." The next day *Izvestiia*'s front page was all about socialist competition in agriculture, and the Bureau report for May 31 reported "nothing of consequence" about all the fronts. A special Bureau report that same day explicitly *denied* any disaster with regard to Kharkiv: capturing it had "not been part of the plan of the command." Instead advancing on Kharkiv had intended to preclude a large enemy offensive "at one of the sectors of the Rostov front," and the "fierce fights" had achieved this goal. The Wehrmacht had lost by death or capture "no less than 90,000 soldiers and officers," while Red Army losses amounted to only "up to 5,000 people killed [and] 70,000 missing in action."[28]

In the last days of June 1942 another, similar attempt to recapture a town failed and received nearly the same media treatment. Launched in January by Vlasov's Second Shock Army, it aimed for Liuban near Volkhov, in an attempt to link up with the Leningrad Front. Almost 160,000 Red Army soldiers died fighting or while attempting to escape encirclement. On June 30 the Bureau denied an almost correct German announcement of two days earlier of the encirclement of three armies. Soviet losses were placed at just 10,000 killed and 10,000 missing.[29]

Under German attack ever since October 30, 1941, the naval city of Sevastopol on the Crimea finally fell on July 4, 1942. Before that outcome, Ehrenburg followed the mandatory optimistic line in calling Sevastopol not just a city but "the glory of Russia, the pride of the Soviet Union," which was "not surrendering." But near the end a *Krasnaia zvezda* correspondent published an imaginary dialogue that opened up the possibility of defeat: "When the Black Sea sailors are asked, will it be possible to hold on to Sevastopol, they reply sadly, 'It's alright, we'll hold on!' They don't say, 'For now, we're holding on.' They don't say, 'We shall hold on.' Here they don't throw words to the wind and don't like to put fate to the test." The initiative came from outside the Bureau: Ortenberg had somehow convinced the censor, the Central Committee's Press Section, and Shcherbakov to allow this text, which they considered demoralizing.[30]

Then, in an exceptional move, the Bureau not only announced the loss but proclaimed it a moral and strategic victory. After "250 days of heroic defense," "on the order of the High Command of the Red Army, on July 3 Soviet troops abandoned the city of Sevastopol." The defenders had performed "miracles of military valor and heroism." Their task had been to chain the German military to the region and to destroy as much personnel and equipment as possible. "In the entire eight months of Sevastopol's defense the enemy lost up to 300,000 of its soldiers as killed and wounded"; in the previous twenty-five days alone casualties numbered "up to 150,000 soldiers and officers, of whom no less than 60,000 killed." (The statement mentioned no figure of Red Army losses during the entire period, but since June 7, it said, 11,385 Red Army members had been killed, 21,099 had been wounded, and 8,300 had gone missing.) The "main organizers" of the defense, such as Deputy Admiral Filipp Oktiabrskii and Major General Ivan Petrov, were mentioned by name—the first defenders of any lost city to receive this acknowledgment. And the news was unusually timely: on the very day Sevastopol fell. Ehrenburg now kept silent, but Tolstoi spoke of a Pyrrhic victory for the Germans.[31] Thus came about the single Soviet equivalent to the British and German glorification of their own military disasters of World War II, Dunkirk and Stalingrad. Available sources cannot explain what exactly produced the Soviet case.

With the city of Rostov, reporting swung back fully to its default position of silence and obfuscation. The official line was that the battle near Kharkiv had precluded a large German offensive toward Rostov, but the ancient Russian "capital of the Don," already briefly occupied in November 1941, soon found itself again on the front line. Part of the Red Army's Southern Front fled from the city in panic (as well as from Novocherkassk), thus opening a German path to the North Caucasus. Thus fell Rostov for the second time, on July 27, but this was not reported at all. The next day Stalin let an order of his be read out to every soldier. He declared that Rostov had surrendered without a fight, and he reminded them of the existence—not the formation, for they dated back to 1920—of the "defensive detachments," military police who were authorized to shoot alleged panic-mongers and cowards on the spot and to transfer commanders to penal battalions. Veterans and historians alike disagree about the impact of this order; one historian even believes that it *lowered* morale.[32]

The media acknowledged neither the order nor the existence of the military police. For one thing, Stalin's statement and order contradicted the propaganda line that panic and insubordination were rare. For another, here the censors followed the rule that nothing could be said about the prosecution of Red Army troops except for "instructive" and isolated cases involving sergeants (in central and front papers) or privates (in army and division papers).[33] Still, fierce editorials hinted at the order. *Pravda* demanded "Not a step back!" and "iron discipline." Major German advances in "the south" notwithstanding, the enemy was "not as strong as some terrified panic-mongers imagine." It warned that Soviet soldiers "must be ready to die a hero's death rather than stepping back from their duty to the motherland." *Krasnaia zvezda* stated, "He who does not observe order and discipline is a traitor, and must be mercilessly destroyed" and "Every officer and political worker can, with the powers given him by the State, see to it that the very idea of retreating without orders becomes impossible." The Panfilovites, mythical heroes discussed below, were reported to have shot a "coward" on the spot.[34] The paper also carried "The Renegade," a story by the writer and film director Oleksandr (Alexander) Dovzhenko in which an elderly Ukrainian fisherman insulted retreating soldiers. Stalin appreciated this, as Malenkov told the author over the phone.[35] The hortatory tone did not last: on August 9, in a reversal in line with Stalin's new wish to limit the shooting of officers by army commissars, *Krasnaia zvezda* warned the latter, "Sometimes you come across people who need your temporary support; after that they will firmly take themselves in hand."[36]

More failed offensives followed. From mid-August until late September 1942 an offensive led by Zhukov attempted to remove the threat to Moscow by capturing Rzhev and Viazma. The first public reference to offensive operations in the central sector of the Soviet-German front came on August 27, when the Bureau declared that at the Western and Kalinin Fronts, namely "in the Rzhev and Ghzatsk-Viazma directions," the enemy defense had been breached for a 115-kilometer stretch. The failed offensive ended with at least 300,000 Red Army dead—60 percent of the fighting forces involved. It was *entirely* covered up. On November 25, 1942, probably in another attempt to realize Stalin's dream for the year 1942, the Red Army launched another great grasp for Rzhev. Again there came disaster and a total cover-up. Thus in these cases no special Bureau reports appeared, probably because the one about Kharkiv had produced consternation.[37]

Stalingrad and New Setbacks

The battle for the highly symbolic city of Stalingrad began in mid-June 1942. It ended in a Soviet victory on February 2, 1943. Despite the relative frankness of the reports as compared to the summer and fall of 1941, it was still difficult to get a clear picture. There was talk of fighting "in the approaches of Stalingrad" when the invader was already waging battle within the city. Only on September 22 did *Krasnaia zvezda* carry a detailed article on house-to-house fighting. From that month on, reports spoke of "heroic Stalingrad." In late October the propaganda became optimistic. The Agitprop leader Aleksandrov wrote in *Pravda* that the defense had held up the Germans for three months and robbed them of "the most precious time they had this year for offensive operations." On November 6 Stalingrad's defenders swore an oath to Stalin personally. Many citizens probably concluded that the invocation of his prestige made a Soviet retreat unlikely. Stalin that day also sounded confident in his speech: "There will be a holiday on our street, too."[38]

On the first day of the new year the Bureau released figures for German losses in the previous six weeks of fighting at "the outskirts of Stalingrad": 175,000 had been killed and 137,650 had been captured. On January 25 Stalin, omitting the number of Germans killed, said that during the previous two months the Red Army had captured "over 200,000" prisoners. Five days later reports claimed that in just three days of fights, the Red Army had killed up to 12,000 and captured more than 14,000 German troops. Stalin added the adjective *German* to the drafts, thereby obscuring the Germans' many allies.[39]

"Our Troops Have Completely Finished the Liquidation of the German-Fascist Troops Encircled in the Stalingrad Region," was the Bureau's headline on February 3. The fighting from January 10 through February 2 had been "one of the largest battles in the history of wars." Here 91,000 German soldiers and officers had been captured. The announcement, which Stalin put through four drafts, gave no figures for enemy wounded or deaths.[40] In early February front pages carried a large photograph of the German general Friedrich Paulus undergoing questioning by Artillery Marshall Nikolai Voronov and Lieutenant General Konstantin Rokossovskii. The whole world recognized, *Pravda* declared, the degree to which the outcome of this battle would decide the war. A laconic item about Goebbels's "total war" speech of February 18 was relegated to the back pages.[41]

On the second anniversary of the German invasion, Stalingrad officially became the war's *turning point*, and in November 1943 Stalin laid down the line that nothing after that point could be of great military consequence. "Stalingrad marked the fall of the German-fascist army. It is known that after the bloody battle of Stalingrad, the Germans could no longer recover." He did not refer to the results of the three-months-long offensive begun on July 12 of that same year, deeming them disappointing, and cut a planned article about them.[42] Yet he felt confident enough to allow superficial reports that Kharkiv and Zhytomyr were again lost to the Germans that year.

In an offensive ordered by Stalin in person, the Red Army rushed forward and recaptured Kharkiv on February 16, 1943. Using a blue pencil, the leader personally edited the special Bureau announcement. *Radianska Ukraïna* spoke of a "new victory of the brilliant Stalin strategy" that the people of the already "reviving" city would forever consider historic.[43] Yet the Wehrmacht regrouped and struck back hard: in the last week of February the Red Army lost everything it had retaken in two months, including the Northern Donets region. It found itself back at its position of December 1942. On March 15 therefore the Red Army abandoned Kharkiv for the second time during the war. This time the Bureau did not attempt to hide the retreat. The report for that evening stated, "On March 15, our troops, after many days of fierce fighting, on the order of Command evacuated the city of Kharkiv." Because there were no newspapers on March 16, this report appeared in print on March 17.[44] Ehrenburg wrote that Kharkiv's second fall had increased "our hatred of the Germans."[45]

Another acknowledgment of failure involved one of the last Red Army setbacks on Soviet territory. After Red Army soldiers entered the town of Zhytomyr west of Kiev late on November 12, 1943, this success became the first item of the next Bureau report and the topic of a detailed article. But seven days later the troops were pushed out again, not to return until the very last day of the year. The Bureau report for November 18 said vaguely that the Red Army had inflicted "enormous losses in living force and technique" as it repulsed a fierce German attack near Zhytomyr, but the next day's report, released on the 20th, said explicitly, "Our troops abandoned the city of Zhytomyr and took up more lines more favorable to defense." The High Command had ordered the move because the Soviet positions were "disadvantageous."[46] The acknowledgment of the new losses of Kharkiv and Zhytomyr, on the face of it demoralizing, showed that overall Stalin's confidence was running high.

Controlling Military Data, Generals, and "Negativity"

Moscow's censors barred items of military importance that every warring state would want to hide, such as the presence below ground on the Hanko Peninsula (leased from Finland in 1940 but abandoned in December 1941) of an airport, hospitals, a radio station, artillery batteries, and cars; the location of an air force school; and the location and capacity of an artillery factory. Also barred was a reference to the use of dogs to blow up German tanks, as were tales about medical personnel participating in the fighting as liaison officers or soldiers, a practice in contravention of the Geneva Conventions.[47]

Sadchikov warned his colleagues that newspapers no longer should mention what he considered revelations of defense fortifications, such as antitank ditches in specific places, even if the local party organization had ordered them to be readied. Thanking a battalion for doing so in a local newspaper also was out of the question.[48] After the fact censors noticed the disclosure in letters read on the radio in December 1941 and January 1942 of the stationing of three artillery regiments and other units and of the location of military schools.[49] In early 1942 implementation of the censorship rules became almost total.

The few, sometimes major digressions that slipped through included the following. *Izvestiia* wrote in February of one campaign, "Many of the Baltic mine-sweepers made up to sixty war cruises; every one destroyed over 100 mines." This supposedly enabled Germany to estimate the impact of its mines and the number of Soviet minesweepers. The paper reported expeditions from Arkhangelsk to the Arctic meant to safeguard the northern sea route; all censors were now warned that the Naval Censorship Department had to approve reports of anything about that route.[50] In October 1942 *Krasnaia zvezda* wrote about the Reserve Artillery of the High Command. "No one" had allowed its publication, Ortenberg later told Shcherbakov, or so he claimed in his memoirs. Actually Aleksander Vasilevskii, the chief of the General Staff, had read it in advance, and he confirmed Ortenberg's explanation to an angry Stalin. The Germans had already known about those reserves, he added.[51] During the German encirclement at Stalingrad, *Pravda* quoted an intercepted German radio telegram, thereby revealing that the USSR possessed the German codes.[52]

The censors were instructed to ban photos of "cities, individual streets, squares and buildings: factories, dams, floodgates, bridges, electricity stations, railroad stations, and the like," so when *Krasny flot* carried photographs of Sevastopol and a plane there in March 1942, censors in hindsight called it a lapse.[53] As for maps of the front situation, initially they did not appear at all, but eventually papers published full-page maps, personally approved by Stalin. They indicated the Soviet territory recaptured in specific periods.[54]

The Red Army employed a multiple rocket launcher (BM-13) that could deliver over four tons of explosives in ten seconds and that inspired terror precisely because it was inaccurate. For some reason the device was nicknamed the Katiusha; as a result an uplifting march and a song about a girl with that name became very popular. Descriptions of the weapon itself were not allowed. In March 1942 a radio broadcast of a meeting of Stakhanovites of the Sverdlovsk oblast accidentally reported that the Katiusha was produced in a Sverdlovsk factory directed by one Miagkov. After the Battle of Stalingrad Shcherbakov allowed a few exceptions, in poetry and song and in the documentary film *Stalingrad*, which showed the device while a voice-over said, "The Katiushas are shooting." That notice of the withdrawal from Stalingrad of a Rocket Launcher Regiment was removed from a radio text was not surprising, however.[55]

When Germany invaded, tens of thousands of women volunteered for the army, but that year only 300 were actually mobilized, into air combat regiments near Moscow. The regime neither encouraged nor prohibited women from becoming soldiers. In March and April 1942, however, the Komsomol organized the mobilization of women as antiaircraft fighters and for a host of noncombat functions such as radio operation and secretarial work. A massive second mobilization began in October 1942. During the entire war around 520,000 field army members were women, and around 120,000 of these were soldiers whose primary role was to engage the enemy. Censors as a rule cut prospective reports about military units staffed by women. The press and poster propaganda followed the prewar line in being inconsistent about women and war: although women's desire to fight came through and reports in 1942 suggested that Moscow wanted them to master military skills, enticing women to pick up arms was and remained taboo, as was the role of the state in enlisting them. Meanwhile reports did celebrate and photos did show individual women, such as Liudmila Pavlichenko the sniper and Mariia Baida the machine-gunner, and *Pravda* even wrote that thousands of women were celebrating Women's Day in 1943 "in the flames of combat and on the battlefields, shoulder to shoulder with men soldiers."[56]

Perhaps some 25,000 children served in the Red Army, assisting, for instance, in minesweeping operations. This topic was totally taboo. Thus censors prohibited a secretary of the Moscow city party from saying on the radio that there were more than 1,500 (male)

Komsomol members in a rifle battalion and a newspaper from reporting that a machine-gunner was only sixteen.[57]

Of great but arbitrary interest to Stalin was the coverage devoted to generals. Late in August 1941 *Krasnaia zvezda* reported the "successes of the units of commander Konev," referring to General Ivan Konev, commander of the 19th Army. Stalin phoned Ortenberg, said, "That's enough printed about Konev," and put down the receiver. In January 1942 all generals were decorated and gained favorable publicity, except for Zhukov, whom Stalin struck from the list, murmuring that the general "still has everything ahead of him."[58]

Konstantin Rokossovskii was one of several generals who published articles. Once, in *Krasnaia zvezda* on December 18, 1941, he even revealed that he reported over the phone to Stalin; Stalin's personal secretary gave him permission to print the information, also over the phone. Whenever they assumed the command of an entire front, Stalin barred generals from publishing articles, seemingly because of his paranoid fear that traitors among them might pass on coded messages to the Germans. Thus Rokossovskii and Nikolai Vatutin stopped publishing after taking command, respectively, of the Briansk and Voronezh Fronts in July and May 1942. Zhukov cleverly devised a way to continue to influence the media after he took charge of the Western Front: at least two *Krasnaia zvezda* editorials were directly inspired by conversations he had with Ortenberg. One, on November 2, 1941, announced correctly the beginning of the "most serious" phase of the battle for Moscow; another, on January 9, 1942, cautioned against unrealistic optimism.[59]

Stalin considered "negative" information dangerous because his subjects might act on it to his detriment, and because Nazi propaganda might benefit. That was why censors always cut "negative" statements about the Red Army and Fleet taken from foreign sources. But the definition of negativity was much broader. When a broadcast text for preschool children on Azerbaijan radio in February 1942 commented that the Red Army was getting help from the winter, it supposedly implied that the army *needed* this season to gain victories, and the item was removed. In a text about Stalingrad, the writer Vasilii Grossman recorded a German's cry, "Hey

Rus, I'm cold, let's exchange gun for cap!" This had to go because such a verbal exchange supposedly was impossible and implied that the Germans had arms to spare. Flame-throwing by whichever side, deemed demoralizing, could not be mentioned either, so when another Grossman report described Germans doing so and also employing poison gas, it was taken out as well.[60]

For a military unit to lose its banner was a sin punishable by disbandment and a court marshal. The media were not supposed to report such cases, but in June 1943 *Krasnaia zvezda* wrote that the banner of the 43rd Regiment was lost near Rostov. Happily, the report went, a Russian peasant had hidden it. He had been given a medal and made an honorary member of the regiment. The censor had banned the article, but Ortenberg disobeyed. Personally absolving the typesetter of responsibility with a comment on the page proofs, he produced a rare specimen: a central Soviet newspaper without a censor number. Summoned by a furious Shcherbakov that evening, Ortenberg said the alternative had been not to publish the paper at all. A month later he was unceremoniously dismissed.[61]

Concern about not "pleasing Goebbels" also showed up in other cases. In the summer of 1943 *Krasnaia zvezda* described a new Hero of the Soviet Union named Aleksei Maresiev. Early in 1942 his plane was shot down near Novgorod, but he crawled for eighteen days to reach the Soviet side. Even though his legs had to be amputated, he resumed flying and downing German planes. But it was indicative of the propaganda's main trend that Stalin refused to give *Pravda* the green light for its article on Maresiev, commenting in the margins of the page proofs of Boris Polevoi's article that Goebbels might use the case to claim that the Red Army was exhausted.[62]

Just one work of fiction was allowed to describe the deadly Soviet disasters of 1941: Grossman's novel *The People Immortal*, serialized in *Krasnaia zvezda* in July and August 1942. But Stalin personally excluded the work from contention for the Stalin Prize, perhaps because of author's Jewish background, but more likely because the main character dies. In general, however, Grossman was relatively untouched by censorship; in July 1943 Ortenberg managed to save a passage in another text by him about shell-shocked and dying soldiers, four months after a censor disallowed the writer Konstantin Simonov from referring to the "remainders" of a regiment and a soldier's sadness because "half of his division had perished."[63]

When the first pictures of American soldiers killed in action appeared in the American press in the fall of 1942, many contemporaries believed they assisted in the drive for U.S. War Bonds. The Soviet media never carried photos of dead Red Army soldiers, unless they were prisoners of war: choosing to die on duty might be unavoidable and could make for an inspiring story, but Stalin believed the sight of soldiers killed in action would demoralize the people; he also never signed any of the few obituaries. Ortenberg believed that his reasoning could be summarized as follows: "There are too many losses. We're not going to make Hitler glad."[64]

In line with a Russian tradition not to systematically record one's own military losses, Moscow obtained the first realistic report of Red Army losses only in early 1942.[65] But such figures were publicized several times. In the middle of July 1941 the Bureau announced that in the first three weeks of the war the Red Army had lost "no more than 250,000 people killed, wounded, and missing in action." When the German command claimed to have taken 895,000 Red Army prisoners in the first six weeks, the official Soviet retort referred only to people killed, wounded, and missing in action. In these and almost all subsequent statistics, the capture of Red Army troops never happened. Officially Red Army losses in those first six weeks came to "around 600,000." The propaganda simply denied any and all German figures on this topic—as, for example, of the capture of 380,000 Red Army members near Kiev by September 1941.[66]

The published figure for the first two months was 700,000, and for the first time the figure was broken down: 150,000 Red Army members had been killed, 440,000 had been wounded, and 110,000 had gone missing. (In drafts all four figures were higher.)[67] Responding to a radio speech by Hitler of October 3, 1941, Shcherbakov acknowledged 1,128,000 Red Army losses, of which 230,000 were killed, 720,000 wounded, and 178,000 missing.[68] In November 1941, in surveying the first four months of the war, Stalin mentioned

350,000 killed, 1,020,000 wounded, and 378,000 missing, thus implying a total loss of 1,748,000. Later that month, when the German command claimed to have inflicted a tremendous loss of eight million (including 3,725,600 prisoners), the Bureau, while referring to "laughable fabrications of the Hitlerite counterfeiters," greatly exceeded Stalin's most recent figure: it became official that in five months of war, 490,000 were killed, "up to" 1,112,000 were wounded, and 520,000 were missing, producing a total loss of 2,122,000.[69]

Seven months later, in June 1942, total Red Army losses were officially twice as high: 4,500,000 killed, wounded, or taken captive. This statistic was unusual in replacing the category of the "missing" with those captured as prisoners. The Soviet citizens and others were told that due to the vast difference in the quality of medical provisions, as many as 70 percent of the Soviet wounded returned to army service, whereas a mere 40 percent of the German wounded did. In October, the General Staff calculated that the losses were 10,406,079, of which nearly 6.4 million wounded (most of whom said to have recovered) and 1,526,712 killed, but the media reported no official total then, nor at the end of 1942 or even in February 1943, when the Bureau spoke of a "false invention by the German-fascist rogues" of Red Army losses (namely 12,800,000 killed or wounded and 5,400,000 prisoners), a count it called incompatible with Germany's heavy losses.[70]

Only in June 1943, for the first time in a whole year, did Stalin sanction the release of a new Soviet figure. Red Army losses in two years had been 4,200,000 "killed and missing in action." No one dared ask why wounded or captured soldiers were not mentioned, or how this could be squared with the previous year's 4,500,000. One year later the figure of total losses was said to include Red Army members "killed, imprisoned, and missing in action." Thus again the wounded went unmentioned, but the prisoners were back. This three-year total was put at 5,300,000.[71]

The Bureau also issued figures for German military losses along the entire Soviet-German front, meaning dead, wounded, and prisoners. During the first three weeks those losses were "no less than a million"; three weeks later the number had risen to "over 1,500,000." *Pravda*'s front page quoted an American radio commentator as mentioning secret German statistics that matched these figures. The American had spoken of 1,250,000 German military losses in the first month, or one-third of all of the German military employed against the Red Army.[72] Published Soviet statistics for the first two months mentioned "over 2,000,000" German losses (as compared to the "up to 2,000,000" from a draft). And Shcherbakov, responding to Hitler's radio announcement of October 1941 that 2.5 million Red Army members had been killed, said that the German army losses on the Eastern Front amounted to "over 3,000,000 killed, wounded, and prisoners," thus equaling German losses "in the past world war on all fronts during two years of military activities." Ehrenburg repeated that figure with reference to the first fifteen weeks of war.[73]

Stalin himself gave an estimate at the end of 1941. Surveying the previous four months, he mentioned "over 4.5 million" on November 6 and "4.5 million" the next day. The Bureau's claim about the first five months, issued soon thereafter, came to "about 6,000,000."[74] The highest of all the Soviet figures of German losses appeared in June 1942. In one year of fighting, a special Bureau statement said, the Red Army had inflicted "about 10,000,000" German losses. Now for the first time a Soviet figure specified the German death toll: "no less than 3,500,000." But the 10 million mark did not stand. By November 1942, in Stalin's words, the Red Army had "removed from service over eight million enemy soldiers and officers," and in February 1943 he spoke of "up to nine million German-fascist soldiers and officers, of whom no less than four million were killed on the battlefield."[75] Numerous times that year Stalin or the Bureau also mentioned figures for German losses in shorter periods.[76]

In June 1943, two years after the German invasion, Stalin once more took the liberty of lowering the announced figure. "Germany and its allies" had lost 6,400,000 people through killing or wounding; for some reason Stalin did not mention prisoners. That he personally lowered the figure is beyond doubt, for Shcherbakov's drafts referred to 9,300,000 (of whom "no less than 4,300,000" were dead).⁷⁷ This statement also stood out as the one and only Soviet figure openly including non-Germans fighting on the German side. The last public reference during the war to a total was made on the invasion's third anniversary. The count of German soldiers and officers killed or captured—this time excluding the wounded—was "over 7,800,000."⁷⁸

In short, after 1941 the propaganda did not offer figures of Red Army members killed, but total "losses" were provided often and were higher than one would expect: more than 2.1 million in the first five months, 4.5 million in June 1942, 4.2 million in June 1943, and a staggering 5.3 million in June 1944.⁷⁹ Providing such high figures seemed safe to Stalin because the Germans supposedly lost many more. Separate totals for German dead, thus excluding other kinds of "losses," were released once: a minimum of four million, proclaimed in February 1943. Meanwhile the figures for total enemy "losses," almost always without reference to Germany's allies, climaxed at about 10 million in mid-1942, to be downgraded thereafter to more than eight million (November 1942), up to nine million (February 1943), and 6.4 million (June 1943). In the final wartime count, in June 1944, the figure stood at more than 7.8 million, well above the equally fictional 5.3 million "losses" of the Red Army. As noted, sometimes numbers for the wounded or prisoners were mentioned, sometimes not; consistency was lacking.

Dying as Normal and Heroic

During the Great War that began in 1914, Russian propaganda glorified soldiers who performed a feat of arms and survived. Such men also appeared in the Soviet propaganda beginning in 1941. Particularly numerous were those downing German planes with a rifle shot.⁸⁰ But in general the propaganda justified the loss of life and eventually came to glorify it as sacrificial. A typical early case was Konstantin Simonov's poem "Scorn of Death," first published in *Krasnaia zvezda* in July 1941. Commemorating a gunner who stopped four tanks until a fifth one crushed him, it quoted him as saying, "We Bolsheviks have hearts forged from steel." It concludes, "Learn, comrade, to act as Poliakov did! Learn how it is necessary to scorn danger in battle, and if need be, to die for your Motherland." An anonymous report supposedly from the Western Front in February 1942 describing the start of a successful counterattack was also typical: "Lieutenant Golovanov, having appraised the full complexity of the situation that had come about, addressed the fighters: 'Comrades! There's very few of us, the forces of the enemy, as you see, supersede ours many times, but we must defend this line or die.' 'We shall die, but we won't retreat!' the fighters replied in unison."[81]

Steadfastness including death by choice was presented as natural because imprisonment by the Germans or their allies was "worse than death"—it would mean only suffering. But that prospect always remained auxiliary to the notion of obedience; reports brought home the message that it was a crime to even *consider* surrender or retreat. A declared hero once explained on the radio how he set off a mine that initially failed to explode. The risks were not worth thinking about: "When going out on a military mission one must forget about oneself and the fear of death, and devote all one's will, all one's thoughts and energy, to the execution of the order."[82] Fiction such as Dovzhenko's "The Renegade" offered the same message. In most people's definition, heroism goes beyond ordinary obligations and cannot be demanded. And yet this was precisely what Soviet propaganda did. As *Pravda*'s editorial warned shortly after Rostov's second fall, all soldiers "must be ready to die a hero's death."[83]

Officially, of course, as the press also wrote, writers merely had to use the bountiful facts at hand—the "thousands of occurrences of individual and collective heroism shown by the Red Army and Fleet"—and "create generalizations from these facts." Stalin was not pleased with the results, however, and on August 13, 1942, the Central Committee secretly warned the central press that reports by front correspondents suffered from two flaws: they disclosed either too much (using staff reports) or too little (repeating Bureau statements). The main task of the front correspondents became to show admirable *individuals*. These soldiers and commanders were capable, staunch, obedient, courageous, smart, and full of hate for "the

Germans." And they displayed "selflessness" (*samootverzhennost*); that is, they gave a low priority to their own life.[84] After the warning, the media such as radio's *Latest News* began emitting an ever larger stream of interchangeable tales of military heroism and feats. The Bureau joined in and during the war mentioned a numbing 14,400 names of Soviet soldiers.[85]

Still, the central papers, whether military or civilian, were obliged to "reduce to a minimum" the mention of names of commanders of units and formations, and to omit not only their location but also the entire Red Army front in question. Civilian republican, krai, and oblast papers never published such information (except in published letters received from the front, where commanders might be named). Thus phrases such as the "fighters of unit X" were used.[86] Soviet troops could not be identified by name at all if they had relatives in occupied territory. The effect was surreal in the case of Jewish army members. A battalion commander named Leonid Gofman had left family in Kiev; censorship replaced that city with "territory occupied by the Germans" so as "not to expose Comrade Gofman's family to repression." It was 1943.[87]

The instructions of August 1942 to report about individuals did not imply artistic license. Censors could and did remove unlikely elements. One manuscript article in early 1943 included the following: "The machine-gunner was already dead, but his hand machine-gun continued shooting until the last cartridge dropped from the disc. The Komsomol man killed the hated enemies even when he was dead." The military censor deleted it.[88]

That said, from the beginning canonical tales appeared about military men who died for their comrades. Also intended to cover up military disasters and setbacks, their core message was that these deaths had produced the deaths of a higher number of enemy soldiers, and thus had advanced the march toward victory.[89] One of the first such tales involved Captain Nikolai Gastello, a pilot who upon being hit did not use a parachute but crashed his plane on German tanks on June 26, 1941. The first mention was in the Bureau report for July 5, 1941: "Squadron Commander Captain Gastelo [*sic*] accomplished a heroic feat. An enemy antiaircraft shell hit his plane's gasoline tank. The fearless commander directed his flaming plane into a concentration of enemy cars and gasoline tanks. Dozens of German cars and cisterns exploded along with the hero's plane." He quickly became a Hero of the Soviet Union. Soviet Belarusian propaganda called him "Nikalai Hastelo," unforgettable and fearless "son of the Belarusian people." The three other members of the crew received only the Order of the Patriotic War, Second Degree. There were many crash landings on enemy infantry, especially in the beginning of the war, but Gastello consistently received the most attention, obviously because someone decided that he was a role model.[90] The pilot Viktor Talalikhin, whom Soviet Belarusian propaganda was also allowed to claim as Belarusian, one night in August 1941 heroically crashed into a German bomber and put it out of operation. He spoke on the radio and died in action two months later. But Gastello remained more prominent.[91]

The best known heroes in infantry were the "Panfilovites," a group of soldiers from the 316th Infantry Division commanded by Major General Ivan Panfilov. On November 16, 1941, at the railroad junction of Dubosekovo, east of Volokolamsk, two groups of German tanks attacked and in several hours of fierce fighting left hundreds of dead, wounded, and missing in action among the division's 1075th Regiment. The next day, before news of the setback at Dubosekovo had made its way up the ranks, at General Zhukov's request the division was renamed the 8th Guards Division in view of its staunchness. On November 18 General Panfilov was killed and became one of a handful of fallen commanders to be granted an obituary. The mythical tale that then developed was probably designed to cover up the contradiction between the staunch public image of the division and the crushing defeat of one of its regiments.

The first reports about the events relating to the German attack appeared in print at the end of November 1941, at the apparent initiative of the correspondents of the papers *Komsomolskaia pravda* and *Krasnaia zvezda*. The Komsomol paper on November 26 mentioned "a group of Red Army men headed by political officer [*politruk*] Diev," who had stopped a German tank advance for over four hours. *Krasnaia zvezda* did not mention any details either, except that eighteen of an alleged fifty-four German tanks had been destroyed by the soldiers, who had fought to the death. The next day the paper carried an editorial by the literary editor Aleksandr Krivitskii that proclaimed there had been "twenty-eight fallen heroes." He and Ortenberg had invented the figure. Diev had led the men, Krivitskii claimed, and declared during the fight, "Not a step back!" All of them "perished but did not let the enemy go through." One other Soviet soldier, however, had "raised his arms. Several guardists simultaneously, without prior agreement, without any order, shot the coward and traitor."[92]

An article that soon became canonical appeared on January 22, 1942, again in *Krasnaia zvezda*. Krivitskii now listed twenty-eight names. So as to make it more likely that the German casualty rate had exceeded the Soviets', he added the presence of German infantry. He also described the German tanks as heavily armored and identified a low-ranking Soviet soldier as the commander, so as to hide the 1075th Regiment's awkwardly small size. Krivitskii explained that Diev had been the nickname of Vasilii Klochkov, the junior political officer of the regiment's 4th Company, who had actually said the following: "Russia is great, but there's nowhere to retreat: behind us is Moscow." Using an ancient mythological motif, Krivitskii claimed to have heard this from a dying survivor of the battle who had reached his own side after wandering for days. In fact the names of the other dead of November 16 were then—and still are—unclear: in March 1942 Klochkov's body and just five others were found at the site. The grave of the alleged dying survivor was never found.

Other newspapers also started writing about what had become the "Panfilovites." The timing was right, for the Red Army had just retaken all of the Moscow oblast. *Pravda* noted, "Among them were Russians, Ukrainians, and Kazakhs—the living embodiment of the Leninist-Stalinist friendship of the peoples of the Soviet Union."[93] On July 21, 1942, the twenty-eight were made Heroes of the Soviet Union. The writer Nikolai Tikhonov published a poem about them, and more publications followed. The division commissar who had survived probably knew that the facts were wrong, but it was not in his interest to protest. The former commander and the commissar of the regiment were even less likely to resist the myth, for it saved them from execution; immediately after the battle they had been discharged for allowing heavy losses and an enemy advance.

Over the course of 1942 Moscow discovered that five of the named men were still alive. Two Panfilovites had been taken from the battlefield, treated in hospitals, and sent back to army service. Shcherbakov was asked to sanction a radio broadcast about this, but he declined.[94] Two others were taken prisoner by the Germans; by August 1942 Soviet investigators were questioning them. The fifth living Panfilovite, Private Daniil Kozhubergenov, spent just a few days as a POW and then managed to rejoin the Red Army. Arrested in the spring of 1942, he was placed in a penal battalion and sustained severe injuries near Rzhev. To cover up the official shame of having been captured alive, already in January 1942 the regiment commander replaced his name with the similar name of a dead soldier, Askar Kozhubergenov. The message remained that twenty-eight men had fought and died at one place and time.

There was an analogous myth with regard to the actions near a Crimean village of five marines from Sevastopol. On November 7, 1941, October Revolution Day, these men, led by the political officer Nikolai Filchenkov, supposedly strapped on grenades and threw themselves under approaching German tanks, destroying ten, and "stopped the enemy." One, Vasilii Tsibulko, supposedly told others about the event just before dying of his wounds. It is unknown whether the Red Army command ever encouraged such attacks on tanks. (The Japanese army trained for them in 1945.) But leaving aside the question of why they did not just *throw* the grenades, their opponent, the 11th German Army, had no tanks at all at that time. The bodies of the marines and Tsibulko's grave were never found. Particularly after October 23, 1942, when the five were made Heroes of the Soviet Union, the myth of the marines evidently was meant to suppress the memory of the recent enforced retreat from the entire Crimean Peninsula. Their fame grew further when the writer Andrei Platonov published a story about them.[95]

In the following year came another story about a suicide attack. Most likely the following had happened. One day in February 1943, near the village of Chernushka, near Velikie Luki, Private Aleksandr Matrosov managed to approach the ventilation opening of a pillbox manned by two German machine-gunners and tried to kill them. He was shot and fell on the ventilation opening. As one German pushed him away, the other temporarily ceased fire. During that spell Red Army men advanced, and the Germans fled. Matrosov's comrades found his dead body before the embrasure. A legend was born in the press that he had deliberately covered and thus silenced the machine-gun, enabling his comrades to approach and kill the Germans manning it. The platoon commander wrote in a front-line newspaper that Matrosov's blood "choked" the German gun. The alleged suicide attack story ignored that even a mere rifle shot throws a person to the ground. *Pravda*'s editorial claimed that self-sacrifice was an eternal trait of Russian soldiers, who had always been acclaimed for it.[96]

In June 1943 Matrosov was declared a Hero of the Soviet Union, and on September 8 Stalin personally and publicly underlined his significance. It had all happened on the twenty-fifth anniversary of the Red Army, February 22, 1943, so Stalin claimed. (There is no documentary evidence that February 27, mentioned in earlier reports, was the real date.) Stalin's special order said, "Comrade Matrosov's feat should serve as an example of fighting courage and heroism for all Red Army soldiers." Indeed it was official that there were *hundreds* of such cases, some actually predating Matrosov's. Probably due to undeclared competition between army units, every soldier found dead near an enemy pillbox was declared a hero. But Stalin's intervention incomparably elevated one of them in particular.[97]

By and large Stalin's propaganda successfully controlled the coverage of the fighting. If the Bureau said nothing about a setback or success at the front, the entire propaganda system stayed silent, unless special permission was given. It was an extreme case of the underreporting endemic to modern war machines. At first the absence of real reporting on battles placed countless military and civilians in danger.[98] The key question, perhaps unanswerable, is whether the draconian controls over war reporting not only helped maintain Stalin's control over the country but also contributed to mobilizing it.

Ehrenburg thought such silence was counterproductive, referring to general bafflement at "not being told." So did an early letter by an engineer, also sent to the Bureau, that called the coverage disrespectful. But Soviet citizens expected far less from the government than their Western counterparts did. A study of the United Kingdom at war has argued, "Lies themselves were not important: few on the Home Front would have argued that they needed to know everything, or denied that it was sometimes necessary to publicise lies in order to fool the enemy. What damaged morale was the suspicion that the government was holding back facts because it either distrusted the Home Front or thought it not worth informing." It would be unwise to assume that the same applied to most citizens of the USSR. Although they might want to be informed, they did not expect to be.[99]

Stalin's other key interventions were his mistaken public prediction of final victory by the end of 1942 and the order to glorify alleged suicide attacks. It seems likely that within the Red Army the war hero stories lowered the value of human lives, confirming commanders in their view that saving soldiers was not important.[100] As for the impact on the rest of the population, Ehrenburg's memoirs, which skirt the issue of the veracity of the reports, state that he and "all those whom [he] came across" always were deeply moved by "self-sacrifice, the death of the soldier who gives up his life voluntarily to save his comrade." Ortenberg recalled the deep impact of certain articles about heroes; many readers' letters responded to Dovzhenko's story "The Renegade," and "pilgrims" began visiting the home of the peasant who had saved the regimental banner.[101] In 1942 an American journalist born in Belarus visited a woman friend in Kuibyshev, whose husband had been killed near Leningrad. She had heavily marked up a newspaper article about the Sevastopol marines.

> "With their own lives," said Natasha, "the dear ones broke up a tank attack—with their own lives." Slowly, devoutly, as

if reciting a prayer, she read the names of the five marines.... She paused, her eyes on the paper, on the names she had just recited. Then she added, "You see why I'm hopeful? We have millions like them—millions, I tell you. In the end, no matter what the Germans do to us now, we shall win. We must win. We won't be conquered."

In his diary Vsevolod Vishnevskii, a writer overseeing colleagues in the Baltic Fleet, also mentioned the marines without any skepticism.[102] Indications that the civilians might have been skeptical about this hero propaganda are hard to find.

Some Western scholars conclude that the propaganda about individual feats, true or not, "bolstered morale," "played an important if not crucial part in propaganda warfare, enabling the Soviet people to stop Hitlerism," and "inspired other similar suicides of men who were moved to emulate [Matrosov's] heroism."[103] Only few Russian historians question in writing the Matrosov and Gastello tales, and virtually all believe those resonated. They had a "strong emotional impact on large masses of people, especially young people," one writes; they "provoked a general desire, on the one hand, to take revenge on the enemy for the death of one's comrades and, on the other hand, to be just like those comrades and fight with ever-greater courage and energy.... An overwhelming majority of the Soviet people responded to the symbols of heroism exactly as the propaganda machine intended them to do."[104] Even a generally skeptical historian, referring to one letter, concludes that contemporaries believed the story of the Sevastopol marines, and that the stories about self-sacrificing soldiers such as these contributed greatly to the mobilization.[105] It seems best to conclude that many Soviet citizens were probably inspired by stories that they suspected were partly or wholly untrue. But given the scarcity of the evidence (and the lack of access to NKVD surveillance reports), it would be unwise to accept this for a fact.

3

A Single Forced Labor Camp

For the hinterland, the slogan "Everything for the Front" described well what was expected of the people there. Through a range of laws and regulations, some predating the German invasion, Stalin subordinated the entire unoccupied Soviet space to the interests of the armed forces. Virtually all the citizens were "mobilized" into forced labor; they had to work, and they had no say about the place and duration. If one wishes to deal with the key goal here—establishing the role that the press and the radio were supposed to play in the militarization of life and the extent to which they played it—it is necessary first to get a sense of the decrees and orders that impacted industrial workers and peasants.

Before the German invasion, close to two-thirds of the population of the Soviet Union lived in villages. Thereafter far less than half did, for many able-bodied villagers departed for work in the city or joined the army: of the initial 35.4 million able-bodied adult peasants (including those who later fell under German occupation), only 15 million remained two years later. In the east of the country, the number of workers and employees increased by about 20 percent, but the number of able-bodied peasants dropped by the same measure or still more, as in the Urals and western Siberia.[1]

Ordinary citizens heard Stalin say something about the *tyl*, or hinterland, on just five occasions: in July 1941 and during the October Revolution anniversaries. On the first occasion he announced that the interests of the Red Army would always have priority. The key issue in the rear was *discipline*, he said: "we" had to "mercilessly" combat "disorganizers," deserters, and "panic-mongers," and to "destroy" spies and saboteurs. He did not cite a need for special measures or new laws.[2]

Forced Labor All Around

Various repressive labor measures had been imposed before 1941, most likely in preparation for war. In June 1940 it became a criminal offense for persons with a regular job at a state company to miss all or part of the working day, for example by arriving more than twenty minutes late (punished by up to six months of "corrective" labor at the enterprise and up to a 25 percent loss of pay), or by quitting without permission (two to four months' imprisonment). Before, to dismiss delinquent workers had been mandatory; the 1940 law eliminated this practice, as the goal became to preclude people's escape from punishment.[3] But if the oppression meant to intimidate, the first results were meager. Many people disobeyed the decree, and managers, trade union officials, and local People's Court judges ignored it for months. All the same, in the first six months after the law went into force, 1.77 million people were convicted for absenteeism and more than 321,500 for illegally quitting.[4] In the fall of 1940 teenagers began to be conscripted for the so-called industrial labor reserves, which amounted to de facto forced labor. In the five years that followed, between 800,000 and one million were called up for either a two-year trade or railway trade school (for boys ages fourteen and fifteen) or for a six-month factory training school (for boys and girls sixteen and seventeen). Simply removing the teenagers from their parents, the state placed them in barracks. Officially by 1942 there were close to 815,000 such labor reserve students. A new Chief Administration of Labor Reserves assigned those who graduated to four years at factories, mines, building projects, or railroads, where their workday began with an early bugle call or drum and military drills.[5] That these rules were already in place made it seem unnecessary to introduce more than a lengthening of the working day by three hours one week after the start of the German invasion.[6]

But discontent ran high. In textile factories in the Ivanovo oblast, the wages of many workers, who were mostly women, fell by 30 to 50 percent; they could not meet their "norms," or daily production targets, because of changes in production and a lack of supplies and qualified personnel due to the army draft. Moreover there was less to eat, and use of the factory canteen increased tenfold. When, in the middle of October 1941, without any announcement, authorities began dismantling factory machines and, it was rumored, taking away all the bread, the dissatisfaction came out into the open. Vandalism began and factory party leaders, a director, and even two NKVD officers were beaten up. Workers shouted things like "We won't allow the machines to be dismantled, let them remain for Hitler and we shall work for him," and went on strike. "We won't allow the Communists to kill us with famine," some workers said. In the end four prominent rebels received the death penalty (commuted in one case), and some fifteen others were sentenced to eight to ten years.[7] It is not known if other industrial regions saw similar unrest; certainly no decree or law was introduced in response to it.

A new law in December 1941 dealt with the military industry, which was entirely (except for airplane factories) run by the NKVD. Now this industry was itself militarized: the law declared people working there to be mobilized and renamed their bosses "commanders." Unsanctioned departure became desertion, punishable by five to eight years of imprisonment. Those guilty of absenteeism received a lower bread ration. As the war wore on, every site that supplied the armed forces was declared to be part of the defense industry, and thus subject to the law: the coal mines (June 1942), textile factories (October 1942), synthetic rubber and tire factories (July 1943), and the gas industry (March 1944).[8] Until August 1943 not even women who had no one to take care of their young children were exempt from the rules. The harsh law also applied to young people who had managed to avoid the labor reserve schools and work sites, even (from August 1942) those under sixteen.[9]

Other labor measures went into force in February 1942. A decree mobilized city dwellers for work in industry or construction. Applying to males sixteen to fifty-five and females sixteen to forty-five (except for the labor reserve children and the women with children under eight without family members who could stay with them), it stated that those refusing would be sentenced to forced labor at their place of residence for up to a year.[10] Peasants who supposedly underperformed also became criminals. A required minimum amount of work by the *kolkhozniks*, or collective farm members, measured in so-called labor days, had existed since 1939, but beginning on February 15 those who without a proper explanation did not meet the minimum faced severe penalties: up to six months of forced labor, confiscation of up to 25 percent of their daily pay, expulsion from the farm, and hence the loss of their garden. Farm officials who did not report offenses faced prosecution. Moreover the minimum of labor days was raised, depending on the region, to 100, 120, or 150 (up from 60, 80, and 100), and regional and local authorities were allowed to raise (or lower) them by 20 percent. Children of collective farmers ages twelve to sixteen now had to work fifty labor days. Every year on average around 160,000 peasants were prosecuted under this law. Almost a quarter of the more than 151,000 cases initiated within five months in 1942 were dismissed, and it seems that in the industrial regions, where the minimums were lowest and thus easier to attain, the maximum penalty was applied to only about 15 percent of the violators.[11] But none of this made the threat of severe punishment less acute.

Two months later the one remaining source of labor was enlisted: city dwellers and (nonpeasant) inhabitants of villages. Now republican and provincial administrations could draft males among them ages fourteen to fifty-five and females fourteen to fifty for labor.[12]

The overall result of the various regulations was that all civilians became forced laborers, and thus Stalin could indeed proclaim on May Day 1942 the existence of a single *lager*, or camp, in the hinterland. The word sounded ominous.[13]

There also existed a practice called "labor duty," whereby men and women ages sixteen to fifty-five guarded railways, roads, and canals or worked at construction sites. In August 1942 regulations were issued. Labor duty differed from mobilization into nonmilitary industry in three ways: its duration was limited (to a maximum of two months), workers and peasants were outsourced from work they already had, and shirkers faced military tribunals of the NKVD or of the army.[14] Finally, in April and May 1943, it was decided that transportation by rail and water fell under the regulations of the *state of war*, "deserters" from which faced three to ten years of labor camp, if not worse.[15]

Despite the severe penalties and the dependence of workers on food rations supplied by their employers, the severe labor laws were widely violated, mainly because of appalling conditions at work or at home. Hours of waiting at canteens were not exceptional. Many village teenagers found it hard to adjust to the regularity of industrial work and instead wanted to help with the harvest back home.[16] In three years military tribunals sentenced more than 814,000 "deserters" from defense enterprises and transport work sites to labor camps, and close to 625,000 "willful quitters" (according to the June 1940 law) to two to four months of prison. Many of those sentenced in this way went into hiding. Most convictions—over 3,129,000—were for absenteeism.[17] But there were also prisoner amnesties, simply because Stalin's state needed workers. In the first year of war with Germany, amnesty was granted to those convicted of quitting factory jobs and juveniles with sentences of less than two years. More amnesties followed near the end of the war, of people convicted under the law of December 1941 who had returned to their place of work (December 1944) and of pregnant inmates and female inmates with infants (January 1945).[18]

Gulag convicts composed about 3 percent of the total civilian working population. At the time of the German invasion there were

2.3 million prisoners inside the eighty-five large corrective labor camps and the many other Gulag sites—the prisons, labor colonies, and special settlements. In three years, when more than a million were drafted into the Red Army and prisoners died at rates far above prewar levels (in 1942, one in four), the number was nearly halved, to 1.2 million. This official forced labor detention system hardly contributed to the Soviet Union's most intense mobilization ever. An economic and administrative burden, it contributed very little output in return.[19]

Even more than in industry, centralization and militarization in agriculture knew no bounds and pushed laborers to the brink of famine. Every locality, however small, retained a Communist Party apparatus in place to supervise the integrity of the collective farm system. Local party members joined the army in 1941, but thousands of others moved in from cities and towns, and many village soviet chairmen were appointed as local party representatives. Although late in 1942 not even one in five collective farms had a party organization, three out of four did have a representative of the Komsomol, the party youth organization. The local authorities, themselves privileged with special rations, closed distribution rooms, and special hospitals, became harsher then ever. The information available suggests that many even established the times peasants had to get up, go to the field, and feed the horses.[20]

The delivery to the state of grain, potatoes, and other agricultural products took precedence over payment in kind for the labor days. Often also stocks and seeds were taken away. As historians put it, this "literally emptied" the villages; "up to the last kernel was taken from the peasants."[21] Ruthless extraction was official policy. Even late in 1944 local agencies of the People's Commissariat of Supplies Procurement imposed sanctions on farms with small arrears and facing transportation problems or labor shortages. The deputy people's commissar of agriculture demanded that requisitions be "relentless." Wherever gardens supplied peasants a bare minimum of food, this served as the pretext to confiscate the farm harvest almost in full for hardly any compensation.[22] Not until the very last weeks of the war were collective farms or their individual members allowed to sell bread at the market.[23]

The producers of the harvests, mostly women, received almost nothing in return: per day on average a cup of grain and one potato, and next to no milk or meat. In the Russian, Ukrainian, and Belarusian republics payment in kind was two to three times less than before the invasion. Meanwhile payment in rubles was savaged by the high inflation.[24] More than ever the peasants' own gardens became their lifeline—but even these tiny plots were included in state delivery plans, and the cultivators were ordered to surrender meat, milk, eggs, potatoes, vegetables, and wool. And many peasants became not just morally in debt to the state (as the propaganda stated), but also financially so.[25]

In short, forced labor proliferated. It no longer remained concentrated on the detention sites but was imposed on virtually all civilians. Peasants faced more obligations than ever, and the workers, being officially mobilized, could be and were sent to destinations exclusively determined by the authorities.[26]

Desertion and Selflessness

The secretiveness became intense. It used to be that only laws governing "political" offenses were classified, but the criminal labor laws of the years 1940 to 1943 were entirely secret, and ordinary citizens did not know what was in them.[27] The texts of the December 1941 law on the military industry and the August 1942 decree about "labor duty" did not appear in the media either. The amnesties remained secret as well (except for the one affecting exiled Polish citizens), and censorship disguised most of the formalized child labor.[28] Even the very concept of labor duty, though not top secret, hardly ever appeared in print.[29] Probably more than one reason explained the secrecy: amnesties replenished the Red Army, the labor policies were deemed demoralizing, and Stalin felt that the enemy might benefit, in his propaganda or otherwise, and that the United States and other allies might disapprove.

The single media source from which citizens could hear about the laws of June 1940 and December 1941 were notices on *Trud*'s back page. In the town of Izhevsk, one article reported, an "inveterate labor deserter" and "production disorganizer," whose previous infraction had been his failure to return after recovering from illness, had been sentenced to eight years. Elsewhere a worker posted to a military factory who failed to show up had also been sentenced to eight years. A specialist and two workers who had left their evacuated factory and returned to Moscow had received either six or eight years. Typically following such reports was condemnation of poor implementation elsewhere; for example, a public prosecutor had "established that at a number of enterprises, the record of the workforce is badly kept and that there is insufficient control over the severe maintenance of the working time schedule, which creates the possibility for transgressors of labor discipline to shirk accountability and to remain unpunished," and a shop leader had been sentenced to one year of corrective labor for inadequate record keeping and for "delay in handing over deserters' cases to the justice organs."[30]

A *Trud* editorial later in the year demanded legal and moral judgments on supervisors' toleration of "desertion from the labor front": "A commander who shows indulgence to a deserter and does not hand him over to the court, breaks discipline in his collective and commits a crime against the motherland. Such a commander must himself be sentenced with the full severity of the law. He shall get a strong condemnation from every honest worker." Soon came a report of the prison or forced labor sentences imposed on a deputy factory director, a personnel department head, a shop leader, and a director.[31]

But evidently not all judges were as harsh as Moscow wished. That same month, following an unpublished Supreme Court resolution (and shortly before Stalin was to give upbeat comments on the selfless conduct of people in the hinterland), the People's Commissariat of Justice made it known that "many" judges were losing the fight against "disorganizers." Over a third of the "cases" in the Kuibyshev, Penza, and Sverdlovsk oblasts were investigated too late. There were "many cases of disgraceful red tape among leaders of enterprises and offices, who often for weeks do not pass on materials about the absentees to the court. Not infrequently, people's judges are also guilty of red tape." Therefore, *Trud* reported, the judges had been ordered to handle unauthorized departure within seventy-two hours and absenteeism within forty-eight hours; sentences were to be implemented at once.[32]

The media did publish the decrees of February 1942, mobilizing for work in industry or construction and criminalizing underperforming peasants. The latter decree appeared after a delay of two months alongside references to the raised minimum labor days and the agricultural mobilization of nonpeasants.[33] There were also reports on the overall results. Moscow's trade unions had "organized a mass exodus of housewives to the field of Moscow region state farms." A typical headline was "Hundreds of Thousands of City Dwellers Selflessly Work the Fields: Let Us Help the Collective and State Farms to Quickly Gather the Harvest."[34] The regional press reported that collective farm chairmen went to court for releasing too much grain for the internal needs of the farm and were sentenced to five or ten years, and it published warnings by oblast and raion party committees against leniency.[35]

Izvestiia asserted in July 1943 that the raised minimum number of labor days had been a success: the vast majority of *kolkhozniks* were meeting them.[36] In reality the farms' unpopularity and inefficiency, an irrational increase in the area under cultivation, and a shortage of hands combined to make for small harvests. According to calculations not corrected for territorial losses to Germany, the collective farms of the Russian Federative Republic supplied almost half the grain in 1942 than two years earlier. The next year the proportion was still less than 40 percent. As for potatoes and milk, in 1942 the state received from all the Soviet republics at best half of the amounts of 1940.[37] (That the state did receive far more meat was mainly because of the slaughter of animals who could not be fed.)[38]

These actual conditions were the setting for denunciations of the "enemy" of the *kolkhoz*: the "loafer and idler."[39] Already in April 1942 *Pravda* implied that there were more than a few egoistic peasants, "a certain proportion of backward collective farmers who, hiding under the collective farm, use the privileges provided to the collective farms and the collective farmers to make their personal farm the main thing, and the general—secondary. Shirking from work, the lazy ones are becoming parasites of the collective farms, and essentially live off the honest collective farmers."[40] The press also often demanded severe punishment of grain thieves.[41]

Every July there appeared long joint government and party statements on the upcoming harvest. That was also the debut in print of "last year's mistakes." In 1942 it was said that "in a number of oblasts, krais, and republics, as a result of bad preparation, the harvest [of 1941] took excessively long," resulting in quantitative and qualitative losses.[42] In 1943 the government and party published an even harsher statement, and *Pravda* demanded harvest work take place "in a military fashion."[43] Last year's mistakes included a failure by "several" local officials and party leaders to arrange the timely repair and productive use of combines. "Many" had been deficient in the use of horse-drawn machines, in the organization of manual mowing, and in the binding of wheat into sheaves. The mistakes of the leaders of various regions where the plan had not been met were "serious." One error was not to "organize the delivery of the grain to the state from the very beginning of the harvest," another an "underestimation of the need for all the collective farmers to be involved and used in field work and of the mobilization of the able-bodied population of the cities and the raion centers." In order words, the grave error had been to leave the peasants with some grain and to absolve some people from working. The July 1943 document also gave detailed instructions: local leaders should inform farm leaders that much grain was left behind after threshing; from every brigade, a day guard and a night guard had to be appointed, as well as "patrols under the direct subordination of the collective farm chairman, no later than ten to fifteen days after the ripening of the grain." The "justice organs" had to severely punish "theft" of grain and the like, "up to application of the law of August 7, 1932 about the preservation of social [socialist] property"—which could mean death penalties. (Whether it did so in practice is unclear.)

On July 28, 1942, the Central Committee, bypassing the formal government, sent a sharply worded secret letter about grain losses to all raion party secretaries, political departments of state farms and machinery and tractor stations (MTS), and to raion, oblast, and krai newspapers. The papers were ordered to "develop a wide press coverage of the matter of the struggle against losses and to show by vivid examples how one must and how one must not supervise the harvest collection."[44] An enthusiastic reaction was orchestrated; collective farm chairmen in one offending oblast sent an open letter to Stalin saying, "We must justify the great faith of the Motherland and are justifying it!"[45] But most coverage of the harvest was very stale, as in the following radio fragment:

> Listen to a speech by Academy Member Ivan Viacheslavovich Iakushkin, "Let's Gather a Rich Harvest Quickly and without Losses." Attention! Academy Member Iakushkin is at the microphone. [*Iakushkin:*] In the resolution of the Sovnarkom of the USSR and the CC of the VKP(b), "About the Gathering of the Harvest and Procurements of Agricultural Produce in 1942," are listed the main conditions that must be implemented everywhere in order to carry out the harvest of all crops in short periods and without losses. Every agricultural worker and every collective farmer is obliged to bring about these main conditions on his plot. The resolution of the party and government obliges all collective farms, state farms, and MTS to compile plans for harvest work, while dividing the terrain into those for harvesting with combines, those with simple sickles, and those by hand. It is a matter of course that to the combines must be allotted the best and most weed-free terrain, so that one can put the combines to the best use possible, as productively as possible.[46]

The notion that not all were working to capacity in 1942 appeared in reports about industry as well, in editorial warnings that "all workers must fulfill the norms," calls on factory trade unions to "verify the fulfillment of obligations every day," and assertions that "everything is important—there are no 'details.'"[47] In January a correspondent in the Omsk oblast reported a seemingly fictional shaming of a worker.[48] At an evacuated factory, the tale went, everyone chose to stay on for a second shift after the meal, working late in the evening to get parts ready for military machines. Everyone, that is, except the planer Goriainov. The next morning, one worker reproached him. He muttered something.

> Then resounded the word—the verdict—that dozens of people had been thinking and mulling over since yesterday. The word sounded like a shot. That was how strongly and bitterly the old worker Vasilii Kuzmich Ignatev pronounced it. He spit on the ground and repeated:
>
> "Deserter!"
>
> Goriainov was dumbfounded. The workers gathered around. It was still fifteen minutes before the whistle. Master Spitsyn opened a brief production meeting.
>
> "Are you not abusing him too sharply, Uncle Vasia?" he softly asked Ignatev. "Goriainov worked through his shift, he fulfilled the norm. As for the second shift—it's up to him, we cannot force him."
>
> "What's this?" objected Gorianov's neighbor, the planer Iablochkin. "It's OK if he wants, it's OK if he doesn't. What if it went like this at the front?"
>
> "That's the front," Goriainov exclaimed indignantly. "What kind of front do we have here?" He looked at the faces around him and searched for support. But all looked at him severely, like judges.
>
> "Let me tell him what kind of front we have," Ignatev said. He turned to Goriainov and said intensely,
>
> "Do you really not know that over there, at the outermost positions, our people are fighting the enemy with weapons that we—*we*," he proudly repeated, "are forging here? Yes, you know! And what does our section mean to the factory as a whole? You know! . . . We cannot allow things to lag because of our section. We shall work as much as needed and shall not keep the others from working. . . . Goriainov, you have

deeply insulted us. You left the ranks. Frankly, you deserted from the battlefield. But Soviet people, actual patriots, don't run away—they advance and smash all difficulties."

Shouts of approval followed, after which the "deserter" stepped forward and, eyes downcast, softly confessed his guilt. Thus failure to work overtime was desertion from the front and unpatriotic, if not treasonous.

"We Shall Not Tolerate Loafers and Simulators in Our Midst" was the headline near an open letter ascribed to a metal worker. "Today every worker must fulfill the norm; if he can fulfill two norms, then he is obliged to also do that," he wrote. "We demand from the factory director comrade Gorshukov, from the production commanders, [and] from the trade union organization that they tighten the labor discipline and call to order those who do not want to be aware of their duty to the motherland."[49]

The Soviet Union had lost its main coal mining region, Ukraine's Donbas, or Donets Basin, to the Germans and was barely able to exploit its other European coal region, the Pechora mines near Arctic Vorkuta, partly because the prisoners there revolted.[50] All eyes were now on Asian mines, in the Kuzbass near Kemerovo in the Novosibirsk oblast, in Kazakhstan near Karaganda, and in the Urals near Sverdlovsk and Cheliabinsk. When the first two regions did not fulfill their plans in September 1942, Stalin personally demanded the local party sections to improve their work. *Pravda* journalists arrived and began publishing local newspapers specifically for these miners.[51] The central media did not mention the resolutions, but something close to a panic did erupt, with *Trud* screaming, "Miners of the Kuzbass and Karaganda, the Country Demands Better Work from You!" At the last minute a Politburo member, Andrei Andreev, removed from an editorial for *Pravda* a passage that nearly equated "disorganizers" among the Kuzbass miners with enemy accomplices.[52] At first the Urals were said to do well—a half-year report to Stalin from the Sverdlovsk oblast, allegedly signed by close to 1.3 million citizens, stated that arms and ammunition production as promised had been doubled or tripled—but in September *Trud* warned Cheliabinsk miners who had allowed production to be interrupted. They were "obliged to liquidate lagging, repay the debt to the country!"[53]

The public signs of trouble made it less surprising that Stalin's October Revolution anniversary speech of November 1942 began with the topic of "organization work in the hinterland." The real surprise was its upbeat tone: "Never before has our country had such a strong and organized hinterland." Factories and farms were working "satisfactorily" because there were few remaining "scatterbrains and sloppy people devoid of a sense of civic duty." People's mind-set had also improved: they had become aware of their "indebtedness." Prewar propaganda had also mentioned this notion, but the debt then—so immense as to be permanent—had been to the state and, above all, Stalin. The new indebtedness was to the "Motherland" and its Red Army. Stalin added the notion that the people of the hinterland were working "selflessly," which recalled the self-denial propagated with regard to the allegedly successful completion of the First Five-Year Plan of the early 1930s. No one said so, but Stalin's two notions were not fully compatible. Whereas "indebtedness" turned people into objects, "selflessness" gave them a choice, namely to sacrifice themselves.[54]

In May 1943, for the first and only time in any speech or order, Stalin sounded concerned about the rear as a whole. Everyone there should work twice as hard and as precisely as a clock. Lenin had said once that the slightest lack of energy and discipline was punishable according to the law of wartime, and this still applied, Stalin grumbled. That year the media devoted much attention to discipline in the hinterland. Workers had a "city duty": "In the hinterland, neither a single enterprise, nor a single shop, nor a single brigade has the right not to fulfill the state plan. Negligent workers who evince a conciliatory attitude to production inadequacies that hinder the successful fulfillment of tasks commit a crime against the motherland." "Deserters" at the Stalin plane construction factory were judged in show trials that were transmitted over the factory's radio. The practice, repeated in 1944, was probably not unique to this place.[55]

But Stalin's upbeat tone returned in November 1943, a festive occasion on which he said more about the hinterland than ever. *All* of its people now were working "selflessly." The "labor heroism" of the workers ensured that the Red Army had no "serious shortages" of armaments and military supplies. There were even nice words for the peasants (although they were never praised by the leader for labor heroism): they had demonstrated their commitment to the war, which they realized was also about their "life and freedom." Addressing the food supply for the first and last time, Stalin said that the army and the country had been fed "without serious holdups," thanks to both the patriotism of the peasants and the collective farm system.

There was also praise for transport workers, the "Soviet intelligentsia," the "friendship of the peoples of our country," and the Communist Party, which, supposedly closer to the people than ever, inspired and organized the national struggle. Best of all, the political system and the state were more solid than ever. The Soviet system had proven to be "the best form of mobilization."[56] That is, the ubiquitous selflessness ultimately had political reasons.

Everything Stalin said or did was followed by promises and reports of actual feats. Peasants and workers always vowed that a particular speech, message, or decree of his "obliges us to work even better." This case was no exception. Within days central radio broadcast a prerecording of a farmer from the Moscow region who reported her pride, joy, and understanding of the tasks ahead. Anna Stoliarova read out a stilted text:

> The speech by comrade Stalin was heard by all the *kolkhozniks* of our collective farm "New Life" with great attention. Everyone tried to sit closer to the loudspeaker, in order not to accidentally miss any single word. When we heard the speech, much became clear at once. When Comrade Stalin said that without the collective farm system, without the selfless labor of the *kolkhoz* men and women, we could not have solved food supply questions, our hearts were filled with pride. The words that we demonstrated the strength

and vitality of the collective farm system and the patriotism of the *kolkhoz* peasantry not only imbued us with a feeling of deep joy and gratefulness for the high evaluation of the work of the collective farms, but also compelled us to understand once more the necessity of further application of force, of further struggle for the rise in harvest yield, for further manifold aid to the front.[57]

That praise received always amounted to an order to do even better was also evident in the words ascribed to a foreman at the motorcycle factory in Moscow. Stalin had inspired the entire hinterland with "a feeling of satisfaction, pride, and confidence and belief in the approaching victory against the fascist German gangs." This particular shop had adopted various new "socialist obligations," such as early plan fulfillment and extra work. Radio listeners heard noises from the Burevestnik shoe factory, and how its director suggested that reporters speak to a "front brigade" worker. The following artificial dialogue with this Dusia Monakhova ensued:

"Does your brigade make many shoes?"

"You can judge for yourself. Our brigade was organized in March this year. Since then we have provided 25,000 pairs of shoes over and above the plan. And I personally completed my year plan already in September."

"Which task do you now set yourself?"

"In response to Comrade Stalin's speech, all of us in the brigade have decided to complete 35,000 pairs of shoes over and above the plan before the new year. We know that this is no easy task, but once decided, we shall achieve it without fail. Now is not the time for bad work. That is shameful. Our Red Army is beyond Kiev. My husband is also fighting. He must know that we in the hinterland are working in a front-line way."[58]

In December 1943 Stalin began publicly congratulating hardworking or anniversary-celebrating factories, ultimately three dozen of them. The favorite, congratulated four times, was the metal factory in Cheliabinsk, also the site of an unmentioned labor camp. (Reports did say that the NKVD was in charge of the factory.)[59] Again these congratulations reportedly sparked local production booms.[60] In short, the sequence of act and praise was reversed.

In 1944 Moscow's statement about the harvest was comparatively confident. Last year's mistakes included "several" leaders' carelessness toward seeds. As usual, Moscow addressed not ordinary peasants but their leaders and demanded that they mobilize the entire "working force" and guarantee "unconditional" and timely deliveries by every single farm. All able-bodied persons from the age of fourteen had to be put to work. Collective farms should fine shirkers by striking part of their recorded labor days and depriving them of the right to advance payment in kind. The mobilized additional harvesters had to work at least forty to fifty days in collective farms (and fifty to sixty "day targets" in state farms); for schoolchildren, the minimums were twenty to thirty.[61]

In May of that year Stalin's public order marking Labor Day singled out women, whose "selfless" labor he praised. The women had "courageously" withstood the "difficulties of wartime" and were an inspiration to Red Army members.[62] Praise for selfless behavior befell everyone once more in November 1944. Now, for the first and only time, the leader mentioned actual hardship: "The Soviet people denied themselves many necessities and consciously accepted serious material privations, in order to give more to the front." That "great feat" had truly made them heroic. For instance, the peasantry, "actively and fully conscious of its duty to the Motherland," had helped the Red Army by providing enough food. Women and children in factories and farms had carried "the main burden" at the home front and "turned out to be worthy of their parents and sons, husbands and brothers who are defending the Motherland from the German-fascist monsters." Lest anyone draw the wrong conclusion, Stalin repeated the old message that none of this could have been possible without vital preconditions: the socialist system, the Soviet state, and people's love for that system and state—Soviet patriotism. And, as usual, although Stalin said that the women had shown they *deserved* their fathers, brothers, husbands, and sons, this surely was no reason to rest, but quite the contrary. As a worker named Elena Bondareva, who had just improved on her production record, told them, the leader's praise "obliged" them to do more.[63]

Records and Competitions

"Socialist competition" was a partly illusory phenomenon among workers and peasants that began in the 1930s. Some of it focused on individual feats, such as by the Donbas miner Aleksei Stakhanov, who in six hours in 1935 supposedly dug 102 tons of coal, or 10 percent of the entire mine's daily output. The "Stakhanovite movement" hardly raised production and was unpopular on many shop floors. Other competition focused on less glamorized "shock workers."[64] Little extant documentation shows the authorship of local worker "initiatives" and "appeals" for hard work, innovation, and competition, but most of the texts were likely ghostwritten by journalists and writers. These materials were both supposed to inspire workers and to justify raising production targets.[65]

The German invasion spoiled the All-Union Socialist Competition in industry, announced on June 16, 1941.[66] Cancellation would not have surprised anyone, but it did not happen, although in the first ten months of the war with Germany this propaganda was less about the usual collectives than about individuals. These men and women supposedly produced *more* than others, worked *faster* than others, and worked at *more tasks*.

Young Stakhanovites called "two-hundreders" inflicted a double blow on "fascism" by also producing in the name of "the comrade who left for the front." Then the propaganda mentioned people who fulfilled norms three, five, or many more times.[67] The first person who achieved *ten* norms was Dmitrii Bosy, a milling machine operator in Nizhnii Tagil (at the Urals Wagon Factory, which censorship omitted). By February 1942 he had reached 1,480 percent of his quota and sparked a "mass movement" of "thousanders." As he told *Trud* two months later, his love (of his bench, the motherland, and Stalin) and hatred (of the enemy) increased his strength. If words could not express how much his Stalin Prize inspired Bosy, his new record did: *twenty* norms. A year later he supposedly reached 6,200 percent.[68]

Other forms of individual Stakhanovism received less attention. Certain steel forgers were "going-fasters," another prewar term.[69] In January 1942 *Trud* carried an open letter by the worker Vasilii Shalaev calling on his fellow construction workers to master many professions. He was himself a roofer, glazier, concrete worker, plasterer, and electric welder. *Trud* reported receiving many supportive letters in response and proclaimed that every construction worker should become a "Shalaevite."[70] By order of the People's Commissariat of Communications, much was said about the analogous "movement" initiated in 1940 by a locomotive driver with ideas about how people like him should make repairs.[71] And there was some publicity about the prewar phenomenon of multitasking by "multibenchers."[72]

Only one large-scale propaganda campaign about labor focused on an individual peasant working outside of a team, and it was short-lived. In the spring of 1942 reports said that V. A. Nagorny, a seventeen-year-old in the Krasnoiarsk krai, plowed four hectares in one day, a total distance of some 120 kilometers. He used two pairs of horses and a groom, ate in the field, and worked for eighteen hours straight. Local authorities spoke of a new Stakhanov movement, and in January 1943 the Party Committee of the Chita oblast, apparently acting on its own initiative, proposed to implement this method on all collective farms. The Osh oblast committee even created schools to teach Nagorny's method and in the Tajik SSR conferences of "Nagornovite" plowmen were convened. Several newspaper articles described all of this.[73] Yet in March 1943 Agitprop found flaws and brought the "movement" to an inglorious end.[74]

By April 1942 nearly two in three industrial workers were on the books as participants in socialist competitions, either individually or as members of "collectives." Stalin still deemed this insufficient, and on May 7, 1942, *Pravda* carried invitations for a round of the All-Union Socialist Competition. These allegedly originated from the I. V. Stalin Kuznetsk Metallurgical Industrial Complex, a plane factory, and a motor factory. Now began the high tide of *collective* competition, covering all branches of the economy and more territorially focused than ever, with competition between raions, oblasts, and republics. It involved close to 80 percent of all industrial workers by the fall of 1943.[75] Among them were experienced shock workers who assisted teenagers and "housewives."[76] "Youth brigades"—a phenomenon already known before 1941—that consistently overfulfilled the plan by at least 150 percent were renamed "front youth brigades."[77] In November 1943, in a particularly unlikely media campaign, some of these brigades asked their directors to reallocate them to other tasks and thus, in words ascribed to the twenty-three-year-old Ekaterina Baryshnikova from Moscow, "allow" them to "fulfill their tasks with a smaller quantity of workers." The Stakhanovite's bright idea to saddle everyone with more work quickly blossomed into an almost entirely fictional "large patriotic movement of Soviet youth," missing even the veneer of competition.[78]

Important wartime innovations in socialist competition were that the outcomes appeared in the newspapers and that the winners were awarded "traveling" Red Banners.[79] There were also public reprimands. In April 1943, for instance, *Trud* noted that the Magnitogorsk Metallurgical Complex had "again" fallen behind its competitor in the Kuzbass. It was "time, high time" for the country's largest metallurgical factory to "overcome its lagging and return its former glory."[80]

In March 1944, for reasons unstated and unclear, the propaganda tide swung back toward personal feats. Indeed the keyword became "individual competition." A plenary session of the Trade Union Council ordered the unions to develop the program. Workers could compete for honorary titles such as "best steeler."[81]

As for the countryside, in 1940 over half of the collective farms and MTS had participated in socialist competition.[82] Early in 1942 the newspaper *Sovetskaia Sibir* reported appeals from farmers that ushered in competition among three Siberian raions.[83] *Sotsialisticheskoe zemledelie*, the main paper on agricultural affairs, carried an open letter, allegedly written at a collective farm and an MTS in the Altai krai, that challenged fellow *kolkhozniks* in the Volga region, the

Urals, Siberia, Central Asia, and Kazakhstan to compete for "the best aid to the front and the best performance in spring sowing." The "initiative" was praised by the central authorities.[84]

First in on the competition launched in May 1942 were the state farmers, who were officially not peasants but "workers" and, like industrial workers, toiled for daily targets. The call was supposedly issued by a farm near Omsk. The purpose was evident in this headline: "Let Us Give the Front and the Country More Grain, Meat, and the Industry More Raw Materials!" There were just seven signatures, although other milkmaids and pig-tenders supposedly had signed as well. The oblast party committee had selected the farm; a combined effort of the People's Commissariat of State Farms, Agitprop, and the central newspaper for state farms had produced a draft letter that was shortened twice.[85] Calls for competition such as these always included deadlines.[86]

Female tractor drivers received special attention; in 1942 680 won medals as an "exemplary worker of socialist agriculture." The media declared that a tractor brigade in Kazakhstan led by Pasha Angelina (who back in 1933 had organized the country's first all-female tractor brigade) had overfulfilled not just its spring sowing plan (by 200 percent) but its entire year plan (by 2,210 hectares).[87] There was also "pre-October" competition on the eve of October Revolution Day and again supposedly a local initiative.[88] And there were competitions in which schools whose children did the best field work won cash prizes.[89]

Most agricultural competition dealt with harvesting, where winners also received "traveling" Red Banners. Early in October 1942 the Radio Committee proposed to Shcherbakov to broadcast speeches from five people in the Moscow oblast: a Moscow city party secretary, the director of the political department of an MTS, a female tractor brigade leader, a female *kolkhoznik*, a combine driver, and a collective farm chairman. Of course there was the usual observation that "the successes that we achieved oblige us to work even better and more systematically." But the combine driver boasted about exchanging telegrams with Shcherbakov, and the chairman vowed that his farm would win the raion's traveling Red Banner. Shcherbakov granted the request, provided modesty was inserted in the speeches.[90]

Because the first-ever All-Union competition in agriculture was held while the Soviet state was at war, it was not surprising that the winning oblasts were declared very late, in April 1943. Peasants from various regions challenged one another to work hard in spring sowing; that would be a good way to mark the competition's upcoming first anniversary.[91] And on it went: in July tractor and combine drivers in the Chkalov oblast reportedly initiated competition among colleagues in that year's harvest.[92] The harvest competition results for 1944 appeared on time, in August of the same year; thirty raions received a banner and a financial reward.[93]

By then an important purpose of the public competition was to focus attention on oaths of loyalty to Stalin and his system, which, in the case of agriculture, meant the state and collective farms. In 1942 Soviet Ukraine's leaders seemed to have promised reform or even abolition of these hated institutions, declaring, "The rich Ukrainian land is waiting for its owner—the free farmer."[94] In 1944 all reverted to normalcy, as evident in a declaration from the Kiev oblast, a region recaptured a year earlier and already proclaimed the winner of a harvest competition. This public letter to Stalin, "signed by 441,589 people" after having been "discussed and unanimously adopted at meetings of collective farmers, MTS and state farm workers, and specialists of agriculture," expressed above all indisputable ideological steadfastness, even among those who just recently might have been heretics: "Now we all see and understand that only the collective farm and only the Stalin school of free labor helped Ukrainian woman to go through all the horrors and trials of war with honor." The rest of the media belabored the point that it would have been "impossible to wage a war on the scale of the Patriotic war based on the individual peasantry."[95]

Seeds of Failure

Slogans for socialist competition such as "All for the Front, all for Victory!" and "How Did You Help the Front?" were less formulaic then prewar predecessors such as "We shall carry out the decisions of the ... plenary meeting!" had been. But that did not necessarily make them effective (or, as various contemporary Russian historians believe, realistic representations of what was happening).[96] Most of the pledges to worker harder and better were phrased in a single, very dry style. To give another example, in December 1943, one week after the Tehran conference, a foreman at the Kirov Dynamo Factory was quoted as saying, "It says in the Declaration of the Conference of the three allied States: Our offensive will be merciless and growing. We, the workers of the hinterland, are obliged to also work at increasing speed. I pledge to finish the December program five days before time." This received "universal agreement. Right there at the meeting, new obligations were taken up. The shop would fulfill the December plan on the 25th, produce 3,000 units over the plan, raise productivity of work compared to November by 4 percent, and improve the quality of the production turned out."[97] But the problem ran deeper than slogans and artificial vows. The entire propaganda for labor carried the seeds of its failures to mobilize.

One of the key flaws was the artificial letters from citizens read out on the radio. In the first five months of 1943 the Radio Committee received on average 13,000 letters per month from the front, and twice as many that were meant for the people at the front. Then a sharp drop occurred, and by December the count stood at 8,000 and 16,000, respectively. On central radio in 1943, more than 12,000 letters were read "from the front" and more than 27,000 "to the front." If done right, such letters might have been inspiring. But next to nothing was natural in the way they were written, obtained, and edited. Unsolicited—that is, actual—letters were often stilted and impersonal because the writers considered it improper to write about themselves and their family. Editing squeezed out any lingering spontaneity. To obtain for broadcasting a letter from a particular wounded soldier, a journalist would chat beside his hospital bed and obtain a signature on brief notes. At the office he or she embellished the notes beyond recognition. The ugliness of such broadcast letters even caused the Radio Committee leader Dmitrii Polikarpov to complain to the Letters Department. A staff member admitted at a staff meeting, "We know why we are being called names." Agitprop also noted that the initial writers "quite often" failed to recognize themselves. As for the actual voices of the loved ones or colleagues, central radio broadcast them in 1943 just 172 times; worse, a mere eighteen of those carrying the title of Hero of the Soviet Union read a letter on the air that year.[98]

The main obstacle to labor mobilization through the media was the outlandish severity of the censors. Early in 1942 the chief censor Sadchikov issued two booklets, *Some Questions about the Work of Censorship during the War* and *Guard Tightly the Secrets of the Socialist State*. They put his subordinates on notice that censorship constituted the "counterweight to enemy intelligence," so it was better to do too much than too little. The censors had to excise not only items on the black list, but "all data that might indirectly allow conclusions revealing military secrets to be drawn."[99] For instance, the names of enterprises (which, Sadchikov wrote, had appeared far too often) could assist "spies, saboteurs, and enemy aviation." As for the locations of factories, they were allowed to appear only in reports on socialist competitions.[100]

He added that the republic, oblast, and local press (where details might have made the propaganda more appealing) were allowed to do even less. If the central press mentioned the name of a factory director, the noncentral press was to abstain from doing so and should omit the factory's identification number; it could name only the factory. Conversely, if the central press mentioned the factory number, the local press could name only the director. If, as often happened, the central press mentioned both the director's name and the factory number, then the local press could say nothing whatsoever—it had to call the factory X (*N-skii*) and refer only to "production." Even though the factory papers (*mnogotirazhki*) did not circulate they were barred from *ever* mentioning a location, director, number, or product. Only if the central press mentioned not just the director's name and the factory number but also the *location* was the secret considered "out" and the local press allowed to follow the precedent. Even so, it had to omit the factory's purpose, the thing it was producing.[101]

The number of workers, whether at enterprises, people's commissariats, branches of industry, or regions, was always entirely secret.[102]

This was reasonable enough, but as censors applied this rule, they went to extremes. When the paper *Gorkovskaia kommuna* wrote in February 1942 that more than 27,000 workers at the Molotov factory were taking part in socialist competitions, Sadchikov complained that this disclosed the *total* number of workers.[103] In practice, labor shortages also became taboo, supposedly because these said something about the scale of the army draft. In hindsight therefore Sadchikov considered it inappropriate for the *Uralskii rabochii* to report that 40 percent of all workers at a factory had joined the armed forces and that 75 percent of those learning how to use a tractor were novices.[104]

The government—that is, Stalin—could choose to mention production figures in official statements. Professional censors could allow absolute figures on the *over*fulfillment of plans by nonmilitary factories only if lack of clarity remained about the monthly, quarterly, or yearly plan. For instance, it could be reported that the Magnitogorsk Metallurgical Complex had produced, in any particular month, "21,000 tons of cast iron over and above plan."[105]

It was also wrong, Sadchikov wrote, to report specific shortcomings. For instance, *Sovetskaia Sibir* had revealed that the Kuznetsk Metallurgical Industrial Complex had not met February's smelting plan due to bad organization, delayed deliveries, poor coal quality, and furnace defects. Nor should the newspaper have been allowed to report the bad work of the open hearth and blast furnace shops and the shortages of consumer goods. Likewise the paper *Gorkovskaia kommuna* should not have revealed that factory machines stood idle for many hours, or that Mikhail Rodionov, the party secretary of the oblast and city, had commented that local factories had worked worse in March 1942 than during the prior month.[106] Spurred on by Sadchikov, in early 1942 censors began banning such reports, and also items about railroad mishaps such as low speed, underutilized and damaged rolling stock, lack of personnel, and poor discipline.[107]

As noted, reports on socialist competitions were the only ones allowed to provide the location of a particular factory. This could not prevent them from being tedious and vague, however. *Latest News* reports on the All-Union competition gave no inkling of how many people were involved and usually omitted the names of the participants. They offered only lists of often anonymous factories, percentages, and directors.[108]

Censorship became equally pervasive with regard to agricultural affairs. In a war situation, it was reasonable that harvest failures were kept top secret. Only special government statements, and nothing else, might refer to the yields in any region or republic, let alone the entire country. Figures on the agricultural deliveries on levels above the raion were equally secret. The noncentral press was not allowed to generalize in any way about land use; here it might offer only "select" data about particular oblasts and autonomous republics.[109] In the end even Aleksandrov considered this too severe. Early in 1943 he reported to the Central Committee his dissatisfaction with the absence of reporting of real problems in the sowing. Many reports, the chief of Agitprop noted, derived from nothing but phone conversations with optimistic raion leaders who obscured the actual situation.[110] But his complaint changed nothing.

Many regional authorities and newspaper editors objected to the censorship, as Sadchikov reported early in 1942. "Rather often," he noted, "one has to listen to the naïve questions of some simpletons from editorial offices: 'what's the secret when, for example, it is mentioned that factories of the city of Gorkii are learning to handle new types of army vehicles. Everybody in our town knows this.'"[111] The editor of *Bolshevistskaia stal* from Stalinsk near Novosibirsk complained that the paper could say nothing about the reconstruction of evacuated factories; therefore it could not highlight good and bad practices. Meanwhile city meetings named the factories, and street announcements were saying that workers were needed. This editor also complained that censors crossed out references to decorations and medals received by workers.[112]

A particularly strong complaint came from Rostov, after Sadchikov demanded that an oblast-level editor be prosecuted for negligence, and even reports about the bread factory were banned simply because it supplied soldiers. The regional leaders wrote angrily to the Central Committee, "Thanks to censorship, our *Molot* has turned into a pious old crazy woman—you won't find in it anything whatsoever that reflects our work in strengthening the city's defense. Our descendents will wonder: for sixteen months, the enemy stood at the gates of Rostov, people fought them with and without success, and *Molot* says nothing about it, nothing whatsoever, because censorship cuts so deep, far, and wide that any academic would be envious."[113] But the colorful letter from Rostov was ineffective.

All through the war the demands of the censor baffled local officials—party and state leaders, factory directors, and party organizers. They often assumed that banning the identification number of factories or the names of their directors was not required if the central press did not omit them. In the Molotov oblast early in 1943 an engineer read a speech on the radio and simply added the factory number. (The censor informed the NKVD and the factory director).[114] Such acts said one thing: the comprehensive scale of the censorship hampered the mobilization of workers—and the people who protested and amended the speeches were in the right.

The propaganda also failed entirely in achieving any semblance of dialogue between the peasants and the authorities, local or central. It was not a bad idea of Party Secretary Rodionov when, in August 1943, he began printing in the newspaper of the Gorkii oblast telegrams to specific raion leaders asking them to greet and congratulate the farmers on his behalf. This was in order, he added, because those farmers had overfulfilled the delivery plan and thus significantly strengthened the country's military might. The Central Committee put an end to the initiative. No reason was given, but it was likely the appreciation expressed. Stalin had framed society around indebtedness and obligation. Peasants had to obey the party-state, and like all Soviet citizens, they were "selfless" subjects who owed everything to the authorities. If any leader were to acknowledge their efforts (let alone *thank* them), it had to be Stalin.[115] That was why obligation was paramount in an open letter in the fall of 1944, ascribed to Ukraine's peasants and directed at all Soviet peasants: "To us ... the interests of the state, the interests of the front supersede everything else."[116]

Forced labor became the norm for virtually all: the workers were mobilized, which meant they could be sent anywhere, and the peasants had fewer rights and more obligations than ever. In that sense, the description of the hinterland that Stalin introduced, "a single camp," was quite appropriate. Meanwhile, whereas before 1940 only the laws against "political" offenders had been secret, the criminal labor laws of the years 1940 to 1943 also were and remained entirely classified, including a decree about "labor duty." Stalin probably felt that the United States and other allies might disapprove and, above all, that the enemy might use this information. Indeed Nazi propaganda in Russian did jump on some of the publicized measures—the USSR's drafting of nonpeasants into agricultural work and the raised targets for peasants—as signs that famine was near.[117] Still, the Soviet media did offer a sense of the other measures in reports on their allegedly insufficient implementation.

Overall the media were ambiguous about the workers and the peasants. On the one hand, they were severely warned against "desertion" and told to be obedient. Stalin himself expressed this forcefully in May 1943. On the other hand, most workers and peasants were portrayed as consciously selfless patriots engaged in public campaigns for records and primacy, in collective and individual competitions. Male workers and farmers in the United Kingdom, one historian has argued, accepted propaganda claims that they were as essential as soldiers, and even likened themselves to heroes.[118] Whether or not this also applied in the Soviet case cannot be established at this stage of the research. The appeals, pledges, and letters to and from the front might have inspired or mobilized, but their bone-dry style and sparse content likely hampered the cause, although Stalin himself, unlike some of his subordinates who complained about the extreme censorship, seemed to think otherwise. He also valued labor propaganda's unofficial aims: to create settings and occasions for increases in production targets and vows of loyalty to him and his system. The sources do not indicate any concern of his that the propaganda was failing to mobilize for labor.

4

Material Privations

Abolished in 1935, rationing returned to Moscow on July 17, 1941, and then to other cities. As always, peasants were excluded from the system, which they supposedly did not need. An important novelty was that the rations imposed not minimum but *maximum* levels of consumption. To assist in distribution and control, in February 1942 factories established workers' supply departments that eventually served about half of all ration receivers.[1]

The rations never offered enough calories to live on.[2] The key problems were the collective farm system, which guaranteed that the peasants worked little and inefficiently, and the state's great reluctance to donate food to civilians, even if supplies were nearby. As for financial aid, in 1942 and 1943, 55 and 50 million rubles were set aside in the RSFSR for one-time aid to needy people, but those funds often did not reach them.[3] Thus uncounted millions in the hinterland died from famine. Already in the first winter many citizens suffered from malnutrition.

A translator for the Soviet Information Bureau recalled that even in Moscow, privileged as to food, many acquaintances starved to death because of their meager bread rations. Meanwhile the elite in the capital had no problem getting enough to eat nor, it seems, enjoying this food to the full. For some months in 1942 Bureau translators had access to the Central Committee canteen at Old Square: "I couldn't believe my eyes when I saw the mountain of white bread in the middle of the table, the pitcher of rich sour cream served with a borshch so full of nutrients that it alone sufficed for a meal. There was a wide choice of dishes on the menu: goose stuffed with apples, tender pork chops, beef Stroganoff, stewed fruit, ice cream."[4]

Outside Moscow the food situation was often disastrous. About half of the population of Leningrad starved to death after the Germans surrounded the city. Famine also struck the Siberian steppes, where a drought had ended all supplies. Beginning in the winter of 1942–1943 famine spread all over Siberia, but Moscow did not send in food from the Caucasus and Uzbekistan. Even peasants began eating moss. In at least one region in northwestern Russia, peasants died in the vicinity of sacks of grain destined for the front.[5] Famine raged still harder in the winter of 1943–1944, and cannibalism appeared. One Russian researcher estimates that (apart from Leningraders) about 1.5 million civilians starved to death during the entire war.[6]

How did the media deal with this calamity, which struck hardest at refugees, family members of combat soldiers, invalids, and children? In principle it was not given special coverage. For, with one exception—a reference by Stalin in November 1944 to "serious material privations"—censors and other supervisors of the media banned all "generalized negative information about the material situation of the population and about the provision of the families of Red Army draftees."[7] But total silence was to prove impossible to maintain.

Food, Gardens, Theft, and Public Inspection

Rationing did not appear on Glavlit's blacklist, but it was unmentionable in practice. The only public admission of its existence was references to *kartochki*, or cards, as in reports that blood donors were rewarded with them, and articles about the punishment of those who stole them.⁸ Probably responding to a large drought in the Volga region, Stalin decided in November 1943, the very month of his optimistic October Revolution Day speech, to lower the daily bread rations by a third, to 300 grams for adults and 200 grams for children and elderly dependents. The evacuee ration was cut in half, to 200 grams. Leningrad was exempted. If residing in Moscow, recipients were allowed 100 grams of bread extra. Everywhere else the bad news continued: raion authorities were now allowed, depending on their estimation of citizens' income from gardens, to give even less to workers living in villages and nothing at all to the dependants these people might have. All this was kept out of the Soviet (and Allied) media. Not finding any reports, those affected often put the blame on local authorities.⁹

The state preferred to tell another story: that it no longer accepted full responsibility for the supply of food to city dwellers. Every factory or city would become "its own food base," declared *Pravda* as early as July 1941, and the message was often repeated. All the same the Soviet authorities did help a significant number of city dwellers to survive. On March 7, 1942, the Trade Union Council published a resolution that referred to a decision two months earlier in support of private ("individual") gardening. Now the council's presidium obliged factory and local committees to register all workers who wished to have a garden. Garden committees also had to be formed.¹⁰

On April 7 the Communist Party issued an important decision with regard to city dwellers, "On the Allocation of Lands for the Subsidiary Farms and Vegetable Gardens of the Workers and Employees." Already before the war various companies had administered and cultivated lands as subsidiary farms. Now the local authorities could cede fallow lands near cities and towns and unused collective farm fields to companies, institutions, army units, and individual workers and employees. Thus some 10,000 new subsidiary farms emerged that year.¹¹ The media only hinted at the resolution about the subsidiary farms, as when *Pravda* carried a letter, supposedly written in a factory in Saratov, that signaled that some factories no longer *wanted* "the state" to satisfy their needs for "a number of products from centralized funds." The subsidiary farms and private gardens would step in. Unfortunately, the letter added, not everyone knew that such gardens were legal.[12]

Published instructions for the garden committees specified that this activity would have to take place in their members' free time and at their own expense.[13] *Pravda* ran a call from the Stalingrad city party secretary for attention to the matter of the "food base." Private farming was becoming more widespread than ever before: as many as 95,000 families in Stalingrad, three times as many as in 1941, had requested a garden. In 1940 and 1941 there had been thirty-four subsidiary farms and five large state farms around Stalingrad; now, he said, some sixty more subsidiary farms were "being organized." In the previous year, he continued, there had been "errors" with the farms, and even today "the leaders of some factories strive only to receive as much land as possible without worrying about their proper cultivation."[14]

Moscow evidently considered such warnings against bad or absent cultivation relevant for the whole country, and, judging from other reports, it had good reasons for doing so. *Trud* editorials up to the very end of the war cited the alleged lack of "labor" at the subsidiary farms, the "threat of the spoilage" of vegetables (thousands of tons around the Kyrgyz capital of Frunze in September 1942), and the carelessness at "some" enterprises about the upcoming harvest.[15]

The individual gardens were declared "of state importance." Reports revealed the key problems were aloof or obstructive officials, hesitant prospective cultivators, and theft. Declaring that "every worker and employee must have his own garden," a Trade Union Council secretary complained that some factories had done nothing but compile lists.[16] *Trud* also published a letter allegedly written by two villagers who admitted that their raion had not sown enough, thus playing the "unenviable role of dependant and parasite"; worse, city authorities were not supportive of gardens and subsidiary farms.[17] Another author accused the Sverdlovsk authorities of deceitfully allocating land located in villages or forests.[18]

Later in 1942 Moscow decided to "grant" the gardens to the people cultivating them for a number of years. In the media the gist of this decision became evident only when an agronomist proposed in

September to consolidate the current situation "for a long period."[19] The resolution itself was not published, and no specific period was mentioned. Later the media repeated the confusing notion of "granting" the gardens to the gardeners, now with reference to "five to seven years."[20] This propaganda was supposed to assure people that despite the state's continuing ownership the gardens were worth cultivating.[21]

Earnest and detailed advice was provided on the increase of garden yields. *Trud*'s rubric "For the Benefit of the Worker-Gardener" and occasionally other articles spread across one or two full pages and benefited many. Sometimes a high-placed agriculture or State Planning Committee official gave advice about planting, sowing, and—particularly useful for evacuees without places to store crops—the drying of vegetables and potatoes.[22] The radio had a special program for gardeners, broadcast a hundred times in 1943 alone. On the afternoon of August 20, 1944, its eight minutes included a talk about building a storehouse and responses to listeners' letters. Movie theaters that year showed a ten-minute educational film, *Spring Work in Gardens*.[23] Trofim Lysenko, an amateur biologist and the scourge of geneticists, wrote many times about planting potato tops rather than entire tubers. This increased his popularity—the potato was the main garden crop—for this traditional wisdom proved useful. (Dispatches also cited him approvingly when the topic was the flawed idea of *vernalization* of plant seeds or tubers.)[24]

There were many reports about theft from the private gardens. The published instructions for the garden committees already included a requirement to organize surveillance, and the matter of protection reappeared in the media every August and September. A man from the Sverdlovsk oblast, for instance, said to have complained about local authorities before, referred to "lovers of easy gain" who repeatedly spoiled and stole from his garden. "Amateur" monitoring was needed, and the local soviets, factory trade unions, and garden committees should promote it. The letter also referred to an unpublished Supreme Court resolution to prosecute people who "attempted" to steal from gardens. *Trud* agreed that "those desiring to live off other people's property" could "always be found."

The paper reported on a conference of Moscow factory unions and garden committees, under the heading "Guard the Workers' Gardens with Vigilance." The Trade Union Council had recently decided to allow payments to induce people to serve as watchmen. In a society that disallowed individuals to hire and thus "exploit" labor, this was highly unusual.[25]

And *Trud* demanded severe penalties. True, the court of the Kuntsevo raion, adjacent to Moscow, had sentenced a worker to two years for stealing from others' gardens, but in general Judge Tumanova and Judge Ivanova were "too liberal." Many cases lay dormant, such as those of "Dmitriev, Ruslov, Proshin, and Nanaev, who stole onions from gardens and sold them at speculative prices." In an interview Konstantin Gorshenin, the people's commissar of justice of the RSFSR, complained that "far from all" justice organs were tough enough. He was sending staff members into the raions to check on the battle against "harvest thieves."[26]

It even became apparent that the guards themselves were unreliable. They must not abandon their posts under any pretext, a trade union leader warned. A named gardener during his once-a-month shift went home for dinner, leaving no one behind. When he returned many potatoes were gone. An eloquent sketch of the situation outside Nizhnii Tagil, a city with endless rows of gardens, noted, "Workers visit the factory committees and garden committees ceaselessly, worrying about one and the same thing—they fear that their harvest will be plundered. These fears are well-founded! At night, uninvited guests visit the gardens. Dozens of cases of theft have been registered." In one factory the watchmen were under suspicion. Worse, a pass system for policing access to the collective gardens did not work because gardeners also coveted each other's harvest. Some organizations had organized around-the-clock surveillance, but this journalist demanded "one or two show trials, to be widely covered in the local press."[27]

Warnings reappeared in 1943 and 1944, when far more people became involved in gardening. In 1944 officially more than 15 million had taken up the pursuit. *Trud* carried a complaint against the garden committee of the Krasny Bogatyr factory in Moscow. Its head, the paper added cryptically, had failed to investigate why the district militia did nothing with reports about thieves caught red-handed. The committee itself was told to draft gardeners or their relatives as guards. A correspondent in an unidentified city said that one Gusarova was caught stealing potatoes and would face a factory "show trial," but that other factories were negligent. In all these reports there was nothing but contempt for the "lovers of easy gain." They were "degenerates who don't want to work." No motive other than laziness was mentioned.[28]

Much was also said about food being stolen elsewhere. A correspondent in Magnitogorsk reported 877 cases of food theft from the local trust, but its director failed to notice and did not read the canteen supervisor's labor booklet, which mentioned his dismissal as a thief from two other jobs. When told, this Giterman was amazed and, the report went on, "suddenly denounced the inspector for personnel registration. A typical dialogue followed: 'Why did you overlook it, Comrade Bariakin?' 'You had the labor booklet, Comrade Giterman!' 'How can I go through all the labor booklets?!'"[29]

The media printed brief, usually anonymous notices of sentences that were supposed to intimidate potential thieves. Thus in a mining settlement near Tula a trust director, food supply head, and accountant were sentenced to, respectively, ten, eight, and five years; the director also saw all his property confiscated. Some notices concerned the theft of food from trains. One M. S. Vorobev was reportedly sentenced to be shot for stealing a bag of meal and boxes of butter from a train; so was one M. E. Shpionov. Even if the story was not entirely fictional, the last names—"Sparrow" and "Spy" in English— must have been. According to another report, the cook and supervisor of the dining car of the train to Novosibirsk were sentenced to eight and ten years.[30] There were many reports of problems at canteens. "Intolerable indifference" among union leaders in Sverdlovsk supposedly explained why hundreds of people at the electric welding machine factory had to use a canteen that could serve only sixty. The "vast majority" of the canteens in Ufa were also in chaos.[31]

On February 1, 1943, shortly after the State Defense Committee passed an unpublished resolution on theft, the trade union organization formalized the preexisting phenomenon of "public inspectors."[32] The media called for the election of these people, whose job was to verify workers' supply departments and canteens. By way of example, a report described how one day, the store at the Kompressor factory failed to put up for sale some announced products: "Inspector Comr. Savich went to the storage room of the store and established that the products were there. Upon the inspector's demand, the products were put up for sale."[33] Articles also directly addressed the inspectors:

> When entering a store, the first things to check are: Is there a price list? Does it hang at a visible spot? Are the prices on it correct? Do the prices on it match the prices indicated on the invoice? Pay attention: What kind of price list is it? Are all of the goods being sold mentioned on it? Remember: every item must have a label mentioning the price and quality. ENSURE that the store serves buyers in a precise and civilized manner.

The trade unions were urged to support the inspectors. In April 1944 the media carried a union resolution for taking control over the "squandering" in "many" canteens, stores, and subsidiary farms. Every canteen must have forty to fifty "merciless" inspectors, who had to work at most three times per week and four to six hours per shift. Increasing the numbers was probably meant to reduce the authority of individual inspectors.[34]

Overall the media gave ample reason to believe that the inspectors hardly made a dent, and officials tended to be blamed. At the Magnitogorsk Complex, for example, the trade union ignored warnings from inspectors; elsewhere public prosecutors and local judges connived to treat offenders "liberally."[35]

Voluntary Duties

On October Revolution Day, New Year's Day, Red Army Day, and May Day, food, clothing, and other gifts were collected for the Red

Army. These gifts were not useful for propaganda because their destination was classified (not to mention that they rarely reached the front line and often were dispersed as standard allowances).[36] The real bright spots in the propaganda were donations by ordinary citizens of money and overtime labor. A huge system of financial loans and donations was set up, with the covert aim of giving vital support to the Soviet treasury.[37]

Already before 1941 Soviet citizens had been urged to purchase state bonds. Some were lottery loans with periodic drawings for cash prizes, while others, exclusively available in the countryside, were "percentage" loans with interest. November 1941 saw a lottery draw related to the pre-1941 bond for the "strengthening of the defense of the USSR"; eighteen days later the press announced the results. Most people lacked the means to buy bonds, and plenipotentiaries exerted enormous psychological and even physical pressure on them.[38]

Participants in the war bond of 1942, announced on April 14 of that year, surrendered three or four weeks' worth of income. Although "completely voluntary," it was also a "matter of honor and patriotic duty of every worker, employee, and *kolkhoznik* in our country." It was also official that everyone was enthusiastic; even front-line soldiers supposedly rushed to subscribe. On April 18 the media reported that the ten-billion-ruble bond had been oversubscribed by 68 million. Whether these figures approximated reality is unknown. Another bond subscription drive, for 12 billion, started on June 5, 1943, and supposedly reached 14,561,000 within twenty-four hours, and over 20 billion within a week. The next year the goal was 25 billion rubles.[39]

Although *Pravda*, *Izvestiia*, and *Trud* published the lottery drawing results, many prizes were not collected, probably due to embezzlement, the death of winners, and simple ignorance. Urged by the people's commissar of finance to give the results more publicity, the Central Committee allowed abbreviated announcements in other papers. Still the central press frequently published the results too late or even not at all. There were eleven drawings in early 1944, but *Pravda* reported only four outcomes and *Izvestiia* only eight.[40] This showed that the authorities cared little about the veneer of private gain masking this tax increase.

Special funds were created and announced to which every citizen was urged to contribute with money or labor. The Defense Fund started in June 1941, at the request of "working people." Reports, often published letters, spoke of *voskresniki*, or voluntary Sunday work, for this fund. In 1943 even members of the armed forces were said to contribute.[41]

In December 1942 Stalin publicly greeted and thanked a civilian for the first time during the war. He said that Ferapont Golovaty, a collective farmer from the Saratov oblast, had donated 100,000 rubles in personal savings toward the construction of a war plane, and thus had initiated a new round of fundraising for the Red Army. It was ignored that his savings stemmed from the illegal sale of honey.[42] The media mentioned a telegraph to Stalin from the Saratov oblast party secretary with the news that farmers had donated from their personal savings a total of 33.5 million rubles toward the construction of military planes. Stalin's one-sentence reply asked the secretary to pass on the Red Army's "brotherly greeting and gratitude."[43] Countless public acknowledgments by Stalin to other donors followed. Marking the beginning of 1943, Soviet president Kalinin said that a recent "spontaneous" campaign had produced money, extra grain, meat, and other produce and thousands of telegrams to Stalin. Typically, he said, "the collective farmers of the national republics and distant oblasts strive not only to keep up with the central oblasts, but often exceed them in sums of their donations."[44]

There were also republican fund drives. Red Army successes and the twenty-fifth anniversary of the Ukrainian Soviet Socialist Republic in December 1942 reportedly inspired fundraising for a tank column named *For Soviet Ukraine*. This, the republican leaders told Stalin, was "a vivid demonstration of the deep love and selfless devotion of the Ukrainian people to its great Soviet Motherland and to You, dear Joseph Vissarionovich." By late February 1943 Soviet Ukraine's "working people" reportedly had supplied 9,643,933 rubles in cash and 952,470 in state bonds. The donors included evacuees, people in the "liberated regions," and even people in the Rivne and Sumy oblasts, which were still under Nazi rule. Reporting on this participation was meager, however, even in the Soviet Ukrainian press.[45] Analogous reports dealt with other republics, such as the Latvian SSR, for a tank column and a plane squadron, both called *Latvian Rifleman*; the Lithuanian SSR, for a plane squadron called *Soviet Lithuania*; and Uzbekistan, for tanks and fighter planes called *Collective Farmer of Uzbekistan*. Unlike the republican press, the central press spoke merely of "citizens" of particular republics, not of Latvians, Lithuanians, and the like.[46]

Early in 1943 appeared the Fund for the Health of the Defenders of the Motherland, consisting of milk donations to wounded soldiers, officially launched in the Cheliabinsk region, and the Fund of the Main Command of the Red Army, originating in Kuibyshev. Also called the Red Army Fund, the latter mostly involved industrial production on top of the plan. On May 1, 1943, Stalin reported that it had raised over seven billion rubles in donations. This demonstrated that the war was truly *obshchenarodnaia*, or national.[47]

Partisans in the Vitsebsk oblast reportedly gathered over 2.5 million rubles from the population.[48] And there came a "movement for aid to the liberated regions": soon after the Red Army recaptured a region, the survivors of war and Nazi terror somehow had rubles and food to spare and surrendered them. As *Pravda* stated, "The last salvos near Stalingrad had barely thundered away when the workers, engineers, and technicians of Factory Number 347 already gathered the first hundred thousand rubles for the [regional] fund for the restoration of the heroic city." The farmers of seven recaptured raions in the Mykolaïv oblast supposedly gathered in one month 15 million rubles for a tank division to be named after the oblast. A letter from recaptured Ukraine in April 1944 reported a cash donation of 1.2 million toward a plane squadron named after the Vasylkiv raion, as well as a donation of more than 200,000 poods of grain, 150,000 poods of potatoes, and 27,000 poods of meat.[49]

Early in 1943 it was also reported that writers had donated 852,000 rubles "from their personal accounts" and 500,000 rubles of theatrical royalties for the *Moscow*, *Press Worker*, and *For a Soviet Ukraine* tanks.[50] Convict labor was secret, but in December 1942 "working men and women, engineering-technical workers, and employees" in Magadan supposedly collected 4.8 million rubles for the construction of bombers. And to celebrate the twenty-fifth anniversary of the Red Army, another 16 million had been donated from personal savings, which the local leaders of Dalstroi asked to be allocated for a tank column named after the founder of Lenin's Cheka, Feliks Dzerzhinskii.[51]

The gifts were supposedly voluntary, but the state and then Stalin took the credit. The first directives about these "patriotic movements" were presented as acts by the Soviet government or at least as joint resolutions of the government and party—evidently Stalin believed this was more effective than drawing attention to his person. But later he used the donations as occasions to orchestrate public declarations of fealty to him. At a certain stage, the editors of *Pravda*, *Izvestiia*, and *Krasnaia zvezda* collectively proposed that in order to save space, they would report just the donations, omitting the ritualized exchanges with Stalin. They dropped the idea for Shcherbakov stared at them without uttering a word.[52]

From the very beginning the Orthodox Church urged believers to raise funds for the Red Army, and in December 1942 it could open a bank account for this purpose. Benefit concerts by religious communities were held. But the media never mentioned this; the notion that nonstate groups might publicly collect was strictly taboo.[53]

Refugees and Evacuees

In 1941 between 12 and 17 million people left the western regions of the expanded Union as refugees or, in Soviet parlance, evacuees. The central authorities did not stimulate this migration, considered detrimental to willingness to fight the Germans to the death. Foreseeing correctly that famine was more likely in villages, most refugees tried to go to cities, but they had little say in their destination. Once the NKVD randomly rounded up refugees in Tashkent and sent them to Siberia for agricultural labor and tree logging operations, joining what people called the "labor army."[54]

Some migrants declined to work on farms, and some spouses of evacuated officials and army commanders disdained the locals. Most able-bodied evacuees and refugees did eventually work, however, even though some employers refused to hire them, believing that they would not stay for long. Early in 1942 some Cossacks in the Kuban were hostile to Leningraders, as the alleged accomplices of a regime they hated for having deported their relatives to faraway places before the war. To generalize on the basis of such anecdotal evidence is risky. Early in 1943 in the Urals almost one in ten people were evacuees, often underage. According to one historian, most were treated normally, but there were accusations of cowardice and spying. Another historian gives this sensible evaluation: "In the absence of clear and coherent signals from the center regarding the status of evacuees, it was all too easy for authorities at all levels to treat them as marginals."[55]

As noted earlier, the maximum daily bread ration for evacuees was downgraded to 200 grams in late 1943. That winter their overall food supply sharply deteriorated.[56] Sometimes Moscow released food from "special funds" for all evacuees or for specific groups, such as Leningraders, "former" citizens of Poland, relatives of party and government officials, and Red Army commanders and other members. But at the major evacuation reception point of Tashkent most aid did not come from the state, but from real volunteers.[57] No media publicity surrounded these state and volunteer measures.

If the propaganda of most of the second half of 1941 is to be believed, there was no evacuation under way at all. Then, on November 25, 1941, the Soviet Information Bureau suddenly declared that the "main" part of the population had evacuated to the country's eastern regions.[58] Equally secret at first was the evacuation of factories. When *Sovetskaia Sibir* revealed in early 1942 that the Novosibirsk oblast had become a large industrial center and the destination of many evacuated (and now troubled) industrial enterprises, censors were reprimanded. Industrial evacuation could be reported only vaguely, as in statements such as "History has no parallel to the immense magnitude of the industrial evacuation we have achieved within so brief a period. Hundreds of enterprises have been transferred from territories temporarily seized by the enemy deep into our rear, thousands of kilometers away from the battlefield."[59]

By then the propaganda often emphasized the hospitality and friendship offered by the people in the Urals, Siberia, and other distant regions. That many newcomers were Jews (in official figures, over a quarter by the end of 1941) was left unsaid. Later in the war evacuees waxed enthusiastically in a regional paper, "We came to Uzbekistan from Bessarabia, Belorussia, and Ukraine. None of us knew the Uzbek language, and the people of the collective farm where we stayed did not know our language. But that did not prevent us from feeling as among close friends on the very first day of our arrival."[60] On special occasions evacuees from particular republics were singled out. In December 1942, for instance, the Saratov oblast party secretary praised the Ukrainian newcomers' labor, and a Ukrainian from the Kryvy Rih basin praised the coexistence of his people with the people of the Urals.[61] The Turkmen press praised the "best people of the Ukrainian intelligentsia," for whom Turkmenistan had become "a new paternal home"; they had arrived "not as guests, but as Soviet people enjoying full rights."[62] The Soviet Ukrainian press meanwhile displayed little interest in the evacuees.[63]

The central media also published examples of endemic problems, but presented them as minor. *Trud* reported in late 1941 that farmers were meeting and assisting the newcomers with "joy and typically Russian hospitality," but "individual" peasants (and some work-shy evacuees) were unhelpful. A correspondent wrote that the authorities in one city had never visited the new factory since its arrival three months earlier. "Part" of the newly arrived workers were still living in a hostel; the factory kitchen could not be installed, resulting in long waits that forced the workers to keep working after their shift. The city bathhouse was packed, and most day care centers did not open until 9 A.M., although workers left home at 7 A.M. Another story described a female worker and her children in Omsk suffering from the indifference of a factory director, a party secretary, and a union leader. Now her problem with fuel had been solved, but those three remained unpunished.[64]

The issue of abandoned apartments and property received some attention early in 1942. The public prosecutor in Moscow had been instructed to bring "all persons guilty of stealing property of evacuated citizens" before a military tribunal, according to a tiny report mentioning names and sentences ranging from five years to (in the case of people who had also stolen food cards) the death penalty. Then the media reported a government order concerning abandoned homes that evacuees used to rent back home from local soviets and enterprises. Those would now be rented out to others. The former tenants were allowed to sell items they had left behind or to retrieve them by mail, but this did not make them any less dissatisfied with the order.[65]

It is likely that there was little surprise about articles in which evacuees vowed to stay put. Later reports suggested that they might never be allowed back. "It is understandable that people from Moscow, Leningrad, Kiev, or the Donbas love their native cities," *Pravda* wrote in September 1944. "But because a process of parallel restoration of factories is going on in the liberated regions, the interests of the Socialist State demand that evacuated enterprises remain in the East. This means that all conditions must be created for the evacuated workers and office employees to settle down in the new places—to settle down permanently and feel satisfied." People anxiously asked at propaganda meetings whether they might eventually return. (Most eventually did.)[66]

Other Vulnerable Groups

Family members of combat soldiers had the right to a small allowance provided certain conditions were met. Some were spelled out in documents distributed to certain party members and the chairmen of soviets. On August 16, 1941, Stalin ordered that the families of Red Army members who surrendered (in practice, who ended up in Germany captivity or whose corpse was lost) be deprived of social benefits, and, if the "malicious deserters" were commanders or political workers, arrested. (To what extent such arrests took place is unclear.) In June 1942 the State Defense Committee defined who belonged to the family of a "traitor of the Motherland" and therefore had to be exiled. None of these rules appeared in the media. The message there was that even though there was a right to undefined "care," the families had to show that they were deserving of it. *Trud* put it as follows: "Surrounded by the care of the entire Soviet people, the family members of the defenders of the motherland strive to be worthy of that care."[67]

During the war with Germany *Pravda* received approximately 400,000 letters. One in five came from the hinterland, and those often were requests or complaints by family members of servicemen. Red Army members who wrote also often addressed the issue of their families. After an editorial in February 1943 on local aid to families of *frontoviki*, or "front-line people," *Krasnaia zvezda* also received many letters from soldiers furious at local officials who seemed indifferent to the starvation of their families and responded evasively or not at all to anxious letters. There were also letters from soldiers' wives about the better treatment of the families of what they called *tyloviki*, "hinterland people." Aleksandrov was informed, but none of this information became public.[68]

Ilia Ehrenburg wrote, "Millions and millions of Soviet people in the hinterland burn with one desire: to ease and embellish the life of the wives, parents, and children of the front-line soldiers." But he also hinted at problems, citing a letter from a senior sergeant whose wife, now with a newborn, was not getting any help. Some people, Ehrenburg commented, were "shielded from emergency, love, and anger by the impenetrable skin of egoism. The fire that has enveloped our country has not chased these bureaucratic badgers from their holes.... In one city, bureaucrats don't want to help evacuated families of privates; in a second, the housing department is an unassailable pillbox; in a third, the secretary of the city soviet does not think of the children of front-line soldiers." But Ehrenburg was allowed more leeway than most other publicists. Censors were instructed to ban "generalizing negative" information about benefits to the families.[69]

The thrust of published reports on family letters was and remained that only a minority faced problems. *Trud* reported late in

1943 on "dozens" of letters from wives of military men mentioning the help they received. "Here and there, one encounters indifferent people who treat the questions of families of front-line men bureaucratically," the paper wrote, but "such irresponsibility does not remain unpunished." The "semi-annual report of the Uralians" to Stalin of July 1944, "signed by 1,608,411 people," vowed that they were carrying out his "directive" to care for the families of Red Army members: "Now we have twice as many children's institutions as there were before the war; and first place in them is reserved for the children of front-line soldiers. The families of the fighters and commanders received the best plots and seeds for gardens. Now we take care to repair their apartments before the winter, to stock fuel, clothes, shoes."[70]

The millions of war invalids embodied the terrible cost of the war. Ever since the early 1930s, the single aim of benefits and care for invalids had been to enable them to get back to work. Level of disability, prior wage, and military rank were taken into account, but the benefits were not enough to live on. Even in the case of invalids demanding full-time care the state assumed that they had families who could help in supporting them. During the war with Germany, the state faced an increased demand for labor and decided to reduce spending on invalids. It chose the following solution, late in 1941: those people's right to work became a duty. For two years Moscow pushed for a sharp reduction in the number of people recognized as partly able-bodied invalids. In the fall of 1943 it focused on removing people from the middle category of disability: those not needing full-time care yet unable to work. Hundreds of thousands suddenly faced the obligation to work. Beginning in 1944 all disabled were further humiliated by a requirement to appear before commissions once a year. The measures created resentment that rarely surfaced. If it did, it often assumed the shape of anti-Semitic slurs.[71]

As with the families of servicemen, a concern about promoting laziness explained why the propaganda about invalids hardly ever mentioned the benefits and instead praised their nearly total mobilization for labor. It was reported that the "former monastery" in Zagorsk, near Moscow, was teaching them trades and that heavily disabled veterans received help in newcraft cooperatives working at home. "'At first it seemed to me that I was not needed, a lost man,' writes the disabled comr. Zhdanov, 'for I could no longer work as a cook and had no education for something else. But the party and government did not abandon me. I received a new specialization.'" There also appeared stories about invalids who rose to become well-paid high achievers. Fiction did not lag behind in presenting a glowing picture. The youngest son portrayed in Boris Gorbatov's novel *Taras' Family* (later retitled *The Unsubdued*), serialized in *Pravda* in 1943, is physically unable to fight after sustaining wounds at Stalingrad. But as he walks west in the army's rear, Nikifor not only finds hospitality all around but senses that he shall soon shed his crutches and join in the festive economic recovery.[72]

A Fund for Aid to Children supported by financial donations, *voskresniki*, and campaigns for unpaid labor lasting ten days or a month gained some attention in February 1942, when *Komsomolskaia pravda* carried a proposal, allegedly from drafted Komsomol members, to donate part of their salary to it. But propaganda related to children generally evinced a desire for tight control over and tangible gratitude from them. In a radio talk on August 30, 1941, Arkadii Gaidar, a writer of children's books, warned the "child laborers" listening, "You will have to work hard.... The country always took care of you, it raised, educated, consoled, and partly even pampered you. The time has come for you to show—not in words but in deed—how much you esteem, cherish, and love her." Shirkers of dirty or mundane work should be treated with "friendly, cold disdain." *Trud* wrote, "One must be demanding toward children, fight against slackers and raise discipline at school and in pioneer detachments." Their labor tasks included recycling metal, collecting fuel for schools, and working in gardens and factory shops. At a ceremony in Leningrad late in 1943 a large group of schoolchildren received medals "for the defense of Leningrad." Reports cited the speech of one child, who introduced the notion of replacement: "Having received a medal, I want to say that we school children must become worthy replacements of our fathers and brothers." It was an anomaly that, from the middle of 1943 (a time when labor camps for unsupervised children were reintroduced), some reports appeared on the need to allow summer holidays for children and teenagers.[73]

The ultimate top secret was that many children either received no adult care at all or were treated as criminals. The militia calculated having arrested more than 200,000 unsupervised children and teenagers in 1942 and thought that child crime rose by 55 percent. The number of unsupervised children grew still more after the ethnic deportations of early 1944. When it was decided in June 1943 to send children ages eleven to sixteen who had committed minor crimes to the NKVD's new labor and education camps for children, officially no one knew. The media hardly ever mentioned problems at orphanages and were silent when orphans without an adoptive parent were sent on to new military schools.[74]

Media focused on the vanishing of orphans—"There will be no orphans among us"—as a result of allegedly massive adoption. The most famous wartime poem in Uzbek dealt with the topic. Published in Russian in *Pravda*, Gafur Guliam's "You Are Not an Orphan" is about an adoptive father reassuring a young boy separated from his parents. A typical report mentioned a female worker at Moscow's Krasny bogatyr factory named Elena Ovchinnikova. She had four children of her own, but was going to adopt an orphan. Her alleged initiative supposedly sparked a "veritable pilgrimage" to the factory committee and the party bureau—indeed a countrywide "movement for the adoption of orphans." Farms reportedly decided to raise orphans collectively; for instance, Moscow oblast radio reported that the members of the Krupskaia farm in the Kuntsevo raion had decided to "take in" five children orphaned by the "fascist monsters." And almost every collective farm in the Mozhaisk raion was raising one or two orphans.[75]

From the very beginning, the regime declared that it no longer accepted full responsibility for the supply of food, but it barred references to rationing, the maximum food amounts to which citizens were entitled. The only causes of food problems were supposed to be laziness and greed. If everyone did as they were told, there would be enough for all.

Meanwhile a system of financial loans and donations was set up. The gifts were supposedly voluntary, but the state and then Stalin took the credit. In the unlikely event that citizens did not experience hardship themselves, media reports would have enlightened them, for only the prospect and presence of famine could convincingly explain the numerous media references to public inspectors, guards, embezzlers, and thieves. But people's own experiences told them that the propaganda was wrong to blame laziness and greed.

The central media gave examples of problems with regard to evacuees, but presented them as minor; overall there was friendship and helpfulness between the refugees and the locals. Although families of servicemen, war invalids, and children had a public right to undefined "care," the media left no doubt that these vulnerable groups had to show that they deserved it, and falsely claimed that it was adequate. The press and radio praised a nearly total integration into labor of the disabled. As for children, the authorities expected not just the usual gratitude but also tight control, which hinted at the severity with which they treated minors. In an echo of the glossy portrayal of the invalids, the media also suggested that all orphans would be adopted. The realities citizens saw themselves in the street diverged sharply from these claims.

The articles on gardens, which offered practical advice, possibly raised morale. But overall, as with the campaign to mobilize for labor, the reports about food and vulnerable groups of people could hardly inspire.

5

Monstrous Atrocities

The Nazis and their foreign and local allies murdered millions of Soviet and other citizens. Jews were highest on their agenda, but countless others were killed as well. The killing was not just by hanging, shooting, or gassing, but also through enforced famine. Just before the invasion Nazi planners anticipated the starvation of "x million" of "superfluous" Soviet citizens. Hitler and his followers deemed this necessary for feeding the homeland and thus for victory, and felt it would help rid them of people, imagined as all being Russians, who had been "Bolshevized" and hence were dangerous, expendable, or both. These secret plans were implemented in various ways. One month into Barbarossa the Nazi goal became to seal off Leningrad, not to conquer it, and by the end of the year German artillery were shelling bread factories, central food supply institutions, and traffic into the city. German soldiers were under orders to shoot refugees, and around the city it was official occupation policy to prevent the civilian population from getting food. Perhaps about half of Leningrad's population starved to death—1 to 1.3 million people. The Nazis also deliberately created famine in occupied cities such as Kiev and Kharkiv. And they starved millions of Soviet war prisoners to death in a very short period.[1]

The Soviet propaganda apparatus faced an unprecedented situation. Millions of Soviet citizens who were supposed to be under Moscow's protective wing, or had been enlisted in their country's defense as soldiers, now faced an immediate threat to their lives, and many were killed. Could the countless killings be reported without lowering morale, or might reports actually bolster it?

Intelligence Reports and Public Statements

On July 19, 1941, Stalin received the first known NKVD report about atrocities in the occupied Soviet regions. Early in 1942 information gathering was streamlined by an NKVD order for all relevant documents relating to Nazi war crimes, whatever their provenance, to be sent to its Bureau of State Records.[2] The Red Army's Main political administration (the party organization controlling it) ensured that a great deal of information arrived. In July 1942, it complained that its subsections had practically ceased to supply material about enemy atrocities and ordered them to gather and regularly forward photographs of victims and destroyed buildings, survivor testimonies, documents discovered on enemy military, and comments by Red Army soldiers about atrocities.[3] The next month the Central Committee ordered editors and front-line correspondents to devote the "most serious attention to the gathering and publication of materials about the atrocities and looting of the Germans in the [Soviet] territory occupied by them."[4]

In line with how military intelligence had reached him before the war—largely as unprocessed data bereft of interpretation—the available archival record suggests that Stalin received few reports with generalizations or analytical comments. It was typical that when Pavel Sudoplatov, a high-ranking NKVD officer, used refugee accounts and intelligence and partisan reports to prepare a long report about German cruelties in Soviet regions the result was simply what he called a "list of facts." Soviet intelligence agencies also wrote few surveys about the entire Soviet space subject to Nazi rule. A rare exception, which surely landed on Stalin's desk, was prepared by the Main Intelligence Administration of the Red Army in the middle of 1943.[5] Regardless of the extent to which Stalin and his inner circle comprehended German policies, the intelligence reports revealed much of the nature of Nazi violence and murder: all ethnic groups were listed as suffering, but there were also many references to Nazi deliberation—the singling out of specific groups, namely disabled people, psychiatric patients, POWs, Communist Party officials, and Jews.[6]

Stalin was interested almost exclusively in citizens who offered armed resistance and prevented German exploitation, and suspected the other people no longer living under his control of betraying him. (In a way he was right, for many of them did not want his rule.) But eventually he did publicly acknowledge the dangers faced by all. His radio speech of July 1941 referred to a matter of "life and death of the peoples of the USSR," defined by reference to historical precedent: the fascists aimed to "Germanize" the Soviet population by restoring "tsarism" and reinstalling the "rule of the landlords," so as to obtain "slaves [for] German princes and barons." At risk was "the national culture and the national statehood of the Russians, Ukrainians, Belarusians, Lithuanians, Latvians, Estonians, Uzbeks, Tatars, Moldavians, Georgians, Armenians, Azerbaijanis, and the other free peoples of the Soviet Union."[7] Thus Stalin said the main threat was not death but enslavement.

Thereafter Stalin mentioned mass killings several times. In his October Revolution Day speech in November 1941 he said the invaders "kill and violate the peaceful inhabitants of our country, with no mercy toward women, children, and elderly." Quoting Hitler, he referred more broadly to a "war of extermination with the peoples of the USSR," with a special reference to "the great Russian nation" and "the Slavic peoples." It was confusing that he also declared the "Hitlerite" regime "essentially a copy of the reactionary regime which existed in Russia under tsarism." For instance—and this became Stalin's one and only personal wartime reference to Jews—"the

Hitlerites organize medieval Jewish pogroms just as eagerly as the tsarist regime used to do."[8]

Viacheslav Molotov was assigned the task of publicly providing lengthy characterizations and overviews of Nazi crimes. In several detailed notes the foreign commissar listed such crimes perpetrated east of the 1941 Soviet border. These notes were directed at the countries with which the USSR had diplomatic relations, but the Soviet media printed them. As with all Soviet publications about the German atrocities, the goal was less to expose crimes than to mobilize. These materials were supposed to develop hatred and ready the mind for merciless vengeance.[9] Molotov's first note appeared in November 1941 and dealt with Soviet war prisoners. A long note in January 1942 described the "wholesale robbery, despoliation of the population, and monstrous atrocities," all part of the Nazi plan for "annihilation of peace-loving peoples."[10]

Molotov's third note, in April 1942, described "monstrous villainies, atrocities, and outrages" and declared the German leadership responsible for them. There existed German "plans and orders," he reported, for the "extermination of the Soviet population, prisoners of war, and partisans by bloody violence, torture, executions, and mass murders of Soviet citizens, irrespective of their nationality, social standing, sex, or age." More than any other leading Soviet statement before or since, this document called the Nazi killings indiscriminate. Why they were committed remained unclear; most acts, Molotov said, were committed "above all to intimidate or directly exterminate Soviet people." As for the victims, he referred to "the Russian, Ukrainian, Belarusian, and other peoples of the Soviet Union."[11] Stalin's May Day 1942 message briefly referred to the German-fascist invaders who "violate and kill the peaceful population of Estonia, Latvia, Lithuania, Belorussia, Ukraine, and Moldavia."[12]

On October 15, 1942, a public announcement to the "governments of Czechoslovakia, Poland, Yugoslavia, Norway, Greece, Belgium, Holland and Luxembourg, and the French National Committee" appeared, signed by "the Soviet government." It fully agreed with an Allied declaration concerning punishment for war crimes. Expressing a desire for an international tribunal, Moscow "confirmed" that the crimes were "universal and deliberate," though the Soviet Union, it implied, suffered the most: the German government and its accomplices "have also made it their aim to carry out the direct, physical extermination of a considerable section of the population of the [Soviet] territories captured by them."[13] In his October Revolution Day speech the next month, Stalin himself took the unusual step of speaking at length about the crimes:

> The Hitlerite scoundrels have made it a rule to torture Soviet prisoners of war, to kill them by the hundreds, to condemn thousands of them to a death by starvation. They violate and kill the civilian population of the occupied territories of our country—men and women, children and elderly, our brothers and sisters. They have made it their aim to enslave or exterminate the population of Ukraine, Belorussia, the Baltic republics, Moldavia, the Crimea, and the Caucasus. Only villains and bastards devoid of honor and fallen to the level of animals, can permit themselves such outrages against innocent unarmed people.

Moreover they were raging elsewhere too: they had "covered Europe with gallows and concentration camps."[14]

December 1942 was also extraordinary because in that month the Soviet leadership specifically referred to just one non-Jewish group as being victimized and also referred at length to the Holocaust. On December 25 Stalin and Molotov placed a message on *Pravda*'s front page on the occasion of the twenty-fifth anniversary of the Ukrainian Soviet Republic. Eliding Jews and others, they said that Nazi Germany had "exterminated and tortured to death hundreds of thousands of Ukrainian men, women, and children." Subsequent articles marking the anniversary also Ukrainianized the human suffering taking place in that republic: *Pravda*'s editorial mentioned *only* Ukrainian victims, and *Krasnaia zvezda*'s editorial spoke of the killing of "hundreds of thousands of peaceful Ukrainian inhabitants.... The enemy is carrying out their monstrous plan for the physical extermination of millions of Ukrainians and the total robbery of the Ukrainian people."[15] The Kremlin's short-lived Ukrainian focus helps explain why, in an appeal to the Ukrainian people that same month, republican leaders Nikita Khrushchev, Mykhailo Hrechukha, and Leonid Korniiets said Nazi Germany was implementing "Hitler's devilish project to physically exterminate the Ukrainians and all of the Slavs." Korniiets's published speech referred to the killing of "over two million peaceful Ukrainian inhabitants."[16]

The Ukrainianization should be seen against the backdrop of statements about Jews. Earlier that month a long, joint Allied condemnation of the extermination of Europe's Jews had appeared in the Soviet media, followed by a long Soviet explication that referred to the extermination of "various nationalities."[17] Stalin evidently had decided, in this time of comparative centrality of Jewish victims, to publicly assure the Soviet Union's second-largest nationality, ethnic Ukrainians, that their suffering was not being overlooked.

The next year deportation to Germany became a key theme. In May Stalin referred to "deportation to German slavery and extermination," and Molotov issued a note (which was to be his final one) about the deportations and the living conditions of Germany's Soviet slave laborers.[18] In November 1943 Stalin made his last wartime reference to Nazi killing. "Hundreds of thousands of our peaceful people have been exterminated by the Germans in the regions captured by them," he said, while ordering the partisans to "save Soviet people from extermination and deportation to slavery in Germany."[19]

An Extraordinary State Commission to investigate crimes committed by the German invaders and their accomplices, headed by the trade union leader Nikolai Shvernik, had been founded in November 1942. Like Molotov's notes and the other official statements, its reports reached Soviet citizens even though they were primarily intended for the Allies. Their main goal, as a historian has put it, was "to give international legal legitimacy to documentary materials that had been both collected and created by the institutions of Soviet power about Nazi war crimes, in order to use them as one of their long-term tools in the ideological and political struggle for the future of postwar Europe and the USSR." This helps explain why almost no government or party officials were on the commission's staff.[20]

That the commission did not primarily mean to inform or convince Soviet citizens of anything explains also why publication of its findings (as booklets and press articles) began only in April 1943, and why fully half of its reports, including those on the Crimea, Moldavia, western Ukraine, and Leningrad, never appeared in print at all. In 1943 nine reports appeared dealing with killings, relating to the RSFSR (towns in the Smolensk and Kalinin oblasts, a hospital in the Kursk oblast, Krasnodar, Stavropol krai, Orel oblast, and the city of Smolensk) and to Ukraine (Kupiansk, Stalino oblast, and Kharkiv).[21] In early 1944 there appeared, apart from government reports about the death camps Majdanek and Auschwitz (discussed in the next chapter), thirteen reports dealing, in whole or in part, with killings of civilians or of POWs known to have been killed by Nazi Germany or its allies. One from March 1944, broadly titled "Directives and Orders of the Hitlerite Government and German Military Command Concerning the Extermination of Soviet Prisoners of War and Civilians," stated that preliminary data indicated that "about two million" Soviet citizens and Soviet POWs had been murdered, gassed, or tortured to death.[22] The other publications were two reports dealing with the RSFSR (on the Novgorod oblast and Karelia), five on Ukraine (on Kiev, the oblasts of Rivne, Odessa, and Lviv, and the POW camp in Slavuta), two on Belarus (on Minsk and the concentration camps near Azarichi), and one each on Estonia, Latvia, and Lithuania.[23] All of these official reports provided a long list of crimes by German, Romanians, Finns, and others.

Worse Than Death

Apart from the prominent reports about the criminal plans and acts, a flood of other materials appeared in print about them.[24]

Captured German policy documents, diaries, and letters were easy to adapt for propaganda use, provided the chief of staff agreed. When the SS magazine *Das Schwarze Korps* stated in August 1942, "Our duty in the East is not Germanization in the former sense of the term—that is, to impose German language and laws upon the population—but to ensure that only people of pure German blood inhabit the East," the Soviet media merely had to provide a summary. One year later an article titled "Hitler's War of Extermination" in *Pravda* described Nazi killings and enforced famine in various countries. Conquering the world through extermination had been a goal of the Nazis from the start, but now they were "making haste to physically exterminate the population of the conquered lands, so that the Allies shall go to the cemetery of peoples." Naturally it also referred to the SS magazine.[25] Photographs found on the bodies of Germans provided equally damning ready-made material. One was a self-portrait of German company commanders sitting behind a large sign saying, "The Russian Must Die, So That We Can Live." Snapshots of beatings, hangings, and shootings were also reproduced.[26]

In addition German war prisoners and Soviet survivors were questioned, and there were the corpses of the victims themselves: early in the war, Germans in retreat often left out in the open their victims killed. Soviet images of these corpses provided vivid evidence of the Nazi goal of extermination. The atrocity propaganda defined various victim groups: captured soldiers, civilians killed, victims of rape, and citizens deported to Germany.

In the first year of the war with Germany, well over two hundred items about the Soviet prisoners of war appeared in the central papers. Coverage began almost immediately: in the second week of July 1941 *Krasnaia zvezda* and the Soviet Information Bureau reported the stabbing of wounded prisoners.[27]

The propaganda could quote numerous captured German documents—orders, personal letters, and photographs—that described how these prisoners were deliberately mistreated, tortured, and murdered. The German order of June 6, 1941, to shoot the military commissars did not appear in the media, but many orders did, in Russian translation. In one early regiment's order, prisoners were simply to be shot. More general orders strove to inspire a merciless attitude in the German soldier; to ban humanity toward the prisoners, to use them to clear mine fields, and to sew a special badge on their clothes.[28] Widely promoted was the ban, issued on October 10, 1941, by Walter von Reichenau, commander of the German 6th Army, against supplying food to the vast majority of Soviet prisoners, namely those not working for the Wehrmacht. Obtained by the USSR early in 1942, the Bureau published a translation.[29]

Krasnaia zvezda quoted unsent private letters from soldiers while printing facsimiles of the German originals. One writer described shooting a Red Army soldier even though he surrendered: "The first Russian. Since then I have shot hundreds. I have such a rage. Since then, I took only one Russian prisoner, a German." Another text described how an entire unit took no prisoners.[30] There appeared German photographs of what were called prisoners of war who had been killed, as well as Soviet reports about such killings, sometimes also reprinted as leaflets.[31]

Molotov's first note, of November 25, 1941, condemned the "appalling atrocities committed by the German authorities against Soviet prisoners of war": they were barely fed, were treated brutally in camps and at work sites, and often were shot. In short, Molotov accurately noted, the Germans were "striving for mass extermination of the Soviet prisoners of war," in flagrant breach of the Hague Convention of 1907. (He did not mention the Geneva Conventions, which the USSR had not signed.)[32] Molotov's second and third notes stated that the Germans had begun treating the entire population in this way, forcing them to work and putting them into camps. Moreover, seeking to avenge recent military defeats, the German command had "introduced the universal practice of physical extermination of Soviet war prisoners." The foreign commissar approvingly cited a memorandum received from the Polish government-in-exile: "The treatment of Soviet war prisoners presents perhaps the vilest page of German barbarism."[33] The third note, like media reports from other sources, claimed that the danger was just as acute for prisoners of non-Germans, such as the Finns.[34] Molotov did not, but other reports referred to the Germans' shooting of women and children for feeding war prisoners.[35]

The descriptions were often headlined with the notion that captivity was "worse than death."[36] Mikhail Sholokhov's short story "The Science of Hatred," published first in *Pravda* in June 1942 to mark the first anniversary of the German invasion, became well known, and was reprinted and translated. Among other atrocities, Sholokhov's story realistically portrayed the shooting of prisoners for being or looking Jewish or for lagging during marches.[37]

With the recapturing of areas where POWs had been held in camps, a new phase of reporting began. Referring to the sites as "death camps," correspondents supplied texts and photos, such as from Khorol near Poltava in November 1943. A published Extraordinary State Commission report about the camp in Slavuta concluded that about 150,000 people had been deliberately killed there.[38]

Civilians Killed

As for Soviet civilians, the media said they were shot, used as human shields, bombed, starved, subjected to biological warfare, and gassed—and in most cases, as with war prisoners, the reports were fairly accurate. Various instances of shootings were reported early in the war on the basis of local investigations after the return of the Red Army. Photographs and films of corpses produced powerful media material. German units that included an SS Panzer division occupied Rostov on the Don on November 20, 1941, but they were pushed out again eight days later. Soviet military commissars and political leaders (*politruks*) spoke with locals and wrote down their tales.[39] The NKVD also assembled materials. There was much to investigate: the streets were full of shot and hanged corpses. Overall the invaders had killed hundreds, including Jews for being Jews. Investigators discovered that some shootings were random, while others struck dozens of men and boys by way of reprisal for a lethal partisan grenade or the provision of shelter to Red Army men.[40]

Some Rostovans mentioned that Germans invaded homes asking who was Jewish, and that some Jews had been shot.[41]

Many press articles in the first half of December described the murders. The intent to mobilize was clear, if only because of references to the locals' horror, indignation, and vengefulness. *Krasnaia zvezda*'s very first report described a gathering amid corpses where a women called upon the army to kill the fascists, described as "wild beasts." While *Komsomolskaia pravda* referred to more than 2,500 shot and hanged civilians and POWs, and *Pravda* to hundreds, other articles sensibly calculated the dead only at certain localities. Two reports stated that the forty-eight shot near the Railway Administration were the victims of reprisals for a nearby shooting of a German. There were striking tales about two boys shot on sight for releasing pigeons or for refusing to surrender them, illustrated with a still picture from the *Union Cinema Journal* for December 23. According to the press attaché of the Polish embassy, moviegoers in Kuibyshev seeing this and other victims erupted in "shouts of indignation and then of wild, cruel hate." Molotov also referred to one of these boys in January 1942.[42]

Izvestiia reported:

> As everywhere, Jews received special attention from the Germans. They were subjected to special humiliation and degradation. They could only walk the streets from 6:00 A.M. to 2:00 P.M. (the others from sunrise to sunset).... First [the Germans] ordered all the Jews to sew on their sleeves little green stars and to paint such stars on their apartment doors.... Then they declared a total registration of all the Jews of Rostov. The mass killings of the Jews in Kiev and Odessa also began with total registration. In Rostov too, the fascist pogromists prepared another extermination of ten thousands of people. Fortunately, they were unsuccessful.[43]

When Rostov was lost to the Germans again in late July 1942, Nazi terror resumed, climaxing in the mass murder of the local Jews. Afterward a long description of the "crimes of the German-fascist cannibals" in the city included photographs of a dead boy and a prison yard full of dead adults.[44]

Other early on-site reports came from Kaluga and Kerch, cities where most of the victims were Jewish. Located near Tula, southwest of Moscow, Kaluga was occupied on October 13, 1941. Here arose Nazi Germany's easternmost ghetto, holding some 150 Jews. During the Soviet counterattack Germans, in an apparent attempt to kill all these Jews, set the ghetto on fire and began shooting. But most Jews survived thanks to the Red Army's arrival on December 30. Almost immediately reports appeared: an article mentioned the Jews as targets and a photograph by Samarii Gurarii in *Izvestiia* on January 1 showed some of those shot—possibly the first published Soviet image of shot Soviet Jewish civilians. On December 31, 1941, the Red Army recaptured the Crimean city of Kerch. Within a week *Pravda* quoted a local who had discovered "heaps of corpses of shot Jews" at the cemetery. "Among them were many elderly, women, and children. Many corpses were with severed heads, arms, and twisted jaws." Photographs of these corpses were flown to Moscow and published in the February issue of the magazine *Ogonek*. The captions did not mention that most victims were Jewish; they gave the Jewish name Kogan but said the victims included "Russians and Tatars, Ukrainians and Jews," all killed "indiscriminately." The photo from Kaluga was captioned likewise in referring to "peaceful inhabitants of Kaluga."[45]

Early in the war an author with a German-sounding name claimed that during the previous war in 1914, the Spanish Civil War in 1936, and elsewhere, whenever possible the Germans used women and children as shields. Stories about human shields, invented or not, now reappeared about the current war. When Stalin edited a brief *Pravda* report in September 1944, he kept unchanged the statement that in August 1941 German attackers shielded themselves with the population of the Belarusian town of Dobrush. He added, "Death for death! Blood for blood!"[46]

German bombing posed another deadly threat. The Bureau reported early on that German planes had bombed Moscow twenty-four times, killing 736 people and wounding thousands. "Naturally," the agency added, the Soviet command retaliated for these "beastly raids" on peaceful civilians with "systematic raids on military and industrial targets in Berlin and other German cities. Thus it will remain." Whereas Soviet bombers used to avoid Berlin so as to preclude "serious" civilian casualties there, now Moscow no longer felt constrained by what it called the "laws of war."[47] Later in the war there were also reports of Britons killed in German bombings.[48]

The media also rightfully accused Berlin of creating deadly famines. Having captured the relatively unimportant "Green Folder" of June 1941 (which implicitly approved the starvation policy), Molotov and others discussed it in April 1942.[49] The media sometimes mentioned the Leningrad famine. In July 1942 *Izvestiia* described the city as "half-starving." In mid-August 1942 the radio broadcast an accurate brief description of the events by the director of the city's Physiological Laboratory: the Nazis "thought they could kill Soviet people through famine," he recalled. "It was monstrous! Hunger death entered the heroic city. We saw it." Famine in the region surrounding Leningrad was also described.[50]

Soviet Ukrainian radio broadcast a text, said to be written by a division commissar, that accused Germany of deliberately imposing famine on Ukraine's city dwellers.[51] The paper *Krasny flot* wrote of a great famine in Kharkiv from which escape was punished with shootings. *Pravda* wrote in 1943 that in that eastern Ukrainian city, "hundreds and thousands died from hunger, cold, and the sickness and exhaustion associated with them, in particular the Kharkiv intelligentsia.... For months, dead bodies lay in the basements of homes. They were buried in courtyards by the hundreds and buried in graves without coffins."[52]

As for Kiev, *Pravda* referred to the confiscation of food at the outskirts from peasants who wanted to sell it inside the city. This was in July 1942, while this policy was actually in full swing. *Krasnaia zvezda* reported that month's German threat to shoot on sight those who moved in or out of the city on unofficial pathways. In 1943, some months before the Red Army regained the city, *Trud* reported that tens of thousands had starved to death in Kiev. Even at the time of writing, in early September, "famine causes Kievans to wander the nearby and distant villages, bartering their last possessions for a few cups of grain or buckwheat. But many already have nothing left to exchange."[53] Overall these reports were fairly accurate—unlike one sweeping accusation in the same year that "about 300 million" inhabitants of "continental Europe" might starve from the consequences of an "organized" famine that had already killed hundreds of thousands.[54]

Near the Belarusian village of Azarichi (or Ozarichi), the retreating Wehrmacht organized three open-air concentration camps for one week in March 1944. There it kept and ultimately abandoned old, sick, and very young people, thereby killing perhaps 13,000 non-Jews, mostly Belarusians. The main site was immediately investigated and described as a death camp. An open letter to Stalin was "adopted" at meetings. Supposedly signed by more than 10,000 of the 33,434 survivors including 15,960 children, it gave "warm thanks to You, dear father," for serving as their inspiration before they were rescued, and for actually rescuing them. They would work selflessly in return. According to the writer Iakub Kolas, Azarichi testified to the German plan for "premeditated extermination of the Belarusian people." Unusually quickly, a state commission report appeared in print that declared the placement in the camps of people with typhus as part of that plan. Even though evidence of this intent was absent, it became official that in this way the Wehrmacht attempted to kill the uninfected inmates.[55]

Other accusations of biological warfare, to date unsubstantiated by researchers, referred to deadly "experiments" and blood transfusions. Ilia Ehrenburg wrote of hundreds of laboratories in Ukraine for criminal experiments: "Now that the Germans have exterminated the Jews, they are carrying out experiments on the Ukrainians," such as gassing, forced impregnation, sterilizations, and—a passage omitted from a reprint—the "production of soap from human fat."[56] In 1943 and 1944 German soldiers were accused of stealing children's blood and then killing them. This was said to happen in Poland (where Hitler had "decided to destroy the Polish people by destroying Polish children") and Belarus.[57]

The claim most likely to be greeted with skepticism, gassing in mobile or stationary gas chambers, of course was true. *Krasny flot* on January 25, 1942, apparently provided the first public Soviet reference to it. According to the article, refugees from the occupied Russian city of Taganrog had reported that the Gestapo was gassing civilians.[58] The first public Soviet reference to gassings in a camp seems to have appeared on July 30 of that year, when TASS reported that a Polish prisoner of "the concentration camp near Tarnów" (a town near Kraków with a prison and ghetto) had told his visiting wife of experiments with poison. One experiment concerned poisoned clothes. "'Last year,' the prisoner declared to his wife, 'in this camp were carried out experiments with poison substances. On the night of September 5 [in 1941] one thousand prisoners were chased into a room under the ground, into which were injected gasses. All of the prisoners died and the next day other prisoners removed their corpses.'" Historians accept close to the same date for the very first gassing murders in Auschwitz, which killed Soviet Jews and members of the Soviet Communist Party.[59]

What may have been the first public Soviet reference to the gas vans, operational in Soviet territory beginning in late 1941, was a radio broadcast of a recording made in Moscow in early 1943. It was an open letter by a woman from the Krasnodar region who mentioned the vans to her son-in-law.[60] In April 1943 Ehrenburg wrote that 1,500 Jews in Minsk had been "poisoned" in hermetically sealed vans. While a description of the gas van used in Krasnodar was censored from the cinema newsreel for March 25, gassing in vans filled with carbon monoxide did feature in reports on the tribunals in Krasnodar in July, in an article about the North Caucasus by Aleksei Tolstoi, and in a Bureau report that for months that year vans had been used daily to gas Kharkivans: "Late in February, during one of its 'journeys,' the car broke down on the road and halted on Moscow Street. They towed the 'dushegubka' to a garage for repairs. When garage workers opened the door, they saw that the car was packed with corpses. The swollen faces of the corpses were unrecognizably distorted. It was clear that the people had died under excruciating torture." The topic also appeared in reports on the tribunal in Kharkiv in December 1943.[61]

The reports of systematic extermination were not limited to Soviet citizens, but also referred to Poles and other non-Soviet peoples as victims. The concept of "Germanization" often appeared here, as synonymous with murder.⁶² Meanwhile German claims of Soviet mass murder were vehemently denied. In April 1943 Nazi Germany publicly launched an investigation into the mass graves of Polish victims of the NKVD found in the Katyn Forest near Smolensk and linked them to a new wave of propaganda against "Jewish Bolshevism." The Nazis wanted to discredit Moscow in the eyes of the Western Allies and seemingly timed the announcement of their discovery to drown out British and American media reports of the imminent German destruction of the Warsaw ghetto and the killing of its last inhabitants.⁶³ A special Bureau statement quickly denounced the "foul fabrications of the German-fascist hangmen." Stalin had personally edited it. (Thus the Soviet claim became that the Polish officers had been engaged in construction work in 1941, not 1940, and "Goebbels's slanderers" replaced the original "Goebbels's propaganda.") In January 1944 a long state commission report about Katyn also blamed the Germans. "The Russian people helped us to find the truth," a Polish army major was quoted as saying at the Katyn graves. These reports were typical in emphasizing that the Nazis were killing all Slavs—as victims the Poles were not special.⁶⁴

Other Nazi Crimes

Apart from the dead, the propaganda acknowledged victims of rape, deportation, and "fascist penal servitude"—all this was also deemed to incite hatred. Rape became a theme early on. *Pravda* spoke of mass rape at the classical writer Leo Tolstoy's estate and elsewhere. Konstantin Simonov's poem "Kill Him!" urged soldiers to kill "if you don't want the Germans / To take her by force, clutched in a corner, / To crucify her, three at a time / Naked, on the floor." A caricature showed a German dragging off a woman, implying that she would be raped, and Ehrenburg denounced the "fornicating Fritzes."⁶⁵

Radio Soviet Ukraine mentioned a group of peasants who traveled under SS supervision to Berlin, where they saw exhausted and famished Soviet citizens who were making military uniforms. The report was unusual in specifying the work done by the forced laborers; usually censors cut out such references. In May 1943 Molotov liberally quoted from letters from deportees. His note said they were humiliated, tortured, and "doomed to hunger and slow and painful death." The deportations were part of a devious plan to enslave citizens from many countries.[66] Later media stories told of their gratitude for their liberation and the "warm care and attention" they received upon returning home.

The enemy was also blamed for wanton destruction of cultural heritage sites. There were reports of the desecration by the "descendants of the Vandals" of the homes of Leo Tolstoy, Anton Chekhov, and Pyotr Chaikovsky, the grave of the Ukrainian writer Taras Shevchenko, and the statue in Lviv of the Polish writer Adam Mickiewicz.[67] Various published reports of the Extraordinary State Commission dealt with nothing else. In reality some of this damage was due to the Soviet scorched-earth policy of 1941 or, in the case of the main university building in Kiev, indiscriminate Red Army artillery fire. Near the end of the war the Red Army destroyed much property in East Prussia, but the Bureau cited German prisoners who claimed the destruction was the work of Germans who had donned Red Army uniforms.[68]

Early in 1942 Soviet authorities arranged visits by survivors of Nazi rule in the regions near Moscow to unaffected areas and let them talk about their experiences to workers and farmers. For example, three peasant women from the Istra raion told a series of horrors. The Germans shot three POWs. They evicted the women from their homes, into the freezing cold, forced them to cook, while killing their cattle; later they forced them to leave their village. Women and children spent eight days and nights in a wood, without food. Three villagers who attempted to return, if only to dig up some potatoes, were shot. Two babies were born dead. Over half of the homes in one village were burned down, the others deliberately vandalized. *Izvestiia* was probably accurate in reporting about these women's visit to textile workers that one tearful survivor asked the listeners to work hard so as to help the Red Army, and that the women listening were moved as well.[69] Groups of similar "delegates" also toured the Saratov oblast, reportedly addressing 44,500 villagers and factory workers. In western Siberia in 316 meetings over twenty-two days, five peasants in two groups spoke to 71,000. The Agitprop leader Aleksandrov reported in April 1942 that these meetings stimulated hatred, patriotism, productive labor, and donations, so he proposed setting up twenty such groups from the Moscow oblast, who would visit the Kalinin, Leningrad, Orel, Smolensk, and Tula oblasts.[70]

But apparently the proposal was not adopted. Aleksandrov's superiors probably reasoned that more speaking tours were not necessary because the print and visual propaganda largely was up to the task. And in this they were right. Stalin had given the green light for extensive reporting about Nazi atrocities, rightly foreseeing that this would raise morale. Overall the Soviet media skillfully used the abundant materials made available, and the mass of largely truthful information drowned out the cases of outright forgery, such as in the case of Katyn.

Most Soviet reports of German crimes had a solid basis in reality, and people became aware of this. The propaganda was immensely aided by the crimes so many Germans committed and their own statements and photographs documenting them. When a Soviet newspaper wrote in the middle of 1942 that "the Germans have condemned the population of the occupied oblasts to extinction" and that "mass extermination of the population" without precedent was under way, Soviet readers realized that this was not an exaggeration, even if this statement should refer only to non-Jews.[71]

6

A Bestial Plan for Physical Extermination

In the mass murder of the Jews of Europe, known today as the Holocaust or Shoah, Germans, Hungarians, Romanians, and many others, including local auxiliaries, murdered millions. Among the dead were virtually all of those Jews living in the USSR who had not left in time—in Ukraine alone, approximately 1.5 million. Most were shot to death or killed in gas vans.[1] Moscow had to decide whether to inform its citizens that the occupying forces had a special policy of rapidly killing all Jews. What it ultimately did—the way Soviet propaganda dealt with the mass murder of Europe's Jews—reveals the relative weight of Communist ideology, concerns about the Allies, and anti-Semitic prejudice.

There was a precedent in the Soviet public record about Nazi anti-Semitism. On November 30, 1936, *Pravda* reported Viacheslav Molotov's speech of five days earlier on the occasion of the new Soviet Constitution. Condemning fascism for its hostility toward Jews, Molotov cited a previously unpublicized comment by Stalin that "anti-Semitism, like any form of racial chauvinism, is the most dangerous vestige of cannibalism," and he added that "brotherly feelings for the Jewish people" would "define our attitudes toward anti-Semites and anti-Semitic atrocities wherever they occur." The Soviet press also covered the staged "Kristallnacht" pogroms in Germany two years later, referring to the "massacre of a defenseless Jewish population." Two Jewish filmmakers released *Professor Mamlock*, the first Soviet film depicting the persecution of German Jews.[2] After the German invasion, explicit media reports about the mass murder of the Jews began appearing. These tended to be buried among other materials but—contrary to what many scholars have assumed—there was no Soviet policy to remain silent or vague.[3]

Reports about Jewish Victims Received by Stalin

Stalin personally became aware of the Nazi aim of killing all Jews—or at least all *Soviet* Jews—no later than August 1941. In the middle of that month Panteleimon Ponomarenko, the first secretary of the Communist Party of Soviet Belarus, informed him in writing that Jewish villagers in that republic were "being subjected to merciless annihilation."[4] On August 26 Aleksandr Shcherbakov received a revealing NKVD report on occupied Ukraine stating that the "physical extermination of the Jewish population in German-occupied regions of the Zhytomyr, Kamianets-Podilsky, and Vinnytsia oblasts is not abating." In the first oblast, "pogroms of the Jewish population with bloody victims do not cease," it read; on August 9 twenty-seven Jews were killed on Zhytomyr's outskirts, and on the night of August 13-14 up to 200 Jews had been shot three kilometers outside the town of Berdychiv. Early in the same month, the NKVD reported, up to 400 Jews from various regions, mostly women and children, had been gathered in the city of Kamianets-Podilsky and "destroyed," ending up in pits dug by Soviet prisoners of war. The phrases "not abating" and "do not cease" strongly suggest even earlier reports about killings targeting Jewish civilians. A report by NKVD officer Pavel Sudoplatov on December 14 included numerous instances of the killing of Jews.[5]

In January 1943 the Central Staff of the Partisan Movement compiled an explicit report specifically about German crimes against

Jews in Soviet territories, and sometime later that year military intelligence described the "anti-Jewish terror" clearly and accurately: "mass extermination of the Jews began during the first days of occupation" and a "new wave of Jewish pogroms and executions began in the summer and fall of 1942." The agency mentioned shootings and lethal injections and added, in an apparent reference to Treblinka, "There are reports that Jews are taken to a concentration camp near Białystok and are killed there with electric current." (Polish Białystok was considered Soviet territory because it had been incorporated into Soviet Belarus at the time of the pact with Germany.) The report added curtly, "The Gypsies are being subjected to the same mass extermination."[6]

As I discuss below, the Kremlin soon captured Nazi documents that bespoke a lethal anti-Semitism. Along with the Soviet intelligence reports, this means that early on, Stalin and his associates were told by various sources that the Nazis were exterminating all Jews and Gypsies (Roma and Sinti). They had no lack of information.

Statements by Prominent Jews

In January 1942 prominent Soviet Jews were recruited to join the Jewish Anti-Fascist Committee in the USSR. Created by Agitprop, the group convened "representatives of the Jewish people" in Moscow. These events were directed at foreign, particularly American Jews, but the Soviet reports were not just sent abroad; they were published in *Eynikayt*, a Soviet weekly in Yiddish, and through central radio broadcasts and newspaper reports reached large Russian-speaking Soviet audiences as well. *Pravda*, *Izvestiia*, and other newspapers reported that at a meeting on August 24, 1941, Solomon Mikhoels, the chairman, warned that Hitler was after the "total destruction of the Jewish people." An open letter to the Jews of the world raised the alarm: "If in the enslaved countries bloody fascism introduced its 'new order' with the assistance of the knife and gallows, with the assistance of fire and violence, with regard to the Jewish people bloody fascism has planned a gangster-like program of the total and unconditional destruction of the Jews with all the means at the fascist butchers' disposal."[7]

Reports on the second meeting of Jewish "representatives" held on May 24, 1942, reproduced an open letter to Stalin that called the current persecution of the Jews unprecedented, and another letter to all Jews that presented Jews as most at risk:

> The Jewish people have a great sorrow. In the cities that they have seized, the Hitlerites condemn Jewish men, Jewish women, Jewish children, Jewish old people to an excruciating death. Before killing them, the Hitlerites torture the Jews, rape the women, kill children under their mothers' eyes. They bury people alive and desecrate the graves. There are cities and villages where Jews worked the benches and tilled the soil and where now not a single Jew remains—neither old people nor infants: all have been killed at Hitler's demand.[8]

On Red Army Day, February 23, 1943, allegedly ordered by the Second Plenary Meeting of the entire Jewish Anti-Fascist Committee, Mikhoels and Shakhno Epstein sent Stalin a letter that was also published. This time it was unclear whether the Nazis were singling out the Jews: "Millions of our brothers and sisters, just as the sons and daughters of other peoples who fell under the yoke of the cannibal Hitler, bleed profusely. The suffering of the Jewish popular masses knows no bounds. Ruin and destruction hang over their heads. The grief of the mothers and the story of the children buried alive shock the world."[9]

On April 2, 1944, the committee organized another meeting, which was broadcast on the radio and extensively reported in *Eynikayt*.[10] While *Izvestiia* and *Trud* printed only a brief item ten days later that summarized Epstein's words on Jewish war heroes, *Pravda* carried a long report. *Eynikayt* reported Mikhoels's statement that in recent years "four million" Jews had been murdered in Europe, or "a quarter of the Jewish people," but *Pravda* omitted this passage. (It retained Mikhoels's pride in the "sons of the Jewish people" who were fighting for "our Soviet motherland," "inspired and united by the great Russian people," and alongside "representatives of all the peoples of the USSR.") *Pravda*'s quotations from another speech, by Itsik Fefer, omitted the statement "The ashes of Babi Yar are searing our hearts." Yet despite the cuts no doubt remained about a specific Nazi policy against the Jews: "The fascists do not only want to exterminate our people. They want us to disappear from the face of the earth with a coward's mark on our forehead. It did not happen!" Jews were fighting hard in the Red Army, Fefer explained.[11]

In August 1941 Ilia Ehrenburg wrote that Hitler "hates us [Jews] more than anything," but within weeks he preferred to de-emphasize this, suggesting to Shcherbakov that the central press let a well-known Russian figure denounce the "fairy tale" that "Hitler is only angry at the Jews." Eventually only he himself published such a denial. The Germans, he wrote in October of that year, hated all non-Germans and wanted to annihilate one half of the people of the Soviet Union and to enslave the other half: "They say, 'We are against the Jews.' It's a lie. They've got Jews of their own, whom they favor. These Jews have their passports marked with the letters 'W.J.,' which means 'Valuable Jew.'" In July 1942 he even wrote that Germans hated the Russians the most. Publications by other Soviet Jews, though less explicitly, also tended to contextualize or "universalize" the mass murder.[12]

Yet later Ehrenburg also published several articles that left little doubt that all of the Jews were being killed, implying that the Nazis treated Jews differently. Late in 1942 he wrote, "Hitler wanted to turn the Jews into a target." Jewish Red Army soldiers wanted to avenge the Jewish girls and old people killed by the Germans. In July 1943 he stated unambiguously that the Germans had "exterminated the Jews" of Ukraine. Likewise *Pravda*'s report on the 1944 Jewish meeting quoted his words about resistance: "The Germans thought that the Jews were a target. They have seen that the target shoots. Not a few dead Germans could talk about how the Jews are fighting." This came after a statement about Jewish victims: "There are no more Jews in Kiev, in Warsaw, in Prague, in Amsterdam. But in the [Ukrainian] village of Blahodatne 30 Jews were saved. At the risk of his own life, the *kolkhoz* accountant Pavlo Serhiiovych Zinchenko saved them."[13]

Early in August 1944, when the Red Army reached the old German state border, Ehrenburg reminded his readers of the "death factories" and gas vans near Minsk and in Bełżec and Sobibór. Here as elsewhere "trains with Jews arrived from France, Holland, Belgium." Large numbers of non-Jews, he added, had also been shot and gassed.[14] As late as December 1944 he could mention the murdered Jews of Europe in *Pravda* and even number them: six million. True, not only Jews had suffered; those indoctrinated by "nationalism" had "decided to put to the wall large, talented, strong peoples." Ehrenburg then made the following, remarkable statement about what we now call the Holocaust:

> In the countries and regions captured, the Germans killed all the Jews: elderly people, babies. Ask a captured German on what ground his compatriots destroyed six million innocent people and he will answer: "They are Jews. They are black-haired (or red-haired). They have different blood." This began with stupid jokes, with the shouts of street kids, with graffiti, and it led to Majdanek, Babi Yar, Treblinka, and ditches filled with children's corpses. If before of Treblinka anti-Semitism could seem an everyday deviation, then now this word is soaked with blood, and the Polish poet Julian Tuwim is right to say, "Anti-Semitism is the international language of the fascists."

Ehrenburg's next sentences barely removed the emphasis on the Jews: "Now the whole world sees the results of racial and national arrogance. The ovens of Majdanek, in which the Germans burned people of thirty nationalities only because they were Russians, French, Poles, or Jews, these terrible ovens did not emerge immediately; they were prepared by a long education based on misanthropy."[15]

In short, many statements by Soviet Jews that made it past the censor of Russian-language publications did say that all the Jews of Europe were being killed.

Reporting on Soviet Jews and Ignoring Other Jews

Although Stalin's July 1941 speech had not mentioned Jews, soon media reports began describing Soviet Jews as victims with some frequency, though never as a matter of routine. In its report for the evening of August 16, 1941, the Soviet Information Bureau placed the following sentence in a long report on German robberies and killings: "In some raions of the Zhytomyr oblast, the Germans have committed bloody Jewish pogroms. In Iemilchyne the fascists buried thirty-two Jews alive." Two weeks later the word was that "in the town of Kamianets-Podilsky, the fascists gathered 400 Jewish refugees from various regions, mainly women and children, and shot all of them." When, early in September 1941, the Red Army entered the town of Elnia in the Smolensk oblast and held on to it for two days, *Izvestiia* and *Trud* immediately described the shooting of several locals "just because they were Jews."[16]

An article of mysterious provenance, "The People's Hatred" by "N. Petrov" in *Izvestiia* on September 27, gave the severest warning of the danger facing all Jews since the first meeting of "Jewish representatives." Stalin's records in the Moscow archives state in passing that this Petrov was actually the Soviet head of state, Mikhail Kalinin, and indeed a postwar Soviet study ascribed this particular article to him. (Neither source gives an explanation for the pseudonym.) Whether Kalinin really wrote the article is unclear; perhaps Aleksei Tolstoi was the ghostwriter. In any event, "Petrov" argued that according to the "fascist" ideology, "the Jews, who, fascism claims, bring disasters to Germany, must be destroyed."[17]

For that same month the first deliberate, if incomplete, omission of known Jewish victims can also be documented. The Bureau statement for the evening of September 22 included translations from the diary of "Emil Goltz," said to be a German soldier and Nazi Party member. One passage (supposedly written in Modlin, northeast of Warsaw, in June 1941) went as follows: "We have been put up in the Jewish district. When you see these loitering figures, one feels like pulling the trigger and shooting the rabble. Well, just wait, we'll get you!" By mistake, the Soviet Union provided foreign media with another, more explicit translation: "Passing through a town, I participated together with Walther in cleansing a Jewish store." The version used within the Soviet Union omitted the Jewish aspect: "Passing through Slonim together with Walther, I participated in the cleansing of stores and homes." The "internal" version also omitted a July reference to searches of "abandoned Jewish homes."[18] By whom these early omissions were made is unclear, but it was evidently an attempt to universalize the event.

In his October Revolution Day speech on November 6, 1941, when he personally mentioned mass killings for the first time, Stalin referred to Jews. The "Hitlerite hordes" engaged in certain activities "just as eagerly as the tsarist regime did," such as "arrang[ing] medieval Jewish pogroms." *Trud* commented that Lenin had known that anti-Semitism served only one purpose: to distract the masses. Now the "Hitlerite pogromists" had broken a record in killing "tens of thousands of people." The context made it evident that this referred to Jews.[19] At this stage of the war, the notion that not only Jews but all the Soviet peoples were targeted for extermination did not bar reports focusing on Jews. For example, *Pravda* reported (accurately) that on October 23 the Romanian army in Odessa had committed "one of the biggest mass murders of Jews in history." The paper put the death toll at 25,000. Stalin himself had removed from the draft what had preceded the massacre: the killing of more than 200 Romanians by a Soviet mine. This means that he personally allowed the word "Jews" to remain.[20]

Similarly, citing TASS in New York, *Pravda* and *Izvestiia* reported on November 19 that "the Germans executed in Kiev 52,000 Jews—men, women, and children." Ten days later *Pravda* referred to the "pogrom" in Kiev that killed 52,000, adding for some reason that Ukrainians and Russians also died in it. After the Red Army recaptured the eastern Ukrainian town of Lozova in January 1942, *Pravda* reported that the "Hitlerites" had shot all the Jews residing there.[21] Molotov's note of January 1942 followed Stalin's line of the previous November in speaking of a Nazi plan for "the annihilation of peace-loving peoples," while also referring to Jews as victims. The Nazi killings in Ukrainian towns, he said, were "particularly directed against unarmed defenseless Jewish working people."[22]

Also in January 1942 Stalin obtained, perhaps for the first time, German documents confirming the killing campaign specifically directed against Jews. Walter von Reichenau, commander of the German 6th Army, had issued instructions on October 10, 1941, on "the conduct of the troops in the East." Among other things, the Nazi general meant to suppress concerns among the German military about the mass murder of the Jews, such as that committed recently at Kiev's Babi Yar. "The main goal of the campaign against the Jewish-Bolshevik system is the total smashing of the state power and the extermination of the Asiatic influence on European culture," he explained. This was a "mission to liberate the German people once and for all from the Asiatic-Jewish danger." German mass murder in the "East" was both in retaliation and for the sake of security. There the German soldier of necessity was an avenger of "bestialities" committed against Germans and congeneric peoples and thus ought to have "full understanding of the necessity for the harsh but justified revenge on Jewish subhumanity." Killings were also needed to suppress uprisings in the army's rear, "which as experience shows always were incited by Jews." Soviet officers discovered the instructions in the recaptured town of Kalinin (now Tver), and on January 14 the NKVD leader Lavrentii Beria sent Stalin and Molotov a photocopy and a generally accurate Russian translation.[23]

Stalin saw to it that *Pravda* published the document the next day. There was a facsimile of the entire document but also a faulty translation that omitted all the anti-Semitic passages except "Asiatic-Jewish danger." Readers with some knowledge of German could see the deviation from the original. *Pravda*'s editorial, probably written by Stalin, did not mention the Jews at all, stating that Reichenau's Hitler-approved order aimed for the extermination of the "male population" of the occupied Soviet territories. It simultaneously claimed that "peaceful inhabitants"—*not* just males—were under threat and that at issue was "the physical extermination of the Russian people, the Ukrainians, the Belarusians, and all the other peoples inhabiting the Soviet Union."[24] It so happened that Reichenau died of a stroke on January 17. In the media response, Stalin again removed from reports the lethal anti-Semitism and added that Reichenau's order had aimed for the extermination of "the peaceful Soviet population."[25] These reports about Reichenau to date are the only known documented cases of Stalin's personally ensuring the removal of the Jewish background of Soviet victims.

A similar case of inconsistent removal occurred the next month. The Soviet authorities found telling documents in the headquarters of the 1st SS Cavalry Brigade, including a report about a "Pripet Action" conducted between July 27 and August 11, 1941. Thousands of civilians died in that campaign of mass murder, the vast majority of them Jews. The report included this passage: "Driving women and children into the marshes did not have the required result, for the marshes were not deep enough to allow for drowning. At a depth of one meter in most cases one reached solid ground (probably sand), so that drowning was impossible." An article in *Izvestiia* in February 1942 attributed to a battalion commissar quoted all of this without clarifying that the victims were Jews.[26] The writer or his censor also omitted an explicit passage about "gathering the Jews" and the comment "Jewish looters were shot. Only a few artisans, who had been put to work in repair shops of the Wehrmacht, were left aside." Yet the removal of Jews was inconsistent, for the article quoted accurately the following from another captured report, about the "pacification" of the Belarusian townlet of Starobin: "It was ordered to shoot all Jewish males without exception, which was carried out.... The auxiliary police carried out a number of executions and arrests." The German report was signed by one Magill, but *Izvestiia* (and later Molotov) called him "von Magill."[27]

Krasny flot several times reported the murder of Jews in southern cities; *Sovetskaia Ukraina* described the shooting of the Jews of Mariiupol and Artemivsk in Ukraine's Donbas (Donets Basin); and *Pravda* wrote, "Almost the entire Jewish population of Minsk has been exterminated."[28] In contrast, a report about Dnipropetrovsk omitted the Jewish ancestry of the 16,000 people shot there on two days in September 1941.[29] That deceptive report paved the way for the public proclamation of a "non-Jewish" line, Molotov's note of April 1942, which called the killings indiscriminate and totally omitted Jews.[30]

Yet even after this statement there came reports on Soviet Jews that referred to them as Jews. According to TASS in June 1942, the Federation of Jewish Philanthropic Organizations in London heard from a refugee that "the Hitlerites and their agents killed 25,000 Latvian Jews in the first four days of the occupation of the Latvian SSR. The Hitlerite pogromists terrorized the population of the Jewish quarters and confiscated from them literally all their belongings. 29,000 Jews have been herded in a ghetto in Riga, where they are living in horrifying conditions."[31] The Russian writer Mikhail Sholokhov could be anti-Semitic—he said once that "Abram is doing business in Tashkent"—but "The Science of Hatred," a story with his rendition of the tale of a Siberian lieutenant in the Red Army, vividly depicted the shooting of Jewish prisoners of war. The possibly fictional Gerasimov related that immediately after he and his comrades were captured, they were lined up. Then the following happened:

> A German lieutenant asked in poor Russian if there were any commissars and commanders among us. Everyone was silent. Then he said again, "Commissars and officers, two steps forward." No one left the line. Walking by slowly, the lieutenant picked out about sixteen people who looked like Jews. He asked each one, "*Jude*?" and without waiting for a response, ordered them out of line. Among those selected were Jews, Armenians, and simply Russians with a dark complexion and black hair. Before our very eyes, all of them were taken aside and shot with submachine guns.

The story was reprinted often, and it also appeared in twenty-one other languages.[32]

Reports on the June 1942 session of the Supreme Soviet provide further evidence of inconsistency about Jewish suffering, and indeed reveal unwillingness among some officials to fully adopt Molotov's line. Speakers from Belarus, Estonia, and Lithuania followed him in omitting Jews but singled out the threat to just one other non-Russian nationality. The Russian-born Ponomarenko probably disliked Jews, for he had reported to Stalin in July 1941 that Jewish refugees were "seized by a deadly fear of Hitler, and don't fight but flee." Now he did not simply Belarusianize the victims of Nazi murder in "his" Soviet republic: they were the "sons and daughters of the Belarusian people.... Never in its entire national history have the Belarusian people been subjected to such a danger. At stake was and is the life and death of the entire people."[33] Johannes Vares, chairman of the Estonian Supreme Soviet, told his audience that "in Estonia the Hitlerites killed in a beastly fashion many thousands of peaceful citizens—women, children, and old people," but added, as if in conclusion, "The German fascists want to destroy the Estonian people, erase [them] from the face of the earth." His Lithuanian colleague Justas Paleckis declared that the Germans were "systematically carrying out the Germanization and extermination of the Lithuanian people." His was the only speech not reported to get extensive or loud applause, probably because Paleckis asserted that throughout history, "no other people in the world has suffered so much from German invaders as the Lithuanian people."[34] In contrast, two other speakers reportedly mentioned the Jews. Vilis Lācis, a writer and the head of the government of Soviet Latvia, mentioned the mass murder of the Jews and "completely innocent people," and Leonid Korniiets, chairman of Soviet Ukraine's Council of People's Commissars, identified the nationalities who had been murdered in Ukrainian cities by the hundreds of thousands as "Ukrainians, Russians, Jews."[35]

Thus scrutiny of reports on Soviet Jews well into 1942 reveals two things: Stalin's involvement, beginning no later than January 1942, in stripping Nazi Germany's Jewish victims of their Jewishness, and a lingering inconsistency in application of this line, even among Soviet leaders, probably because there was no central directive specifically dealing with the media portrayal of the Jews. Once, early in November 1942, a party bureaucrat named Arkin did tell Ehrenburg, "It's better not to say that the Germans are killing Jews," but there is no evidence that Georgii Aleksandrov and other high-ranking party officials issued such statements.[36]

All the while the media took a different approach in discussing Jews in Europe who were not Soviet citizens. Although mentioned initially, they quickly disappeared from sight. On July 19, 1941, a brief notice referring to an interview by United Press with the former Chilean ambassador to Romania said, "In Romania, under pressure from the Germans mass persecutions of Jews are being carried out." The diplomat had "seen on gallows the bodies of citizens whose only crime was that they were Jews."[37] *Sovetskaia Ukraina* carried a play by Oleksandr Korniichuk in which a partisan read from a captured German diary about the burning alive of Jews in Rotterdam.[38] This kind of publicity about non-Soviet Jews soon became exceptional. In the first year of the war with Germany, the Soviet media's treatment of Jews victimized elsewhere in Europe was consistent; these Jews merited little or no attention.

Important reports from Poland made headlines in the United Kingdom and the United States and probably reached the Kremlin. In May 1942 the socialist Jewish Bund in Warsaw informed the London-based Polish government-in-exile that a transition toward the mass murder of all Jews was under way. In articles on June 25 and 30 the British *Daily Telegraph* said that "more than 700,000 Polish Jews have been slaughtered by the Germans in the greatest massacres in the world's history," and headlined "More than 1,000,000 Jews Killed in Europe," in what it called a campaign designed to "wipe the race from the European continent." The Bund report contained "the most gruesome details of mass killings even to the use of poison gas." The *New York Times* republished the articles (on June 30 and July 2), the BBC paid attention, and so did the Polish underground paper *Rzeczpospolita Polska* (on July 2).[39] Until December 1942 the Soviet media completely ignored all of this. They also neither mentioned nor used the references in the Polish underground *Biuletyn Informacyjny* in April, June, July, and August 1942 about gassings in specific death camps (Chełmno, Bełżec, and Treblinka-II).[40] Perhaps the bulletin did not reach Moscow at that stage; even if did, it seems unlikely it would have been used.

Then, without any sign that this might be coming, on December 18, 1942, all the major Soviet papers published a long, joint Allied condemnation of the "extermination of the Jewish population of Europe."[41] The next day a long statement placed this extermination into its supposedly proper perspective. The text was attributed not to Molotov but to the "Information Bureau" of the People's Commissariat of Foreign Affairs, a fictional entity never heard of before or since. Stalin evidently deemed it inappropriate for a Soviet leader to be personally associated with the statement. According to one Russian researcher, the draft of the document referred to the dangers of anti-Semitism; however that may be (the archival reference is incomplete), the final version did not do so.[42] The perspective instead was that of a larger planned assault on many peoples, not just the Jews: "Recently, throughout the territories of the countries of Europe occupied by the German-fascist invaders, a new intensification of the Hitlerite regime of bloody massacre of the peaceful population has been observed." The "criminal Hitlerite rulers" had various reasons: they wanted to "drown in the blood of innocent people their animal fear of approaching doom and retribution," and they realized that they could not break the "will of the peoples of Europe for the restoration of their independence and freedom." Hence they now were "putting into practice a bestial plan for the physical extermination of a considerable part of the civilian population of German-occupied territories—absolutely innocent people of various nationalities, social positions, views and creeds, and of all ages."

Only then did Jews specifically enter the stage, and in boldface: "In doing so, the Hitlerites and their associates are putting into practice at an accelerated rate their special plan for *the total extermination of the Jewish population in the occupied territory of Europe*." But the specific "atrocities against the Jews" and (especially, so Moscow seemed to argue) the "fanatical propaganda of anti-Semitism" were smokescreens: Hitler and his associates wished to "divert the attention of the German people from the disaster which is facing fascist Germany" and to "drown their own innumerable crimes against the peoples of Europe." Less authoritative comments focused on the Jews even less. One in *Trud* claimed that the "fascist 'philosophy' justifies the extermination of entire peoples, *especially the Slavs*." As a result, "about three million Poles" were dead.[43] Thus, even in December 1942, there was an attempt to weaken the focus on Jews by converting their ordeal into the prototype for the universal threat of Nazism.

However, this attempt should not obscure the appearance of the joint Allied document and other explicit articles, even though relegated to the fourth and final page of newspapers and to the very end of radio news broadcasts. On December 13 the media summarized two alarming foreign reports. One was a document received by President Roosevelt from American Jewish organizations: "Hitler has ordered the destruction of all the Jews in the occupied regions [of Europe]. Two million Jewish men, women, and children have already been killed. Five million more are under threat of similar destruction."[44]

The other summary was explicitly based on a Polish government-in-exile note of December 10 that, according to TASS, mentioned Nazi Germany's "intention to exterminate the Polish people," as well as that "the German authorities aim with systematic deliberation at the total extermination of the Jewish population in Poland." "Over a third" of Poland's 3,130,000 Jews had died in the past three years. The Polish note, TASS wrote, included "details of Himmler's March 1942 decree about the extermination of 50 percent of the total of Polish Jews by the end of 1942." TASS did omit some important elements. The original note referred to total extermination of "the Jewish population of Poland and of the many thousands of Jews whom the German authorities deported to Poland from Western and Central European countries and from the German Reich itself." Nor did TASS note that the trains were sent to "three localities: Tremblinka [sic], Belzec and Sobibor," thereby missing another opportunity to refer to such camps.[45]

A little later in December it was reported that a Swedish newspaper had demanded the opening of the Swedish border to Norwegian Jews, who otherwise would be shipped to their death in Poland, and that Canadian officials had said that Nazi Germany had killed at least two-thirds of Europe's 6.5 million Jews.[46]

Soviet Jewish Victims

In the beginning of 1943 a paradoxical development came into focus. Whereas Soviet Jewish victims were identified as Jews far less often than before, the Soviet Russian-language media often identified Jewish victims in Poland and elsewhere beyond the Soviet Union as Jews. A good example of the neglect of Soviet Jews was a report about crimes committed in Rostov, published in March 1943 after Stalin's personal perusal; it spoke of *citizens*, not Jews.[47] Stalin twice publicly reconfirmed the trend that year, calling the victims of extermination "Soviet citizens" (on May 1) and "our peaceful people" (on November 6).[48]

The rare exceptions usually involved Soviet Jews from cities close to the advancing front line. In January 1943, less then two weeks before the Red Army retook the Russian town of Velikie Luki, TASS reported, "From the very first day of their arrival in the town the Germans started to shoot groups of inhabitants," and gave a very specific example:

> One night, they chased twenty-eight Jewish families to the town fortress and subjected them to excruciating torture. Then they forced the condemned to dig a pit. On order of the officers, the soldiers stripped the men and women naked and started beating them with birch branches. Those who resisted were beaten with rifle butts and stabbed with bayonets. The execution was monstrous. Goaded on by bayonets, the victims of the Hitlerite hangmen approached the pit one by one. There were terrible scenes. A mother saw her daughter being shot, a son witnessed the execution of his father, a brother of his sister.[49]

Articles in the month of Kiev's recapture, November 1943, also mentioned the Jews. *Krasnaia zvezda* said those murdered at Babi Yar had been "Jews, Communists, and the workers of a range of Soviet establishments." *Izvestiia* extensively quoted a witness, Dmitrii Orlov, who began by mentioning the Jews and then supposedly shifted his focus to "the people."[50]

Reports about recaptured Kharkiv more typically omitted Jews entirely. A favorable review of Oleksandr Dovzhenko's documentary *The Battle for Our Soviet Ukraine*, released in October 1943, two months after Kharkiv's recapture, quoted the voice-over accompanying footage of an unearthed mass grave: "Look, living ones, do not turn away from our terrible pits.... There is a great multitude of us in Ukraine. Do not forget us. Seek vengeance against Germany for our sufferings." Likewise Nikolai Tikhonov wrote not of Jews but of 14,000 killed "Kharkivans." As for the regular Bureau reports, they had already stopped identifying victims as Jews in late 1941. This line continued, except in one November 1944 reference to Latvian forests as the setting for mass shootings of "peaceful Soviet inhabitants—Russians, Latvians, Belarusians, and Jews."[51]

The archival record of the Extraordinary State Commission was inconsistent in its treatment of Jewish victims, but the published commission reports set forth a pattern that would endure for years: ethnic distinctions among the victims were ruled out or obscured, and the extent of Jewish suffering and death was severely underplayed.[52] There were few exceptions. The commission reported the following about the German military commander of the town of Sychevka in the Smolensk oblast: "On January 7, 1943, he chased together about 100 Jews—women, elderly, and children. First he beat them up, then he took them to the city outskirts and shot them." According to the report about the Stavropol krai, "the German occupiers carried out with incredible hatred a bloody slaughter of the Jewish population of the city of Kislovodsk." Some 2,000 had been taken by train to Mineralnye Vody, walked to an antitank ditch, and shot. Also shot there were "thousands of Jews" from Essentuki and Piatigorsk. An exhumation supposedly conducted by Aleksei Tolstoi produced a body count of 6,300 "Soviet citizens."[53]

In "The Brown Drug," a long *Pravda* article of his own published on the same day as the state commission report, Tolstoi was outspoken: "In the North Caucasus, the Germans killed the entire Jewish population, most of whom had been evacuated there during the war from Leningrad, Odessa, Ukraine, and the Crimea." He added, "The Germans began preparing for the mass murder from the very first days of the occupation." Quoting various survivors and witnesses, he told a horrific tale of shooting and the gas van murder of Jews and a limited number of Russians. He admitted his incomprehension: "How could the German people fall so low that its army committed acts that humanity will remember for a thousand years with loathing and horror?"[54] Perhaps decisive in these reports about the North Caucasus was Tolstoi's standing with Stalin as a member of the state commission and as a writer similar to Ehrenburg in both his usefulness to propaganda and his popularity. Already one month into the war, he had written in *Izvestiia* that Hitler had won the support of the "petty bourgeois" through anti-Semitic agitation and desired to "exterminate the peoples that he does not need."[55]

From early 1944 on there appeared, apart from government reports about the death camps Majdanek and Auschwitz discussed below, eleven commission reports dealing, in whole or in part, with the killings of Jews. Five of these entirely failed to mention those Jews. The first omission concerned Nazi crimes in Kiev. On December 25, 1943, the commission chairman Nikolai Shvernik asked Aleksandrov to approve the long draft report. It was returned only on February 8, 1944, six week weeks later. Editorial comments by Aleksandrov replaced the Jews—already mentioned only sparsely—with "citizens." The final version (approved by Khrushchev and others) read, "On September 29, 1941, the Hitlerite bandits chased thousands of peaceful Soviet citizens to the corner of Melnik [sic] and Dokterev [sic] Streets. They brought them to Babi Yar, took away all their valuables, and then shot them."[56] The reports about the Novgorod oblast, Karelia, the Odessa oblast, and Estonia also omitted Jews. The Soviet Estonian report, for example, described the hasty murders committed at the camp at Klooga just months before, but provided no ethnographic detail about the 2,000 victims, most of whom were Jewish.[57]

But six other commission reports mentioned the Jews in some way. A March 1944 report on German orders with regard to war prisoners and Soviet citizens cited and included a facsimile of Reinhard Heydrich's guidelines of October 1941 on the "exposure" of "the Soviet Russian intelligentsia *and Jews*, in so far as this concerns professional revolutionaries or politicians, writers, editors, Comintern officials, and so on."[58] The report about the Rivne oblast quoted a witness of open-air shootings referring to "Soviet citizens—Ukrainians, Russians, Poles, Jews." The report on the Lviv oblast, released in December, described the suffering and death of the Jews—thus identified—of Lviv, partly in a statement by a French witness. Immediately thereafter came this passage: "During the ghetto's existence from September 7, 1941 to June 6, 1943, the Germans exterminated over 133,000 people, part of whom were shot in the ghetto itself, part in the Janowska camp, and the remainder sent for extermination to the German death camp in Bełżec (Poland)."[59]

The report on Minsk described the SS camp in Maly Trastsianets (or Maly Trostinets) and failed to mention the Jews, but did mention the Jews in another context: "The Germans kept up to 100,000 Jews in a special ghetto camp in the western part of the city of Minsk.... The assistant commandant of the ghetto camp, Gottenbach, drank toasts to the annihilation of the Jews and forced the doomed people to sing and dance, and personally shot prisoners." The report on Lithuania was deceptive about the extent of Jewish suffering, but mentioned Jews with regard to the city of Kaunas, albeit last in a line of victims. Finally, the report on Latvia of April 1945 omitted them in places but contained a section entitled "Massacre of the Jewish Population of the Latvian SSR by the Germans" that could not have been more explicit: "From the very first days of the occupation, the Germans began to massacre the Jewish population of the Latvian republic."[60]

These commission reports notwithstanding, more typical of Russian-language media reports after 1942 concerning Soviet Jewish victims was the publication in *Trud* in October 1944 of a speech by Shvernik's successor as trade union leader, Vasilii Kuznetsov. Speaking to a British audience about the "special cruelty" of Germans against people "merely because they were free Soviet citizens," he was quoted as stating:

> In every [Soviet] populated area, there are mass graves where there lie the burned corpses of hundreds and thou-

sands of completely innocent Soviet citizens who were tormented and killed. In every village you can see terrible places of torture and death, from whence no one sent there ever returned alive. Ukraine and Belarus, Moldavia, and other places where the Hitlerite cutthroats spent time were flooded with blood of completely innocent women, children, and elderly. Millions and millions of Soviet citizens fell victim to the Hitlerite terror.

In Kiev they had murdered almost 200,000 and in and around Minsk almost 300,000, Kuznetsov said. He did not mention Jews.[61]

Thus some state commission reports referred to Soviet Jews, and the Russian papers published some other explicit articles. But the general trend of reports about Soviet Jews after 1942 was omission of the words "Jews" and "Jewish."

The Murder of Jews in Poland

In 1943 and 1944 a lack of media attention to Soviet Jews coexisted with increasing publicity about non-Soviet Jews. To begin with, TASS issued without comment a two-sentence item on March 12, 1943: "As Reuters agency reports, the English minister of foreign affairs, [Anthony] Eden, has told the House of Commons that to judge from available reports, the mass murders of Jews in Poland are not abating. Eden added that a large number of people belonging to the Polish and Yugoslav nationality are also being subjected to mass extermination."[62]

The Katyn affair sparked a small increase in Soviet media attention to the Jews, to hammer home the Germans' atrocities. The Jews were being deported to "certain death" in Poland and Bulgaria, and "this organized destruction of the Jews is calling forth indignation among the Bulgarian people." An editorial in *Pravda* on April 19 expressing anger against "Hitler's Polish accomplices" who wanted to investigate Katyn spoke of atrocities against "the defenseless peaceful population, especially Jews." Aware of "the enormous anger of all progressive humanity" about these atrocities, the "Hitlerites" were "trying with all their might to turn gullible and naïve people against the Jews. For this purpose the Hitlerites invent some mythical Jewish 'commissars,' who allegedly participated in the killing of 10,000 Polish officers." It was analogous, *Pravda* said, to the Nazi lies in 1941 about NKVD victims in Lviv. A separate TASS item made it known to the world—Soviet citizens knew it already—that the editorial reflected the opinion of the Soviet leadership.[63]

Pravda also carried an explicit article about the Jews of Europe. I. Sergeeva reported on April 21 that according to Jan Masaryk, the Czech foreign minister-in-exile, Germany had officially admitted to the disappearance of 1,600,000 Polish Jews. She commented, "The German barbarians see their task as to completely exterminate the entire Jewish population of not only Poland but also the other European countries." Sergeeva quoted at length from an underground Polish radio report about Treblinka, thus making what was most likely the first published Soviet reference to the camp. Efficient killing of "people" with "steam" was taking place there, she said. Yet she concluded by calling the people killed in Poland Slavs, as if there were no more Jews to kill. This went on "day in day out, according to a plan, with premeditated intent, fully in accord with the misanthropic theories about the extermination of the Slavic peoples."[64] This proclamation—that Europe's Jews and Slavs were all suffering from the same extermination—may have been the author's sincere if mistaken opinion.

Already a few times in 1941 the Soviet media had reported starvation and other cruelties imposed on Warsaw's Jews.[65] Late in May 1943 *Pravda* said that "the Hitlerites had decided to erase the [Warsaw] ghetto from the face of the earth and to kill the hundreds of thousands of people who are on the inside." But they had been meeting fierce resistance for a month: "The surrounded people of the ghetto are fighting with great bitterness; they lack arms, and they take up stones; they blow up buildings that German gendarmes enter; they have turned the ghetto into a fortress. Many German gendarmes and Gestapo men have already found their death in its siege. The Polish population is helping the Jews in the fight against the common enemy."[66]

The media attention in April and May 1943 to the Jews in Poland probably came about mainly because Stalin believed—and with reason—that the Western Allies would not question the morality of the anti-Nazi alliance. He tried to alienate them from the Polish government-in-exile by allying it with anti-Semites.[67] This is also clear from the case of Vinnytsia, a revelation that was similar to Katyn's but lacked a recognized government-in-exile to embarrass. A public Nazi investigation of and propaganda campaign about the NKVD mass graves in that Ukrainian city began in late May 1943, accompanied by another wave of anti-Semitic propaganda. But only in August 1943 did the Bureau deign to respond to "the next provocation from the fascist cannibals."[68]

On July 24, 1944, the Red Army for the first time liberated a Nazi death camp, Majdanek near Lublin. It had been mentioned in passing at least once before: "In the concentration camp in Majdanek, at least 200 people die every day," a review of the foreign press in *Trud* had reported in January, adding that prisoners were being "killed in gas chambers."[69] Vasilii Grossman was available, but although he provided, on August 6, the first published reference to Sobibór—as part of a report on both the "massive mechanized murder of the Jewish population of Poland" and the "concerted, gradual extermination of the Poles"—he was replaced at Majdanek by the non-Jewish Konstantin Simonov.[70]

His article "Extermination Camp," serialized in *Krasnaia zvezda* on August 10, 11, and 12 and read on the radio on three evenings at 8:40, defined the camp as Europe's largest death factory. The name "Majdanek" was absent; Simonov followed official Nazi usage in naming the camp after Lublin, as Majdanek denoted the suburb. According to the writer, in the spring of 1942 large numbers of Jewish prisoners began arriving, first from Lublin and nearby ghettos, then from Czechoslovakia, Oświęcim (Auschwitz), and Warsaw. When discussing the mass shootings of November 3, 1943, however, he did not mention that all 18,000 victims (an accurate figure) were Jews. (See also the statement "We know of such places as Sobibór and Bełżec, where trains brought people condemned to death along a narrow-gauge track to an empty field located in a remote corner, where they were shot and burned.") In summing up, Simonov did mention the Jews, noting that most of the Majdanek dead were Poles, followed by Russians and Ukrainians and an equally large group of Jews from throughout Europe. Today's estimate is that 20,000 non-Jews, mostly Poles, Russians, Ukrainians, and Belarusians, and many more Jews—60,000—were murdered in the camp.[71] Overall, however, the description was remarkably accurate for its time, especially when compared with other Soviet reports.

The long eyewitness accounts in other papers, accompanied by vivid photographs, mentioned the Jews only in passing. Evgenii Krieger in *Izvestiia* called Majdanek a death factory and noted that the term "distinguishes it from all other German camps for prisoners of war and prisoners that we saw up to now in three years of war." The people were gassed and killed "without distinction of nationality, religion, conviction, sex, and age." During 1943 these were "Russians, French, Serbs, Dutchmen, Jews, Poles, Ukrainians, Greeks," and more.[72]

Pravda's correspondent Boris Gorbatov had more questions than answers about the reason for the camp, but he knew that "only Germans are capable of this." Hitler evidently aspired to "exterminate everything humane in occupied Europe." The survivors he quoted had also been in Dachau, Buchenwald, even Auschwitz, but they called Majdanek the worst. There were ample details about the gassings, the sorting of victims' clothes and shoes, and the sadistic tortures. One man from Lublin, Gorbatov reported, had seen an SS man with a baby face crush a young Jewish man with a sixty-kilogram pipe. Gorbatov mentioned among the victims Jews from Warsaw and Lublin. His manuscript named seventeen nationalities incarcerated in Majdanek, including Russians and Germans, but excluding, for some reason, Jews, Ukrainians, and Belarusians. When Shcherbakov received the text from *Pravda*'s editor in chief, Petr Pospelov, for review, he added them to the list (and struck out the Turks and Chinese). Thus the publication mentioned the Jews third, after Poles and Russians.⁷³ This archival find shows that even as late as August 1944 there was no top-level decision to fully omit Jews from media reports about the victims of the Nazis.

Other Soviet publications about Majdanek support this conclusion. When a Polish-Soviet commission was founded to investigate the place, TASS completely omitted the Jews from its brief items about it, but *Izvestiia* did not remove them from the translated text of a Polish press communiqué. The commission report that appeared in September 1944 emphatically declared Majdanek a "place for the mass extermination of various nationalities of Europe," of whom only a minority were "Jews brought from various ghettos set up by the Gestapo in Poland and various cities of Western Europe" (and not, this implied, Soviet Jews). Through shooting and gassing, "about 1.5 million" people were killed at Majdanek, including a "large mass of Jews."⁷⁴

The long report also offered the first elaborate official Soviet statement since December 1942 about Nazi extermination in Europe in general. The "Hitlerites" were using concentration camps in Poland—"in Lublin, Dęblin, Oświęcim, Chełm, Sobibór, Biała Podliaska, Treblinka, and other places"—to murder "people it held to be undesirable, in the first place the intelligentsia of the occupied countries of Europe, Soviet and Polish prisoners of war, and Jews." It had all begun with anti-*Slavic* plans: "The mass extermination of the civilian population of the countries of Europe, including Poland and the occupied oblasts of the USSR, constituted a policy of Hitlerite Germany that derived from plans for the enslavement and extermination of the leading and active part of the Slavic peoples." The placement in Poland of these "extermination camps" had been meant to conceal the crimes. Only then did the authors say, as if this was secondary, "These camps, including the 'extermination camp' in Majdanek, were also the place for the total annihilation of the Jewish population."⁷⁵

Editorials in *Pravda, Izvestiia,* and *Trud* also added "and Jews" to the list of Majdanek's victims.⁷⁶ The point here, however, is that despite a transparent effort to de-emphasize the Jews murdered in Poland, they were not always omitted. A December 1944 report on a trial in Lublin mentioned that 40,000 Warsaw Jews had been gassed in Majdanek in just three weeks.[77]

In Auschwitz-Birkenau, about one million Jews and 100,000 others, mainly Poles and Gypsies, were murdered. The first public Soviet report naming the place appeared on March 10, 1943, well after reports in the British, American, and underground Polish press. "Thousands of Polish patriots" had been sent to the camp in Oświęcim, TASS reported. There were executions every day, and six "special ovens" disposed of the dead.[78] The press agency reported early the next month that almost three million men, women, and children had died from "hunger and epidemics" in camps in Poland. Of these, tens of thousands of Poles—"blamed, as a rule, for being a member of the Polish nation"—perished in concentration camps such as Auschwitz.[79] Then, on April 14, possibly to focus on Jews in view of the Katyn affair, *Pravda* reported the news it said Reuters in London had received: "The Hitlerites have started to 'liquidate' the Jewish ghetto in Kraków by exterminating its population. Agents killed over 1,000 Jews within three days, and they are sending the rest on trucks to the concentration camp in Auschwitz, where they are put to death with gasses and electric current."[80]

The next year, reporting from Lublin on October 25, 1944, while giving escaped inmates as sources, TASS mentioned Auschwitz's Jewish victims again, probably for the first time since April 1943. "From all corners of Europe," the report went, "the Germans send tens of thousands of people of various nationalities—Czechs, French, Poles, Jews, and so on—to the camp of Auschwitz, with the aim of destruction. The Hitlerite cannibals also direct Soviet POWs here." Although this suggested nothing particular about the treatment of the Jews, the report added that the Nazis "scoff especially at Jews; during the 'check' they must kneel with their arms in the air for hours."[81]

In November 1944 the War Refugee Board at the Executive Office of the President in Washington, D.C., published a mimeographed report entitled *German Extermination Camps—Auschwitz and Birkenau*. It included the testimonies of Rudolf Vrba and Alfred Wetzler, two Slovak Jews who had escaped earlier that year, and specifics

A BESTIAL PLAN FOR PHYSICAL EXTERMINATION

about the gas chambers and the numbers of Jews murdered in them since April 1942. The *New York Times* of November 26 quoted extensively from it. Three days later *Pravda* and other Soviet papers, citing TASS from New York, also wrote about and quoted from the American official report, even on page 3 instead of 4. Little was left to the imagination:

> In the course of about two years, 1,700,000 Jews were killed with poison gas.... At the moment, there are active in Birkenau four crematoria, consisting of ovens, gas chambers, and auxiliary rooms. Every day, 6,000 corpses pass through the crematoria. At Birkenau, as at Majdanek, groups of prisoners are locked in a hermetically sealed room. Thereafter gas is inserted through an opening in the ceiling. Then the corpses are taken to the crematorium and burned. At the opening of the first crematorium in March 1943, high-level guests from Berlin were present. The "program" consisted of the poisoning and burning of 8,000 Jews from Kraków.[82]

There also appeared at least one item about the murder of non-Soviet Jews that did not mention Auschwitz. Reporting from Washington in July 1944, TASS implicitly dealt with the camp, however, quoting U.S. Secretary of State Cordell Hull: "Reliable reports from Hungary confirm the terrible news of the mass murder of the Jews by the Nazis and the Hungarian Quislings. The scale and form of these beastly crimes are enormous. The entire Jewish community in Hungary, numbering one million people, is threatened by extermination."[83]

The Last Months of the War

The next year saw coverage shift yet again. On February 2, 1945, *Pravda* carried an emotional report from Auschwitz, which the Red Army had liberated five days earlier. The correspondent Boris Polevoi mentioned the separation of deportees into those put to forced labor and those—"elderly, children, sick people"—immediately sent to the gas chambers. But he attempted no explanation for the events, and the words "Jew" and "Jewish" were completely absent, as indeed were all ethnic markers. Editorials on the occasion of the official investigation into Auschwitz in May 1945 likewise did not identify any of Auschwitz's victims by ethnicity. They were simply "over four million people—Soviet citizens, citizens of Poland, France, Belgium, Holland, Czechoslovakia, Yugoslavia, Romania, Hungary, and other countries, including women, elderly people, and children."[84] (The figure of four million remained official at the former camp until 1990.)

Even so, some voices still referred to the Jews. In January and February 1945 Ehrenburg wrote in *Krasnaia zvezda* that the Germans had killed the "entire Jewish population" of all of the towns they occupied, and that in Germany itself he saw people of various nationalities but no Jews, for "the Germans killed them all." On April 11 he still could note, "In our country the Hitlerites killed not one, but millions of innocent Jews."[85] The state commission report on Latvia, with its lengthy discussion of the mass murder of the Jews, appeared that same month.

Throughout the war Stalin and his associates heard from various sources that the Nazis were deliberately killing all the Jews they could get their hands on. Soviet propaganda often toned down this fact, and it is even possible to document Stalin's personal involvement in this undertaking. The main media hardly ever highlighted the Nazi killing campaign against the Jews and, from today's Western perspective, "buried" it. Most articles mentioning Jewish victims were brief and located on page 3 or 4, and they rarely explained the importance of anti-Semitism in Nazi racism.

Coverage of the mass murder of the Jews was pale compared to at least one non-Russian-language Soviet periodical. The Soviet Yiddish-language newspaper *Eynikayt* often wrote during the war about the Nazis' mass murder of Jews, Soviet and non-Soviet. For example, it carried an article by Grossman stating, "The Germans have exterminated a whole people in Ukraine—one million children, women, and old people, for the sole reason that they were

Jews."[86] The Soviet newspapers in Polish and German may also have been more explicit than the Soviet mainstream: *Wolna Polska* (Free Poland) published the call for help from the Warsaw ghetto insurgents, and *Freies Deutschland* (Free Germany) described how, in November 1941, Heinrich Himmler, dissatisfied with the number of Jews shot by the SS attached to Army Group Center, ordered his subordinate there to follow the practices of the SS at Army Group North.[87]

But burying the Holocaust in the mainstream Soviet media was rarely complete and consistent, let alone a conspiracy of silence or some other policy. Statements by Soviet Jews that passed the censor of Russian-language publications did say that all the Jews of Europe were being killed. From early 1943 until early 1945 the media rarely identified Soviet Jewish victims as Jews, but those Jews remained visible in various pieces, published documents, and investigative reports. Moreover, by that time Europe's other Jews, generally killed later than the Soviet Jews, in a sense had replaced them. Jewish victims beyond the Soviet Union were often identified as such, for example in articles on Majdanek and Auschwitz. The media also mentioned the other death camps and the Jews murdered there, and bit by bit standard Russian transliterations of their names evolved.

Comparison with wartime British and American journalism reveals similarities. Like the main Soviet media, BBC domestic radio and American newspapers also tended to universalize the victims of Nazi crimes. Of the twenty-six front-page stories about the persecution and mass murder of European Jews in the *New York Times* from September 1939 until May 1945, only six identified them as the Nazis' primary victims.[88] But positioning hardly mattered in Soviet newspapers, as opposed to their Western counterparts: the back or penultimate page (and the end of radio broadcasts) was the standard position for items about foreign countries. Many Soviet citizens realized that important issues were wholly or partly "buried," searched them out, and read and listened between the lines.

The next question is how to explain the nature of the Soviet reporting about Jewish victims. Some researchers consider the relationship with the Allies to have been crucial: just to placate the

British and Americans, they believe, the Soviet media occasionally referred to the murder of the Jews.[89] This factor cannot fully explain everything, but it probably did play its part during the Katyn affair, and one can speculate that Moscow referred to a report about Auschwitz by the U.S. presidential administration with the aim of bolstering the credibility of Soviet reports presented to the Allies.[90] By the same token, the absence of a perceived foreign (and domestic) constituency probably produced the seemingly total silence about the mass murder of the Roma and Sinti. To the Kremlin, the Gypsies, subject to "the same massive extermination" as the Jews (as Stalin was told in 1943), were politically worthless.

A large part of the tentative answer to the question should be anti-Semitism, both within the Central Committee and as a mindset among Soviet citizens. Stalin disliked the Jews, but during the war he preferred to hide this. The antipathy of others has left a small but revealing trail in contemporary archival documents and postwar recollections. Already in May 1942 Ehrenburg wrote in his private notebook of "anti-Semitism among party bureaucrats." There was talk among party members that Jews were too prominent. In August 1942 a Central Committee official named Bolshakov proposed barring an actress from Sergei Eisenstein's forthcoming film *Ivan the Terrible* simply because of her "prominently" Semitic face. When some of Bolshakov's colleagues attempted to remove Aleksandr Fadeev as president of the Writers' Union by listing "politically dubious" employees of the newspaper *Literatura i iskusstvo*, most on the list had Jewish names.[91]

Jews remained barred from diplomatic service, as they had been since 1939, and many Jewish journalists were dismissed from positions during the war, such as *Izvestiia*'s editor in chief, L. Ia. Rovinskii. It is even likely that only the wartime shortage of qualified non-Jewish journalists precluded the dismissal of all of them. David Ortenberg was first ordered to use the more Russian-sounding pseudonym Vadimov (an order he and other editors of Jewish descent had first received in the mid-1930s), but in late July 1943 Shcherbakov told him out of the blue, "The CC has decided to appoint [Nikolai] Talenskii as editor of *Krasnaia zvezda*. What is your opinion of him?" Thus Ortenberg knew that he was dismissed. Neither then nor later was he given a reason but he wisely did not belabor the point—the threat of arrest loomed over him no less than over other citizens.[92]

Unpublished words were spoken at the Second Plenary Meeting of the Jewish Anti-Fascist Committee about anti-Semitism in the Soviet hinterland. Ehrenburg even called fighting anti-Semitism the body's "main" task. In June 1943 the Bureau official blamed for allowing Ehrenburg to speak out was replaced by N. I. Kondakov, a bully who soon reported to Shcherbakov about the committee's "nationalistic line." He also warned Ehrenburg that year that it was "bragging" to mention the heroism of Jewish soldiers.[93] It was in line with this attitude that the January 1943 issue of the party monthly *Bolshevik* relegated the Jews to insignificance. Jewish soldiers had not been refused awards (on the contrary), but here the chairman of the Presidium of the Supreme Soviet of the RSFSR gave the specific number of military awards received only for Russians, Ukrainians, and Belarusians. Actually in fourth place, Jews were mentioned at the very end of a long, unspecified list of other nationalities.[94]

Higher up the party hierarchy, Kondakov's immediate superior, Aleksandrov, was an important exponent of Russian chauvinism. There are indications that he also disliked all Jews. As early as December 1941 he referred in *Pravda* to the incitement against Jews in Germany but omitted that most of the "over 400,000 Germans" evicted from Germany were Jewish. In August 1942 he warned the Central Committee (Georgii Malenkov, Andrei Andreev, and Shcherbakov) that "non-Russians (in particular Jews)" dominated Russian cultural life and cultural journalism. In May 1944, when he warned Shcherbakov that many students at the Writer's Union's Literary Institute were "anti-Soviet," he identified the worst offenders as Jews. Earlier that year he had removed the Jews from the state commission report about Kiev; in 1947 he was to write to Politburo member Andrei Zhdanov, despite all the evidence to the contrary, that the Nazis had persecuted all Soviet peoples "equally."[95]

Shcherbakov's son recalled never once hearing at home "talk or jokes directed against any particular nationality," but a Russian historian has called Shcherbakov the "most ardent opponent of the 'over-emphasizing' of the Jewish theme in the propaganda," and even explained, unconvincingly, the long references to Jews in the commission reports on Lviv and Latvia as being enabled by Shcherbakov's illness.[96] The head of the Soviet Information Bureau did not reveal what he thought, but certainly carried out anti-Semitic policies. He told Ortenberg in the late spring of 1943 that there were too many Jews at *Krasnaia zvezda*. Ortenberg responded that he was the only Jew there and named eight Jewish correspondents who had died at the front. As noted, Shcherbakov dismissed the editor in chief later that year. On the other hand, two Americans assert that at a party meeting in Moscow later that year, he demanded an end to anti-Jewish purges.[97]

In January 1944 the World Jewish Congress asked for another public Soviet statement against the mass murder. Solomon Lozovskii, deputy leader of the Bureau and deputy foreign commissar, believed such words would be counterproductive for the Jews. The Germans would "respond by killing every single Jew in Europe," he wrote. Shcherbakov wrote in the margin to Lozovskii's note that this view was mistaken, but did not elaborate. His only motivation to decline the request was "We already have declared enough in both word and deed."[98] Most relevant here is that, as revealed above, later that year he *added* Jews to Gorbatov's article about Majdanek, which at the very least shows that his actions were not consistently anti-Semitic.

In the Soviet hinterland almost immediately after the start of the war with Germany one could hear anti-Semitic comments and epithets. They spread and grew in intensity, due to both the difficult living conditions and Nazi propaganda. Soviet Jewish refugees, among whom were officials who drove up market prices, aroused antipathy, as did Polish Jewish refugees (some of whom also recalled kindness), partly because they looked different and were unfamiliar with Soviet life.[99]

It seems that early in the war with Germany many non-Jews in unoccupied Soviet regions somehow fell under the influence of Nazi propaganda, believing the invader was not killing everyone but "merely" Communists and Jews. There was such "hostile" talk (as a Communist Party report put it), along with verbal threats to Communists, at many Moscow factories in early September 1941. Evidence for the perception that only Jews were threatened, often with verbal approval of the idea, also exists for places such as Rostov in August 1941 and August 1944, front-line villages in the fall of 1942, and a village in the Kyrgyz SSR in 1943.[100]

In various places there were accusations that Jews were shirking their duty to fight, often accompanied by physical attacks on them, for instance in Stalingrad as early as 1941 ("You damned Yids, the time of reckoning will come in the end!"), in Moscow in October 1941, and in the Uzbek and Kazakh Soviet Republics in August 1942.[101] Demobilized wounded soldiers were key promoters of anti-Semitism, but they were not alone. Leningraders also made anti-Jewish remarks, and Dovzhenko and apparently many other members of Soviet Ukraine's Writer's Union resented that it was headed by the Jewish Ukrainian novelist Natan Rybak.[102]

It seems likely that Stalin concluded that many of his subjects reacted positively to Nazi anti-Semitic propaganda about "Judeo-Bolshevism" and the Nazi killing of Jews. If the director of the Tropical Institute ordered Jews dismissed from the editorial board of a journal while saying that "Hitler is throwing leaflets and points out that Jews are all over the USSR," the Soviet leader must have been all the more aware of the appeal to many Soviet citizens of the anti-Semitic nature of Nazi propaganda and actions. Therefore by early 1942 he probably thought that the risk was smallest if the media reduced the focus on Jewish victims.[103] This again reminds one of British and American journalists: many feared that reports on Jews would foment or strengthen anti-Semitism—a fear shared by many British and American Jews.[104]

Stalin was aware that many of his associates and subjects were anti-Semitic, and he assumed that telling the country about the Nazi policy to exterminate the Jews would hurt the war effort. That was why after 1941 he himself did not say openly what he knew as a fact, namely that all Jews were targeted for immediate extermination. Yet, as noted, the media did not follow any particular policy of reporting on what today is known as the Holocaust because the leadership—meaning, ultimately, Stalin—did not choose one. Key factors in the indecision were the Communist ideology (which wanted Jews to assimilate in the long run but did not preclude wartime Jewish references to "the Jewish people")[105] and the continued desire for military and other support from the Allies, in particular the United States. Had Stalin informed his inner circle that he wanted media silence about the Jews, then many would have rushed to implement a decision they had favored all along.

The key point, however, is that despite the media's tendency to bury the knowledge that the Jews were targeted for total mass murder, Soviet readers and radio listeners who *wanted* to know were able to find references to that Nazi campaign. And some anecdotal evidence suggests that they found them. During the Battle of Kursk in 1943 a refugee from Poland visited a neighbor in a town in the Kyrgyz SSR for a chat. The man looked up from his newspaper and cried out, "You see what Hitler is doing to the Jews!" (He was pleased: his eyes were "shining with delight.") But it seems even more likely that, just as in the world at large, the full dimensions of the Holocaust remained beyond the imagination, even among Jewish refugees in the Soviet hinterland.[106]

7

Hatred with All the Might of the Soul

During the Second World War domestic broadcasts by the BBC blurred the distinction between Germans and Nazis, and the British Ministry of Information gave the impression that everything German always would be abhorrent. American radio dehumanized the Japanese.[1] Various studies of this phenomenon exist, but even today many Britons and Americans find it difficult to acknowledge that in a past war their countries emitted hate speech—language encouraging or inciting racial hatred, discrimination, or violence.[2] Today's Russia is even more reluctant. For lack of interest, courage, or both, its historians do not study Soviet hate propaganda in depth. They call it "justified and objectively necessary" and underplay its anti-German nature. "For all its bitterness and excesses," a biographer of Ilia Ehrenburg writes, the hatred incited was mainly against the "fascist conquerors." Another approach is to state that the slogan "Kill the German" was necessary and yet not so much created as *reflected* a sentiment, vaguely identified as "hatred for the enemy," which may mean—it is not spelled out—that the media successfully registered popular anti-German sentiment and then magnified and directed it.[3] It generally takes a foreign historian to write that the propaganda "debased the enemy to such an extent that he was scarcely human," played an "active part" in shaping Red Army men's perceptions and conduct, and thus helped bring about mass atrocities such as serial rape of German girls and women.[4]

As noted in prior chapters, one goal of Soviet war propaganda was to strengthen or, unofficially, to *create* resolve for opposing the German armed forces and their allies, primarily for fighting at the front, but also for disciplined and selfless labor. Moscow came to believe that hate propaganda had a role to play here. This propaganda was remarkably self-reflective about its own importance. The purpose of this chapter is to present an overview of its object, trends, and scope, and to offer some observations about its impact.

The First Year

According to some sources, in 1939 and early 1940, the first period of the Molotov-Ribbentrop pact, Soviet citizens sympathized with the Germans and were pleased with their military successes.[5] The nature of this sympathy is still unclear. There is insufficient evidence for the statement that propaganda "succeeded in convincing many Soviet citizens that ordinary Germans, unlike their capitalist and episodically warmongering leaders, were friendly to the workers' state." It seems more likely that peasants in particular considered the Germans potential *liberators* from Stalin's state. Even many Jews may have thought along these lines. In Kharkiv just before the German occupation, none of the local Jews believed reports about German cruelties, a non-Jewish emigré wrote. An elderly, intelligent woman named Sara Borisovna said the Germans were civilized, and even if unfriendly their arrival would improve life. Similar evidence exists for Jews in other cities.[6]

During the pact with Nazi Germany, the Soviet media had been far from anti-German; newsreels showed friendly visits by Khrushchev to Kraków and by Molotov to Berlin.[7] But to make a radical switch, turning friend into foe, had many Soviet precedents, and probably surprised less than the Molotov-Ribbentrop pact had.

And this time the switch began gradually. On July 3, 1941, Stalin defined the invader as *germanskii fashizm*. This Germanic or German fascism—the propaganda did not acknowledge a difference with the adjective *nemetskii*—wanted to "Germanize" the Soviet peoples, by which Stalin seemed to mean enslavement by "German princes and barons." But happily, unlike their leaders the German people were supporting the Soviet Union. This was in line with Molotov's radio statement that "this war was not foisted on us by the German people—not by the German workers, peasants, and intelligentsia," but by the "clique of bloodthirsty fascist rulers."[8] This generous view began to fade only in November, when Stalin explicitly denied that the "Hitlerite" regime was nationalist. While this had been the case in the past, when Germany annexed Austria, the regime had lost this trait as soon as it began attacking "foreign countries." Because of this dogmatic statement, modified only in the final months of the war, nothing in Soviet propaganda could denounce German *nationalism*. Still, in a radical formulation of the required Soviet response, Stalin referred to "the Germans":

> All right, if the Germans want to have a war of extermination, they shall have one. From now on, our task, the task of the peoples of the USSR, the task of the fighters, commanders, and political workers of our army and our fleet will be to exterminate all Germans, to a man, who forced their way into our motherland as occupiers. Absolutely no mercy for the German occupiers! Death to the German occupiers![9]

His audience reportedly burst into "stormy applause" and shouted "That's right!" and "Hurrah!" The listeners were not in a position to question Stalin's confusing description of Nazi aims—"destruction of the great Russian nation [*natsiia*]," to "evict and exterminate the Slavic peoples," and to wage a "war of extermination with the peoples of the USSR"—or the paradox that the "Hitlerite" regime pursuing this mass murder was nothing new, but "essentially . . . a copy of the reactionary regime that existed in Russia under tsarism."

Stalin attributed exterminatory designs to "the Germans," but neither then nor later did he order the killing of all or even most of them; only those Germans who had crossed the 1941 Soviet border as "occupiers" should be exterminated. Thus on Red Army Day, February 23, 1942, Stalin responded to what he called foreign claims that the Soviet people and the Red Army wanted to "exterminate the German people": "History teaches us that Hitlerites come and go, but the Germanic people and the Germanic state remain." This ruled out the abolition of German statehood. (And even for the Nazi leaders there were two possible fates: destruction or "eviction.") The Soviet war aim was merely to liberate the Soviet territories. Then he made what was to remain his only public allowance for German prisoners: "If they surrender, the Red Army takes German soldiers and officers captive and keeps them alive."[10]

Likewise in May 1942 Stalin was ruthless about the German occupiers but remarkably generous about the German people: "We can and must continue to beat the German-fascist invaders until their total extermination," he said. Referring to "Hitlerite scoundrels," "German fascists," "German-fascist oppressors," "German oppressors," and "German occupiers," this time he scrupulously avoided saying "Germans" or "German people" except to give good news: that "the German people realize with growing clarity" that their "only way out" was Germany's liberation from "the adventurist Hitler-Göring clique."[11] No Allied leader at the time talked in this way.

The propaganda reflected Stalin's approach. For many months the media offered articles by or about "good" Germans. The first Soviet photograph of a German prisoner appeared in *Pravda* on June 27, 1941; he was a defector named Alfred Liskow, and he was quoted as calling upon the Germans to overthrow "fascism." The next day his meeting with "Kievan workers" was reported. TASS quoted a Swiss journalist's claim that the overwhelming majority in Germany and Austria was pro-Soviet. When two German writers and refugees spoke at the first All-Slavic Meeting in Moscow in August 1941, the media translated their speeches, which asserted that the "best elements of the German people" did not hold racist views and that "many tens of thousands of the best representatives of the German people" were languishing in Nazi captivity. "Hitler is not the German people! And the day shall come when the German people shall wash away the brown shame!" The press also published speeches at Moscow meetings by Communist emigrés and a call by the German Communist Party that spoke of the need to liberate the German people.[12]

The tendency coincided with sparse media treatment of the Soviet Union's own citizens of German descent. In mid-July 1941 there appeared a declaration of loyalty by the largest group of Soviet citizens of German origin, adopted by a meeting of Volga Germans and calling upon "Germany's farmers" to remove the "gang of Hitlerite murderers." The Soviet Information Bureau reported that thousands of Volga Germans volunteered for army service.[13] But they were not heard from again, and on August 28 the Presidium of the Supreme Soviet decreed "On Resettling the Germans Living in the Volga Region." It referred to "scores and thousands of agents and spies among ethnic Germans residing in the Volga region, who are to carry out explosions in districts populated by the Volga Germans following a signal delivered from Germany." None of the Volga Germans had informed the Soviet authorities. In order to prevent "bloodshed," all of them would be "resettled" to "other regions." The deportation decree appeared on August 30 both in *Nachrichten*, the German-language paper for the Volga German ASSR, and in the central Russian-language periodical *Bolshevik*, though not in central newspapers (and the decision to abolish the ASSR was not mentioned anywhere).[14]

No other Soviet deportation of alleged aliens, including Germans from Leningrad, Ukraine, and the Caucasus, was ever to appear in the wartime Soviet media, and neither did the decisions to turn ethnic German residents east of the Urals into "special settlers" and to move ethnic German Red Army members to NKVD labor battalions. Efforts were made to keep this all secret.[15] Unlike the Volga Germans, the other Soviet Germans thus became neither loyal nor disloyal but simply disappeared from view. Being of German ancestry had become incompatible with being Soviet. Not all these people needed to be dead, but all of them had become foreigners.

"N. Petrov" warned in *Izvestiia* in mid-August 1941 that "far from all" Soviet citizens fully realized the danger facing them. Presenting a desired situation as a given, the author also claimed that among all honest citizens, "holy" hatred for "the enemy" was growing. In another article in late September 1941 Petrov was specific: "Every Soviet citizen who has just a drop of hot blood must burn with a fierce hatred for the oppressors of man's cultural freedom. Our feeling of hatred must rise to the level of supreme people's heroism." After the war the head of state, Mikhail Kalinin, was declared to be the author of the articles.[16] But during the war Stalin evidently considered it undignified for Soviet leaders to incite hated.

After November 1941 incitement against Germany intensified. Agitprop's leader, Aleksandrov, wrote in *Pravda* that Germany's former admirers now were its mortal enemies and that the Germans had become a "nation to which thousands and thousands of curses are sent from all corners of the earth." In instructing the raion newspapers in early 1942 to warn against the threat of extermination and slavery, Agitprop referred to "German scoundrels."[17] One gets the sense that had Stalin lashed out against "the Germans," Aleksandrov would have applauded him sincerely. Germany's rulers had managed to "turn the German youth into robbers and pillagers," *Trud* noted. There also came criticism of the German population in Germany. The satirical journal *Krokodil*, for example, reproached German women for wearing clothes "robbed or stripped from the bodies of murdered people."[18]

German spokespersons joined in the new trend. In January 1942 German emigrés in the Soviet Union issued an accusatory statement. Germans in Germany did not believe the news about the crimes committed at the Eastern Front against "Russian workers and peasants." Should they fail to rise up, they would be to blame—and "woe to Germany if Hitler shall be defeated without our people's participation." *Pravda* carried a full translation. Two months later TASS publicized a statement by the U.S.-based emigrés Heinrich Mann, Leon Feuchtwanger, and Bertolt Brecht in which they reproached the Germans for tolerating the Nazis.[19]

Allegedly responding to Molotov's January 1942 statement on Nazi crimes, the "first conference of imprisoned young officers of the German army" of "late February 1942" spoke up to confirm its veracity. *Pravda* printed a facsimile and Russian translation of their appeal to the German army and people. German "officers and soldiers" misbehaved because Hitler's state system and the army supreme command "consciously let loose the lowest instincts" and "poisoned us with boundless and beastly hatred toward the freedom-loving and democratic great Soviet people." The *Pravda* report also quoted from speeches—even including one by an NCO of an SS infantry regiment—condemning the "Hitlerite army" and the *natsisty*, or Nazis, a term otherwise rare in Soviet usage. Other open letters (including partial facsimiles of the German originals) by German and Austrian prisoners provided details about the treatment of the Soviet POWs and the occupied Soviet regions.[20]

The Shift in May 1942

In February 1942 Stalin disputed what he called foreign claims that "Soviet people hate the Germans precisely as Germans." Thanks to the way its members had been educated, the Red Army did *not* feel a "hatred for everything German," and it was "free of the feeling of racial hatred," all manifestations of which, he added, were illegal in the USSR.[21] He did not say whether the army and society felt any other kind of hatred, and whether that might be useful. That happened the following May. While not revealing then (or on any other occasion) whether he himself hated the "German-fascist invaders," he reported that the men and women of the Red Army had learned to "really hate" them. The soldiers now "understood that one cannot beat an enemy without having learned to hate him with all the might of the soul." This last sentence, taken from Aleksei Tolstoi (who spoke them behind closed doors in August 1941), became Stalin's firm conviction, which was why *Pravda*'s editorial belabored the point: "Our country is going through a great school of patriotic hatred." As to its source, the paper focused not on enemy criminality (in marked contrast to later propaganda), but on *love*: "Burning, holy hatred for the mean enemy arises from passionate, selfless love of the Soviet motherland, one's family, one's people, one's dear ones." In turn hatred was producing invincible strength and heroism.[22] In short, it was official that a positive emotion—love—was the wellspring of everything else.

During the Red Army's disasters in the weeks that followed, the demand for hatred became more prominent and more anti-German. Stalin personally approved a review of a book about Aleksandr Suvorov that called the tsarist general "an enemy of the Germans."[23] *Pravda*'s editorial on June 6 simply *ordered* all citizens to feel nothing but hate. A Soviet patriot was "a person who everywhere, even in the most distant hinterland, sees the hated enemy before him, senses his terrible breath—and kills him." An editorial on July 11 appealed to all citizens to defend "our motherland" from the "fascist dogs" who were "frantically trying to break through to the life-giving centers of the country." Now, within weeks, patriotism, love, and even faith lost much of their prestige, for the war became a struggle "not for life, but to the death." The Red Army was staunch because above all it hated the Germans. Civilians should follow the example: "And in the entire Soviet hinterland may holy hatred for the enemy become our main, only feeling. This hatred combines a burning love of the motherland, anxiety for our families and children, and an unshakable will for victory. May hatred for the enemy become such a force as to lift mountains, work wonders of labor at the bench and in the field."[24]

Special prominence was gained by a literary work published in *Pravda* on the first anniversary of the German invasion: Mikhail Sholokhov's "The Science of Hatred."[25] Lieutenant Gerasimov, thirty-two, is telling the narrator about a recent battle when some German prisoners come into view and his calm face is "instantly transformed: his swarthy cheeks grew pale, the swellings under his cheek bones were drawn inward, and his eyes, that were fixed in front of him, flamed up with such inextinguishable, ferocious hatred that I involuntarily turned away from his gaze." A party member from Siberia, Gerasimov explains that he used to wonder how such an "industrious and talented people" could tolerate the Hitlerite regime, "but that was, after all, their own affair." Before he even arrived at the front he "began to feel a quiet hatred for the Germans." But he never expected the "German army" to be such "shameless scum." In Ukraine he saw burned villages, hundreds of murdered women, children, and old people, the mutilated bodies of war prisoners, and raped and savagely murdered women, girls, and adolescents. "You understand that we went wild when we saw all that the Germans had done. What else could one expect? We all understood that we were not dealing with people but with canine degenerates with some satanic lust for blood." In September 1941 Gerasimov lost consciousness and was taken prisoner. He saw how prisoners were shot for being Jewish or for failing to keep up during a long march. His German guards were "inveterate scoundrels." Gerasimov killed one, joined the partisans, and was taken across the front line. War sharpens feelings, he tells the narrator:

> It might seem that love and hatred cannot be put side by side; you know that they say, "you cannot harness a horse with a deer." But with us they are harnessed together and they pull together wonderfully. I deeply hate the Germans for all they have done to my motherland and to me personally, and at the same time, I love my people with all my heart and don't want them to suffer under the German yoke. It is this which forces me, indeed all of us, to fight so fiercely— and these very feelings, united in action, will lead us to victory.

Hate speech typically dehumanizes. Nazi propaganda went furthest in this, but the Soviet portrayal of the German occupiers, particularly on posters but also in texts, certainly participated. Adherence to the Communist ideology precluded calling enemies poison, rats, or maggots. "Poison" was used as a metaphor for the "fascist" ideology, not for humans. But while texts rarely equated humans with rodents or insects, the propaganda did so in caricatures of Nazi leaders (and their foreign allies, such as the leaders of Vichy France). There were references to fascist vermin (*gady*) and spiders.[26] Stalin's favorite terms, "beast" and "cannibal," became particularly common, often with the addition that occupiers were "not human." Published poetry often referred to them as wolves.[27]

Aleksei Tolstoi declared that the leading sentiment among Soviet citizens "must be and will be" hatred, but he did not fully step into line, usually referring to a "beast" or "fascist," not the German.[28] Meanwhile his Polish colleague Wanda Wasilewska wrote and published *The Rainbow,* a naturalistic novel full of racist hatred. A Russian translation of the story about a fictional Ukrainian village was serialized in *Izvestiia* in 1942 (and made into a film in 1944). Its characters refer to German paws and beastly mugs, and to Germans as cockroaches. Her body, a rape victim knows, has become the "nest" of a "wolf-cub." She is expecting "not a child" but "German dung" from the "race of wolves." People know about the rape and feel sorry for her, yet already treat her like a leper; she has been contaminated. Should they find out that she was pregnant, they would step aside "from utter disdain, from a fear to touch her, a German mattress with a Fritz in her belly." No one would help her give birth. She herself would actually "strangle it with her own hands."[29] Eventually killed (by a German), she smiles, because death offers the only honorable outcome. No voice in the novel disagrees.

The Germans represent an unredeemable lineage of murder, sadism, and lice-ridden filth. "Never could anything good, any happiness, come from German hands," one woman believes, and a man who lost a son to them in 1918 says, "That's why he is a German, to kill."[30] Again nothing in the novel contradicts these prejudices. All the villagers "cursed the Germans and spoke of the day when all would be avenged." In the future "there won't be any Germans," one woman says, followed by another's agreement: "There would be no justice in this world if we did not cut down the whole tribe of hellhounds to the last." An elderly man would like to see "the last German on gallows in Kiev." No other widely published novel broke the law against incitement of national hatred so thoroughly.

Contrary to the logic of the work, though in keeping with Stalin's public line, the speaker who mentions the gallows explicitly spares those Germans who "twisted ropes for our necks" in Germany: they must be brought to the USSR for forced labor. Equally inconsistently, one woman warns another that German war prisoners must not be killed without procedure: "Do you think there is no judge wiser than you? ... Let him live to hear his own wife curse him and his own children repudiate him! ... Let him beg death to come for him and let him beg in vain, let even death turn away from this German carrion!"[31]

Konstantin Simonov's play *Russian People,* serialized in *Pravda* beginning on July 13, 1942, also propagated hate: a woman who is about to be executed says she would want to kill the Germans' mothers if they did not curse their sons. The work became well-known; for instance, a brigade commissar quoted it approvingly in a radio talk on hatred. Simonov also published, in *Krasnaia zvezda* and *Komsomolskaia pravda* on July 18 and 19, 1942, the long poem "Kill Him!" Addressing Soviet citizens under arms, it declared that one's love and patriotism could be proven only by the death of "the German": "If your brother kills a German, / If your neighbour kills a German— / This is your brother's and neighbor's vengeance, / You—you have no excuse."[32]

Aleksei Surkov published so many "poems of hatred" that a booklet with this title could be published. Depicting scenes of desolation and death, particularly of infants and revealing the cause—enemy rampages—they called for revenge. "I Hate," for example, published in *Krasnaia zvezda* in August 1942, stated:

> My grievances and memories are countless
> With these hands of mine
> I have lifted the corpses of little children.
> ....
> I hate them deeply
> For those hours of sleepless gloom.
> I hate them because in one year
> My temples have grown white.
> My house has been defiled by the Prussians,
> Their drunken laughter dims my reason.
> And with these hands of mine
> I want to strangle every one of them.

Here the target was specific ("the Prussians"), but Surkov's other poems could call the enemy a "drunken beast" that "cackles, baring yellowed fangs."[33]

Meanwhile reasonable Germans all but disappeared for a year. There were no German speakers at the second women's and youth meetings in May and June 1942, and participants of the latter meeting told Germans that the Red Army was not fighting them as a people but added, "Death awaits you as long as you are robbing our land, as long as you are linking your fate with Hitler." An article by an author with a German name gave up on German young people, millions of whom had been "turned by the Hitlerite gang into wild, rabid beasts. It has rooted out of them anything resembling thought and conscience, has bereft them of human feelings, a human appearance."[34] Even the periodical *Propagandist* expressed the racist sentiment, stating, in late 1942, that a German officer had been able to throw a baby into a burning cottage "only because he was a German." "German soldiers must now not be divided into workers, peasants, intelligentsia: all of them are robbers and beasts." Thus "the more German corpses there will be, the less *human* corpses there will be."[35]

When no weapon is available, Surkov wrote,

> Then with your teeth will you clutch his throat.
> You will bite and tear and strangle
> Until he will turn whiter than chalk,
> Until his murderous soul,
> A reptile's soul, will quit his body.

The method of killing by biting through the victim's throat even appeared in a report in *Pravda* under the heading "Hatred," about a soldier who ran out of ammunition.[36] Such vitriol was now expected, and failure to propagate it quickly attracted attention. Even *Pravda*'s editor and censors were collectively rebuked early in 1943 for a report of the German surrender at Stalingrad that failed to incite hatred, and the correspondent in question was removed from the front.[37]

In November 1942 Stalin himself referred to the German armed forces as "the Germans," but as usual he ruled out the abolition of German statehood: the "Hitlerite" army and state had to go, but "to destroy Germany is impossible." His message of February 1943 defined the enemy in qualified terms such as "Hitlerite armed forces,"

"German-fascist scoundrels," "German-fascist hordes," "German invaders," and "fascist beast," but also sweepingly as "the Germans." On May Day 1943 he referred to "the Germans" in a call to continue to "mercilessly exterminate the German invaders, without pause chase them from the Soviet land." Of the slogans he proclaimed on this occasion, last and thus with the most emphasis came "Death to the German occupiers!" His published response to two American correspondents' questions some days later identified the main enemies as "the Germans."[38]

Early in that same year there were even unambiguous calls for the killing of "the" German. The poet Semen Kirsanov wrote rhymed stories about the fictitious soldier Foma Smyslov, read on state radio's *Red Army Hour*. The January 13, 1943, episode proclaimed "every German" a criminal, a rotten fascist who had to be exterminated.[39] In March the radio broadcast a letter from a woman in Kislovodsk. "Kill the German vermin, kill the swastika-marked scum," she begged her drafted son. Another woman, addressing her brother in Ukrainian (even while referring to "us Russians") on the radio, seemed to be dizzy with lethal hatred: "I tremble all over when pronouncing the word German. They must be destroyed. For every life of us they must pay with hundreds of their own filthy lives." She would "ask for my children to be placed in a children's home. I shall go to the front myself and kill Germans not any worse than men. I will avenge Katenka, my daughter, and hundreds of other children!"[40]

Radianska Ukraïna often blamed "the Germans" of the current war for crimes: "Wherever the German went, there are ruins, famine, blood, homeless elderly, lonely orphans"; "We shall pay the Germans back with death!" The Ukrainian historian Mykola Petrovsky asked, "Who could treat humans more cruelly than the Germans?" Ukrainians had been killing these "eternal enemies" like flies for centuries, so nothing much was new.[41]

"Free Germany" and the "German Beast"

In July 1943 the propaganda again shifted dramatically. Out of the blue there appeared a facsimile and a full and accurate translation of the foundational document from the Soviet hinterland of the National Committee of "Free Germany." Soviet citizens read and heard translations of Free Germany's call for the overthrow of the Nazi regime, a ceasefire, and an "immediate peace." Its slogan was "Long Live a Free, Peaceful, and Independent Germany!" In September 1943 the press proceeded likewise with regard to the new Union of German Officers.[42] *Pravda* attempted to reconcile the contradiction with the hate propaganda by defining the committee's main "political meaning" in an increase in the number of "opponents of the Hitlerite tyranny."[43] In reality the committee was mostly used to pressure the United States and the United Kingdom. During four days in November and December 1943 Stalin conferred with the Americans and Britons in Tehran and was satisfied with the extent of their support. Now the Soviet Union joined the longstanding Allied demand that Germany surrender unconditionally, and this sharply reduced the usefulness of the Free Germany Committee. Although it was not the last German-to-German call to appear in the Soviet Russian media, the committee faded from view.[44]

The publicity about Free Germany had only modestly reduced the agitation against Germans. When the Red Army reached and crossed the 1941 Soviet border and patriotism alone seemed less likely to mobilize, Stalin evidently felt the need to urge the soldiers on with hatred for the Germans. Thus when, in August 1943, the leader read the draft of the Bureau statement about the mass graves in Vinnytsia exploited by Nazi propaganda, he changed "fascist butchers" into "German butchers." In November he declared that the Red Army's advances had revealed that "hundreds of thousands of our peaceful people have been exterminated by the Germans in the raions invaded by them. Like medieval barbarians or the hordes of Atilla, the German villains trample fields, burn down villages and cities, destroy industrial enterprises and cultural establishments." These "German criminals" (and "fascist pogromists") would be severely punished. On May Day 1944, the moment when he finally declared the new Soviet war aim of liberating "our brethren the Poles, Czechoslovaks, and other people of Western Europe allied with us," Stalin even referred to a wounded and fleeing "*German* beast." To avert the lingering danger of "enslavement," one had to "finish it off in its own lair."[45]

In September 1944, after Pope Pius XII called for an end to hatred, Stalin himself ordered the press to quote indignant Londoners.[46] Death camps also were blamed on the Germans. The Belarusian survivors of the Azarichi camp denounced the "German cannibals"; reports blamed the dead at the Klooga camp on "the Germans"; and according to *Izvestiia*, Majdanek revealed the cruelty of "the contemporary German": "Humanity demands retribution on the Germans, a mad beast. This retribution will be merciless!" Also in reference to Majdanek, Simonov wrote in *Krasnaia zvezda* that "the nation [*natsiia*] that gave birth to" those who killed there would be held fully accountable.[47]

On July 17, 1944, *Pravda* carried a small notice that on that day German war prisoners would march through Moscow. "Any outbursts" against the prisoners on the announced route were forbidden, the commandant of the city militia added. A convoy of tens of thousands of Germans captured in Belarus was paraded through the streets of the capital. Reports were unambiguously anti-German, though not bloodthirsty. What Leonid Leonov wrote in *Pravda* was typical:

> Disgusting green mold gushed from the hippodrome onto Leningrad Avenue, which is always so clean and festive, and it was strange to see that this motley, two-legged riffraff had backs, even arms along the sides, and other secondary humanoid characteristics. It flowed for a long time down the Moscow streets, the rabble whom a maniac had convinced that it was the best part of humanity, and the Moscow women sat down for a rest, wearied by disgust rather than the monotony of the spectacle.

These prisoners were "living mechanisms with springs instead of souls." But, Leonov added, "my people do not go over the limits of reason or lose their hearts when angered.... We do not burn war prisoners, we do not mutilate them: we are not Germans." Mostly there was a "disdainful silence." The journalist Boris Polevoi also wrote that whistles and curses were rare, and most onlookers were "taciturn, angry, hateful." (Palpably hateful silence in the presence of Germans was a trope in both reports and fiction.)[48]

In November 1944 Stalin once more changed his own public stance on the Germans. He implicitly withdrew the previous May's reference to a *German* beast and, for reasons that are unclear, his three-year-old denial that the problem was German nationalism. The task, he said now, was to finish off a *fascist* beast, and he denounced the Nazis for the first and only time for their "misanthropic race theory" and "beastly nationalism." He also repeated that the Soviet people hated "the German invaders." In fact the entire "so-called 'chosen German race' has become the object of universal hatred." But this worldwide hatred was because of the suffering they had produced, not "because they are people of a foreign nation." He cited the popular saying that a wolf is not killed because he is gray, but because he ate the sheep. He left it up to his audience to conclude that although the media had deliberately fanned that very "universal hatred" of Germans, now such "general hatred" was no longer desirable.[49]

"We Shall Kill Them All"

The most prominent Soviet voice of hatred was Ilia Ehrenburg, who requires special attention. The Jewish Russian writer had a long history of journalism, beginning with contributions to White newspapers in Kiev during the Civil War and the Ukrainian war for independence. Lenin's Cheka arrested him but released him for reasons unknown, and by 1938 he was writing for *Izvestiia* about the show trial of his former schoolmate, the Bolshevik Nikolai Bukharin. He lived in Paris for some years and saw the German occupation in 1940. On the way home with the benefit of diplomatic immunity, he saw anti-Jewish signs on stores and restaurants in Berlin. Because Germany was an ally, censors blocked a poem sympathetic to the Londoners during the Blitz and part of his novel about the fall of

Paris; but in April 1941 Stalin unexpectedly made a phone call to him and suggested that he write about the "German fascists."⁵⁰

Well into the new war, at a session of the War Commission of the Writers' Union in January 1943, Ehrenburg was to recall that because he knew Germany already, "from the beginning of the war, I was deeply convinced that we are fighting not just against the Hitlerites, but also against the Germans."⁵¹ His public hatred was racist, denouncing Germans of all times as inherently bad—and the solution he demanded was killing or some other kind of destruction.

That Ehrenburg came to believe this is almost certain. In December 1943 he attended the tribunal in Kharkiv (though not the public hanging that immediately followed it). As another writer testified in his diary, Ehrenburg told other attendees that "all Fritzes ages sixteen to thirty-five" had to be killed. Tolstoi went even further: all of them had to be exterminated. In the train back to Moscow foreign correspondents conversed with both men. Edmund Stevens of the *Christian Science Monitor* recalled that "nothing could alter [Ehrenburg's] conviction that Nazi cruelty was an atavism of a people who had always been barbarians."

> "I once knew a good German," Ehrenburg remarked between puffs of his pipe, "but I lost track of him many years ago. I don't even know if he's still alive—I seriously doubt it.... If you only knew," he added, "how sick and tired I am of Germans, Germans, Germans! When in the name of heaven will we have time to think and talk of something besides Germans? After all the suffering they've caused, after all the towns they've destroyed, no punishment ever devised would be severe enough. The trouble is that our Russians are too kind-hearted. Even if you tried, you couldn't order our Russian soldiers to do any of the things to German civilians that the German soldiers have done to ours. It's a pity in a way."

He ridiculed as sentimentalism the distinction between the Germans and the Nazis, Stevens recalled, who "objected for the sake of argument: 'But suppose the Germans overthrew Hitler of their own free will and welcomed the advancing Red Army by getting out the old red flags and singing the *Internationale*?' 'Those,' said Ehrenburg, 'would be the first people we should shoot.'"[52]

Ehrenburg's writings after the Germans invaded were fierce. On the very first day of the war he described the "German fascists" as robbers and child killers, and in July 1941 wrote that the "Hitlerites" were "not human beings" but "brown lice," "awful parasites crawling in order to devour us. They must be destroyed."[53] In August 1941 he complained about the censors of the Soviet Information Bureau, to which the Central Committee reacted with a document stating, "Do not correct Ehrenburg." This probably also applied to his use of the word "Germans" instead of "German occupiers" or "German fascists," for later, addressing his fellow writers in 1943, he recalled that in the beginning, "every time, the word German was corrected into Hitlerite. But gradually it became customary and won out."[54] Not entirely: censorship may explain why some of his later articles condemn the "Hitlerites" or "fascists," but in general his writings denounced Germany and the Germans. "Germany [was] the tyrant of the twentieth century" undeserving of mercy. "The Germans" were trying to hide that they "hate all peoples except the Germans, and despise all races except the German race."[55]

Several weeks after Stalin's proclamation of a "war of extermination," Ehrenburg agreed with such a response. "We have decided," he wrote, "to kill all Germans who burst into our country. We don't want to torment or torture them. We simply want to destroy them. This is a humane mission, it fell to our people's lot. We are continuing the work of Pasteur, who discovered a serum against rabies. We are continuing the work of all the scientists who found the means to destroy deadly microbes." He outdid Stalin in dehumanizing the invaders and in condemning *all* Germans: the "Hitlerites" descended from the "wild Teutons" and Germany's foreign minister Joachim von Ribbentrop was the "representative" of a "tribe [*plemia*] that has destroyed millions of people."[56] This was more than censors granted to other writers at the time. Glavlit watched lest reports inspired by Stalin's speeches fail to copy his exact wording—

German invaders or *German occupiers*—correcting, for example, the wording "Germans who are in our land."[57] The care stemmed from the master himself; his speech to the Red Army on Red Square of November 7, 1941, broadcast live to the country, referred to "our enemies" and "German tyranny," but when Stalin published it, he replaced these words with "German invaders."[58]

Likewise in various articles the next January Ehrenburg wrote that Hitler had "really removed the Germans' conscience." Before the invasion "naive people supposed that Germany was a country, but it had become a huge criminal organization. They thought that the Germans are a people, but they had become a multimillion-man gang." Now "the Germans achieved a wonder: they squeezed pity from the Russian heart and gave birth to a mortal hatred. Even old people have just one wish: 'kill them all.'" In addressing an imaginary Nazi German reader, he wrote, evidently referring to Germans, "We want just one thing—to destroy your Hitlerite tribe."[59]

Only somewhat less sweeping was the article "Hatred" in May 1942, which declared that "the Hitlerites" were "not human beings, but murderers, executioners, moral degenerates and cruel fanatics.... A German soldier with a rifle in his hand to us is not a human but a fascist. We hate him. We hate every one of them for all that they have done in accord." (At this stage he denied that the Red Army wanted revenge.) The article "The Justification of Hatred," later that same month, railed against "the German fascists," "the Hitlerites," and indeed "the Germans": "We are fighting not against human beings, but against robots which resemble human beings but do not have a grain of humanism in them.... To the Germans, murder is not a manifestation of an unsound mind, but a methodical activity. Having murdered thousands of children in Kiev, one German wrote, 'We are killing the small representatives of a terrible race.'" Another article called the German invaders vermin.[60]

Ehrenburg's article "Patriotism" in *Pravda* on June 14, 1942, an ode to Russia, declared that "the outlook of a German formed by Hitler" was not patriotism for it rested on "contempt for other peoples." By banning works such as by the classical writer Heinrich Heine, the

"Hitlerites" had "lopped off and degraded the national culture of the German people." "Hitler contributed to a national animalization of Germany," a country that "lost its face and its soul." "We do not transfer our hatred for fascism to races, peoples, or languages. No crimes of Hitler will make me forget the modest little house in Weimar where Goethe lived and worked," he wrote, but followed this with the ominous comment that it was "not accidental" that the "Tyrolean bloodsucker managed to turn millions of Germans into the soldiers of a bloodthirsty and marauding army." The version included in the collection *War*, issued in large numbers, elaborated that "ninety percent of German youth is poisoned with the poison of fascism, which affects the organism like syphilis." And the problem was even more fundamental, for older: "We can boldly say that the Hitlerites had fathers and grandfathers." Seventy years earlier the French writer Guy de Maupassant described Prussian misbehavior, and Ehrenburg had seen the Germans in France in 1915.[61] This was not included in the *Pravda* version; Stalin did not want the country's most prestigious newspaper to blame successive generations.

One month later Ehrenburg blamed "the Germans" for deceit and murder. "Kill them all," he wrote, because "the German of 1942 is an oaf, an ignoramus, a self-satisfied imbecile."[62] Particularly strident was "Kill," published in *Krasnaia zvezda* on July 24, 1942, and as a separate leaflet. (Whether it was read on domestic radio is unclear.) Evidently using Stalin's May Day license to hate, Ehrenburg firmly placed all Germans outside humanity:

> We have understood that the Germans are not human. From now on, the word "German" is to us the most terrible curse. From now on, the word "German" unloads a firearm. We won't speak. We won't be indignant. We shall kill. If on a day you did not kill even just one German, that day is wasted. If you think about the fact that for you the German shall kill your neighbor, you have misunderstood the threat. If you do not kill the German, the German will kill you. He will take away your dear ones and torture them in his

damned Germany. If you cannot kill the German with a bullet, kill the German with the bayonet. If there is quiet at your section of the front, if you are waiting for the battle, kill a German before the battle. If you keep the German alive, the German will hang a Russian man and disgrace a Russian woman. If you have killed one German, kill another one—we enjoy nothing more than German corpses. Do not count days. Do not count *versts*. Count one thing: the Germans you killed. Kill the German! The old mother asks for this. Kill the German! The children beg you for this. Kill the German! The native soil cries out for this. Don't miss the chance. Don't let it slip. Kill![63]

The call received various Nazi German replies, including a leaflet in Russian directed at the Red Army and supposedly authored by "the Vlasovites." Defiantly accepting on Germany's behalf Ehrenburg's accusation of mass murder, it was more specific about the victims: "Yes! The Germans did mercilessly exterminate the Yids."[64]

Under the heading "The Accursed Seed," Ehrenburg vowed in August 1942 that "the Germans" would never again be able to reduce France and Russia to ashes "every quarter century": "We shall finish off the future warmongers." There was "only one way to save Russia—to kill the Germans":

> One can bear anything—plague, hunger, and death. But one cannot bear the Germans. One cannot bear these fish-eyed oafs who contemptuously snort at everything Russian and who have crawled from the Carpathian Mountains to the foothills of the Caucasus, over land that was always ours. We cannot live as long as this gray-green vermin is alive. . . . Now there are no books, no love, no stars—only one thought: kill the Germans. Kill them all. Bury them. . . . We must no longer say, "Good morning" or "Good night." In the morning we must say, "Kill the German," and at night, "Kill the German." The Germans took our life away from us. We want to live. And we must kill the Germans. . . . We are killing them, everyone understands that. But they must be

killed sooner, or else they will ravage all of Russia and torture to death millions more people.⁶⁵

The people of what he called Russia disagreed about many things, but "one feeling links all: kill the German."⁶⁶ "When you see a Hitlerite soldier you don't believe that this is a human, it seems that he was fed not with mother milk but with machine oil." "We must now put aside all thoughts, all feelings but one—destroy the Germans." And indeed everyone was joining in the carnage:

> Not only at the front are people killing Germans. All of Russia's valiant children are killing Germans. The peasant women gathering ears cut off the heads of Germans. The women workers who are weaving cloth for our fighters are weaving Germany's shroud. The engine-drivers who are taking heavy loads to Kazakhstan are killing Germans with bread, oil, and cotton. The women who take care of the wounded, who surround the fighters with the care of a family, who launder soldiers' underwear or nurse orphans are doing the same high deed: they are killing Germans.⁶⁷

In December he declared, "'Kill the German'—these words have long moved from the newspaper columns to the leaves of letters. Mother writes them. Children write them, in naive scribbles. The beloved woman writes them with longing and hope, and the fighter rereading these words feels warm breath on his face even in a strong frost."⁶⁸ His strong words even appeared in the pages of *Bolshevik*, the theoretical and political journal of the Central Committee, with a much smaller circulation than *Pravda*. "The Germans" would "perish like a savage tribe," he wrote. "We no longer replace the word German with the word fascist: we realized that they are synonyms."⁶⁹

Thus not only the armed forces, but *all* Soviet citizens wanted the Germans to be killed. They wanted this because of German misdeeds—the "Fritzes" had been murdering millions—and because the Germans were nonhumans. "We can learn from the Germans how to fight. But we won't learn from them how to live. To us they are two-legged beasts that have mastered to perfection the technique of war." The next year Ehrenburg wrote again that "to call the German a wild animal means aggrandizing the German.... We are not fighting people with a more or less developed intellect, but peculiar machines that have risen up against man."[70]

The anti-German incitement was no less strong in late 1943, early 1944, and thereafter. "Through their crimes the Germans have excluded themselves from the family of peoples. A severe retribution awaits them. We know that not a few but millions are guilty of the crimes committed by the German army." "If you're feeling bad, if there's a stone on your breast—kill a German. If you want to go home as soon as possible—kill a German." Take Berlin and preclude an attack by the next generation of Germans: "it is time to finish off the Germans." They were a "nation for which a military campaign is man's highest purpose," rehearsing for war "from the cradle." In August 1944, when the Red Army was about to cross the old German state border, Ehrenburg wrote in *Pravda* of the need to traverse Germany "with sword in hand to beat from the Germans for centuries their love of the sword." Lunatics could be tolerated but not "the inventors of the gas chamber." During and after the Yalta conference, he wrote of the need for retribution and a "trial against Germany," both all the more needed because "Germans will be Germans."[71]

In March 1945 he wrote, "By the blood and tears of beloved Russia we vow: there won't be a Germany at the Oder or at Stettin!" He listed the reasons why "we" despised the enemy: their "conceit, cruelty, cult of the exterior, cult of the 'colossal,' they are morally and physically shameless and dull (they are unable to think critically), the absence among them of basic dignity."[72] His *Pravda* article "Enough!" of April 9, 1945, offered nothing new: "There is no Germany. There is only a gigantic robbers' gang that falls apart as soon as the question is raised who is responsible" for things such as the murder of "millions of innocent Jews." It warned Americans and Britons against mildness.[73]

Aleksandrov told Ehrenburg he liked that article, but on April 14 the leader of Agitprop himself appeared in *Pravda* with a long article entitled "Comrade Ehrenburg Is Oversimplifying." Here he told Soviet citizens and the world, "If one were to recognize the point of view of Comr. Ehrenburg as correct, then one has to consider that the entire population of Germany must share the fate of the Hitlerite clique." But, Aleksandrov said, Stalin and "the Soviet people" had never equated the Germans with the Hitlerites. He added that the Yalta conference had ruled out "extermination of the German people."[74] It was a situation without precedent: the Soviet Union's main propaganda outlet implicitly agreed with the Nazis that a prominent Russian Soviet writer and self-identified Jew wanted to exterminate the Germans. Contemporaries understood that Ehrenburg was a scapegoat; others had published similar works, and none of them would have been possible without Moscow's consent.

Front-line soldiers, who were to launch a final assault on Berlin two days later, were indignant and sent in supportive letters and telegrams. Fearful of the consequences when unknown Muscovites shook his hand, Ehrenburg stayed home.[75] In a letter to Stalin he denied that his writings about the Germans had stood out. "I expressed not any line of my own, but the feelings of our people, and others who are politically more authoritative did the same." That must have been why, up to that point, "neither the editors nor the Press Department told me that I was writing incorrectly." He also denied ever advocating extermination of the Germans.

> The article in *Pravda* says that it is incomprehensible for an antifascist to call for the total destruction of the German people. I did not call for this. In the years when the invaders were trampling our land I wrote that it was necessary to kill the German occupiers. But at that time I emphasized that we are not fascists nor executioners. And upon my return from East Prussia I emphasized in several articles ("Knights of Equity" and others) that we treat the civilian population with a different yardstick than the Hitlerites did. In this regard my conscience is clear.

Did "the interests of the state" require him to stop publishing altogether, he asked Stalin.[76] No reply came, but the NKVD did not arrest Ehrenburg. His return to grace was marked by his article "The World in the Morning" in *Pravda* on May 10, 1945. With Aleksandrov's consent, it silently quoted from some of Ehrenburg's earlier articles that called revenge foreign to the Red Army—thus implicitly countering Stalin's February 1943 description of an "army of avengers"—and foresaw a future for the German people.[77] These recycled earlier qualifications merit a closer look.

Ehrenburg had denied in some wartime articles that his stance was xenophobic or racist: "Racial and national hatred is alien to us. We hate the Germans not because they were born German, but because, having deluded themselves they were the world's premiers, they soaked the world in blood. We hate them because they are fascists." To support this view, he noted that German classical music, philosophy, and literature still were esteemed in the Soviet Union.[78] But that his stance was anti-German he never denied. A more detached look actually shows that it was also racist.

According to Ehrenburg's own memoirs, the writer Vasilii Grossman often reproached him for saying "Germans" instead of "Hitlerites" or "fascists" in his descriptions of the crimes of the occupiers. Grossman added, "An epidemic should not be called national character. 'Karl Liebknecht was also German.'" But Ehrenburg wrote once that there were *no* favorable exceptions: "Of course, there are good and bad people among the Germans, but the psychic qualities of this or that Hitlerite are beside the point. The good German fellows, those who at home give way to sentimentalities, give pickaback rides to their kids and feed German cats morsels of their rationed hamburgers, murder Russian children with the same pedantry as do the bad ones." He claimed an ability to recognize German generals in a bathhouse and German colonels by their face.[79] He also wrote, in late 1944, "We despise the German women for who they are—mothers, wives, and sisters of hangmen." The conquest of Germany "won't end well for the blond witch."[80] Regardless of whether "Germans" to Ehrenburg meant only German occupiers (as his memoirs stated), the fact remains that he preached hatred for all Germans.[81]

Another matter is whether he demanded (or supported) killing all of them. A senior German historian considered him equally guilty of criminal incitement to genocide as the prominent Nazi Julius Streicher, who was hanged at Nuremberg for publishing anti-Semitic ramblings. Ehrenburg's American biographer writes that the writer "never advocated the extermination of the German people or the destruction of Germany as a country."[82] Neither qualification is correct. In September 1942 Ehrenburg himself granted that he promoted indiscriminate killing. "Of course, there are in this army individual people who think and feel, but these are a few among the millions, ladybugs on the back of an elephant gone insane. We don't have time or desire to deal with ladybugs. We must shoot the mad elephant. Now we understand fully that the only school for the Germans is the grave." In a front-line newspaper in May 1944 he went as far as declaring what he seemingly wanted: "A living Germany is death lurking beside a cradle. *No Germans will remain alive.*"[83] Bluntness of this kind was impossible in the main press.

Ehrenburg almost never supported taking German war prisoners. But in May 1942, possibly with Stalin's Red Army Day statement in mind, he wrote, "If a German soldier will lay down his weapon and surrender, we will not lay a finger on him—he will live. Perhaps a future Germany will reeducate him and turn the dumb killer into a worker and human." But this future was now irrelevant: "Let the German pedagogues think about this." It was also exceptional when he wrote, "The German people, too, shall live, having purged itself of the terrible crimes of the Hitler decade."[84]

And he rarely exempted civilians from the Red Army's killing campaign. He wrote in January 1942, "We do not want to shoot sixty-two-year-old German schoolteachers. We will not bother twelve-year-old girls."[85] But soon the only German civilians his writings specifically spared were children: the Red Army would never kill them. By 1945 he seemed to believe that they could easily be reeducated.[86] That Ehrenburg even had to write that children should be spared shows how extreme his writings were. Only in March 1945 did he add women, and indeed male adults: "After the war we have to start educating the human-like ones, we have to raise them, if only to the level of backward people." He wanted nothing to do with it, however. "Let specialists teach the Germans so that they become human or at least resemble humans."[87]

Agitprop's ungrateful rebuke of April 1945 must partly be seen in the context of the Red Army's actual behavior and Ehrenburg's reaction to it. In late March Stalin was informed that on the 5th Ehrenburg had spoken to editors of *Krasnaia zvezda* about plunder, senseless destruction, and heavy drinking by Red Army troops in East Prussia. They were also not shunning, in his words, German women, a veiled reference to rapes. He repeated his concerns in an address at the Frunze Academy on March 21.[88] Stalin felt it was time to intimidate the prominent and popular writer.

But the main reason for the public rebuke seems to have been Stalin's concern with Nazi propaganda, which referred to Ehrenburg not only as a Jew (and thus a murderer), but also as "Stalin's number one war correspondent." Even Hitler mentioned Ehrenburg in his first order for the year 1945, in an attempt to underline the threat of extermination he claimed the Germans were facing. On May Day that year Stalin was to denounce Nazi propaganda claims, saying, "As if the Allied nations want to exterminate the German people. To destroy the German people is not the task of the Allied nations." That was why the allied military authorities would not "touch Germany's peaceful population" if it loyally carried out demands.[89] That is, two weeks earlier Aleksandrov's *Pravda* article was addressing above all a foreign audience. Stalin could not do so yet, for deviating from his ever sparse speaking schedule would overexpose the matter. The Germans had to be told, quickly, that the Kremlin no longer tolerated acts of revenge and that Germans residing west of the Oder and Neisse Rivers need not flee. And focusing on Ehrenburg had the added perceived benefit of signaling that Bolshevism, contrary to what the Nazis and many other Germans believed, did not equal Jewish rule.

Germany's Allies

Stalin's public statements always ignored the presence in Soviet territory of citizens of states allied with Germany. He thought, probably correctly, that his own citizens preferred to conceive of the enemy as one. Ehrenburg once made this explicit. "We do not add anything to the oath 'Death to the German occupiers,'" he wrote, because Italian, Romanian, Finnish, Spanish, French, and Belgian hirelings were "not representatives of other peoples." They were "the very same German occupiers, 'second rate.'"[90] Still, non-German invaders were mentioned and to varying degrees included in the campaign for hate.

Romanians had been vilified for years, and in the middle of 1940 the Soviet media raged against "Romanian boyars and gendarmes" oppressing Bessarabia and northern Bukovina.[91] After the German invasion, real or attributed crimes by Romanians were often identified as such. The Bureau quoted a captured order by a Romanian divisional commander to shoot food hoarders; Romanians in Chișinău (Kishinev) were said to have shot several locals and to have blamed the Bolsheviks; *Pravda* reported the killing of 25,000 Jews in Odessa by the Romanian army; and *Krasny flot* reported that Romanians had taken all the Jews of the Crimean town of Sudak to the seashore and tortured them for hours before shooting all of them.[92] Ehrenburg demanded payback to the Romanian army "for Odessa," where, among other things, the population supposedly was forced to speak Romanian. Romanian peasants might be starving and suffering, but "we also know what the Romanians did to our cities and villages." In the time of reckoning to come, "the jackals shall get what they deserve. They will get what they came to us for."[93]

In early 1942 the media provided translations of protest letters by Romanian war prisoners, but no such Romanian voices (or reports of them) appeared thereafter—not even when, in September 1943, Ana Pauker, Emil Bodnăraș, and 200 Romanian inmates of the POW camp at Krasnogorsk founded a Romanian National Committee, which eventually created a Romanian military formation.[94] Meanwhile the crimes of the "German-Romanian invaders" were often described. On the occasion of the Extraordinary State Commission's report on the Odessa oblast *Pravda* wrote, "We know the horrors of the Drobytsky Iar near Kharkiv, the horrors of Babi Yar in Kiev.... It seemed that the limit of criminality had been reached. But that which took place in Odessa supersedes also these cruelties." The task ahead was to rid the "future generations of the Romanian people" of the "fascist stupidity."[95] In August 1944, when King Michael of Romania accepted the Soviet Union's armistice conditions, the anti-Romanian propaganda came to an abrupt halt.

With another major German ally the situation was more clear-cut. Although the media provided some statements by Hungarian civilians and POWs, Hungarians generally were and remained enemies, if only because the Communist Mátyás Rákosi could not agree with Krasnogorsk prisoners about a national committee, let alone a Hungarian military unit.[96]

Finland was another very specific opponent. Propaganda against Finland's rulers dated back to the Soviet attack of November 1939. That invasion, to which the Finns capitulated in March 1940, had officially been a defense striving to "wipe the brazen Finnish bandits from the face of the earth." The media denounced the "Finnish pigs," "reptiles," "insects," "bandits," and "warmongers"; the Soviet Union was "ready to destroy the enemy on his own territory." A poem by Vasilii Lebedev-Kumach, who was much more outspoken than any party or government official, railed against Finnish "war mongers," "traitors," "rabid dogs," and "bloody clowns." That these evildoers were officially separate from the Finnish people could easily be overlooked.[97] Finland declared war on the USSR on June 25, 1941, in what it called the "Continuation War." But under American pressure and despite German urging, it initially did not cross the Finnish-Soviet border of 1939,[98] retained full diplomatic relations with the United States until mid-1944, and declared neutrality in September of that year. Meanwhile Finnish rule was lethal for Russian civilians, particularly in the town of Petrozavodsk.

When in August and September 1941, and again in March and April 1942, Soviet Finnish civilians were deported and removed from the front line, the Soviet media were silent.[99] Friendly Finnish voices included organized war prisoners whose appeal appeared in translation, but such voices were rare. The propaganda denounced again "Finnish robbers," "Finnish fascists," "Mannerheimites," and—a new term—"Finnish Hitlerites." There were eventually also words simply against "the Finns," as in an article about the treatment of war prisoners and Petrozavodsk.[100] Three films called the Finnish enemy cruel and insidious. In short, in their perceived traits and actions the Finns came very close to the German mortal and eternal enemy, and it is reasonable to consider it anti-Finnish hate speech.[101]

In total contrast, the Italians received a good press, even though they also joined the Germans on Soviet territory (and no pro-Soviet Italian military unit was formed). Not just the usual text of a prisoner conference appeared, but even praise of the Italians as a people. Thus the paper *Trud* in December 1941 gave an audience to one author's confidence that "the Italian people, faithful to its best own traditions of love of freedom, the people that gave birth to Garibaldi, shall manage to throw off the chains of slavery in which its worst enemies—Hitler and Mussolini—have forged it." There was some criticism of the "royal musketeers," who were "robbing the Ukrainian people with the same frenzy and cruelty as the Germans."[102] Still Ehrenburg was more typical when assuring readers that the people from the cradle of fascism did not wish to serve "the German baron" and were "not cowards": "We don't confuse the Italian people with the Italian fascists and semi-fascists." The book version of his essay "Patriotism" even declared, "I love the Italian people, and when talking with Italian imprisoned soldiers, I am always pleased: fascism in Italy has not managed to penetrate the heart of the people, it has remained a skin disease, a repulsive eczema."[103]

Further research is needed to clarify the coverage of these and Germany's other European military allies: Croatia, Slovakia, Denmark, Norway, and Spain. As for Japan, the Soviet Union adhered to its neutrality pact with that country until August 1945. Well before then publications denounced Japan as an aggressor, but to Soviet citizens it must have seemed irrelevant until November 6, 1944, when Stalin mentioned the country for the very first time during the war with Germany.[104]

Little research has been done on the mentality in the Soviet hinterland and recaptured territories, and far too few surveillance reports by the NKVD have been declassified. Therefore, although it would seem likely that hatred there became widespread, researchers have not demonstrated, let alone analyzed this. That there was hatred is clear. Various testimonies by survivors of Nazi rule written down by Red Army commissars, for instance in Rostov in late 1941, call the Germans animals, dogs, and vermin who must be exterminated. As noted in an earlier chapter, at least some viewers of film footage with corpses in that city uttered hateful cries. An American journalist fluent in Russian encountered in Leningrad a "deep hatred" of the Germans and the "White Guard Finns." When Germans were hanged in a public square in Kharkiv in December 1943, boys whistled and others applauded. Anti-German hatred also developed in central Ukraine.[105]

But other evidence points in another direction. In early 1943 a woman went to the recaptured city of Voronezh and spent many nights in hostels, without disclosing that she was working for *Pravda*. Secretly reporting about her frank conversations with the young women living there, she noted the absence of "real hatred" of the Germans. The women spoke "calmly" about them, "and some even called them good." They remembered joint dances and, "with a smile, entirely carelessly, how Franz walked, how Willy sang, how George 'womanized,' et cetera." The reporter "asked if there had been any atrocities here. They respond no. One says, 'They say they mostly kill Jews, but we are all pure Russians.'" She also asked how they could dance with Germans even as war prisoners were dying in the nearby camp. After a silence someone said, "You were far away, but we had to live with them."[106]

Foreigners and unpublished Soviet reports also nuance the stance of the onlookers during the subsequent public marches of war prisoners—Germans who had not faced a tribunal yet. Alexander Werth's testimony about the march through Moscow in July 1944 rings true: "Youngsters booed and whistled, and even threw things at the Germans, only to be immediately restrained by the adults; men looked on grimly and in silence; but many women, especially elderly women, were full of commiseration (some even had tears in their eyes) as they looked at these bedraggled 'Fritzes.'" The correspondent of the *Christian Science Monitor* was told by a Russian woman he knew that several female onlookers cried out of pity for the Germans.[107] The same mixed response was apparent at a march through Kiev in August 1944; secret reports referred to both hateful shouts and pitiful comments, and there were even helpful gestures: a woman threw an apple (and was arrested), and someone else threw bread and tobacco.[108]

It was possible for Soviet citizens to hold contradictory views: to want, for example, for one's son to create orphans in many German families without feeling hatred for German war prisoners one had gotten to know. This duality matches the recollections of ethnic Germans who survived the Soviet deportations, which refer to popular hatred for the "fascists" and acts of kindness toward themselves.[109]

Stalin's own statements about the way to deal with and think about the Germans were less clear than might have been expected. They were in some ways mild and in other ways radical, and their character changed over time in both directions. He demanded the "total" extermination of the "German occupiers" of Soviet territory (November 1941, May 1942, November 1942, May 1943), a call that seemed to exclude other Germans, as he indeed confirmed twice (February 1942, May 1945). "The German people" thought differently from Hitler, he said more than once (July 1941, May 1942); a German state would remain (February and November 1942); and for much of 1943 he toyed with the notion of a "Free Germany," deciding only near the end of that year to demand Germany's unconditional surrender. On the other hand, sometimes Stalin described "the Germans" negatively, calling them possessed by exterminatory designs (November 1941), or used "the Germans" as shorthand for "German occupiers" and other epithets (November 1942, February 1943, May

1943, November 1943). Early in 1944 he even publicly called upon the Red Army to finish off the "German beast."

Righteous anger at declared enemies had long been a staple of Soviet public life. But although Stalin allowed his subjects to express emotions, he wanted to retain a core of rationality. This was contrary to Nazi propaganda, which glorified blind faith and instinct and gave the emotions of hatred and love a free rein. Thus the prewar Soviet criminal code prescribed up to two years of detention for "propaganda or agitation directed at the incitement of national or religious hatred or discord."[110] The rational core also helps explain why it took almost a year for Stalin to call hatred a precondition for victory and for propaganda to begin denouncing the Germans as a people. Stalin and his representatives did not openly sanction ethnic hatred; the only *official* targets were not the Germans in general but the "German-fascist invaders." There were also still performances of classical German music and theater; sometimes writers such as Goethe were presented as totally unlike the Nazis; and young people were encouraged to learn the German language.[111]

But unlike with Germany's foreign allies—treated as enemies for the moment—Moscow did encourage others to blur and occasionally erase the distinction between "fascists" and Germans. Publications in the most prestigious papers of Sholokhov's, Wasilewska's, and other writers' fiction, Ehrenburg's essays, and many other items about sadists, bloodthirsty beasts, and inhuman robots made Soviet citizens understand that their rulers were giving them a license to hate all the Germans.[112] The more perceptive ones realized that the license was a tool for mobilization that might be withdrawn. Meanwhile considerations of foreign policy best explained the sudden rise and fall of the propaganda about a "Free Germany" and the public rebuke to Ehrenburg near the end of the war.

When Stalin noted the existence of hatred in the Red Army and (in 1944) among the entire population, the only reason he mentioned were German crimes. This was and remained the public line. No Soviet reports or other writings, but enemy actions produced tremendous hatred.¹¹³ No Soviet leader ever said in public that the hatred supposedly pervading Soviet life had been primarily or even partly the doing of Agitprop and the media. Nor has an archival document or memoir been found in which a member of the Central Committee evaluated the overall nature of the hate propaganda and its impact.

Foreign correspondents, whose almost single source of information was the Soviet press, were uncertain about the significance of the hate propaganda as compared to the impact of the Nazi crimes. It was typical that Alexander Werth deemed "profound" the impact of Sholokhov's "The Science of Hatred," but felt that Ehrenburg's "near racialist" writings merely "grasped by intuition what the ordinary Russian really felt."¹¹⁴ Lev Kopelev, a Germanist of Jewish descent, produced German-language Soviet front propaganda. At first nearly ashamed for not having a personal score of dead Germans, he gradually became concerned. In the summer of 1942 he complained to Ehrenburg about his articles, which he evidently believed to be influential, telling him he had witnessed Red Army members shoot Germans who tried to surrender. Kopelev was arrested in 1944, in his view because superiors who had supported Red Army plunder and violence in East Prussia feared he would denounce them.¹¹⁵ His postwar memoirs published abroad raised painful questions: "We wrote, shouted about holy revenge. But who were those avengers and on whom did they avenge? Why did so many of our soldiers turn out to be bandits who gang-raped women and girls in the snow and in house entrances, killed unarmed people, shattered, fouled, and burned everything they could not take along? And they destroyed senselessly, just to destroy. How did all of this become possible?" Western translations of the Russian original continue with a specific answer about who was responsible: "Had we not raised them, the political workers, the journalists, the writers—Ehrenburg and Simonov and hundreds of thousands of other industrious, ambitious, but also talented agitators, teachers, and instructors, genuine preachers of the 'holy revenge'? We taught them to hate, convinced them, that the German was bad merely for being German. We glorified murder in poetry, prose, and drawings: 'Daddy, kill the Germans!'"¹¹⁶

Vsevolod Vishnevskii, a writer and official overseeing fellow writers at the Baltic Fleet, has recalled something similar: "In 1941–1942, we writers gave the people a monstrous charge of hatred for the enemy."[117] But to what extent the hate propaganda achieved its unstated goal of creating, magnifying, and distributing hatred actually remains unclear. The Nazi crimes themselves, reported extensively, may well have been more influential.

8

The Motherland and Its People

In the years before the German invasion a strong focus on the beneficial qualities of the Russian people had pervaded Soviet public life, including a heavy emphasis on their role as the "elder brother" to the USSR's non-Russians. The reasons were perhaps mostly pragmatic: the country was supposed to function in an integrated way in military, political, and economic matters, and Russian national heroes, myths, and imagery might popularize the dominant Communist ideology, which since the Great Terror lacked a usable Soviet past to enliven it. Scholars disagree as to which term best describes the public trend—Russian nationalism, Russification, or Russocentrism—and not all believe that a Russian national character was praised.[1]

It was not surprising that the trend, called Russocentrism here, increased in force during the war. In July 1941 *Pravda* did something it had never done before by proclaiming the Russians more equal than others. The Russian people were the "first among the equal peoples of the USSR."[2] In his October Revolution speech on Red Square that year, Stalin hoped not only that "the great Lenin's banner" would shield the soldiers, but also that the soldiers would be "inspired" by the "manly image of our great ancestors Aleksandr Nevskii, Dmitrii Donskoi, Kuzma Minin, Dmitrii Pozharskii, Aleksandr Suvorov, and Mikhail Kutuzov." All were Russians, and all had defended the old regime. Notably absent here, and also from most wartime publications, for reasons unknown, were Ivan IV, "the Terrible," who had been rehabilitated a few years before, and Peter I, "the Great."[3]

Ilia Ehrenburg began praising the Russians almost immediately. In August 1941 he freed them from blame for the anti-Jewish pogrom he had seen in Kiev as a young boy. In fact in that "Russian city," he said, "Russian people hid Jews." In the current fight "not a single Russian" had stepped out of line. "Disdain of other peoples has always been alien to the Russians," he repeated the next year, a time when he also noted that "the elder brother of the Soviet family, the Russian people, gained the respect of the other peoples not by self-assertion, but by selflessness: they went ahead and are going ahead of the others along the road where man is met not only by flowers, but also with bullets." The Russians were great (as the birth of Leo Tolstoy proved), humane, and peaceable.[4] By 1943 there appeared articles by others that were simply entitled "We Are Russians." Non-Russian-language Soviet media also praised the "unyielding spirit of the Russian people" and the "creative force of their genius."[5]

Russocentrism pervaded many published works of literature and their reviews. In a widely read poem, "Do you remember, Alesha, the roads near Smolensk...," Konstantin Simonov described his discovery of the Russian countryside, the "country lanes traversed by our grandfathers / With the simple crosses of their Russian graves." The author was "full of pride that I had been born a Russian."[6] His play *Russian People*, serialized in *Pravda* in July 1942, the best-known play from the war period and turned into a film called *In the Name of the Motherland* (1943), gave the message that all Russians, including even a former tsarist officer, were as one against their foreign enemy. Set on both sides of the Southern Front, it featured ordinary people whose modest bravery and contempt of death were typically Russian. One paper's review was joyful: "Never before has the name of the Russian man sounded this proudly as in our days, when it has become to all freedom-loving peoples the symbol of heroism, selflessness, and patriotism.... The whole world reveres the valor of the Russians, who have managed to withstand the weight of the most crippling blows that no other state has withstood. The Russians of our days have resurrected and immensely compounded the battle glory of their ancestors, the dreaded glory of the mighty Russian weapon."[7]

Pravda was a stage for similar works of fiction. In September 1942 it published installments of Aleksandr Tvardovskii's poem "Vasilii Terkin," which emphasized the man's Russian identity.[8] The next year it serialized *Taras' Family*, later retitled *The Unsubdued*, which also appeared as a book in a print run of 200,000. Although the novel by Boris Gorbatov, a *Pravda* correspondent, explicitly takes place in Ukraine, its main character, Taras, calls the setting "Russian," and a Jewish man deeply loves the "Russian land" with its "Russian" climate. As in Ehrenburg's glorification of Kiev's Russians, Ukrainians are fully absent—except when a young man explains how, faced with German propaganda about the Russians and the "Ukrainian nation," he opts for "Bolshevism, Russia, the Komsomol." An unknown person is *rodnoi*, "familiar," to Taras because of the man's "unsubdued, beautiful Russian soul." *Izvestiia*'s review referred to the "greatness and nobility of the Russian man's soul—a soul bright and proud, humane and indomitable."[9]

In principle the Russians could do no wrong. There were no public references to those Russian Cossacks who defected to the Germans. Instead the propaganda offered loyalty statements, such as from the Kuban region.[10] The public references to Russians who supported the German cause, such as the war prisoner and defector General Andrei Vlasov, were far fewer than those to their non-Russian counterparts—and unlike with them, the long list of these Russians' misdeeds never included nationalism.

Soviet quotations of German and Allied statements inadvertently contributed to the Russocentrism. Throughout the war most foreigners spoke of "Russia" and "the Russians," not of the Soviet Union and Soviet citizens. The Extraordinary State Commission's report on Kiev quoted German prisoners referring to the "massacres of the Russian civilian population" committed there. Soviet readers found out that the head of the American Committee to Support Russia admired "the brave Russian people," that a Stockholm paper proclaimed that the name "Stalingrad" would forever commemorate the bravery of "the Russians," and that the British and Canadian press described the Red Army's capture of Orel and Belgorod as indicative of the offensive superiority of "the Russians."[11]

Told by Shcherbakov in June 1944 to improve a draft greeting from the Union Komsomol to Ukraine's Komsomol, Aleksandrov replaced "all brotherly peoples of the Soviet Union" with "its elder brother, the Russian people."[12] By then it was typical for that year's Jewish Meeting to include a toast to "the great Russian people—the inspirer of the struggle of all the peoples of our glorious Motherland"; for Aleksei Tolstoi to entitle a front story simply "The Russian Character"; and for *Pravda* to declare in an editorial about the classical writer Anton Chekhov that "the people who founded such literature are great!"[13] A professor talked for half an hour on the radio about the world's "general recognition" not only of the Russian soldier, but of all Russians, with their "bravery, physical endurance, assiduity, readiness for self-sacrifice, devotion to its own people, hatred of oppression, and love of the Motherland." That other Red Army soldiers had adopted the centuries-old qualities did not make them any less "nationally Russian," he added.[14]

Publications and archival documents show that the Russocentrism could have become even more pervasive. Some leading propagandists were in favor of much more extravagant praise. When, in October 1941, a regiment commissar requested a new and specifically Soviet Russian patriotic paper, Agitprop and the propagandist Emelian Iaroslavskii supported the idea. In December 1941 Iaroslavskii wrote in *Pravda* that the Bolsheviks had cherished the "great cultural heritage of the Russian people," people (*narod*) who worked hard and each were a "versatile artist," a "great builder," a "persistent investigator," a "bold reformer," and a "bold innovator."[15] But Shcherbakov was more ambiguous. This member of Stalin's inner circle said at the commemoration of Lenin's death in January 1942, according to the published text, that the "first among the equals" were "bearing the main burden of the struggle with the German occupiers," a notion immediately copied by other articles.[16] But he apparently did not want to glorify the Russian *past*. In Shcherbakov's one and only meeting with Western correspondents, early in 1943, a British journalist mentioned to him a Russian tradition of military bravery. "Don't talk to me about the Russian soul," Shcherbakov retorted. "Let me recommend you to study the Soviet man."[17]

Stalin made the decision to impose restraint by omission; his speeches and published orders referred to Russian primacy and leadership only rarely when compared to the prewar years. He implied this leadership only in a passing reference to "the English, Americans, and Russians" made late in the war, on November 6, 1944.[18] Stalin's and Shcherbakov's restraint was why Russocentrism remained a tendency and did not become a policy. It usually lacked the notions of prerevolutionary military aid to non-Russians and of Russian cultural leadership in the past and the present.[19] The idea for a Russian patriotic paper was shelved, despite Agitprop's support for it. Not one of the countless meetings of "representatives" of Soviet peoples was held for the Russian people alone. And, as shown below, propaganda in the republics was allowed to celebrate local heroes.

It was official from the start that the war was *great*, but Stalin himself did not publicly call the war great until November 1944.[20] It was also *patriotic*—to be precise, *of the fatherland*, but unlike in the United Kingdom and the United States the key word for the belligerent did not become "Russia" but "the Soviet Union" and, with far more emphasis than before 1941, the *rodina*, or motherland. Stalin used the last word in July 1941, and he consistently capitalized it beginning in November 1942, often preceding it with "Soviet." The choice of *rodina* was brilliant: conveniently vague about the territory it covered, it demanded more than the equally traditional word "fatherland," *otechestvo*. At least some contemporaries considered the latter term to be more political than *rodina*, which one could love unconditionally.[21]

Late in 1943 the concept of a "Soviet system" (*sovetskii stroi*), virtually absent until then, resurfaced, and the nature of the war officially became not a Russian but a *Soviet* achievement. Stalin publicly praised the Soviet system, and others explained that a new state anthem was needed because the current one failed to reflect "the socialist essence of the Soviet state."[22] Sovietness was not simply *Russian*, even though discussions of "Soviet patriotism" tended to include remarks that Lenin had felt a "justified pride when talking about the Russian people."[23] In November 1944 Stalin again cleared away any misunderstanding; one of many sources of the forthcoming victory, Soviet patriotism comprised not just vertical ties—"profound devotion and loyalty" to the Soviet Motherland—but also horizontal ones: "fraternal cooperation" of its "nations and peoples."[24]

The central imposition of restrictions on Russocentrism was also evident from Soviet propaganda's continued reluctance to employ the Orthodox Church. The religious term "holy war" was introduced by the writer Vasilii Lebedev-Kumach in a song that was broadcast over and over, but the Orthodox Church, whose leaders immediately came out in support of the war against Germany, remained absent from the media for a long time. On the day of the German invasion, Metropolitan Sergii of Moscow and Kolomna, the Patriarchal Locum Tenens, prepared a call to "the Russian people" for defense; it was read out in churches but entirely ignored in the media. The same happened to Sergii's message in November 1941, that true Russian patriots would "not hesitate to exterminate the fascist invaders," and his many other appeals. On the night of April 5, 1942, Moscow's curfew was lifted, and midnight Easter services were allowed, but the media were silent.[25]

Sergii first came into view only on November 9, 1942, on the occasion of the twenty-fifth anniversary of the Soviet Union. In two sentences on *Pravda*'s back page, he assured Stalin that he and his flock knew him as the "god-chosen leader of our military and cultural forces.... May god bless Your great feat for the Motherland with success and glory." There also appeared greetings from Metropolitan Nikolai (Mykola) of Kiev and Galicia, Catholikos Georg of the Armenian Orthodox Church, and—the precedent on November 7—Catholikos-Patriarch Kalistrate of the Georgian Orthodox

Church. Church greetings reappeared in February 1943, such as by the First Bishop of the Orthodox of the Renovationist Churches. This media presence baffled regional Agitprop workers.[26]

On September 4, 1943, *Pravda*'s front page reported a meeting without precedent in Stalin's time: he had received Sergii and Bishops Aleksii and Nikolai. Some days later a small piece announced the formation of a Holy Synod and the election of Sergii as patriarch. The Church was reportedly grateful but its own letter was not published.[27] Months later the media reported congratulations to Stalin (with the October Revolution and the successes of the Red Army) from various Orthodox bishops. The Exarch of Ukraine, Nikolai, was quoted as asking the Lord to prolong Stalin's life.[28]

On May 16, 1944, the media reported the death of Sergii and his forthcoming burial, and afterward the Synod was allowed to use the media to thank people for their condolences. A published letter from the Patriarchal Locum Tenens, Aleksii, assured Stalin that the deceased had felt the "sincerest love of You and devotion to You as the wise, God-given Leader." Aleksii would be just as faithful to "the Motherland and the Government headed by You," whereby coordination with the Council for the Affairs of the Russian Orthodox Church would preclude "mistakes and incorrect steps." When Orthodox leaders received the medal "For the Defense of Moscow," Nikolai was quoted as recalling that the city's clergy had stood with the country, both in holy hatred and holy thirst to fully destroy "Hitlerism."[29]

But throughout this new time of media exposure, authorities at all levels obstructed church openings and, near the end of the war, furthered closures. A new journal of the Moscow Patriarchate was allowed, but the state did not distribute it. (When shown a copy by a foreign correspondent, Russians were amazed.) Unlike before 1941, works of fiction tolerated religious faith; in Wanda Wasilewska's *The Rainbow*, for instance, someone defends the right to pray, and Gorbatov's novel mentions icons, prayer, and expressions such as "For God's sake." But Taras in *The Unsubdued* warns his wife that if she wants to pray she should do so at home: "Don't go to a German [*sic*] priest!" Gorbatov's novel, like virtually all published greetings by church leaders, pointedly did not capitalize the word "god." By the fall of 1944 it was not surprising that the party leader of the Stavopol krai, Mikhail Suslov, complained in *Komsomolskaia pravda* about the teaching of religion and stated that "the party's relationship with religion" had "not changed."[30]

Thus overall the rapprochement with the leaders of religious denominations was meager. It was primarily meant to influence the Allies, who were told much more about it, and those citizens who were and had been living under German rule.[31] Otherwise considered virtually useless, what could have been an important contribution to mobilization was not employed extensively in the media.

Younger Brothers

Scholars have described the Soviet state's promotion of ethnic particularism in the 1930s, 1940s, and 1950s, a policy coexisting with the notion of Russian dominance.[32] When the war with Germany broke out the central media largely ended this campaign. The main problem, from a non-Russian perspective, soon became a lack of visibility of ethnic difference in military affairs; the central media did not systematically cover non-Russian war heroes (historical or contemporary) and hardly ever identified the ethnicity of such contemporaries. War correspondents tended not to write of "Uzbeks," "Ukrainians," and so on, but of soldiers, civilians, and the Motherland.[33] Although *Zviazda*, the main Belarusian-language paper, claimed Captain Nikolai Gastello, the Soviet Union's main air force hero, as a "fearless son of the Belarusian people," and a poem read on Kazakh radio identified the "Panfilovite" Tulegen Tokhtarov as Kazakh, the *central* Soviet media hardly ever were this precise. There, although the Panfilovites were a Central Asian unit including Russians, Ukrainians, Kazakhs, Kirgizians, and Karelians, their mythological rallying call was Russocentric: "Not a step back! Russia may be vast, but there is nowhere to retreat! Moscow is at our backs!"[34] It was a concession to non-Russian patriotism that numerous "national" military formations (Latvian, Kuban Cossack, Azerbaijani, and others, though not Belarusian or Ukrainian) were in existence beginning in 1941, but the central media did not mention them.

In marked contrast to this caution, in early February 1944 the propaganda reported a constitutional change and a speech by Molotov about it. Without any prior signals, it became known that each Soviet republic would have its own army and commissariats of defense and foreign affairs. Stalin also mentioned the creation of "new military formations in the Union republics" on Red Army Day.[35] These announcements likely had nothing to do with any wish to mollify non-Russians and everything to do with Stalin's desire for sixteen seats in the new United Nations. The Politburo also set in motion the creation of republican "state anthems." (After the war they were retained, unlike the largely fictional separate armies and commissariats.)

Pravda and other central papers carried some materials in the original Belarusian, Ukrainian, or Uzbek languages, and they sometimes emitted and supported non-Russian ethnic pride. The Belarusians and Ukrainians benefited the most; they were special in having been declared "great" people in late 1939, mainly in an attempt to justify the annexation of regions from Poland where they numerically predominated. The adjective had faded before the German invasion, but, in an evident attempt to mobilize these populations, it made a comeback.[36]

In August 1943 an open letter to the partisans of Belarus and indeed to all Belarusians appeared, allegedly discussed by 25,000 Belarusian Red Army members. It declared that the Belarusian people had always been aware of the "blood unity with the Russian and Ukrainian peoples."[37] Yet in central newspapers it was possible to add that in the eighteenth century an ancient town such as Homel had "united" with Russia, not "reunited," and to celebrate not just the twenty-fifth anniversary of "Belarusian statehood" but also the Belarusian people, to the exclusion of everyone else. The Belarusian writer Mikhas Lynkou praised Belarusians in *Izvestiia* as heroic "partisan people" fighting for their "independence." The chairman of the republican Supreme Soviet reported that the Germans were systematically exterminating Belarusians, while omitting mention of all non-Belarusians. Stalin and Molotov also excluded them from their congratulatory note.[38] At the same time, the republican government and party also put the Belarusians in their proper place. With all their greatness, they owed eternal gratitude not only to Stalin and the Red Army but also to the great Russian people and the other brotherly peoples.[39]

The Ukrainians also had a Russian superior but in practice were more equal to them than others, which was hardly surprising given the large number of these fellow eastern Slavs. From July 1941 to the end of the war, a dozen Ukrainian patriotic appeals to the Ukrainians or occupied Ukraine were made, three of them adopted at meetings of Ukrainian "representatives" in Saratov (November 1941 and August 1942) and Moscow (May 1943). The appeal of April 1942 addressed "you, the great, freedom-loving, warlike Ukrainian people," fortunate to have seen the realization of their "eternal dream" of "reunification of all Ukrainians in one great Ukrainian state." In December 1942 the chairman of the republic's government, Leonid Korniiets, declared that the Ukrainians had "given" the country Aleksei Stakhanov and other pioneers of the prewar production record "movement" named after him.[40] *The Rainbow*, the Ukrainian patriotic novel that was promoted the most heavily, including a debut in *Izvestiia* in August and September 1942, talked about Ukrainian history and quoted Ukrainian slave songs. Now Ukraine was suffering worse than it had done under the Tatar slave raids, "Turkish slavery," and—in a reference to Polish rule—"Lord Potocki."[41]

The media called Lviv a Ukrainian city and placed Poland's eastern border well to the west of what Polish representatives were demanding. In response to the claim by the Polish government-in-exile on Ukrainian and Belarusian regions that the Soviet Union had annexed from the Polish state in 1939, Wasilewska's Ukrainian husband, Oleksandr Korniichuk, attacked a straw man by claiming that Polish "noblemen" were disputing the Ukrainian right to statehood: "Why? On what grounds? In what sense are the Ukrainian people worse that any other people united within the confines of a state of their own?" Initially published in the Soviet Ukrainian press, Aleksandrov arranged for a reprint of the angry rebuke in *Pravda* and *Izvestiia*.[42]

In April and May 1943 Stalin deemed such materials crucial enough to publish them first in *Pravda* and other central papers. The Ukrainian writer Maksym Rylsky defended Ukraine's "freedom, honor, independence, and unity" against Polish claims: "The Ukrainians won't hand over their freedom to anyone." Some of these polemics were not against Poles but against the Ukrainian Canadian Committee; the Academy member Oleksandr Bohomolets (in an article checked by Stalin) and the writer Pavlo Tychyna asserted that Ukrainian independence, which "traitors" and emigrés such as these were demanding, already existed as the Ukrainian SSR.[43]

Central propaganda of Soviet Ukrainian patriotism peaked in the fall of 1943. Inspired by Oleksandr Dovzhenko, Khrushchev proposed to Stalin the idea of the Order of Bohdan Khmelnytsky, and Stalin approved. The only Soviet military order named after a non-Russian historical personality, it could exist because of Khmelnytsky's role in the unification of Ukrainian lands with Moscow. Stalin also allowed Khrushchev to celebrate, in January 1944, the 290th anniversary of the Pereiaslav Agreement. Intended to mark the liberation of Ukraine from the Nazis and to counter Nazi and Ukrainian nationalist propaganda, this was the very first Soviet commemoration of the formation of the "eternal union of the Ukrainian and Russian peoples." But Khrushchev's other proposals, for a special army banner "of the Ukrainian Soviet Socialist Republic" and a medal "For the Liberation of Ukraine," were rejected.[44]

On the day the Khmelnytsky Order was introduced, and a few days before the Red Army retook the Ukrainian city of Zaporizhzhia, Soviet radio broadcast a letter, supposedly from four named front-line soldiers, including one woman. Addressing their fellow "Zaporozhians" in Russian, they waxed rhapsodic about the "Ukrainian land." Centuries ago the Zaporozhian Cossacks had made their mark. Recently one Red Army soldier had crawled on his own toward the Germans to hurl a call of defiance at them, in Ukrainian and in the name of these Cossacks' "grandchildren." On the following evening he and others successfully made a daring raid. In a blood-and-soil image, the letter referred to the mythological Greek giant Antaeus, who had been invincible provided he stayed in touch with the land. The descendants of the Cossacks of Zaporizhzhia should draw strength from their "beloved Ukrainian land" and from the "Cossack force." The author here may have been Iurii Ianovsky, a writer who some time later eulogized the Ukrainians' "immortal spirit" in *Izvestiia*, adding, "What a joy to be the son of such people!"[45]

Ianovsky and others also composed a letter "from the Ukrainian People to the Great Russian People," adopted by acclamation at an open-air rally in Kiev on November 27, 1943. It implied that through the centuries the two brother peoples had achieved all their victories together, as if the Russians could not do without the Ukrainians. And in the Soviet Union both "gave the example, went ahead, and helped all the peoples of the USSR." At this time Aleksandr Fadeev was writing virtually the same in the country's party monthly, and the Ukrainian letter appeared in the Soviet Ukrainian press. The writers probably were shocked that Aleksandrov, noting correctly the absence of the Russians' status as "elder brother," barred its full publication in the central press and allowed only an inaccurate summary.[46] Agitprop's leader also must have been responsible for the disappearance from the central press around this time of the "great Ukrainian people," a concept that lingered in the Soviet Ukrainian press.[47] But he could not preclude all countrywide resonance of Ukrainian pride, for Stalin deemed some of it appropriate. Responding to Khrushchev's speech to the republican Supreme Soviet in March 1944, *Pravda* editorialized that his figures and facts "call forth a feeling of pride for the Ukrainian people. Love of the motherland, hatred of the enemy, courage and bravery in battle—these qualities, which have always distinguished the Ukrainian, in the days of the Patriotic war are coming out in a legendary grandeur and beauty."[48]

In mid-October 1944 propaganda in praise of what was called the total liberation of Soviet Ukraine declared that the Ukrainians had always fought for freedom and "independence." Now they had justified Stalin's hopes. Then began a republicwide campaign to obtain, by force if necessary, signatures under an *Epistle to the Great Stalin from the Ukrainian People*, which was published three months later. The regime apparently hoped in this way to gain and bolster popular support. At least some citizens refused to sign, but more than 9.3 million did, if only because abstention would be held against them.[49]

As part of diplomatic wrestling, Soviet Belarusian and Ukrainian leaders were allowed to express radical territorial demands. Belarusians demanded a return into their fold of the "Belarusian city" of Białystok, annexed to Soviet Belarus in 1939. Mykhailo Hrechukha, chairman of the presidium of Ukraine's Supreme Soviet, and then Khrushchev proclaimed Ukrainian disagreement with Moscow's proposal to arbitrate Poland's eastern border according to the Curzon Line and demanded several districts west of it, with the towns of Chełm, Hrubieszów, Jarosław, and Zamość. Ultimately Białystok was returned to Poland and no Kholm oblast was created.[50] The proposals would have placed the postwar Polish-Soviet border even farther west than the line to which Churchill and Roosevelt had agreed at a conference in Tehran late in December 1943. But Stalin probably considered such voices useful, both in his continued bargaining with the Allies and in the propaganda war against anti-Soviet Ukrainian nationalists.

For of all the Nazi-oriented nationalists, the Ukrainians publicly concerned Moscow the most. The First Ukrainian Meeting of November 1941 put a death warrant on the "yellow-blue bandits, Ukrainian nationalists" who were helping the invaders. By early 1942 this small minority was more hated than German fascism or typhoid lice. The Ukrainians who should "tremble," Hrechukha declared in 1943, were those "yellow-blue killers and looters who betrayed their native fatherland, who trade with the soul and body of the Ukrainian people." Khrushchev also excoriated what he called "Ukrainian-German nationalists," and Ukrainian press articles commemorating the Pereiaslav Agreement of 1654 denounced "today's attempts of the Hitlerite lackeys and loathsome mercenaries of the Bandera, Melnyk, and Bulba type to disunite the eternal friendship of the Russian and Ukrainian peoples."[51]

Particularly fiercely attacked were prominent Soviet-educated writers and intellectuals who supported the German cause. Soviet Ukraine's Radio Shevchenko denounced Arkadii Liubchenko as a writer who had always been a "reptile" and now was dancing to the tune of Goebbels; the reckoning with this "enemy of the Ukrainian people" would be severe. Volodymyr Kubiiovych, head of the Ukrainian Central Committee in the General Government, was a heartless and soulless slave. Soviet propaganda gave such nationalists, named or not, this much attention because of their prominence, and perhaps also because they were not entirely alien: no matter how tightly controlled, no Soviet Ukrainian identity could be totally devoid of nationalist elements.[52]

It testified to Moscow's concern with Ukrainian nationalism that the media repeatedly offered not just the stick but also the carrot. In March 1944 *Pravda* published an amnesty offer to certain Ukrainian nationalists, made in a speech two weeks earlier by Khrushchev. It specifically mentioned the Organization of Ukrainian Nationalists (OUN), the largely fictional Ukrainian National Council, the Ukrainian Insurgent Army (UPA), and the Ukrainian National Revolutionary Army (UNRA) of Taras "Bulba" Borovets, adding—accurately—that they "act with arms against the Soviet Ukrainian partisans, slaughter the Polish population, and destroy all Ukrainians who do not support the nationalists." But Soviet Ukraine's Supreme Soviet Presidium and government had guaranteed members of the UPA and UNRA who "honorably break off all ties with the Hitlerites-OUNites . . . full forgiveness of their mistakes." It seemed hardly accidental that an Extraordinary State Commission report released that month cited a German order of late 1941 to the subunits of SS Einsatzgruppe C to secretly shoot all activists of the OUN's Bandera faction.[53]

Another amnesty offer appeared in the Soviet Ukrainian press in December. Calling on UPA and OUN members and Ukrainians in German service to emerge from hiding and confess, it added that most had joined the nationalist organizations assuming that they would be fighting the Germans. Soviet intelligence already possessed German intelligence reports of British weapon supplies to the UPA, but this made no impact on the propaganda at this stage, possibly at least partly because so few quantities were involved.[54]

The Non-Slavs

Stalin publicly gave the Soviet Union's non-Slavs little attention. In July 1941 he only mentioned the Moldavians, the Baltic peoples, and, probably randomly, two Caucasian Christian peoples (the Georgians and Armenians), and three Muslim peoples (the Azerbaijanis, Tatars, and Uzbeks).[55] But as in the case of the Belarusians and Ukrainians, propaganda's Russocentric tendency did not bar acknowledgments that these non-Russian soldiers might be fighting at least in part for their own non-Russian homelands. For example, the chairman of Kazakhstan's Council of People's Commissars, Nurtas Undasynov, told the defenders of Stalingrad on Kazakh radio, "In defending the great Russian river Volga, you are defending your own sunny Kazakhstan."[56]

Occasionally there appeared proclamations of the ancient, independent ethnogenesis of the non-Slavs. In late 1943, for example, *Izvestiia* reported that the chairman of the Uzbek branch of the Academy of Sciences had asserted, "The culture of the Uzbek people, like that of the other peoples of Central Asia, developed completely separately from earliest times." Moscow's biggest headache was that all non-Russian heroes in Central Asia and the Caucasus of the past three centuries had been fighting Russians. Some wartime works of history even failed to exonerate Russia, as Aleksandrov noted angrily in 1944 in a report about Kazakhstan. But such criticism, also leveled against the Tatar and Bashkir party organizations, remained behind closed doors.[57]

As for Islam, Moscow evidently considered it mainly a nuisance. Only citizens who paid close attention would not miss reports on Muslim affairs, such as that all Soviet Muslims received, de facto in June 1942 and de jure one year later, a mufti (interpreter of Islamic law), Abdurrahman Rasulev. In 1944 *Pravda* carried a letter to Stalin from a conference of Muslims held in Dagestan on June 20 that stated, "May Allah curse the despicable Hitlerites."[58] Moscow did ensure that each Muslim national group sent at least one "national" letter to "its" own front-line fighters. If the Uzbeks had been deported during the war, than the open letter to the Uzbek soldier, published in *Pravda* on October 31, 1942, in both Russian and Uzbek, might in hindsight have been considered the warning sign: "Should you in the difficult days not support your elder and younger brothers—the large and small peoples of the USSR—then you can remain lonely and a severe fate awaits you.... We curse cowards [and] deserters, in our sunny Uzbekistan there will be no place for them. Never shall their mother, the Motherland, forgive them. Such an unworthy son does not have the right to return and knock on the door of his native home."[59]

Beginning in late 1943 various groups shared the fate of the Soviet Germans and Finns. Moscow uprooted and deported almost 95,000 citizens from Georgia, some 90,000 Kalmyks, more than 600,000 people from the North Caucasus, and some 225,000 Crimean Tatars. They were the Karachais from Georgia (November 1943); the titular people from Russia's Kalmyk ASSR (December 1943); the Chechens and Ingushi from their ASSRs (February 1944); the Balkars from Georgia (April 1944); and, just weeks after the Crimea was recaptured, the Crimean Tatars (May 1944). All but the predominantly Buddhist Kalmyks were Muslims. But deportation in 1944 also befell, besides two more Muslim groups in the Caucasus (the Kurds and Meskhets), three Christian populations: Crimea's Armenians, Bulgarians, and Greeks. Although the secret deportation orders claimed that "many" among the people in question had betrayed the motherland, the process of blacklisting was impulsive and illogical—Karelians and Russian Cossacks were not deported, for example—and in this resembled the Great Terror of the late 1930s.[60]

On August 13, 1942, at the beginning of the German Caucasus offensive, a large antifascist meeting took place in Ordzhonikidze (today's Vladikavkaz), the capital of North Ossetia, featuring Chechen, Ingush, and Balkar speakers, and it was reported.[61] Soviet radio in the Crimean Tatar language directed at the peninsula denounced the "bourgeois nationalists" and other Soviet citizens in the Crimea who assisted the Germans. There appeared a few such reports in Russian as well. Perhaps those contributed to the idea of excluding all Tatars from the "friendship of peoples," but whether this was intended is doubtful.[62] Tens of thousands of deported Crimean Tatars died within a few months, which one survivor ascribed mainly to the initially hostile treatment from the local Uzbeks influenced by "anti-Tatar propaganda."[63] Whichever form such verbal propaganda might have taken, it did not appear in the media. Stalin and his inner circle considered the deportations urgently necessary, but also deemed the requirement a stain on the record of the country of Soviets. In short, the media neither foreshadowed nor reflected the deportations.

Jews received special treatment. In October and November 1941 Stalin toyed with the idea of setting up an international Jewish antifascist committee, but then he ordered the arrest of the two Polish Jews involved, Henryk Erlich and Viktor Adler, and in December gave the nod to Agitprop's idea of a purely Soviet committee. Its purpose was to mobilize foreign Jewish support for the Soviet Union; without the large numbers of Jews in North America, the committee probably would not have been created. It met its goal brilliantly, particularly through foreign travel. Meanwhile, failing to grasp that just one role had been reserved for them, its leaders believed they represented six million Jews. They attempted to combat anti-Semitism in the Soviet Union and, their greatest heresy from Stalin's perspective, early in 1944 requested a Jewish socialist republic in the Crimea.[64]

Well before then Stalin's leading officials were highly suspicious of the Soviet Jews. Had Aleksandrov gotten his wish, a large campaign against what he coined "cosmopolitanism," a code word for rootless Jews, might have begun early in 1943, for that was when he complained to his superiors about a "cosmopolitan" article in the newspaper *Literatura i iskusstvo*. Ehrenburg evidently found out and quickly stepped in line, writing, "Outside national culture there is no art. Cosmopolitanism is a world in which things lose their color and shape, and words are bereft of their significance." The newspaper's editor, Konstantin Fadeev, now also condemned "cosmopolitanism" (along with nationalism) in a journal, but newspaper summaries omitted this. The matter was shelved for the duration of the war.[65]

Traditionally Jewish names appeared in published listings of military Heroes of the Soviet Union (as in lists of awarded industrial workers), and Jews appeared in some reports about brothers in arms.[66] But the central press limited Jewish *pride* to reports on the meetings of the "representatives of the Jewish people," with their specific purpose of mobilizing foreigners: Ehrenburg's happiness in being a Jew because "Hitler hates us most of all. And this makes us look well" (August 1941); references to the "best sons of the Jewish people" and all the Jews, defending the country as one (May 1942); and reports that Jewish valor was evident from the more than 32,000 military awards granted to Jews and the one hundred Jewish Heroes of the Soviet Union (April 1944).[67] The poor visibility of Jewish pride was not incidental in being both sanctioned from above and adhered to by many non-Jewish creators. Mikhail Sholokhov's well-received novel *They Fought for the Motherland*, serialized in *Pravda* beginning in May 1943, and other fiction about battles studiously avoided mentioning Jews.[68]

Real promotion of a tangible Soviet Jewish identity or a sense that there existed a Jewish community was possible only in Yiddish, and only because the Jewish Committee existed. The first request to Moscow for a Soviet Jewish newspaper, understood to mean a paper in Yiddish, came in July 1941 from five Jewish writers in Moscow. (By that time there was actually a Yiddish newspaper in faraway Birobidzhan.) A Politburo member, Andrei Andreev, declared it "inexpedient," but Jews asked again in September 1941 and in early 1942, each time using the unconvincing argument that most Jewish evacuees knew only Yiddish.[69] Finally, on June 7, 1942, a new Yiddish newspaper called *Eynikayt* (Unity) appeared in Kuibyshev as the Jewish Committee's official weekly. Its circulation was 10,000; thirty-nine issues were published in 1943, fifty-two the next year, and sixty-two in the first half of 1945.⁷⁰ The vast majority of Soviet citizens could not access these materials and, forced to rely on the Soviet mainstream, received a distorted picture of the ways Jews contributed to the fighting.

The European war had ended when, on May 25, 1945, the media reported that at a Kremlin reception the previous day Stalin raised a toast to the health of the Soviet people that included two remarkable items. For the first time Stalin declared the Russians the leaders of the country, and he implied that the non-Russians had proven to be less reliable than they. His toast was addressed "most of all, to the Russian people," who had earned "general recognition" as the country's "leading force." Russians constituted "the most outstanding nation," with a "clear mind, staunch character, and patience." These traits were evident: the Russians had always "believed in the correctness of the policy of their Government." And they were crucial: Russian faith had been "decisive" for victory. The toast indicated an ethnic hierarchy in the portrayal of heroism that was to remain obligatory for decades.⁷¹

That same month TASS distributed worldwide what became one of the best-known pictures of World War II, showing a hoisting of the Soviet flag over the German Reichstag, supposedly on April 30. The main actor was identified as one Mikhail Egorov, evidently a Russian, and his assistant as the Georgian Meliton Kantaria. In reality the raising was staged on May 2. The NKVD intimidated the actual hero, a Ukrainian named Oleksii Kovaliov, into a silence that lasted half a century, for, as the photographer Evgenii Khaldei recalled years later, Stalin demanded that one Russian and one Georgian be found and awarded for the flag raising.⁷²

Stalin's proclamations of Russian leadership and comparative unreliability of non-Russians significantly modified the trend of the wartime propaganda, which navigated among various tendencies. During the war there was Russocentrism, or Russian primacy, whereby most non-Russian war heroes, contemporary and historical, either were ignored or not identified as non-Russian. But the key concepts were and remained the *motherland* and its imagined community of "Soviet people," even though Stalin and others rarely mentioned and never clearly defined them. For instance, what was really Soviet in *Pravda*'s definition in mid-1942 of Soviet patriotism as "subordination of one's whole life to the fight for the motherland"?[73]

The Russians did stand out in the wartime media because of their numerical majority and because of the attitude of leading propagandists and society as a whole.[74] And the outside world supported their prominance; Western Allies and German prisoners routinely referred to the country, its inhabitants, and its army as Russian. Yet, as shown here, the central media were not as Russocentric as might have been expected. Praise to the Russians usually did not go to extremes simply because Stalin did not give it the green light, sensing that the Belarusians, Ukrainians, and other non-Russians were needed to achieve victory. He also attempted to mobilize those non-Russians by allowing the central media to praise them as national groups. Framing the overall struggle as one for the "motherland" enabled this. That in reality Stalin suspected many non-Russians of disloyalty was another matter. As for the Jews, a propaganda campaign against them, for which some in his inner circle were readying themselves, was blocked, if only because Stalin still felt it contradicted the notion of "national" unity.

Had Stalin been less cautious, the central media would have worked harder along the Russocentric, xenophobic, and anti-Semitic lines he was to let loose with his sensational toast in May 1945. Doing so might have been more effective in mobilizing Russians, but it would have contravened the mobilization of the vitally important non-Russians. From Stalin's perspective, to focus instead on the motherland was indeed the best option. Ideological concerns mostly explained why, for a long time, the propaganda ignored the patriotic rallying cries of Orthodox hierarchs, even though these likely would have influenced large numbers of Russians and non-Russians alike—here an opportunity was missed.

The propaganda did probably contribute to the formation of ethnic Russian consciousness. Even though the meager attention to the non-Russian identity of war heroes usually did not mean to denigrate, many Russians likely concluded what Stalin was to say out loud later: that the non-Russians could not be trusted. The impact of total omission of Jewish heroes was even more profound: it bolstered a preexisting popular prejudice that Jews were shirking the fight.[75] Countering this view consumes the energy of Russian-speaking Jews to this day.

9

Immortal Avengers and Enemy Accomplices

It was official that only a minority of the original inhabitants of the occupied regions fell under German rule. The regime's officials and journalists were and remained highly suspicious of them: Why had they not left, and why had they not died?[1] *Krasnaia zvezda*'s editor, David Ortenberg, rejected an article about a recaptured Russian site because of its description of an engineer who made repairs beneficial to both Germans and locals and a city administration typist with three children to feed. The sympathy they received from the author, Konstantin Simonov, supposedly implied that collaboration would go unpunished. Those people should not have worked at all; in fact they were guilty simply for not retreating with the Red Army.[2]

David Zaslavskii, a prominent commentator who specialized in public denunciation of intellectuals (and like Ortenberg of Jewish descent), was able to visit the sites of the murder of the Jews of Kharkiv in December 1943. "Those killed were the less solid and worthy part of Soviet Jewry, the part that more and more lost both personal and national dignity," he wrote in his private diary. Many had even deserved to die: "Any Jew who, for whatever reason, remained with the Germans and did not kill himself condemned himself to death. And when, in addition, he, for private gain, kept his children with him and thus doomed them to death, he is a traitor."[3] The question is to what degree newspapers and radio broadcasts reflected the ideological establishment's suspicion and condescension.

Death as Deliverance

Works of fiction serialized in the media portrayed the people in question as loyal, in action or at least in spirit. Wanda Wasilewska's *The Rainbow* features the occasional fearful peasant, but no one doubts that "our people will come." The villagers gather to wave at a Soviet plane, and their "inflexible, stubborn, silent resistance" frustrates the Germans' plans.[4] Boris Gorbatov's novel *The Unsubdued* was set in the fictional Donbas town of Kamenny Brod. Much of the content derived from the author's visit to his native city of Voroshilovhrad (today's Luhansk), where he spoke with acquaintances and read the notes made by a former underground activist. The novel describes life and death after the arrival of the Germans and Italians in July 1942. Taras Iatsenko is a sixty-year-old metalworker with a strong faith in the USSR. His three sons have left home: Stepan is carrying out a party order to conduct underground work; Andrei is a former war prisoner who rejoins the Red Army; and Nikifor is wounded at Stalingrad. Stepan's truthful leaflets fight the main threat, which is not death but fear and disbelief. At first considering "the people" shamefully "silent," Stepan then realizes that they are like a dry tree that only needs a spark to blaze into a vengeful fire. The notion that the people deserve credit reappears when the wounded son visits a bookstore in a liberated city. The books will be stolen because the shop window is broken, Nikifor worries, but the salesman disagrees: under the Germans the people were "not deluded by their promises. How can one now insult them by doubt? One can believe in our people."[5]

Some of the propaganda dealt with non-Jews who felt sorry for the Jews and helped them. *Izvestiia* reported in August 1941 on the

Podolian town of Antoniny, where "fascists" had been unable to force Ukrainians to bury the local Jews. The first Germans had looted and raped and had murdered three officials; a second German group (obviously an SS death squad) singled out the Jews:

> In the town square in the presence of the inhabitants the Germans forced four Ukrainians to dig a pit. Then they separated out four Jews and threw them in. An order came: "Bury them!" No one moved. People froze on the edge of the grave they dug. "You don't want to? All right!" The Jews were ordered to climb out of the pit. "Lie down!" the corporal shouted at the Ukrainians. Again there came an order to fill in the pit. No one threw a handful of soil into the grave with living people at the bottom. Threats to shoot everyone at once did not work either. Waving with his sub-machine gun, the corporal nudged the people numb from horror: "Fill it in!" From someone's feet a lump of earth broke loose and fell down. It was what the torturers had been waiting for. They pulled the Ukrainians from the pit and told them, "See, the Jews want to bury you alive. Pay them for this in the same way." But still no one raised a finger in support of this vile crime. Then the Germans took up the spades themselves. Four Jews were buried alive.[6]

The Soviet Information Bureau released a similar account about a concentration camp near Minsk, quoting an eyewitness. Indeed according to the Foreign Affairs Commissariat statement of December 1942 about the mass murder of the European Jews, non-Jews were displaying strong "solidarity" with the Jews in Czechoslovakia, France, the Netherlands, Norway, Sweden, and even in "foreign regions adjacent to Soviet territory," where "racial prejudices" had been strong. As for the topic of Soviet citizens aiding Jews, it was probably accidental that only Russians, Belarusians, and Lithuanians were mentioned.[7]

The statement by the commissariat did not usher in more accounts about such solidarity, however, and that was one reason why, in 1943, Gorbatov's novel stood out. Although Kamenny Brod is a place where people fear even meeting each other, Taras bows deeper than ever upon greeting Dr. Fishman, who is now wearing a Star of David. One morning Taras sees Jews being herded somewhere by auxiliary policemen and German submachine-gunners. These Jews "don't know and don't believe" that they are to be murdered that day—except for one, about whom Taras says to himself, "Goodbye Doctor Aron Davidovich! Don't condemn me; I cannot save you. We ourselves are awaiting execution." Even so, some Jews who escape are hidden by "Russian families": "Russian people eagerly, without fear, saved the martyrs: it was a duty of conscience." Taras and his family do precisely this, sheltering a six-year-old girl (and suffering no consequences when an auxiliary policeman finds out). Here, as in almost all other materials, the Jewish victims are presented as largely passive, but they are not condemned for this. Entirely lacking is the postwar notion that Jews might betray their own by working in Jewish councils or as policemen.[8]

The Kremlin was aware of the involvement of Poles, Ukrainians, Lithuanians, and others in anti-Jewish pogroms, and it captured SS documents claiming that non-Jews demanded harsh measures against the Jews. The media mentioned some of the pogroms. The one in Lviv of July 1941 appeared more than once. Aleksei Tolstoi wrote within weeks of a "night of the long knives" there against "many thousands of people—large and small"; Wasilewska wrote that the "Hitlerites" organized a pogrom under the slogan "Beat the Jews and the Poles," killing about 400 people; and Molotov in January 1942 also made a reference. A few articles, such as one by Iaroslav Halan, the main propaganda writer for Soviet Ukrainian radio, reported that the Nazis first presented corpses as victims of NKVD killings, which, he added, was a lie. Missing from all such accounts was the participation of locals in the pogroms.[9]

A cited way of betrayal was supplying the Germans with food. The villagers in *The Rainbow* had lacked the time to give all their grain to the retreating Red Army, so they buried the remainder in a distant pit. To give it to the Germans was more than disobedient: it meant, readers were warned, acknowledging German rule over the Ukrainian land and "repudiating the motherland, selling oneself to the enemy, betraying those who were dying in this war and in the civil war, in 1918, and even earlier—betraying all those who had ever fought for liberty of man and attained it with their hearts' blood."[10] This followed the line, expressed particularly forcefully in May 1942, that "any indifference" among Soviet citizens in occupied territories or elsewhere constituted "state treason."[11] Death-defying resistance was not merely honorable but *required*; even unarmed civilians, reports implied, acted out of the same moral obligation as soldiers.

The dogma explained the removal from a story by Vasilii Grossman of the anxious cries by women whom German soldiers used as human shields: the censor argued that they seemed "prepared to betray the motherland to save their lives."[12] In *The Rainbow* a woman's husband is taken hostage, but she is fatalistic about both his and her own life: "What will be, will be. If it's his fate, they'll kill him. If not, he'll stay alive. And if it comes to that, the sooner we die the better, rather than live under the Germans." Actually "death would be a happy deliverance" for the hostages, and if it were certain that the Germans would stay, she would take her own life. When the Red Army returns and fighting ensues around a cottage that has a baby inside, the mother admonishes the Soviet soldiers to burn it down: "You must not all perish because of my baby." There are also no tears when it turns out that not fire but the Germans inside killed the child: "It must have cried in its cradle and the scum killed it with their rifle butts. . . . See? And you didn't want to burn the house down. You felt sorry for a dead child. Two men were hurt because of this. . . . I won't cry. Just give me a rifle please."[13]

Gorbatov's *The Unsubdued* mentions "traitors, those who renounced the party and the people, betrayed comrades, and served the German," and "cowards." The novel adds that predicting who would fall into this category is impossible. As a fellow party member tells Stepan, the underground activist, every citizen is undergoing a great test, a great "cleansing," and the outcome is never certain. But one surely fails when placing survival over loyalty to the Soviet state. Stepan's father, Taras, is a stern Bolshevik who believes that one should worry only about saving one's "soul." Stepan "feared neither gallows nor death, he believed in our victory, and was glad to give up his life for it." He admonishes another person, "Death does not exist. It is an invention. It's *kaputt* for cowards and immortality for heroes—there is no middle ground."[14]

Resistance Fighters

Partisans and underground fighters were the most likely to become immortal, but for a long time Moscow discouraged popular participation in partisan activity, let alone initiatives for it. Change came only in September 1942, when Stalin secretly disseminated his conclusion that preconditions for the quick development everywhere of a partisan struggle "of the entire people" were in place and that therefore "all the wider layers of the population," even in the cities, had to get involved. The propaganda apparatus now encountered problems. From the very beginning the media had declared not only that there was a large "partisan movement," but also that most participants were ordinary people. As Agitprop now told Shcherbakov, the press was "very bad" and "extremely cautious" in portraying them. Hardly any article explained their significance for the struggle against the German army or told Soviet citizens in occupied regions that it was their duty to join the "movement." The agency planned twenty-eight such articles. The media marked the policy change when *Pravda* stated that Stalin had demanded a new, "broader" partisan movement.[15] Twice in 1943 the propaganda again mirrored the existence of new directives, this time in public statements by Stalin himself in May and November 1943 that partisans had to save Soviet people from deportation and extermination, which matched secret orders, given to the partisans in the spring of that year, to save lives and material resources.[16]

It was an unwritten rule that reports could ascribe to partisans personal, regional, and non-Russian patriotic motives but also had to emphasize all-Union ones (perhaps also to broaden the way the partisans thought of themselves). Formal rules on the depiction of partisans, put to paper early in 1942, banned a host of details: first and last names of commanders and commissars; last names of other partisans; places and raions (instead, formulations such as "the partisans of the Smolensk oblast" should be used); photographs revealing identities or locations; wordings such as "partisan brigade" revealing the structure and size of units; weaponry; methods of communication with civilians and the Red Army; reconnaissance for the Red Army; the use of children and elderly people; and the presence in German service of people following partisan (or Soviet underground) directives. Scrutiny of such materials intended for the central press took place in Moscow at both the Bureau and the Central Staff of the Partisan Movement. The reported dates of partisan attacks were also easily adjusted. If intended for newspapers of oblasts and republics near the front, the texts were checked by the relevant partisan staff or military council. In October 1942 the Central Staff also began banning reports that might increase German repression.[17]

In principle no reports of diversion and sabotage in occupied cities and towns were possible, but one big exception was allowed. The Nazi in charge of the White Ruthenia district of the Reichskommissariat Ostland, General Commissar Wilhelm Kube, was killed in Minsk in September 1943 by a Soviet mine, placed under his bed by a cleaning woman who had been forced to cooperate with activists. The Soviet press reported the killing within two days and did not shy from adding that the Nazis were killing countless innocent people by way of revenge.[18] No other action by the Soviet underground during the war was this spectacular, which probably explained the publicity.

Reports on the partisans emphasized above all that their deeds were selflessly heroic, a heroism that came naturally thanks to their hatred of the invaders, their local and Soviet patriotism, and their loyalty to Stalin. They were willing without a moment's hesitation to give up their own lives and that of relatives and other loved ones, including children.[19] The Kalinin oblast partisans were typical in promising Stalin, "Each of us is prepared to carry out any of Your military orders," and in being inspired by an eighty-six-year-old farmer near Pskov who, as reported in early 1942, guided 250 German soldiers into a Red Army ambush in which he died along with them. (This kind of action later was called *Susaninite*, after an early seventeenth-century peasant who supposedly did the same to Polish invaders.)[20]

A young woman who, like many others, was dispatched across the front to burn front-line villages and did not survive became the biggest of all Soviet war heroes.[21] On January 27, 1942, *Pravda* carried an article by the correspondent Petr Lidov, "Tania," with a story set in the recently recaptured village of Petrishchevo in the Moscow oblast. Here, early in December 1941, an eighteen-year-old Komsomol member from Moscow who called herself Tatiana cut German field communication lines and burned down stables and seventeen horses in use by the local German military. That evening she was arrested. What happened next was known, Lidov wrote, thanks to unnamed locals and the owner of the house that served as a German prison. Despite vicious beatings, the young woman remained silent except in response to mockery of Stalin. "Stalin is at his post," she retorted. Before her hanging, as the "few" locals who had obeyed the order to attend remembered, she told the Germans to surrender: "There are 200 million of us and you can't hang us all. My vengeance will be taken for me." To the locals, she proclaimed courage and faith: "Hey, comrades! Why are you looking so sad? Be brave, continue the struggle, beat the Germans, burn them, poison them! . . . I'm not afraid to die, comrades. It's a great joy to die for your people. . . . Farewell, comrades! Keep up the struggle, don't fear! Stalin is with us! Stalin will come!" On New Year's Eve "drunken fascists" stripped the corpse and "vilely defiled" it. The woman was buried on New Year's Day. Lidov was certain that Stalin would think of her and that millions would love her. After all, Tania had "accepted the death of a martyr like a heroine, like the daughter of great people who cannot ever be broken by anyone! Her memory shall live forever! . . . And her undying glory will reach all corners of the Soviet land, and millions of people will think about a distant snowy grave with love, and Stalin's thoughts will go to his faithful daughter's gravestone."[22]

Another war correspondent investigated the case at the same time and wrote about it in *Komsomolskaia pravda*.[23] But Lidov's article took the limelight because of its location in *Pravda*, its style, and a stunning photograph of the corpse, said to have been taken by a Soviet photo correspondent. (There was no explanation of the apparent contradiction with a burial.) In marked contrast to standard Soviet depictions of women as warriors or mothers, the photograph revealed a bare breast and a face as serene as a Christian saint's. The photograph inspired a colorful poster, "Kill the Fascist Fanatic!," showing a gleeful SS man wearing a monocle.[24]

On February 17, 1942, a decree was published and broadcast about the woman heretofore known as Tania. Now identified as Zoia Kosmodemianskaia, she became the first woman Hero of the Soviet Union. The text was on *Pravda*'s front page, along with a large portrait and a long caption. Her mother spoke on the radio. Published by *Pravda* on the next day (accompanied by another article by Lidov), the woman's statement expressed a proud grief and called for revenge. Lidov's articles were reprinted as a brochure, of which more than 1.5 million copies were printed in a few months. Until the end of the war at least twenty different publications were to appear about the female partisan.[25]

In February 1942 locals recalled to a commission of the Moscow Komsomol the words of the hanged partisan, which resembled the published ones: "Stalin is at his post" and "There are 170 million of us." But they also made clear that because Kosmodemianskaia had set homes on fire, some of the villagers had been very angry with her. One owner of a burned house apparently had hit her even as the young woman was being hanged. The Soviet authorities sentenced her and another local woman to death. None of this was publicized.[26]

The Zoia myth was of a Communist hero who, probably inspired by the striking photograph, unintentionally was given the traits of a Christian saint. From early childhood she had been faithful, selfless, diligent, loving, and loyal to authority—her mother, the Communist Party, and the country—and she seemed to have sensed her fate, telling her mother that she would become a hero, come what may.[27] In the fall of 1943 a full page in *Pravda* was devoted to five photographs of her walking to and hanging on the gallows, said to have been found on a dead German officer. A commemoration took place at her new grave in Moscow; the papers said that among the speakers was her partisan instructor, whose real name was provided. She was remembered in a long poem by Margarita Aliger and in a song, "Tania," which Pioneers sang to wounded soldiers. In August 1944 the media reported the capture of two Germans who had participated in her hanging. The next month a feature film about her with music by Dmitrii Shostakovich premiered. In a practice familiar from earlier films about Lenin, its final image—to the words "Stalin will come!"—was of a smiling Zoia high in the sky, dead yet alive.[28]

Girls and women also figured prominently in other reports and stories about partisans. In this way those came to resemble the entire occupied population, people whom the propaganda often feminized as realistic or allegorical women awaiting liberation.[29] In Wasilewska's *The Rainbow* the Ukrainian partisan Olena Kostiuk returns to her native village to give birth. Arrested, she confesses to blowing up a bridge but betrays no one. Her German captors roar with laughter as they make her run naked and stab her with bayonets. Soon after she gives birth, without any help, her interrogators threaten the life of the newborn. But Olena says that in the forest she has many more "sons." The Germans shoot the baby in the face and use a bayonet to toss him into an ice hole in a frozen river. Olena is stabbed to death and also vanishes into the water. These became the most memorable scenes of the movie version of late 1943.[30] Such fictional and supposedly real women acting heroically on territory marked by the failure of the regular and male-dominated Red Army and implicitly—though unintentionally—calling the adequacy of males into question also appeared in *She Defends the Motherland* (May 1943) and other films.[31]

The biggest story about resistance in the underground was set in eastern Ukraine's Donets Basin. German, Italian, and Romanian military controlled the town of Krasnodon there after July 1942.

After several months young teenagers who believed in Soviet Communism founded an underground group called the Young Guard. Eventually including perhaps over a hundred members (the actual number of members, dead, and survivors will likely always remain in doubt), the group distributed leaflets, hoisted red flags on buildings on October Revolution Day, and burned down the labor office. In January and early February 1943 the German authorities tortured and executed more than seventy members and threw many into a mine shaft. After the Red Army returned in the middle of February, the NKVD concluded without any apparent foundation that the Young Guard perished because of treason. The agency blamed some thirty outsiders and one of its leaders, Viktor Tretiakevich, who had died from a German bullet.[32]

Ukrainian newspapers produced the first report related to the group. Without mentioning the Young Guard or indeed any young people, *Radianska Ukraïna* stated on June 16, 1943, that thirty-two people who had been arrested by the Germans in Krasnodon turned out to have been buried alive in a mine. Some weeks later *Sovetskaia Ukraina* said that fifty-five members of what it called the Young Guard had been thrown alive into a mine shaft. Late in July the Komsomol completed a report with the goal of getting the activists posthumously awarded. Khrushchev signed it without reading it and forwarded it to Stalin early in September, who at once told Kalinin to work on it. Published in the central and republican media on September 15, Kalinin's decrees claimed that there had been just five leaders, all of whom were now promoted to Heroes of the Soviet Union. Forty-five others and the mother of one activist received Orders. Meanwhile uninterested officials, and therefore also the media, fully ignored two other dead leaders (apart from Tretiakevich) and the dozens of survivors who had left the city, often as new Red Army members.[33]

The very first issue of Soviet Ukraine's revived Komsomol periodical was entirely devoted to the group. A *Pravda* editorial called them "the Stalinist Tribe" and quoted their vow to "mercilessly avenge the burned, razed cities and villages, the blood of our people.... And if my life is needed for that revenge, I shall give it up without a minute's hesitation." Just before she died, the newspaper claimed, one of the women leaders shouted, "We shall die for the motherland. Kill the German vermin!" Aleksandr Fadeev spoke to the few survivors still in Krasnodon and read the flawed Komsomol report. He wrote in *Pravda* that older people had been unable to organize resistance to the Germans, for those designated to do so had been exposed and killed or forced to hide. Some Young Guardists had created "diversions and terrorist acts," such as the hanging of policemen. The Young Guard, he wrote, had also included in its vow the following: "If I break this holy pledge under torture or from cowardice, let my name and my relatives be cursed forever, and let me be punished by the severe hand of my comrades." On the one hand, the activists were of a special kind, with "a temperament of such spiritual beauty that it will inspire many generations of young people to come." On the other hand, their morals and behavior merely expressed "the best features of a people tempered in the Leninist-Stalinist forge." The dead were "immortal, because their spiritual character is that of the new Soviet man, of the people of the land of socialism." Fadeev began publishing in *Komsomolskaia pravda* and in magazines parts of what in 1945 became a canonical novel.[34]

Labor and Other Treason

When the war with Germany broke out, the Soviet media immediately warned against enemy agents: "The insidious and cunning enemy is spreading false rumors and strives to disorganize our interior. Workers of the interior! Do not give in to provocations! Be on the alert! More orderliness and Bolshevik vigilance! Destroy the spies, saboteurs, and enemy parachutists!"[35] According to a high-ranking emigré, thousands of civilians were executed in the first six months in Moscow alone, but this is not confirmed by available data. It is known, however, that on October 15, 1941, Stalin ordered the relatives of executed "enemies of the people" remaining in Moscow moved to Kuibyshev for execution. The next month the NKVD had almost 10,500 people on death row, almost all of whom it shot. (Formally, confirmation by higher judicial organs was required, but Stalin agreed with Lavrentii Beria's request to ignore this.) In 1942 the NKVD's so-called Special Committee reviewed 77,500 such cases; by 1944, 27,400. Meanwhile censors barred details about such arrests and executions.[36]

Early in 1944 Shcherbakov told a Bureau meeting that an article by the Jewish Anti-Fascist Committee about a Belarusian who murdered Jews was inappropriate for foreign propaganda. "Why should we present to the outside world that we have traitors, that they kill Jews, Russians, and Ukrainians? We should not present such an article to the outside world. For our point has been that it is the Finns and Germans who are the beasts." But such articles were "entirely appropriate" for publication inside the Soviet Union, he added. By then Soviet propaganda and literature had an impressive track record in referring to treacherous individuals—"traitors of the motherland" and enemy "accomplices" and "underlings."[37] In line with Stalin's paranoia, this norm never surprised anyone.

Ilia Ehrenburg was among those who mentioned traitors, writing in January 1942 that there were only "several thousand" of them, who would get the death penalty. The citizens involved—mayors, village elders, prison wardens, and informers—were Judases on whom "no court will be too severe." The next year he identified specific cases: the deputy mayor of German-ruled Kursk, an abusive village elder in the Kursk oblast, a peasant woman who housed a German, "Russian traitors" in Kiev, and "Ukrainian traitors headed by some kind of 'hetman'" in the Orlov oblast. He even reproduced his conversation with a Russian who had killed civilians. But of such people there were only a "handful," and besides, "every family has a depraved member."[38]

Perhaps to remove the stain of failure and imprisonment from dead heroes, almost all tales about them paired them with treacherous individuals. A man who had accompanied Zoia Kosmodemianskaia returned to partisan headquarters in February 1942, possibly with actual German spy training. The propaganda mentioned him by his real name as the one who had betrayed Zoia. (He had confessed, but he was innocent.) *Pravda*'s editorial about the Young Guard said the group had been betrayed. Fadeev first blamed "less steadfast" members of the large group, but his novel blamed one villain, "Stakhovich," easily recognizable as Tretiakevich, the eighth group leader, who had been innocently blamed by the NKVD.[39] Even if Stalin's inner circle received evidence that individuals had been publicly shamed as traitors without reason, it refrained from correcting the story—the "organs" officially never made mistakes. Thus when once Shcherbakov heard that *Komsomolskaia pravda* had been wrong about a case of betrayal by named people in the town of Shakhty, the political police told him that this new information was classified.[40]

Traitors came in various categories: war prisoners, women befriending Germans, passive members of the party or Komsomol, village elders and agronomists, and auxiliary policemen. As noted in an earlier chapter, propaganda did refer to the cruelty and murder that befell Soviet war prisoners. But German imprisonment officially concerned small numbers, so censors removed realistic estimates from descriptions of German POW camps.[41] In August 1941, in a statement read to the troops, Stalin threatened the families of Soviet war prisoners with reprisals, including arrest in the case of commanders and political workers. Thus Red Army soldiers fought not simply for their country, but also to ward off such vengefulness (which perhaps was not often implemented). But Stalin, who did not apply the rule to himself when his son Iakov was captured, did not allow the media to mention the threat.[42]

In late 1941 it was still possible for *Pravda* to quote a former POW by name who had escaped from Kiev. Beginning in the middle of 1942, however, former war prisoners, and even soldiers who had narrowly escaped from German encirclement, were treated with suspicion and cut from the headlines. *Pravda* wrote, "During the civil war, Lenin used to say, 'He who does not help the Red Army wholeheartedly and does not observe its order and iron discipline is a traitor.' "[43] According to the propaganda, the only honorable way for former war prisoners to erase their shame was to join the partisans, who would be very cautious. The escaped prisoner in Mikhail Sholokhov's story

"The Science of Hatred" says, "At first they treated me with a certain amount of mistrust, although I produced my party card from my coat, where I had managed to hide it in the camp." According to Wasilewska's *The Rainbow*, all war prisoners are doomed to die in disgrace. A woman says of her enlisted son, "Let him put a bullet in his brain, blow himself up with a grenade, only not this, not this!" She admonishes her youngest son, five years old, "If you should ever have to choose between dying and being taken by the Germans—choose death."[44]

Stepan in Gorbatov's *The Unsubdued* helps some—not all—escaped POWs to reach the partisans. His brother Andrei gets out of a German death camp because a woman claims him as a relative, but back home no one sympathizes with his experience. His wife denies for a while that Andrei is her husband and her hair turns gray. A furious Taras never tires of saying he should not have been saved—this son betrayed "Russia." The narrator agrees: "his life now had neither meaning, nor justification, nor even a purpose." Suddenly deeply ashamed of his former lack of faith and fear of dying because "slavery is worse than death," Andrei understands that he must "pay back his guilt toward his father and the army." He also is consumed by an insatiable hatred of the Germans even stronger than his newfound faith. Killing many Germans as he crosses the front, he rejoins the Red Army, where the Special Section interrogates him for a long time and severely but "not as severely as he had so often interrogated himself." This particular POW has redeemed himself; he drops off a bravery medal at home.[45]

Particularly despised in works of fiction were women who had affairs with Germans and Communists who behaved passively. Probably spies, they were definitely traitors. *The Rainbow*'s most loathsome character is a Red Army officer's wife who, already before the war, was shunned by her sister because she refused to do the laundry, scrub floors, drive a tractor, or bear children. Even the married German who moved in with her is repelled by her laziness, capriciousness, and whining. Children run away at the sight of this "black rat" whose "insipid smile" does not even vanish at the sight of suffering war prisoners. The only thing barring another woman from "taking this little dark creature resembling a rat in a corner by the throat and throttling and then crushing her underfoot" is the "repugnance beyond belief at the thought of touching that frail and feeble body, the repugnance of a healthy, normal being toward something perverted and diseased." The people will not forgive her, she is told: "You will be sorry a hundred times over that it was not you [the Germans] hanged on the gallows, not you they stabbed with bayonets, not you they shot dead!" When Red Army men arrive, one of them recognizes her as his wife. He trembles but shoots her.[46] Gorbatov's novel features a similar woman, Liza Lukich, who symbolically renounces Soviet citizenship by calling herself Luiza. This woman, who accepts a grisly German gift (a bloodstained coat), looks eccentric: "Everything about her was not Russian, not German, but ape-like." Taras knows that *nashi*, "our people," won't forgive women like her.[47]

Moscow knew that many party and Komsomol members destroyed their membership card at the approach of the Germans. It considered this an unforgivable transgression. Registration with the German authorities was even worse. Betrayal by members of the Communist Party did not appear explicitly in public reports, however, and the verification of the conduct of party members (in southern Russian regions in early 1943, in Ukrainian regions beginning in November 1943) remained top secret. But fiction could be outspoken. Gorbatov's Stepan, for instance, rebukes a fellow party member who wishes to save his life by burying his party card and reporting himself to the Gestapo, and he writes in his testament that others should also condemn this man.[48]

In line with a November 1942 directive by the leader of the Central Staff of the Partisan Movement, Soviet propaganda in the German zone promised defectors a chance to "atone for their sins." In March 1943 *Radianska Ukraïna*, a newspaper primarily for occupied Ukraine, published a call by Soviet Ukraine's rulers that "the Hitlerites are lying that Soviet power will punish all those who one way or another were forced to work for the Germans." The Red Army and Soviet authorities actually "know under what threats the German oppressors forced you into unfree labor"; for example, famine had forced the "intelligentsia" to work in German offices. Later that year these republican authorities repeated their denial of future punishment of "those who were forced to work under the Germans." This central policy was eventually implemented and it met with success.[49]

In contrast, the propaganda for the hinterland generally kept insisting that working in one's own country for German pay—working at all under German rule—was tantamount to treason. Gorbatov's novel put it bluntly: "Now labor was treason. Now to go hungry meant not to submit." Unrealistically Taras and others are drafted for forced labor from their homes every morning. One day they must repair tanks, a problem that vanishes after their German supervisor believes their false claim to be unqualified for the job. Those who do work should always expect the worst. That is why a metalworker whom Stepan orders to sabotage steamboats says that he will be killed by the foremen, who don't know his work is a cover. How unemployed workers were to avoid starving to death remained unclear. In another marked contrast, reports about citizens who had been taken to Germany and put to work there did not denounce them, and censors barred references to cases of voluntary migration to work in Germany.[50]

Hinterland propaganda initially was full of venom against village elders (mayors), farm accountants, and similar native officials under foreign rule. In line with Stalin's public demand of July 1941 for the destruction of all the enemy's "accomplices" (*posobniki*), *Pravda* reported that partisans were exterminating elders and the like, "dirty renegades and petty kulak carrion that [had] forever broken with the feelings, honor, and traditions of its own great [Russian] people." A public call to the Ukrainians denounced the elders as "White-Guardist-Petliurite scoundrels, kulaks, thieves, and bandits" deserving of extermination. A story in *Trud* described a former "kulak" who, serving as a village elder, turned in partisans and enabled the Germans to shoot the family members of Red Army men. At dawn there was a knock on his door, and soon "neighbors ran over because of his wife's shrieking. The fascist agent was lying dead on the floor of his home. And next to him they found a note: 'There's no place for traitors in the Ukrainian land.' 'That was Hanna,' the Ukrainians told each other," referring to an evidently fictional partisan.[51]

In *The Rainbow* ordinary villagers are licensed for such killings. The Germans arrest a Ukrainian partisan woman who came to the village to give birth, hang a boy who wants to become a partisan, take five hostages, and starve hungry children to death. The elder is responsible. Four women and a man take him blindfolded to a "court of law" that unceremoniously finds him to be a "kulak" and former soldier under Symon Petliura. He had escaped from prewar Soviet imprisonment. The "freak," "stooge," "son of a bitch," "muck," and—above all—"snake" and "reptile" meekly confesses to his lifelong opposition to "Soviet rule." Revolted by his begging for mercy, the villagers hang him and dump his corpse into a dry well.[52] Gorbatov's novel was mild in comparison. Stepan visits a village elder who asks if he recognizes him. Did I "dekulakize" him, Stepan wonders. The answer is no, but before the war the man had refused to join the collective farm. Without explaining why, the elder now no longer wants private land and supports "Soviet rule." Ashamed of his job, which his fellow villagers forced upon him, he is fighting the Germans by hiding things. How can I help the partisans, he now asks. Stepan apologizes for having thought badly of him. But that suspicion was the right thing. Even the convert says, "All elders are animals and exploiters, kulaks."[53]

Early on the Kremlin knew that Nazi mass murder involved participation by local non-Jewish policemen. For instance, the NKVD reported in August 1941 that the "Ukrainian police participated in the shootings" of Jews near Berdychiv. Hinterland propaganda acknowledged the presence of those working as auxiliary policemen, whom it usually called *politseiskie,* even though they were generally called *politsai*. And it was clear that they all deserved the death penalty. Reports of actual policemen were at best superficial; even the media reports in July 1943 about the tribunal in Krasnodar of eleven non-German defendants focused on their German overlords. Again fiction gave a strong hint of what had really happened. When Gorbatov's Stepan orders a man to join the police as an informant, both know that he risks being killed as a traitor.[54]

Again there was a contrast with the propaganda meant for the occupied territories. But not consistently: some partisan leaflets included in their threats the relatives of policemen, but often those policemen were offered promises. One leaflet told Russian police that if they turned against the Germans, the Motherland would forgive them. Radio Soviet Ukraine said that policemen who killed the Germans and joined the partisans could avoid being lynched or forced into shameful flight. They could "return to the honest Soviet people," and if they earned their respect, the Red Army—the NKVD was not mentioned—would not punish them. The Third Ukrainian Meeting of May 1943 made it known that 120 auxiliary policemen had gone over to the Soviet partisans, and the government and party of Soviet Ukraine called on not just elders but also policemen and "Cossack" soldiers to change sides.[55]

At an early stage *Izvestiia* reported the death sentence by a tribunal of a village agronomist who voluntarily helped the Germans. But in general the Soviet treatment of those real-life individuals after capture was reported only modestly. The execution of Vasilii Klubkov, Kosmodemianskaia's alleged nemesis, was not reported. When, on April 19, 1943, the Politburo demanded the hanging not only of "German fascist criminals" who had killed or tortured Soviet citizens and POWs but also "spies," "accomplices," and "traitors of the Motherland" with Soviet citizenship, the relevant Supreme Soviet decree was kept secret. Late in 1943 the Supreme Court warned military courts, in an apparent effort to curb the excessive mistrust, that they should convict workers and low-level employees only for crimes committed—an order that was kept secret as well. Censors barred a picture of the hanging of a "traitor" by partisans and a letter about the investigation of a village woman near Voronezh for treasonous conduct and the need for her to be put on a "show trial." Likewise there was near-total silence about the often-applied law against Soviet citizens everywhere who failed to report "treason" or "counterrevolutionary activity."[56]

This hesitancy in referring to the verdicts suggests Stalin's discomfort with the scope of the disloyalty; perhaps he had expected less of it. Betrayal of the Motherland had to be framed as minor. Only late in the war did a public hint at a serious problem appear, when *Pravda* wrote that the German invaders "tried by every method to poison the consciousness of Soviet men and women and to confuse them," promoting "anti-collective farm and anti-state tendencies." It was urgently necessary to "implant in the population a socialist attitude toward labor and public property." This was in October 1944, after secret party resolutions about the matter with regard to Belarus and western Ukraine had been issued on August 9 and September 27.[57] The unusual public reference to the huge task ahead probably meant to underline its importance to the party's rank and file.

In and around Stalin's inner circle suspicion of the citizens who lived under occupation ran high, but up until the fall of 1944 the central media gave little or no clue of this. If the propaganda was to be believed, few strayed from the Soviet cause in thoughts or actions; officially the vast majority loyally supported all kinds of resistance to the Germans, and few citizens had not evacuated east. A minority of this minority were traitors, vividly described and vilified, just as they were in the propaganda released by other combatants in World War II. But most of the tribunals were not publicized, and Moscow's unthinking suspicion of the occupation survivors did not spill over into the newspapers and the radio. Nor did those media refer to the prewar and wartime rules about the need to deport the family members of traitors.[58] Soviet public culture did declare all civilians' duty to sacrifice their lives for others, and this was unlike anywhere else in Europe at the time.[59] It seems unlikely that the severe code was accepted by many.

It is not possible to state conclusively how ordinary citizens in the Soviet hinterland responded to the propaganda about compatriots who had temporarily slipped from under Stalin's control. Women befriending Germans were probably widely condemned; this was the pattern throughout Europe, independent of propaganda.

The stories about resistance fighters probably attracted people, even if they might doubt the details. Hard evidence is elusive here: few letters by nonmilitary people about Kosmodemianskaia survive in Lidov's personal papers, and if, as the *Pravda* journalist told his colleagues, her mother received hundreds of letters within months, then the question (as with all Soviet citizens' letters) remains: Who took the initiative and who wrote them? But it may well be that most ordinary people admired, even loved this young woman, even when suspecting that they were not getting the full story. They kept loving her for decades after the war.[60]

10

Allies Who Must Join the Action

Before and during the pact with Nazi Germany, caricatures showed Uncle Sam and John Bull sitting on money bags. The United States was not only criticized for unemployment and racism but also praised for its efficiency and advanced technology.[1] But the United Kingdom and France were denounced as warmongers. On the occasion of the additional Boundary and Friendship Pact of September 28, 1939, Germany and the Soviet Union jointly declared, "The end of the war between Germany on the one hand and Britain and France on the other would be for the good of all nations. Yet if despite this fact the efforts of the two governments fail, it will be proof that the responsibility for the continuation of the war must rest with Britain and France." Addressing the Supreme Soviet on October 31, Molotov called the British government "criminal" in striving for "nothing less than the defeat of Hitlerism. In other words, this is an ideological war, a sort of holy war like those waged during the Middle Ages." One could "sympathize with Hitlerism or be disgusted by it," but every intelligent person had to "realize that an ideology cannot be eliminated by war. A war 'for the destruction of Hitlerism,' under the false slogan of a struggle for democracy, is therefore nonsense and even criminal."[2] When the League of Nations expelled the Soviet Union because of its invasion of Finland in the winter of 1939–1940, Soviet citizens were told that the body had degenerated into an "instrument of the Anglo-French bloc to support and incite war in Europe."[3]

The other major enemies before 1941 were the Polish state and its Polish inhabitants. This antagonism even led to the revival of Mikhail Glinka's nineteenth-century opera *A Life of the Tsar*, a glorification of partisan struggle against Polish invaders, under the new title *Ivan Susasin*.[4] In September and October 1939 the press quoted without comment speeches by Hitler that blamed the Poles for the war. Moscow itself said that a Polish state built on "the bones of Germans and Russians" had no right to exist, and Molotov described Poland in terms identical to Hitler's traditional refrain, as a "monster" spawned by the Treaty of Versailles.[5] Newspaper articles and poems appeared with titles such as "Holy Hatred," written by, among others, Aleksandr Tvardovskii. These called Poland a site where a few Polish "nobles" had oppressed the non-Polish "us" or "the people." Verbal propaganda in the annexed regions even denied the existence of a Poland. Feature films in 1938 and 1939 implicitly rejected the Comintern's notion that there were not just bad (*pan*, or "lord") Poles but also good ("Jan") ones—*all* the Poles there represented danger and treason.[6]

After as before the German invasion, information about the outside world was meager. Even in 1943 TASS supplied editors often with just eight or nine foreign stories per day, and at most 20 percent of radio news bulletins concerned foreign affairs.[7] The degree to which Soviet citizens were interested is hard to establish. John Lawrence, the press attaché at the British embassy, found that most citizens did want to know what was happening in the rest of the world: "The average reader, after reading the Sovinformbureau communiqué and glancing at the headlines, turned first to the foreign news on the back page. This he read all through, looking for meaning between the lines and noting the position of each item on the page. Next he would turn to the front page for more war news or home front news, after which he would look at the two middle pages, which gave more background to the news on the front page."⁸ There was always a line for *Britanskii Soiuznik*, the periodical by the embassy with a print run of 25,000, later doubled; it sold for one ruble at kiosks and when resold at markets fetched up to sixty.⁹ After the Allied invasion of Normandy, an American correspondent noticed, militiamen were needed to control the crush at newsstands.¹⁰

To this must be added that public disinterest said little about citizens' actual state of mind. Many made an effort to shun international affairs in public, rightly considering any interest risky.¹¹ In Kazakhstan in 1943 a man told his physician from Lviv that people did not even wish to be seen reading the back pages of papers and thus betraying interest in foreign affairs. Now this Galician Ukrainian medic understood why two years earlier no one had said a word after a loudspeaker at a train station gave the news of the Japanese attack at Pearl Harbor.¹² In general it is a sensible working assumption that Soviet citizens followed whatever was reported eagerly but discretely.

Polish Friends and Enemies

On August 13, 1941, the media in one sentence announced an "amnesty" for those "Polish citizens in prisons in the territory of the USSR" being held as war prisoners or on "other sufficient grounds." Whereas in 1940 the Ukrainian poet Maksym Rylsky had praised the removal of the "lords," now *Izvestiia* carried a poem of his admiring Polish culture. Censors removed references to the anti-Polishness of Nikolai Gogol's story "Taras Bulba." But the media also warned against Polish claims to the pre-1939 state border.¹³

Persons claiming to speak for the Poles appeared in a "radio meeting" of "representatives" of the Polish people in Saratov. On December 4, 1941, at 6:30 P.M., the radio broadcast a speech in Polish, published in Russian in next day's newspapers, by General Władysław Sikorski, identified as "the chairman of the Council of Ministers of the Polish Republic." He was quoted as calling the Soviet people heroes in the ongoing war "between democracy and totalitarianism," and accurately noting that Poland had been the first to fight Germany—concepts that never before or since appeared in the Soviet media.[14]

Meanwhile the propaganda ignored Soviet claims and actions with regard to Polish citizenship. In December 1941 the Kremlin renounced the stance it had taken toward prewar Polish citizens since the Polish-Soviet military agreement of mid-August and returned to its view that those of Belarusian, Ukrainian, and Jewish descent had become Soviet citizens in late 1939. In mid-January 1943 Stalin was to strengthen his claim to former eastern Poland by arguing that even ethnic Poles from there were, since 1939, Soviet citizens. Even they had to exchange their Polish documents for Soviet ones. Refusal to do so resulted in denial of bread cards, dismissal from work, eviction from apartments, imprisonment, and placement of one's children in children's homes.[15] The media were silent.

The military agreement enabled Władysław Anders, a recently released prisoner, to create and lead a Polish army in the USSR, which Moscow allowed only non-Communist ethnic Poles to join. Though closely watched by the NKVD, it was formally independent.[16] Central and regional newspapers reported the formation, and *Pravda* carried an interview with its commander. After a while General Anders concluded that it was best to leave the USSR, in view of its sparse food supply. To his amazement, Stalin (who had plans with Polish Communists) granted his wish, and from April to June 1942 the army evacuated to British-controlled Iran, followed in the months thereafter by other Poles. Anders's force eventually joined the British 8th Army in Italy. These developments did not appear in the Soviet media either.[17]

Anxious to preserve good relations with the Soviet Union, the Polish government-in-exile said nothing in public about the thousands of Polish officers who had been missing after being imprisoned by the Soviet occupier. This stance became untenable after April 13, 1943, when Germany announced that it had found many of them in mass graves near Katyn. On April 15 and 16 Soviet radio and newspapers carried a statement blaming the Germans. The Poles announced that they would ask the Red Cross to investigate. They withdrew this plan on May 1, but it was too late: on April 27 Molotov reported the breaking off of diplomatic relations. Soviet censorship barred all further statements by the Polish ambassador to the USSR.[18]

In May 1943 the Soviet government curtly announced in the media that it would create a military formation open to Polish volunteers. The next month the Union of Polish Patriots in the USSR was declared to exist. Chaired by Wanda Wasilewska, it was reportedly open to all "regardless of political, social, and religious views." The report came months after the first issue of the union's Polish-language weekly, *Wolna Polska* (Free Poland), edited by Wasilewska and nine Poles of Jewish descent. Its print run was now increased.[19] Soon the Soviet media carried an address to Stalin (in Polish and in translation) by the new formation's Polish commander, Lieutenant Zygmunt Berling. It was a Polish vow of loyalty and eternal gratitude to Moscow:

> In the name of the Tadeusz Kościuszko Polish Division and of ourselves, I ask you, Citizen Marshall, to accept warm gratitude for the greeting sent. We are deeply convinced that our hopes for the resurrection of a strong and independent Poland will materialize only with the aid of the Soviet Union. We vow to fulfill honestly and carefully our duty in the defeat of the common enemy. A fierce desire for Soviet-Polish friendship has sunk deep in our hearts. We vow to You, Citizen Marshall, that we shall give all our strength to strengthen this friendship and will never forget our duty of gratefulness for the aid given to us by the Soviet Union in the resurrection of a strong and independent Poland.

The unit's oath, publicized one month later, was not to any constitution, but to "the Polish land" and "the Polish people," as well as "faithfulness to the Soviet Union." Formally if not explicitly separate from the Red Army, the Kościuszko Division began fighting in October, and by the middle of 1944, when it joined up with other armed Poles in the homeland, it had some 90,000 members, including Russians and Ukrainians.[20]

In the first half of 1944 Moscow both proclaimed its friendship with Poland and published numerous reports that were highly critical of Polish opponents. A reported call to Poles on the occasion of a "festive session devoted to the 150th anniversary of the Polish uprising for national liberation led by Tadeusz Kościuszko" naturally ignored his opposition to the Russian Empire. The future "democratic" Poland would again possess its "eternal lands that once were forcibly taken from her by the Prussians." But Poles loyal to the London government claiming former eastern Poland were "accomplices of German fascism who, in the interests of borderland magnates, attempt to inflame a fratricidal fight between the Poles and the Belarusians, Ukrainians, and Russians."[21] In April Stalin assumed that a visitor from Massachusetts, Father Stanislaus Orlemanski, represented Polish Americans. He printed pictures of their meeting on front pages and allowed Orlemanski to call him, on Soviet radio, a friend of the Poles and the Roman Catholic Church.[22] Back in the United States, the priest was reprimanded by his bishop; in the Soviet Union the mistake was forgotten.

Meanwhile, usually with reference to foreign sources such as the *New York Times*, the media reported allegedly widespread mistreatment of non-Poles and pro-Soviet Poles within Anders's troops in Iran. They were being "tortured." Worse, the entire Polish expatriate community there was "governed by totalitarian principles," and a member of the U.S. Congress had "exposed the anti-Semitism in the Polish army." Poles based in Scotland were also vilified: Ukrainian, Belarusian, and Jewish allies were deserting from them because of the Poles' "mockeries" and anti-Semitism. A rally in London had condemned this "racial persecution."[23]

In May 1944 the Union of Polish Patriots reported that there existed in Poland an underground National Council whose leader had met with Stalin. The next month the media carried the thanks by council representatives just about to leave "the land of the Ukrainian republic." They had received extraordinary hospitality and friendship from Khrushchev, the Ukrainian Soviet government, and the entire Ukrainian people. In July the formation of the Polish Committee of National Liberation was prominently reported.[24]

On July 29, 1944, the Union of Polish Patriots said on Soviet radio that the Red and Polish armed forces were near Warsaw and called for an uprising inside the city. The Soviet-sponsored Radio Kościuszko added that aid would be offered. In fact Moscow's soldiers were still across the Vistula River, as a map published on August 3 showed, but contemporaries could easily expect, probably unrealistically, that Warsaw could and would be captured within days. With that in mind, Warsaw's non-Communist underground launched an uprising. It failed in its main objective, to greet the Red Army as Polish representatives, and the brutal German response left thousands dead and a city in ruins. What precisely motivated Stalin to impose media silence about the uprising, which in a letter to Churchill he called the work of "power-grabbing criminals," is not fully clear. Its failure mattered, of course. (The failed uprising in Slovakia later that year was also ignored.)[25]

During many years of the war the Soviet media did not even rule out that ultimately all Polish territory might be incorporated into the Soviet Union. After all, "independence" as a concept was also used with regard to Ukraine and other republics, all of which would surely remain in one state under Moscow. Asked in May 1943 by American correspondents whether the Soviet government wanted a "strong and independent" Poland, Stalin replied affirmatively, but added that it was up to "the Polish people" to decide if the relationship with the Soviet Union might become similar to the anti-German alliance, thus allowing the option of a Polish "request" to be unified with the USSR. Clarity came only in the fall of 1944, with reports of the population exchange of "Polish citizens" from the Lithuanian Soviet Republic and the "Lithuanian population" from "the territory of Poland."[26]

The "Second Front"

When, on November 6, 1941, Stalin asked out loud what explained the Red Army's "temporary setbacks," he himself gave two reasons: numerical inferiority in tanks and planes and the isolation of the

Soviet Union in the "war of liberation," given the "absence in Europe of a second front against the German-fascist troops." To loud applause, he demanded that such a front appear in the "near future." (He seemingly felt this need from the very beginning: on August 30, 1941, he warned the Soviet ambassador in London that if this front did not materialize in the next four weeks, "we and our allies can lose this business.")[27] Throughout the world, with the exception of the BBC, the term "second front" became a resounding propaganda success, even though the Soviet Union had been aggressive itself (against Poland, Finland, and the Baltic countries) and had joined the anti-German war fourth in line, after Poland (1939), western Europe (1940), and southern Europe (1941).[28]

Stalin also ensured that the media remained Eurocentric, himself not mentioning the Japanese attack on the United States at Pearl Harbor until November 1944. To him and thus everyone else "the war" meant fighting in Eurasia west of the Ural Mountains. Whatever other countries might be doing in Asia, it was not a "front." *Pravda* often made this explicit. One year after the Soviet Union joined the United Kingdom in the war against Germany, Aleksei Tolstoi claimed that "for twelve months, the Red Army has been bearing the total weight of the world war, while allowing England and the USA to arm themselves."[29]

On May 26 and June 11, 1942, respectively, came military agreements with the United Kingdom and the United States. The agreements and their ratification by the Supreme Soviet on June 18 were reported unemotionally; there was only an article by Ehrenburg on British steadfastness. On June 11 a communiqué added that "full understanding" had been reached "with regard to the urgent tasks of creating a second front in Europe in 1942." This set off a new flood of propaganda on the need for that year to become the war's final year. From the British and American perspective, agreeing to this text was a mistake.[30]

Stalin publicly emphasized for a long time how important the second front was. The various statements that followed showed a constant interplay between anger and optimism. Informed in confidence by Churchill in August 1942 that no landing in western

Europe would take place that year, he ordered the media to return to an anti-British tone and to quote optimistic words about the second front by President Roosevelt's representative Wendell Wilkie, who came to visit that same month. Photos of him meeting Stalin and Molotov appeared in every newspaper. On October 3 Stalin told the Associated Press that the Allied aid was "still little effective compared to the aid that the Soviet Union gives the Allies by drawing the main forces of the German fascist armies on itself." Allied aid would only "widen and improve" if the those giving it "fulfilled their obligations in a complete and timely way," by opening a second front. Three days later *Pravda* carried a cartoon with General Guts and General Decision alongside the evidently British generals What-if-they-lick-us, What's-the-hurry, and Why-take-risks.[31]

On November 6 Stalin mentioned the existence of the "progressive rapprochement" of the three states, indeed their unification into a "single military union," but an entire section of his speech was devoted to "the matter of the second front in Europe." Its "absence" explained why Germany could throw "all of its reserves" against the Soviet Union, take the initiative, and achieve "serious tactical successes." But the second front would appear "sooner or later," for the Western Allies realized that otherwise the war could "end badly for all the freedom-loving countries." A while later Stalin mentioned American and British military action outside Europe for the first time. As he told the Associated Press on November 13, in a report naturally also carried in the Soviet media, the Allied campaign in North Africa was an "outstanding fact of great importance."[32]

On Red Army Day, February 23, 1943, it became clear that victory at Stalingrad had not softened Stalin's public stance on the Allies. On the contrary, he was colder than ever. Ignoring the Allied campaign in Africa, he repeated his long-standing point that "in view of the absence of a second front in Europe the Red Army is bearing the full weight of the war." There was also no word of the Allied deliveries.[33] Later that year the Western Allies landed in southern Europe, so emotions on May Day were positive: the Allied armies had defeated the Italian and German forces "near Libya and Tripolitania" and were now fighting "near Tunisia." On May 9 Stalin publicly congratulated Churchill, Roosevelt, and the British and American troops for the victory that had resulted in the liberation of Bizerta and Tunis. Still, the Soviet Information Bureau's look back on June 22, 1943, declared that German defeat was "impossible" without a second front. Many Soviet citizens seem to have been skeptical about this statement, which may have reflected Stalin's genuine nervousness.[34]

On November 6, 1943, Stalin again sounded optimistic. The past year's Allied operations in North Africa, the Mediterranean, and southern Italy had "supported" the Red Army, and together with Allied bombings and deliveries, this had "considerably facilitated the successes of our summer campaign." "Of course," he added, those Allied operations in southern Europe did *not* constitute the second front, even though they resembled it. But that front—which would "considerably hasten" the victory over Germany—was "not far off." As the very first slogan of the day he offered, "For the Victory of the Anglo-Soviet-American Military Alliance!"[35]

The impatience felt on Red Army Day returned the next year. It was time, Stalin said in February 1944, for "the main forces of our Allies" to *"join the action."* Only that could ensure German defeat: "History shows that Germany has always won wars when she fought on one front, but that she has always lost wars when she was forced to fight on two fronts." The Allies appeared in only one of the forty-nine official slogans marking Red Army Day ("Long live the victory of the Anglo-Soviet-American military union over the enemies of humanity—the German-fascist enslavers").[36]

Eventually 1944 became the year when Stalin gave the British and the Americans the most praise. In May, while repeating that for Germany's final defeat, a combined attack from east and west was required, he did grant that Red Army successes since Stalingrad had been "significantly" facilitated by "our great Allies, the United States of America and Great Britain, who are maintaining a front in Italy against the Germans and diverting a considerable number of German troops from us, supply us with very valuable strategic raw materials and armaments, subject German military targets to systematic bombing and are thus undermining the latter's military might."[37]

Details about Allied warfare were not provided. In fact no article during the war described how the British, Americans, and others were fighting; articles on the Allies' activities were brief and appeared under tiny headlines, only sometimes accompanied by a small map, and never with pictures. A contemporary observation by the British correspondent Paul Winterton was correct: "Never in the history of joint military operations have the spectacular and decisive achievements of a country's allies been so deliberately, consistently and dishonestly hushed up as have the Anglo-American efforts by the Soviet authorities in this war." This propaganda line often led to diplomatic friction: in March 1943 the American ambassador openly complained. Seemingly in response, the press for a while mentioned Allied efforts a bit more. Thus citizens were told that the U.S. War Department had reported that the U.S. Army lost "63,958 people, including 7,528 killed, 17,128 wounded, 22,687 missing in action, and 16,615 fallen into captivity." There were also specifics for North Africa, the Pacific Ocean, Europe, and elsewhere.[38]

Aid and Bombing

General Georgii Zhukov told Konstantin Simonov after the war that the Soviet military and fuel industry was so inadequate that the Red Army could not have stopped Germany without imports from the United Kingdom and North America, known at the time as Lend-Lease. A Russian researcher of the war rare in his skepticism of Soviet figures agrees. In his calculations those quantities compared very favorably to Soviet production or even surpassed it. Lend-Lease sugar was around 42 percent of Soviet production; canned meat, 18 percent; copper, almost 83 percent; aluminum, 125 percent; gasoline, 140 percent. American armored steel amounted to around 47 percent of the average Soviet monthly production in the year 1942. Lend-Lease motor vehicles were 150 percent of Soviet production and constituted close to a third of all Red Army vehicles by May 1945. Railway transport would have ground to a halt without imported locomotives, which were 240 percent of Soviet production, or even, in the case of diesel-electric locomotives, 1,100 percent. Almost half of the railroad tracks in use was imported from the United States. Explosive materials were 53 percent of Soviet production, combat aircraft about 30 percent, and tanks and self-propelled guns almost 25 percent.[39]

In July 1941 Stalin told his radio audience that the British and Americans had promised to help "our country," which "can only call forth a feeling of gratefulness among the peoples of the Soviet Union."[40] Although he would mention this aid on other occasions, he never repeated that thanks were due and barred others from expressing them. In September 1941, interviewed by *Pravda* about the British Trade Unions' decision to found a committee to coordinate Soviet aid, the Soviet trade union leader Nikolai Shvernik simply followed Stalin's radio speech in saying that the British decision could only call forth a "feeling of sincere gratitude." Personally editing the draft text, Stalin replaced this with a "feeling of satisfaction" and belittled the aid as a "response to the most serious aid that the Soviet Union gave and is still giving to England by drawing off the main force of the Germans to the east and saving the English isles from invasion by the Hitlerite gangs and London from bombing by German planes."[41]

Well into 1942 Stalin publicly referred to a *koalitsiia* (coalition) with Great Britain and the United States—indeed a "friendship." The former country had been delivering "rare" (*defitsitnye*) goods such as aluminum, lead, tin, nickel, and rubber for some time, he said in November 1941, and "as is known, we have already begun receiving tanks and planes." As for the United States, it recently had offered a "bond" worth one billion dollars. In May 1942 he said those two allies were giving "more and more military aid." Then, for a year and a half, Stalin refrained from specifically mentioning the deliveries, probably because he was suspicious, angry, and cautious because surveillance reports that informed him that various citizens interpreted references to the aid as confirmation of Soviet weakness.[42]

The propaganda gave disproportionate attention to food deliveries, which usually were portrayed as "gifts of the workers and peasants" of the United States and the United Kingdom, sometimes even as Soviet purchases. It seems that when Stalin found out that the press was referring to the use of American fighter planes he expressed his disapproval. A British Matilda tank once appeared in *Izvestiia*, but the caption called it a burning German tank. According to one memoirist, Shcherbakov exiled the photographer to a front-line penal battalion after the British discovered the misidentification.[43]

In March 1943 the American ambassador complained at a press conference about an "ungracious" Soviet attitude toward American donations, including silence about the *private* aid received from the American Red Cross and Russian War Relief. Several days later Soviet papers published a detailed statement by U.S. Secretary of State Edward Stettinius on the Lend-Lease supplies, and in June *Pravda* marked the anniversary of the American-Soviet agreement by almost thanking the United States for its shipments: "The Soviet people not only know about them, but they highly value the support coming from the great republic beyond the ocean." As if in reward for the Normandy landing that same month, some days later *Pravda* published its first-ever list of British and North American deliveries.[44] But as before, public enthusiasm about the deliveries was neither orchestrated nor encouraged.

As for Soviet exports of raw materials to the United States, Canada, and the United Kingdom, their nature and scale were (and still are) treated as completely secret. The press only referred to them in statements such as the one by U.S. Ambassador Averell Harriman, published on *Pravda*'s front page in early October 1941, in which he and Lord Beaverbrook confirmed receipt of "large deliveries of Russian raw materials that will significantly help the arms production in our countries."[45]

When *Pravda* carried an article about the British sailors who traveled to and from Arkhangelsk, this was deemed a mistake, if only because of the reference to a "friendship" they were establishing with

Soviet colleagues. A decree awarding medals to twelve of the sailors was published, but Aleksandrov deemed it "inexpedient" to describe their exploits. British pilots received slightly more coverage.[46] But this paled in comparison to the attention lavished on "Normandy," a squadron of French pilot volunteers for service against Germany in the east. Arriving in late 1942, it first saw action as a part of the Soviet armed forces in early 1943. Ehrenburg praised them, squadron members were decorated, and by 1944 they were Heroes of the Soviet Union. Their names or portraits were not provided, but only because of censorship guidelines concerning the presence of family members in German-held territories.[47]

Late in the war the idea arose to let American planes fly sorties from bases in Italy, bomb Hungarian and Romanian targets, and then land at new U.S. bases in Soviet-recaptured Ukraine, after which they would return on another bombing mission. Between June and mid-September 1944 there were indeed such bases at Poltava, Pyriatyn, and Myrhorod. The first "Operation Frantic" mission by the 15th Air Force began on June 2, 1944, days before the Allied invasion of Normandy. But a German spotter trailed the bombers to Poltava, where the Soviet anti-aircraft guns lacked radar, and on the night of June 21 German war planes attacked the base by surprise and unhindered, destroying forty-nine U.S. planes on the ground and killing thirty-two people, including two Americans and three Soviet journalists. Both Soviet and Allied journalists had been able to report about American planes in Soviet territory before, but now Soviet and American censors naturally barred this bad news.[48]

Stalin mentioned the Allied bombing of Germany three times in 1943 and 1944, describing the targets as "military," "industrial," or both. In May 1943 he said the "valiant Anglo-American air force is striking shattering blows at the military and industrial centers of Germany and Italy," which "foreshadowed" Europe's second front. On November 6, 1943, he reported that over the previous year "the Allies subjected and continue to subject important German industrial centers to heavy bombing and thus considerably weaken the enemy's military strength." In May 1944 he said they "subject military targets in Germany to systematic bombing and thus undermine the latter's military might." Thus each time Stalin added that the Allied actions were weakening Germany.[49]

In late September 1941 Ehrenburg complained to Shcherbakov, with good reason, that the Soviet media said nothing about the (still limited) British bombing of Germany. Beginning in early 1942, when British bombing was intense and civilian casualties in Germany rose sharply (eventually reaching around half a million by May 1945), Soviet reporting became more frequent, timely, and often detailed, although as always with foreign news it was relocated to the last page of newspapers and at the end of radio reports. Headlined "Actions of the Allied Air Force" or "Actions of the Air Force of the Allies," these items often referred to Allied news agencies, the British Ministry of Aviation, and the U.S. Bureau of War Information. Thus citizens became aware that unlike the Soviet command, the British and American commands frequently stated how many of their own planes were lost.[50]

One of the first major bombings was of the harbor city of Lübeck, on March 29, 1942. The British attack killed 320 people. TASS issued a brief report that referred not to casualties but to the loss of twelve bombers. Cologne was next, on May 30, 1942; the attack left 469 people dead, and Churchill publicly called it "the herald of what Germany will receive, city by city, from now on." TASS reported that according to Reuters, more than 1,000 British planes had carried out "the largest operation ever carried out by English aviation," and that Radio London reported that in ninety minutes, 10,000 bombs were dropped on the city's "military targets," producing many large fires.[51]

In March 1943 an operation in the Ruhr region started. Ongoing for months on end, it climaxed first with the flooding of the Ruhr River on May 17, which left 1,200 dead. That this bombing produced gigantic floods that "destroyed everything along the way" was quickly revealed, if only because Stalin had just underlined the importance of bombing. German morale was seriously lowered, *Trud* wrote. A Swiss man told a British correspondent that when he crawled out of his bomb shelter in Duisburg after one bombing in May, fires were all around and all buildings had been destroyed. "Everything literally had been razed to the ground," he was quoted as saying. Unofficial figures from the House of Commons had placed the total loss of bombers departing from the United Kingdom at 699. In a Swedish newspaper a visitor to Germany had described the flooding that resulted from the dam bursts on the Main River and near Edertal as causing "many miners" to die in shafts, and "according to eyewitnesses, the entire central part of the city of Dortmund has been erased from the earth." The *New York Times*, the Soviet media stated in June, had reported from Berlin a recent "mass flight" from the Ruhr and Rhine areas. Most of these people were "forced to roam around the country." The lack of firefighters, despite the drafting of women in that role, made the damage "extraordinarily great."[52]

Operation Gomorrah against Hamburg from July 25 to 28 produced a firestorm that killed more than 8,000 people. The bombing of Germany's second-largest city was reported to be very effective; the British Ministry of Aviation said that over 77 percent of the city's buildings had been destroyed: "Enormous white spots one hundred, in some cases 150 meters wide indicate sites of total devastation where bombs weighing 1,800 and 3,600 kg. came down." The four British nighttime raids and the one American daytime raid had flattened nine square miles of the city.[53]

The killing of people in Hamburg was only implied, but with regard to Berlin, from the beginning casualties also appeared in reports, first in early 1943. A cartoon had Hitler, Göring, and Goebbels rushing into a bomb shelter, and TASS reported from New York that the Associated Press had heard from diplomats that recently 890 Berliners had died in bombings. A Swedish correspondent had referred to deaths "in many families." The Nazi capital was subjected to more than one hundred raids in late 1943 and early 1944. "At Berlin train stations and metro stations one can meet thousands of people who have become homeless," Reuters had reported, according to the Soviet media. After a first smaller attack, Berliners came out of their shelters, but then heavy bombers showed up that "dropped bombs of large explosive power and incendiary bombs." There was a body count: according to a Swedish correspondent, "25,000 people were believed to have been killed" in one night alone.

By late December about 1.5 million of Berlin's four million inhabitants were reported to be homeless.[54]

The German missile attacks on London starting in 1944 were also reported, often with praise for the bravery of those enduring them. A Conservative member of Parliament wanted the British government to warn that his country would bomb historic cities if Germany continued to employ rockets "against England's civilian population." The British minister of foreign affairs, Anthony Eden, reportedly rejected the threat, asserting that targets were chosen on the principle of "how to liquidate Germany's capability to wage war as quickly as possible." There was "no comparison" between what the United Kingdom and Germany did or could do.[55]

The most notorious Allied bombing was that of February 13 and 14, 1945, on Dresden, which created a large firestorm and killed between 35,000 and 40,000. Soviet coverage was meager, possibly because of a suspicion that the attack was also meant to intimidate Moscow. In tiny items on February 16 and 17 TASS referred to Reuters in reporting that the main targets of two raids had been Dresden and, unlike German and British reports, it said nothing about the lethal consequences.[56]

There were also articles on the Allied bombing of targets outside Germany, such as Rotterdam (its harbor), Paris (the Renault car factories), Palermo (its harbor), and the Amsterdam region (the Fokker plane factory and Schiphol Airport).[57] In all, for most of the war the Soviet media reported fairly accurately on Allied bombings.[58] (As for *Soviet* bombings, there was no consistency in the reporting.)[59]

Allied Leaders and Their Societies

The media carried what were purported to be full texts of speeches by British and American leaders and representatives. On the evening of June 22, 1941, Churchill spoke on British radio. The next day's *Pravda* placed a text based on it on page 5, including the leader's refusal to negotiate with Hitler, his vow to bomb Germany day and night, and his promise of assistance to "Russia and the Russian people," who were defending their "native soil." Omitted in the *Pravda* transcript was the notion that the civilized world had allowed Germany to build a "terrible military machine"; that the invasion was the fourth turning point in a war that began with the conquest of France; that the United Kingdom had stood alone against Germany and had warned Stalin about the invasion; and that no one had been a more consistent opponent of Communism than Churchill for the past twenty-five years, of which he would "unsay no word."[60] The next year *Pravda* cut Churchill's comment that the British supply of raw materials, tanks, and aircraft to the Soviet Union was a heavy sacrifice in view of the danger of German invasion.[61] Not all such texts were cut, but it was telling that the Soviet media censored the Allied leaders. President Roosevelt also appeared often in the Soviet press. When he ran for reelection in November 1944, it praised him—and it did so still more when he died in April 1945, calling him an "outstanding fighter for the cause of democracy and progress."[62]

Like Stalin, the media referred to the "freedom-loving" countries of the United Nations, where the broad masses were jointly fighting "fascism" and the workers felt obliged to support their government. The term "proletarians" became taboo, and in May 1943 this was emphasized by the public dissolution of the Communist International.[63] But the change in the public portrayal of former enemies was far more modest than in the United Kingdom and the United States, where the propaganda appealed to emotion, for example asserting that "the Russians" were saving "democracy." (And most British citizens were indeed pro-Russian.) In Soviet propaganda Allied flags appeared, but almost never images of the Allies themselves. Whereas an American poster showed a Russian soldier and called him "your friend," an analogous Soviet portrait of the Allies never materialized. In Stalin's public line the coalition had certain common interests—even "vital and long-lasting" ones, as he noted in November 1944—but sympathy was inappropriate. In September 1942 the Agitprop chief Aleksandrov rejected a proposal for ten days of celebration of the "friendship" between the young people of the USSR, the United Kingdom, and the United States. He gave no reason, but unease with the continued lack of the "second front" must have been on his mind. Even late in the war the detention of Americans of Japanese descent in "concentration camps" in the United States was not censored.[64]

Meanwhile verbal propaganda, harder to trace by Allied observers, for most of the war remained almost as critical of American and especially British policies as before the German invasion. Agitators on the ground expressed suspicion about the material aid and declared at meetings that the reasons for the absence of the "second front" were purely political. Criticism was also vented in the new biweekly journal *War and the Working Class*; although secretly edited by Molotov, critical foreign diplomats were told that it was not a government but a trade union publication.[65]

The British government gave little publicity to its treatment of captured German war criminals, mainly because it feared retaliation against British war prisoners. When it applied this policy to Hitler's associate Rudolf Hess, who escaped to the United Kingdom in 1942, *Pravda* demanded to know whether he was regarded as a criminal or as a "plenipotentiary of the Hitlerite government in England, with all the privileges of immunity." Alexander Werth, who noticed that the editorial "stirred up a great deal of anti-British feeling in Russia," surmised that Stalin, aware of the preparations for Allied landings in North Africa, wished to disorient Germany, or wished to provide a vent for frustration with the tense situation near Stalingrad.[66] But it is just as likely that he was simply suspicious.

From November 28 to December 1, 1943, Stalin convened with the Allied leaders in Tehran. To Soviet citizens it was sensational that he had traveled abroad. On the eve of the meetings, the media made much of the tenth anniversary of Soviet-U.S. diplomatic relations, and afterward the line was that the entire Soviet people enthusiastically approved the decisions taken. There were reports of pledges to finish the December work schedule ahead of time, to raise production quality and productivity, and to donate earned wages.[67] But one of Tehran's secret agreements was that there would not be a "second front" until late May 1944.

Then a brief item in *Pravda* on January 17, 1944, under a Cairo dateline and supposedly from the newspaper's correspondent, said that usually well-informed sources had reported that in a coastal town on the Iberian Peninsula, Britain and Germany had been engaged in negotiations for a bilateral peace. No other central Soviet paper carried the story and it was not sent abroad, but regional papers reprinted it. American correspondents noticed that even people who "never saw a newspaper or followed events" had heard about it. A while later the papers reported the vigorous denial by Anthony Eden. Stalin himself had unilaterally created the Free Germany Committee in 1943, but he perhaps planted the report from the fictitious correspondent because of his irritation with Churchill, who had resisted Soviet plans for Poland and been noncommittal about invading western Europe. He may also have wished to dampen the actual goodwill for the Allies that his own media had reported. And suspicion of the British played its usual part. Four weeks later *Pravda* carried a German war prisoner's confession that he had been captured earlier in North Africa by the British, who then exchanged him for British prisoners.[68]

The Final Year

The invasion that began on June 6, 1944, received far less attention than had its absence in earlier years. Although the operation missed the morning papers, the radio mentioned it that day, and for the first time ever the evening paper *Vechernaia Moskva* scooped the central press. That evening the heads of the U.S. and British military missions to Moscow spoke on the radio, the latter even in broken Russian. The next day's *Pravda* pictured General Dwight Eisenhower and his order referring to a "great crusade." Most remarkable was the TASS item "Prayer by Roosevelt," directed to "God Almighty." But no Soviet-produced report on the landing and invasion appeared, even though the invaders provided facilities for Soviet correspondents. There were only dry reports and, on June 11, an article in which Ehrenburg praised above all the French Resistance for facilitating the invaders. On June 14 Stalin explained, allegedly in response to a question from a *Pravda* correspondent, that neither Napoleon nor Hitler had ever crossed the Channel. He said of the invasion, "The history of war knows no other undertaking resembling its breadth of design, its grandness of scale, and its mastery of execution." But he did not use the words "second front." The film footage that the Allies rushed to Moscow was shown only to high-ranking officers and court intellectuals.[69]

Moreover the media minimized or cast in the least flattering light subsequent Allied military achievements. The capture of Rome that same month was called a victory, but Italy's surrender many months later appeared in tiny headlines and was largely ascribed to the previous summer's successes of the Red Army. At a time when the Soviet media declared that in modern wars cities (such as Warsaw) could not liberate themselves, the French capital inexplicably became an exception: its liberation on August 26 was credited to the French Resistance.[70]

The implied dogma was that Allied invasion of western Europe was easy but reluctant. Only *Komsomolskaia pravda* took a different line, with a commentary on the "force and speed of the offensive of the Allies. In July, Marshall Rokossovskii covered 640 kilometers from the Dnieper to the Vistula in thirty days. In August, General Patton covered almost 640 kilometers from Avranches to the Saar, also in thirty days. Marshall Malinovskii covered 480 kilometers, from Iași to Craiova in two weeks. General Patch covered 370 kilometers from the French Riviera to Mâcon, in less then three weeks." Aleksandrov complained that this inflated the performance of British and American armies, which did "not encounter serious military resistance," and denigrated the "decisive role of the attack of the Red Army, which is fighting against the main forces of the German army." At Andrei Zhdanov's order he verbally reprimanded the paper.[71]

Commentators pretended not to understand why the Allied armies were slowed for a while on the German-French border, where they supposedly faced only fifteen to twenty German divisions (compared to the hundreds facing the Red Army). After the Allies attacked and took one million POWs, these commentators did not admit that their figure had been wrong and only reluctantly conceded that German divisions had arrived from the east.[72] The disastrous landing at the Dutch city of Arnhem on September 17 was all but ignored, and reports on the fierce fighting near Koblenz in March 1945, at a time of comparative quiet on the war's Eastern Front, were short, inspired by Stalin's silence on Allied military action after his praise in November 1944 for the Allied liberation of France and Belgium.[73] On April 27 American and Soviet armed forces met at Torgau on the Elbe River. That event did receive significant coverage and became the topic of a May Day slogan.[74]

On May 2, 1945, the Red Army took control of Berlin. On the evening of May 4 the German armed forces in northwestern Europe agreed to surrender the next morning. It was the third hour of May 7 when Colonel General Alfred Jodl, chief of the General Staff of the German armed forces, placed his signature on two English documents at the Supreme Headquarters of the Allied Expeditionary Forces in Rheims, France, thereby agreeing to end all hostilities on May 9 at 12:01 A.M. against the United States, the United Kingdom, and the Soviet Union, which was represented by an officer. Jodl had no command authority over the entire Wehrmacht but agreed that the German Supreme Command would ratify the surrender the next day, in the presence of the Soviet Supreme Command. This measure was intended to preclude a German stab-in-the-back legend and to reassure Stalin. Western radio reported the capitulation later on May 7. On the afternoon of May 8, ignoring Stalin's request to wait until the ratification, Churchill spoke about it on British radio.

The ratification was planned for that day, but although all were present in the afternoon, hours went by before a complete Russian text arrived from Moscow and could be compared with the other texts. That was why the signing ceremony, dominated by General Keitel and General Zhukov, ended fifteen minutes past the designated local time for implementation, midnight. In the western European time zone it was still May 8, 11:15 P.M., but in Moscow (and Kiev) it was 2:15 A.M. on May 9.

Soviet citizens still knew nothing; the radio broadcast hours of opera music. Shortly after 2:00 A.M. it was announced that in several minutes "important news" would be provided. At ten past the hour Levitan declared that on May 8 Germany had signed an unconditional surrender. There followed a sound recording of the event with commentary by a Soviet journalist. Many citizens had been waiting around street loudspeakers, but not everyone found out that night, and even in Moscow, according to a British observer,

> thousands went to work that morning without knowing what had happened. They were told to go home and take a holiday. No formal parades had been arranged and at first it seemed that no one quite knew what to do. Then, suddenly, at noon, it all began. The people of Moscow took things into their own hands. Huge crowds swarmed into the centre of the city, halting all traffic. Children drove about in trucks waving red flags.

Many hours later, at 8 P.M., Stalin appeared on the radio. In an unemotional speech worlds apart from his "brothers and sisters" address of July 1941, he referred to the "final act of surrender." The first in the Soviet Union to refer accurately to the Rheims "preliminary protocol on surrender," he left unsaid which armed forces had signed that earlier document and only implied that the Soviet Union had been party to those first talks.[75]

During the war the media dropped the anti-Polish, anti-American, and anti-British shrillness of the 1930s. It was a real change, but the slightest complication with the Allies immediately showed in a sharper tone. A historian has called the public presence of the British and American allies in the USSR "faint but real," but contemporaries would likely have said real but faint.[76] For, as noted, Stalin gave the Red Army, the Soviet Union, and ultimately himself all the credit for Germany's defeat and ensured that the media minimized reports of Allied material aid and warfare.

The turbulent developments with Poland probably baffled many citizens. To make sense of them often seemed impossible. Red Army soldiers who saw the Anders army in a Turkmen town exclaimed, "They told us, and we have read in the papers, that Poland does not exist, and yet there you are. A Polish Army dressed like staff officers, well fed. To hell with it! They always lie to us!" At least one agitator was asked in December 1943 whether there would be war with Poland, as the creation of the Khmelnytsky Order suggested to the questioner.[77] The actual stance of Russians, Ukrainians, and Kazakhs toward the Polish exiles in their midst varied, partly mirroring the media treatment of the Poles. Some exiles who survived have recalled insults (mostly from Komsomol members and mostly at the time of Anders's departure), envy because of food aid received by Poles, and exploitation. But at least as many survivors recall sympathy and selfless aid, particularly from locals who had in years past themselves arrived as exiles.[78]

The impact of the propaganda about the other allies seems to have been ambiguous. With regard to the material aid, tangible reality nullified whatever the media said. Secret informers noted statements by writers and journalists to the effect that the Soviet Union (or Russia) could not withstand the Germans without Allied aid, or that Allied pressure would change the Soviet system.[79] How many people held such views, and at what stage of the war, cannot be determined. But according to the press attaché at the U.S. embassy, American material aid loomed large in "popular consciousness." He was told by "Soviet friends" that the food and clothing were particularly important to the Red Army, and "Russians often told Americans they would have starved without lend-lease food." This great impression was possible because the evidence of that aid was "omnipresent": "In all parts of the Soviet Union in which I lived or traveled, I saw American foodstuffs, clothing, and other products on sale in government stores, on the black market, or in use in Soviet homes."[80]

The propaganda generally portrayed the Red Army as fighting the Germans alone. Perhaps here it was really effective in its coverage—or more precisely, its omission. After the first months following the German invasion, references to the first "two years of the war" disappeared. Usually the years 1939 and 1940 were ignored, including the battles fought in western Europe. Real war, the "Great Patriotic War," began on June 22, 1941, and not a day earlier. A woman whose job it was to translate TASS reports into English recalled, "We understood the events surrounding World War II strictly through what we were told by the Soviet media. What had taken place in Europe prior to the attack on the Soviet Union seemed unreal and was not to be compared with Russia's struggle. The German conquest of Europe had been swift and presented in the Soviet press in a neutral, not to say favorable, light. We had only a vague idea of what the bombing of Britain had wrought." The American entry into the war made little impression for that reason.[81]

Many citizens seemingly shared this mind-set. The American journalist William White traveled throughout the Soviet Union for six weeks in the summer of 1944, accompanying the president of the U.S. Chamber of Commerce and conversing with foreign colleagues. "The average Russian," he concluded, "firmly and logically believes that his government has until recently borne, not most of the war burden, but all of it." When Stalin said that the fascist bear could not be crushed in its lair without Allied aid, the average person "probably dismissed it as the kind of perfunctory gesture which all statesmen occasionally make."[82] Many foreign observers drew this conclusion during or shortly after the war. The former correspondent Paul Winterton also believed that the authorities succeeded to a great extent in creating a popular belief that the Soviet Union was fighting and winning the war almost unaided. And he made an accurate prediction: that Russian history books of the future would reflect this view.[83]

Conclusion

When the war with Nazi Germany began, Stalin immediately organized a central information bureau and made censorship tighter than ever. His goal was both mobilization of his subjects and total control of the information provided to them. Such extreme centralization, as both an ideal and a practice, had no equal in wartime Europe. And nothing exemplified Stalin's goal better than the unique general confiscation of radio receivers. In late 1939 the Nazis criminalized listening to foreign radio (including broadcasts from allied or neutral countries), but they allowed the sale of receivers.[1] As for the practice, not even Nazi Germany's propaganda structure was as singularly united as the one at Stalin's disposal. Goebbels was the Reich minister of enlightenment and propaganda, but he consistently faced competition from other German agencies. Unlike Stalin, he did not have a clear monopoly on propaganda strategy and output.[2] Stalin aimed for control and secrecy out of a range of fears: that his citizens might become less loyal to "Soviet rule," that Nazi propaganda might benefit, and that American citizens or other allies might reconsider the aid they were supplying to the Soviet Union.

Besides disinformation, readers and listeners received a specifically Stalinist message: each one of them had to be willing to accept death. If dying was needed to avoid German captivity or simply to contribute to the war, then there was nothing else to do or say. As before 1941, the key was obedience, not individual initiative. Dying heroes did as they were told, and they were not called special. The tales about this most radical form of selflessness only made sense from a highly unrealistic perspective, namely that it was treason to fall alive into enemy hands. No other state in Europe imposed this bipolar view. Even Nazi hero propaganda preferred to praise pilots, tank drivers, and submariners who managed to stay alive. In fact in this regard the only European equivalent to Moscow's demand was found in the ideology of the SS.[3]

The press and other media did show corpses of the hanged partisan Zoia Kosmodemianskaia and of murdered civilians. But, as in other belligerent countries, the propaganda allowed for little grief, and sometimes self-consciously opposed it. It was typical that the fictional villagers in Wasilewska's *The Rainbow* who bury people killed by Germans felt "no grief in their heart, only a solemn triumph," for the victims died "for their own land.... Such was the scheme of things that the land was defended with the blood and lives of the people who were born of it and lived on it." A woman who buried her teenage son tells a tearful bystander, "It's no use being sorry, the time is not right. Mitia is gone, but there's Viktor. Our people are strong, well rooted in the earth. Cut down a pear-tree and before you know it, a fresh shoot comes out of the ground and drives upward toward the sun."[4]

The propaganda about industry and agriculture was unappealing and, above all, evasive, failing even to publish laws militarizing workers and regulations of the practice of labor duty. It was also typical that factory newspapers did not mention the products or name the directors. There was ceaseless talk of competition and production records, but an equally nagging refrain that not all workers and peasants were working to capacity. Meanwhile their actual harsh experience told people that the propaganda was wrong to blame food shortages only on laziness and greed. Their only possible inspiration was reports on vegetable gardens, which resembled the morale-boosting "kitchen front" campaign in the United Kingdom and were one of the media's least Soviet items.[5]

Early on, Moscow decided to publicize the Nazi atrocities extensively. By and large Agitprop made skillful use of the evidence, which was also provided by the Germans themselves in captured policy documents, personal letters, photographs, and testimonies. The media did not highlight the Nazi killing campaign against the Jews but, from today's Western perspective, "buried" it. The main reason was anti-Semitism, in two senses: as a sentiment in and near Stalin's inner circle and as a mind-set among Soviet citizens who, Stalin feared, would be encouraged in their anti-Semitism by reports on Jews. There was little Soviet about this: both the nature of the reporting and the reasons for them were essentially the same as in the United Kingdom and the United States.

Stalin wanted his citizens and soldiers to hate the enemy, which suggests that he realized that loyalty, discipline, and patriotic fervor were not plentiful and strong enough. He made the decision to promote ethnic hatred rationally, and only many months after the war began.[6] Meanwhile the propaganda was ambiguous about the need to stimulate hatred. Stalin said the enemy could not be defeated without this sentiment. But another dogma, often repeated, held that the hatred stemmed exclusively from enemy crimes: the media were simply informing the citizens. The propaganda blurred and sometimes erased the distinction between "fascists" and "Germans." British propaganda did the same, but in the Soviet world Germanophobia was a heresy tolerated by the party hierarchy. In 1945 the Communist Party's leading full-time propagandist signaled its end by publicly reprimanding the writer who most actively espoused it.

Whether the hate speech worked as intended is another matter. There exist some credible references to sincere hatred by ordinary people. In January 1942 a Polish citizen just released from the Gulag spoke to seven women on a train to Sverdlovsk who were evacuating with their factory from Moscow. He was touched by their "sincere and touching expression of patriotism" and hatred:

The women outdid each other in telling me stories of the courage and sacrifice of the people of besieged Moscow, of their own work, which often continued, with short breaks, during whole days and nights, of the readiness with which they now abandoned their homes and families in order to rush to the Urals at the call of "the Government and the Party"; the gleam of hatred and enthusiasm in their eyes was unfeigned as they assured me that they would not hesitate to give up their lives in the defense of the Fatherland against the German invader.[7]

There is some information that civilians in the unoccupied parts of the Soviet Union, influenced by the media and rumors, developed a hatred of the Germans that did not run deep, and perhaps was less enthusiastic than the hatred felt by Red Army soldiers at the front.[8]

Stalin framed the war as *patriotic*. From the very start it was about a "motherland" to which unquestioning allegiance was due. A Communist Party monthly set the tone: nothing in the world was better than Soviet citizenship, but those in possession of this precious gift had to place the "interests of the Soviet land" above everything, and they had to prove their loyalty with concrete examples of their patriotism.[9]

British war propaganda was Anglocentric, despite a sincere intention not to antagonize the Irish, Welsh, and Scots.[10] Likewise in the Soviet Union, because most members of the intended audience of the "motherland" propaganda were Russians, the large majority of the population, some kind of Russocentric bias was inevitable. But the Soviet leader of Georgian descent restrained those leading propagandists who wanted to go further. Had Stalin given his toast to the Russian people *during* the war, the propagandists and the central media would have expressed Russocentrism, xenophobia, and anti-Semitism much more forcefully.[11] For most of the war, however, praise for the Russian "elder brother" and his special character did not go to extremes. In an odd twist, the notion that the war was about "Russia" and "the Russians" did pervade the propaganda of the Allies. Such an approach might work in countries where most people were ignorant of the existence of non-Russians in Stalin's country, but in the Soviet context, as its leader seems to have realized, easily antagonized the non-Russians who had to fight alongside the Russians.

Propaganda has unintended effects, and Stalin's media were no exception. Although Russian chauvinism was restrained, the newspapers and radio broadcasts probably still contributed to it and also created suspicion. The prominent theme of dying for one's country most likely helped to strengthen Russian pride; social psychologists have demonstrated that simply thinking about one's own mortality tends to make people more positive about their outlook on the world.[12] The meager attention to the non-Russian identity of war heroes generally did not mean to denigrate, but many Russians probably concluded what Stalin was to say only after the war: that they should not rely on the non-Russians.

Stalin and his circle suspected *all* the citizens who temporarily left the Soviet orbit and experienced German rule of treason. Yet, as this study has shown, the propaganda did not deliberately encourage this sentiment and instead portrayed those citizens as overwhelmingly loyal. Partisan heroes were sustained by their faith in Communism and Stalin, but also by a generally supportive environment. The stories about specific resistance fighters probably attracted people, even if details might have seemed questionable.

In no other modern case of joint military warfare were the achievements of allies as hidden from public view as in the Great Patriotic War proclaimed by the propaganda. The contributions of the British, Americans, Canadians, and Poles were vastly underestimated; the Red Army supposedly was fighting the Germans almost on its own. Stalin and his media had said for years that the world's first socialist society needed no foreign aid, and now the Red Army and the Soviet Union did get virtually all the credit. Reports about the former enemies were mostly bland and never appealed to emotion—friendship constituted a danger. With regard to the material aid that was received, the tangible reality overrode the propaganda, but the sense that the Soviet Union was the only real force fighting Germany did become widespread. Thus in this one case omission gave Stalin what he wanted.

In short, the war propaganda of the Soviet Union somewhat resembled that of other belligerent states. There too the media searched for and found heroes, promoted gardening, gave meager attention to the Holocaust, denigrated an entire people, and vilified those called traitors. On the whole, however, the Soviet propaganda output stood out with traits of its own: condescending omission of facts known abroad, at the expense of lives and morale; the simplistic dilemma of death or treason; willful neglect of the suffering of one's own citizens in the hinterland; open support for the view that everyone had to and did hate the invader; restraint on chauvinism; and denigration of the military efforts of allied states. All of these traits had been put in place well before 1941, and they all stemmed from Stalin's tight control.

The propaganda must also be compared to earlier and later decades in Russian and Soviet history. Various intellectuals during the war with Germany and observers after it noted that the war eased living under Stalin a little because, for once, the authorities and most of the rest of the population had a common cause. In discussing Soviet films, one historian has referred to a comparative "oasis of freedom. The regime allowed a measure of artistic experimentation.... During the war directors made films on subjects about which they themselves cared, expressing genuine and deeply felt emotions."[13] But the findings presented in this book do not support the notion of a breathing space. Censorship became tighter than ever. Moscow did allow deviations from the official line expressed by Stalin and the Soviet Information Bureau, such as forebodings concerning the German threat to Kiev and Moscow and anti-German hate speech, but many citizens realized that these were heresies whose authors were liable for punishment as soon as Stalin or his entourage decided to restore orthodoxy.

The themes of selflessness and indebtedness were not innovations but modifications of prewar lines. Before the early 1930s the press propagated selfless labor for the implementation of the First Five-Year Plan; in the years just before the German invasion it mentioned an immense and permanent debt of all to the state and ultimately Stalin. For a while after June 1941 Stalin stepped aside somewhat and people were declared to be indebted to the motherland and the soldiers of the Red Army. Continuity was particularly striking in the propaganda about heroism: prewar hero worship was equally contradictory in that each feat was unique yet also representative of mass heroism.[14]

During World War I the press of the Russian Empire (as did the press of almost every belligerent country) had campaigned against enemy aliens. Racist plays and propaganda declared assimilation of Russians of German descent a mask for German treason and murderous impulses, and sympathy for these people was ethnic blindness. And in general, righteous anger at internal and external "enemies" had been a staple of Soviet public life. The real difference beginning in 1941 was that now the foreign targets of hatred were fewer. The media were far less anti-Polish, anti-British, and anti-American than in the 1930s, simply because the Poles, the British, and the Americans had become allies. As for patriotic pride, the tsarist regime also attempted to mobilize through appeals to Russian patriotism, but it was too little and too late to have tangible effects. Already in the Soviet 1930s, however, there were expressions of pride in great names and events from the past, although with some hesitation. The war propaganda could build on this precedent.[15]

Writings about Soviet propaganda during World War II abound with poorly supported statements about its impact. One Russian populist view holds that the propaganda did not matter that much, because from the very beginning people were patriotic and willing to sacrifice themselves; thus the term "holy war" expressed a preexisting mentality.[16] Other Russian researchers are of the view that the propaganda played a large if not crucial role, and some foreign scholars agree that it was "enormously effective."[17] Some scholars used to believe that the same thing happened to Stalin as happened to Churchill: the Soviet leader gained widespread popularity and his words inspired. But NKVD surveillance reports in Leningrad and Moscow show that support for Stalin and his entourage consistently sat side by side with a strong current of skepticism.[18]

To fruitfully discuss to what degree the propaganda succeeded or was effective, one first needs to establish its goals. As argued here, wartime Soviet propaganda's basic goal was to control the population and to make it do as it was told.

Most Soviet citizens probably thought that the propaganda did not inform them, except in the sense of telling them what they were supposed to think and do. Old people in particular had an attitude of *pozhivem, uvidim:* "We'll see about that."[19] Labor and behavior in the hinterland were shaped less by the media (or even foreign radio broadcasts) than by other factors: the militarization of labor and other policies affecting daily life; the endless cruelties of Nazi Germany and its allies; and conversations with refugees, evacuees, railway employees, hospitalized soldiers, and others. That rumors circulated was not always easy to observe, and some foreigners even believed that Soviet citizens almost never spoke their minds to strangers. For instance, a Polish man recalled in 1942, just after leaving the USSR, that talk in trains and canteens usually concerned the current interpretation of events provided by *Pravda* or *Izvestiia* and simply ended whenever someone proclaimed, "Stalin said so." But the war did loosen tongues at markets, stores, trains, canteens, polyclinics, bathhouses, barbershops, and shopping queues, where social barriers lost their meaning. People talked even though prison or worse loomed if their dissent was denounced, and even though they could be convicted for telling uncomfortable truths—that Leningraders were eating cats, that Stalin's own son was in German captivity, and that the slogans "Beating the enemy on his own territory" and "With little blood" had failed, for example.[20]

In an American interview project in 1950 and 1951 with citizens who had recently left the Soviet Union, an overwhelming majority said that the population trusted rumor more than the Soviet press. The interviewees differed about the impact of the war propaganda. Some called it of great consequence, agreeing that it succeeded in getting people to fight for the regime and calling the Bolsheviks masterful propagandists. Others said that an intitial consensus that there was nothing to defend vanished simply because of German conduct, and did not ascribe any role in this to propaganda. Still others referred to a combination of propaganda and German misdeeds, saying, "Soviet propaganda could do a lot if it had facts on which to base itself" and "[It] became very important." Although early media reports of atrocities were disbelieved, conversations eventually made it clear that the atrocity propaganda was at least partly true.[21]

Soviet journalists themselves realized that their propaganda was uninformative and disliked. A radio editor complained to an acquaintance, "Our propaganda is stupid and bland. I cannot read the newspapers, the Soviet Information Bureau reports, the things we broadcast over the radio without anger." A commission of inquiry into the *Latest News* broadcasts noted in the middle of 1942, "Every one of us often observes the following: having carefully listened to the Bureau bulletin with reports from the fronts and international information, the listeners walk away from the loudspeakers, usually saying, 'We know that already.'" Even the chief of Agitprop, Aleksandrov, referred to the "serious shortcomings" of a press full of official documents and TASS reports.[22] And because of scarcity, technical problems, and poor distribution, many people often did not even see or hear the print and radio propaganda. (Newsreels and films fared little better; in 1943 the Russian republic had only 6,550 sites where they could be viewed.)[23]

In short, with his own citizens, Stalin faced an uphill propaganda battle. The key problem was the extreme centralization. Nazi Germany ultimately lost the war, but Nazi propaganda for the German population was effective in many ways, such as in demonizing Jews and discrediting alternatives to Nazi rule, and perhaps largely because it was not totally uniform.[24] In Stalin's orbit the Soviet propaganda did not fail entirely. The notion of a fight for the motherland against murderers and virtually without outside help resonated. But the successes in the battle for hearts and minds were smaller than less tightly controlled propaganda might have been. What saved Stalin's day was less his propaganda than the reality: Hitler's regime offered no livable alternative to Stalin's. Most Soviet citizens probably came to believe that their life under the Germans would be worse than under Stalin. That awareness, deriving not just from the propaganda but also from rumors, was the key reason people rallied around the state and its armed forces.

After the European war, the propaganda—no longer directed by Shcherbakov, who died on May 10, 1945, at the age of forty-four—both changed and stayed the same. Censorship became even more vigilant, and the celebration of Russianness, having finally received Stalin's open support, blossomed. But hatred of Germans largely left the stage, and quickly. The official purpose of all but one of the public events in recaptured Kiev between 1943 and 1954 was to celebrate and express positive emotions (love for the motherland and gratitude to Stalin), not hatred. The ethnic heresy was corrected, aided by the creation of a Soviet-friendly German zone of occupation, which eventually became the German Democratic Republic. Reprints of wartime propaganda customarily replaced "German" with "fascist." Still, for several decades most Russians and other Soviet citizens were hostile to Germans. By the new millennium this group had shrunk to a minority.[25]

The main continuities in propaganda after 1945 concerned the war heroes, the heroes of labor, the "fascist" crimes, and the capitalist countries. Canonical hero tales were never rectified, even if contrary evidence literally rose from the dead. In the fall of 1945 a veteran discovered a large statue of himself in his Kyrgyz town of Tokmak. It turned out that he was considered a dead Panfilovite. But Sergeant Ivan Dobrobabin had been imprisoned by the Germans. This was followed by an escape, return to his native village near Kharkiv, a second imprisonment, a bribery-induced release, and enlistment with the local auxiliary police. When the Red Army retook the area he became a soldier again, then, after the war, he was sentenced to fifteen years of hard labor. He was released in 1954, one year after Stalin's death. None of this received any publicity.[26]

This was because the Panfilov story had to remain pure and because during the war and for decades after it, officials and others kept following Stalin in denouncing former POWs as treacherous deserters. By late 1943 the military tribunals were treating assistance offered to Germans by citizens as treason, in contravention of a Supreme

Soviet decree distinguishing accomplices from traitors. In real life the propaganda about the mostly loyal masses under foreign occupation had no impact, except perhaps in raising suspicion that the opposite was true. Until the very end of Communist rule, all citizens had to write on job questionnaires whether they or a relative had been a war prisoner, or had even lived in territory under German occupation. If they themselves, or a German stamp in their identity document, confirmed this, officials barred them from professions such as teaching. Most citizens who had worked in Germany were allowed to return home, but they too were unthinkingly stigmatized.[27]

Labor feats continued to be glorified. Meliton Kantaria, the designated Georgian aide to the Russian flag-hoister of May 1945, reportedly overfulfilled the postwar plan in a mine shaft by 300 percent.[28] Public portrayal of the Holocaust largely remained inconsistent, and the Allied role in the war remained obscure—just one country had saved humanity, on its own.[29] These continuities help explain why today most Russians still do not know what to think about the Holocaust and the Allied war effort.

The veneration of war heroism also continued. For years many Soviet citizens venerated the official heroes, particularly Zoia. Even decades later, new Russian books described the acts of more than four hundred soldiers, all like Matrosov's ending in selfless death. Many recent Russian films and publications depict heroic soldiers who perish under enemy fire.[30] One reason such stories keep circulating is that selflessness is not just an invention; in all wars some soldiers do sacrifice themselves for their brothers in arms.

Another reason is that commemorating heroes is comparatively easy. Commemorating victims is hard work, for their death has no clear meaning. Russians today generally venerate the dead of what they still call the Great Patriotic War but prefer to ignore the mass mortality in the hinterland that does not fit the heroism scheme. And most find it difficult to imagine a war in which their leaders would attempt to limit casualties not just in propaganda but also in reality. To them war seems a natural disaster in which mass death is unavoidable.[31] That too is a belief stemming largely from the Soviet Union's war propaganda.

Notes

Introduction

1. Lev Gudkov, "The Fetters of Victory: How the War Provides Russia with Its Identity," http://www.eurozine.com, May 3, 2005; A. E. Videneeva, ed., *"Byla voina . . .": Sbornik dokumentov i vospominanii o Rostove v period Velikoi Otechestvennoi voiny 1941–1945 godov. 55–letnemu iubileiu Velikoi Pobedy posviashchaetsia* (Rostov, 2001). In source references in the endnotes, transliteration follows the standards of the Library of Congress, with minor modifications. In the main text, transliterations that are more readable or traditional are used. Thus, whereas source references have *Il'ia Erenburg*, the main text has *Ilia Ehrenburg*. With the exception of Kiev, geographical locations in Ukraine according to its current borders are transliterated from the Ukrainian; thus, it is Zhytomyr and Kharkiv, not Zhitomir and Kharkov. With locations in Belarus, transliteration is from the Belarusian; thus, it is Vitsebsk, not Vitebsk. The few Yiddish words are spelled in accordance with usage by the YIVO Encyclopedia of Jews in Eastern Europe Online at http://www.yivoencyclopedia.org/.
2. The website is "1941–1945. Khronika Pobedy," initially at http://www.pobeda-info.ru, and as of June 2011 at http://www.pobeda-vov.ru.
3. On Russian historiography, see Boris Sokolow, "Von der 'deutschen Schuld' zur 'sowjetischen Schuld': Russische Literatur über den Zweiten

Weltkrieg," in Dagmar Herrmann et al., eds., *Traum und Trauma: Russen und Deutsche im 20. Jahrhundert* (Munich, 2003), 314–360. On Ukraine, see Wilfried Jilge, "The Politics of Memory and the Second World War in Post-Communist Ukraine (1986/1991–2004/2005)," *Jahrbücher für Geschichte Osteuropas* 54, no. 1 (2006): 50–81. A thorough recent German study also using Slavic sources is Dieter Pohl, *Die Herrschaft der Wehrmacht: Deutsche Militärbesatzung und einheimische Bevölkerung in der Sowjetunion 1941–1944* (Munich, 2008). On English-language scholarship, see Amir Weiner, "Saving Private Ivan: From What, Why, and How?," *Kritika* 1, no. 2 (Spring 2000): 305–336. One of several notable exceptions is Catherine Merridale, *Ivan's War: The Red Army 1939–1945* (London, 2005).

4. Jeffrey Brooks, *Thank You, Comrade Stalin! Soviet Public Culture from Revolution to Civil War* (Princeton, N.J., 2000), especially chapter 7; I. I. Shirokorad, *Tsentral'naia periodicheskaia pechat' v gody Velikoi Otechestvennoi voiny: 1941–1945* (Moscow, 2001).

5. On posters, see, for example, Larisa Kolesnikova, *"OKNA TASS" 1941/1945: Oruzhie pobedy* (Moscow, 2005); Peter Kort Zegers and Douglas W. Druick, eds., *Windows on the War: Soviet TASS Posters at Home and Abroad, 1941–1945* (Chicago, 2011); Mark Edele, "Paper Soldiers: The World of the Soldier Hero according to Soviet Wartime Posters," *Jahrbücher für Geschichte Osteuropas* 47, no. 1 (1999): 89–108; Jörg Ganzenmüller, "'Polnischer Pan' und 'deutscher Faschist': Die nationale Komponente sowjetischer Feindbilder im Krieg," in Silke Satjukow and Rainer Gries, eds., *Unsere Feinde: Konstruktionen des Anderen im Sozialismus* ([Leipzig], 2004), 421–436. Full-color reproductions of 209 posters are in Rossiiskaia gosudarstvennaia biblioteka, *Plakaty voiny i pobedy* (Moscow, 2005). On documentaries and films, see, for example, Peter Kenez, *Cinema and Soviet Society, 1917–1953* (Cambridge, U.K., 1992), 186–206; V. I. Fomin, ed., *Kino na voine: Dokumenty i svidetel'stva* (Moscow, 2005); Denise J. Youngblood, *Russian War Films: On the Cinema Front, 1914–2005* (Lawrence, Kan., 2007), 55–81.

6. Frank Ellis, "The Media as Social Engineer," in Catriona Kelly and David Shepherd, eds., *Russian Cultural Studies: An Introduction* (Oxford, 1998), 197; Peter Kenez, *The Birth of the Propaganda State: Soviet Methods of Mass Mobilization, 1917–1929* (New York, 1985), 2, 10.

7. The definition has been adapted from Garth S. Jowett and Victoria O'Donnell, *Propaganda and Persuasion*, 3rd ed. (Thousand Oaks, Calif., 1999), 6, 45, 290. The former definition is from "State of Deception: The Power of Nazi Propaganda," special exhibition at the U.S. Holocaust Memorial Museum, http://www.ushmm.org/propaganda/.

8. To the Nazis, the word *agitation* was pejorative. Daniel Weiss, "Stalinistischer und nationalsozialistischer Propagandadiskurs im Vergleich: Eine erste Annäherung," in Holger Kuße, ed., *Slavistische Linguistik 2001: Referate des XXVII. Konstanzer Slavistischen Arbeitstreffens. Frankfurt/Friedrichsdorf, 11.–13.9.2001 = Slavistische Beiträge,* 422 (Munich, 2003), 318.
9. Brooks, *Thank You, Comrade Stalin*, 150.
10. Ellis, "The Media as Social Engineer," 197-198, 200; Kenez, *The Birth of the Propaganda State*, 7-8.
11. Erik van Ree, "Stalinistische propaganda: Theorie, praktijk, resultaten," *Leidschrift* 16, no. 3 (2001): 9-11; Peter Kenez, "Black and White: The War on Film," in Richard Stites, ed., *Culture and Entertainment in Wartime Russia* (Bloomington, Ind., 1995), 157; Kenez, *The Birth of the Propaganda State*; David Brandenberger, *Propaganda State in Crisis: Soviet Ideology, Indoctrination, and Terror under Stalin, 1927–1941* (New Haven, Conn., 2011).
12. The quotation is from Kenez, *The Birth of the Propaganda State*, 8, 10. Compare Brooks, *Thank You, Comrade Stalin*, 15-16, 54-55.
13. TsDAHOU, 1/23/67/19/17: Upravlenie propagandy i agitatsii TsK VKP(b), *O rabote raionnykh gazet*, March 3, 1942 (first quotation); A. Puzin, *O nekotorykh zadachakh pechati v dni otechestvennoi voiny* (Moscow, 1942), 5, 8-9.

1. Stalinist Propaganda as a System for Control

1. Peter Kenez, *The Birth of the Propaganda State: Soviet Methods of Mass Mobilization, 1917–1929* (New York, 1985), 4.
2. Frank Ellis, "The Media as Social Engineer," in Catriona Kelly and David Shepherd, eds., *Russian Cultural Studies: An Introduction* (Oxford, 1998), 199-201.
3. This paragraph derives from David Brandenberger, *Propaganda State in Crisis: Soviet Ideology, Indoctrination, and Terror under Stalin, 1927–1941* (New Haven, Conn., 2011), 15-16, 24, 69-71, 73-74, 85-88, 95-97.
4. Ibid., 99, 101-102, 116-118.
5. Ibid., 118-119, 136-140. On the spell-binding Soviet ethos and effort to "speak Bolshevik," see also Stephen Kotkin, *Magnetic Mountain: Stalinism as a Civilization* (Berkeley, 1995), esp. chapter 5; Jochen Hellbeck, *Revolution on My Mind: Writing a Diary under Stalin* (Cambridge, Mass., 2006).
6. Brandenberger, *Propaganda State in Crisis*, 179-180, 185, 197, 233-235, 248, 252-253.
7. This paragraph uses and quotes Jeffrey Brooks, *Thank You, Comrade Stalin! Soviet Public Culture from Revolution to Civil War* (Princeton, N.J., 2000), 150-152.

8. Ellis, "The Media as Social Engineer," 201–202; Ben-Cion Pinchuk, "Soviet Media on the Fate of the Jews in Nazi-Occupied Territory (1939–1941)," *Yad Vashem Studies* 11 (Jerusalem, 1976): 223.
9. Brooks, *Thank you, Comrade Stalin*, 152.
10. Ibid., 156.
11. Ibid., 154; A. Anatoli (Kuznetsov), *Babi Yar: A Document in the Form of a Novel*, trans. David Floyd (New York, 1970), 134 (the quotation). Another Russian witness recalls that Hitler's face was actually blacked out; see Hoover Institution on War, Revolution, and Peace, Stanford, Calif., B. I. Nicolaevsky collection, series no. 178, box 232, folder 10, fol. 43: [Lev Vladimirovich] Dudin, "Velikii Mirazh: Sobytiia 1941–1947 godov v ponimanii sovetskogo cheloveka" (n.p., 1947).
12. Vladimir Nevezhin, "Soviet War Propaganda, from Anti-imperialism to Anti-fascism: Shifts and Contradictions," in Silvio Pons and Andrea Romano, eds., *Russia in the Age of Wars, 1914–1945* (Milan, 2000), 264. See also V. A. Nevezhin, *Sindrom nastupatel'noi voiny: Sovetskaia propaganda v preddverii "sviashchennykh boev," 1939–1941* (Moscow, 1997); Vladimir Nevezhin, *"Esli zavtra v pokhod...": Podgotovka k voine i ideologicheskaia propaganda v 30-kh–40-kh godakh* (Moscow, 2007).
13. Aleksander Topolski, *Without Vodka: Adventures in Wartime Russia* (South Royalton, Vt., 2001), 200–201.
14. Viktor Cherepanov, *Vlast' i voina: Stalinskii mekhanizm gosudarstvennogo upravleniia v Velikoi Otechestvennoi voine* (Moscow, 2006), 23, 34; "Vystuplenie po radio Zamestitelia Predstavitelia Soveta Narodnykh Komissarov Soiuza SSR i Narodnogo Komissara Inostrannykh Del tov. V. M. MOLOTOVA," *Pravda*, June 23, 1941, 1.
15. Elena Skrjabina, *Siege and Survival: The Odyssey of a Leningrader*, trans. Norman Luxemburg (Carbondale, Ill., 1971), 4; K. S. Karol, *Solik: Life in the Soviet Union 1939–1946*, trans. Eamonn McArdle (London, 1986), 75; Viktoriia Babenko-Vudberi, *Obratno k vragam* (Kiev, 2003), 92.
16. Wanda Lidia Smereczańska-Zienkiewicz and Witold Jan Smereczański, *Krajobraz niewoli: Wspomnienia z Kazachstanu* (Lublin, 2005), 71.
17. Brandenberger, *Propaganda State in Crisis*, 23; TsDAHOU, 1/23/67/19/21v: Upravlenie propagandy i agitatsii TsK VKP(b), *O rabote raionnykh gazet*, March 3, 1942.
18. RGASPI, 17/125/57/1: N. Pal'gunov, i.o. zav. Otdelom Pechati NKID, to Aleksandrov, [Moscow], January 4, 1941 (on reports in 1940); V. P. Iampols'kii et al., comps., *Organy gosudarstvennoi bezopasnosti SSSR v Velikoi Otechestvennoi voine: Sbornik dokumentov*, vol. 2, book 1: *Nachalo: 22 iiunia–31 avgusta 1941 goda* (Moscow, 2000), 17–23 (the quotation). Distribution lists are at RGASPI,

17/125/III/23, 24-25 (July 8, 1942), 17/125/191/14-16, 17-19 (July 3 and 2, 1943). Samples of *Vestnik* issues from 1943 are at RGASPI, 558/11/209. At first there was also a bulletin by the Press and Agitation Department with translated foreign radio broadcasts; an example dated August 16, 1941, is at RGASPI, 17/125/73/38-43.

19. Stalin's epithet was *svoloch*. RGASPI, 558/11/208/75: Vestnik instrannoi sluzhebnoi informatsii TASS, report by General Hüseyin Erkilet in *Cumhuriyet*, November 1941 to early 1942. Stalin briefly quoted Erkilet's account in his speech on November 6, 1942.
20. Iampols'kii, *Organy gosudarstvennoi bezopasnoti SSSR v Velikoi Otechestvennoi voine*, vol. 2, book 1, 63-64; RGASPI, 88/1/998/20: "Stenogramma zasedaniia Sovinformbiuro 17 ianvaria 1944 goda" (on staff size); N. Iu. Nikulina and Z. N. Soroka, "Sovetskoe Informatsionnoe Biuro v gody Velikoi Otechestvennoi voiny (Analiz istochnikov)," in V. I. Gal'tsov, ed. in chief, *Problemy istochnikovedeniia i istoriografii* (Kaliningrad, 1999), 59; G. A. Kovalev, "Sovinformbiuro v gody Velikoi Otechestvennoi voiny," *Voprosy istorii*, no. 6 (June 1987): 16, 23. On the meeting with Shcherbakov, see Nadezhda Ulianovskaia and Maiia Ulianovskaia, *Istoriia odnoi sem'i* (Moscow, 1994), 159-160. The one Western study of the Bureau deals with the postwar period: Wolfram Eggeling, "Das Sowjetische Informationsbüro: Innenansichten einer sowjetischen Propagandainstitution, 1945-1947," *Osteuropa* 50, no. 2 (February 2000): 201-214. Its regular reports are available at Nasha pobeda, "Ot Sovetskogo Informbiuro," http://9may.ru/inform/ (last accessed February 20, 2011).
21. RGASPI, 17/125/60/88-90: Ia. Khavinson to Shcherbakov, [September 30, 1941], draft letter, with a draft of a Central Committee resolution.
22. RGASPI, 17/125/191/89: report of TASS otdel sviazi, [probably June 1943].
23. RGASPI, 17/125/196/11: Ia. Khavinson to A. A. Puzin, Moscow, October 16, 1942. For various reasons (weak or absent short-wave receivers, a lack of receivers of any kind, a lack of electricity, and a lack of local capacity to receive medium waves), newspaper editors in recaptured Soviet regions or in armies at the front also often failed to obtain items from TASS. See RGASPI, 17/125/295/133-134: N. Pal'gunov, otvetstvennyi rukovoditel' TASS, to A. S. Shcherbakov, Moscow, August 19, 1944.
24. Larisa Kolesnikova, *"OKNA TASS" 1941/1945: Oruzhie pobedy* (Moscow, 2005), 187, 189; "OKNA TASS (svodnyi katalog). K XX-i godovshchine pobedy Sovetskogo Soiuza v Velikoi Otechestvennoi voine," in Gosudarstvennaia ordena Lenina Biblioteka SSSR imeni V. I. Lenina, *Trudy* 8, ed. in chief I. P. Kondakov (Moscow, 1965), 163-371.

25. The Russian word for the newsletters was *mnogotirazhki*. K. I. Propina, ed., *Pechat' SSSR za 25 let: 1918–1942 gody: Statisticheskie materialy* (Moscow, 1942), 52–53, cited from a copy with written corrections held at the Rossiiskaia knizhnaia palata, Otdel statistiki, Moscow. The totals are not reliable, for adding the figures listed in another table produces other totals; for the year 1937, for instance, the total becomes 8,570. See 61–62.
26. Rossiiskaia knizhnaia palata, Otdel statistiki, file "Pechat' SSSR za period Velikoi Otechestvennoi voiny 1941–1946 (gazety)" (hereafter RKP file), Solovtseva, April 28, [1944], and Solovtseva, April 19, 1945. Details about the All-Union Book Chamber during the war are in B. A. Semenovker, *Gosudarstvennaia bibliografiia Rossii XVIII–XX vv.: Moskovskii period. Vypusk II, 1934–1945* (Moscow, 2000), 145–244.
27. RGASPI, 17/125/115/4: [P.] Bulanov, chief of political department of the Gulag, to Otdel pechati of UPA, Moscow, May 6, 1942; RGASPI, 17/125/264/9–10 (May 1942); RGASPI, 17/125/265/14–15: Bulanov, "O tirazhe, periodichnosti i shtatakh mnogotirazhnykh gazet lagerei i stroitel'stv NKVD SSSR na 1944 g.," n.p., n.d.
28. RKP file, Solovtseva, April 28, [1944].
29. The Russian terms were *molnii* and *boevye listki*. I. I. Shirokorad, *Tsentral'naia periodicheskaia pechat' v gody Velikoi Otechestvennoi voiny: 1941–1945* (Moscow, 2001), 43; RGASPI, 17/125/264/3, 4: L. Shaumian to Malenkov, Sverdlovsk, January 14, 1944, and G. Aleksandrov to G. M. Malenkov, n.p., March 28, 1944.
30. The Russian term for the practice was *vyezdnaia redaktsiia*. Semen Gershberg, *Zavtra gazeta vykhodit* (Moscow, 1966), 356–377.
31. M. M. Kozlov, ed., *Velikaia Otechestvennaia voina, 1941–1945: Entsiklopediia* (Moscow, 1985), 746 (the year 1942); RKP file, [Solovtseva], "Dopolnenie k ob"iasnitel'noi zapiske po gazetam za 1944 g.," [1945]. N. I. Kondakova, *Dukhovnaia zhizn' Rossii i Velikaia Otechestvennaia voina 1941–1945 gg.* (Moscow, 1995), 29, deduces different figures from the RKP file. Shirokorad did not study this file; citing statistics published in 1990, she arrives at numbers for regions "untouched by military activities" that are higher than mine (8,806 paper titles in 1940; 7,218 in 1941; 4,561 in 1942; 4,762 in 1943; 6,072 in 1944; and 6,455 in 1945). Shirokorad, *Tsentral'naia periodicheskaia pechat'*, 36. The figures for 1937 are from Propina, *Pechat' SSSR za 25 let*, 52.
32. RGASPI, 17/3/1041/84: reference to Politburo resolution 381 of August 20, 1941.
33. RGASPI, 17/3/1041/84: reference to Politburo resolution 381 of August 20, 1941; Kozlov, *Velikaia Otechestvennaia voina*, 546 (*Smena*); RGASPI,

17/125/60/93-95: N. Mikhailov to Aleksandrov, October 5, 1941; RGASPI, 17/125/193/6: Puzin to Shcherbakov, March 1, 1943; RGASPI, 17/125/262/118-119, 120: N. Mikhailov to Shcherbakov, April 26, 1944, and Aleksandrov and P. Fedoseev to Shcherbakov, June 14, 1944; RGASPI, 17/125/264/29: G. Aleksandrov and P. Fedoseev to Malenkov, n.p., October 26, 1944.

34. RGASPI, 17/125/121/158-159: T. Aleksandrov to I. V. Stalin, copy, n.p., n.d. See also Shirokorad, *Tsentral'naia periodicheskaia pechat'*, 34.
35. L. V. Maksimenkov, ed., *Bol'shaia tsenzura: Pisateli i zhurnalisty v Strane Sovetov, 1917–1956* (Moscow, 2005), 536–537; RKP file, Solovtseva, April 28, [1944].
36. RGASPI, 17/125/112/179: Puzin; TsDAHOU, 1/70/128/21-28v: booklet by Narodnyi komissariat sviazi Soiuza SSR, Tsentral'noe upravlenie rasprostraneniia i ekspedirovaniia pechati, *Katalog gazet i zhurnalov na 1943 god* (Moscow, [podpisano k pechati 14/XII-42 g.]).
37. RKP file, passim, Solovtseva, April 28, [1944], and Solovtseva, April 19, 1945.
38. As claimed in G. D. Komkov, "Politicheskaia propaganda i agitatsiia v gody Velikoi Otechestvennoi voiny," *Istoriia SSSR*, no. 4 (July–August 1972): 103. On prewar circulation, see *Izvestiia TsK KPSS*, no. 5 (May 1990): 194.
39. To be precise, in 1942, 1,313,00; in 1943, 1,054,000; in 1944, 1,113,000; and in the first half of 1945, 1,151,000. Propina, *Pechat' SSSR za 25 let*, 52; RKP file. I have rounded the RKP file figures. The precise prewar figures for *Pravda* were 2,010,000 (1940), 1,978,000 (1939), and 1,914,000 (1938). Shirokorad, *Tsentral'naia periodicheskaia pechat'*, 32–33, overestimates the prewar print runs of the central papers and thus concludes wrongly that those declined by half during the war. The quotations are from RGASPI, 17/3/1041/84: reference to Politburo resolution 194 of October 17, 1941.
40. Propina, *Pechat' SSSR za 25 let*, 52; RKP file. I have rounded the RKP file figures.
41. Shirokorad, *Tsentral'naia periodicheskaia pechat'*, 100, with my modification of the figure mentioned there for *Izvestiia*, and taking into consideration a printing error for *Pravda*'s circulation.
42. Propina, *Pechat' SSSR za 25 let*, [61–62].
43. In the entire year of 1943, 284.5 million (or 12 percent of the total for that year) of newspaper issues came out in non-Russian languages, and the next year the figure jumped to 509 million (or 18.9 percent). RKP file, [Solovtseva], "Dopolnenie," [1945].
44. RKP file, Solovtseva, October 1945.
45. A. Puzin, *O nekotorykh zadachakh pechati v dni otechestvennoi voiny* (Moscow, 1942), 13.

46. RKP file, Solovtseva, April 19, 1945.
47. RKP file, Solovtseva, April 28, [1944]; RKP file, Solovtseva, April 19, 1945.
48. RGASPI, 17/125/115/7-8: G. Aleksandrov and A. Puzin to Andreev, Malenkov, and Shcherbakov, n.p., June 5, 1942 (on booklets); Shirokorad, *Tsentral'naia periodicheskaia pechat'*, 63-65.
49. TsDAHOU, 1/23/67/19/17-21v: Upravlenie propagandy i agitatsii TsK VKP(b), *O rabote raionnykh gazet*, March 3, 1942.
50. RGASPI, 17/125/196/8-9, 10: G. Aleksandrov and A. Puzin to Shcherbakov, n.p., March 13, 1943, and G. Aleksandrov to Ia. S. Khavinson, n.p., March 20, 1943.
51. *Radio v dni voiny: Ocherki i vospominaniia vidnykh voenachal'nikov, izvestnykh pisatelei, zhurnalistov, deiatelei iskusstva, diktorov radioveshchaniia*, rev. and exp. 2nd ed., comps. M. S. Gleizer and N. M. Potapov (Moscow, 1982), 296 (on one channel); James von Geldern, "Radio Moscow: The Voice from the Center," in Richard Stites, ed., *Culture and Entertainment in Wartime Russia* (Bloomington, Ind., 1995), 46 (on talk shows); Ewa M. Thompson, "Nationalist Propaganda in the Soviet Russian Press, 1939-1941," *Slavic Review* 50, no. 2 (Summer 1991): 387 (on the Central Committee); TsDAVOV, 4915/1/10/4: Ia. Sirchenko to N. S. Khrushchev, "O nedostatkakh v rabote ukrainskogo radiokomiteta i respublikanskogo radioveshchaniia," n.p., January 29, 1945 (on salaries).
52. RGASPI, 17/125/295/150: Narkom sviazi K. Sergeichuk and A. Puzin to G. M. Malenkov, "O dvadtsatiletii sovetskogo radioveshchaniia," [Moscow], October 3, 1944; Siân Nicholas, *The Echo of War: Home Front Propaganda and the Wartime BBC, 1939–45* (Manchester, U.K., 1996), 12, 71; von Geldern, "Radio Moscow," 45. On Moscow, see *Radio v dni voiny*, 140. Figures on Soviet Ukraine are at TsDAVOV, 4915/1/4/240: "Spravka ob itogakh vosstanovleniia radiofikatsii i radioveshchaniia v Ukrainskoi SSR na 1/XII-1944 goda," n.p., n.d.
53. RGASPI, 17/125/295/140-142: A. Puzin to A. A. Zhdanov, G. M. Malenkov, and A. S. Shcherbakov, [Moscow], September 7, 1944.
54. F. Pihido-Pravoberezhnyi, *"Velyka Vitchyzniana viina"* (Winnipeg, 1954), 29-30; Abraham A. Kreusler, *A Teacher's Experiences in the Soviet Union* (Leiden, 1965), 35, 37.
55. RGASPI, 17/3/1041/27-28: reference to Politburo resolution 119 of June 25, 1941; Iampols'kii, *Organy gosudarstvennoi bezopasnoti SSSR v Velikoi Otechestvennoi voine*, vol. 2, book 1, 75-76; Victor Kravchenko, *I Chose Freedom: The Personal and Political Life of a Soviet Official* (New York, 1947), 358; private archives of M. S. Petrovskii (Kiev): Nachal'nik Kievskogo Obl[astnogo] Upravleniia Sviazi Sviridov to M. Z. Goshon of 30/19 Levashivs'ka Street,

"Izveshchenie." On excessive confiscation, see RGASPI, 17/125/73/99: D. Polikarpov to A. S. Shcherbakov, n.p., October 5, 1941, with draft resolution, also cited in Richard J. Brody, *Ideology and Political Mobilization: The Soviet Home Front During World War II*, The Carl Beck Papers in Russian and East European Studies, no. 1104 (Pittsburgh, 1994), 8.

56. TsDAHOU, 1/23/89/7-9: Savchenko, VRIO NKVD USSR, to Korotchenko, Luhans'k [Voroshilovhrad], July 4, 1942 (a list); Xavier Pruszyński, *Russian Year: The Notebook of an Amateur Diplomat* (New York, 1944), 160–161 (on reception in Kuibyshev); O. Horodys'kyi, "Z shchodennyka perekladacha (Prodovzhennia z poperedn'oho ch. zhurnalu 'Visti')," *Visti Bratstva kol. Voiakiv 1 UD UNA* 11, no. 104 (Munich, December 1961): 109 (on Taganrog).

57. T. M. Goriaeva, comp., Ia. I. Zasurskii, ed. in chief, *Istoriia sovetskoi radiozhurnalistiki: Dokumenty. Teksty. Vospominaniia 1917–1945* (Moscow, 1991), 35.

58. Ibid., 69; RGASPI, 17/125/295/140-142: A. Puzin to A. A. Zhdanov, G. M. Malenkov, and A. S. Shcherbakov, [Moscow], September 7, 1944; RGASPI, 17/125/295/203: G. Aleksandrov to G. M. Malenkov and A. S. Shcherbakov, n.p., November 11, 1944.

59. GARF, 6903/1/70/1-4: "K otchetu redaktsii 'Poslednikh izvestii' za 1942-i god," n.p., [1943]; GARF, 6903/1/82/35-36: E. Skleznev, "Otchet redaktsii 'Poslednikh Izvestii' za 1943 god," n.p., n.d. For the estimate of 18 million listeners, see RGALI, 631/15/584/13: Viktor Gusev in "Stenogramma Zasedaniia Prezidiuma Soiuza Sovetskikh pisatelei (Po voprosu ob uchastii pisatelei v radioveshchanii), 29.VII.1942 goda." Well into the war, Soviet on-site recordings were made with the unreliable Shorinophone, a heavy device that recorded sound on celluloid from old movies or on discarded X-ray pictures. The *Latest News* correspondents at the Southern Front in 1941 shared one. Later, recordings were also made on varnished glass "Presto" discs, which broke easily. *Radio v dni voiny*, 19, 70–71, 167; von Geldern, "Radio Moscow," 49. In the newsreel *Soiuzkinozhurnal* there was no direct sound at all, even when leaders were seen to be speaking; all sound was added in the studio. Valérie Pozner, "Les actualités soviétiques de la Second Guerre Mondiale," in Natacha Laurent, ed., *Le cinéma "stalinien": Questions d'histoire* (Toulouse, 2003), 135.

60. GARF, 6903/1/62/83, 17, 27: "Stenogramma zasedaniia rabotnikov tsentral'nogo veshchaniia pri predsedatele VRK 7-go ianvaria 1943 g." and "Stenogramma soveshchaniia po voprosam Soiuznogo veshchaniia ot 8 ianvaria 1943 g. (vtoroi den')"; GARF, 6903/1/70/59-61: "Vyvod komissii o rabote redaktsii 'Poslednikh Izvestii' za iiul' mesiats," n.p., [not earlier than July 1942].

61. GARF, 6903/1/82/35-37: Sklezlnev, "Otchet redaktsii 'Poslednikh Izvestii' za 1943 god."
62. GARF, 6903/1/65/11: "Spravka o materialakh, peredannykh redaktsiami za avgust 1942 g."; GARF, 6903/1/68/16: report for the first quarter of 1943.
63. RGASPI, 17/125/295/140-142: A. Puzin to A. A. Zhdanov, G. M. Malenkov, and A. S. Shcherbakov, [Moscow], September 7, 1944; TASS, "20 let sovetskogo radioveshchaniia," *Trud*, December 10, 1944, 2.
64. RGASPI, 17/125/295/13-14: list of announcers; *Radio v dni voiny*, 178, 186; Erskine Caldwell, *All-Out on the Road to Smolensk* (New York, 1942), 85.
65. *Radio v dni voiny*, 25; GARF, 6903/1/62/83v-84: "Stenogramma zasedaniia rabotnikov tsentral'nogo veshchaniia pri predsedatele VRK 7-go ianvaria 1943 g."
66. *Radio v dni voiny*, 284-285. On Kalinin, see 276, 286, 290.
67. Ibid., 275, 284; A. Ia. Livshin and I. B. Orlov, comps., *Sovetskaia propaganda v gody Velikoi Otechestvennoi voiny: "Kommunikatsiia ubezhdeniia" i mobilizatsionnye mekhanizmy* (Moscow, 2007), 505. On disinterest among writers, see RGALI, 631/15/584/48: Aleksandr Fadeev in "Stenogramma Zasedaniia..., 29.VII.1942 goda." Compare RGALI, 631/15/532/4v: Viktor Gusev in "Soiuz sovetskikh pisatelei. Stenogramma zasedaniia prezidiuma ot 2-go oktiabria 1941 g."; RGALI, 631/15/576/40-41: Viktor Gusev, speech, January 26, 1942; RGALI, 631/15/584/2: "Otchet o literaturnykh peredachakh s 1-go ianvaria do 1-go iiulia 1942 goda."
68. Brody, *Ideology and Political Mobilization*, 21-23.
69. *Radio v dni voiny*, 15-16.
70. Ibid., 135-136; Propina, *Pechat' SSSR za 25 let*, 51. A sound recording is available at http://www.wilsoncenter.org.
71. GARF, 6903/1/82/70-75: "Tsentral'noe muzykal'noe radioveshchanie," report for D. A. Polikarpov, January 12, [1944]; *Radio v dni voiny*, 199, 279, 284; TASS, "Pervoe otkrytoe ispolnenie Sed'moi simfonii Shostakovicha," *Trud*, March 7, 1942, 4.
72. RGASPI, 17/125/73/98: D. Polikarpov to A. S. Shcherbakov, n.p., October 5, 1941, with draft resolution; Brody, *Ideology and Political Mobilization*, 9 (on the Sverdlovsk oblast).
73. RGASPI, 17/125/73/100: D. Polikarpov to A. S. Shcherbakov, n.p., October 5, 1941, with draft resolution.
74. RGASPI, 17/125/215/13-14, 16-17, 20, 24-26: G. Aleksandrov, "O nedostatkakh v raionnom radioveshchanii," n.p., n.d., note of May 19, [1943] to A. S. Shcherbakov, and D. Polikarpov to A. S. Shcherbakov, n.p., June 7, 1943; *Radio v dni voiny*, 289; Livshin and Orlov, *Sovetskaia propaganda*, 510-512; Brody, *Ideology and Political Mobilization*, 35, n. 19.

75. Shirokorad, *Tsentral'naia periodicheskaia pechat'*, 95 (on the ban); RGASPI, 17/125/350/1-5: N. Beliaev, Altai krai committee secretary, to Malenkov, n.p., April 8, 1945; Brody, *Ideology and Political Mobilization*, 11.
76. John Lawrence, *Life in Russia* (London, 1947), 117; Herman Carmel, *Black Days, White Nights* (New York, 1984), 226; Tadeusz Kiersnowski, *Moje spostrzeżenia o Rosji Sowieckiej (1940–1942)* (Warsaw, 1997), 57. Compare A. Gaev, "Kak 'Pravda' dokhodit do chitatelia," *Vestnik instituta po izucheniiu istorii i kul'tury SSSR*, no. 7 (Munich, October–December 1953): 51 (an unconvincing emigré statement that papers were left unsold due to disinterest).
77. Shirokorad, *Tsentral'naia periodicheskaia pechat'*, 100-102; Brody, *Ideology and Political Mobilization*, 10-11, 36, n. 24; Livshin and Orlov, *Sovetskaia propaganda*, 235, 519; TsDAHOU, 1/70/242/183-184: Strel'tsov to the Viddil Propahandy i Ahitatsiï in Kiev, "Dopovidna zapyska. Pro stan rozproviudzhennia ta dostavku presy v Zhytomyrs'kii oblasti," [Zhytomyr], June 12, 1944; U. Zhukovkin, "Gazety ne dokhodiat do sela (Ot korrespondenta 'Pravdy' po Voronezhskoi oblasti)," *Pravda*, July 23, 1943, 3.
78. RGASPI, 17/3/1042/53: reference to Politburo resolution 194 of October 17, 1941.
79. *Radio v dni voiny*, 112; RGASPI, 17/125/264/33, 35: Kuznetsov to Malenkov, n.p., November 26, 1944, and Aleksandrov and Fedoseev to Malenkov, December 14, 1944; RGASPI, 17/125/349/15: Pegov, secretary of the Primorskii krai committee, to Malenkov, Vladivostok, April 23, 1945; Brody, *Ideology and Political Mobilization*, 11.
80. Shirokorad, *Tsentral'naia periodicheskaia pechat'*, 109.
81. Ibid., 95, 103-104.
82. *Radio v dni voiny*, 138-141.
83. RGASPI, 17/125/295/148-149: Narkom sviazi K. Sergeichuk and A. Puzin to G. M. Malenkov, "O dvadtsatiletii sovetskogo radioveshchaniia," [Moscow], October 3, 1944. On inaudible sound from street loudspeakers, see RGALI, 631/15/584/55: Azakh at "Stenogramma Zasedaniia . . . , 29.VII.1942 goda."
84. RGASPI, 17/125/374/53-54, 56: Zhelezova, nachal'nik Veshchatel'nogo Otdela Tsentral'nogo upravleniia radiosviazi i radioveshchaniia Narkomsviazi, to I. V. Stalin, "O sostoianii sovetskogo radioveshchaniia," n.p., n.d. [no later than May 1945].
85. See, for example, A. Il'iushin, "O proizvodstve reproduktorov," *Trud*, July 11, 1944, 3.
86. RGASPI, 17/125/374/53, 55: Zhelezova, nachal'nik Veshchatel'nogo Otdela Tsentral'nogo upravleniia radiosviazi i radioveshchaniia Narkomsviazi, to I. V. Stalin, "O sostoianii sovetskogo radioveshchaniia," n.p., n.d. [no

later than May 1945]. On Rostov, see RGASPI, 17/125/73/29-30: B. Dvinskii, secretary of the Rostov obkom, to Shcherbakov, Rostov-na-Donu, July 11, 1941. On Leningrad, see Vsevolod Vishnevskii, *Leningrad: Dnevniki voennykh let. 2 noiabria 1941 goda–31 dekabria 1942 goda* (Moscow, 2002), 1: 61; Livshin and Orlov, *Sovetskaia propaganda*, 164-165.

87. Livshin and Orlov, *Sovetskaia propaganda*, 245, 512-514, 516. On Agitprop's departments, see Cherepanov, *Vlast' i voina*,, 361.
88. G. V. Kostyrchenko, "Sovetskaia tsenzura v 1941-1952 godakh," *Voprosy istorii*, nos. 11-12 (1996): 87, 89; A. V. Blium, *Sovetskaia tsenzura v epokhu total'nogo terrora. 1929–1953* (St. Petersburg, 2000), 24, 31.
89. Blium, *Sovetskaia tzenzura*, 145; T. M. Goriaeva, *Politicheskaia tsenzura v SSSR: 1917–1991* (Moscow, 2002), 276-277.
90. Shirokorad, *Tsentral'naia periodicheskaia pechat'*, 90. See also Livshin and Orlov, *Sovetskaia propaganda*, 258.
91. RGASPI, 17/3/1046/16: reference to Politburo resolution 63 of December 5, 1942.
92. The figures, for December 31, 1943, were rounded off from Livshin and Orlov, *Sovetskaia propaganda*, 255. The Russian terms were *vypusk v svet* and *posleduiushchii kontrol'*. [Anon.], *Instruktsiia tsenzoru* (Moscow, 1942), number 7 of ninety-four-page booklet by Glavlit, filed at RGASPI, 17/125/117/98-146v.
93. Shirokorad, *Tsentral'naia periodicheskaia pechat'*, 93. See, for example, RGASPI, 17/125/187/86-101v: Sadchikov, "Svodka iz"iatii tsenzury iz predstavlennykh i pechati i peredache po radio materialov i oshibok pechati, obnaruzhennykh posleduiushchim kontrolem za vremia s 10 iiunia po 15 avgusta 1943 goda" (copy sent to Aleksandrov), no later than August 20, 1943. For an example of a regional report, see TsDAHOU, 1/70/243/31-34: E. Barlanitskii, nachal'nik Glavlita USSR, "Tekstovaia svodka vycherkov predvaritel'noi tsenzury s 1-go avgusta po 20 avgusta 1944 goda, no. 183s," n.p., August 22, [1944].
94. Goriaeva, *Politicheskaia tsenzura*, 281, 283-284; Kostyrchenko, "Sovetskaia tsenzura," 89, citing RGASPI, 17/125/117/64v and 17/116/126/83.
95. TsDAHOU, 1/70/243/18: Barlanitskii, nachal'nik Glavlita USSR, to the Otdel agitatsii i propagandy of the CC of the CP(b)U, Kiev, October 11, 1944: "Otchet o rabote Glavlita Ukrainskoi SSR za 9 mesiatsev 1944 goda."
96. [Anon.], *Instruktsiia tsenzoru*. On the *Latest News*, see Tat'iana Goriaeva, "Informatsiia, vera, nadezhda. Sovetskoe radio v gody voiny," in Karl Eimermacher et al., eds., *Rossiia i Germaniia v XX veke*, vol. 1: *Obol'shchenie vlast'iu: Russkie i nemtsy v Pervoi i Vtoroi mirovykh voinakh* (Moscow, 2010), 402.
97. GARF, 9425/1/108/61: "Svodka vazhneishikh iz"iatii...."

98. David Ortenberg, *Stalin, Shcherbakov, Mekhlis i drugie* (Moscow, 1995), 19, 159; see also 127.
99. RGASPI, 17/125/112/64: T. Aleksandrov to Shcherbakov, February 28, 1942; RGASPI, 17/125/112/181-183: plan, December 22, 1942.
100. Ortenberg, *Stalin*, 97, 127; Kostyrchenko, "Sovetskaia tsenzura," 88-89, citing RGASPI, 17/125/129/3-5; Lazar' Brontman, *Voennyi dnevnik korrespondenta "Pravdy": Vstrechi. Sobytiia. Sud'by. 1942–1945* (Moscow, 2007), 95.
101. Goriaeva, *Politicheskaia tsenzura*, 281, 283, 285-286; GARF, 9425/1/207/3-105: Sadchikov, "Perechen' svedenii, sostavliaiushchikh voennuiu i gosudarstvennuiu tainu na vremia voiny," May 18, 1944.

2. Selfless Obedience and Heroism at the Front

1. On cases of transgression of the first rule in *Krasnaia zvezda* and *Pravda*, see RGASPI, 17/125/187/22v, 43: polkovnik Cherstvoi, nach. otdela voennoi tsenzury NKO, to general-maior Shikin, zam. nach. GlavPURKKA, with a copy to Puzin, "Svodka" for February 17-28, 1943, Moscow, April 2, 1943, and "Svodka" for April 21-30, 1943, Moscow, May 8, 1943; RGASPI, 17/125/187/52: Cherstvoi, "Otchet otdela voennoi tsenzury NKO za aprel' mesiats 1943 goda." On oblast and krai papers, see RGASPI, 17/125/117/158: I. Belousov of Krasnodar Krailit to Seleznev, secretary of Krasnodar Krai committee, Sochi, October 5, 1942. On morale, see GARF, 9425/1/207/34: Sadchikov, "Perechen' svedenii, sostavliaiushchikh voennuiu i gosudarstvennuiu tainu na vremia voiny," May 18, 1944.
2. On Stalin's disregard, see David E. Murphy, *What Stalin Knew: The Enigma of Barbarossa* (New Haven, Conn., 2005); Constantine Pleshakov, *Stalin's Folly: The Tragic First Ten Days of WWII on the Eastern Front* (New York, 2005). The quotation is from Victor Kravchenko, *I Chose Freedom: The Personal and Political Life of a Soviet Official* (New York, 1947), 359.
3. L. D. Dergacheva, "Istochnikovedcheskie problemy sovetskoi zhurnalistiki voennogo vremeni (1941-1945 gg.)," *Vestnik Moskovskogo universiteta, Seriia 8, Istoriia*, no. 2 (March-April 1999): 14.
4. RGASPI, 17/125/48/30-31: Zlobin, lieutenant general and nach. operativnogo upravleniia gen. shtaba KA, report for the evening of July 3, 1941; "Ot Sovetskogo Informbiuro (vechernee soobshchenie)," *Pravda*, July 4, 1941, 1; RGASPI, 17/125/48/40-42: General-Maior Vasilevskii, zam. nach. operativnogo upravleniia Genshtaba KA, report for the morning of July 5, 1941.
5. Dergacheva, "Istochnikovedcheskie problemy," 13.
6. RGASPI, 17/125/48/43-44, 48-53, 56-63, 67-68, 70-75, 77-83: reports for the evening of July 5 through the morning of July 11, 1941; "Ot Sovetskogo

Informbiuro," *Pravda*, July 16, 1941, 1; Jeffrey Brooks, *Thank You, Comrade Stalin! Soviet Public Culture from Revolution to Cold War* (Princeton, N.J., 2000), xvii, 161, 250, n. 15 (on the fall of Smolensk); Dergacheva, "Istochnikovedcheskie problemy," 13-14 (on Novgorod and Dnipropetrovsk).

7. Kravchenko, *I Chose Freedom*, 358; Volodymyr Pasika, *U krutezhi shalu* (Toronto, 1979), 109. See also F. Pihido-Pravoberezhnyi, *"Velyka Vitchyzniana viina"* (Winnipeg, 1954), 31.

8. Karel C. Berkhoff, *Harvest of Despair: Life and Death in Ukraine under Nazi Rule* (Cambridge, Mass., 2004), 22-23; Alexander Werth, *Russia at War, 1941–1945* (New York, 1964), 185.

9. David Ortenberg, *Stalin, Shcherbakov, Mekhlis i drugie* (Moscow, 1995), 102-104; RGASPI, 17/125/59/86, 87-92: D. Ortenberg to A. S. Shcherbakov, n.p., n.d., and manuscript Aleksei Tolstoi, "Dneprovskaia plotina," n.p., September 30, 1941. On plans for Moscow, see Berkhoff, *Harvest of Despair*, 34.

10. RGASPI, 17/125/187/39v: polkovnik Cherstvoi, nach. otdela voennoi tsenzury NKO, to general-maior Shikin, zam. nach. GlavPURKKA, with a copy to Puzin, "Svodka" for 1 po 10 April 1943, Moscow, April 15, 1943 (at issue was S. Borzenko, "Dva ordena," *Komsomol'skaia pravda*, April 4, 1943); akademik B. E. Vedeneev, "Vnov' zazhgutsia ogni Dneprogesa," *Sovetskaia Ukraina*, October 17, 1943, 3, also in Ukrainian in *Radians'ka Ukraïna* of the same date; I. Kandalov, "Dneprostroi," *Pravda*, September 22, 1944, 2; I. Kandalov, "Dneproges vozrozhdaetsia," *Trud*, October 14, 1944, 3. On Kiev's great fire, see Berkhoff, *Harvest of Despair*, 29-32.

11. A. Krasnov, "Geroicheskaia oborona stolitsy Ukrainy," *Pravda*, September 6, 1941, 2; I. Lysenko, "Kiev est' i budet sovetskim," *Pravda*, September 11, 1941, 2.

12. TASS, "Govorit Kiev: Radioperedacha iz stolitsy Ukrainy," *Izvestiia*, September 13, 1941, 1. A shorter text in Ukrainian from the Soviet Ukrainian Telegraph Agency is "Radioperedacha, prysviachena oboroni Kyieva," *Komunist*, September 14, 1941, 4; this issue has not been preserved, but a retyped copy is at TsDAHOU, 1/70/849/30-32.

13. TASS, "Radiopereklichka trekh gorodov: U mikrofona—Leningrad, Kiev, Moskva," *Pravda*, September 15, 1941, 1; A. Anatoli (Kuznetsov), *Babi Yar: A Document in the Form of a Novel*, trans. David Floyd (New York, 1970), 141, 147 (on posters); Boris Lapin and Zakhar Khatsrevin, "Kiev in Those Days" ["September 18, 1941"], in S. Krasilshchik, ed., *World War II: Dispatches from the Soviet Front*, trans. Nina Bous (New York, 1985), 17-20; Il'ia Erenburg, *Liudi, gody, zhizn': Vospominaniia v trekh tomakh*, revised and expanded ed. (n.p., 1990), 2:243.

14. "Ozhestochennye boi pod Kievom," *Pravda*, September 19, 1941, 1.

15. RGASPI, 17/125/59/60, 61-63: Ortenberg to Shcherbakov, n.p., September 18, 1941, and D. Ortenberg, "Polozhenie v Kieve. Kiev, 18 sentiabria. (Po telegrafe ot nash. spets. korr.)"; "Boi za Kiev," *Izvestiia*, September 19, 1941, 2. On ghostwriting, see also Semen Gershberg, *Zavtra gazeta vykhodit* (Moscow, 1966), 29, 413-414.
16. RGASPI, 17/125/35/89-91, published in A. Ia. Livshin and I. B. Orlov, comps., *Sovetskaia propaganda v gody Velikoi Otechestvennoi voiny: "Kommunikatsiia ubezhdeniia" i mobilizatsionnye mekhanizmy* (Moscow, 2007), 309-311; "Ot Sovetskoe Informbiuro: Vechernee soobshchenie 21 sentiabria," *Pravda*, September 22, 1942, 1.
17. Brooks, *Thank You, Comrade Stalin*, 162 (on Stalin's order); RGASPI, 17/125/59/71, 72-73: D. Ortenberg to Shcherbakov, n.p., [no later than September 28, 1941], and manuscript of I. Erenburg, "Kiev"; I. Erenburg, "Kiev," *Krasnaia zvezda*, September 27, 1941, 3; Ortenberg, *Stalin*, 60; Joshua Rubenstein, *Tangled Loyalties: The Life and Times of Ilya Ehrenburg* (London, 1996), 191.
18. Werth, *Russia at War*, 231; Ortenberg, *Stalin*, 61-62.
19. Ortenberg, *Stalin*, 62-63; quotation from Rubenstein, *Tangled Loyalties*, 192; Werth, *Russia at War*, 232.
20. V. P. Iampols'kii et al., comps., *Organy gosudarstvennoi bezopasnoti SSSR v Velikoi Otechestvennoi voine: Sbornik dokumentov*, vol. 2, book 2: *Nachalo: 1 sentiabria–31 dekabria 1941 goda* (Moscow, 2000), 207; Brooks, *Thank You, Comrade Stalin*, 162; Werth, *Russia at War*, 233, 238; Rebecca Manley, *To the Tashkent Station: Evacuation and Survival in the Soviet Union at War* (Ithaca, N.Y., 2009), 61-63, 107-117; Gershberg, *Zavtra gazeta vykhodit*, 55-56.
21. "Postanovlenie Gosudarstvennogo Komiteta Oborony," *Pravda*, October 20, 1941, 1, also in *Izvestiia*, October 21, 1941, 1. On bombings, see "Nalet nemetskikh samoletov na Moskvu," *Izvestiia*, October 24, 1941, 3, October 25, 1941, 3, and October 29, 1941, 3. Compare RGASPI, 558/11/490/1-3: [Sovinformbiuro,] "O rezul'tatakh naletov nemetskikh samoletov na Moskvu v noch' na 22, 23 i 24 iiulia s 22 iiulia po 6 avgusta." On portraits, see Brooks, *Thank You, Comrade Stalin*, 162-163; Ortenberg, *Stalin*, 147-148.
22. Il'ia Erenburg, "Chudo," *Krasnaia zvezda*, February 8, 1942, reprinted in Il'ia Erenburg, *Voina (Iiun' 1941–aprel' 1942)* (Moscow, 1942), 350.
23. "Otstuplenie fashistskikh voisk ot Moskvy (Snimok dostavlen s Mozhaiskogo napravleniia)," *Pravda*, December 31, 1941, 2; Deutsch-Russisches Museum Berlin-Karlshorst, *Beutestücke: Kriegsgefangene in der deutschen und sowjetischen Fotografie 1941–1945* (n.p., 2003), 58, 106.
24. I. Stalin, *O Velikoi Otechestvennoi voine Sovetskogo Soiuza*, 4th ed. (Moscow, 1944), 20, 36.

25. "God razgroma nemetskikh zakhvatchikov," *Trud*, January 1, 1942, 1. For the letter, see 2.
26. Stalin, *O Velikoi Otechestvennoi voine Sovetskogo Soiuza*, 54; "Novyi period otechestvennoi voiny," editorial, *Izvestiia*, May 6, 1942, 1; "God voiny," editorial, *Pravda*, June 22, 1942, 1 (the quotation); "Vrag budet razgromlen v 1942 godu," editorial, *Izvestiia*, June 21, 1942, 1; Aleksei Tolstoi, "Ubei zveria!," *Pravda*, June 23, 1942, 2.
27. For the draft and the final version, see RGASPI, 558/11/490/23-24. On travel to Voronezh, see Boris Ol'shanskii, *My prikhodim s Vostoka (1941–1951)* (Buenos Aires, 1954), 71-74.
28. E. Kriger, "Vrag neset bol'shie poteri," *Izvestiia*, May 24, 1942, 1; V. Safonov, "Ogromnye poteri nemetsko-fashistskikh voisk na Izium-Barvenkovskom napravlenii," *Izvestiia*, May 26, 1942, 1; M. Ruzov, "Upornye boi na Izium-Barvenkovskom napravlenii," *Izvestiia*, May 29, 1942, 2; Brooks, *Thank You, Comrade Stalin*, 164, 289, n. 44; "O boiakh na Khar'kovskom napravlenii," *Pravda*, May 31, 1942, 1.
29. B. I. Gavrilov, "V Miasnom Boru, v 'Doline smerti,'" *Otechestvennaia istoriia*, no. 3 (May–June 2004): 3-13.
30. Werth, *Russia at War*, 375; Ortenberg, *Stalin*, 86.
31. Werth, *Russia at War*, 376; Ortenberg, *Stalin*, 84; Sovinformbiuro, "250 dnei geroicheskoi oborony Sevastopolia: Nashi voiska ostavili Sevastopol'," *Pravda*, July 4, 1942, 1; Aleksei Tolstoi, "Flag Sevastopolia," *Izvestiia*, July 5, 1942, 2.
32. A. A. Cherkasov, "O formirovanii i primenenii v Krasnoi armii zagradotriadov," *Voprosy istorii*, no. 2 (2003): 174-175; Nina Tumarkin, *The Living and the Dead: The Rise and Fall of the Cult of World War II in Russia* (New York, 1994), 103; Catherine Merridale, *Ivan's War: The Red Army 1939–1945* (London, 2005), 134, 136. For views, see John Barber, "The Image of Stalin in Soviet Propaganda and Public Opinion during World War 2," in John Garrard and Carol Garrard, eds., *World War 2 and the Soviet People: Selected Papers from the Fourth World Congress for Soviet and East European Studies, Harrogate, 1990* (New York, 1993), 46; Ol'shanskii, *My prikhodim s Vostoka*, 92. The one historian is B. V. Sokolov, *Tainy vtoroi mirovoi* (Moscow, 2001), 432.
33. RGASPI, 17/125/186/101: "Perechen' svedenii, sostavliaiushchikh voennuiu tainu (na voennoe vremia). Proekt," [1943?]; GARF, 9425/1/207/32-34: Sadchikov, "Perechen' svedenii."
34. Quotations from Werth, *Russia at War*, 392-393, and *Pravda*, July 30, 1942, 1.
35. Ortenberg, *Stalin*, 89-91.
36. Werth, *Russia at War*, 393-394. On 1941, see Viktor Cherepanov, *Vlast' i voina: Stalinskii mekhanizm gosudarstvennogo upravleniia v Velikoi Otechest-*

vennoi voine (Moscow, 2006), 56–57; Sokolov, *Tainy vtoroi mirovoi*, 429–431.

37. S. A. Gerasimova, "Pervaia Rzhevsko-Sychevskaia nastupatel'naia operatsiia 1942 goda (novyi vzgliad)," *Voprosy istorii*, no. 5 (2005): 16–29; David M. Glantz, *Zhukov's Greatest Defeat: The Red Army's Epic Disaster in Operation Mars, 1942* (Lawrence, Kan., 1999); Werth, *Russia at War*, 369 (on consternation).

38. Werth, *Russia at War*, 450, 456–458; Deutsch-Russisches Museum Berlin-Karlshorst, *Stalingrad erinnern: Stalingrad im deutschen und im russischen Gedächtnis* (n.p., 2003), 31.

39. Sovinformbiuro, "Itogi 6-nedel'nogo nastupleniia nashikh voisk na podstupakh Stalingrada," *Pravda*, January 1, 1943, 1; RGASPI, 558/11/490/33–40: draft sent by Shcherbakov to Stalin on December 31, 1942. For Stalin, see Stalin, *O Velikoi Otechestvennoi voine Sovetskogo Soiuza*, 79. For January 30, see "V poslednii chas. Uspeshnoe nastuplenie nashikh voisk zapadnee Voronezha," *Pravda*, January 30, 1943, 1. One draft dated January 29 spoke of "up to 2*015*.000" "enemy" military killed; another of "over 1*514*.000" "enemy *German* soldiers and officers" taken captive. The parts in italic are handwritten modifications and additions. See RGASPI, 558/11/490/43–46.

40. Sovinformbiuro, "V poslednii chas: Nashi voiska polnost'iu zakonchili likvidatsiiu nemetsko-fashistskikh voisk, okruzhennykh v raione Stalingrada," *Pravda*, February 3, 1943, 1; also "Moskva, Verkhovnomu Glavnokomanduiushchemu tovarishchu STALINU," *Pravda*, February 3, 1943, 1. For the four drafts, see RGASPI, 558/11/490/52–63.

41. *Trud*, February 3, 1943, 1 (the photograph); "Istoricheskaia pobeda Krasnoi Armii," editorial, *Pravda*, February 4, 1943, 1, cited in *Stalingrad erinnern*, 28; "Gitlerovskie glavari vstrevozheny: Vystuplenie Gebbel'sa v Berline," *Trud*, February 20, 1943, 4.

42. Sovinformbiuro, "Dva goda Otechestvennoi voiny Sovetskogo Soiuza (Ko vtoroi godovshchiny Otechestvennoi voiny)," *Trud*, June 22, 1943, 1; Stalin, *O Velikoi Otechestvennoi voine Sovetskogo Soiuza*, 104; *Stalingrad erinnern*, 28–29; RGASPI, 558/11/491/60, 61–67: "Itogi trekhmesiachnogo nastupleniia Krasnoi Armii (s 12 iiulia po 12 oktiabria 1943 goda)."

43. A. S. Iakovlev, *Tsel' zhizni: Zapiski aviakonstruktora*, 5th revised and expanded ed. (Moscow, 1987), 273; editorial, *Radians'ka Ukraïna*, February 17, 1943, 1; "Misto vidrodzhuiet'sia," *Radians'ka Ukraïna*, February 24, 1943, 1.

44. "Ot Sovetskogo Informbiuro," *Pravda*, March 17, 1943, 1.

45. Il'ia Erenburg, "Khar'kov," *Krasnaia zvezda*, March 16, 1943, reprinted in Il'ia Erenburg, *Voina (Aprel' 1942–mart 1943)* (Moscow, 1943), 284–285. After Kharkiv was definitely retaken on August 23, 1943, Ehrenburg ascribed

its second loss to stretched supply lines, bad roads, and fatigue. Il'ia Erenburg, "Khar'kov," *Krasnaia zvezda*, August 24, 1943, reprinted in Il'ia Erenburg, *Voina (aprel' 1943–mart 1944)* (Moscow, 1944), 323-325.

46. "Ot Sovetskogo Informbiuro: Operativnaia svodka za 13 noiabria," *Trud*, November 14, 1943, 1; "Zhitomir nash!," *Trud*, November 14, 1943, 2; "Ot Sovetskogo Informbiuro: Operativnaia svodka za 18 noiabria," *Trud*, November 19, 1943, 1; "Ot Sovetskogo Informbiuro: Operativnaia svodka za 19 noiabria," *Trud*, November 20, 1943, 1.

47. See, respectively, GARF, 9425/1/108/20: Sadchikov, "Svodka No 1 vycherkov, proizvedennykh tsenzorami v poriadke predvaritel'nogo i posleduiushchego kontrolia, po materialam na 15-e ianvaria 1942 goda"; GARF, 9425/1/108/2; RGASPI, 17/125/187/100v: Sadchikov, "Svodka iz"iatii tsenzury iz predstavlennykh i pechati i peredache po radio materialov i oshibok pechati, obnaruzhennykh posleduiushchim kontorlem za vremia s 10 iiunia po 15 avgusta 1943 goda" (copy sent to Aleksandrov), no later than August 20, 1943; RGASPI, 17/125/187/103: Sadchikov, "Svodka iz"iatii tsenzury iz predstavlennykh i pechati i peredache po radio materialov, a takzhe iz"iatii iz inostrannoi literatury za vremia s 15 avgusta po 5 sentiabria 1943 goda" (copy sent to Aleksandrov), September 15, 1943; GARF, 9425/1/108/63: "Svodka vazhneishikh iz"iatii" (on a cut made in March 1942).

48. N. G. Sadchikov, *Strogo khranit' tainy sotsialisticheskogo gosudarstva* (Moscow, 1942), 6, filed at RGASPI, 17/125/117/39v. On the battalion, see GARF, 9425/1/43/7: "Otchet o rabote Otdela posleduiushchei tsenzury Soiuza SSR za 1-i kvartal 1942 g."

49. GARF, 9425/1/43/7: "Otchet o rabote Otdela posleduiushchei tsenzury Soiuza SSR za 1-i kvartal 1942 g."

50. Sadchikov, *Strogo khranit' tainy*, 3, filed at RGASPI, 17/125/117/38, with regard to Vsev. Azarov, "Slovo baltiitsev," *Izvestiia*, February 23, 1942, 4; GARF, 9425/1/108/115-116: "Svodka . . . ," July 29, 1942, with regard to "Ekspeditsiia v Arktiku," *Izvestiia*, July 14, 1942, 3.

51. Ortenberg, *Stalin*, 151.

52. Gershberg, *Zavtra gazeta vykhodit*, 28-29.

53. GARF, 9425/1/207/51: Sadchikov, "Perechen' svedenii"; Sadchikov, *Strogo khranit' tainy*, 31-32, filed at RGASPI, 17/125/117/52-52v.

54. For example, "Razmery territorii, osvobozhdennoi Krasnoi Armiei ot nemetskoi okkupatsii za period s 12 iiulia po 5 noiabria 1943 g.," *Izvestiia*, November 5, 1943, 2; *Trud*, November 5, 1943, 2; RGASPI, 558/11/204/68, 69: Shcherbakov to Stalin, August 2, 1944, and map; "Razmery okkupirovannoi nemtsami territorii, osvobozhdennoi Krasnoi Armiei ot nemetskikh

i finskikh zakhvatchikov s 23 iiunia po 2 avgusta 1944 goda," *Pravda*, August 3, 1944, 2.

55. Tumarkin, *The Living and the Dead*, 39, 228; Suzanne Ament, "Sing to Victory: The Role of Popular Song in the Soviet Union during World War II" (Ph.D. dissertation, Indiana University, 1996), 13-14; Richard Overy, *Why the Allies Won* (New York, 1996), 76. On the broadcast, see RGASPI, 17/125/117/147v-148: N. Sadchikov to G. F. Aleksandrov, August 7, 1942. About exceptions, see RGASPI, 17/125/187/20: Prikaz Otdela voennoi tsenzury NKO, no. 3, Moscow, March 5, 1943; G. V. Kostyrchenko, "Sovetskaia tsenzura v 1941-1952 godakh," *Voprosy istorii*, nos. 11-12 (1996): 90. For the removal, see GARF, 9425/1/192/4v: A. Burtakov, "Svodka tsenzorskikh vmeshchatel'stv po otdelu radiotsenzury za fevral' 1943 goda." About another excision, see RGASPI, 17/125/187/100: Sadchikov, "Svodka iz"iatii tsenzury."

56. Anna Krylova, *Soviet Women in Combat: A History of Violence on the Eastern Front* (Cambridge, U.K., 2010), 61-62, 65, 82, 89, 101, 104-107, 112-113, 119, 143, 146, 158-159, 168-169, 217, 222-225, 227; Euridice Charon Cardona and Roger D. Markwick, "'Our Brigade Will Not Be Sent to the Front': Soviet Women under Arms in the Great Fatherland War, 1941-45," *Russian Review* 68, no. 2 (April 2009): 242-243, 247. For the censorship rule, see RGASPI, 17/125/186/98: "Perechen' svedenii"; GARF, 9425/1/207/21: Sadchikov, "Perechen' svedenii." For a cut with regard to radio, April 9, 1942, see GARF, 9425/1/108/67-68: draft, "Iz"iatiia svedenii, sostavliaiushchikh voennuiu tainu."

57. Olga Kucherenko, *Little Soldiers: How Soviet Children Went to War, 1941–1945* (Oxford, 2011), 2; GARF, 9425/1/108/1: P. Galdin, zam. nachal'nika Glavlita, "Svodka No 1 vycherkov, proizvedennykh tsenzorami GLAVLITA v poriadke predvaritel'nogo kontrolia nad pechatnoi produktsiei g. Moskvy"; RGASPI, 17/125/187/102: polkovnik Cherstvoi, nach. otdela voennoi tsenzury NKO, to general-maior Shikin, zam. nach. GlavPURKKA, with copies to Puzin and Sadchikov, "Svodka" for August 21-31, 1943, Moscow, September 6, 1943.

58. Ortenberg, *Stalin*, 145-146, 148-149.

59. Ibid., 72-76.

60. GARF, 9425/1/207/75: Sadchikov, "Perechen' svedenii" (on the rule); GARF, 9425/1/108/72: "Svodka vazhneishikh iz"iatii" (on Azerbaijani radio); RGASPI, 17/125/187/3: Cherstvoi of Otdel voennoi tsenzury NKO to Zam. nach. GlavPURKKA, January 19, 1943, with regard to Grossman in *Krasnaia zvezda*, January 1, 1943; RGASPI, 17/125/187/80-80v: polkovnik Cherstvoi, nach. otdela voennoi tsenzury NKO, to general-maior Shikin,

61. zam. nach. GlavPURKKA, with copies to Puzin and Sadchikov, "Svodka" for June 21-30, 1943, Moscow, July 6, 1943; RGASPI, 17/125/187/79v (on Soviet use of flamethrowers).
61. B. Galin, "Znamia vernulos' v polk," *Krasnaia zvezda*, June 9, 1943; RGASPI, 17/125/187/64-64v: Cherstvoi, nach. of the Otdel voennoi tsenzury NKO, to Shcherbakov, nach. of GlavPURKKA, original, Moscow, June 9, 1943; for a copy, see RGASPI, 17/125/186/70-70v; Ortenberg, *Stalin*, 63-67.
62. Ortenberg, *Stalin*, 120-121; O. A. Rzeshevskii, ed., *Kto byl kto v Velikoi Otechestvennoi voine 1941–1945: Liudi, sobytiia, fakty. Spravochnik*, expanded 2nd ed. (Moscow, 2000), 164. An interview with Maresiev conducted in Moscow in 1999 is in Albert Axell, *Russia's Heroes* (New York, 2002), 187-192.
63. Vasilii Grossman, "Narod bessmerten," *Krasnaia zvezda*, 1942, nos. 168-170, 172-177, 180-188, translated as "The People Immortal" in Vassili Grossman, *The Years of War (1941–1945)*, trans. Elizabeth Donnelly and Rose Prokofiev (Moscow, 1946), 9-151; *A Writer at War: Vasily Grossman with the Red Army, 1941–1945*, ed. and trans. Antony Beevor and Luba Vinogradova (London, 2005), 211, 235-236, 269. On the cut from K. Simonov, "Syn Aksin'i Ivanovny," *Krasnaia zvezda*, March 27, 1943, see RGASPI, 17/125/187/38: polkovnik Cherstvoi, nach. otdela voennoi tsenzury NKO, to generalmaior Shikin, zam. nach. GlavPURKKA, with a copy to Puzin, "Svodka" for 21 po 31 March 1943, Moscow, April 2, 1943.
64. Vicki Goldberg, *The Power of Photography: How Photographs Changed Our Lives* (New York, 1991), 196, 198-199; Ortenberg, *Stalin*, 167-168.
65. Marina Sorokina, "People and Procedures: Toward a History of the Investigation of Nazi Crimes in the USSR," *Kritika* 6, no. 4 (Fall 2005): 812; A. N. Ponomarev, *Aleksandr Shcherbakov: Stranitsy biografii* (Moscow, 2004), 214-215.
66. "Ot Sovetskogo Informbiuro (vechernee soobshchenie 13 iiulia)," *Pravda*, July 14, 1941, 2; "Arabskie skazki nemetskogo verkhovnogo komandovaniia ili shestinedel'nye itogi voiny," *Pravda*, August 8, 1941, 1; *Pravda*, September 26, 1941, 1.
67. Respectively, 830,000; 170,000; 510,000; and 150,000. "Dvukhmesiachnye itogi voiny mezhdu gitlerovskoi Germaniei i Sovetskim Soiuzom," *Pravda*, August 23, 1941, 1; RGASPI, 88/1/989/16, compare 3, 7, 22, 26, 38: drafts of the Sovinformbiuro statement for the evening of August 22, 1941.
68. A. S. Shcherbakov, "Gitler obmanyvaet nemetskii narod," *Pravda*, October 5, 1941, 1. These figures are also in the unpublished draft document filed at RGASPI, 88/1/991/6: "Tri mesiatsa boev protiv nemetsko-fashistskikh voisk."

69. Stalin, *O Velikoi Otechestvennoi voine Sovetskogo Soiuza*, 18; Sovinformbiuro, "Smekhotvornye izmyshleniia gitlerovskikh fal'shivomonetchikov o poteriakh sovetskikh voisk," *Pravda*, November 26, 1941, 1.
70. Sovinformbiuro, "Politicheskie i voennye itogi goda Otechestvennoi voiny," *Pravda*, June 23, 1942, 1; Sergei Kudriashov, ed. in chief, *Vestnik Arkhiva Prezidenta Rossiiskoi Federatsii: Voina, 1941–1945* (Moscow, 2010), 197–198; Sovinformbiuro, "Lzhivaia vydumka nemetsko-fashistskikh moshennikov," *Trud*, February 25, 1943, 1.
71. Sovinformbiuro, "Dva goda Otechestvennoi voiny Sovetskogo Soiuza (Ko vtoroi godovshchiny Otechestvennoi voiny)," *Trud*, June 22, 1943, 1; "Tri goda otechestvennoi voiny Sovetskogo Soiuza (voennye i politcheskie itogi)," *Pravda*, June 22, 1944, 1. A first draft for the second article referred to 5.3 million "killed and missing in action" (strikethroughs on the original). See RGASPI, 558/11/491/97: "Tri goda otechestvennoi voiny Sovetskogo Soiuza (voennye i politcheskie itogi)."
72. "Ot Sovetskogo Informbiuro (vechernee soobshchenie 13 iiulia)," *Pravda*, July 14, 1941, 2; "Arabskie skazki nemetskogo verkhovnogo komandovaniia ili shestinedel'nye itogi voiny," *Pravda*, August 8, 1941, 1; "V poslednii chas. Amerikanskii radiokommentator o germanskikh poteriakh na vostochnom fronte," *Pravda*, August 8, 1941, 1.
73. "Dvukhmesiachnye itogi voiny mezhdu gitlerovskoi Germaniei i Sovetskim Soiuzom," *Pravda*, August 23, 1941, 1; RGASPI, 88/1/989/3, 6, 12, 19, 27, 34: drafts of Sovinformbiuro statement for the evening of August 22, 1941; A. S. Shcherbakov, "Gitler obmanyvaet nemetskii narod," *Pravda*, October 5, 1941, 1; Il'ia Erenburg, "Na cherepakh," [*Krasnaia zvezda*], October 7, 1941, reprinted in Erenburg, *Voina (Iiun' 1941–aprel' 1942)*, 99. Not published was RGASPI, 88/1/991/6: "Tri mesiatsa boev protiv nemetsko-fashistskikh voisk," which also mentioned "over three million" German losses.
74. Stalin, *O Velikoi Otechestvennoi voine Sovetskogo Soiuza*, 18, 36; Kostyrchenko, "Sovetskaia tsenzura," 88; Sovinformbiuro, "Smekhotvornye izmyshleniia gitlerovskikh fal'shivomonetchikov o poteriakh sovetskikh voisk," *Pravda*, November 26, 1941, 1.
75. Sovinformbiuro, "Politicheskie i voennye itogi goda Otechestvennoi voiny," *Pravda*, June 23, 1942, 1; Stalin, *O Velikoi Otechestvennoi voine Sovetskogo Soiuza*, 75, 84. In October 1942, the Red Army's General Staff put the German losses at 9,330,000, including 3,188,000 killed; see Kudriashov, *Vestnik Arkhiva Prezidenta Rossiiskoi Federatsii*, 197–189.
76. In February 1943 Stalin and a Bureau statement claimed that during the previous three months at all sectors of the front (not only at Stalingrad),

the Red Army had killed "over 700,000" and captured "over 300,000" enemy military. See Stalin, *O Velikoi Otechestvennoi voine Sovetskogo Soiuza*, 84; Sovinformbiuro, "Lzhivaia vydumka nemetsko-fashistskikh moshennikov," *Trud*, February 25, 1943, 1. One month later the Bureau said that at least 52,000 German soldiers and officers had been killed in recent fighting between the Northern Donets and the Dnieper Rivers. (The report obfuscated the Soviet loss of the Northern Donets region, but added that from the Red Army 36,722 were killed or went missing in action—a suspiciously precise count.) See Sovinformbiuro, "Eshche odna fal'shivka gitlerovskogo komandovaniia," *Pravda*, March 24, 1943, 1. In April 1943 the Bureau looked back at the Red Army's winter campaign and noted that from November 10, 1942, through March 1943 "over 850,000" enemy soldiers and officers were killed and 343,525 were captured. See Sovinformbiuro, "Itogi zimnei kampanii Krasnoi Armii (s 10 noiabria 1942 goda po 31 marta 1943 goda)," *Pravda*, April 3, 1943, 1; RGASPI, 558/11/490/86–98: drafts with the figures 800,000 and 403,525. In September German losses in the two months since July 5 were declared to be "no less than 1,500,000" killed and wounded, of whom the dead were "over 420,000." The Red Army had taken 38,600 prisoners. See Sovinformbiuro, "Poteri nemetsko-fashistskikh voisk na sovetsko-germanskom fronte za vremia s 5 iiulia po 5 sentiabria," *Pravda*, September 8, 1943, 1; RGASPI, 558/11/491/55, 57, 59: drafts with other figures. In November Stalin declared that 147,200 German military and only 46,700 Red Army members had been "buried" after Stalingrad and that just within the previous year the German armed forces at the Soviet-German front had lost "over four million," including "no less than 1,800,000 killed." See Stalin, *O Velikoi Otechestvennoi voine Sovetskogo Soiuza*, 103–104, 119.

77. Sovinformbiuro, "Dva goda Otechestvennoi voiny Sovetskogo Soiuza (Ko vtoroi godovshchiny Otechestvennoi voiny)," *Trud*, June 22, 1943, 1; RGASPI, 558/11/491/27, 15, 34: two drafts of Sovinformbiuro statement "Dva goda Vel. Ot. voiny Sov. Soiuza," with accompanying notes by Shcherbakov to Stalin dated June 15 and 20, 1943, and a note by Stalin.

78. A draft mentioned "over 8,000,000." "Tri goda otechestvennoi voiny Sovetskogo Soiuza (voennye i politcheskie itogi)," *Pravda*, June 22, 1944, 1; RGASPI, 558/11/491/97: "Tri goda otechestvennoi voiny Sovetskogo Soiuza (voennye i politcheskie itogi)," draft.

79. In 1946 Stalin was to speak in public of seven million Soviet dead, including civilians. To his inner circle he seems to have spoken of 30 million, two-thirds of whom Russians. Brooks, *Thank You, Comrade Stalin*, 163; Cherepanov, *Vlast' i voina*, 151. On the problems with counting how

many Soviet soldiers (and civilians) died in the war, see V. G. Pervyshin, "Liudskie poteri v Velikoi Otechestvennoi voine," *Voprosy istorii*, no. 7 (2000): 116–122; Sokolov, *Tainy vtoroi mirovoi*, 219–272; Michael Haynes, "Counting Soviet Deaths in the Great Patriotic War: A Note," *Europe-Asia Studies* 55, no. 2 (May 2003): 303–309; the discussion by Mark Harrison and Michael Haynes in *Europe-Asia Studies*, no. 6 (September 2003): 939–947; and Niels Bo Poulsen, "The Soviet Extraordinary State Commission on War Crimes: An Analysis of the Commission's Investigative Work in War and Post-War Stalinist Society" (Ph.D. dissertation, Copenhagen University, 2004), 333–337.

80. S. V. Kormilitsyn and A. V. Lysev, comps., *Lozh' ot Sovetskogo Informbiuro* (St. Petersburg, 2005), 14.
81. Katharine Hodgson, *Written with the Bayonet: Soviet Russian Poetry of World War Two* (Liverpool, 1996), 149; "'Umrem, no ne otstupim!,'" *Trud*, February 13, 1942, 2.
82. GARF, 6903/1/82/107–109: Hero Sergei Ivanovich Shershavin to his brother, broadcast text for 8:45 A.M., December 1, 1943.
83. Berel Lang, *The Future of the Holocaust: Between History and Memory* (Ithaca, N.Y., 1999), 123 (on the definition); editorial, *Pravda*, July 30, 1942, 1.
84. "Mesto literatora v Otechestvennoi voine," *Literaturnaia gazeta*, August 20, 1941, 1, quoted in Hodgson, *Written with the Bayonet*, 149; V. A. Zolotarev et al., eds., *Russkii arkhiv: Velikaia Otechestvennaia*, vol. 17-6 (Moscow, 1996), 162–163.
85. GARF, 6903/1/100/31–33: "Stenogramma soveshchaniia u predsedatelia vsesoiuznogo radiokomiteta po voprosu o rabote 'Poslednikh izvestii' 15 maia 1944 goda," n.p., n.d.; G. A. Kovalev, "Sovinformbiuro v gody Velikoi Otechestvennoi voiny," *Voprosy istorii*, no. 6 (June 1987): 16.
86. In original usage, *boitsy N-skoi chasti*. The press also did not publish the names of population points of military significance, even if located in the hinterland. The rules for the military press were as follows: all localities were anonymous; army and division papers could mention the names, ranks, and postings of commanders of battalions or smaller units; and front and military district (*okrug*) papers could mention the names, ranks, and postings of commanders of regiments. N. G. Sadchikov, *O nekotorykh voprosakh raboty tsenzury vo vremia voiny* (Moscow, 1942), 7–9, 12–13, filed at RGASPI, 17/125/117/61v–62, 63v–64. See also the report at RGASPI, 17/125/127/22–25.
87. GARF, 9425/1/207/77: Sadchikov, "Perechen' svedenii." On Gofman, see "Zrelost' komandira," *Krasnaia zvezda*, June 19, 1944; and RGASPI, 17/125/187/71: polkovnik Cherstvoi, nach. otdela voennoi tsenzury NKO,

to general-maior Shikin, zam. nach. GlavPURKKA, with copies to Puzin and Sadchikov, "Svodka" for June 11-20, 1943, Moscow, June 27, 1943.
88. RGASPI, 17/125/187/55: Cherstvoi, "Otchet otdela voennoi tsenzury NKO za aprel' mesiats 1943 goda," with regard to Iu. Rodichev, "Posledniaia ochered' pulemetchika D'iachenko."
89. Sokolov, *Tainy vtoroi mirovoi*, 410, 419.
90. "Ot Sovetskogo Informbiuro (vechernee soobshchenie 5 iiulia)," *Pravda*, July 6, 1941, 1 (the long quotation); "Obrashchenie voinov-belorussov k partizanam i partizankam, ko vsemu belorusskomu narodu," *Pravda*, August 8, 1943, 3; H. Shcharbatau, "Hastelautsy," *Zviazda*, July 25, 1944, 4; Rzeshevskii, *Kto byl kto*, 66–67; Elena S. Seniavskaia, "Heroic Symbols: The Reality and Mythology of War," *Russian Studies in History* 37, no. 1 (Summer 1998): 73, 86, n. 86.
91. Rzeshevskii, *Kto byl kto*, 243; Seniavskaia, "Heroic Symbols," 73, 86, n. 18; Tat'iana Goriaeva and Aleksandr Sherel', "Vnimanie, govorit pobeda! Sovetskoe radio v gody Velikoi Otechestvennoi voiny," *Televidenie i radioveshchanie*, no. 4 (1985): 11; "Obrashchenie . . . ," *Pravda*, August 8, 1943, 3. For a contemporary interview with Talalikhin by a correspondent of CBS Radio (through an interpreter), see Erskine Caldwell, *All-Out on the Road to Smolensk* (New York, 1942), 127–130. The British case of the pilot Ray Holmes, acting in defense of London in September 1940, possibly explains the lack of skepticism in the account of Soviet air ramming in Axell, *Russia's Heroes*, 121–132.
92. V. Chernyshev, "Slava besstrashnym patriotam," *Komsomol'skaia pravda*, November 26, 1941; V. Koroteev, "Gvardeitsy Panfilova v boiakh za Moskvu," *Krasnaia zvezda*, November 27, 1941. The obituary is "Pamiati general-maiora I. V. Panfilova," *Krasnaia zvezda*, November 21, 1941. Apart from these sources and those mentioned below, my discussion of the Panfilovites is based on N. Petrov and O. Edel'man, "Novoe o sovetskikh geroiakh," *Novyi mir*, no. 6 (1997): 144–149; G. K. Kumanev, *Podvig i podlog: Stranitsy Velikoi Otechestvennoi voiny, 1941–1945 gg.* (Moscow, 2000), 125–137, 155, 158–159, 161; Sokolov, *Tainy vtoroi mirovoi*, 379–395, 406. On Klochkov's words, see also Boris Efimov, *Desiat' desiatiletii: O tom, chto videl, perezhil, zapomnil* (Moscow, 2000), 337–338.
93. "Moskovskaia oblast' ochishchena ot gitlerovskogo zver'ia," editorial, *Pravda*, January 27, 1942, 1. See also *Izvestiia*, January 22, 1942.
94. GARF, 6903/1/60/18: Polikarpov to Shcherbakov, n.p., October 27, 1942.
95. Sokolov, *Tainy vtoroi mirovoi*, 395–407.
96. Ibid., 408–409, 411; "Velikii podvig Aleksandra Matrosova," editorial, *Pravda*, March 6, 1943, 1, summarized in I. I. Shirokorad, *Tsentral'naia*

periodicheskaia pechat' v gody Velikoi Otechestvennoi voiny. 1941–1945 (Moscow, 2001), 119.

97. Sokolov, *Tainy vtoroi mirovoi*, 409; Rzeshevskii, *Kto byl kto*, 166–167; Seniavskaia, "Heroic Symbols," 74, 86, n. 86; "Prikaz Narodnogo Komissara Oborony," *Trud*, September 11, 1943, 1; Rosalinde Sartorti, "On the Making of Heroes, Heroines, and Saints," in Richard Stites, ed., *Culture and Entertainment in Wartime Russia* (Bloomington, Ind., 1995), 181.
98. As also noted in Brooks, *Thank You, Comrade Stalin*, 162.
99. I owe this insight to David Brandenberger. For the study, see Siân Nicholas, *The Echo of War: Home Front Propaganda and the Wartime BBC, 1939–45* (Manchester, 1996), 199. For the engineer's letter, see Livshin and Orlov, *Sovetskaia propaganda*, 587.
100. Sokolov, *Tainy vtoroi mirovoi*, 424.
101. Ilya Ehrenburg, *The War: 1941–1945* (Cleveland, 1964), 78, quoted in Tumarkin, *The Living and the Dead*, 78; Ortenberg, *Stalin*, 63–67, 89.
102. Maurice Hindus, *Mother Russia* (London, 1943), 16, quoted from a different edition in Lisa A. Kirschenbaum, "'Our City, Our Hearts, Our Families': Local Loyalties and Private Life in Soviet World War II Propaganda," *Slavic Review* 59, no. 4 (Winter 2000): 829; Vsevolod Vishnevskii, *Leningrad: Dnevniki voennykh let. 2 noiabria 1941 goda–31 dekabria 1942 goda* (Moscow, 2002), 1:184.
103. See, respectively, James von Geldern, "Radio Moscow: The Voice from the Center," in Stites, *Culture and Entertainment*, 51; Sartorti, "On the Making of Heroes," 190; Tumarkin, *The Living and the Dead*, 78.
104. Seniavskaia, "Heroic Symbols," 81–83 (the quotations); E. S. Seniavskaia, *Protivniki Rossii v voinakh XX veka: Evoliutsiia "obraza vraga" v soznanii armii i obshchestva* (Moscow, 2006), 96–97.
105. Sokolov, *Tainy vtoroi mirovoi*, 407.

3. A Single Forced Labor Camp

1. V. T. Aniskov, *Krest'ianstvo protiv fashizma. 1941–1945: Istoriia i psikhologiia podviga* (Moscow, 2003), 20–21, 360, 364; V. F. Zima, *Mentalitet narodov Rossii v voine 1941–1945 godov* (Moscow, 2000), 211.
2. I. Stalin, *O Velikoi Otechestvennoi voine Sovetskogo Soiuza*, 4th ed. (Moscow, 1944), 12–13.
3. Peter H. Solomon Jr., *Soviet Criminal Justice under Stalin* (Cambridge, U.K., 1996), 300–301.
4. Ibid., 307; Donald Filtzer, *Soviet Workers and Late Stalinism: Labour and the Restoration of the Stalinist System after World War II* (Cambridge, U.K., 2002), 161, 163.

5. Victor Kravchenko, *I Chose Freedom: The Personal and Political Life of a Soviet Official* (New York, 1947), 406-407; Filtzer, *Soviet Workers*, 34, 36.
6. *Pravda*, June 27, 1941.
7. S. V. Tochenov, "Volneniia i zabastovki na tekstil'nykh predpriiatiiakh Ivanovskoi oblasti osen'iu 1941 goda," *Otechestvennaia istoriia*, no. 3 (May–June 2004): 42-47. A publication of two of the relevant documents, from RGASPI, 17/88/45/12-36, 37-50, is A. Ia. Livshin and I. B. Orlov, comps., *Sovetskaia povsednevnost' i massovoe soznanie: 1939–1945* (Moscow, 2003), 37-54.
8. Filtzer, *Soviet Workers*, 161-162; John Barber and Mark Harrison, *The Soviet Home Front, 1941–1945: A Social and Economic History of the USSR in World War II* (London, 1991), 164-165, 173; "Trudovaia distsiplina v gody voiny," *Istoricheskii arkhiv* 8, no. 2 (2000): 122.
9. Filtzer, *Soviet Workers*, 35; V. A. Somov, *Po zakonam voennogo vremeni: Ocherki istorii trudovoi politiki SSSR v gody Velikoi Otechestvennoi voiny (1941–1945 gg.). Monografiia* (Nizhnii Novgorod, 2001), 32, 51.
10. "Ukaz Prezidiuma Verkhovnogo Soveta SSSR: O mobilizatsii na period voennogo vremeni trudosposobnogo gorodskogo naseleniia dlia raboty na proizvodstve i stroitel'stve," *Pravda*, February 14, 1942, 1. Also in *Izvestiia*, February 14, 1942, 1, and *Trud*, February 15, 1942, 1.
11. "V Sovnarkome SSSR i TsK VKP(b)," *Pravda*, April 17, 1942, 1; also in *Izvestiia*, April 17, 1942, 1, and *Trud*, April 18, 1942, 1. For the prior minimum labor days, see Barber and Harrison, *The Soviet Home Front*, 168. On prosecution, see Jean Lévesque, *Exile and Discipline: The June 1948 Campaign against Collective Farm Shirkers*, The Carl Beck Papers in Russian and East European Studies, No. 1708 (Pittsburgh, 2006), 10; M. A. Vyltsan, "Command and Homily: Ways of Mobilizing Village Resources during the War," *Russian Studies in History* 37, no. 1 (Summer 1998): 27-28; Barber and Harrison, *The Soviet Home Front*, 168-169.
12. "V Sovnarkome SSSR i TsK VKP(b)," *Pravda*, April 17, 1942, 1; also in *Izvestiia*, April 17, 1942, 1, and *Trud*, April 18, 1942, 1.
13. Stalin, *O Velikoi Otechestvennoi voine Sovetskogo Soiuza*, 47. On November 6, 1941, he had implied that this camp was still in the making. See 20, 33.
14. The Russian term is *trudovaia povinnost'*. Somov, *Po zakonam voennogo vremeni*, 34, 55-56, 80-81, 124.
15. Filtzer, *Soviet Workers*, 162.
16. Zima, *Mentalitet narodov Rossii*, 209; A. V. Zakharchenko, "Sotsial'no-bytovoi aspekt zhizni rabochikh aviatsionnykh zavodov Povolzh'ia v gody Velikoi Otechestvennoi voiny," *Otechestvennaia istoriia*, no. 2 (March–April 2005): 83-85.

17. Filtzer, *Soviet Workers*, 162–163. See also Solomon, *Soviet Criminal Justice*, 324.
18. Filtzer, *Soviet Workers*, 162, 164; Solomon, *Soviet Criminal Justice*, 421, 36.
19. Steven A. Barnes, *Death and Redemption: The Gulag and the Shaping of Soviet Society* (Princeton, N.J., 2011), 127–128.
20. Aniskov, *Kres'ianstvo*, 56–57, 60, 62. On authorities, see I. E. Zelenin, book review, *Istoriia SSSR*, no. 6 (November–December 1991): 169–170.
21. Zima, *Mentalitet narodov Rossii*, 216, 222; Viktor Cherepanov, *Vlast' i voina: Stalinskii mekhanizm gosudarstvennogo upravleniia v Velikoi Otechestvennoi voine* (Moscow, 2006), 381.
22. Vyltsan, "Command and Homily," 26, 30; Aniskov, *Krest'ianstvo*, 369. See also "'Vera v zhiznesposobnost' sotsialisticheskogo stroia poluchila znachitel'nyi ushib': Dva pis'ma perioda Velikoi Otechestvennoi voiny," *Istoricheskii arkhiv* 13, no. 3 (2005): 66.
23. Zima, *Mentalitet narodov Rossii*, 219–220.
24. Aniskov, *Kres'ianstvo*, 390–392.
25. Ibid., 402; Vyltsan, "Command and Homily," 31; Zima, *Mentalitet narodov Rossii*, 229, 237.
26. Filtzer, *Soviet Workers*, 8, 35, 40.
27. Solomon, *Soviet Criminal Justice*, 418.
28. The next public amnesty, to those serving sentences of less than three years, came in July 1945, "in connection with the victory over Hitlerite Germany." Over a third of those eligible had been convicted under the law of December 1941, close to 235,000 Gulag prisoners. Solomon, *Soviet Criminal Justice*, 421; Golfo Alexopoulos, "Amnesty 1945: The Revolving Door of Stalin's Gulag," *Slavic Review* 64, no. 2 (Summer 2005): 280. As an example of censorship of child labor, an article about unwilling fourteen-year-olds at a military factory was cut entirely from *Izvestiia*. RGASPI, 17/125/187/105–105v: Sadchikov, "Svodka iz"iatii tsenzury iz predstavlennykh v pechati i peredache po radio materialov, a takzhe iz"iatii iz inostrannoi literatury za vremia s 15 avgusta po 5 sentiabria 1943 goda" (copy sent to Aleksandrov), September 15, 1943.
29. Somov, *Po zakonam voennogo vremeni*, 23.
30. "Zlostnyi dezertir truda," *Trud*, July 5, 1942, 4; "V Prokurature Soiuza SSR," *Trud*, February 8, 1942, 4.
31. "Strozhaishe, po-voennomu bliusti distsiplinu truda," *Trud*, October 22, 1942, 1; "V Prokurature Soiuza SSR," *Trud*, November 3, 1942, 4.
32. "Dela o progulakh rassmatrivat' nemedlenno: Prikaz narodnogo komissara iustitsii SSSR," *Trud*, November 1, 1942, 4. On the resolution, see Somov, *Po zakonam voennogo vremeni*, 53.

33. The precise date of the decree on labor days, February 15, was first mentioned only in *Pravda*, July 20, 1944, 1-3.
34. "Gorozhane, vykhodite na sovkhoznye polia! Sleduite primeru profaktiva promyshlennykh i torgovykh predpriiatii stolitsy," *Trud*, August 6, 1942, 2; "Sotni tysiachi gorozhan samootverzhenno trudiatsia na poliakh: Pomozhem kolkhozam i sovkhozam bystro ubrat' urozhai," *Trud*, 21 August 1942, 2.
35. Zima, *Mentalitet narodov Rossii*, 217.
36. *Izvestiia*, July 13, 1943, quoted in Somov, *Po zakonam voennogo vremeni*, 99-100.
37. Zima, *Mentalitet narodov Rossii*, 223, 225.
38. Ibid., 223-224.
39. For an instruction to this effect, see RGASPI, 17/125/114/6, 11, 17-18: Upravl. prop. i agit. TsK VKP(b), "O nedostatkakh v osveshchenii voprosov se. kh. oblastnoi gazetoi 'Tambovskoi pravdy,'" n.p., n.d. See also Aniskov, *Krest'ianstvo*, 65, citing *Propagandist*, no. 3 (1942): 43.
40. "V interesakh gosudarstva, kolkhozov i vsekh chestnykh kolkhoznikov," editorial, *Pravda*, April 18, 1942, 1.
41. For example, *Pravda*, December 4, 1942, 3, cited in William Moskoff, *The Bread of Affliction: The Food Supply in the USSR during World War II* (Cambridge, U.K., 1990), 174-175.
42. "V Sovete narodnykh komissarov Soiuza SSR i Tsentral'nom komitete VKP(b): Ob uborke urozhaia i zagotovkakh sel'skokhoziaistvennykh produktov v 1942 godu," *Pravda*, July 12, 1942, 1-2; also published in other papers.
43. "V Sovnarkome Soiuza SSR i TsK VKP(b): Ob uborke urozhaia i zagotovkakh sel'sko-khoziaistvennykh produktov v 1943 godu," *Pravda*, July 18, 1943, 1-3; "Uborka urozhaia provesti po-voennomu!," editorial, Pravda, July 18, 1943, 1; Moskoff, *The Bread of Affliction*, 175-176.
44. K. U. Cherchenko and M. S. Smirtiukov, comps., *Resheniia partii i pravitel'stva po khoziaistvennym voprosam*, vol. 3: *1941–1952 gody* (Moscow, 1968), 69-72.
45. "Pis'mo predsedatelei kolkhozov Penzenskoi oblasti tovarishchu I. V. STALINU," *Pravda*, July 28, 1943, 1; also in *Trud*, July 28, 1941, 1.
46. GARF, 6903/12/24/262: broadcast of July 22, 1942, 8:00-8:19 P.M.
47. "Vse rabochie dolzhny vypolniat' normy," editorial, *Trud*, March 4, 1942, 1; "Fabzavkomy, povsednevno proveriaite vypolnenie obiazatel'stv!," *Trud*, June 13, 1942, 3; "Voennaia minuta," editorial, *Trud*, September 13, 1942, 1.
48. D. Rubezhnyi, "Slovo patriotov," *Trud*, January 15, 1942, 3.

49. Grigorii Perfil'ev, "Ne poterpim lodyrei i simuliantov v svoei srede: Pis'mo stakhanovtsa," *Trud*, September 30, 1942, 3.
50. Barnes, *Death and Redemption*, 134–135; G. Solov'ianov, "Bol'shaia Vorkuta—zapoliarnyi ugol'nyi bassein," *Trud*, November 22, 1944, 3; V. Rogov, "Geroicheskii trud shakhtërov Vorkuty," *Trud*, December 14, 1944, 3.
51. S. V. Roginskii, ed., *SSSR v Velikoi Otechestvennoi voine 1941–1945 gg. (Kratkaia khronika)* (Moscow, 1964), 259; A. G. Kushnir, "Izmeneniia v administrativno-territorial'nom delenii SSSR v gody Velikoi Otechestvennoi voiny," *Istoriia SSSR*, no. 1 (January–February 1975): 130; Semen Gershberg, *Gazeta zavtra vykhodit* (Moscow, 1966), 372.
52. "Shakhtery Kuzbassa i Karagandy, strana trebuet ot vas luchshei raboty!," editorial, *Trud*, September 26, 1942, 1; A. Litvak, "Za Donbass!," *Trud*, September 30, 1942, 3; RGASPI, 17/1215/112/39–40: Pospelov to Andreev, Moscow, September 6, 1942.
53. "Industriia Urala kuet oruzhie dlia fronta: Slovo, dannoe vozhdiu,—nerushimoe slovo. Raport ural'tsev tovarishchu STALINU," *Trud*, July 21, 1942, 2; G. Nemanov, "Gorniaki Cheliabinskuglia obiazany likvidirovat' otstaivanie, vernut' dolg strane!," *Trud*, September 23, 1942, 3. One measure was not reported: the creation early in 1943 of the mining oblasts Kemerovo and Kurgan; see Kushnir, "Izmeneniia," 130.
54. Stalin, *O Velikoi Otechestvennoi voine Sovetskogo Soiuza*, 57–58; 75. On prewar Soviet propaganda of self-sacrifice and permanent indebtedness, see Jeffrey Brooks, *Thank You, Comrade Stalin! Soviet Public Culture from Revolution to Cold War* (Princeton, N.J., 2000), 83–84, 127–128, 183.
55. Stalin, *O Velikoi Otechestvennoi voine Sovetskogo Soiuza*, 93; "Grazhdanskii dolg rabotnikov tyla," editorial, *Trud*, May 28, 1943, 1; A. V. Zakharchenko, "Sotsial'no-bytovoi aspekt zhizni rabochikh aviatsionnykh zavodov Povolzh'ia v gody Velikoi Otechestvennoi voiny," *Otechestvennaia istoriia*, no. 2 (March–April 2005): 83.
56. Stalin, *O Velikoi Otechestvennoi voine Sovetskogo Soiuza*, 106–111.
57. GARF, 6903/12/66/282: *reportazh* "Doklad Stalina vdokhnovliaet na novye uspekhi," November 10, 1943, 6:20–6:40 P.M.
58. GARF, 6903/12/66/280–281.
59. Stalin, messages dated January 27, 1944, May 11, 1944, August 23, 1944, and January 7, 1945, [Gosudarstvennaia biblioteka SSSR imeni V. I. Lenina], "Vystupleniia, prikazy, privetstviia I. V. STALINA za vremia Velikoi Otechestvennoi voiny 1941–1945 gg. (Khronologicheskii perechen')," *Partiinoe stroitel'stvo*, nos. 9–10 (Moscow, May 1945): 83, 85, 88, 90. On the NKVD, see Cherepanov, *Vlast' i voina*, 211.

60. For an example, on the Stalin Artillery Factory, see "V otvet na privetstvie tovarishcha Stalina," *Trud*, August 25, 1944, 2.
61. "V Sovnarkome SSSR i TsK VKP(b): Ob uborke urozhaia i zagotovkakh sel'skokhoziaistvennykh produktov v 1944 godu," *Pravda*, July 20, 1944, 1–3.
62. Stalin, *O Velikoi Otechestvennoi voine Sovetskogo Soiuza*, 133.
63. Ibid., 144–146; Cherepanov, *Vlast' i voina*, 136–137; "Vydaiushchaiasia proizvodstvennaia pobeda zheny frontovika: Otvet sverdlovshchitsy Eleny Bondarevoi na doklad tovarishcha Stalina," *Trud*, December 5, 1944, 2; Elena Bondareva, "Moi otvet na doklad vozhdia," *Trud*, December 8, 1944, 3.
64. The Russian term is *udarniki*. R. W. Davies and Oleg Khlevniuk, "Stakhanovism and the Soviet Economy," *Europe-Asia Studies* 54, no. 6 (September 2002): 867–903; L. H. Siegelbaum, *Stakhanovism and the Politics of Productivity in the USSR, 1935–1941* (Cambridge, U.K., 1988), 295; M. M. Kozlov, ed., *Velikaia Otechestvennaia voina, 1941–1945: Entsiklopediia* (Moscow, 1985), 674; Mary Buckley, *Mobilizing Soviet Peasants: Heroines and Heroes of Stalin's Fields* (Lanham, Md., 2006), 2.
65. David L. Hoffmann, *Stalinist Values: The Cultural Norms of Soviet Modernity, 1917–1941* (Ithaca, N.Y., 2003), 29. A rare archival record with the genesis of such a call during the war period is at RGASPI, 17/125/348/1, 2–6: L. Mel'nikov, secretary of Stalino obkom, to Malenkov, n.p., [no later than January 25, 1945]: request for permission to publish in *Pravda* the enclosed call for socialist competition by the Stalin Novo-Kramatorsk factory of heavy machine-building. The text was written with D. S. Korotchenko's consent. Permission to publish is granted.
66. Kozlov, *Velikaia Otechestvennaia voina*, 185.
67. The Russian word is *dvukhsotniki*. Ibid., 232–233.
68. The Russian word is *tysiachniki*. Ibid., 235; O. A. Rzheshevskii, ed., *Kto byl kto v Velikoi Otechestvennoi voine, 1941–1945: Liudi. Sobytiia. Fakty. Spravochnik*, expanded 2nd ed. (Moscow, 2000), 47; Dmitrii Bosyi, "Eto vozmozhno lish' v nashei strane," *Trud*, April 12, 1942, 3; A. Aristov, "Bogatyri trudovogo fronta," *Trud*, May 17, 1942, 2.
69. Kozlov, *Velikaia Otechestvennaia voina*, 233; "Skorostniki—mastera voennykh tempov," *Trud*, April 3, 1943, 1.
70. "'Nado byt' masterom na vse ruki': Pomoch' vsem stroiteliam stat' shalaevtsami!," *Trud*, February 12, 1942, 3; Rzheshevskii, *Kto byl kto*, 277. See also "Rastit' novykh shalaevtsev! Ko vsem rabochim, stakhanovtsam i inzhenerno-tekhnicheskim rabotnikam stroek," *Trud*, March 6, 1942, 3.

71. Rzheshevskii, *Kto byl kto*, 155–156; Kozlov, *Velikaia Otechestvennaia voina*, 421. For examples, see GARF, 6903/17/1/716: Moscow oblast radio, May 29, 1942; T. Murav'ev, "Voennaia chetkost' Luninskoe depo stantsii Danilov," *Trud*, July 19, 1942, 3; K. Sokolov, "Na prifrontovoi magistrali," *Trud*, June 20, 1942, 3.
72. The Russian word is *mnogostanochniki*. Kozlov, *Velikaia Otechestvennaia voina*, 452. For examples, see the photographs of and commentary on two female weavers in *Trud*, October 31, 1942, 3, and *Trud*, December 19, 1942, 3.
73. Examples are M. Saratovskii, "Kak ia dognal Nagornogo: Rasskaz molodogo nagornovtsa Mikhaila Pshenichnikova," *Komsomol'skaia pravda*, September 8, 1942, 1; A. Medvedev, "Nagornovtsy Tul'koi oblasti," *Komsomol'skaia pravda*, September 10, 1942, 1; "Nagornovtsy Tadzhikistana. TsK KP(b) Tadzhikskoi SSR vynes reshenie o rasprostranenii nagornovskogo metoda truda v kolkhozakh," *Komsomol'skaia pravda*, September 12, 1942, 1; I. Sip, "Po-delovomu pomogat' nagornovtsam," *Sotsialisticheskoe zemledelie*, October 10, 1942, 3.
74. RGASPI, 17/125/115/44–45: G. Aleksandrov and A. Puzin to Andreev, March 15, 1943, with draft of a resolution by the Central Committee.
75. Kozlov, *Velikaia Otechestvennaia voina*, 674; Roginskii, *SSSR v Velikoi Otechestvennoi voine 1941–1945 gg.*, 186.
76. Kozlov, *Velikaia Otechestvennaia voina*, 738; Rzheshevskii, *Kto byl kto*, 232; S. V., "Sleduiut primeru patriota," *Trud*, May 21, 1942, 3.
77. Kozlov, *Velikaia Otechestvennaia voina*, 364, 764–765.
78. A. Kharlamov, "Molodëzhnye frontovye brigady," *Trud*, April 15, 1944, 3; Rzheshevskii, *Kto byl kto*, 35.
79. Kozlov, *Velikaia Otechestvennaia voina*, 185, 553–554. For an example of outcome publications, see this report for July 1943: "V TsSPS i Narkomles SSSR," *Trud*, August 18, 1943, 2.
80. "Vse sily nashei promyshlennosti na sluzhbu frontu!," editorial, *Trud*, April 8, 1943, 1.
81. Kozlov, *Velikaia Otechestvennaia voina*, 674; L. Borisov, "Individual'noe sorevnovanie," *Trud*, March 9, 1944, 3. See also *Trud*, March 14–18, 1944.
82. Aniskov, *Krest'ianstvo*, 101.
83. *Sovetskaia Sibir'*, January 22, 1942, and February 15, 1942, both cited in Aniskov, *Krest'ianstvo*, 98.
84. *Sotsialisticheskoe zemledelie*, February 14, 1942, cited in Aniskov, *Krest'ianstvo*, 98–99.
85. RGASPI, 17/125/112/104–110, 103, 111: draft of "Dadim frontu i strane . . . ," Aleksandrov and N. Itskov to Andreev, "Spravka," n.p., May 19, 1942, and

response by Andreev. For the published version, see *Pravda*, May 26, 1942, 1–2.

86. Failure to add deadlines (and to promote advanced farmers) was why the Agitprop workers in the Altai krai reprimanded a raion newspaper and even blamed it for the raion's production lag. RGASPI, 17/125/197/11–11v: I. Krutov, secretary of the Altai krai party committee, to unidentified raion secretary and raion newspaper editor, "Sotsialisticheskoe sorevnovanie na vesennem seve," n.p., May 15, 1943.
87. *Pravda*, June 28, 1942, and *Pravda*, December 1, 1942, both cited in Aniskov, *Krest'ianstvo*, 102–103.
88. *Pravda*, October 4, 1944, cited in Aniskov, *Krest'ianstvo*, 107.
89. Zima, *Mentalitet narodov Rossii*, 214.
90. RGASPI, 17/125/125/28–37v: D. Polikarpov to A. S. Shcherbakov, n.p., October 7, 1942, and text of radio speeches.
91. Aniskov, *Krest'ianstvo*, 106–107, citing, among others, *Pravda*, April 15, 1943.
92. "Traktoristy i kombainery! . . . ," *Pravda*, July 28, 1943, 2.
93. "Ob itogakh Vsesoiuznogo sotsialisticheskogo sorevnovaniia raionov po provedeniiu vesennikh sel'skokhoziaistvennykh rabot i razvitiiu kolkhoznogo zhivotnovodstva v 1944 godu," *Trud*, August 3, 1944, 1.
94. "K ukrainskomu narodu," *Pravda*, January 21, 1942, 2.
95. "Ot kolkhoznikov i kolkhoznits, rabochikh i rabotnits MTS, sovkhozov i spetsialistov sel'skogo khoziaistva Kievskoi oblasti: Marshalu Sovetskogo Soiuza, vozhdiu i luchshemu drugu ukrainskogo naroda tovarishchu STALINU," *Trud*, October 8, 1944, 2; "Patrioticheskii prizyv trudiashchikhsia sel'skogo khoziaistva Ukrainy," editorial, *Trud*, October 11, 1944, 1. This propaganda has mesmerized generations of Soviet and post-Soviet historians and even today few doubt that the collective farm system helped win the war. Even those highly critical of that system assert that most peasants were "loyal" to it and ignore the fact that the most frequently circulated rumor during the war was that the collective farms would be dissolved. It is all in striking contrast to the wartime observations by foreigners inside the Soviet Union. For traditional Russian views, see Zima, *Mentalitet narodov Rossii*, 238; Aniskov, *Krest'ianstvo*, 485. For exceptional recent voices, see Vyltsan, "Command and Homily," 23, 31; M. A. Vyltsan, *Krest'ianstvo Rossii v gody bol'shoi voiny 1941–1945: Pirrova pobeda* (Moscow, 1995); I. E. Zelenin, book review, *Istoriia SSSR*, no. 6 (November–December 1991): 168–172. For a Polish observation, written in London in 1942, see Tadeusz Kiersnowski, *Moje spostrzeżenia o Rosji Sowieckiej (1940–1942)* (Warsaw, 1997), 46.
96. See, for example, N. I. Kondakova, *Dukhovnaia zhizn' Rossii i Velikaia Otechestvennaia voina 1941–1945 gg.* (Moscow, 1995), 31.

97. TASS, "Ves' sovetskii narod goriacho odobriaet resheniia konferentsii rukovoditelei trekh soiuznykh derzhav," *Trud*, December 8, 1943, 1.
98. For the monthly averages of letters received, see GARF, 6903/1/82/114: "Postuplenie pisem za 1943 god," n.p., n.d. (Unconvincingly high averages for mid-1942 of the number of letters received—30,000 *daily* or "in certain months" even twice as many—are at GARF, 6903/1/66/5: K. Zaitsev, "Vyvody Komissii o rabote otdela pisem na front i s fronta za period s 15 iiulia po 15 avgusta 1942 goda," n.p., n.d.) For the number of letters read on air, and the actual voices, see GARF, 6903/1/82/76, 79, 81, 85: V. Kabluchko, "Otchet otdela pisem na front i s frontov Otechestvennoi voiny (za iavar'-dekabr' 1943 goda)," n.p., January 4, 1944. On obtaining letters, see GARF, 6903/1/101/11: "Stenogramma soveshchaniia [on October 19, 1944] u predsedatelia komiteta tov. Puzina A. A." (hospital visit) and Ark. Gaev, "Sovetskaia pechat' na voine," *Vestnik Instituta po izuchenii istorii i kul'tury SSSR*, no. 1(8) (Munich, January–February 1954): 48. On editorial distortion, see RGALI, 631/15/584/51, 55: "Stenogramma Zasedaniia Prezidiuma Soiuza Sovetskikh pisatelei (Po voprosu ob uchastii pisatelei v radioveshchanii), 29.VII.1942 goda"; GARF, 6903/1/66/6–7: Zaitsev, "Vyvody Komissii"; GARF, 6903/1/62/80v-81, 84: "Stenogramma zasedaniia rabotnikov tsentral'nogo veshchaniia pri predsedatele VRK 7-go ianvaria 1943g."; RGASPI, 17/125/295/206: K. Kuzakov and N. Sakontikov, UPA, to G. M. Malenkov and A. S. Shcherbakov, "O raspisanii radioperedachi," n.p., n.d. [1944]. Compare James von Geldern, "Radio Moscow: The Voice from the Center," in Richard Stites, ed., *Culture and Entertainment in Wartime Russia* (Bloomington, Ind., 1995), 51, who states that beginning in 1942 the letters were read on air "without 'correction.'"
99. N. G. Sadchikov, *O nekotorykh voprosakh raboty tsenzury vo vremia voiny* (Moscow, 1942), filed at RGASPI, 17/125/117/57-96v; N. G. Sadchikov, *Strogo khranit' tainy sotsialisticheskogo gosudarstva* (Moscow, 1942), filed at RGASPI, 17/125/117/37-56v (quotation from *Strogo khranit' tainy*, 13; folio 43).
100. Sadchikov, *O nekotorykh voprosakh*, 33.
101. Ibid., 37–38.
102. GARF, 9425/1/207/66: Sadchikov, "Perechen' svedenii, sostavliaiushchikh voennuiu i gosudarstvennuiu tainu na vremia voiny," May 18, 1944.
103. Sadchikov, *O nekotorykh voprosakh*, 30.
104. Ibid., 21–22, 32–33.
105. GARF, 9425/1/207/65: Sadchikov, "Perechen' svedenii."
106. Sadchikov, *O nekotorykh voprosakh*, 23–24, 28.
107. Examples of bad censorial practices are in Sadchikov, *O nekotorykh voprosakh*, 21–22, 25, 27.

108. GARF, 6903/1/70/59-61: "Vyvod komissii o rabote redaktsii 'Poslednikh Izvestii' za iiul' mesiats," n.p., [not earlier than July 1942].
109. GARF, 9425/1/207/70-71: Sadchikov, "Perechen' svedenii."
110. RGASPI, 17/125/196/17-19: G. Aleksandrov to A. A. Andreev, April 1, 1943.
111. Sadchikov, *O nekotorykh voprosakh*, 29.
112. Sadchikov, *Strogo khranit' tainy*, 9-13.
113. G. V. Kostyrchenko, "Sovetskaia tsenzura v 1941-1952 godakh," *Voprosy istorii*, nos. 11-12 (1996): 89-90, citing RGASPI, 17/125/185/54-55.
114. GARF, 9425/1/117/42-43: "Prodolzhenie soveshchaniia[,] 28.IV-43g."
115. RGASPI, 17/125/196/28-29: A. Puzin to G. M. Malenkov, n.p., n.d., and page from the paper *Gor'kovskaia kommuna*. See also Lewis H. Siegelbaum, "'Dear Comrade, You Ask What We Need': Socialist Paternalism and Soviet Rural 'Notables' in the Mid-1930s," *Slavic Review* 57, no. 1 (Spring 1998): 107.
116. "Obrashchenie kolkhoznikov, kolkhoznits, rabochikh MTS i sovkhozov i spetsialistov sel'skogo khoziaistva Sovetskoi Ukrainy ko vsem kolkhoznikam i kolkhoznits, rabotnikam MTS i sovkhozov, ko vsem spetsialistam sel'skogo khoziaistva SSSR," *Trud*, October 1, 1944, 1.
117. "Golod grozit SSSR," *Novoe Slovo* (Berlin), no. 44(426), June 3, 1942, 1.
118. Sonya O. Rose, *Which People's War? National Identity in Britain, 1939-1945* (Oxford, 2003), 191-192, 196.

4. Material Privations

1. The Russian words for the supply department were *Otdel rabochego snabzheniia*, or *ors*. William Moskoff, *The Bread of Affliction: The Food Supply in the USSR during World War II* (Cambridge, U.K., 1990), 102-103, 136-143; M. M. Kozlov, ed., *Velikaia Otechestvennaia voina, 1941-1945: Entsiklopediia* (Moscow, 1985), 496-497, 522.
2. Moskoff, *The Bread of Affliction*, 146-148, 151.
3. M. N. Potemkina, "Evakonaselenie v ural'kom tylu: Opyt vyzhivaniia," *Otechestvennaia istoriia*, no. 2 (March-April 2005): 92.
4. Suzanne Rosenberg, *A Soviet Odyssey* (Toronto, 1988), 90-91.
5. Jörg Ganzenmüller, *Das belagerte Leningrad 1941-1944: Die Stadt in den Strategien von Angreifern und Verteidigern* (Paderborn, 2005), 254; V. T. Aniskov, *Krest'ianstvo protiv fashizma: 1941-1945. Istoriia i psikhologiia podviga* (Moscow, 2003), 384-387, 404; M. S. Zinich, *Budni voennogo likholet'ia 1941-1945* (Moscow, 1994), 1:25 (on moss); Eva Maeder, book review, *Jahrbücher für Geschichte Osteuropas* 53, no. 2 (2005): 293, reviewing Viktor Berdinskikh, *Krest'ianskaia tsivilizatsiia v Rossii* (Moscow, 2001) (on sacks).

6. M. A. Vyltsan, *Krest'ianstvo Rossii v gody bol'shoi voiny 1941–1945: Pirrova pobeda* (Moscow, 1995), 30, 43 (estimate); V. F. Zima, *Mentalitet narodov Rossii v voine 1941–1945 godov* (Moscow, 2000), 207.
7. I. Stalin, *O Velikoi Otechestvennoi voine Sovetskogo Soiuza*, 4th ed. (Moscow, 1944), 145 (*ser'ëznye material'nye lisheniia*); GARF, 9425/1/207/72: Sadchikov, "Perechen' svedenii, sostavliaiushchikh voennuiu i gosudarstvennuiu tainu na vremia voiny," May 18, 1944.
8. "Donory stolitsy," *Trud*, November 14, 1942, 4. See also Moskoff, *The Bread of Affliction*, 149–150. Another reference to rationing is in *Izvestiia*, November 21, 1944, 1. On an "organization" of card thieves in Moscow, see "Raskhishchenie khlebnykh talonov," *Trud*, July 5, 1942, 4.
9. Zima, *Mentalitet narodov Rossii*, 199–200, 204, 206; Moskoff, *The Bread of Affliction*, 139, 141.
10. Moskoff, *The Bread of Affliction*, 96–97, citing *Pravda*, July 19, 1941. For another example, see Factory Director Dranishchev et al., "Kazhdomu predpriiatiiu—sobstevennuiu prodovol'stvennuiu bazu (Iz pis'ma rabochikh i sluzhashchikh Saratovskogo zavoda imeni Lenina)," *Pravda*, March 3, 1942, 3. On gardens, see "O rasshirenii individual'nogo ogorodnichestva sredi rabochikh i sluzhashchikh v 1942 godu (Postanovlenie Sekretariata VTsSPS)," *Trud*, January 16, 1942, 1; "Postanovlenie Vsesoiuznogo Tsentral'nogo Soveta Professional'nykh Soiuzov ot 3 marta 1942 goda," *Trud*, March 7, 1942, 1.
11. The Russian term is *podsobnye khoziaistva*. Moskoff, *The Bread of Affliction*, 101–102, 106; Kozlov, *Velikaia Otechestvennaia voina*, 566–567; Eugene Zaleski, *Stalinist Planning for Economic Growth, 1933–1952* (London, 1980), 335, cited in Donald Filtzer, *Soviet Workers and Late Stalinism: Labour and the Restoration of the Stalinist System after World War II* (Cambridge, U.K., 2002), 71.
12. Dranishchev et al., "Kazhdomu predpriiatiiu—sobstvennuiu prodovol'stvennuiu bazu."
13. "Polozhenie" dated April 3, 1942, *Trud*, April 8, 1942, 3.
14. A. Vdovin, sekretar' Stalingradskogo gorkoma VKP(b), "Rasshiriaem mestnuiu prodovol'stvennuiu bazu," *Pravda*, April 10, 1942, 3.
15. "Sobrat' vysokii urozhai v podsobnykh khoziaistvakh," editorial, *Trud*, August 13, 1942, 1; "Pomozhem podsobnym khoziaistvam sobrat' urozhai," editorial, *Trud*, September 19, 1942, 1; "Tshchatel'no podgotovit'sia k uborke urozhaia v podsobnykh khoziaistvakh," editorial, *Trud*, August 10, 1943, 1. See also Moskoff, *The Bread of Affliction*, 104.
16. VTsSPS secretary S. L. Bregman, "Kazhdyi rabochii i sluzhashchii dolzhen imet' svoi ogorod," *Trud*, April 11, 1942, 2.

17. F. Brattsev and F. Lomakov, "Poleznaia initsiativa ostaetsia bez podderzhki (Pis'mo v redaktsiiu)," *Trud*, April 10, 1942, 3.
18. D. Nikolaev, "Vopiiushchaia nerazberikha: V Sverdlovske prodolzhaiut zatiagivat' vydelenie zemli dlia individual'nykh ogorodov," *Trud*, April 23, 1942, 4.
19. P. Sigida, agronomist of the Sovetskii raion, Moscow, "Zakrepit' ogorodnye uchastki za rabochimi-ogorodnikami: V poriadke predlozheniia," *Trud*, September 19, 1942, 4. Compare Moskoff, *The Bread of Affliction*, 106.
20. "Zheleznaia distsiplina v tylu," editorial, *Trud*, June 1, 1943, 1.
21. See, for example, A. Stepanov, "Polnost'iu ubrat' i sokhranit' obil'nyi urozhai," *Trud*, August 18, 1943, 3; M. Basin, "Otvety na voprosy ogorodnikov," *Trud*, April 12, 1944, 4.
22. See, for example, Z. Kol'tsova, "Kak podgotovit' semena k posadke," *Trud*, April 10, 1942, 3; "Khochesh imet' ovoshchi—khorosho vozdelai svoi ogorod," *Trud*, April 19, 1942, 3-4; N. Troshina, "Prosteishaia pererabotka ovoshchei," *Trud*, September 4, 1942, 4; "Sushka kartofelia, ovoshchei i zeleni," *Trud*, September 18, 1942, 4; N. Emel'ianov, "Chto vyrashchivat' na ogorode," *Trud*, April 7, 1943, 4; T. Koval', "Chto nuzhno znat' ob ogorodnykh kul'turakh?," *Trud*, May 9, 1943, 4.
23. GARF, 6903/1/82/14: "Otchet Otdela politagitatsii za 1943 god," December 28, 1943; GARF, 6903/12/89/371-375: "Sovety ogorodnikam," August 20, 1944, 4:20-4:28 P.M. See also T. M. Goriaeva, comp., Ia. I. Zasurskii, ed. in chief, *Istoriia sovetskoi radiozhurnalistiki: Dokumenty. Teksty. Vospominaniia 1917-1945* (Moscow, 1991), 267-268. About the film, see N. Shmelev, "'Vesennie raboty na ogorodakh,'" *Trud*, May 14, 1944, 4.
24. Valerii Soifer, *Vlast' i nauka: Istoriia razgroma genetiki v SSSR* (Tenafly, N.J., 1989), 366-367. Articles by Lysenko included "Ogorody—bol'shoe i vazhnoe delo," *Trud*, March 25, 1942, 3; "Nachat' sbor verkhushek klubnei kartofelia," *Trud*, November 24, 1943, 3; "Podgotovka verkhushek klubnei kartofelia k posadke," *Trud*, April 11, 1944, 3. See also Moskoff, *The Bread of Affliction*, 106, n. 53; David Joravsky, *The Lysenko Affair* (Chicago, 1986), 130. On Lysenko and potatoes, see, for example, "Po metodu akademika Lysenko," *Trud*, January 4, 1942, 4; "Vsemerno razvivat' i ukrepliat' ogorodnichestvo rabochikh i sluzhashchikh," editorial, *Trud*, April 10, 1943, 1; "Na sobranii ogorodnikov Moskvy," *Trud*, July 1, 1943, 1. On "vernalization," see, for example, I. Emel'ianov, "Iarovizatsiia kartofelia i semian," *Trud*, 17 April 1943, 4; TsDAVOV, 4915/1/10/14: Ia. Sirchenko to Ostroverkh of the CP(b)U Viddil propahandy, n.p., March 23, 1945.
25. "Polozhenie" dated April 3, 1942, in *Trud*, April 8, 1942, 3; F. Brattsev, "Samodeiatel'naia okhrana urozhaia na ogorodakh," *Trud*, August 5,

1942, 2; "Khorosho podgotovit'sia k sboru ovoshchei na individual'nykh ogorodakh," editorial, *Trud*, August 5, 1942, 1; "Zorko okhraniat' rabochie ogorody: Soveshchanie fabzavmestkomov i ogorodnykh komissii," *Trud*, August 6, 1942, 1.

26. S. Nezamov, "Sluchai na ogorode... O liberal'nykh sud'iakh na Kuntsevskogo raiona," *Trud*, August 14, 1942, 4; "Sokhranit' urozhai ovoshchei na rabochikh ogorodakh," *Trud*, August 15, 1942, 4.

27. D. Tarasov, "Opyt okhrany ogorodov," *Trud*, August 19, 1942, 2. About Nizhii Tagil, see A. Khavin, "Urozhai idet," *Trud*, August 27, 1942, 2. About a guard who stole, see Herman Carmel, *Black Days, White Nights* (New York, 1984), 151–152.

28. See, respectively, M. Kondrashova, "Khorosho organizovat' okhranu ogorodov," *Trud*, August 10, 1943, 3; "Samodeiatel'naia okhrana ogorodov," *Trud*, August 12, 1943, 3; V. Tadevasian and P. Tarasov, "O khishcheniiakh na ogorodakh," *Trud*, September 2, 1942, 2 (the quotations). For the figure, see "Po-boevomu zavershit' ogorodnuiu kampaniiu," *Trud*, September 2, 1944, 1.

29. S. Bursanovskii, "Raskhititelei—k strozhaishei otvetstvennosti," *Trud*, March 12, 1942, 3.

30. "Sud. Raskhititeli produktov," *Trud*, March 17, 1943, 4; "V voennom tribunale: Za khishchenie gruzov—rasstrel," *Trud*, March 25, 1942, 4; "Sud. Khishcheniia v vagon-restorane," *Trud*, February 28, 1943, 4.

31. S. Savin and N. Dyshlovaia, "Neterpimoe ravnodushie," *Trud*, January 18, 1942, 3; "Besporiadok v stolovykh Ufy," *Trud*, March 28, 1942, 3.

32. Moskoff, *The Bread of Affliction*, 175. On the prewar history, see Amy Randall, *The Soviet Dream World of Retail Trade and Consumption in the 1930s* (Basingstoke, U.K., 2008). On the resolution, see Zinich, *Budni voennogo likholet'ia*, 1:46. An early reference to such inspectors was in S. Savin and N. Dyshlovaia, "Neterpimoe ravnodushie," *Trud*, January 18, 1942, 3.

33. "Vybory obshchestvennykh kontrolërov na sobraniiakh rabochikh i sluzhashchikh," *Trud*, February 6, 1943, 3.

34. "Obshchestvennye kontrolëry! Vnikaite v rabotu stolovykh i magazinov!," banner heading, *Trud*, February 12, 1943, 3; "Organizatsiia obshchestvennogo kontrolia nad rabotoi stolovykh i magazinov—vazhneishaia zadacha profsoiuza," banner heading, *Trud*, February 16, 1943, 4 (the long quotation); "Ob usilenii obshchestvennogo kontrolia profsoiuznykh organizatsii nad rabotoi stolovykh, magazinov i podsobnykh khoziaistv: Postanovlenie XII plenuma VTsSPS po dokladu tov. M. P. Tarasova," *Trud*, April 2, 1944, 3; "Otvety na voprosy proaktivistov," *Trud*, April 29, 1944, 4.

35. "Signaly kontrolërov ostaiutsia bez posledstvii: Strannaia pozitsiia zavkoma Magnitorskogo kombinata," *Trud*, April 1, 1943, 3; "Bol'she vnimaniia signalam obshchestvennykh kontrolërov (Obzor pisem v redaktsiiu)," *Trud*, May 5, 1943, 3; "'Obshchestvennykh kontrolerov ne dopuskaiut k proverke,'" *Trud*, April 12, 1944, 3.
36. A. Ia. Livshin and I. B. Orlov, comps., *Sovetskaia propaganda v gody Velikoi Otechestvennoi voiny: "Kommunikatsiia ubezhdeniia" i mobilizatsionnye mekhanizmy* (Moscow, 2007), 610-611, 652-654.
37. Viktor Cherepanov, *Vlast' i voina: Stalinskii mekhanizm gosudarstvennogo upravleniia v Velikoi Otechestvennoi voine* (Moscow, 2006), 419.
38. "Gosud. Zaem Ukrepleniia Oborony Soiuza SSR: Besproigryshnyi vypusk. Ofitsial'naia tablitsa shestnadtsatogo tirazha vyigryshei," *Trud*, December 17, 1941, 4; Zima, *Mentalitet narodov Rossii*, 239.
39. A. Zverev, "Usloviia vypuska Gosudarstvennogo Voennogo Zaima 1942 goda," *Trud*, April 14, 1942, 1; "Gosudarstvennyi Voennyi Zaem," editorial, *Trud*, April 14, 1942, 1; A. Zverev, "Zaem otechestvennoi voiny," *Trud*, April 14, 1942, 3 (the quotations); "Voennyi zaem—eto novyi sokrushitel'nyi udar po vragu," *Trud*, April 17, 1942, 2; "Frontoviki—vzaimy gosudarstvu," *Trud*, April 16, 1942, 2; "Iskliuchitel'nyi uspekh Voennogo Zaima," editorial, *Trud*, April 18, 1942, 1; A. Zverev, "Zaëm perevypolnen v techenie odnikh sutok," *Trud*, June 8, 1943, 1; A. Zverev, "Soobshchenie Narkomfina Soiuza SSR," *Pravda*, June 13, 1943, 1; "V Sovnarkome Soiuza SSR: O vypuske Tret'ego Gosudarstvennogo Voennogo Zaima," *Trud*, May 5, 1944, 1.
40. "Proverka vyigryshei po 2-i denezhno-veshchevoi loteree," *Trud*, April 21, 1943, 4; RGASPI, 17/125/193/129-131, 132: A. Zverev to Shcherbakov, August 14, 1943, and Puzin to Shcherbakov, August 27, 1943; RGASPI, 17/125/262/121: Aleksandrov and P. Fedoseev to Shcherbakov, May 13, 1944.
41. "Trudiashchiesia predlagaiut sozdat' Fond oborony," *Pravda*, June 29, 1941; Kozlov, *Velikaia Otechestvennaia voina*, 761-762; Moskoff, *The Bread of Affliction*, 117.
42. [Gosudarstvennaia biblioteka SSSR imeni V. I. Lenina], "Vystupleniia, prikazy, privetstviia I. V. STALINA za vremia Velikoi Otechestvennoi voiny 1941-1945 gg. (Khronologicheskii perechen')," *Partiinoe stroitel'stvo: Zhurnal TsK VKP(b)*, nos. 9-10 (Moscow, May 1945): 79; O. A. Rzheshevskii, ed., *Kto byl kto v Velikoi Otechestvennoi voine, 1941–1945: Liudi. Sobytiia. Fakty. Spravochnik*, 2d ed. (Moscow, 2000), 72; Cherepanov, *Vlast' i voina*, 418.
43. Komarov, "Moskva: TsK VKP(b) tovarishchu Stalinu," *Trud*, December 12, 1942, 1.
44. "Novogodniaia rech' Predsedatelia Prezidiuma Verkhovnogo Soveta SSSR tov. M. I. Kalinina," *Trud*, January 1, 1943, 2.

45. "Miting predstavitelei ukrainskoi molodëzhi, posviashchënnyi XXV-letiiu Ukrainskoi Sovetskoi Sotsialisticheskoi Respubliki," *Trud*, December 16, 1942, 2; "Za Radians'ku Ukrainu!," editorial, *Sovetskaia Ukraina*, January 14, 1943, 1; N. Khrushchev, M. Grechukha, and L. Korniets, "Tovarischu STALINU," *Trud*, March 3, 1943, 1; TsDAHOU, 1/70/29/16: "Dovidka pro robotu hazet 'Komunist' i 'Sovetskaia Ukraina' za period z 1 hrudnia po 15 sichnia 1943 roku," n.p., n.d.
46. Ia. Kalnberzin, A. Kirkhenshtein, and V. Latsis, "Moskva, Kreml' tovarishchu STALINU," *Trud*, January 27, 1943, 1; Iu. Paletskis, M. Gedvilas, komandir litovskogo national'nogo soedineniia RKKA general-maior Zhemaitis, and brigade commissar Matsiiauskas, "Moskva, Kreml' tovarishchu STALINU," *Trud*, January 27, 1943, 1; Sekretar' TsK KP(b) Uzbekistana Iusupov, "Moskva, TsK VKP(b) tovarishchu STALINU," *Trud*, December 22, 1942, 1.
47. Kozlov, *Velikaia Otechestvennaia voina*, 761; "Na poroge vtorogo kvartala," editorial, *Trud*, April 1, 1943, 1; Moskoff, *The Bread of Affliction*, 118; Stalin, *O Velikoi Otechestvennoi voine Sovetskogo Soiuza*, 93.
48. Stulov, "Moskva: Verkhovnomu Glavnokomanduiushchemu, marshalu Sovetskogo Soiuza tovarishchu Stalinu," *Trud*, April 3, 1943, 1.
49. "Pomoshch osvobozhdennym raionam," editorial, *Pravda*, February 19, 1943, 1; Filippov, "Moskva, Kreml': Tovarishchu STALINU," *Trud*, April 5, 1944, 2 (on the Mykolaïv oblast); Sirotiuk and Mikitenko, "Moskva, Kreml': Iosifu Vissarionovichu STALINU," *Trud*, 30 April 1944, 1.
50. A. Fadeev et al., "Moskva, Kreml': I. V. STALINU," *Trud*, February 13, 1943, 1.
51. Nikishov et al., "Moskva, Kreml': Predsedateliu Gosudarstvennogo Komiteta Oborony tovarishchu STALINU," *Pravda*, February 19, 1943, 2. See also, for instance, "U zolotoiskatelei Kolymy," *Trud*, September 19, 1943, 2.
52. Cherepanov, *Vlast' i voina*, 420. For the proposal, see David Ortenberg, *Stalin, Shcherbakov, Mekhlis i drugie* (Moscow, 1995), 149–150.
53. M. A. Vyltsan, "Command and Homily: Ways of Mobilizing Village Resources during the War," *Russian Studies in History* 37, no. 1 (Summer 1998): 32–34. For two examples from Ukraine, see TsDAHOU, 1/70/243/33–34: E. Barlanitskii, nachal'nik Glavlita USSR, "Tekstovaia svodka vycherkov predvaritel'noi tsenzury s 1-go avgusta po 20 avgusta 1944 goda, no. 183s," n.p., August 22, [1944].
54. Rebecca Manley, *To the Tashkent Station: Evacuation and Survival in the Soviet Union at War* (Ithaca, N.Y., 2007), 74; Potemkina, "Evakonaselenie," 89, 92; On the roundup, see Jack Pomerantz and Lyric Wallwork-Winik, *Run East: Flight from the Holocaust* (Urbana, Ill., 1997), 55, 60, 64–71.

55. Elena Kozhina, *Through the Burning Steppe: A Memoir of Wartime Russia, 1942–1943*, trans. Vadim Mahmoudov (New York, 2000), 11–13 (on Cossacks); Potemkina, "Evakonaselenie," 87, 93–94; Manley, *To the Tashkent Station*, 153.
56. Potemkina, "Evakonaselenie," 88.
57. Ibid., 91 (on releases); Manley, *To the Tashkent Station*, 169–170, 187–188, 210–214.
58. S. V. Kormilitsyn and A. V. Lysev, comps., *Lozh' ot Sovetskogo Informbiuro* (St. Petersburg, 2005), 4–5, 55.
59. N. G. Sadchikov, *O nekotorykh voprosakh raboty tsenzury vo vremia voiny* (Moscow, 1942), 23, filed at RGASPI, 17/125/117/69; Maurice Hindus, *Mother Russia* (London, 1943), 215.
60. *Kommunist* (Andijan), January 18, 1944, quoted in M. V. Koval', *U hornyli viiny (Spivdruzhist' ukraïns'koho narodu z bratnimy narodamy SRSR u roky Velykoï Vitchyznianoï viiny 1941–1945 rr.)* (Kiev, 1972), 84. On Jews as refugees, see Manley, *To the Tashkent Station*, 264.
61. *Kommunist* (Saratov), December 27, 1942, quoted in Koval', *U hornyli viiny*, 107; Aleksei Semivolos, "Nash Ural," *Trud*, December 23, 1942, 3.
62. "Ot kruch Dnepra, ot iasnoi Ukrainy...," *Turkmenskaia iskra* (Ashkhabad), December 25, 1942, clipping filed at TsDAHOU, 1/70/34/1. See also, for example, P. Il'in, "Mastera skorostnykh stroek. Ukraintsy na Urale," *Trud*, February 21, 1943, 3.
63. TsDAHOU, 1/70/29/15: "Dovidka pro robotu hazet 'Komunist' i 'Sovetskaia Ukraina' za period z 1 hrudnia po 15 sichnia 1943 roku," n.p., n.d.
64. "Evakuirovannye v kolkhoze," editorial, *Trud*, December 6, 1941, 1; "Tak li nuzhno zabotit'sia o nuzhdakh evakuirovannykh?," *Trud*, January 29, 1942, 3; D. Rubezhnyi, "Sluchai, kotoryi ne dolzhen ostat'sia beznakazannym," *Trud*, February 12, 1942, 3.
65. "V Prokurature Soiuza SSR," *Trud*, January 24, 1942, 4; "V Sovnarkome SSSR: Ob osvobozhdenii zhiloi ploshchadi mestnykh Sovetov i predpriiatii, zanimavsheisia ranee rabochimi i sluzhashchimi, evakuirovannymi na vostok," *Izvestiia*, February 17, 1942, 3; Manley, *To the Tashkent Station*, 259.
66. E. Michugina, "Ostaius' zhit' na Urale," *Trud*, February 27, 1942, 3; Edmund Stevens, *Russia Is No Riddle* (New York, 1945), 297 (the long quotation, slightly modified); Potemkina, "Evakonaselenie," 95–96.
67. V. P. Iampols'kii et al., comps., *Organy gosudarstvennoi bezopasnoti SSSR v Velikoi Otechestvennoi voine: Sbornik dokumentov*, vol. 2, book 1: *Nachalo: 22 iiunia–31 avgusta 1941 goda* (Moscow, 2000), 485; O. Ie. Lysenko et al., eds., *Kyïv u dni natsysts'koï navaly: Za dokumentamy radians'kykh spetssluzhb. Do*

60-richchia vyzvolennia Ukraïny vid hitlerivs'kykh zaharbnykiv. Naukovo-dokumental'ne vydannia (Kiev, 2003 [2004]), 384; "Boets spokoen za svoiu sem'iu: Obzor pisem," *Trud*, December 24, 1943, 3.

68. I. I. Shirokorad, *Tsentral'naia periodicheskaia pechat' v gody Velikoi Otechestvennoi voiny: 1941–1945* (Moscow, 2001), 65, 67 (letters to *Pravda*); "Pomoshch sem'iam frontovikov," editorial, *Krasnaia zvezda*, February 28, 1943; RGASPI, 17/125/193/69-76: Maksimova, nach. Otdela pisem to Ortenberg, "Dokladnaia," n.p., n.d., and Ortenberg to Aleksandrov, May 13, 1943. Maksimova's report is also in Livshin and Orlov, *Sovetskaia propaganda v gody Velikoi Otechestvennoi voiny*, 621–627.

69. I. Erenburg, "Vysokoe delo," October 16, 1942, reprinted in Il'ia Erenburg, *Voina (Aprel' 1942–mart 1943)* (Moscow, 1943), 315-317; GARF, 9425/1/207/72: Sadchikov, "Perechen' svedenii."

70. "Boets spokoen za svoiu sem'iu: Obzor pisem," *Trud*, December 24, 1943, 3; "Polugodovoi raport ural'tsev: Velikomu Marshalu Sovetskogo Soiuza tovarishchu STALINU," *Trud*, July 23, 1944, 2.

71. Beate Fieseler, "Arme Sieger: Die Invaliden des 'Großen Vaterländischen Krieges,'" *Osteuropa* 55, nos. 4-6 (2005): 207-217; Zinich, *Budni voennogo likholet'ia*, 2:20-39.

72. Fieseler, "Arme Sieger," 215; V. Chuprakova, "Vozvrashchenie k trudovoi zhizni," *Trud*, November 26, 1943, 4 (quotation); An. Mikhailov, "Vozvrashchenie k trudu," *Trud*, September 3, 1943, 4 (book review); "Trudovoe ustroistvo invalidov Otechestvennoi voiny," editorial, *Trud*, May 25, 1944, 1; Boris Gorbatov, *Nepokorënnye (Sem'ia Tarasa)* (Moscow, 1943), 154-159. The key postwar novel with this trend was Boris Polevoi's *Story of a Real Man* (1946), about the pilot Aleksei Maresiev referred to in Chapter 2.

73. Kozlov, *Velikaia Otechestvennaia voina*, 762 (on the Fund); Goriaeva and Zasurskii, *Istoriia sovetskoi radiozhurnalistiki*, 228-229, 269-270; "Zabota o detiakh," editorial, *Trud*, April 9, 1942, 1; "Khorosho organizovat' letnii otdykh detei," editorial, *Trud*, May 18, 1943, 1; "Letnii otdykh detei," editorial, *Trud*, June 1, 1944, 1; "Letnii otdykh rabochikh podrostkov," editorial, *Trud*, July 5, 1944, 1. On the camps, see Lazar' Brontman, *Voennyi dnevnik korrespondenta "Pravdy": Vstrechi. Sobytiia. Sud'by. 1942–1945* (Moscow, 2007), 149.

74. Zima, *Mentalitet narodov Rossii*, 242, 246, 248; GARF, 6903/18/2/52-53: "Retsenziia na obshch.-pol. materialy radioveshchaniia Arkhangel'skogo radiokomiteta," n.p., [January 1946] (a rare case of publicity about problems); Victor Kravchenko, *I Chose Freedom: The Personal and Political Life of a Soviet Official* (New York, 1947), 407 (about military schools). See also Katrin Boeckh, *Stalinismus in der Ukraine: Die Rekonstruktion des sowjetischen Systems nach dem Zweiten Weltkrieg* (Wiesbaden, 2007), 451-475.

75. Gafur Guliam, "Ty ne sirota," *Pravda*, April 27, 1942, 4; Manley, *To the Tashkent Station*, 223; Lisa A. Kirschenbaum, "'Our City, Our Hearts, Our Families': Local Loyalties and Private Life in Soviet World War II Propaganda," *Slavic Review* 59, no. 4 (Winter 2000): 845 (the slogan); Z. Mokhov, "Deti vnov' obretaiut sem'iu . . . ," *Trud*, March 13, 1942, 3; GARF, 6903/17/1/645, 699: Moscow oblast radio, May 23 and 28, 1942.

5. Monstrous Atrocities

1. Timothy Snyder, *Bloodlands: Europe between Hitler and Stalin* (New York, 2010); Alex J. Kay, *Exploitation, Resettlement, Mass Murder: Political and Economic Planning for German Occupation Policy in the Soviet Union, 1940–1941* (New York, 2006); Jörg Ganzenmüller, *Das belagerte Leningrad 1941–1944: Die Stadt in den Strategien von Angreifern und Verteidigern* (Paderborn, 2005); Karel C. Berkhoff, *Harvest of Despair: Life and Death in Ukraine under Nazi Rule* (Cambridge, Mass., 2004), 164-186 (on Kiev); Norbert Kunz, "Das Beispiel Charkow: Eine Stadtbevölkerung als Opfer der deutschen Hungerstrategie 1941/42," in Christian Hartmann et al., eds., *Verbrechen der Wehrmacht: Bilanz einer Debatte* (Munich, 2005), 136-144; A. V. Skorobohatov, *Kharkiv u chasy nimets'koï okupatsiï (1941–1943)* (Kharkiv, 2004), 82-98; Dieter Pohl, *Die Herrschaft der Wehrmacht: Deutsche Militärbesatzung und einheimische Bevölkerung in der Sowjetunion 1941–1944* (Munich, 2008), 201-242 (on POWs).
2. Niels Bo Poulsen, "The Soviet Extraordinary State Commission on War Crimes: An Analysis of the Commission's Investigative Work in War and post War Stalinist Society" (Ph.D. dissertation, Copenhagen University, 2004), 38 (on the report to Stalin); Marina Sorokina, "People and Procedures: Toward a History of the Investigation of Nazi Crimes in the USSR," *Kritika* 6, no. 4 (Fall 2005): 813.
3. David Shneer, *Through Soviet Jewish Eyes: Photography, War, and the Holocaust* (New Brunswick, N.J., 2011), 109.
4. V. A. Zolotarev et al., eds., *Russkii arkhiv: Velikaia Otechestvennaia*, vol. 17-6 (Moscow, 1996), 162-163.
5. On prewar military intelligence, see Niels Erik Rosenfeldt, *The "Special" World: Stalin's Power Apparatus and the Soviet System's Secret Structure of Communication* (Copenhagen, 2009), 1:538. For the first report, see USHMM, RG-22.009M (01.10), holding a photocopy of Arkhiv vneshnei politiki RF, 6/4/papka7/73/70-98: [Pavel] Sudoplatov, nachal'nik 2 otdela NKVD SSSR, "O zverstvakh, grabezhe mirnogo naseleniia, nasilii i beschinstvakh nemetskikh okkupantov na zaniatoi protivnikom territorii," n.p., December 14, 1941. For the exception, see GARF, 7021/148/10/1-52, copy at

USHMM, RG-22.014M, reel 10: "Meropriiatiia germanskikh vlastei na vremenno okkupirovannoi territorii SSSR," Moscow, 1943; also published, from another GARF collection, in *Neizvestnaia Rossia: XX vek*, ed. V. A. Kozlov, book 4 (Moscow, 1993), 235-330.

6. Poulsen, "The Soviet Extraordinary State Commission," 45-47.
7. Yitshak Arad, "Stalin and the Soviet Leadership: Responses to the Holocaust," in *Remembering for the Future: The Holocaust in an Age of Genocide*, vol. 1: *History*, eds. in chief John K. Roth and Elisabeth Maxwell (Houndmills, U.K., 2001), 356, 369 (on Stalin's interest); I. Stalin, *O Velikoi Otechestvennoi voine Sovetskogo Soiuza*, 4th ed. (Moscow, 1944), 11.
8. Stalin, *O Velikoi Otechestvennoi voine Sovetskogo Soiuza*, 17, 26-28.
9. Shneer, *Through Soviet Jewish Eyes*, 109.
10. "Nota Narodnogo komissara inostrannykh del tov. V. M. Molotova: O vozmutitel'nykh zverstvakh germanskikh vlastei v otnoshenii sovetskikh voennoplennykh," *Pravda*, November 26, 1941, 1; "Nota Narodnogo komissara inostrannykh del tov. V. M. Molotova: O povsemestnykh grabezhakh, razorenii naseleniia i chudovishchnykh zverstvakh germanskikh vlastei na zakhvachennykh imi sovetskikh territoriiakh," *Pravda*, January 7, 1942, 1-2. Both are translated in *Soviet Government Statements on Nazi Atrocities* (London, [1946]), 7-24.
11. "Nota Narodnogo komissara inostrannykh del tov. V. M. Molotova: O chudovishchnykh zlodeiianiiakh, zverstvakh i nasiliiakh nemetsko-fashistskikh zakhvatchikov v okkupirovannykh sovetskikh raionakh i ob otvetstvennosti germanskogo pravitel'stva i komandovaniia za eti prestupleniia," *Pravda*, April 28, 1942, 1-3; *Soviet Government Statements*, 24-51.
12. Stalin, *O Velikoi Otechestvennoi voine Sovetskogo Soiuza*, 47.
13. "Zaiavlenie Sovetskogo pravitel'stva ob otvetstvennosti gitlerovskikh zakhvatchikov i ikh soobshchnikov za zlodeiianiia, sovershennye imi v okkupirovannykh stranakh Evropy," *Pravda*, October 15, 1942, 1; *Soviet Government Statements*, 51-55.
14. Stalin, *O Velikoi Otechestvennoi voine Sovetskogo Soiuza*, 71.
15. I. Stalin and V. Molotov, "Tsentral'nomu Komitetu KP(b) Ukrainy. Prezidiumu Verkhovnogo Soveta Ukrainskoi SSR. Sovetu Narodnykh Komissarov Ukrainskoi SSR," *Pravda*, December 25, 1942, 1; "Da zdravstvuet Sovetskaia Ukraina!," *Pravda*, December 25, 1942, 1; "Ukraina byla i budet sovetskoi!," *Krasnaia zvezda*, December 25, 1942, 1.
16. M. Grechukha, L. Korniets, and N. Khrushchev, "K ukrainskomu narodu," *Pravda*, December 26, 1942, 3; "Doklad predsedatelia Soveta Narodnykh Komissarov Ukrainskoi SSR tov. L. R. Korniets na torzhestvennom

zasedanii v Kolonnom zale Doma soiuzov, posviashchennom 25-letiiu Ukrainskoi SSR," *Pravda*, December 26, 1942, 3.

17. See the next chapter.
18. Stalin, *O Velikoi Otechestvennoi voine Sovetskogo Soiuza*, 95; "Nota Narodnogo komissara inostrannykh del tov. V. M. Molotova: O massovom nasil'stvennom uvode v nemetsko-fashistskoe rabstvo mirnykh sovetskikh grazhdan i ob otvetstvennosti za eto prestuplenie germanskikh vlastei i chastnykh lits, eksploatiruiushchikh podnevol'nyi trud sovetskikh grazhdan v Germanii," *Pravda*, May 12, 1943, 1–2, translated in *Soviet Government Statements*, 62–77.
19. Stalin, *O Velikoi Otechestvennoi voine Sovetskogo Soiuza*, 111, 122.
20. Sorokina, "People and Procedures," 812–813, 816.
21. Poulsen, "The Soviet Extraordinary State Commission," 171–172, 175; Sorokina, "People and Procedures," 804. The reports dealing with the RSFSR are in *Pravda*, April 7, 1943, 1–2; June 25, 1943, 1; July 14, 1943, 1; August 5, 1943, 1–2; September 8, 1943, 2; and November 6, 1943, 2–3. The reports dealing with Ukraine are in *Pravda*, June 25, 1943, 1; November 13, 1943, 2–3; and December 13, 1943, 1. English translations of all except for the first and the Smolensk report are in *Soviet Government Statements*, 79–107.
22. "Direktivy i prikazy gitlerovskogo pravitel'stva i germanskogo voennogo komandovaniia ob istreblenii sovetskikh voennoplennykh i mirnykh grazhdan," *Pravda*, March 11, 1944, 2–3, and other newspapers; *Soviet Government Statements*, 143–153.
23. The reports on the RSFSR are in *Pravda*, May 5, 1944, 3, and August 18, 1944, 2. The reports on Ukraine appeared in *Pravda*, March 1, 1944, 1–2; May 7, 1944, 3; June 14, 1944, 3; August 3, 1944, 3; and December 23, 1944, 2–3. The reports on Azarichi, Minsk, and the Baltic republics are in *Pravda*, April 30, 1944, 2; September 20, 1944, 3; November 26, 1944, 2–3; December 20, 1944, 2–3; and April 5, 1945, 2–3. English translations are in *Soviet Government Statements*, 136–143, 153–198, 225–283.
24. The magnitude is evident from published bibliographies and from the filed newspaper articles about atrocities and destruction published in Soviet newspapers from November 1942 through May 1944. See GARF, 7021/148/386–404, available as copies at USHMM, RG-22.-014M, reels 34 and 35.
25. GARF, 9425/1/207/34: Sadchikov, "Perechen' svedenii, sostavliaiushchikh voennuiu i gosudarstvennuiu tainu na vremia voiny," May 18, 1944 (on permission); TASS, "Krovavye plany gitlerovskikh liudoedov: 'Raz"iasneniia' Gimmlera o zadachakh 'germanizatsii Vostoka,'" *Trud*, August 28, 1942, 4; translation modified from Alexander Dallin, *German Rule in Russia, 1941–*

1945: A Study of Occupation Policies, 2nd ed. (London, 1981), 279; A. Leont'ev, "Istrebitel'naia voina Gitlera," *Pravda*, July 26, 1943, 4.

26. "My ne zabudem, otomstim!," *Krasnaia zvezda*, March 19, 1942, 3. For some other photographs, see *Pravda*, January 23, 1942, 3; *Pravda*, February 6, 1942, 2; *Trud*, July 7, 1942, 2; Peter Kort Zegers and Douglas W. Druick, eds., *Windows on the War: Soviet TASS Posters at Home and Abroad, 1941–1945* (Chicago, 2011), 259, reproducing execution photos from *Krasnaia zvezda*, September 8, 1943.

27. P. Pavlenko, "Izvergi i liudoedy," *Krasnaia zvezda*, July 8, 1941; Vasil'ev, "Luchshe smert' v boiu, chem fashistskii plen," *Krasnaia zvezda*, July 10, 1941; Soviet Information Bureau in *Pravda*, July 11, 1941. The estimate is mine, based on *Zverstva fashistskikh varvarov: Ukazatel' faktov, opublikovannykh v pechati* (Moscow, 1943), 29–69.

28. Soviet Information Bureau in *Pravda*, July 30, 1941 (the regiment's order); Soviet Information Bureau in *Pravda*, August 19, 1941 (on propagating mercilessness); *Zverstva fashistskikh varvarov*, 38, quoting *Liudoedy o sebe: Dokumenty, izoblichaiushchie krovozhadnykh fashistskikh varvarov* (Moscow, 1942) (ban on humanity, issued on July 25, 1941). On mine clearing, see T. Lil'chenko, "Chernoe zlodeianie nemetskikh podletsov," *Krasnaia zvezda*, December 5, 1941; "Nemtsy ispol'zuiut plennykh krasnoarmeitsev na raschistke minnykh polei," *Krasnaia zvezda*, January 6, 1942; B. Polevoi, "Chudovishchnyi prikaz nemetskogo generala," *Pravda*, April 8, 1942. On the badge, see "Chudovishchnoe zlodeianie gitlerovskikh izvergov," *Pravda*, August 2, 1943, 3.

29. *Pravda*, January 15, 1942, 2; discussed also in the next chapter.

30. "Dokumenty o krovozhadnosti fashistskikh razboinikov," *Krasnaia zvezda*, November 23, 1941, 3; "Dokumenty o krovozhadnosti i otchaianii nemetskikh soldat," *Krasnaia zvezda*, November 29, 1941, 3.

31. *Krasnaia zvezda*, December 6, 1941, 3 (a photograph); "Rasstrely nemtsami plennykh krasnoarmeitsev," *Krasnaia zvezda*, December 10, 1941; *Russkii arkhiv: Velikaia Otechestvennaia*, vol. 17-6 (Moscow, 1996), 91.

32. *Pravda*, November 26, 1941; *Soviet Government Statements*, 7–10.

33. *Pravda*, January 7, 1942; *Pravda*, April 28, 1942; *Soviet Government Statements*, 47, 50.

34. See, for example, "Zverskoe obrashchenie finnov s plennymi krasnoarmeitsami," *Krasnaia zvezda*, August 18, 1943, 2.

35. See, for example, M. Levin, "Nikogda ne prostim!," *Trud*, February 12, 1942, 2; TASS, "Voroshilovsgradskaia tragediia," *Trud*, April 1, 1943, 2.

36. See, for example, "Fashistskii plen khuzhe smerti," editorial, *Krasnaia zvezda*, July 14, 1942, 1; Krasnoarmeets Fedor Egorushkin, Leningradskii

front, "Luchshe smert', chem fashistskii plen," *Krasnaia zvezda*, August 13, 1942, 3.
37. Mikhail Sholokhov, "Nauka nenavisti," *Pravda*, June 22, 1942, 3, also in *Krasnaia zvezda*, June 23, 1942.
38. A. Surkov, "Po lageriam smerti," *Krasnaia zvezda*, April 10, 1943, 3. On Khorol, see Shneer, *Through Soviet Jewish Eyes*, 149–150. On Slavuta, see *Pravda*, 3 August 1944, 3; *Soviet Government Statements*, 183–189. An early testimony referred to more than 100,000 graves in Slavuta. See USHMM, RG-22.016, folder 4, holding a photocopy of TsAMO RF, 236/2675/134/40.
39. See USHMM, RG-22.016, folders 43, 44, 48, and 49, holding photocopies of TsAMO RF, 32/11302/29/178–189v, 198–209, and 32/11302/30/94–189v.
40. USHMM, RG-22.016, folder 44, holding a photocopy of TsAMO RF, 32/11302/29/208–208b: Protokol no. 53, December 17, 1941; USHMM, RG-22.016, folder 48, holding photocopies of TsAMO RF, 32/11302/30/96–97v, 122–123v: Akt, December 21, 1941, and Akt, December 21, 1941.
41. USHMM, RG-22.016, folder 43, holding a photocopy of TsAMO RF, 32/11302/29/188–189v: Akt no. 42, [December 10, 1941]. On killings of Jews, see USHMM, RG-22.016, folder 49, holding a photocopy of TsAMO RF, 32/11302/30/139–141v: Akt no. 14, December 10, 1941.
42. S. Kochetov, "Chto uvideli nashi boitsy v Rostove," and V. Kozlov, "Rasstrely, ubiistva, pytki," *Krasnaia zvezda*, December 2, 1941, 2; E. Vilenskii, "V osvobozhdennom Rostove," *Izvestiia*, December 2, 1941, 3; A. Kalinin, "V osvobozhdennom Rostove," *Komsomol'skaia pravda*, December 2, 1941, 3; "Rasstrely v Kieve i Rostove," editorial, *Krasnaia zvezda*, December 3, 1941, 1; E. Vilenskii et al., "V g. Rostove: Massovoe ubiistvo mirnykh zhitelei. Akt," *Krasnaia zvezda*, December 6, 1941, 3 (includes a photograph); A. Matskin and V. Sobolev, "Kak khoziainichali nemtsy v Rostove," *Pravda*, December 7, 1941, 2; P. Nikitin, "Na ulitsakh Rostova," *Izvestiia*, December 9, 1941, 2; "Ne zabudem, ne prostim! Fotodokumenty o krovavykh zverstvakh fashistskikh merzavtsev v Rostove-na-Donu," *Krasnaia zvezda*, December 11, 1941, 3 (still pictures); A. Puzin, "Moral'naia degradatsiia nemetskikh zakhvatchikov," *Pravda*, December 16, 1941, 3; "Krovavye prestupleniia gitlerovskikh banditov," *Trud*, January 11, 1942, 2 (photographs). As of October 2011, *Soiuzkinozhurnal*, no. 114, December 23, 1941, was available at http://www.youtube.com/watch?v=6BIlUR1OzCw. On spectators in Kuibyshev, see Xavier Pruszyński, *Russian Year: The Notebook of an Amateur Diplomat* (New York, 1944), 124–126. Molotov evidently used a passage in Sudoplatov, "O zverstvakh, grabezhe mirnogo naseleniia," fol. 86.

43. *Izvestiia*, December 2, 1941, 3. Identified here as a special correspondent, the author was a senior battalion commissar according to *Krasnaia zvezda*, December 6, 1941, 3.
44. "Zverstva nemetsko-fashistskikh liudoedov v Rostove-na-Donu," *Pravda*, March 13, 1943, 3, also that day's *Izvestiia*, *Krasnaia Zvezda*, and *Trud*.
45. On Kaluga, see "Eshche odin document o zverstvakh fashistskikh varvarov," *Izvestiia*, January 1, 1942, 3 (the photograph); Krylov, "Tam, gde byl fashistkii zastenok," *Trud*, January 7, 1942; Martin Dean, "Kaluga," in *The United States Holocaust Memorial Museum Encyclopedia of Camps and Ghettos, 1933–1945*, 2 (Bloomington, Ind., 2012), 1795–1796. On Kerch, see "Krovavye zverstva nemtsev v Kerchi," *Pravda*, January 5, 1942, 2; Shneer, *Through Soviet Jewish Eyes*, 100–106.
46. Viktor Fink, "Blizitsia chas rasplaty," *Trud*, January 20, 1942, 2; RGASPI, 558/11/490/5-7: "Fashistsko-nemetskie merzavtsy"; *Pravda*, September 4, 1944. Another report is N. Rybak, "Golos mesti," *Stalinskii sokol*, May 13, 1944, 4.
47. "Dvukhmesiachnye itogi voiny mezhdu gitlerovskoi Germaniei i Sovetskim Soiuzom," *Pravda*, August 23, 1941, 1.
48. *Trud*, February 28, 1943, 4; *Trud*, May 18, 1943, 4; *Trud*, February 22, 1944, 4.
49. *Pravda*, April 28, 1942; *Soviet Government Statements*, 25–26; D. Leont'ev, "'Zelena papka Geringa,'" *Pravda*, May 4, 1942, 3, and May 7, 1942, 4.
50. *Izvestiia*, July 10, 1942, 3, quoted in William Moskoff, *The Bread of Affliction: The Food Supply in the USSR during World War II* (Cambridge, U.K., 1990), 204; GARF, 6903/12/89/259-261v: broadcast of August 16, 1942, 1-1:09 p.m. On the Leningrad region, see "Pytka golodom," *Komsomol'skaia pravda*, December 17, 1941, 2.
51. TsDAHOU, 1/70/36/54-57: K. Hurov, "Fashysty moriat' holodom i vynyshshuiut' narod Ukraïny," broadcast on March 22, 1942.
52. I. Laponogov, "Zverstva fashistov v Khar'kove," *Krasnyi flot*, June 17, 1942, summarized in *Zverstva fashistskikh varvarov*, 145; *Pravda*, August 28, 1943, 3, cited in Moskoff, *The Bread of Affliction*, 55–56.
53. Ia. Makarenko, "Zverstva gitlerovskikh razboinikov v Kieve. 86 tysiach rasstreliannykh, podveshennykh, zamuchennykh," *Pravda*, July 4, 1942, 3; TASS, "Golod, rabskii trud i smert' nesut gitlerovtsy sovetskim liudiam," *Krasnaia zvezda*, August 4, 1942, 4; K. Sergienko, "Den' v Kieve," *Trud*, September 4, 1943, 2.
54. M. Zhirmunskii, "Golod v Evrope," *Trud*, June 13, 1943, 3.
55. About the camps, see Hans-Heinrich Nolte, "Osariči 1944," in Gerd R. Ueberschär, ed., *Orte des Grauens: Verbrechen im Zweiten Weltkrieg* (Darmstadt,

2003), 187–194; Pohl, *Die Herrschaft der Wehrmacht*, 328–329. For the letter, see "Ot grazhdan Sovetskoi Belorussii, osvobozhdennykh nashei doblestnoi Krasnoi Armiei iz nemetskogo lageria smerti v raione mestechka Azarichi, Polesskoi oblasti: Moskva, Kreml. Tovarishchu STALINU," *Izvestiia*, April 16, 1944, 2. Other media reports included Mikola Sadkovich, "Pust' osenit ikh schast'e," *Izvestiia*, April 16, 1944, 2; Iakub Kolas, "Lager' smerti," *Izvestiia*, April 19, 1944, 4, translated (almost in full) as Yakub Kolas, "Death Camp," in S. Krasilshchik, ed., *World War II: Dispatches from the Soviet Front*, trans. Nina Bous (New York, 1985), 246–249. The commission report is "Istreblenie gitlerovtsami sovetskikh liudei putem zarazheniia sypnym tifom," *Pravda*, April 30, 1944, 2, translated in *Soviet Government Statements*, 153–159. The first Soviet investigations are at USHMM, RG-22.016, folders 16, 38, and 39, holding photocopies of TsAMO RF, 233/2374/20/59–60 and 422/10510/112/83–84, 168–169.

56. Il'ia Erenburg, "Velikii i negasimyi," *Krasnaia zvezda*, July 4, 1943, 3 and *Sovetskaia Ukraina*, July 14, 1943, 4; compare the reprint in Il'ia Erenburg, *Voina (aprel' 1943–mart 1944)* (Moscow, 1944), 288.

57. P. Nikitin, "Sto odin," *Izvestiia*, May 8, 1943, 3; Erenburg, "Velikii i negasimyi"; I. Denisov, "Detoubiitsy," *Krasnyi flot*, July 5, 1944, 2; I. Anufriev, "Nemtsy berut u belorusskikh detei krov' dlia svoikh ranenykh," *Krasnaia zvezda*, July 12, 1944, 3; "Gitlerovskie izvergi v Pol'she," *Trud*, 1 April 1943, 4.

58. Politruk I. Miroshnichenko, "Chudovishchnye zverstva gitlerovskikh merzavtsev v Krymu," *Krasnyi flot*, January 25, 1942, cited in *Zverstva fashistskikh varvarov*, 132.

59. TASS, "Chudovishchnye prestupleniia gitlerovskikh palachei v Pol'she," *Trud*, July 30, 1942, 4; Raul Hilberg, *The Destruction of the European Jews*, 3rd ed. (New Haven, Conn., 2003), 941, n. 58.

60. GARF, 6903/1/82/93–94v: transcript of the tape recording of Ekaterina Mikhailovna Shvetsova, Moscow, [early 1943].

61. Il'ia Erenburg, "Za cheloveka," *Krasnaia zvezda*, April 24, 1943, reprint in *Voina (aprel' 1943–mart 1944)*, 10. Compare Il'ia Erenburg, "Konets Vil'gelma Kube," September 24, 1943, reprinted in Erenburg, *Voina*, 117–118 ("the Germans took Jews from various countries to Minsk and killed them there with gas"). On censorship, see RGASPI, 7/125/187/37: polkovnik Cherstvoi, nach. otdela voennoi tsenzury NKO, to general-maior Shikin, zam. nach. GlavPURKKA, with a copy to Puzin, "Svodka" for March 21–31, 1943, Moscow, April 2, 1943. For reports and articles about the Krasnodar tribunal, including photographs of gassed people, see *Pravda*, July 15–19, 1943; Ilya Bourtman, "'Blood for Blood, Death for Death': The Soviet

Military Tribunal in Krasnodar, 1943," *Holocaust and Genocide Studies* 22, no. 2 (Fall 2008): 256-258. On the North Caucasus, see Aleksei Tolstoi, "Korichnevyi durman," *Pravda*, August 5, 1943, 2. The quotation about Kharkiv is from "Ot Sovetskogo Informbiuro: Operativnaia svodka za 19 oktiabria," *Trud*, October 20, 1943, 1. For reports and articles about the Kharkiv tribunal, see *Pravda*, December 16-20, 1943.

62. See, for example, "Nasil'stvennoe onemechivanie Pol'shi okkupantami," *Trud*, October 23, 1942, 4.

63. This point was first made in Ewa M. Thompson, "The Katyn Massacre and the Warsaw Ghetto Uprising in the Soviet-Nazi Propaganda War," in John Garrard and Carol Garrard, eds., *World War 2 and the Soviet People: Selected Papers from the Fourth World Congress for Soviet and East European Studies, Harrogate, 1990* (Houndmills, U.K., 1993), 213-232.

64. RGASPI, 558/11/490/100-101: marked-up draft Sovinformbiuro statement, "Gnusnye izmyshleniia nemetsko-fashistskikh palachei"; *Pravda*, April 16, 1943; "Soobshchenie Spetsial'noi Komissii po ustanovleniiu i rassledovaniiu obstoiatel'stv rasstrela nemetsko-fashistskimi zakhvatchikami v Katynskom lesu voennoplennykh pol'skikh ofitserov," *Pravda*, January 26, 1944, 2-4; *Soviet Government Statements*, 107-136; "Chudovishchnye zlodeiianiia gitlerovskikh izvergov v Katyni," *Pravda*, 26 January 1944, 1; K. Pukhov, "Kliatva na mogile v Katynskom lesu," *Trud*, 1 February 1944, 3.

65. "Prokliatie i mest' fashistskim varvaram!," editorial, *Pravda*, December 21, 1941, 1; Vera Sandomirsky, "Soviet War Poetry," *Russian Review* 4, no. 1 (Spring 1944): 50; "Otomsti!," *Pravda*, July 19, 1942, 3, reproduced in Jeffrey Brooks, *Thank You, Comrade Stalin! Soviet Public Culture from Revolution to Cold War* (Princeton, N.J., 2000), 179; Susan Brownmiller, *Against Our Will: Men, Women and Rape* (London, 1975), 65.

66. TsDAVOV, 4188/1/146/156-157: "Na hitlerivs'kii katorzi," broadcast on February 8, [1943]; RGASPI, 17/125/187/55v: Cherstvoi, "Otchet otdela voennoi tsenzury NKO za aprel' mesiats 1943 goda"; *Pravda*, May 12, 1943, 1-2; *Soviet Government Statements*, 62-77.

67. A. Surkov, "Gitlerovskie razrushiteli kul'tury," *Pravda*, December 16, 1941, 2; "Prokliatie i mest' fashistskim varvaram!," editorial, *Pravda*, December 21, 1941, 1 (the quotation).

68. "O razrusheniiakh i zverstvakh, sovershennykh nemetsko-fashistskimi zakhvatchikami v gorode Kieve," *Pravda*, 1 March 1944, 2; Berkhoff, *Harvest of Despair*, 30-32; Patricia Kennedy Grimsted, "The Fate of the Kyiv Archive of Early Acts in the Second World War: A Triple Tragedy of Destruction, Plunder, and Propaganda," in Serhii Plokhy and Frank E. Sysyn, eds.,

Synopsis: A Collection of Essays in Honour of Zenon E. Kohut (Edmonton, Canada, 2005), 103-105. On East Prussia, see G. A. Kovalev, "Sovinformbiuro v gody Velikoi Otechestvennoi voiny," *Voprosy istorii*, no. 6 (June 1987): 20.

69. "My budem mstit': Vystuplenie kolkhoznits Istrinskogo raiona na Trekhgorke," *Izvestiia*, January 4, 1942, 3. See also David Carl Spaeder, "Propaganda and the Politics of Community in the USSR, 1941-1947" (Ph.D. dissertation, Indiana University, 1997), 100-101, citing RGASPI, 17/125/104/9-13.

70. Spaeder, "Propaganda and the Politics of Community in the USSR," 101-103; Poulsen, "The Soviet Extraordinary State Commission," 184-185. Both authors cite RGASPI, 17/125/79/2-5. On tours of the Saratov oblast, see V. P. Kiselev, *Ideologicheskaia rabota partiinykh organizatsii sredi truzhenikov tyla v gody Velikoi Otechestvennoi voiny (Na materialakh oblastei i avtonomnykh respublik Povolzh'ia)* (Gor'kii, 1975), 83-84.

71. "V okkupirovannykh raionakh," editorial, *Krasnaia zvezda*, July 8, 1942, 1.

6. A Bestial Plan for Physical Extermination

1. Dieter Pohl, "The Murder of Ukraine's Jews under German Military Administration and in the Reich Commissariat Ukraine," in Ray Brandon and Wendy Lower, eds., *The Shoah in Ukraine: History, Testimony, Memorialization* (Bloomington, Ind., 2008), 251; Alexander Kruglov, "Jewish Losses in Ukraine, 1941-1944," in Brandon and Lower, *The Shoah in Ukraine*, 283, 288.

2. Joshua Rubenstein, "The War and the Final Solution on the Russian Front," in Joshua Rubenstein and Ilya Altman, eds., *The Unknown Black Book: The Holocaust in the German-Occupied Soviet Territories* (Bloomington, Ind., 2008), 19.

3. Solomon M. Schwarz, *The Jews in the Soviet Union* (Syracuse, N.Y., 1951), 334-342, argues that "the very fact of the wholesale extermination of Jews" was "shrouded in silence" and "kept out of the Soviet newspapers." See also S. Shvarts, *Evrei v Sovetskom Soiuze: S nachala Vtoroi Mirovoi voiny (1939–1965)* (New York, 1966), 136-152. Today researchers from various countries still refer to a Soviet wartime conspiracy of silence, even when acknowledging exceptions. See Arno Lustiger, *Rotbuch: Stalin und die Juden. Die tragische Geschichte des Jüdischen Antifaschistischen Komitees und der sowjetischen Juden* (Berlin, 1998), 120-121 ("the murder of the Jews could be reported only in publications that were unavailable to the wider Soviet public"); G. V. Kostyrchenko, *Tainaia politika Stalina: Vlast' i antisemitizm* (Moscow, 2003 [2001]), 225-227, 229-230 (the Soviet leadership "decided . . .

to remove any reference to the cruelties done by the fascists to the Soviet Jews from the open press and radio"); Frank Grüner, *Patrioten und Kosmopoliten: Juden im Sowjetstaat 1941–1953* (Cologne, 2008), 422, 427 (the Soviet media "stopped mentioning the Jews separately as victims"). See also Pavel Polian, "Stalin und die Opfer des nationalsozialistischen Vernichtungskriegs," in Jürgen Zarusky, ed., *Stalin und die Deutschen: Neue Beiträge der Forschung* (Munich, 2006), 90 ("information about the genocide and about the anti-Semitic specificity of the German crimes did not appear on the air or in headlines"); Catherine Merridale, *Ivan's War: The Red Army 1939–1945* (London, 2005), 255 (which asserts that the Soviet media did not mention Auschwitz until May 1945). Important works on the Jewish Anti-Fascist Committee in the USSR and postwar Soviet reactions to the Holocaust that neither accept nor modify the notion of wartime "silence" are Shimon Redlich, *Propaganda and Nationalism in Wartime Russia: The Jewish Antifascist Committee in the USSR, 1941–1948* (Boulder, Colo., 1982); Zvi Gitelman, "Soviet Reactions to the Holocaust, 1945–1991," in Lucjan Dobroszycki and Jeffrey Gurock, eds., *The Holocaust in the Soviet Union: Studies and Sources on the Destruction of the Jews in the Nazi-Occupied Territories of the USSR, 1941–1945* (Armonk, N.Y., 1993), 3–27. Yeshoshua A. Gilboa, *The Black Years of Soviet Jewry 1939–1953* (Boston, 1971), 7–8, refers to a "deliberate attempt to conceal the Jewish tragedy behind general descriptions of German ferocity. Only rarely were massacres of Jewry specifically mentioned." Walter Laqueur, *The Terrible Secret: Suppression of the Truth about Hitler's "Final Solution"* (New York, 1998 [1980]), 71, 202–203, argues that the wartime Soviet media made "no mention of the fact that the [Soviet] Jews were singled out for 'special treatment'"—that is, for indiscriminate mass murder. Like many other studies, this book does not say whether those media treated the murder of non-Soviet Jews in the same manner. See also Laqueur, "Final Solution: Public Knowledge," in Walter Laqueur, ed., *The Holocaust Encyclopedia* (New Haven, Conn., 2001), 203. Jeffrey Brooks, *Thank You, Comrade Stalin! Soviet Public Culture from Revolution to Cold War* (Princeton, N.J., 2000), 164, 173, finds Soviet reports on the killings of Jews "scarce," with even writers of Jewish descent such as Ehrenburg downplaying their "exceptionality." According to the German scholar Heinz-Dietrich Löwe, only journals offered some clarity, and "the Soviet reader . . . hardly ever got a full picture of the extent of the annihilation of Jews by the Nazi regime of terror in Eastern Europe and in the Soviet Union. Neither the importance of Nazi racism, which targeted the Jews in a very special way, nor the methodical character of the killings perpetrated by the SS, SD, and the Wehrmacht, and in particular the 'industrialized' character of the mass exterminations in camps like Auschwitz, were ever fully reported and analyzed." See Heinz-Dietrich Löwe, "The Holocaust in the Soviet Press," in Frank Grüner et al., eds., *"Zerstörer des Schweigens": Formen künstlerischer Erinnerung an die nationalsozialistische Rasse- und Vernichtungskrieg in Osteuropa* (Cologne, 2006), 33.

Possibly, though not explicitly, in contradiction to the above, three authors have written, respectively, that "accessible information about the Germans' anti-Jewish atrocities had returned to the official Soviet media from the very first days of the German-Soviet war"; that "a considerable amount of material about the Holocaust (obviously without using this or any similar description) appeared in the Soviet Union"; and that "as early as October 1941 the mass murder of the Jews throughout Europe and the Soviet Union was publicly exposed." Like most others, these authors cite few newspaper articles and no Communist Party archival collection dealing with newspapers. See Mordechai Altshuler, "Escape and Evacuation of Soviet Jews at the Time of the Nazi Invasion," in Dobroszycki and Gurock, *The Holocaust in the Soviet Union*, 89 (citing *Der Shtern*, Kiev, July 7, 1941; *Krasnaia zvezda*, June 29, 1941; *Pravda*, June 26, 1941; *Pravda*, June 27, 1941; and *Pravda*, August 25, 1941); Lukasz Hirszowicz, "The Holocaust in the Soviet Mirror," in Dobroszycki and Gurock, *The Holocaust in the Soviet Union*, 31 (citing for the war only Molotov's diplomatic note of January 1942); Amir Weiner, *Making Sense of War: The Second World War and the Fate of the Bolshevik Revolution* (Princeton, N.J., 2001), 209 (citing *Sovetskaia Ukraina*, October 12, 1941, which carried Oleksandr Korniichuk's play *Partisans in the Steppes of Ukraine*).

A few authors have explicitly countered the notion that Soviet coverage was deliberately nonexistent or meager from start to end. A "perceptible drop in press items and TASS reports about Jewish pogroms and ghettos" set in only "some time in 1943," Lev Bezymenskii writes, and Ilia Altman finds that Jews as victims were either omitted or renamed "civilians"—but only during the war's "final phase," meaning the period after the Battle of Stalingrad in early 1943. Before then a different situation existed. Joshua Rubenstein agrees that "public references to Jewish suffering came almost entirely in the first years of the war." See Lev Bezymenskii, "Informatsiia po-sovetski," *Znamia*, no. 5 (May 1998): 196; Ilya Altman and Claudio Sergio Ingerflom, "Le Kremlin et l'Holocauste (1933–2001)," in Vassili Petrenko, *Avant et après Auschwitz*, trans. François-Xavier Nérard (Paris, 2002), 250, 259–260; Il'ja Al'tman, "Die Wiederspiegelung der nationalsozialistischen Politik der Judenvernichtung in der sowjetischen Literatur und Politik (1940–1980)," in Grüner et al., *"Zerstörer des Schweigens,"* 17–19; Rubenstein, "The War and the Final Solution on the Russian Front," 21. Corinne Ducey, "The Representation of the Holocaust in the Soviet Press, 1941–1945," *Slavonica* 14, no. 2 (November 2008): 136, says that "many articles were dedicated solely to the persecution and extermination of the Jews," but refers almost exclusively to Ehrenburg.

Yitzhak Arad so far has been the only researcher clarifying to what extent the findings apply equally to reports about Soviet Jews and reports about Jews killed outside "Soviet territory." He concludes that although *Pravda, Izvestiia,* and *Krasnaia zvezda* "constantly concealed the total extermination of the [Soviet] Jews," they did mention the mass murder of *non-*Soviet Jews, in reports in 1943 about Katyn and Warsaw and in one reference in 1944 to the deportation of Hamburg's Jews to Minsk. Overall, however, his verdict is harsh: far too little information was released in a country where "even Soviet Jews could not openly refer to the totality of extermination of Jews and the uniqueness of their fate." Yitshak [Yitzhak] Arad, "The Holocaust as Reflected in the Soviet Russian Language Newspapers in the Years 1941–1945," in Robert Moses Shapiro, ed., *Why Didn't the Press Shout? American and International Journalism during the Holocaust: A Collection of Papers Originally Presented at an International Conference Sponsored by the Elia and Diana Zborowski Professorial Chair in Interdisciplinary Holocaust Studies, Yeshiva University, October 1995* (Hoboken, N.J., 2003), 203–204, 211–212. See also Yitshak Arad, "Stalin and the Soviet Leadership: Responses to the Holocaust," in *Remembering for the Future: The Holocaust in an Age of Genocide,* vol. 1: *History,* eds. in chief John K. Roth and Elisabeth Maxwell (Houndmills, U.K., 2001), 355–370. The findings from Arad's 2003 article are entirely absent from Yitzhak Arad, *The Holocaust in the Soviet Union* (Lincoln, Neb., 2009).

4. Il'ia Al'tman, *Zhertvy nenavisti: Kholokost v SSSR 1941–1945 gg.* (Moscow, 2002), 386. Compare Arad, "Stalin and the Soviet Leadership," 359.

5. RGASPI, 17/125/52/30: [P. M.] Fitin, head of the 1st [Intelligence] Upravlenie NKVD SSSR to Shcherbakov, "O polozhenii v raionakh, okkupirovannykh protivnikom: Po sostoianiiu na 20-oe avgusta 1941 goda," Moscow, August 26, 1941. A shorter quotation from the document is in Niels Bo Poulsen, "The Soviet Extraordinary State Commission on War Crimes: An Analysis of the Commission's Investigative Work in War and post War Stalinist Society" (Ph.D. dissertation, Copenhagen University, 2004), 45. For the other report, see USHMM, RG-22.009M (01.10), holding a photocopy of Arkhiv vneshnei politiki RF, 6/4/papka7/73/70–98: [Pavel] Sudoplatov, nachal'nik 2 otdela NKVD SSSR, "O zverstvakh, grabezhe mirnogo

naseleniia, nasilii i beschinstvakh nemetskikh okkupantov na zaniatoi protivnikom territorii," n.p., December 14, 1941.

6. RGASPI, 69/1/1090/10-11v: Tomenko, "Spravka o zverstvakh nemetskikh okkupantov nad evreiskim naseleniem na vremenno zakhvachennykh imi sovetskikh territoriiakh," n.p., January 11, 1943, copy at USHMM, RG-22.005M, reel 2 (the first report); GARF, 7021/148/10/16-16v, copy at USHMM, RG-22.014M, reel 10: "Meropriiatiia germanskikh vlastei na vremenno okkupirovannoi territorii SSSR," Moscow, 1943, also published (from another GARF collection) in *Neizvestnaia Rossia: XX vek*, ed. V. A. Kozlov, book 4 (Moscow, 1993), 273-275.

7. *Pravda*, August 25, 1941; *Izvestiia*, August 26, 1941; "Brat'ia evrei vsego mira!," *Izvestiia*, August 26, 1941, 3. On the meeting, see Redlich, *Propaganda and Nationalism in Wartime Russia*, 3, 40-41, 193-194, n. 5.

8. "Vtoroi miting predstavitelei evreiskogo naroda," *Izvestiia*, May 26, 1942, 3, and *Pravda*, May 26, 1942, 3. Another English translation of *Pravda*'s rendition of the appeal "To the Jews of the Entire World!" is in *War, Holocaust and Stalinism: A Documented Study of the Jewish Anti-Fascist Committee in the USSR*, ed. Shimon Redlich (Luxembourg, 1995), 202-203. On the meeting, see Redlich, *Propaganda and Nationalism in Wartime Russia*, 42-43.

9. *Trud*, February 24, 1943, 2. This letter is not mentioned in Redlich, *Propaganda and Nationalism in Wartime Russia* or in Redlich, *War, Holocaust and Stalinism*.

10. Redlich, *Propaganda and Nationalism in Wartime Russia*, 51-52, 196, nn. 32-36. Translated excerpts from speeches here by Mikhoels, Fefer, Rabbi Shlifer, and Ehrenburg are in Redlich, *War, Holocaust and Stalinism*, 216-219.

11. "Plenum Evreiskogo antifashistskogo komiteta v SSSR," *Izvestiia*, April 12, 1944, 2, also in *Trud*, April 12, 1944, 3; TASS, "Miting predstavitelei evreiskogo naroda," *Pravda*, April 5, 1944, 2; Lustiger, *Rotbuch*, 145; Dov-Ber Kerler, "The Soviet Yiddish Press: Eynikayt during the War, 1942-1945," in Shapiro, *Why Didn't the Press Shout?*, 243.

12. "Brat'ia evrei vsego mira!," *Pravda*, August 25, 1941, and Il'ia Erenburg, "Vystoiat'!," *Krasnaia zvezda*, both reprinted Il'ia Erenburg, *Voina (Iiun' 1941–aprel' 1942)* (Moscow, 1942), 292, 306-309; "Ugroza," *Krasnaia zvezda*, July 17, 1942, 3, reprinted in Il'ia Erenburg, *Voina (Aprel' 1942–mart 1943)* (Moscow, 1943), 239-243; Kostyrchenko, *Tainaia politika Stalina*, 225. On other Jews, see David Shneer, "From Mourning to Vengeance: Bergelson's Holocaust Journalism (1941-1945)," in Joseph Sherman and Gennady Estraikh, eds., *David Bergelson: From Modernism to Socialist Realism* (Leeds, U.K., 2007), 264.

13. Il'ia Erenburg, "Evrei," *Krasnaia zvezda*, November 1, 1942, 3, reprinted in Erenburg, *Voina (Aprel' 1942–mart 1943)*, 224-226; I. Erenburg, "Velikii i negasimyi," *Krasnaia zvezda*, July 4, 1943, 3, reprinted in *Sovetskaia Ukraina*, July 14, 1943, 4, and in Il'ia Erenburg, *Voina (Aprel' 1943–mart 1944)* (Moscow, 1944), 284-289; TASS, "Miting," 2.
14. The terms used in the text are *Belzhets* and *Sabibur*. Il'ia Erenburg, "Nakanune," *Pravda*, August 7, 1944, 3.
15. The term used in the article is *Tremblinka*. Il'ia Erenburg, "Pomnit'!," *Pravda*, December 17, 1944, 3; Joshua Rubenstein, *Tangled Loyalties: The Life and Times of Ilya Ehrenburg* (London, 1996), 220; Al'tman, "Die Wiederspiegelung der nationalsozialistischen Politik," 23. Compare "Sud nad gitlerovtsami—uchastnikami zlodeianii v Maidaneke," *Pravda*, December 4, 1944, 4, which cites a prosecutor as referring to *Tremblina*.
16. "Ot Sovetskogo Informbiuro: Vechernee soobshchenie 16 avgusta," *Pravda*, August 17, 1941, 1; "Ot Sovetskogo Informbiuro: Vechernee soobshchenie 30 avgusta," *Pravda*, August 31, 1941, 1. On Elnia, see TASS, "V osvobozhdennoi El'ne," *Trud*, September 11, 1941, 2 (the quotation); E. Vorob'ev, "Gorod vozvrashchaetsia k zhizni," *Trud*, October 5, 1941; "My vyrvalis' iz ada. Rasskazy zhitelei El'ni," *Izvestiia*, September 12, 1941, 3.
17. N. Petrov, "Nenavist' naroda," *Izvestiia*, September 27, 1941, 3; RGASPI, 558/11/204/63 (the revelation, made in passing); V. V. Mastikova, "Publitsistika M. I. Kalinina," in S. I. Zhukov and A. L. Mishuris, eds., *Partiinosovetskaia pechat' v gody Velikoi Otechestvennoi voiny (Sbornik statei)* (Moscow, 1964), 10, 12. See also N. Petrov, "Sviashchennaia nenavist'," *Izvestiia*, August 13, 1941, 2; Mastikova, "Publitsistika," 15-16, 18.
18. *Pravda*, September 23, 1941, 1. The differences from the original Russian translation were pointed out in RGASPI, 17/125/47/54-57: M. Burtsev, nachal'nik UP Otdela GlavPURKKA, polkovyi komissar. Dmitrii Manuilskii forwarded the document to Shcherbakov on September 27, 1941, commenting that he had verified it all. This and another case of editing by the Soviet Information Bureau were most likely the ones to which Ehrenburg referred in a letter, probably from October 1941, to Shcherbakov, Lozovskii, and Aleksandrov: RGASPI, 17/125/35/89. He writes here also that he had earlier published one of the original fragments in *Krasnaia zvezda*. Despite the internal awareness, the falsification reappeared in print; see Viktor Fink, "Blizitsia chas rasplaty," *Trud*, January 20, 1942, 2.
19. I. Stalin, *O Velikoi Otechestvennoi voine Sovetskogo Soiuza*, 4th ed. (Moscow, 1944), 17, 26, 28; G. Grigor'ev, "Gitlerovskaia Germaniia—kopiia tsarizma," *Trud*, December 31, 1941, 2.

20. RGASPI, 558/11/208/67: "Vestnik inostrannoi sluzhebnoi informatsii TASS," November 13, 1941, 48; "Rumynskie zverstva v Odesse," *Pravda*, November 16, 1941.
21. "Zverstva nemtsev v Kieve," *Pravda*, November 19, 1941, 4, and *Izvestiia*, November 19, 1941, 4; Altman and Ingerflom, "Le Kremlin et l'Holocauste," 251; Major P. Stepanenko, "Chto proiskhodit v Kieve (Ot spetsial'nogo korrespondenta 'Krasnoi zvezdy')," *Pravda*, November 29, 1941, 3; Ia. Makarenko, "V Lozovoi," *Pravda*, February 4, 1942, 2.
22. "Nota Narodnogo komissara inostrannykh del tov. V. M. Molotova: O povsemestnykh grabezhakh, razorenii naseleniia i chudovishchnykh zverstvakh germanskikh vlastei na zakhvachennykh imi sovetskikh territoriiakh," *Pravda*, January 7, 1942; *Soviet Government Statements on Nazi Atrocities* (London, [1946]), 22–23.
23. V. K. Vinogradov et al., comps., *Lubianka v dni bitvy za Moskvu: Po rassekrechennym dokumentam FSB RF* (Moscow, 2002), 367–70. Two copies of the German original and a translation omitting the key anti-Semitic phrases are at GARF, 7021/148/10/1–5v, copy at USHMM, RG-22.014M, reel 2. For the German original, see *Trial of the Major War Criminals* (Neuremberg, 1949), 35:84–86; for a facsimile, see Hamburger Institut für Sozialforschung, *Verbrechen der Wehrmacht: Dimensionen des Vernichtungskrieges 1941–1944. Ausstellungskatalog* (Hamburg, 2002), 89.
24. Sovinformbiuro, "Chudovishchnyi prikaz gitlerovskogo generala ob unichtozhenii vsekh istoricheskikh i khudozhestvennykh tsennostei i ob istreblenii muzhskogo naseleniia v zakhvachennykh nemtsami sovetskikh raionakh," *Pravda*, January 15, 1942, 2; "Chudovishchnyi prikaz gitlerovskogo komandovaniia," editorial, *Pravda*, January 15, 1942, 1.
25. RGASPI, 558/11/208/70: "Vestnik instrannoi sluzhebnoi informatsii TASS," January 17, 1942; *Izvestiia*, January 18, 1942.
26. Molotov's note of April 1942 (discussed below) did not do so either.
27. L. Dubrovitskii, "Bukhgalteriia palachei," *Izvestiia*, February 4, 1942, 2. See also *Pravda*, April 28, 1942, and *Soviet Government Statements*, 47. On these events, see Martin Cüppers, *Wegbereiter der Shoah: Die Waffen-SS, der Kommandostab Reichsführer-SS und die Judenvernichtung 1939–1945* (Darmstadt, 2005), 164–165, 194.
28. Politruk I. Miroshnichenko, "Chudovishchnye zverstva gitlerovskikh merzavtsev v Krymu," *Krasnyi flot*, January 25, 1942; politruk I. Miroshnichenko, "Chudovishchnye zverstva gitlerovtsev v Taganroge," *Krasnyi flot*, April 15, 1942; GARF, 8114/1/942/54–58: copied typescripts of "Mariupol'skaia tragediia," *Sovetskaia Ukraina*, February 28, 1942, 3, and of A. Podchekaev, "Novye zlodeiianiia nemetskikh fashistov: Chudovishchnyi akt umershchvleniia sovetskikh detei," *Sovetskaia Ukraina*, March 4, 1942, 1. The quo-

tation is in P. Lidov, "Na razvalinakh Minska i Vitebska," *Pravda*, April 15, 1942, 2.

29. Starshii politruk S. Opershtein, "Chto proiskhodit v Dnepropetrovske," *Izvestiia*, April 18, 1942, 3; Pohl, "The Murder of Ukraine's Jews," 37-38.
30. *Pravda*, April 28, 1942; *Soviet Government Statements*, 24-51.
31. "Dikie prestupleniia gitlerovskikh liudoedov," *Izvestiia*, June 20, 1942, 4. Jews are also mentioned in politruk I. Mirochnichenko, "Zverstva nemtsev v Mariupole," *Krasnyi flot*, June 25, 1942.
32. Rubenstein, *Tangled Loyalties*, 205 (on Tashkent); Mikhail Sholokhov, "Nauka nenavisti," *Pravda*, June 22, 1942, 3, also in *Krasnaia zvezda*, June 23, 1942. On translations, see *Novyi mir* 33, no. 2 (February 1958): 189. For another reference to the singling out of Jewish war prisoners for murder, see S. Liubimov, "Mozhaisk snova nash, sovetskii!," *Komsomol'skaia pravda*, January 21, 1942.
33. Kostyrchenko, *Tainaia politika Stalina*, 222-223 (on the July report); *Izvestiia*, June 19, 1942, 2.
34. *Izvestiia*, June 19, 1942, 3-4. See also Iu. Paletskis, "Ne zakabalit' narody Pribaltiki," *Trud*, July 21, 1942, 3.
35. "Rech' deputata Latsisa V.T. (Latviiskaia SSR)," *Trud*, June 19, 1942, 3, and *Izvestiia*, June 20, 1942, 2-3. For Korniiets, see *Izvestiia*, June 20, 1942, 2.
36. Il'ia Erenburg, *Liudi, gody, zhizn': Vospominaniia v trekh tomakh*, revised and enlarged ed. (n.p., 1990), 2:441, n.
37. TASS, "Evreiskie pogromy v Rumynii," *Izvestiia*, July 19, 1941, 4.
38. The play was "Partisans in the Steppes of Ukraine." Weiner, *Making Sense of War*, 209-210.
39. Richard C. Lukas, *The Forgotten Holocaust: The Poles under German Occupation, 1939-1944* (New York, 1990 [1986]), 154-155; Laqueur, *The Terrible Secret*, 73-74; Klaus-Peter Friedrich, *Der nationalsozialistische Judenmord und das polnisch-jüdische Verhältnis im Diskurs der polnischen Untergrundpresse (1942-1944)* (Marburg, 2006), 51.
40. Friedrich, *Der nationalsozialistische Judenmord*, 24-25, 51-52.
41. "Sovmestnaia deklaratsiia pravitel'stv Bel'gii, Velikobritanii, Gollandii, Gretsii, Liuksemburga, Norvegii, Pol'shchi, Soedinennykh Shtatov Ameriki, Soiuza Sovetskikh Sotsialisticheskikh Respublik, Chekhoslovakii, Iugoslavii i Frantsuzskogo Natsional'nogo Komiteta o provodimom gitlerovskimi vlastiami istreblenii evreiskogo naseleniia Evropy," *Pravda*, December 18, 1942, 1, also *Izvestiia*, December 18, 1942, *Krasnaia zvezda*, December 18, 1942, and *Trud*, December 18, 1942, 1.
42. Lev Besymenski, "Was das Sowjetvolk vom Holocaust wußte," in Leonid Luks, ed., *Der Spätstalinismus und die "jüdische Frage": Zur antisemitischen Wende des Kommunismus* (Cologne, 1998), 75-76 (on the draft); Informbiuro

Narkomindela, "Ob osushchestvlenii gitlerovskimi vlastiami plana istrebleniia evreiskogo naseleniia Evropy," *Pravda*, December 19, 1942, 1, also *Izvestiia*, December 19, 1942, 1, and *Krasnaia zvezda*, December 19, 1942, 1; *Soviet Government Statements*, 57–62.

43. N. Matiushkin, "Prokliatie i smert' nemetsko-fashistskim zakhvatchikam!," *Trud*, December 18, 1942, 2. The emphasis is mine.
44. TASS, "Otvet Ruzvel'ta na obrashchenie amerikanskikh evreiskikh organizatsii," *Trud*, December 13, 1942, 4.
45. TASS, "Nota pol'skogo pravitel'stva o zverstvakh gitlerovskikh zakhvatchikov," *Trud*, December 13, 1942, 4; Republic of Poland, Ministry of Foreign Affairs, *The Mass Extermination of Jews in Occupied Poland: Note Addressed to the Governments of the United Nations on December 10th, 1942, and Other Documents* (London, 1945).
46. TASS, "'Otvratitel'noe prestuplenie protiv chelovechestva': Shvedskaia gazeta ob istreblenii gitlerovtsami evreiskogo naseleniia Evropy," *Trud*, December 22, 1942, 4; TASS, "Prisoedinenie Kanady k deklaratsii ob"iedinennykh stran ob istreblenii gitlerovtsami evreiskogo naseleniia Evropy," *Trud*, December 22, 1942, 4.
47. "Zverstva nemetsko-fashistskikh liudoedov v Rostove-na-Donu," *Pravda*, March 13, 1943, 3, also that day's *Izvestiia*, *Krasnaia Zvezda*, and *Trud*; Altman and Ingerflom, "Le Kremlin et l'Holocaust," 260; Polian, "Stalin und die Opfer," 91; RGASPI, 558/11/490/73–74: draft report, with Stalin's permission to Shcherbakov ("Mozhno. St") for publication.
48. Stalin, *O Velikoi Otechestvennoi voine Sovetskogo Soiuza*, 95, 111.
49. I. Denisov, "Chto tvorili gitlerovtsy v Velikikh Lukakh," *Trud*, January 5, 1943, 2.
50. A. Avdeenko and P. Olender, "Babii Iar (Ot spetsial'nykh korrespondentov 'Krasnoi zvezdy')," *Krasnaia zvezda*, November 20, 1943, 3; Evgenii Kriger, Kiev, November 15, "Tak bylo v Kieve... (Ot spetsial'nogo voennogo korrespondenta 'Izvestii')," *Izvestiia*, November 16, 1943, 2, translated as "The Truth Lived on in Kiev," in Evgeny Krieger, *From Moscow to the Prussian Frontier* (London, 1945), 80–83.
51. I. Bachelis, "'Bitva za nashu Sovetskuiu Ukrainu': Novyi dokumental'nyi fil'm," *Izvestiia*, October 22, 1943, 3; Nikolai Tikhonov, "Bitva za nashu Sovetskuiu Ukrainu," *Pravda*, October 20, 1943, 2. On the Bureau, see "Ot Sovetskogo Informbiuro: Operativnaia svodka za 15 noiabria," *Pravda*, November 16, 1944, 1–2; Besymenski, "Was das Sowjetvolk vom Holocaust wußte," 73–74.
52. On the archival record, see Kiril Feferman, "Soviet Investigation of Nazi Crimes in the USSR: Documenting the Holocaust," *Journal of Genocide*

Research 5, no. 4 (December 2003): 592. Compare Katrin Boeckh, *Stalinismus in der Ukraine: Die Rekonstruktion des sowjetischen Systems nach dem Zweiten Weltkrieg* (Wiesbaden, 2007), 286-289. On the pattern, see Weiner, *Making Sense of War*, 213.

53. "O zlodeiianiiakh nemetsko-fashistskikh zakhvatchikov v g.g. Viaz'me, Gzhatske i Sychevke Smolenskoi oblasti i v gor. Rzheve Kalininskoi oblasti," *Pravda*, April 7, 1943, 1-2; "O zlodeiianiiakh nemetsko-fashistskikh okkupantov v Stravropol'skom krae," *Pravda*, August 5, 1943, 1-2. Unlike this second original, *Soviet Government Statements*, 82-90, adds a special section title.
54. Aleksei Tolstoi, "Korichnevyi durman," *Pravda*, 5 August 1943, 2.
55. Kostyrchenko, *Tainaia politika Stalina*, 226-227; Al'tman, "Die Wiederspiegelung der nationalsozialistischen Politik," 23; Aleksei Tolstoi, "Kto takoi Gitler i chego on dobivaetsia?," *Izvestiia*, 17 July 1941, 3.
56. "O razrusheniiakh i zverstvakh, sovershennykh nemetsko-fashistskimi zakhvatchikami v gorode Kieve," *Pravda*, March 1, 1944, 2, and other papers; *Soviet Government Statements*, 141; Bezymenskii, "Informatsiia posovetski," 192-193; Besymenski, "Was das Sowjetvolk vom Holocaust wußte," 78-80; Stefan Brukhfel'd [Stéphane Bruchfeld] and Pol A. Levin [Paul A. Levine], *Peredaite ob etom detiam vashim . . . : Istoriia Kholokosta v Evrope 1933-1945* (Moscow, 2000), 94 (facsimile of the edited passage). The fullest reference to the archival record (GARF, 7021/116/36/97) is in Poulsen, "The Soviet Extraordinary State Commission," 180-181.
57. "O zlodeianiiakh nemetsko-fashistskikh zakhvatchikov v Estonskoi Sovetskoi Sotsialisticheskoi Respublike," *Pravda*, November 26, 1944, 2-3; *Soviet Government Statements*, 239-240. Jews were also missing in I. Osipov, "Kostry u stantsii Kloga (Ot spetsial'nogo korrespondenta 'Izvestii')," *Izvestiia*, September 28, 1944, 2; M. Kurganov and A. Vakhov, "Lager' uzhasa i smerti," *Komsomol'skaia pravda*, October 3, 1944, 2; "Lager' smerti v poselke Kloga," *Krasnyi flot*, October 1, 1944, 3. See also Anton Weiss-Wendt, *Murder without Hatred: Estonians and the Holocaust* (Syracuse, N.Y., 2009), 301-322.
58. The emphasis is mine. "Direktivy i prikazy gitlerovskogo pravitel'stva i germanskogo voennogo komandovaniia ob istreblenii sovetskikh voennoplennykh i mirnykh grazhdan," *Pravda*, March 11, 1944, 2-3, and other newspapers; *Soviet Government Statements*, 147.
59. "O razrusheniiakh, grabezhakh i zlodeianiiakh nemetsko-fashistskikh zakhvatchikov i ikh soobshchnikov v gorode Rovno i Rovenskoi oblasti," *Pravda*, May 7, 1944, 3; "O zlodeiianiiakh nemtsev na territorii L'vovskoi oblast," *Pravda*, December 23, 1944, 2-3 (referring to *Bel'zets*); *Soviet Government Statements*, 170, 248.

60. "O zlodeianiiakh nemetsko-fashistskikh zakhvatchikov v gorode Minsk," *Pravda*, September 20, 1944, 3; "O prestupleniiakh gitlerovskikh zakhvatchikov v Litovskoi Sovetskoi Sotsialisticheskoi Respublike," *Pravda*, December 20, 1944, 2-3; "O prestupleniiakh nemetskikh zakhvatchikov na territorii Latviiskoi Sovetskoi Sotsialistischeskoi Respubliki," *Pravda*, April 5, 1945, 2-3; *Soviet Government Statements*, 227, 260, 278-280.
61. "Sovetskie profsoiuzy sdelaiut vsë neobkhodimoe dlia bystreishego razgroma vraga i obespecheniia prochnogo mira: Rech' rukovoditelia sovetskoi delegatsii, Predsedatelia VTsSPS tov. V. V. Kuznetsova na kongresse britanskikh tred-iunionov v Blekpule," *Trud*, October 21, 1944, 3.
62. TASS, "Iden o massovom terrore gitlerovtsev," *Pravda*, March 12, 1943, 4.
63. TASS, "Vozmushchenie v Bolgarii beschelovechnymi meropriiatiiami vlastei protiv evreiskogo naseleniia," *Pravda*, April 14, 1943, 4; "Pol'skie sotrudniki Gitlera," *Pravda*, April 19, 1943, 1, also quoted in Arad, "The Holocaust as Reflected," 215-216. For the TASS item, see N. S. Lebedeva et al., eds., *Katyn': Mart 1940 g.–sentiabr' 2000 g. Rasstrel. Sud'by zhivykh. Ekho Katyni. Dokumenty* (Moscow, 2001), 455.
64. I. Sergeeva, "Pol'sha—gitlerovskii 'dom smerti,'" *Pravda*, April 21, 1943, 4, also quoted in Arad, "The Holocaust as Reflected," 215-216.
65. Iuliia Barlitskaia, "Gitlerovskie razboiniki v Varshave," *Pravda*, June 26, 1941, 6; Tadeush Krushevskii [Tadeusz Kruszewski], "Nenavist' k germanskim okkupantam bezgranichna: Pis'mo iz Varshavy," *Pravda*, June 27, 1941, 6, both cited in Altshuler, "Escape and Evacuation," 88; "Vashavskoe getto vymiraet," *Izvestiia*, October 16, 1941, 4.
66. B. Ponomarev, "Neprochnyi tyl 'evropeiskoi kreposti,'" *Pravda*, May 29, 1943, 4. See also "Gitlerovskii terror v Varshave," *Pravda*, June 2, 1943, 4.
67. Ewa M. Thompson, "The Katyn Massacre and the Warsaw Ghetto Uprising in the Soviet-Nazi Propaganda War," in John Garrard and Carol Garrard, eds., *World War 2 and the Soviet People: Selected Papers from the Fourth World Congress for Soviet and East European Studies, Harrogate, 1990* (Houndmills, U.K., 1993), 223.
68. Sovinformbiuro, "Ocherednaia provokatsiia fashistskikh liudoedov," *Pravda*, August 12, 1943, also in *Sovetskaia Ukraina*, August 13, 1943, 2.
69. A. Aleksandrova, "Schet krovi: Inostrannaia pechat' ob istreblenii gitlerovskimi palachami naseleniia okkupirovannykh stran Evropy," *Trud*, January 7, 1944, 4. The article uses the words *Maidanik* and *Tremblinka*. The latter misspelling also appeared in the Polish note of November 1942 and probably was its source. Aleksandrova also mentions Auschwitz and gas vans, but no Jews.

70. The Russian spelling used is *Sabibur*. Vas[ilii] Grossman, "V gorodakh i selakh Pol'shi," *Krasnaia zvezda*, August 6, 1944, 3; Brooks, *Thank You, Comrade Stalin*, 173; *A Writer at War: Vasily Grossman with the Red Army, 1941-1945*, eds. and transl. by Antony Beevor and Luba Vinogradova (London, 2005), 281. The translation in Vassili Grossman, *With the Red Army in Poland and Byelorussia (First Byelorussian Front, June-July 1944)*, trans. Helen Altschuler (London, n.d.), 30-36, omits the notion that extermination began with the Jews and then turned to the Poles. On the other hand, it mentions population figures for prewar Lublin and its Jews in particular that are absent from the Russian text, most likely due to censorship. As for Sobibór, two articles appeared specifically about it (now identified as *Sobibur*), but neither mentioned Jews in any way. One was by the former leader of the revolt of 1943, supposedly writing from the "Acting Army"; in reality, he was hospitalized. See A. Rutman and S. Krasil'shchik, "Fabrika smerti v Sobibure," *Komsomol'skaia pravda*, September 2, 1944; A. Pecherskii, "Vosstanie v lagere smerti—Sobibur," *Komsomol'skaia pravda*, January 31, 1945, 2; S. S. Vilenskii et al., eds. *Sobibor* (Moscow, 2008), 140.
71. The Russian spellings used are *Osventsim*, *Sabibor*, and *Belzets*. K. Simonov, "Lager' unichtozheniia," *Krasnaia zvezda*, August 10-12, 1943, 3, republished in 1944 by Voenizdat as a forty-five-page brochure. An English translation is in Ilya Ehrenburg and Konstantin Simonov, *In One Newspaper: A Chronicle of Unforgettable Years*, trans. Anatol Kagan (New York, 1985), 405-430. For the text of the broadcast, see GARF, 6903/12/88/545-547 and 6903/12/89/39-41, 7-9. For today's estimate, see State Museum at Majdanek, "The History of the Camp," http://www.majdanek.pl (last accessed on August 15, 2011). The November 1943 massacre was carried out by Reserve Police Battalion 101, well-known through Christopher R. Browning, *Ordinary Men: Reserve Police Battalion 101 and the Final Solution in Poland* (New York, 1992), and Daniel Goldhagen, *Hitler's Willing Executioners: Ordinary Germans and the Holocaust* (New York, 1996).
72. Evgenii Kriger, "Nemetskaia fabrika smerti pod Liublinom," *Izvestiia*, August 12, 1944, 2, and August 13, 1944, 2.
73. The Russian spelling used is *Os'ventsim*. Boris Gorbatov, "Lager' na Maidaneke," *Pravda*, August 11, 1944, 2, and August 12, 1944, 3. For a translation, see Boris Gorbatov, "The Camp at Majdanek," in S. Krasilshchik, ed., *World War II: Dispatches from the Soviet Front*, trans. Nina Bous (New York, 1985), 287-299; RGASPI, 17/125/262/34-44: Pospelov to Shcherbakov, letter, August 10, 1944, and draft of the first part of the article, Boris Gorbatov, "Lager' na Maidanneke [*sic*]."

74. "Kommiunike agentstva 'Pol'press,'" *Izvestiia*, August 19, 1944, 4; TASS, "Rassledovanie nemetsko-fashistskikh zlodeianii v Liubline," *Izvestiia*, August 19, 1944, 4; TASS, "Zasedanie Chrezvychainoi pol'sko-sovetskoi komissii po rassledovaniiu nemetsko-fashistskikh zlodeianii v Liubline," *Trud*, August 20, 1944, 4; TASS, "Rassledovanie nemetsko-fashistskikh zlodeiianii v Liubline," *Trud*, August 23, 1944, 4; "Kommiunike Pol'sko-Sovetskoi Chrezvychainoi Komissii po rassledovaniiu zlodeianii nemtsev, sovershennykh v lagere unichtozheniia na Maidaneke v gorode Liublin," *Pravda*, September 16, 1944, 2–3, available in English in *Soviet Government Statements*, 210–225.
75. The terms used in the communiqué are *Osventim*, *Sabibur*, and *Treblinka*.
76. "Maidanek," editorial, *Pravda*, September 16, 1944, 1; "Krov' 1.500.000 ubitykh na Maidaneke vopiet o mshchenii!," editorial, *Izvestiia*, September 16, 1944, 1; "Maidanek," editorial, *Trud*, September 16, 1944, 1.
77. TASS, "Sud na palachami Maidaneka," *Pravda*, December 2, 1944, 4.
78. The Russian spelling used is *Osvetsim*. "Chudovishchnye zverstva gitlerovtsev v Pol'she," *Trud*, March 10, 1943, 3.
79. The Russian spelling used is *Osvietsim*. S. Gerasimov, "Stradaniia i bor'ba pol'skogo naroda," *Trud*, April 3, 1943, 4.
80. The Russian spelling used is *Osventsim*, which became the standard Soviet Russian transliteration from the Polish. TASS, "Zverstva gitlerovskikh liudoedov v Pol'she," *Pravda*, April 14, 1943, 4, and *Trud*, April 14, 1943, 4.
81. TASS, "Lager' smerti v Osventsime," *Pravda*, October 27, 1944, 4, also in that day's *Izvestiia* and *Trud*; Arad, "The Holocaust as Reflected," 217.
82. John S. Conway, "The First Report about Auschwitz," *Simon Wiesenthal Center Annual*, 1 (Chappaqua, N.Y., 1984), 134–135, 147; "Soobshchenie amerikanskogo upravleniia po delam bezhentsev o zverstvakh nemtsev v Pol'she," *Pravda*, November 29, 1944, 3.
83. TASS, "Zaiavlenie Khella po povodu zverstv gitlerovtsev," *Trud*, July 16, 1944, 4.
84. B. Polevoi, "Kombinat smerti v Osventsime (Ot voennogo korrespondenta 'Pravdy')," *Pravda*, February 2, 1945; "Chudovishchnye prestupleniia germanskogo pravitel'stva v Osventsime," *Pravda*, May 7, 1945, 1; Arad, "The Holocaust as Reflected," 217. A translation of the Auschwitz report is in *Soviet Government Statements*, 283–300.
85. Il'ia Erenburg, "Krov' i den'gi," *Krasnaia zvezda*, January 19, 1945, 3; Il'ia Erenburg, "V Germanii," *Krasnaia zvezda*, February 23, 1945, 3; Il'ia Erenburg, "Khvatit!," *Krasnaia zvezda*, April 11, 1945, 3.

86. Kerler, "The Soviet Yiddish Press," 221-249; my English quotation from *Eynikayt*, November 25, 1943, and December 2, 1943 is based on Gilboa, *The Black Years of Soviet Jewry*, 8, and on Weiner, *Making Sense of War*, 226.
87. "Druga bitwa o Warszawę," *Wolna Polska*, no. 14, June 8, 1943, 1, filed at RGASPI, 17/125/193/114; Major Bernhard Bechler in *Freies Deutschland*, no. 23, December 19, 1943, 3, quoted in *Das Schwarzbuch: Der Genozid an den sowjetischen Juden*, ed. Wassili Grossman, Ilja Ehrenburg, and Arno Lustiger, trans. Ruth and Heinz Deutschland (Reinbek bei Hamburg, 1994), 987.
88. Peter Novick, *The Holocaust and Collective Memory: The American Experience* (London, 2001), 27-29; Jeremy D. Harris, "Broadcasting the Massacres: An Analysis of the BBC's Contemporary Coverage of the Holocaust," *Yad Vashem Studies* 25 (Jerusalem, 1996): 65-98; Laurel Leff, *Buried by the Times: The Holocaust and America's Most Important Newspaper* (Cambridge, U.K., 2005), 2-3.
89. Kostyrchenko, *Tainaia politika Stalina*, 226-27; Arad, "The Holocaust as Reflected," 215. Arad mentions the foreign policy factor only for the time of the Katyn affair. Kostyrchenko also gives an exaggerated description of Soviet propaganda to foreign countries; from the very first months, it offered the "maximum of information about the tragedy and heroism of Soviet Jewry," and "of course, descriptions of the facts of the Hitlerite genocide of the Jews in Soviet territory in Soviet propaganda material for the West were not subject to censorship, let alone excision." Kostyrchenko, *Tainaia politika Stalina*, 229. This cannot be reconciled with the treatment of the above-quoted passage in Sholokhov's story "The Science of Hatred" about the shooting of Jews; at least one Soviet-sponsored translation omitted the passage. See Mikhail Sholokhov, *The Science of Hatred* (New York, 1943).
90. I owe this insight to Vladimir Solonari.
91. On Stalin, see Erik van Ree, "Heroes and Merchants: Stalin's Understanding of National Character," *Kritika* 8, no. 1 (Winter 2007): 45. The quotation is from Erenburg, *Liudi, gody, zhizn'*, 441. See also Kostyrchenko, *Tainaia politika Stalina*, 271-273; Weiner, *Making Sense of War*, 289. On Bolshakov, see Kostyrchenko, *Tainaia politika Stalina*, 263; full text in G. V. Kostyrchenko, ed., *Gosudarstvennyi antisemitizm v SSSR: Ot nachala do kul'minatsii, 1938-1953* (Moscow, 2005), 30. On the list, see Kostyrchenko, *Tainaia politika Stalina*, 268.
92. L. Liuks [Leonid Luks], "Evreiskii vopros v politike Stalina," *Voprosy istorii*, no. 7 (1999): 45 (on diplomats); I. I. Shirokorad, *Tsentral'naia periodicheskaia*

pechat' v gody Velikoi Otechestvennoi voiny: 1941–1945 (Moscow, 2001), 74–78; David Ortenberg, *Stalin, Shcherbakov, Mekhlis i drugie* (Moscow, 1995), 20–21, 141–143, 187; Brooks, *Thank You, Comrade Stalin*, 154, 171–172; Kostyrchenko, *Tainaia politika Stalina*, 266.

93. Kostyrchenko, *Tainaia politika Stalina*, 246–247; Suzanne Rosenberg, *A Soviet Odyssey* (Toronto, 1988), 88–90. A partial publication of Kondakov's report is in Kostyrchenko, *Gosudarstvennyi antisemitizm v SSSR*, 48–49. On the warning, see Weiner, *Making Sense of War*, 225.

94. Kostyrchenko, *Tainaia politika Stalina*, 245; Kostyrchenko, *Gosudarstvennyi antisemitizm v SSSR*, 35–36.

95. On his chauvinism, see David Brandenberger, *National Bolshevism: Stalinist Mass Culture and the Formation of Modern Russian National Identity, 1931–1956* (Cambridge, Mass., 2002), 125, 159. His article was G. Aleksandrov, "Gitlerovskaia Germaniia lopnet pod tiazhestv'iu svoikh prestuplenii," *Pravda*, December 4, 1941, 3; see also Bezymenskii, "Informatsiia posovetski," 193–194. About August 1942, see Liuks, "Evreiskii vopros v politike Stalina," 44–45; Kostyrchenko, *Tainaia politika Stalina*, 259–61; and the full document in Kostyrchenko, *Gosudarstvennyi antisemitizm v SSSR*, 27–29. About May 1944, see Kostyrchenko, *Tainaia politika Stalina*, 269–271. About 1947, see Redlich, *War, Holocaust and Stalinism*, 366.

96. A. N. Ponomarev, *Aleksandr Shcherbakov: Stranitsy biografii* (Moscow, 2004), 228; Kostyrchenko, *Tainaia politika Stalina*, 227. See also Gilboa, *The Black Years of Soviet Jewry*, 381, n. 6.

97. Brooks, *Thank You, Comrade Stalin*, 189; Gilboa, *The Black Years of Soviet Jewry*, 382, n. 6, citing Harrison E. Salisbury, *To Moscow and Beyond: A Reporter's Narrative* (New York, 1960), 68, and Maurice Hindus, *House without a Roof: Russia after Forty-three Years of Revolution* (Garden City, N.Y., 1961), 311.

98. U.S. Holocaust Memorial Museum archives, RG-22.009 (Selected Records from the Archive of the Ministry of Foreign Affairs, Moscow, 1941–1944), fiche 03*01, holding a photocopy of Arkhiv vneshnei politiki RF, 13/6/papka2/10/65–66: [S.] A. Lozovskii, "Tovarishchu V. G. Dekanozovu," n.p., February 11, 1944.

99. Kostyrchenko, *Tainaia politika Stalina*, 242; Jack Pomerantz and Lyric Wallwork-Winik, *Run East: Flight from the Holocaust* (Urbana, Ill., 1997), 47, 54, 58, 90 (on kindness). For more on Polish Jewish refugees, see Yosef Litvak, "Jewish Refugees from Poland in the USSR," in Zvi Gitelman, ed., *Bitter Legacy: Confronting the Holocaust in the USSR* (Bloomington, Ind., 1997), 123–150.

100. *Rapports secrets soviétiques: La société russe dans les documents confidentiels 1921–1991: Recueil de pièces d'archives provenant du Centre de conservation de la documentation contemporaine, du Centre russe de conservation et d'étude des documents d'histoire contemporaine, des Archives d'État de la Féderation de Russie*, ed. and trans. Nicolas Werth and Gaël Moullec (Paris, 1994), 228–230 (on Moscow); Jörg Baberowski, *Der rote Terror: Die Geschichte des Stalinismus* (Munich, 2003), 221, 219 (on Moscow and Rostov); K. S. Karol, *Solik: Life in the Soviet Union 1939–1946*, trans. Eamonn McArdle (London, 1986), 308 (on Rostov); Kostyrchenko, *Tainaia politika Stalina*, 225 (on front-line villages); Abraham A. Kreusler, *A Teacher's Experiences in the Soviet Union* (Leiden, 1965), 157.

101. Kreusler, *A Teacher's Experiences in the Soviet Union*, 51, 95 (on Stalingrad); Leon Gouré and Herbert S. Dinerstein, *Two Studies in Soviet Controls* (Glencoe, Ill., 1955), 216 (on Moscow); Kostyrchenko, *Tainaia politika Stalina*, 243; full texts in Kostyrchenko, *Gosudarstvennyi antisemitizm v SSSR*, 32–34. For further discussion, see Brandenberger, *National Bolshevism*, 179.

102. On demobilized soldiers, see Brandenberger, *National Bolshevism*, 179; Kostyrchenko, *Tainaia politika Stalina*, 243. On Leningraders, see Nikita Andreevich Lomagin, *Neizvestnaia blokada*, 2nd ed., book 1 (St. Petersburg, 2004), 313–315, 323–324, 327, 351, 359, 367, 372, 390, 393. On writers, see TsDAHOU, 1/23/685/82–87: Sergienko, NKVD U[k]SSR to N. S. Khrushchev, "Spetsial'noe soobshchenie," n.p., March 22, 1943.

103. On the institute, see Kostyrchenko, *Tainaia politika Stalina*, 272–273; full text in Kostyrchenko, *Gosudarstvennyi antisemitizm v SSSR*, 36–37. On Stalin's thinking, see Al'tman, "Die Wiederspiegelung der nationalsozialistischen Politik," 17–19; Arad, "Stalin and the Soviet Leadership," 203, 219; Liuks, "Evreiskii vopros v politike Stalina," 44; Gilboa, *The Black Years of Soviet Jewry*, 300; Lustiger, *Rotbuch*, 121–122; Altman and Ingerflom, "Le Kremlin et l'Holocauste," 271.

104. Novick, *The Holocaust and Collective Memory*, 28–29; Peter Novick, review of Leff, *Buried by the Times*, *Washington Post*, May 1, 2005, BW06; Harris, "Broadcasting the Massacres"; David Cesarani, "Great Britain," in David S. Wyman and Charles H. Rosenzweig, eds., *The World Reacts to the Holocaust* (Baltimore, 1996), 607–608.

105. See Arad, "Stalin and the Soviet Leadership," 356; Arad, "The Holocaust as Reflected," 218; Löwe, "The Holocaust in the Soviet Press," 37–38.

106. Kreusler, *A Teacher's Experiences in the Soviet Union*, 154 (the quotation); Herman Carmel, *Black Days, White Nights* (New York, 1984), 230, 285, 338.

7. Hatred with All the Might of the Soul

1. Siân Nicholas, *The Echo of War: Home Front Propaganda and the Wartime BBC, 1939–45* (Manchester, U.K., 1996), 154–155, 179 (believes that the Germans "never became the explicit focus of hate-propaganda"); Ian McLaine, *Ministry of Morale: Home Front Morale and the Ministry of Information in World War II* (London, 1979), 158; John W. Dower, *War without Mercy: Race and Power in the Pacific* (New York, 1986).
2. Susan Benesch, "Vile Crime or Inalienable Right: Defining Incitement to Genocide," *Virginia Journal of International Law* 48, no. 3 (2008): 487.
3. The latter sentence is the argument proposed in Argyrios K. Pisiotis, "Images of Hate in the Art of War," in Richard Stites, ed., *Culture and Entertainment in Wartime Russia* (Bloomington, Ind., 1995), 152. The quoted Russian historians are, respectively, N. D. Kozlov, *Obshchestvennoe soznanie v gody Velikoi Otechestvennoi voiny (1941–1945)* (St. Petersburg, 1995), 90, repeated in his *Propaganda i obydennoe soznanie v gody Velikoi Otechestvennoi voiny* (St Petersburg, 2002), 191; Aleksandr Rubashkin, *Il'ia Erenburg: Put' pisatelia* (St. Petersburg, 1990), 337; E. S. Seniavskaia, *Protivniki Rossii v voinakh XX veka: Evoliutsiia "obraza vraga" v soznanii armii i obshchestva* (Moscow, 2006), 84–85, 88, 95, 97. For rare Russian acknowledgments that the propaganda was anti-German, see Tatiana Goriaeva, "Ubit' nemtsa: Obraz protivnika v sovetskoi propagande," *Rodina*, no. 10 (Moscow, 2002): 43; Tat'iana Goriaeva, "'Esli zavtra voina...': Obraz protivnika v sovetskoi propagande 1941–1945," in Karl Eimermacher et al., eds., *Rossiia i Germaniia v XX veke*, tom 1: *Obol'shchenie vlast'iu: Russkie i nemtsy v Pervoi i Vtoroi mirovykh voinakh* (Moscow, 2010), 353.
4. Catherine Merridale, *Ivan's War: The Red Army 1939–1945* (London, 2005), 256, 270.
5. See, for example, Boris Ol'shanskii, *My prikhodim s Vostoka (1941–1951)* (Buenos Aires, 1954), 19–20.
6. Jeffrey Brooks, *Thank You, Comrade Stalin! Soviet Public Culture from Revolution to Civil War* (Princeton, N.J., 2000), 170 (the quotation); Liudmyla Hrynevych, "Tsina stalins'koï 'revoliutsiï zhory': Ukraïns'ke selianstvo v ochikuvanni na viinu," *Problemy istoriï Ukraïny: Fakty, sudzhennia, poshuky*, no. 16, pt. 1 (Kiev, 2007): 287–306 (on peasants in the early 1930s); G. Kizilo, "Nemtsy prishli," *Vozrozhdenie*, no. 17 (Paris, September–October 1951): 108–109 (on Kharkiv). For evidence on Rostov and Kiev, respectively, see Mary M. Leder, *My Life in Stalinist Russia: An American Woman Looks Back* (Bloomington, Ind., 2001), 193–194; Karel C. Berkhoff, *Harvest of Despair: Life and Death in Ukraine under Nazi Rule* (Cambridge, Mass., 2004), 61–62.

7. K. S. Karol, *Solik: Life in the Soviet Union 1939–1946*, trans. Eamonn McArdle (London, 1996), 62.
8. I. Stalin, *O Velikoi Otechestvennoi voine Sovetskogo Soiuza*, 4th ed. (Moscow, 1944), 10-11, 14. For Molotov, see *Pravda*, June 22, 1941.
9. Stalin, *O Velikoi Otechestvennoi voine Sovetskogo Soiuza*, 25-28.
10. Ibid., 43-45.
11. Ibid., 45-54.
12. "Rasskaz nemetskogo soldata Al'freda Liskofa," *Pravda*, June 27, 1941, 2, facsimile in Deutsch-Russisches Museum Berlin-Karlshorst, *Beutestücke: Kriegsgefangene in der deutschen und sowjetischen Fotografie 1941–1945* (Berlin, 2003), 104; TASS, "Zarubezhnye otkliki na vystuplenie po radio Predsedatelia Gos. Kom. Ob. I. V. Stalina," *Izvestiia*, July 6, 1941, 4 (on the Swiss claim); Johannes Becher and Friedrich Wolff in *Izvestiia*, August 12, 1941, 1-3; "Zhenshchiny vsego mira—na bor'bu protiv fashizma! Na mitinge v Kolonnom zale Doma Soiuzov 7 sentiabria 1941 goda," *Izvestiia*, September 9, 1941, 3; "Molodezh' mira—na sviashchennuiu bor'bu s gitlerizmom! Vystupleniia na antifashistskom mitinge molodezhe v Moskve," *Izvestiia*, September 30, 1941, 3; Vil'gel'm Pik [Wilhelm Pieck] et al., "Obrashchenie Tsentral'nogo Komiteta Kommunisticheskoi partii Germanii. K nemetskomu narodu i k nemetskoi armii!," *Izvestiia*, October 16, 1941, 3.
13. "Povernite oruzhie protiv bandy gitlerovskikh ubiits! Golos krest'ian Respubliki Nemtsev Povolzh'ia," *Izvestiia*, July 15, 1941, 3, also in *Trud*, July 15, 1941, 2. The Bureau statement is in *Pravda*, July 14, 1941, 2, and *Izvestiia*, July 15, 1941, 2.
14. Deutsch-Russisches Museum Berlin-Karlshorst, *Juni 1941: Der tiefe Schnitt* (Berlin, 2001), 112; J. Otto Pohl, *Ethnic Cleansing in the USSR, 1937–1949* (Westport, Conn., 1999), 34-35; Pavel Polian, *Against Their Will: The History and Geography of Forced Migrations in the USSR*, trans. Anna Yastrzembska (Budapest, 2004), 128-129, 131.
15. Viktor Krieger, "Patriots or Traitors? The Soviet Government and the 'German Russians' after the Attack on the USSR by National Socialist Germany," in Karl Schlögel, ed., *Russian-German Special Relations in the Twentieth Century* (Oxford, 2006), 139, 149-150; Jörg Ganzenmüller, *Das belagerte Leningrad 1941–1944: Die Stadt in den Strategien von Angreifern und Verteidigern* (Paderborn, 2005), 285-286; Robert Conquest, *The Nation Killers: The Soviet Deportation of Nationalities* (London, 1970), 107; Pohl, *Ethnic Cleansing in the USSR*, 32-54; Polian, *Against Their Will*, 126-138; Amir Weiner, *Making Sense of War: The Second World War and the Fate of the Bolshevik Revolution* (Princeton, N.J., 2001), 150. The deportations had a tsarist

Russian precedent during World War I. Mostly involving Slavs, they exceeded other belligerent states' deportations in scope. See Eric Lohr, *Nationalizing the Russian Empire: The Campaign against Enemy Aliens during World War I* (Cambridge, Mass., 2003), 127.

16. N. Petrov, "Sviashchennaia nenavist'," *Izvestiia*, 13 August, 1941, 2, reprinted in M. I. Kalinin, *Stat'i i rechi (1941–1946)* (Moscow, 1975), 20–22; N. Petrov, "Nenavist' naroda," *Izvestiia*, September 27, 1941, 3.

17. Aleksandrov, "Gitlerovskaia Germaniia lopnet pod tiazhestv'iu svoikh prestuplenii," *Pravda*, December 4, 1941, 3; *O rabote raionnykh gazet*, secret booklet dated March 3, 1942, filed at TsDAHOU, 1/23/67/19/21.

18. G. Grigor'ev, "Gitlerovskaia Germaniia—kopiia tsarizma," *Trud*, December 13, 1941, 2; Tatjana Filippowa, "Von der Witzfigur zum Unmenschen—Die Deutschen in den Kriegsausgaben von 'Novyj Satirikon' und 'Krokodil,'" in Dagmar Herrmann et al., eds., *Traum und Trauma: Russen und Deutsche im 20. Jahrhundert* (Munich, 2003), 139.

19. Iogannes Bekher et al., "Obrashchenie obshchestvennykh i politicheskikh deiatelei Germanii k germanskomu narodu," *Pravda*, January 30, 1942, 2; TASS from New York, "Obrashchenie antifashistskikh nemetskikh pisatelei k germanskomu narodu," *Pravda*, March 22, 1942, 4.

20. "Pervaia konferentsiia plennykh mladshikh komandirov nemetskoi armii," *Pravda*, March 19, 1942, 3. For the other letters by Germans, see "Protest nemetskikh voennoplennykh protiv zverskogo obrashcheniia germanskikh vlastei s sovetskimi voennoplennymi: Ianvar' 1942 goda. Mezhdunarodnomu komitetu Krasnogo Kresta," *Pravda*, February 5, 1942; "765 plennykh nemetskikh soldat prisoedinilis' k deklaratsii pervoi konferentsii nemetskikh voennoplennykh," *Pravda*, February 13, 1942, 3, facsimile in *Beutestücke*, 108; "Protest nemetskikh voennoplennykh protiv zverstv i nasilii germanskikh vlastei v okkupirovannykh sovetskikh raionakh: Mezhdunarodnomu Komitetu Krasnogo Kresta. Zheneva (Shveitsariia)," *Izvestiia*, June 4, 1942, 3. On Austrian POWs, see *Pravda*, March 27, 1942; Peter Gosztony, *Stalins fremde Heere: Das Schicksal der nichtsowjetischen Truppen im Rahmen der Roten Armee 1941–1945* (Bonn, 1991), 122–129.

21. Stalin, *O Velikoi Otechestvennoi voine Sovetskogo Soiuza*, 44. About Stalin's lifelong ambiguity about Germans, see Erik van Ree, "Heroes and Merchants: Stalin's Understanding of National Character," *Kritika* 8, no. 1 (Winter 2007): 49–51.

22. Stalin, *O Velikoi Otechestvennoi voine Sovetskogo Soiuza*, 52; Brooks, *Thank You, Comrade Stalin*, 170; "Liubov' k rodine i nenevist' k vragu," *Pravda*, May 18, 1942, 1 (the editorial).

23. RGASPI, 558/11/204/5-22: marked draft and final typing; "Polkovodets Suvorov (Kniga t. Osipova 'Suvorov,' Gospolitizdat, 1942 g.)," *Izvestiia*, August 26, 1942, 4.
24. "Sovetskii patriot," *Pravda*, June 6, 1942, 1; "Nenavist' k vragu," *Pravda*, July 11, 1942, 1, also quoted in Alexander Werth, *Russia at War, 1941–1945* (New York, 1964), 391.
25. Mikhail Sholokhov, "Nauka nenavisti," *Pravda*, June 22, 1942, 3, and *Krasnaia zvezda*, June 23, 1942.
26. On the ideology and metaphors, see Daniel Weiss, "Stalinistischer und nationalsozialistischer Propagandadiskurs im Vergleich: Eine erste Annäherung," in Holger Kuße, ed., *Slavistische Linguistik 2001: Referate des XXVII. Konstanzer Slavistischen Arbeitstreffens. Frankfurt/Friedrichsdorf, 11.–13.9.2001 = Slavistische Beiträge*, 422 (Munich, 2003), 325. On images, see Pisiotis, "Images of Hate," 146, 149. For Vichy leaders, see Boris Efimov, "Utechka gosudarstvennogo apparata," *Trud*, July 8, 1944, 4. On vermin, see, for example, TsDAVOV, 4915/1/4/206: Ukrainian radio, May 1, 1944. On spiders, see "Goriat nenavist'iu k vragu serdtsa sovetskikh liudei," *Izvestiia*, June 28, 1942, 1, an editorial citing a Soviet soldier.
27. P. Antokol'skii, "Eto ne liudi," *Izvestiia*, September 16, 1941, 3; "Smert' detoubiitsam!," editorial, *Pravda*, August 14, 1942, 1 (both on killers as not human); Katharine Hodgson, *Written with the Bayonet: Soviet Russian Poetry of World War Two* (Liverpool, 1996), 139 (on wolves).
28. Aleksei Tolstoi, "Ubei zveria!," *Pravda*, June 23, 1942, 2.
29. The Russian word used for "race" was *otrod'e*. Vanda Vasilevskaia, *Raduga: Povest'*, trans. E. Usievich (Moscow, 1945), 77–78. For other English translations of the passages, see *Rainbow: A Novel by Wanda Wassilewska*, trans. Edith Bone (London, n.d.), 66. The novel appeared in *Izvestia* from August 25 to September 27, 1942.
30. Vasilevskaia, *Raduga*, 77, 88. See also *Rainbow*, 65–66, 75.
31. Vasilevskaia, *Raduga*, 78, 166, 89, 219–220. See also *Rainbow*, 67, 139, 76, 181.
32. Maurice Hindus, *Mother Russia* (London, 1943), 162; GARF, 6903/12/25/154–155: July 22, 1942 (the radio talk); Vera Sandomirsky, "Soviet War Poetry," *Russian Review* 4, no. 1 (Spring 1944): 50 (the quotation). The relevant archival file, GARF, 6903/12/24, does not reveal whether the poem was read on the radio at the time.
33. A. Surkov, *Stikhi o nenavisti* (Moscow, 1943); Werth, *Russia at War*, 387–388 (the long quotations); Hodgson, *Written with the Bayonet*, 61–62.
34. "K zhenshchinam vsego mira," *Izvestiia*, May 12, 1942, 2; "Vtoroi antifashistskii miting molodezhi v Moskve," *Izvestiia*, June 9, 1942, 2; Mikhail Vol'f,

"Fashistskaia sistema razvrashcheniia molodezhi," *Krasnaia zvezda*, July 16, 1942, 4.

35. G. Grigor'ev, "O roli moral'nogo faktora v bor'be za razgrom vraga," *Propagandist*, nos. 13-14 (1942): 35, quoted in Evgenii Dobrenko, *Metafora vlasti: Literatura stalinskoi epokhi v istoricheskom osveshchenii* (Munich, 1993), 309-310.
36. Sandomirsky, "Soviet War Poetry," 51-52; Battalion Commissar Vershinin, "Nenavist'," *Pravda*, September 9, 1942, 1.
37. Semen Gershberg, *Zavtra gazeta vykhodit* (Moscow, 1966), 375-377.
38. Stalin, *O Velikoi Otechestvennoi voine Sovetskogo Soiuza*, 70-71, 82, 93, 96.
39. T. M. Goriaeva, comp., Ia. I. Zasurskii, ed. in chief, *Istoriia soveskoi radiozhurnalistiki: Dokumenty. Teksty. Vospominaniia 1917-1945* (Moscow, 1991), 263, 265.
40. GARF, 6903/1/82/95-96: Tat'iana Mironovna Delitsina, March 3, 1943, 10:25 A.M.; GARF, 6903/1/82/97: Klavdiia Semenovna Kolesnikova, March 7, 1943, 10:25 A.M.
41. "Smert' dushohubam!," editorial, *Radians'ka Ukraïna*, March 3, 1943, 1; Prof. M. N. Petrovs'kyi, "Nimets'ki zaharbnyky—vikonvichni vorohy ukraïns'koho narodu," *Radians'ka Ukraïna*, June 16, 1943, 3.
42. On the committee, see "MANIFEST Natsional'nogo Komiteta 'Svobodnaia Germaniia' k germanskoi armii i germanskomu narodu," *Pravda*, July 21, 1943, 3, also in *Sovetskaia Ukraina*, July 24, 1943, 2; Gerd R. Ueberschär, ed., *Das Nationalkomitee "Freies Deutschland" und der Bund Deutscher Offiziere* (Frankfurt am Main, 1995), 265-268 (the original German text). On the officers, see "Sozdanie Soiuza nemetskikh ofitserov," *Pravda*, September 20, 1943, 3; "Stvorennia Soiuzu nimets'kykh ofitseriv," *Radians'ka Ukraïna*, September 24, 1943, 3; Bodo Scheurig, *Verräter oder Patrioten: Das Nationalkomitee "Freies Deutschland" und der Bund Deutscher Offiziere in der Sowjetunion 1943-1945* (Berlin, 1993), 189-192 (the original German text).
43. "K obrazovaniiu National'nogo Komiteta 'Svobodnaia Germaniia,'" *Pravda*, August 1, 1943, 1.
44. W. L. White, *Report on the Russians* (London, 1945), 131. A late case was "Obrashchenie nemetskikh generalov i polkovnikov: K nemetskomu narodu v armii i na rodine," *Trud*, September 26, 1944, 2.
45. Catherine Merridale, "Culture, Ideology and Combat in the Red Army, 1939-45," *Journal of Contemporary History* 41, no. 2 (April 2006): 319 (on the border crossing); RGASPI, 558/11/491/50-54: draft of the Sovinformbiuro statement, "Ocherednaia provokatsiia fashistsikh liudoedov"; compare the published version in *Pravda*, August 12, 1943 (both on Vinnytsia); Stalin, *O Velikoi Otechestvennoi voine Sovetskogo Soiuza*, 111, 135 (my emphasis).

46. "Otvety chitatelei 'Sandi ekspress' na pis'mo rimskogo papy," *Izvestiia*, September 6, 1944, 4; RGASPI, 558/11/209/23 (Stalin's order).
47. "Ot grazhdan Sovetskoi Belorussii, osvobozhdennykh nashei doblestnoi Krasnoi Armiei iz nemetskogo lageria smerti v raione mestechka Azarichi, Polesskoi oblasti: Moskva, Kreml. Tovarishchu STALINU," *Izvestiia*, April 16, 1944, 2; I. Osipov, acting army, September 27, "Kostry u stantsii Kloga (Ot spetsial'nogo korrespondenta 'Izvestii')," *Izvestiia*, September 28, 1944, 2; Evgenii Kriger, "Nemetskaia fabrika smerti pod Liublinom," *Izvestiia*, August 12, 1944, 2, and August 13, 1944, 2; Seniavskaia, *Protivniki Rossii*, 89, citing K. Simonov, "Lager' unichtozheniia," *Krasnaia zvezda*, August 10-12, 1943, 3.
48. "Izveshchenie ot nachal'nika militsii gor. Mosvky," *Pravda*, July 17, 1944, 4; B. Polevoi, "Oni uvideli Moskvu," *Pravda*, July 19, 1944, 3; Leonid Leonov, "Nemtsy v Moskve," *Pravda*, July 19, 1944, 3; Leonid Leonov, "Germans in Moscow," in S. Krasilshchik, ed., *World War II: Dispatches from the Soviet Front*, trans. Nina Bous (New York, 1985), 278-282. The draft of Polevoi's article is at RGASPI, 17/125/263/9-13. For examples of hateful silence, see Ivan Le, "Vyzvolennia," *Radians'ka Ukraïna*, February 19, 1943, 3, and Boris Gorbatov, *Nepokorennye (Sem'ia Tarasa)* (Moscow, 1943), 27-28.
49. In original usage, *vseobshchaia nenavist'; natsiia*. Stalin, *O Velikoi Otechestvennoi voine Sovetskogo Soiuza*, 147, 154.
50. Thomas Urban, "Ilja Ehrenburg als Kriegspropagandist," in Herrmann et al., *Traum und Trauma*, 245, 249-252.
51. Goriaeva, "Ubit' nemtsa," 42, citing RGALI, 631/16/129/1-18.
52. "I. Erenburg glazami D. Zaslavskogo," *Lekhaim*, no. 7(171) (electronic journal, Moscow, July 2006), at www.lechaim.ru; Edmund Stevens, *Russia Is No Riddle* (New York, 1945), 135, slightly revised.
53. "The First Day," "Brown Lice," in Ilya Ehrenburg, *Russia at War*, trans. Gerard Shelley (London, 1943), 202, 22; I. Erenburg, "Korichnevaia vosh'," July 18, 1941, reprinted in Il'ia Erenburg, *Voina (Iiun' 1941-aprel' 1942)* (Moscow, 1942), 30-33.
54. Goriaeva, "'Esli zavtra voina,'" 351, citing RGASPI, 17/125/47/20-24 (Central Committee document); Goriaeva, "Ubit' nemtsa," 42.
55. For examples with *Hitlerites* or *fascists*, see I. Erenburg, "Khuzhe zverei," September 5, 1941, reprinted in Erenburg, *Voina (Iiun' 1941-aprel' 1942)*, 69-71, and translated as "Worse than Wild Beasts," in Ehrenburg, *Russia at War*, 49-50; Il'ia Erenburg, "Spravedlivost'," 18 December 1943, reprinted in Il'ia Erenburg, *Voina (aprel' 1943-mart 1944)* (Moscow, 1944), 165. For the quotations, see I. Erenburg, "Strakh," *Krasnaia zvezda*, October 9, 1941, 3, reprinted in Erenburg, *Voina (Iiun' 1941-aprel' 1942)*, 104-105, and translated

as "Fear," in Ehrenburg, *Russia at War*, 73-74; Ilia Erenburg, "Vystoiat'!," *Krasnaia zvezda*, October 12, 1941, reprinted in Erenburg, *Voina (Iiun' 1941–aprel' 1942)*, 306-309, and translated as "Hold Out!," in Ehrenburg, *Russia at War*, 219-222.

56. I. Erenburg, "Otvet Ribbentropu," December 3, 1941, reprinted in Erenburg, *Voina (Iiun' 1941–aprel' 1942)*, 118-121.
57. GARF, 9425/1/108/28-29: Sadchikov, "Svodka No 1 vycherkov, proizvedennykh tsenzorami v poriadke predvaritel'nogo i posleduiushchego kontrolia, po materialam na 15-e ianvaria 1942 goda," about an open letter to Stalin signed by collective farmers, scheduled for the radio program *Latest News* (*Poslednie izvestiia*). For a similar correction with regard to Stalin's May 1, 1942, order, see GARF, 6903/1/70/48: [signature illegible] to Polikarpov, "Dokladnaia zapiska ob itogakh proverki sostoianiia raboty v otdele agitatsii," n.p., August 14, 1942, criticizing an essay by one Vasilenko, "Nenavidet' vraga vsemi silami dushi," broadcast on July 22, 1942.
58. Fragments of the recording, in author's possession; Stalin, *O Velikoi Otechestvennoi voine Sovetskogo Soiuza*, 34, 36.
59. I. Erenburg, "Vesna v ianvare," January 14, 1942, "Velikoe odichanie," January 29, 1942, and "Gore ot rasseiannosti," January 25, 1942, reprinted in Erenburg, *Voina (Iiun' 1941–aprel' 1942)*, 329-336, 151-157, 148-151.
60. I. Erenburg, "O nenavisti," *Krasnaia zvezda*, May 5, 1942, 4, reprinted in Erenburg, *Voina (Iiun' 1941–aprel' 1942)*, 178-185, and translated as "Hatred," in Ehrenburg, *Russia at War*, 127-132, and as "About Hatred," in Ilya Ehrenburg and Konstantin Simonov, *In One Newspaper: A Chronicle of Unforgettable Years*, trans. Anatol Kagan (New York, 1985), 143-150; I. Erenburg, "Opravdanie nenavisti," May 26, 1942, reprinted in Il'ia Erenburg, *Voina (Aprel' 1942–mart 1943)* (Moscow, 1943), 3-8. The English translation, published in Moscow in 1942, sometimes replaced the word "German" with "Nazi" or "Hitlerites"; see the reprint in James von Geldern and Richard Stites, eds., *Mass Culture in Soviet Russia: Tales, Poems, Songs, Movies, Plays, and Folklore. 1917–1953* (Bloomington, Ind., 1995), 403, 405. On vermin (*gady*), see "Iiun'," June 21, 1942, reprint in Erenburg, *Voina (Aprel' 1942–mart 1943)*, 286-291.
61. Il'ia Erenburg, "O patriotizme," *Pravda*, June 14, 1942, 2. Compare Erenburg, *Voina (Aprel' 1942–mart 1943)*, 199-200. A partial German translation of the *Pravda* version is in Erwin Oberländer, *Sowjetpatriotismus und Geschichte: Dokumentation* (Cologne, 1967), 75-76. The English translation "On Patriotism," reprinted in Ehrenburg and Simonov, *In One Newspaper*, 171-178, was based on the longer version (wrongly dated *July* 14, 1942) in

Erenburg, *Voina (Aprel' 1942–mart 1943)*, 193-200, but omitted numerous anti-German passages. The omissions and deviations demonstrate the need for a full and critical bibliography of all of Ehrenburg's wartime publications.

62. "Ugroza," *Krasnaia zvezda*, July 17, 1942, 3, reprinted in Erenburg, *Voina (Aprel' 1942–mart 1943)*, 239-243 (on deceit and murder); Il'ia Erenburg, "Orda na Donu," *Krasnaia zvezda*, July 12, 1942, 3. For some reason, the quoted sentence (with, in the original, *nedorosl'*, *nevezhda*, and *kretin*) was omitted from Erenburg, *Voina (Aprel' 1942–mart 1943)*, 16-20.

63. The original words in the first sentence are *nemtsy ne liudi*. Erenburg, "Ubei," *Krasnaia zvezda*, July 24, 1942, 4, reprinted in Erenburg, *Voina (Aprel' 1942–mart 1943)*, 21-23. A facsimile of the leaflet is in *Ilja Ehrenburg und die Deutschen* (Berlin, 1997), 70; a full wartime German translation is in Ortwin Buchbender, *Das tönende Erz: Deutsche Propaganda gegen die Rote Armee im Zweiten Weltkrieg* (Stuttgart, 1978), 305. English translations of the key sentences are in Werth, *Russia at War*, 388; Joshua Rubenstein, *Tangled Loyalties: The Life and Times of Ilya Ehrenburg* (London, 1996), 192. All texts broadcast from July 25 through 30 are missing from GARF, 6903/12/25.

64. *Ilja Ehrenburg und die Deutschen*, 74 ("*Da! Nemtsy bezzhalostno istrebliali zhidov*"). In his memoirs Ehrenburg cites the same sentence, but apparently from another German-sponsored leaflet; see Il'ia Erenburg, *Liudi, gody, zhizn'* (Moscow, 1990), 2:351.

65. Il'ia Erenburg, "Prokliatoe semia," *Krasnaia zvezda*, August 2, 1942, 3, reprinted in Erenburg, *Voina (Aprel' 1942–mart 1943)*, 23-24 (on warmongers); Il'ia Erenburg, "Pomni!," *Krasnaia zvezda*, August 13, 1942, 3, also quoted in Werth, *Russia at War*, 388.

66. I. Erenburg, "Rossiia," August 14, 1942, reprinted in Erenburg, *Voina (Aprel' 1942–mart 1943)*, 213-216. See also, about a political officer (*politruk*), Il'ia Erenburg, "Nenavist' i prezrenie," August 28, 1942, reprinted in Erenburg, *Voina (Aprel' 1942–mart 1943)*, 255-258.

67. "Zhit' odnim," August 21, 1942, reprinted in Erenburg, *Voina (Aprel' 1942–mart 1943)*, 311-315.

68. Il'ia Erenburg, "Lichnoe delo," December 20, 1942, reprinted in Erenburg, *Voina (Aprel' 1942–mart 1943)*, 334-339.

69. Il'ia Erenburg, "Zrelost'," *Bol'shevik*, nos. 19-20 (Moscow, October 1942): 94, 96. This text was first cited in Kozlov, *Obshchestvennoe soznanie*, 102-103.

70. "Sud skoryi i pravyi," September 22, 1942; "Svet v blindazhe," November 10, 1942, both reprinted in Erenburg, *Voina (Aprel' 1942–mart 1943)*, 145-147,

326–332; Il'ia Erenburg, "Za cheloveka," April 24, 1943, reprinted in Erenburg, *Voina (aprel' 1943–mart 1944)*, 5.

71. On retribution, see Erenburg, "Dusha Rossii," November 11, 1943, reprinted in Erenburg, *Voina (aprel' 1943–mart 1944)*, 394, 398. The quoted text is lacking from the translation in Ehrenburg and Simonov, *In One Newspaper*, 362. On feeling bad, see Il'ia Erenburg, "Nashe gore," December 4, 1943, reprinted in Erenburg, *Voina (aprel' 1943–mart 1944)*, 114. On finishing off, see Manfred Zeidler, *Kriegsende im Osten: Die Rote Armee und die Besetzung Deutschlands östlich von Oder und Neiβe 1944/45* (Munich, 1996), 120, quoting "Finish It Properly!," *Soviet War News*, February 25, 1944, 1. On the cradle, see I. Erenburg, "Narod na voine," February 24, 1944, reprinted in Erenburg, *Voina (aprel' 1943–mart 1944)*, 404. On the sword, see I. Erenburg, "Nakanune," *Pravda*, August 7, 1944, 3; Ewa Bérard, *La vie tumultueuse d'Ilya Ehrenbourg: Juif, Russe et Soviétique* (Paris, 1991), 252. On a trial, see Il'ia Erenburg, "V Germanii," *Krasnaia zvezda*, February 23, 1945, 3. For the final quotation, see Erenburg, "Nastalsia rasplata," *Krasnaia zvezda*, January 30, 1945, quoted in Urban, "Ilja Ehrenburg," 261.

72. Il'ia Erenburg, "Dal'she!," *Krasnaia zvezda*, March 8, 1945, 3 (the first quotation); Il'ia Erenburg, "Obosnovanie prezreniia," *Krasnaia zvezda*, March 25, 1945, 3.

73. Il'ia Erenburg, "Khvatit!," *Pravda*, April 9, 1945, also in *Krasnaia zvezda*, April 11, 1945, 3; E. S. Seniavskaia, "Obraz Germanii i nemtsev v gody vtoroi mirovoi voiny glazami sovetskikh soldat i ofitserov," *Voenno-istoricheskii arkhiv*, no. 13 (Moscow, 2000): 29; Rubenstein, *Tangled Loyalties*, 221–222; Urban, "Ilja Ehrenburg," 263.

74. G. Aleksandrov, "Tovarishch Erenburg uproshchaet," *Pravda*, April 14, 1945, 2, also *Krasnaia zvezda*, April 15, 1945, 2, and other newspapers.

75. David Ortenberg, *Stalin, Shcherbakov, Mekhlis i drugie* (Moscow, 1995), 174–175; Erenburg, *Liudi, gody, zhizn'*, 385. For various views on the affair, see Werth, *Russia at War*, 873; Bérard, *La vie tumultueuse*, 252; Brooks, *Thank You, Comrade Stalin*, 189, 294, n. 181; Weiner, *Making Sense of War*, 164; Urban, "Ilja Ehrenburg," 259–260; G. V. Kostyrchenko, *Tainaia politika Stalina: Vlast' i antisemitizm* (Moscow, 2003 [2001]), 248.

76. Two different retypings of the April 15, 1945, letter, both without a signature, are at RGASPI, 558/11/833/23, and RGASPI, 17/125/347/16–17, published in D. L. Babichenko, *Literaturnyi front: Istoriia politicheskoi tsenzury 1932–1946 gg.: Sbornik dokumentov* (Moscow, 1994), 156–157.

77. Erenburg, *Liudi, gody, zhizn'*, 384.

78. Il'ia Erenburg, "Zaria pobedy," June 21, 1943, reprinted in Erenburg, *Voina (aprel' 1943–mart 1944)*, 283-284. A similar statement was "There is not and cannot be among us anything like arrogant and loathsome racism." "Dolg iskusstva," *Literatura i iskusstvo*, July 3, 1943, reprinted in Erenburg, *Voina (aprel' 1943–mart 1944)*, 253.
79. Erenburg, *Liudi, gody, zhizn'* 2, 349. On exceptions, see I. Erenburg, "Opravdanie nenavisti," May 26, 1942, reprinted in Erenburg, *Voina (Aprel' 1942–mart 1943)*, 3-8. On recognition, see Erenburg, "Dusha Rossii," November 11, 1943, and "Narod na voine," February 24, 1944, both reprinted in Erenburg, *Voina (aprel' 1943–mart 1944)*, 394, 405.
80. That Ehrenburg incited to rape was unlikely in a Soviet context to begin with, but Nazi propaganda successfully promoted this notion. A study group at the German Institute for Contemporary History disproved it in 1996. Erenburg, *Liudi, gody, zhizn'* 2, 252; Urban, "Ilja Ehrenburg," 241-243, citing, among others, I. Erenburg, "Progulki po Fritslandii," *Krasnaia zvezda*, November 25, 1944.
81. This is also the conclusion of Urban, "Ilja Ehrenburg," 273.
82. Joachim Hoffmann, *Stalins Vernichtungskrieg 1941–1945*, 3rd ed. (Munich, 1996), 133, 138-139, 202. Compare Rubenstein, *Tangled Loyalties*, 223. See also Brooks, *Thank You, Comrade Stalin*, 140.
83. Il'ia Erenburg, "Fritsy o fritsakh," *Krasnaia zvezda*, September 15, 1942, 4; I. Erenburg, "Dobit' nemtsa!," *Za Otchiznu*, May 5, 1944, cited in Bérard, *La vie tumultueuse*, 252. The emphasis is mine.
84. I. Erenburg, "O nenavisti," *Krasnaia zvezda*, May 5, 1942, 4, reprinted in Erenburg, *Voina (Iiun' 1941–aprel' 1942)*, 178-185; Ehrenburg, *Russia at War*, 127-132; Ehrenburg and Simonov, *In One Newspaper*, 143-150; I. Erenburg, "Opravdanie nenavisti," May 26, 1942, reprinted in Erenburg, *Voina (Aprel' 1942–mart 1943)*, 3-8.
85. Brooks, *Thank You, Comrade Stalin*, 170, citing *Krasnaia zvezda*, January 24, 1942.
86. I. Erenburg, "Opravdanie nenavisti," May 26, 1942, reprinted in Erenburg, *Voina (Aprel' 1942–mart 1943)*, 3-8; Il'ia Erenburg, "Dykhanie rebenka," March 2, 1944, reprinted in Erenburg, *Voina (aprel' 1943–mart 1944)*, 128. On reeducating German children, see a letter of March 14, 1945, in Il'ia Erenburg, *Na tsokole istorii . . . : Pis'ma 1931–1967*, ed. B. Ia. Frezinskii (Moscow, 2004), 336.
87. Ilia Erenburg, "Dal'she!," *Krasnaia zvezda*, March 8, 1945, 3 (on women); Il'ia Erenburg, "Obosnovanie prezreniia," *Krasnaia zvezda*, March 25, 1945, 3.

88. Urban, "Ilja Ehrenburg," 262-263; *Ilja Ehrenburg und die Deutschen* (Berlin: Museum Berlin Karlshorst, 1997), 75. I found no evidence for the notion that Ehrenburg openly denounced rape, which is the view in Rubenstein, *Tangled Loyalties*, 222, and Brooks, *Thank You, Comrade Stalin*, 189.
89. Rubenstein, *Tangled Loyalties*, 220 (quotation from *Völkischer Beobachter*, March 25, 1943); Bérard, *La vie tumultueuse*, 252 (on Hitler); I. Stalin, *O Velikoi Otechestvennoi voine Sovetskogo Soiuza*, 5th ed. (Moscow, 1945), 189.
90. Il'ia Erenburg, "Naemniki," March 11, 1942, reprinted in Erenburg, *Voina (Iiun' 1941–aprel' 1942)*, 215-222; "Hirelings," in Ehrenburg, *Russia at War*, 153-159.
91. Ewa M. Thompson, "Nationalist Propaganda in the Soviet Russian Press, 1939-1941," *Slavic Review* 50, no. 2 (Summer 1991): 397-399.
92. *Pravda*, August 14, 1941; *Pravda*, October 1, 1941; "Rumynskie zverstva v Odesse," *Pravda*, November 16, 1941; Bat. Komissar L. Lagin, "Gazeta krymskikh partizan," *Krasnyi flot*, April 1, 1942, summarized in *Zverstva fashistskikh varvarov: Ukazatel' faktov, opublikovannykh v pechati* (Moscow, 1943), 109.
93. Il'ia Erenburg, "Odessa," *Krasnaia zvezda*, August 9, 1942, 3; Il'ia Erenburg, "Sud'ba shakalov," December 12, 1942; both reprinted in Erenburg, *Voina (Aprel' 1942–mart 1943)*, 136-138, 78-81.
94. "Pervaia konferentsiia rumynskikh voennoplennykh," *Pravda*, January 25, 1942, 3; "1393 plennykh rumynskikh soldata prisoedinilis' k deklaratsii pervoi konferentsii rumynskikh voennoplennykh," *Pravda*, April 29, 1942, 3; Gosztony, *Stalins fremde Heere*, 101-107.
95. "Nemetsko-rumynskie zakhvatchiki ne uidut ot rasplaty!," editorial, *Pravda*, June 14, 1944, 1.
96. "Pervaia konferentsiia vengerskikh voennoplennykh," *Pravda*, February 22, 1942, 3; Bela Balazh [Béla Balázs] et al., "Obrashchenie obshchestvennykh i politicheskikh deiatelei Vengrii k vengerskomu narodu," *Pravda*, April 4, 1942, 3; Gosztony, *Stalins fremde Heere*, 108-115.
97. Brooks, *Thank You, Comrade Stalin*, 156; Thompson, "Nationalist Propaganda in the Soviet Russian Press," 395-396; V. A. Nevezhin, *Sindrom nastupatel'noi voiny: Sovetskaia propaganda v preddverii "sviashchennykh boev," 1939–1941* (Moscow, 1997), 81-95; Seniavskaia, *Protivniki Rossii*, 133-135.
98. Ganzenmüller, *Das belagerte Leningrad*, 27-29.
99. Pohl, *Ethnic Cleansing in the USSR*, 21, 23-24; Polian, *Against Their Will*, 139.
100. "Pervaia konferentsiia finskikh voennoplennykh," *Pravda*, February 18, 1942, 3; G. Kupriianov, "Pod iarmom finskikh razboinikov," *Krasnaia zvezda*, October 9, 1942, 3; *Pravda*, December 10, 1943, 3; *Trud*, December 15, 1943, 2; P. Rysakov, "Neudachnaia maskirovka finskikh gitlerovtsev," *Pravda*, January 3, 1944, 4. For "the Finns," see "Zverskoe obrashchenie

finnov s plennymi krasnoarmeitsami," *Krasnaia zvezda*, August 18, 1943, 2; I. Konovalov, "Na finskoi katorge," *Izvestiia*, December 29, 1943, 4.
101. For another view, see Seniavskaia, *Protivniki Rossii*, 153.
102. Gosztony, *Stalins fremde Heere*, 115–116 (on absence of a military unit); "Pervaia konferentsiia ital'ianskikh voennoplennykh," *Pravda*, June 25, 1942, 3, also in *Izvestiia*, June 25, 1942, 3; Dzhiovanni Dzhermanetto [Giovanni Germanetto], "Italiia segodnia," *Trud*, December 21, 1941, 2; Ia. Makarenko and B. Galanov, "Pogromnye dela ital'ianskikh zakhvatchikov (Ot spetsial'nykh voennykh korrespondentov 'Pravdy')," *Pravda*, November 23, 1942, 2.
103. Il'ia Erenburg, "Petushinye per'ia," April 12, 1942, reprinted in Erenburg, *Voina (Aprel' 1942–mart 1943)*, 64–68; I. Erenburg, "Dva udara," September 10, 1943, reprinted in Erenburg, *Voina (aprel' 1943–mart 1944)*, 331–333; Erenburg, *Voina (Aprel' 1942–mart 1943)*, 199.
104. I. Stalin, *O Velikoi otechestvennoi voine Sovetskogo Soiuza*, 4th ed., 152.
105. On Rostov, see TsAMO RF, 32/11302/29/178-189v, 198-209, and 32/11302/30/94-189v, photocopies of which are at USHMM, RG-22.016, folders 43–44, 48–49. On Leningrad, see Richard E. Lauterbach, *These Are the Russians*, 7th ed. (New York, 1945), 68, 316. On Kharkiv, see "I. Erenburg glazami D. Zaslavskogo." On central Ukraine, see Berkhoff, *Harvest of Despair*, 215-217.
106. "A tak, konechno, oni—gady," *Rodina*, no. 10 (Moscow, 2002): 59.
107. Stevens, *Russia Is No Riddle*, 245-247; Werth, *Russia at War*, 782-783.
108. In a typically Soviet pattern, a more authoritative secret report about the march, signed by the deputy head of the NKVD and the head of the NKVD for Soviet Ukraine, omitted the commiseration. Serhy Yekelchyk, "The Civic Duty to Hate: Stalinist Citizenship as Political Practice and Civic Emotion (Kiev, 1943-53)," *Kritika* 7, no. 3 (Summer 2006): 543-544; M. A. Vyltsan, "Kievskii 'marsh' nemetskikh voennoplennykh: Dokumenty 'Osoboi papki' I. V. Stalina. 1944g.," *Istoricheskii arkhiv* 6, no. 1 (January-February 1997): 66-68.
109. Karol, *Solik*, 307; Irina Mukhina, "'The Forgotten History': Ethnic German Women in Soviet Exile, 1941-1955," *Europe-Asia Studies* 57, no. 5 (July 2005): 743.
110. Sheila Fitzpatrick, "Happiness and *Toska*: An Essay in the History of Emotions in Pre-War Soviet Russia," *Australian Journal of Politics and History* 50, no. 3 (2004): 358. On the law, see *Instruktsiia tsenzoru* (Moscow, 1942), 84, filed at RGASPI, 17/125/117/98-146v. On the difference with Nazi propaganda, see Weiss, "Stalinistischer und nationalsozialistischer Propagandadiskurs im Vergleich," 338-339. A view on Nazi propaganda arguing the total opposite of Weiss is in Mark Edele and Michael

Geyer, "States of Exception: The Nazi-Soviet War as a System of Violence, 1939–1945," in Michael Geyer and Sheila Fitzpatrick, eds., *Beyond Totalitarianism: Stalinism and Nazism Compared* (Cambridge, U.K., 2009), 350–351.

111. Efimov, "'Literaturnyi pryziv' Gebbel'sa," *Trud*, October 24, 1942, 4; Hindus, *Mother Russia*, 164 (on German language).

112. This was also noted by the precursor of the U.S. Central Intelligence Agency; see Office of Strategic Services, Research and Analysis Branch, R & A no. 2185, "The Nature of Soviet National Feeling (Since June 1941)," n.p., June 15, 1944, fol. 49.

113. See, for example, "Pis'ma gneva," *Krasnaia zvezda*, October 28, 1942, 3, a compilation of readers' letters in response to Ehrenburg's quotation from captured German diaries.

114. Philip Knightley, *The First Casualty: The War Correspondent as Hero and Mythmaker from the Crimea to Kosovo*, rev. ed. (London, 2000), 281–282; Werth, *Russia at War*, 386; Urban, "Ilja Ehrenburg," 261.

115. Rubenstein, *Tangled Loyalties*, 194 (on the complaint); Heinrich Böll and Lew Kopelew, *Warum haben wir aufeinander geschossen?* (Bornheim-Merten, 1981), 38.

116. Lev Kopelev, *Khranit' vechno* (Ann Arbor, Mich., 1975), 16; Lev Kopelev, *To Be Preserved Forever*, trans. and ed. Anthony Austin (Philadelphia, 1977), 10; Lew Kopelew, *Aufbewahren für alle Zeit!*, trans. Heddy Pross-Weerth and Heinz-Dieter Mendel (Hamburg, 1976), 17.

117. Kozlov, *Obshchestvennoe soznanie*, 104.

8. The Motherland and Its People

1. Compare David Brandenberger, *National Bolshevism: Stalinist Mass Culture and the Formation of Modern Russian National Identity, 1931–1956* (Cambridge, Mass., 2002), 2, 234; David Brandenberger, *Propaganda State in Crisis: Soviet Ideology, Indoctrination, and Terror under Stalin, 1927–1941* (New Haven, Conn., 2011), 257–258; Erik van Ree, *The Political Thought of Joseph Stalin: A Study in Twentieth-Century Revolutionary Patriotism* (London, 2002), 196, 198.

2. "Velikaia druzhba narodov SSSR," editorial, *Pravda*, July 29, 1941, 1.

3. I. Stalin, *O Velikoi Otechestvennoi voine Sovetskogo Soiuza*, 4th ed. (Moscow, 1944), 37; Lowell Tillett, *The Great Friendship: Soviet Historians on the Non-Russian Nationalities* (Chapel Hill, N.C., 1969), 63; Brandenberger, *National Bolshevism*, 118.

4. Il'ia Erenburg in "Brat'ia evrei vsego mira!," *Pravda*, August 25, 1941, 3; Il'ia Erenburg, "Net tyla," November 4, 1941 (on "not a single Russian"); both reprinted in Il'ia Erenburg, *Voina (Iiun' 1941–aprel' 1942)* (Moscow, 1942),

292 ("Evreiam"), 317. See also "To the Jews," in Ilya Ehrenburg, *Russia at War*, trans. Gerard Shelley (London, 1943), 209. On disdain and respect, see Il'ia Erenburg, "O patriotizme," *Pravda*, June 14, 1942, 2. On Tolstoy and humanism, see, respectively, Il'ia Erenburg, "Sud'ba Rossii," July 28, 1942, and Il'ia Erenburg, "Znachenie Rossii," November 12, 1942, both reprinted in Il'ia Erenburg, *Voina (Aprel' 1942–mart 1943)* (Moscow, 1943), 200-203, 288. On being peaceable, see Il'ia Erenburg, "V Germanii," *Krasnaia zvezda*, February 23, 1945, 3.

5. N. Tikhonov, "My–russkie," *Izvestiia*, April 14, 1943, 4; A. Perventsev, "My–russkie!," *Izvestiia*, May 26, 1943, 3; Iurii Shaporin, "Symfoniia pro rosiis'ku zemliu," *Radians'ka Ukraïna*, November 6, 1943, 2.

6. Katharine Hodgson, *Written with the Bayonet: Soviet Russian Poetry of World War Two* (Liverpool, 1996), 70; Gleb Struve, *Soviet Russian Literature 1917–50* (Norman, Okla., 1951), 308.

7. *Pravda*, July 13-16, 1942; Alexander Werth, *Russia at War, 1941–1945* (New York, 1964), 386-387; Struve, *Soviet Russian Literature*, 206; V. Morozov, "'Russkie liudi': Prem'era p'esy K. Simonova v Moskovskom teatre Lensoveta," *Krasnaia zvezda*, July 14, 1942, 4.

8. *Pravda*, September 20, 23, and 26, 1942; Hodgson, *Written with the Bayonet*, 198.

9. Boris Gorbatov, "Sem'ia Tarasa," later "Nepokorennye (Sem'ia Tarasa)," serialized in *Pravda* from May 17, 1943, 3, to October 11, 1943, 2; Boris Gorbatov, *Taras' Family*, trans. Elizabeth Donnelly (London, 1944, reprint New York, 1946). The quotations are from Boris Gorbatov, *Nepokorënnye (Sem'ia Tarasa)* (Moscow, 1943), 45, 47, 88, 102, 136-137; G. Fedoseev, "Nepokorënnye: O knige Borisa Gorbatova," *Izvestiia*, November 24, 1943, 3.

10. Kenneth Slepyan, *Stalin's Guerillas: Soviet Partisans in World War II* (Lawrence, Kan., 2006), 217; "PIS'MO kazakov i kazachek, rabochikh i intelligentsia Sovetskoi Kubani tovarishchu STALINU I. V.," *Izvestiia*, November 5, 1943, 3. The emphasis on loyalty "implied the opposite," argues Jeffrey W. Jones, "'Every Family Has Its Freak': Perceptions of Collaboration in Occupied Soviet Russia, 1943-1948," *Slavic Review* 64, no. 4 (Winter 2005): 762. But the real issues are whether contemporary readers thought along these lines, and whether Stalin wanted them to do so.

11. I. Erenburg, "Ispoved' vraga," December 29, 1943, reprint in Il'ia Erenburg, *Voina (aprel' 1943–mart 1944)* (Moscow, 1944), 364-375. For the report on Kiev, see *Pravda*, March 1, 1944, 2; *Soviet Government Statements on Nazi Atrocities* (London, [1946]), 142. For the other quotations, see TASS, "'Khrabryi russkii narod spasaet i nashi ochagi,'" *Pravda*, August 24, 1941, 4; TASS, "'Stalingrad budet vechno siiat' kak pamiatnik muzhestva

russkikh': Shvedskie gazety o pobede Krasnoi Armii pod Stalingradom," *Trud*, February 5, 1943, 4; "'Prevoskhodstvo russkikh v oborone prevratilos' v ikh prevoskhodstvo i v nastuplenii'" and "'Velikolepnye boevye kachestva russkikh armii,'" *Pravda*, August 11, 1943, 4.

12. RGASPI, 17/125/260/81-83: N. Mikhailov to Shcherbakov, June 23, 1944, and marked-up draft.

13. TASS, "Miting predstavitelei evreiskogo naroda," *Pravda*, April 5, 1944, 2; Aleksei Tolstoi, "Russkii kharakter: Iz rasskazov Ivana Sudareva," *Krasnaia zvezda*, May 7, 1944, 4, reprinted in *Pravda*, May 10, 1944, 4; GARF, 6903/12/88/668-669: broadcast text, July 15, 1944, with "Velikii pisatel' russkogo naroda," *Pravda*, July 15, 1944, 1.

14. GARF, 6903/12/87/636-649: Professor Konstantin Vasil'evich Bazilevich, "Russkii soldat," July 28, 1944.

15. RGASPI, 17/125/59/94-98, published in A. Ia. Livshin and I. B. Orlov, comps., *Sovetskaia propaganda v gody Velikoi Otechestvennoi voiny: "Kommunikatsiia ubezhdeniia" i mobilizatsionnye mekhanizmy* (Moscow, 2007), 314-316; Em. Iaroslavskii, "Bol'sheviki—prodolzhateli luchshikh patrioticheskikh traditsii russkogo naroda," *Pravda*, December 27, 1941, 3; Tillett, *The Great Friendship*, 61-62; Brandenberger, *National Bolshevism*, 119.

16. Tillett, *The Great Friendship*, 61; "Pod znamenem Lenina: Doklad tov. A. Shcherbakova 21 ianvaria 1942 goda," *Pravda*, January 22, 1942, 2; V. Kruzhkov, "Velikaia sila leninsko-stalinskoi druzhby narodov," *Pravda*, February 21, 1942.

17. Ralph Parker, *Moscow Correspondent* (London, 1949), 152.

18. Van Ree, *The Political Thought of Joseph Stalin*, 194 (the first quotation); Stalin, *O Velikoi Otechestvennoi voine Sovetskogo Soiuza*, 152.

19. Brandenberger, *National Bolshevism*, 118, 120, 131, referring to "the first years of the war"; Tillett, *The Great Friendship*, 66.

20. Viktor Cherepanov, *Vlast' i voina: Stalinskii mekhanizm gosudarstvennogo upravleniia v Velikoi Otechestvennoi voine* (Moscow, 2006), 143; David Ortenberg, *Stalin, Shcherbakov, Mekhlis i drugie* (Moscow, 1995), 160.

21. Melissa K. Stockdale, "What Is a Fatherland? Changing Notions of Duties, Rights, and Belonging in Russia," in Mark Bassin et al., eds., *Space, Place and Power in Modern Russia: Essays in the New Spatial History* (DeKalb, Ill., 2010), 23-48.

22. Stalin, *O Velikoi Otechestvennoi voine Sovetskogo Soiuza*, 110-111; "O gosudarstvennom gimne Sovetskogo Soiuza," *Trud*, December 21, 1943, 1, also in *Pravda*, December 22, 1943.

23. M. Mitin, "Velikaia sila sovetskogo patriotizma," *Pravda*, February 1, 1942, 3.

24. Original usage: *natsii i narodnosti*. Stalin, *O Velikoi Otechestvennoi voine Sovetskogo Soiuza*, 146.
25. Jeffrey Brooks, *Thank You, Comrade Stalin! Soviet Public Culture from Revolution to Civil War* (Princeton, N.J., 2000), 159 (on the song); Cherepanov, *Vlast' i voina*, 13-14; A. I. Perelygin, "The Russian Orthodox Church in the Orel Region during the Great Patriotic War," *Russian Studies in History* 37, no. 1 (Summer 1998): 44; N. D. Kozlov, *Obshchestvennoe soznanie v gody Velikoi Otechestvennoi voiny (1941-1945)* (St. Petersburg, 1995), 49. On Easter, see Steven Merritt Miner, *Stalin's Holy War: Religion, Nationalism, and Alliance Politics, 1941-1945* (Chapel Hill, N.C., 2003), 82-83.
26. The lack of the capital letter in *god* is in accordance with the Russian original, *bog*. *Pravda*, November 7, 1942, 4; *Pravda*, November 9, 1942, 4; *Trud*, November 15, 1942, 4; *Trud*, February 24, 1943, 2. On bafflement, see Daniel Peris, "'God Is Now on Our Side': The Religious Revival on Unoccupied Soviet Territory during World War II," *Kritika* 1, no. 1 (Winter 2000): 114-115.
27. Brooks, *Thank You, Comrade Stalin*, 190; TASS, "Sobor episkopov pravoslavnoi tserkvi," *Trud*, September 9, 1943, 2. The letter is in L. V. Maksimenkov, ed., *Bol'shaia tsenzura: Pisateli i zhurnalisty v Strane Sovetov, 1917-1956* (Moscow, 2005), 541.
28. Three rabbis were also quoted. *Trud*, November 12, 1943, 4; *Trud*, November 16, 1943, 4; *Radians'ka Ukraïna*, November 16, 1943, 1.
29. *Trud*, May 16, 1944, 1; "Pis'mo Patriarshego Mestobliustitelia, Mitropolita Aleksiia Predsedateliu Soveta Narodnykh Komissarov, Marshalu Sovetskogo Soiuza I. V. STALINU," *Trud*, May 21, 1944, 2; "Ot Sviashchennogo Sinoda Pravoslavnoi Russkoi Tserkvi," *Trud*, May 24, 1944, 4; TASS, "Vruchenie medalei 'Za oboronu Moskvy' mitropolitu Nikolaiu i drugim sluzhiteliam russkoi pravoslavnoi tserkvi," *Trud*, October 10, 1944, 2.
30. Perelygin, "The Russian Orthodox Church," 50-51, 53; A. Vyltsan, "Command and Homily: Ways of Mobilizing Village Resources during the War," *Russian Studies in History* 37, no. 1 (Summer 1998): 32-34 (both on obstruction); Edmund Stevens, *Russia Is No Riddle* (New York, 1945), 77 (on amazement); Vanda Vasilevskaia, *Raduga: Povest'*, trans. E. Usievich (Moscow, 1945), 196; Gorbatov, *Nepokorënnye*, 21, 77, 85, 90, 115, 118, 145-146; Peris, "'God Is Now on Our Side,'" 115 (on Suslov).
31. Miner, *Stalin's Holy War*, xiv-xv, 68-83.
32. See, for example, Yuri Slezkine, "The USSR as a Communal Apartment, or How a Socialist State Promoted Ethnic Particularism," *Slavic Review* 53, no. 2 (Summer 1994): 414-452; Amir Weiner, *Making Sense of War: The Second World War and the Fate of the Bolshevik Revolution* (Princeton, N.J.,

2001); Serhy Yekelchyk, "Stalinist Patriotism as Imperial Discourse: Reconciling the Ukrainian and Russian 'Heroic Pasts,' 1939–1945," *Kritika* 3, no. 1 (Winter 2002): 51–80.

33. Brandenberger, *National Bolshevism*, 157–158; Brooks, *Thank You, Comrade Stalin*, 188.

34. H. Shcharbatau, "Hastelautsy," *Zviazda*, July 25, 1944, 4; S. Kozybaev, "Iz opyta radio po voenno-patrioticheskomu vospitaniiu trudiashchikhsia Kazakhstana v gody Velikoi Otechestvennoi voiny," *Zhurnalistika*, no. 5(7) (Alma-Ata, 1975), 171; Brandenberger, *National Bolshevism*, 326–327, n. 58 (battle cry). Ehrenburg did call another Panfilovite, Sultan Khodzhinov, typical for the hard-fighting *dzhigity*, or courageous horsemen from whom Kazakhs descended; see Il'ia Erenburg, "Kazakhi," October 18, 1942, reprinted in Erenburg, *Voina (Aprel' 1942–mart 1943)*, 221–224.

35. Stalin, *O Velikoi Otechestvennoi voine Sovetskogo Soiuza*, 127; RGASPI, 17/3/1049/79, 272: Politbureau resolution 325, February 3, 1944, and draft text, "O gosudarstvennykh gimnakh sovetskikh respublik"; Gerhard Simon, *Nationalismus und Nationalitätenpolitik in der Sowjetunion: Von der totalitären Diktatur zur nachstalinschen Gesellschaft* (Baden-Baden, 1986), 210–213, 216–217; N. A. Kirsanov, "Natsional'nye formirovaniia Krasnoi Armii v Velikoi Otechestvennoi voine 1941–1945 godov," *Otechestvennaia istoriia*, no. 4 (1994): 120–124; Serhy Yekelchyk, *Stalin's Empire of Memory: Russian-Ukrainian Relations in the Soviet Historical Imagination* (Toronto, 2004), 33–34.

36. Brandenberger, *National Bolshevism*, 286–287, n. 61; Yekelchyk, *Stalin's Empire of Memory*, 25.

37. "Obrashchenie voinov-belorussov k partizanam i partizankam, ko vsemu belorusskomu narodu," *Pravda*, August 8, 1943, 3. For drafts, see RGASPI, 17/125/195/33: Ponomarenko to Shcherbakov, July 27, 1943; RGASPI, 558/11/204/53-54: note by Shcherbakov, and page proof. A response "discussed and signed by 120,000 male and female partisans and by over 500,000 inhabitants" did not appear in print: see RGASPI, 17/125/195/48-54: Ponomarenko to Shcherbakov, September 29, 1943, and draft text.

38. Mikhas' Lyn'kov, "Privet rodnomu gorodu," *Izvestiia*, November 27, 1943, 3 (on Homel); Mikhas' Lyn'kov, "Druzhba narodov—istochnik nashei sily," *Izvestiia*, December 5, 1943, 2; N. Natalevich, "Zhivet i boretsia Sovetskaia Belarus'," *Izvestiia*, December 31, 1943, 2; Tsentral'nyi komitet VKP(b) and Sovet Narodnykh Komissarov..., "Tsentral'nomu Komitetu KP(b) Belorussii...," *Pravda*, January 1, 1944, 2.

39. "Obrashchenie Sovnarkoma i Prezidiuma Verkhovnogo Soveta BSSR i TsK KP(b) Belorussii k belorusskomu narodu," *Pravda*, July 7, 1944, 3.
40. A. Bogomolets et al., "K ukrainskomu narodu," *Pravda*, April 2, 1942, 3, also in *Izvestiia*, April 2, 1942; "Doklad predsedatelia Soveta Narodnykh Komissarov Ukrainskoi SSR tov. L. R. Korniets na torzhestvennom zasedanii v Kolonnom zale Doma soiuzov, posviashchennom 25-letiiu Ukrainskoi SSR," *Pravda*, December 26, 1942, 3.
41. Vasilevskaia, *Raduga*, 85, 177-178, 180-181. The English translation, *Rainbow: A Novel by Wanda Wassilewska*, trans. Edith Bone (London, n.d.), omits the passage on Ukrainian history.
42. Oleksandr Korniichuk, "Vozz"iednannia ukraïns'koho narodu v nadrakh svoieï derzhavy," *Radians'ka Ukraïna*, February 19, 1943, 3; A. Korneichuk, "Vossoedinenie ukrainskogo naroda v nedrakh svoego gosudarstva," *Sovetskaia Ukraina*, February 19, 1943, reprinted in *Pravda*, February 20, 1943, 2, and *Izvestiia*, February 21, 1943; RGASPI, 17/125/192/7: Aleksandrov to Molotov, with written comment by Molotov.
43. M. Ryl'skii, "Ukraintsy nikomu ne otdadut svoei svobody," *Pravda*, April 29, 1943, 3; M. Ryl's'kyi, "Ukraïntsi nikomu ne viddadut' svoieï svobody," *Radians'ka Ukraïna*, May 8, 1943, 3; Akad. A. Bogomolets, "Sovetskaia Ukraina i ukrainsko-nemetskie natsionalisty v Kanade," *Pravda*, May 13, 1943, 3, also in *Izvestiia* and *Krasnaia zvezda*; Ukrainian version in *Radians'ka Ukraïna*, May 15, 1943, 3; P. Tychina, "Proch' griaznye ruki ot Ukrainy!," *Pravda*, May 14, 1943, 3, also in *Izvestiia* and *Krasnaia zvezda*; Ukrainian version in *Radians'ka Ukraïna*, May 16, 1943, 3-4. The draft checked by Stalin is at RGASPI, 558/11/204/35-44. On the assertion, see Vladislav Antal'evich Grinevich, "Natsional'nye problemy v Krasnoi Armii v period osvobozhdeniia Ukrainy ot nemetsko-fashistskikh zakhvatchikov (dekabr' 1942-oktiabr' 1944 gg.)" (*kandidat* dissertation, Institut istorii Ukrainy Akademii nauk Ukrainy, Kiev, 1994), 51.
44. Yekelchyk, *Stalin's Empire of Memory*, 35-37; Grinevich, "Natsional'nye problemy v Krasnoi Armii," 44-47.
45. GARF, 6903/1/82/112-113v: radio broadcast text, October 10, 1943; Iurii Ianovskii, "Bessmertnaia Ukraina," *Izvestiia*, November 11, 1943, 4.
46. Weiner, *Making Sense of War*, 352 (on Fadeev); "Ukraïns'kyi narod—velykomu narodovi rosiis'komu," *Radians'ka Ukraïna*, November 30, 1943, 1-2; "Moskva, Kreml': Tovarishchu Stalinu. Ot trudiashchikhsia goroda Kieva," *Pravda*, December 3, 1943, 1; TASS, "Miting v osvobozhdënnom Kieve," *Izvestiia*, December 3, 1943, 2. On Aleksandrov and the letter, see Brandenberger, *National Bolshevism*, 158-159; Yekelchyk, *Stalin's Empire of Memory*, 39-40.

47. See "Promova tov. Bazhana M. P.," *Radian'ska Ukraïna*, December 5, 1943, 2, a speech also unusual for referring to the German persecution of Ukrainian nationalists.
48. "Sovetskaia Ukraina," editorial, *Pravda*, March 17, 1944, 1.
49. M. Hrechukha, N. Khrushchev, and D. Korotchenko, "K ukrainskomu narodu," *Pravda*, October 15, 1944, 2; Serhy Yekelchyk, "The Leader, the Victory, and the Nation: Public Celebrations in Soviet Ukraine under Stalin (Kiev, 1943–1953)," *Jahrbücher für Geschichte Osteuropas* 54, no. 1 (2006): 6–7.
50. N. Natalevich in *Radians'ka Ukraïna*, November 7, 1943 (on Białystok); *Pravda*, February 7, 1944, 3, also in *Izvestiia*, February 8, 1944; Grinevich, "Natsional'nye problemy v Krasnoi Armii," 48–50 (citing Hrechukha in *Radians'ka Ukraïna*, February 15, 1944; on Khrushchev's proposal for a Kholm oblast); Yekelchyk, *Stalin's Empire of Memory*, 48, citing *Radians'ka Ukraïna*, April 30, 1944, 2.
51. M. S. Hrechukha et al., "Do ukraïns'koho narodu," *Komunist*, November 29, 1941, 1, cited from the retyped text filed at TsDAHOU, 1/70/849/37–40; A. Bogomolets et al., "K ukrainskomu narodu," *Pravda*, April 2, 1942, 3, also in *Izvestiia*, April 2, 1942; "Bezzhalostno istrebliat' zhelto-blakitnykh predatelei," *Sovetskaia Ukraina*, May 5, 1942, filed at TsDAHOU, 1/70/30/63 (on lice); "Na vyrishal'ni boï vstavai, narode Ukraïny! Vstupna promova Holovy Prezydiï Verkhovnoï Rady Ukraïns'koï RSR Mykhaila Serhiiovycha Hrechukhy," reprinted in *Ukraïna bula i bude radians'koiu: Tretii mitynh predstavnykiv ukraïns'koho narodu* ([Moscow], 1943), 10; *Radians'ka Ukraïna*, January 18, 1944, quoted in Grinevich, "Natsional'nye problemy v Krasnoi Armii," 46–47.
52. TsDAHOU, 1/70/36/58–63: Semen Skliarenko, "Hadyna," March 23, 1942 (on Liubchenko); TsDAVOV, 4188/1/146/150–151v: Iaroslav Halan, "Kreatury," broadcast on January 31 and February 1, [1943]; Yekelchyk, *Stalin's Empire of Memory*, 31.
53. N. S. Khrushchev, speech in *Pravda*, March 16, 1944, 2; "Direktivy i prikazy gitlerovskogo pravitel'stva i germanskogo voennogo komandovaniia ob istreblenii sovetskikh voennoplennykh i mirnykh grazhdan," *Pravda*, March 11, 1944, 2–3, also in other newspapers, including a partial facsimile; *Soviet Government Statements*, 147–148.
54. Katrin Boeckh, *Stalinismus in der Ukraine: Die Rekonstruktion des sowjetischen Systems nach dem Zweiten Weltkrieg* (Wiesbaden, 2007), 343; Lew Shankowsky, "Soviet and Satellite Sources on the Ukrainian Insurgent Army," *Annals of the Ukrainian Academy of Arts and Sciences in the U.S.* 9, nos. 1–2(27–28) (1961): 250. On intelligence, see Jeffrey Burds, *The Early Cold*

War in Soviet West Ukraine, 1944–1948, The Carl Beck Papers in Russian and East European Studies, No. 1505 (Pittsburgh, 2001), 22-24.
55. Tillett, *The Great Friendship*, 60; Stalin, *O Velikoi Otechestvennoi voine Sovetskogo Soiuza*, 11.
56. Kozybaev, "Iz opyta radio po voenno-patrioticheskomu vospitaniiu trudiashchikhsia Kazakhstana," 164-165.
57. T. N. Kary-Niiazov, "Prazdnik uzbekskogo naroda: Otkrytie Akademii nauk Uzbekskoi SSR," *Izvestiia*, November 5, 1943, 3; Brandenberger, *National Bolshevism*, 125; Tillett, *The Great Friendship*, 79-80.
58. Patrik von zur Mühlen, *Zwischen Hakenkreuz und Sowjetstern: Der Nationalismus der sowjetischen Orientvölker im Zweiten Weltkrieg* (Düsseldorf, 1971), 221. For the letter, see "Ot s"ezda musul'manskogo dukhovenstva i veruiushchikh Severnogo Kavkaza. Moskva, Kreml': Predsedateliu Soveta Narodnykh Komissarov SSSR, Verkhovnomu Glavnokomanduiushchemu Marshalu Sovetskogo Soiuza Iosifu Vissarionovichu STALINU," *Pravda*, 23 June 1944, 2, also in *Trud*, 23 June 1944, 2. For an earlier Muslim message, see *Izvestiia*, October 19, 1943.
59. Azhibaev et al., "Özbek khalkining zhangchilariga ularning el-iurtlaridan maktub" and the translation, "Pis'mo boitsam-uzbekam ot uzbekskogo naroda," *Pravda*, October 31, 1942, 3.
60. Alexander Statiev, "The Nature of Anti-Soviet Armed Resistance, 1942-44: The North Caucasus, the Kalmyk Autonomous Republic, and Crimea," *Kritika* 6, no. 2 (Spring 2005): 317-318; Cherepanov, *Vlast' i voina*, 79-80. Deporting Muslims had a regional precedent; the Russian Empire deported thousands of them during World War I; see Eric Lohr, *Nationalizing the Russian Empire: The Campaign against Enemy Aliens during World War I* (Cambridge, Mass., 2003), 150.
61. Von zur Mühlen, *Zwischen Hakenkreuz und Sowjetstern*, 216-217; *Pravda*, September 1, 1942, 3.
62. GARF, 6903/1/81/148: Bolat, "Otchet o rabote Krymsko-Tatartskoi redaktsii s 1-go ianvaria 1943 g. po 1-e ianvaria 1944 goda," n.p., n.d.; Slepyan, *Stalin's Guerillas*, 208.
63. Brain Glyn Williams, "The Hidden Ethnic Cleansing of Muslims in the Soviet Union: The Exile and Repatriation of the Crimean Tatars," *Journal of Contemporary History* 37, no. 3 (July 2002): 337.
64. RGASPI, 17/125/112/83-84: Mikhoels to Shcherbakov, March 4, 1942 (the figure); G. V. Kostyrchenko, *Tainaia politika Stalina: Vlast' i antisemitizm* (Moscow, 2003 [2001]), 232-236; G. V. Kostyrchenko, ed., *Gosudarstvennyi antisemitizm v SSSR: Ot nachala do kul'minatsii, 1938–1953* (Moscow, 2005), 45-48.

65. RGASPI, 17/125/193/140-146: Aleksandrov and N. Shatalin to Andreev, Malenkov, and Shcherbakov, "O gazete 'Literatura i iskusstvo,'" n.d.; A. V. Fateev, *Obraz vraga v sovetskoi propagande 1945-1954gg.* (Moscow, 1999), 16, 21; Il'ia Erenburg, "Dolg iskusstva," *Literatura i iskusstvo*, July 3, 1943, reprinted in Erenburg, *Voina (aprel' 1943-mart 1944)*, 250, 252-253; "'O sovetskom patriotizme i natsional'noi gordosti narodov SSSR': Na lektsii pisatelia A. Fadeeva," *Izvestiia*, November 4, 1943, 3, abridged version in *Trud*, November 4, 1943, 4.
66. See, for example, "Ukaz Prezidiuma Verkhovnogo Soveta SSSR: O prisvoenii zvaniia Geroia Sovetskogo Soiuza generalam, ofitserskomu, serzhantskomu i riadovomu sostavu Krasnoi Armii," *Izvestiia*, November 2, 1943, 3; B. Iagling, "Druzhba," *Trud*, December 30, 1942, 3.
67. *Pravda*, August 25, 1941, *Izvestiia*, August 26, 1941, and reprinted in Erenburg, *Voina (Iiun' 1941-aprel' 1942)*, 291-293; "Vtoroi miting predstavitelei evreiskogo naroda," *Izvestiia*, May 26, 1942, 3; "Plenum Evreiskogo antifashistskogo komiteta v SSSR," *Izvestiia*, April 12, 1944, 2, and *Trud*, April 12, 1944, 3.
68. Mikhail Sholokhov, "Oni srazhalis' za Rodinu," *Pravda*, May 5, 1943, and subsequent issues; Ewa Bérard, *La vie tumultueuse d'Ilya Ehrenbourg: Juif, Russe et Soviétique* (Paris, 1991), 242. Similarly just one film, *Wait for Me* of 1943, showed a Jew as contributing heroically to the war effort. See David Shneer, *Through Soviet Jewish Eyes: Photography, War, and the Holocaust* (New Brunswick, N.J., 2011), 233-235.
69. RGASPI, 17/125/59/29 (five writers), 41-42, 76-77; RGASPI, 17/125/112/83-84, 127: Mikhoels to Shcherbakov, March 4, 1942, and Shakhno Epstein, May 1942.
70. TsDAHOU, 1/70/128/6: *Katalog gazet*; RGASPI, 17/125/262/85-86: N. Kondakov to Shcherbakov, n.p., January 14, 1944; RKP, file "Pechat' SSSR za period Velikoi Otechestvennoi voiny 1941-1946 (gazety)."
71. Van Ree, *The Political Thought of Joseph Stalin*, 194; Brandenberger, *National Bolshevism*, 130-131; V. A. Nevezhin, ed., *Zastol'nye rechi Stalina: Dokumenty i materialy* (Moscow, 2003), 470-473, which includes the original stenographic report corrected by Stalin. On the long-term significance, see Weiner, *Making Sense of War*, 208, 222.
72. *Witness to History: The Photographs of Yevgenii Khaldei*, biographical essay by Alexander Nakhimovsky and Alice Nakhimovsky (New York, 1997), 11; Ernst Volland and Heinz Krimmer, *Das bedeutende Augenblick: Jewgeni Chaldei. Eine Retrospektive* (Leipzig, 2008); O. A. Rzeshevskii, ed., *Kto byl kto v Velikoi Otechestvennoi voine 1941-1945: Liudi. Sobytiia. Fakty. Spravochnik*, expanded 2d ed. (Moscow, 2000), 91.

73. Van Ree, *The Political Thought of Joseph Stalin*, 195 (on Stalin); "Sovetskii patriot," editorial, *Pravda*, June 6, 1942, 1.
74. See also Brandenberger, *National Bolshevism*, 131.
75. On Russian chauvinism, see ibid., 176-178, 180. Two memoirs, K. S. Karol, *Solik: Life in the Soviet Union 1939-1946*, trans. Eamonn McArdle (London, 1996), 281-282, and W. L. White, *Report on the Russians* (London, 1945), 135-136, both simplify in explaining anti-Semitic sentiments by the propaganda alone.

9. Immortal Avengers and Enemy Accomplices

1. Catherine Merridale, *Ivan's War: The Red Army 1939-1945* (London, 2005), 217.
2. David Ortenberg, *Stalin, Shcherbakov, Mekhlis i drugie* (Moscow, 1995), 140-141.
3. Pavel Polian, "Stalin und die Opfer des nationalsozialistischen Vernichtungskriegs," in Jürgen Zarusky, ed., *Stalin und die Deutschen: Neue Beiträge der Forschung* (Munich, 2006); 91, Russian original text published in "I. Erenburg glazami D. Zaslavskogo," *Lekhaim*, no. 7(171) (electronic journal, Moscow, July 2006), at www.lechaim.ru.
4. Vanda Vasilevskaia, *Raduga: Povest'*, trans. E. Usievich (Moscow, 1945), 129, 150-152.
5. The activist was a regional party official named Stepan Stetsenko. *Pravda*, May 17 to October 11, 1943; Boris Gorbatov, *Nepokorënnye (Sem'ia Tarasa)* (Moscow, 1943); Boris Gorbatov, "O sem'e Tarasa," *Pravdist*, no. 33, November 6, 1943, 6, filed at RGASPI, 629/1/89/14v. The quotations are from *Nepokorënnye*, 118-119, 158.
6. I. Osipov, special correspondent, "Chudovishchnye zlodeianiia fashistov," *Izvestiia*, August 20, 1941, 3.
7. "Ot Sovetskogo Informbiuro: Utrennee soobshchenie 9 avgusta," *Pravda*, August 10, 1941, 2; *Pravda*, December 19, 1942, 1; *Soviet Government Statements on Nazi Atrocities* (London, [1946]), 60-61.
8. Gorbatov, *Nepokorënnye*, 44-46; Tanja Penter, "Collaboration on Trial: New Source Material on Soviet Postwar Trials against Collaborators," *Slavic Review* 64, no. 4 (Winter 2005): 784.
9. Aleksei Tolstoi, "Kto takoi Gitler i chego on dobivaetsia?," *Izvestiia*, July 17, 1941, 3; Vanda Vasilevskaia, "Pytki i smert', nadrugatel'stva i nasilie—vot chto nesut gitlerovtsy," *Pravda*, September 13, 1941 2; Molotov, January 6, 1942, cited from the translation in *Soviet Government Statements*, 19; Iaroslav Halan, "L'viv pid fashysts'koiu p"iatoiu," *Radian'ska Ukraïna*, May 21, 1943, 2.
10. Vasilevskaia, *Raduga*, 94.

11. "Liubov' k rodine i nenevist' k vragu," editorial, *Pravda*, May 18, 1942, 1.
12. RGASPI, 17/125/187/80-80v: polkovnik Cherstvoi, nach. otdela voennoi tsenzury NKO, to general-maior Shikin, zam. nach. GlavPURKKA, with copies to Puzin and Sadchikov, "Svodka" for June 21-30, 1943, Moscow, July 6, 1943. For a typical condemnation of "treasonous" POWs in such a predicament, see L. Vilkomir, "Tak gibnut predateli," *Krasnaia zvezda*, November 23, 1941, 3.
13. Vasilevskaia, *Raduga*, 69-70, 77, 193.
14. Gorbatov, *Nepokorënnye*, 22, 107-110, 113-114, 124.
15. RGASPI, 17/125/112/164-167: G. Aleksandrov and A. Puzin to A. S. Shcherbakov, n.p., October 15, [1942], also published in A. Ia. Livshin and I. B. Orlov, comps., *Sovetskaia propaganda v gody Velikoi Otechestvennoi voiny: "Kommunikatsiia ubezhdeniia" i mobilizatsionnye mekhanizmy* (Moscow, 2007), 426-427; V. A. Zolotarev et al., eds., *Russkii arkhiv: Velikaia Otechestvennaia*, vol. 20-9 (Moscow, 1999), 133-134; Kenneth Slepyan, *Stalin's Guerillas: Soviet Partisans in World War II* (Lawrence, Kan., 2006), 23-24, 48-50. For two similar complaints about Soviet Ukrainian papers in December 1942, see TsDAHOU, 1/70/29/14-15, 21-22.
16. Slepyan, *Stalin's Guerillas*, 157; I. Stalin, *O Velikoi Otechestvennoi voine Sovetskogo Soiuza*, 4th ed. (Moscow, 1944), 95, 122.
17. On the unwritten rule, see Slepyan, *Stalin's Guerillas*, 149, 153. For the formal rules, see N. G. Sadchikov, *Strogo khranit' tainy sotsialisticheskogo gosudarstva* (Moscow, 1942), 31, filed at RGASPI, 17/125/117/52; RGASPI, 17/125/112/164-165: G. Aleksandrov and A. Puzin to A. S. Shcherbakov, n.p., October 15, [1942]; RGASPI, 17/125/186/99-100: "Perechen' svedenii, sostavliaiushchikh voennuiu tainu (na voennoe vremia). Proekt," n.d. [1943?]; GARF, 9425/1/207/26-28: Sadchikov, "Perechen' svedenii, sostavliaiushchikh voennuiu i gosudarstvennuiu tainu na vremia voiny," May 18, 1944. Three examples of military censorship of details from *Pravda* and *Komsomolskaia pravda* issues in April and May 1943 are at RGASPI, 17/125/187/51v, 61v, 62. The genesis of five Sovinformbiuro statements about partisans in Ukraine and the RSFSR in March 1943, with modification of the dates or the number of German deaths, can be found at RGASPI, 17/125/161/36, 38, 39, 40. On October 1942, see Slepyan, *Stalin's Guerillas*, 340, n. 127.
18. Aleksei Popov, *NKVD i partizanskoe dvizhenie* (Moscow, 2003), 122-132; Bogdan Musial, *Sowjetische Partisanen 1941-1944: Mythos und Wirklichkeit* (Paderborn, 2009), 253; Kondrat Krapiva, "Palach kaznen," *Pravda*, September 24, 1943, 4.

19. "Privetstvie pervoi partiinoi konferentsii Partizanskogo kraia tovarishcham I. V. Stalinu i A. A. Zhdanovu," *Pravda*, July 3, 1942, 1, also in *Trud*, *Izvestiia*, and *Krasnaia zvezda*; "Pis'mo partizan Orlovskoi oblasti tovarishchu Stalinu," *Izvestiia*, May 6, 1942, 1; "Otkrytoe pis'mo partizan Kalininskogo fronta Iosifu Vissarionovichu Stalinu," *Izvestiia*, May 1, 1942, 1; Slepyan, *Stalin's Guerillas*, 157, 163.
20. "Otkrytoe pis'mo partizan Kalininskogo fronta Iosifu Vissarionovichu Stalinu," *Izvestiia*, May 1, 1942, 1; B. Polevoi, "Podvig Matveia Kuz'mina," *Pravda*, February 26, 1942, 3; I. I. Shirokorad, *Tsentral'naia periodicheskaia pechat' v gody Velikoi Otechestvennoi voiny: 1941–1945* (Moscow, 2001), 119.
21. On the order, see M. M. Gorinov, "Zoia Kosmodem'ianskaia (1923–1941)," *Otechestvennaia istoriia*, no. 1 (January–February 2003): 79–80.
22. P. Lidov, "Tania," *Pravda*, January 27, 1942, 3. For an English translation (with the wrong date), see James von Geldern and Richard Stites, eds., *Mass Culture in Soviet Russia: Tales, Poems, Songs, Movies, Plays, and Folklore, 1917–1953* (Bloomington, Ind., 1995), 341-344. Unrecognizably garbled and lacking Stalin is this translation: Pyotr Lidov, "Tanya," in S. Krasilshchik, ed., *World War II: Dispatches from the Soviet Front*, trans. Nina Bous (New York, 1985), 65-74.
23. S. Liubimov, "My ne zabudem tebia, Tania," *Komsomol'skaia pravda*, January 27, 1942; Elena S. Seniavskaia, "Heroic Symbols: The Reality and Mythology of War," *Russian Studies in History* 37, no. 1 (Summer 1998): 76; Gorinov, "Zoia Kosmodem'ianskaia (1923–1941)," 87.
24. As noted in Rosalinde Sartorti, "On the Making of Heroes, Heroines, and Saints," in Richard Stites, ed., *Culture and Entertainment in Wartime Russia* (Bloomington, Ind., 1995), 184-185; *Victor Deni: Ein russischer Karikaturist im Dienst der Propaganda* (Hamburg, 1992), 130.
25. "Ukaz Prezidiuma Verkhovnogo Soveta SSSR...," *Pravda*, February 17, 1942, 1; "Vystuplenie po radio D. T. Kosmodem'ianskoi—materi Geroia Sovetskogo Soiuza Z. A. Kosmodem'ianskoi (radioperedacha dlia molodezhi)," *Pravda*, February 18, 1942, 3; P. Lidov, "Kto byla Tania," *Pravda*, February 18, 1942, 2; Seniavskaia, "Heroic Symbols," 76; Sartorti, "On the Making of Heroes," 183-184; K. I. Propina, ed., *Pechat' SSSR za 25 let: 1918–1942 gody: Statisticheskie materialy* (Moscow, 1942), 51 (on the brochure).
26. Seniavskaia, "Heroic Symbols," 76-77, referring to the personal archives of Lidov's widow; Gorinov, "Zoia Kosmodem'ianskaia (1923–1941)," 82, 84.
27. Sartorti, "On the Making of Heroes," 182-183.
28. Ibid., 184, 186; A. Dovzhenko, "Smotrite, liudi!" and P. Lidov, "Piat' nemetskikh fotografii," *Pravda*, October 24, 1943, 3; TASS, "Na mogile

Zoi Kosmodem'ianskoi: Traurnyi miting molodëzhi Moskvy," *Trud*, October 30, 1943, 4; Vadim Kozhevnikov, "Vozmezdie," *Pravda*, August 25, 1944, 3; movie advertisement in *Trud*, October 4, 1944, 4; Peter Kenez, "Black and White: The War on Film," in Stites, *Culture and Entertainment in Wartime Russia*, 168.

29. Slepyan, *Stalin's Guerillas*, 201; Victoria E. Bonnell, *Iconography of Power: Soviet Political Posters under Lenin and Stalin* (Berkeley, 1997), 260-261.

30. Vasilevskaia, *Raduga*; Kenez, "Black and White," 167-168.

31. Lisa A. Kirschenbaum, "'Our City, Our Hearts, Our Families': Local Loyalties and Private Life in Soviet World War II Propaganda," *Slavic Review* 59, no. 4 (Winter 2000): 834; Denise J. Youngblood, "A War Remembered: Soviet Films of the Great Patriotic War," *American Historical Review* 107, no. 3 (June 2001): 841-842. Examples of items on female partisans are the letters from the Briansk region in *Pravda*, March 18, 1942; V. Aleksandrov, "Mstitel'nitsy," *Trud*, September 14, 1943, 2; and "Gorod Lenina vstrechaet partizan," *Trud*, March 2, 1944, 2.

32. N. K. Petrova, "Vspomnim . . . (eshche raz o molodezhnoi podpol'noi organizatsii 'Molodaia gvardiia')," *Otechestvennaia istoriia*, no. 3 (May-June 2000): 33-40; I. A. Ioffe and N. K. Petrova, eds., *"Molodia gvardiia" (g. Krasnodon): Khudozhestvennyi vymysel i istoricheskaia real'nost'* (Moscow, 2003), 3; Hiroaki Kuromiya, review of Ioffe and Petrova, *"Molodia gvardiia," Kritika* 6, no. 3 (Summer 2005): 658.

33. Dm. Lisovyi, "Tse bulo v Krasnodoni," *Radians'ka Ukraïna*, June 16, 1943, 3; A. Serpilin, "Nasha molodezh' (Ot spetsial'nogo korrespondenta 'Sovetskoi Ukrainy')," *Sovetskaia Ukraina*, July 9, 1943, 3; "Ukaz Prezidiuma Verkhovnogo Soveta SSSR: O prisvoenii zvaniia Geroia Sovetskogo Soiuza organizatoram i rukovoditeliam podpol'noi komsomol'skoi organizatsii 'Molodaia Gvardiia,'" and other decrees, *Pravda*, September 15, 1943, 1-2; Petrova, "Vspomnim."

34. Petrova, *"Molodaia gvardiia,"* 101, 5; "Stalinskoe plemia," *Pravda*, September 15, 1943, 1; A. Fadeev, "Bessmertie," *Pravda*, September 15, 1943, 3. The translation in von Geldern and Stites, *Mass Culture in Soviet Russia*, 387-392, lacks the part of the oath, "If I break. . . ." An utterly incomplete and garbled translation is Alexander Fadeev, "Immortality," in Krasilshchik, *World War II*, 208-213.

35. V. A. Zolotarev et al., eds., *Russkii arkhiv: Velikaia Otechestvennaia*, vol. 17-6 (Moscow, 1996), 37.

36. Victor Kravchenko, *I Chose Freedom: The Personal and Political Life of a Soviet Official* (New York, 1947), 356; Jörg Baberowski, *Der rote Terror: Die Geschichte des Stalinismus* (Munich, 2003), 234 (on Kuibyshev executions); "Po

zakonam voennogo vremeni: Iiun'-dekabr' 1941 g.," *Istoricheskii arkhiv* 8, no. 3 (2000): 39–41, 34. For censor's cuts of the discovery of a "serious bandit-kulak formation" in Novosibirsk and the names of German spies arrested in Moscow, see GARF, 9425/1/108/14, 28: "Svodka tsenzury po dannym, postupivshim v tsentral'nyi apparat Glavlita (2 dekabria 1941 goda)" and Sadchikov, "Svodka No 1 vycherkov, proizvedennykh tsenzorami v poriadke predvaritel'nogo i posleduiushchego kontrolia, po materialam na 15-e ianvaria 1942 goda."

37. RGASPI, 88/1/998/6–7: "Vystuplenie A. S. Shcherbakova na zasedanii Sovetskogo Informbiuro. 17 ianvaria 1944 g." The original usage for the epithets was *predateli rodiny* (or *izmenniki rodiny*), *posobniki*, and *prisluzhniki*.
38. I. Erenburg, "Smert' predateliam," January 4, 1942, reprinted in Il'ia Erenburg, *Voina (Iiun' 1941–aprel' 1942)* (Moscow, 1942), 202–204; I. Erenburg, "Vernost'," March 5, 1943, reprinted in Il'ia Erenburg, *Voina (Aprel' 1942–mart 1943)* (Moscow, 1943), 334–339; Erenburg, "Chërnyi spisok," August 6, 1943, reprinted in Il'ia Erenburg, *Voina (aprel' 1943–mart 1944)* (Moscow, 1944), 311–315.
39. On Zoia's betrayal, see V. K. Vinogradov et al., comps., *Lubianka v dni bitvy za Moskvu: Po rassekrechennym dokumentam FSB RF* (Moscow, 2002), 182–192. Various other texts from the Klubkov file at the FSB archives are cited in Gorinov, "Zoia Kosmodem'ianskaia (1923–1941)," 84–86. For the publicity, see P. Lidov, "Novoe o 'Tane,'" *Pravdist*, no. 4(119), May 5, 1942, 5, filed at RGASPI, 629/1/89/5; Ia. Miletskii, "Kto predal Taniu," *Krasnaia zvezda*, April 22, 1942, cited in Seniavskaia, "Heroic Symbols," 76.
40. Boris Kovalev, "Shakhtinskaia tragediia," *Komsomol'skaia pravda*, November 4, 1942; RGASPI, 17/125/190/19, 24: Kobulov, deputy NKGB, to Shcherbakov, Moscow, October 15, 1943 and Puzin to Shcherbakov, n.p., October 29, 1943.
41. RGASPI, 17/125/187/40v: polkovnik Cherstvoi, nach. otdela voennoi tsenzury NKO, to general-maior Shikin, zam. nach. GlavPURKKA, with a copy to Puzin, "Svodka" for April 1–10, 1943, Moscow, April 15, 1943 ("900" replaced with "many," in A. Surkov, "Po lageriam smerti," *Krasnaia zvezda*, 10 April 1943, 3); RGASPI, 17/125/187/41v: polkovnik Cherstvoi, nach. otdela voennoi tsenzury NKO, to general-maior Shikin, zam. nach. GlavPURKKA, with a copy to Puzin, "Svodka" for April 11–20, 1943, Moscow, April 22, 1943 (on Demiansk, in "Biulenen' v pomoshch' agitatoram," *Krasnaia zvezda*, April 14, 1943); RGASPI, 17/125/187/124: Polkovnik Berezin, nach. Otdela voennoi tsenzury GSh KA, "Svodka" on November 1–30, 1943, n.p., December 20, 1943 (on "Mshchenie i smert' nemetsko-fashistskim zakhvatchikam!," editorial, *Krasnaia zvezda*, November 13, 1943).

42. Baberowski, *Der rote Terror*, 230. For the full text of the order, see Sergei Kudriashov, ed. in chief, *Vestnik Arkhiv Prezidenta Rossiiskoi Federatsii: Voina, 1941–1945* (Moscow, 2010), 63–66.
43. *Pravda*, December 25, 1941; Amir Weiner, *Making Sense of War: The Second World War and the Fate of the Bolshevik Revolution* (Princeton, N.J., 2001), 161.
44. Mikhail Sholokhov, "Nauka nenavisti," *Pravda*, June 22, 1942, 3; Vasilevskaia, *Raduga*, 165–166.
45. Gorbatov, *Nepokorënnye*, 54–58, 69–73, 149–153.
46. Vasilevskaia, *Raduga*, 16, 28, 43, 143–144, 163, 183–184.
47. Gorbatov, *Nepokorënnye*, 17–19, 36. See also Jeffrey W. Jones, "'Every Family Has Its Freak': Perceptions of Collaboration in Occupied Soviet Russia, 1943–1948," *Slavic Review* 64, no. 4 (Winter 2005): 760–763.
48. "A tak, konechno, oni—gady," *Rodina*, no. 10 (Moscow, 2002): 59; Jones, "'Every Family Has Its Freak,'" 759; Weiner, *Making Sense of War*, 86–87; Gorbatov, *Nepokorënnye*, 109–110, 113.
49. On the central policy, see Alexander Statiev, *The Soviet Counterinsurgency in the Western Borderlands* (Cambridge, U.K., 2010), 197–199. The first Ukrainian text inadvertently suggested that there were no Ukrainians in the Red Army or in the Soviet hinterland. "Do narodu Ukraïny," *Radians'ka Ukraïna*, March 2, 1943, 1; TsDAHOU, 57/4/3/52: retyping by Vinnytsia obkom of M. Hrechukha, L. Korniiets', and N. Khrushchev, "Ukraïns'kyi narode! Dorohi braty i sestry!," Kharkiv, September 25, 1943.
50. Gorbatov, *Nepokorënnye*, 38, 60, 63–67. On deported citizens, see, for example, RGASPI, 17/125/187/38v: report, April 2, 1943, with regard to A. Surkov, "On byl v Brandenburge," *Krasnaia zvezda*, March 31, 1943.
51. Stalin, *O Velikoi Otechestvennoi voine Sovetskogo Soiuza*, 13; A. Filippov, "Narodnye mstiteli," *Pravda*, November 23, 1941, 2; M. Grechukha, L. Korniets, N. Khrushchev, "K ukrainskomu narodu," *Pravda*, January 21, 1942, 2; V. Sysova, "Ganna," *Trud*, March 8, 1942, 2.
52. Vasilevskaia, *Raduga*, 29, 52, 132–139; *Rainbow: A Novel by Wanda Wassilewska*, trans. Edith Bone (London, n.d.), 26, 45–46, 111–116.
53. Gorbatov, *Nepokorënnye*, 114–118.
54. RGASPI, 17/125/52/30: Fitin, head of the 1st [Intelligence] Upravlenie NKVD SSSR to Shcherbakov, "O polozhenii v raionakh, okkupirovannykh protivnikom: Po sostoianiiu na 20-oe avgusta 1941 goda," Moscow, August 26, 1941; Ilya Bourtman, "'Blood for Blood, Death for Death': The Soviet Military Tribunal in Krasnodar, 1943," *Holocaust and Genocide Studies* 22, no. 2 (Fall 2008): 257; Gorbatov, *Nepokorënnye*, 125.

55. On the partisan threat, see Aleksandr Gogun, *Partyzanci Stalina na Ukrainie: Nieznane działania 1941–1944*, trans. Witold Stefanowicz (Warsaw, 2010), 287-288 (on the threat to relatives); "Politseiskii!," in Livshin and Orlov, *Sovetskaia propaganda*, 416; TsDAVOV, 4188/1/146/133-134v: Syrchenko, "Politsaiu," broadcast by Radio Soviet Ukraine on February 7, 9, and 13, [1943] (using the words *sud hromady*); Porfyrii Khomych Kumanek in "Tretii mitynh predstavnykiv ukraïns'koho narodu," *Radians'ka Ukraïna*, June 2, 1943, 1-3, also in *Ukraïna bula i bude radians'koiu: Tretii mitynh predstavnykiv ukraïns'koho narodu* ([Moscow], 1943), 16; "Zvernennia do naselennia okupovanykh raioniv Ukraïny," *Radians'ka Ukraïna*, June 5, 1943, 1-2. A Komsomol call in 1943 to those in German military service also promised forgiveness; see Livshin and Orlov, *Sovetskaia propaganda*, 489.
56. On the agronomist, see "Izmennika rodine—k rasstrelu," *Izvestiia*, September 26, 1941, 4. On hangings, see RGASPI, 17/3/1047/34, 232-233: resolution, April 19, 1943, and decree, also published in V. A. Zolotarev et al., eds., *Russkii arkhiv: Velikaia Otchestvennaia*, vol. 13-3 (Moscow, 2002), 282-283. On the Supreme Court, see Kiril Feferman, "Soviet Investigation of Nazi Crimes in the USSR: Documenting the Holocaust," *Journal of Genocide Research* 5, no. 4 (December 2003): 591. On the picture, see RGASPI, 17/125/187/40: polkovnik Cherstvoi, nach. otdela voennoi tsenzury NKO, to general-maior Shikin, zam. nach. GlavPURKKA, with a copy to Puzin, "Svodka" for April 1-10, 1943, Moscow, April 15, 1943. On the village woman, see Livshin and Orlov, *Sovetskaia propaganda*, 656. On duty to report, see Katrin Boeckh, *Stalinismus in der Ukraine: Die Rekonstruktion des sowjetischen Systems nach dem Zweiten Weltkrieg* (Wiesbaden, 2007), 209.
57. Weiner, *Making Sense of War*, 301; Gerhard Simon, *Nationalismus und Nationalitätenpolitik in der Sowjetunion: Von totalitären Diktatur zur nachstalinschen Gesellschaft* (Baden-Baden, 1986), 244-245.
58. On tribunals and rules, see Sergey Kudriashov and Vanessa Voisin, "The Early Stages of 'Legal Purges' in Soviet Russia (1941-1945)," *Cahiers du monde russe* 49, nos. 2-3 (2008): 275-277.
59. Compare Berel Lang, *The Future of the Holocaust: Between History and Memory* (Ithaca, N.Y., 1999), 122-124, which argues that no society has ever declared this imperative.
60. On letters, see Lidov, "Novoe o 'Tane'"; RGALI, 1865/1/111 and 113. On popularity, see Nina Tumarkin, *The Living and the Dead: The Rise and Fall of the Cult of World War II in Russia* (New York, 1994), 76-77; Kirschenbaum, "'Our City, Our Hearts, Our Families,'" 829, 832; Sartorti, "On the Making

of Heroes," 182–183, 187, 190; Seniavskaia, "Heroic Symbols," 81–83; N. D. Kozlov, *S volei k pobede: Propaganda i obydennoe soznanie v gody Velikoi Otechestvennoi voiny* (St. Petersburg, 2002), 204.

10. Allies Who Must Join the Action

1. Vladimir Nevezhin, "Soviet War Propaganda, from Anti-imperialism to Anti-fascism: Shifts and Contradictions," in Silvio Pons and Andrea Romano, eds., *Russia in the Age of Wars, 1914–1945* (Milan, 2000), 254; Victor Kravchenko, *I Chose Freedom: The Personal and Political Life of a Soviet Official* (New York, 1947), 334; Frederick Barghoorn, *The Soviet Image of the United States: A Study in Distortion* (New York, 1950), 26, 28.
2. Ben-Cion Pinchuk, "Soviet Media on the Fate of the Jews in Nazi-Occupied Territory (1939–1941)," *Yad Vashem Studies* 11 (Jerusalem, 1976): 224–225.
3. Jeffrey Brooks, *Thank You, Comrade Stalin! Soviet Public Culture from Revolution to Civil War* (Princeton, N.J., 2000), 150; E. S. Seniavskaia, *Protivniki Rossii v voinakh XX veka: Evoliutsiia "obraza vraga" v soznanii armii i obshchestva* (Moscow, 2006), 135.
4. David Brandenberger, *National Bolshevism: Stalinist Mass Culture and the Formation of Modern Russian National Identity, 1931–1956* (Cambridge, Mass., 2002), 86.
5. Ewa M. Thompson, "Nationalist Propaganda in the Soviet Russian Press, 1939–1941," *Slavic Review* 50, no. 2 (Summer 1991): 389–390; Pinchuk, "Soviet Media," 224–225.
6. Thompson, "Nationalist Propaganda," 392; Ewa M. Thompson, "Soviet Russian Writers and the Soviet Invasion of Poland in September 1939," in Ewa M. Thompson, ed., *The Search for Self-Definition in Russian Literature* (Amsterdam, 1991), 160, 165; Volodymyr Pasika, *U krutezhi shalu* (Toronto, 1979), 54–55 (on verbal propaganda); V. A. Tokarev, "'Kará panam! Kará!': Pol'skaia tema v predvoennom kino (1939–1941 gody)," *Otechestvennaia istoriia*, no. 6 (November–December 2003): 47–59.
7. GARF, 6903/1/82/44: E. Skleznev, "Otchet redaktsii 'Poslednikh Izvestii' za 1943 god," n.p., n.d.
8. John Lawrence, *Life in Russia* (London, 1947), 117.
9. Edmund Stevens, *Russia Is No Riddle* (New York, 1945), 279–281.
10. Ibid., 277.
11. In the Gulag this attitude predated the German-Soviet war. For instance, in the spring of 1941 the tiny minority of inmates at one labor colony who did read *Pravda* and *Izvestiia* did so "with impassive faces, shuffling

their feet sideways without glancing left or right lest the reader's face betray his politically incorrect reactions to the news content and he be denounced to the Cultural and Educational Section." Aleksander Topolski, *Without Vodka: Adventures in Wartime Russia* (South Royalton, Vt., 2001), 201.
12. Pasika, *U krutezhi shalu*, 118, 197.
13. "Ob amnistii ... ," *Izvestiia*, August 13, 1941, 1; Thompson, "Soviet Russian Writers," 163. For the cut from a factory newspaper, see GARF, 9425/1/108/126: "Svodka ... ," August 1, 1942. On warnings, see Alexander Werth, *Russia at War, 1941–1945* (New York, 1964), 191; Peter Gosztony, *Stalins fremde Heere: Das Schicksal der nichtsowjetischen Truppen im Rahmen der Roten Armee 1941–1945* (Bonn, 1991), 34.
14. "Sluchaite, brat'ia poliaki!," *Pravda*, December 2, 1941; "Vystuplenie po radio Predsedatelia Soveta ministrov Pol'skoi respubliki generala Vl. Sikorskogo," *Trud*, December 5, 1941, 4.
15. Keith Sword, *Deportation and Exile: Poles in the Soviet Union, 1939–48* (Houndmills, U.K., 1996 [1994]), 133; Stanisław Ciesielski, *Polacy w Kazachstanie. 1940–1946: Zesłańcy lat wojny* (Wrocław, 1997), 265–266.
16. This was unlike the Polish Red Army division that had been foreseen in plans in early June 1941, as an analogy to events on the eve of the Finnish War of November 1939, and bespeaking Soviet offensive intent. Boris V. Sokolov, "The Role of Lend-Lease in Soviet Military Efforts, 1941–1945," *Journal of Slavic Military Studies* 7, no. 3 (September 1994): 583.
17. *Pravda*, December 6, 1941 (Anders interview); Topolski, *Without Vodka*, 239 (regional paper); Gosztony, *Stalins fremde Heere*, 34-46. Gosztony states that Soviet propaganda mentioned the departure and called it desertion, but gives no source reference.
18. W. L. White, *Report on the Russians* (London, 1945), 107–108; Werth, *Russia at War*, 594–595.
19. From its initial 18,000 to 28,000. Klaus-Peter Friedrich, "Von der polnischen Kriegspropaganda in der Sowjetunion zur Machtübernahme der Kommunisten in Polen (1942-1944)," *Zeitschrift für Geschichtswissenschaft* 54, nos. 7–8 (2006): 667–668; RGASPI, 17/125/193/116–117: Wasilewska to Shcherbakov [June 1943].
20. "Pis'mo lichnogo sostava divizii im. Tadeusha Kostiushko—Marshalu Sovetskogo Soiuza, Predsedateliu Gosudarstvennogo Komiteta Oborony I. V. STALINU," *Trud*, June 29, 1943, 2; "Priniatie prisiagi v pol'skoi divizii im. Tadeusha Kostiushko," *Trud*, July 17, 1943, 2; Gosztony, *Stalins fremde Heere*, 81, 84, 88–91, 137, 80, 84–85.

21. "Obrashchenie torzhestvennogo zasedaniia, posviashchennogo 150-letiiu pol'skogo natsional'no-osovoboditel'nogo vosstaniia pod rukovodstvom Tadeusha Kostiushko," *Trud*, March 26, 1944, 4.
22. Werth, *Russia at War*, 766–768; *Pravda*, April 28, 1944, 1; *Trud*, April 29, 1944, 1.
23. On Poles in Iran, see TASS, "Srednevekovye pytki v armii Andersa," *Trud*, March 21, 1944, 4; TASS, "Svidetel'stvo inostrannogo zhurnalista o deiianiiakh pol'skikh vlastei v Irane," *Trud*, March 29, 1944, 4; TASS, "Chlen kongressa SShA razoblachaet antisemitizm v pol'skoi armii," *Trud*, May 23, 1944, 4. On Poles in Scotland, see TASS, "Obstoiatel'stva aresta gruppy pol'skikh soldat—vykhodtsev iz Zapadnoi Ukrainy," *Trud*, April 4, 1944, 4; TASS, "'Reinol'ds n'ius' o polozhenii belorussov i ukraintsev v pol'skoi armii," *Trud*, April 4, 1944, 4; TASS, "Angliiskaia pechat' ob izdevatel'stvakh nad predstaviteliami natsmenshinstv v pol'skoi armii," *Trud*, April 28, 1944, 4; TASS, "Izdevatel'stva nad belorussami i ukraintsami v pol'skoi armii," *Trud*, April 28, 1944, 4; TASS, "Protest meksikanskikh poliakov protiv antisemitizma v pol'skoi armii," *Trud*, May 16, 1944, 4; TASS, "Miting protest protiv rasovykh gonenii v pol'skoi armii," *Trud*, May 17, 1944, 4.
24. Werth, *Russia at War*, 770–771; "Telegramma upolnomochennykh Natsional'nogo Soveta Pol'shi tov. N. S. Khrushchevu," *Trud*, June 11, 1944, 2; "Obrazovanie Pol'skogo Komiteta Natsional'nogo Osvobozhdeniia," *Trud*, July 25, 1944, 3.
25. RGASPI, 17/125/296/52: G. Aleksandrov to A. S. Shcherbakov, "Spravka," September 23, 1944 (on radio); Werth, *Russia at War*, 790, 792, 825.
26. I. Stalin, *O Velikoi Otechestvennoi voine Sovetskogo Soiuza*, 4th ed. (Moscow, 1944), 96; "Podpisanie soglasheniia mezhdu Pravitel'stvom Litovskoi Sovetskoi Sovetskoi Sotsialisticheskoi Respubliki i Pol'skim Komitetom Natsional'nogo Osvobozhdeniia ob evakuatsii litovskogo naseleniia s territorii Pol'shi i pol'skikh grazhdan s territorii Litovskoi SSR," *Trud*, September 26, 1944, 2.
27. Stalin, *O Velikoi Otechestvennoi voine Sovetskogo Soiuza*, 22–23. On Stalin's sense of urgency, see B. V. Sokolov, *Tainy vtoroi mirovoi* (Moscow, 2001), 172, citing RGASPI, 558/11/59.
28. On the BBC, see Siân Nicholas, *The Echo of War: Home Front Propaganda and the Wartime BBC, 1939–45* (Manchester, U.K., 1996), 208.
29. Stalin, *O Velikoi Otechestvennoi voine Sovetskogo Soiuza*, 152 (the mention); Aleksei Tolstoi, "Ubei zveria!," *Pravda*, June 23, 1942, 2.
30. Sarah Davies, "Soviet Perceptions of the Allies during the Great Patriotic War," in Cathryn Brennan and Murray Frame, eds., *Russia and the Wider*

World in Historical Perspective: Essays for Paul Dukes (Houndmills, U.K., 2000), 175; Werth, *Russia at War*, 359-360; Barghoorn, *The Soviet Image of the United States*, 62.

31. Werth, *Russia at War*, 451-453; Stalin, *O Velikoi Otechestvennoi voine Sovetskogo Soiuza*, 55-56.
32. Stalin, *O Velikoi Otechestvennoi voine Sovetskogo Soiuza*, 62-66, 69-70, 77.
33. Ibid., 82; Werth, *Russia at War*, 580-581.
34. Stalin, *O Velikoi Otechestvennoi voine Sovetskogo Soiuza*, 90, 97; Werth, *Russia at War*, 614 (both on May); Sovinformbiuro, "Dva goda Otechestvennoi voiny Sovetskogo Soiuza (Ko vtoroi godovshchiny Otechestvennoi voiny)," *Trud*, June 22, 1943, 1; Davies, "Soviet Perceptions of the Allies," 183; Werth, *Russia at War*, 618.
35. Stalin, *O Velikoi Otechestvennoi voine Sovetskogo Soiuza*, 112-113, 116; Werth, *Russia at War*, 786.
36. My emphasis. In original usage, *kogda vstupiat v deistvie*. Stalin, *O Velikoi Otechestvennoi voine Sovetskogo Soiuza*, 125. On the slogans, see A. V. Golubev, "Sovetskoe obshchestvo i 'obraz soiuznika' v gody Vtoroi mirovoi voiny," *Sotsial'naia istoriia: Ezhegodnik 2001/2002*, Moscow, 2004, 433.
37. Stalin, *O Velikoi Otechestvennoi voine Sovetskogo Soiuza*, 132, 135; Werth, *Russia at War*, 765.
38. Paul Winterton, *Report on Russia* (London, 1945), 26, 28-29; Golubev, "Sovetskoe obshchestvo," 433; "Poteri amerikanskoi armii," *Trud*, June 27, 1943, 4.
39. Sokolov, "The Role of Lend-Lease," 568 (on Zhukov), 571-575, 578-581, 583. The Russian version of the article is in Sokolov, *Tainy vtoroi mirovoi*, 198-218.
40. Stalin, *O Velikoi Otechestvennoi voine Sovetskogo Soiuza*, 14.
41. RGASPI, 558/11/203/197-198: clipping of "Ob"edinennymi silami na bor'bu s gitlerizmom: Beseda s sekretarem VTsSPS tov. N. M. Shvernikom," *Pravda*, September 7, 1941, and an untitled typed manuscript.
42. Stalin, *O Velikoi Otechestvennoi voine Sovetskogo Soiuza*, 31, 51; Golubev, "Sovetskoe obshchestvo," 431-432, 438.
43. On attention, see Golubev, "Sovetskoe obshchestvo," 432-433. More balanced was "Zaiavlenie Kroula ob amerikanskh postavkakh Sovetskomu Soiuzu," *Pravda*, March 1, 1944, 4. On planes, see David Ortenberg, *Stalin, Shcherbakov, Mekhlis i drugie* (Moscow, 1995), 146-147; "Na amerikanskom istrebitele 'Aerokobra,'" *Trud*, March 28, 1942, 4. On the tank, see Niels Bo Poulsen, "The Soviet Extraordinary State Commission on War Crimes: An Analysis of the Commission's Investigative Work in War and post War Stalinist Society" (Ph.D. dissertation, Copenhagen University,

2004), 157; M. Koriakov, "Sovetskaia zhurnalistika," *Novoe Russkoe Slovo* (New York), October 17, 1948, 2.

44. Werth, *Russia at War*, 574-575, 577, 617, 776; Barghoorn, *The Soviet Image of the United States*, 57; "O postavkakh Sovetskomu Soiuzu vooruzheniia, strategicheskogo syr'ia, promyshlennoho oborudovaniia i prodovol'stviia Soedinennymi Shtatami Ameriki, Velikobritanii i Kanadoi," *Pravda*, June 11, 1944, 1. *Trud*'s publication of this article was followed by a highly unusual rectification of one figure; see "Popravka," *Trud*, June 13, 1944, 4.
45. V. F. Zima, *Mentalitet narodov Rossii v voine 1941–1945 godov* (Moscow, 2000), 101; "Rech' g. Garrimana na zakliuchitel'nom zasedanii konferentsii predstavitelei SSSR, Velikobritanii i SShA," *Pravda*, October 2, 1941, 1.
46. On sailors, see A. Dunaevskii, "O-Kei, Britaniia!," *Pravda*, January 16, 1942, 2; GARF, 9425/1/43/8: "Otchet o rabote Otdela poseleduiushchei tsenzury Soiuza SSR za 1-i kvartal 1942 g."; *Pravda*, September 8, 1942, 1; RGASPI, 17/125/112/158: Zaitsev, head of the Foreign Relations Department of the People's Commissariat of the Military Fleet, to Aleksandrov, Moscow, September 23, 1942, with written comment dated October 1. On British pilots, see *Pravda*, November 28, 1941, 1; *Trud*, March 29, 1942, 2-3; *Trud*, May 24, 1944, 1; *Trud*, July 29, 1944, 4.
47. Gosztony, *Stalins fremde Heere*, 130-134; Il'ia Erenburg, "Frantsuzy," January 6, 1943, reprinted in Il'ia Erenburg, *Voina (Aprel' 1942–mart 1943)* (Moscow, 1943), 106-109; A. Bulgakov, deistvuiushchaia armiia, "Letchiki 'Normandii,'" *Sovetskaia Ukraina*, July 4, 1943, 4; *Pravda*, July 3, 1943; *Pravda*, August 26, 1943; *Pravda*, February 5, 1944; *Trud*, February 22, 1944, 4; *Trud*, October 28 1944, 1; *Trud*, December 10, 1944, 1; *Pravda*, February 24, 1945; RGASPI, 17/125/187/58v: polkovnik Cherstvoi, nach. otdela voennoi tsenzury NKO, to general-maior Shikin, zam. nach. GlavPURKKA, with a copy to Puzin, "Svodka" for May 1-10, 1943, Moscow, May 14, 1943.
48. Philip Knightley, *The First Casualty: The War Correspondent as Hero and Mythmaker from the Crimea to Kosovo*, rev. ed. (London, 2000), 287; Werth, *Russia at War*, 773-774; White, *Report on the Russians*, 142, 144, 152, 161; Lazar' Brontman, *Voennyi dnevnik korrespondenta "Pravdy": Vstrechi. Sobytiia. Sud'by. 1942–1945* (Moscow, 2007), 332; Glenn B. Infield, *The Poltava Affair: A Russian Warning. An American Tragedy* (New York, 1973), 228, 251-252. Infield, a former U.S. pilot, states unconvincingly (230, 233) that Stalin had already decided he no longer wanted the bases and therefore tipped off the Germans about the presence that night of American planes at Poltava.
49. Stalin, *O Velikoi Otechestvennoi voine Sovetskogo Soiuza*, 90, 113, 132.

50. Christoph Kucklick, *Feuersturm: Der Bombenkrieg gegen Deutschland* (Hamburg, 2003); RGASPI, 17/125/35/89: Il'ia Erenburg to Shcherbakov, Lozovskii, and Aleksandrov, n.p., n.d. [late in September 1941]; "Poteri angliiskoi i amerikanskoi aviatsii nad Germaniei i Severnoi Evropy v 1943 g.," *Trud*, February 18, 1944, 4.
51. TASS, "Ozhestochennye bombardirovki Liubeka," *Pravda*, March 30, 1942, 4; Charles Eade, comp., *The End of the Beginning: War Speeches 1942 by the Right Hon. Winston S. Churchill C.H., M.P.*, 2nd ed. (London, 1943), 112 (the Churchill quotation); TASS, "Svyshe 1.000 angliiskikh bombardirovshchikov nad Kel'nom: 10.000 bomb v 90 minut," *Pravda*, June 1, 1942, 4.
52. "Sinkler o bombardirovkakh germanskikh promyshlennykh tsentrov," *Trud*, May 23, 1943, 4; S. Matveev, "Rur pod udarami angliiskoi aviatsii," *Trud*, May 20, 1943, 4 (on morale); "Deistviia soiuznoi aviatsii," *Trud*, May 30, 1943, 4 (Swiss witness); "Posledstviia razrusheniia damb na Mene i Eder," *Trud*, June 8, 1943, 4 (Swedish newspaper); "Massovoe begstvo germanskogo naseleniia iz Rura," *Trud*, June 18, 1943, 4.
53. "Deistviia aviatsii soiuznikov: Nalët angliiskikh bombardirovshchikov na Gamburg. Podrobnosti bombardirovki Essena," *Trud*, July 29, 1943, 4; "Deistviia aviatsii soiuznikov: Razrusheniia v Gamburge," *Trud*, September 22, 1943, 4.
54. "Rezul'taty angliiskoi bombardirovski Berlina," *Trud*, January 26, 1943, 4; "Berlinskii iubilei," *Pravda*, February 1, 1943, 4; "Posledstviia bombardirovki Berlina," *Trud*, March 6, 1943, 4 (on families); "Deistviia aviatsii soiuznikov," *Trud*, November 25, 1943, 4 (on Reuters); "Opustoshitel'nye posledstviia bombardirovki Berlina," *Trud*, November 27, 1943, 4 (the body count); "Nalët angliiskikh bombardirovshchikov na Berlin," *Trud*, December 25, 1943, 4 (on homeless).
55. TASS, "Unichtozhenie nad Angliei germanskikh samoletov, upravliaemykh po radio," *Trud*, June 20, 1944, 4; "Vpechatleniia sekretaria komiteta 'Fond pomoshchi Rossii' Mabel' Dzhonson ot poseshcheniia Leningrada," *Trud*, November 12, 1944, 4; E. Sidorenko and M. Kuznetsov, "V gostiakh u angliiskikh rabochikh," *Trud*, December 10, 1944, 2; "Vozdushnye nalety na Angliiu," *Trud*, January 10, 1945, 4; "Otvet Idena...," *Trud*, December 13, 1944, 4.
56. "Krupnye nalëty aviatsii soiuznikov na Germaniiu," *Trud*, February 16, 1945, 4; "Voennye deistviia v Zapadnoi Evrope," *Trud*, February 17, 1945, 4.
57. See, respectively, *Trud*, February 11, 1942, 2; March 10, 1942, 4; March 28, 1943, 4; July 27, 1943, 4.

58. German reporting of the Allied bombings wavered. Sometimes Goebbels warned the press not to describe its impact (October 1940, April 1942, March 1943, August 1943), but sometimes he ordered more realistic reporting (September 1941) and even frankness, combined with admiration for German civilian heroism (August 1942, June 1943). He apparently hoped that such occasional candid coverage would increase hatred of the British and strengthen popular support, and possibly believed himself (in June 1943) that a massive retaliation on British cities was imminent. Gerald Kirwin, "Allied Bombing and Nazi Domestic Propaganda," *European History Quarterly* 15, no. 3 (July 1985): 341–362.

59. Some reports were cut because they targeted Soviet and other non-German cities. See, for example, RGASPI, 17/125/187/41v, 60v: polkovnik Cherstvoi, nach. otdela voennoi tsenzury NKO, to general-maior Shikin, zam. nach. GlavPURKKA, with a copy to Puzin, "Svodka" for April 11–20, 1943, Moscow, April 22, 1943, and "Svodka" for May 11–20, 1943, Moscow, May 27, 1943. But compare, for example, "Ot Sovetskogo Informbiuro," *Trud*, September 15, 1944, 1. In contrast, censors rigidly enforced the ban on reports of submarine actions, and thus also omitted the Red Fleet's most deadly torpedo attack, of January 30, 1945, which sank the German *Wilhelm Gustloff*. (The biggest shipping catastrophe in history, in 1990 it served as the reason for declaring the submarine commander Aleksandr Marinesko a Hero of the Soviet Union.) Sokolov, *Tainy vtoroi mirovoi*, 418; Heinz Schön, "Flucht über die Ostsee: Die größte Rettungsaktion der Seegeschichte," in *Flucht und Vertreibung: Europa zwischen 1939 und 1948. Mit einer Einleitung von Arno Surminski* (Hamburg, 2004), 105–106; I. I. Shirokorad, *Tsentral'naia periodicheskaia pechat' v gody Velikoi Otechestvennoi voiny: 1941–1945* (Moscow, 2001), 92.

60. "Vystuplenie Cherchilla po radio," *Pravda*, June 23, 1941, 5; Charles Eade, comp., *The Unrelenting Struggle: War Speeches by the Right Hon. Winston S. Churchill C.H., M.P.*, 3rd ed. (London, 1943), 176–180. Compare Werth, *Russia at War*, 169, which implies that the entire text was available. As Winterton, *Report on Russia*, 54 notes, foreign correspondents were not allowed to report that cuts were made.

61. "Rech' Cherchilla v palate obshchin," *Pravda*, January 29, 1942, 4; Eade, *End of the Beginning*, 14–15.

62. Mikhail N. Narinsky et al., "Mutual Perceptions: Images, Ideals, and Illusions," in David Reynolds, Warren F. Kimball, and A. O. Chubarian, eds., *Allies at War: The Soviet, American, and British Experience, 1939–1945* (Houndmills, U.K., 1994), 312.

63. Werth, *Russia at War*, 615; Stalin, *O Velikoi Otechestvennoi voine Sovetskogo Soiuza*, 98-99; RGASPI, 17/125/197/13-13v: I. Krutov of the Altai krai committee to Pupynina, editor of the paper *Bol'shevik* of the Krasnoshchekovo raion, printed copy for editors of raion and city newspapers, n.p., May 18, 1943.
64. Golubev, "Sovetskoe obshchestvo," 431; Siân Nicholas, "'Partners Now': Problems in the Portrayal by the BBC of the Soviet Union and the United States of America, 1939-45," *Diplomacy and Statecraft* 3, no. 2 (July 1992): 243-271; Stalin, *O Velikoi Otechestvennoi voine Sovetskogo Soiuza*, 150; A. Ia. Livshin and I. B. Orlov, comps., *Sovetskaia propaganda v gody Velikoi Otechestvennoi voiny: "Kommunikatsiia ubezhdeniia" i mobilizatsionnye mekhanizmy* (Moscow, 2007), 387-389 (Aleksandrov); "Otvety Ruzvel'ta zhurnalistam na press-konferentsii," *Trud*, November 23, 1944, 4 (on camps).
65. Werth, *Russia at War*, 449, 454; Kravchenko, *I Chose Freedom*, 468; Barghoorn, *The Soviet Image of the United States*, 47, 58. See also, on a speech by E. Iaroslavskii, N. D. Kozlov, *Obshchestvennoe soznanie v gody Velikoi Otechestvennoi voiny (1941-1945)* (St. Petersburg, 1995), 67. On the journal, see Golubev, "Sovetskoe obshchestvo," 435.
66. "Prestupnuiu gitlerovskuiu kliku k otvetu!," editorial, *Pravda*, October 19, 1942, 1; Ariel J. Kochavi, "Anglo-Soviet Differences over a Policy towards War Criminals, 1942-1943," *Slavonic and East European Review* 69, no. 3 (July 1991): 475-476; Werth, *Russia at War*, 454-455. On November 6, 1941, Stalin had been laconic about Hess; see Stalin, *O Velikoi Otechestvennoi voine Sovetskogo Soiuza*, 19.
67. Golubev, "Sovetskoe obshchestvo," 434; Stevens, *Russia Is No Riddle*, 153; TASS, "Ves' sovetskii narod goriacho odobriaet resheniia konferentsii rukovoditelei trekh soiuznykh derzhav," *Trud*, December 8, 1943, 1.
68. Stevens, *Russia Is No Riddle*, 158-161 (the quotation); Werth, *Russia at War*, 690, 700; White, *Report on the Russians*, 53; "Zaiavlenie nemetskogo voennoplennogo Gerkharda Makhensa Glavnomu Komandovaniiu Krasnoi Armii," *Pravda*, February 17, 1944; RGASPI, 558/11/204/61-62 (also at 17/125/262/7-8): letter by Shcherbakov to Stalin and page proofs.
69. Winterton, *Report on Russia*, 28; Stevens, *Russia Is No Riddle*, 277; Werth, *Russia at War*, 774-776; White, *Report on the Russians*, 55, 131; Davies, "Soviet Perceptions of the Allies," 184; Stalin, *O Velikoi Otechestvennoi voine Sovetskogo Soiuza*, 137.
70. Davies, "Soviet Perceptions of the Allies," 184 (on Rome); Winterton, *Report on Russia*, 28; Werth, *Russia at War*, 776-777; Barghoorn, *The Soviet Image of the United States*, 65, 67.

71. RGASPI, 17/125/262/132: Aleksandrov and P. Fedoseev to Zhdanov, "Ob oshibke v 'Mezhdunarodnom obzore' gazety 'Komsomol'skaia pravda' za 14 sentiabria 1944 goda," n.p., September 14, 1944.
72. Winterton, *Report on Russia*, 24-25.
73. "Vysadka krupnogo aviadesanta soiuznikov v Gollandii," *Trud*, September 19, 1944, 4; Winterton, *Report on Russia*, 26-28; Stalin, *O Velikoi Otechestvennoi voine Sovetskogo Soiuza*, 157-158.
74. *Pravda*, April 28, 1945, 1, 5.
75. Peter Jahn, "Das Ende der nationalsozialistischen Herrschaft: Die Kapitulation in Berlin-Karlshorst am 8. Mai 1945," in Museum Berlin-Karlshorst, *Erinnerung an einen Krieg* (Berlin, 1997), 40-44; "Kriegsende Mai 1945—Legenden über die Kapitulationen am 7. und 8. Mai," at http://www.museum-karlshorst.de; Tat'iana Goriaeva and Aleksandr Sherel', "Vnimanie, govorit pobeda! Sovetskoe radio v gody Velikoi Otechestvennoi voiny," *Televidenie i radioveshchanie*, no. 4 (1985): 32, without source reference; "Podpisanie akta o bezogovorochnoi kapituliatsii germanskikh vooruzhennykh sil: Akt o voennoi kapituliatsii," *Krasnaia zvezda*, May 9, 1945, 1; I. Stalin, *O Velikoi Otechestvennoi voine Sovetskogo Soiuza*, 5th ed. (Moscow, 1945), 192. On Kiev, see Serhy Yekelchyk, "The Leader, the Victory, and the Nation: Public Celebrations in Soviet Ukraine under Stalin (Kiev, 1943-1953)," *Jahrbücher für Geschichte Osteuropas* 54, no. 1 (2006): 8. The long quotation is from Alaric Jacob, *A Window in Moscow. 1944-1945* (London, 1946), 306.
76. A. V. Golubev, "'Tsar' Kitaiu ne verit...': Soiuzniki v predstavlenii rossiiskogo obshchestva 1914-1945 gg.," in A. V. Golubev, ed. in chief, *Rossia i mir glazami drug druga: Iz istoriia vzaimovospriiatiia. Vypusk pervyi* (Moscow, 2000), 337; Brooks, *Thank You, Comrade Stalin*, 193 (the quoted historian).
77. Topolski, *Without Vodka*, 380-381, slightly revised; Livshin and Orlov, *Sovetskaia propaganda v gody Velikoi Otechestvennoi voiny*, 677 (the citizen).
78. Ciesielski, *Polacy w Kazachstanie*, 255-276; Wanda Lidia Smereczańska-Zienkiewicz and Witold Jan Smereczański, *Krajobraz niewoli: Wspomnienia z Kazachstanu* (Lublin, 2005), 67; Szczepan Wiesław Nalepiński, *Syberyjski szlak*, 3d ed. (Lublin, 2006), 57-58.
79. Andrei Artizov and Oleg Naumov, eds., *Vlast' i khudozhestvennaia intelligentsiia: Dokumenty TsK RKP(b)–VKP(b)–VChK–OGPU–NKVD o kul'turnoi politike. 1917–1953 gg.* (Moscow, 1999), 488-489, 491, 494-494, 499. On pressure, see 488, 492.
80. Barghoorn, *The Soviet Image of the United States*, 236.
81. Mary M. Leder, *My Life in Stalinist Russia: An American Woman Looks Back* (Bloomington, Ind., 2001), 239-240. Compare V. Kruzhkov, "Dva goda

voiny," *Pravda*, August 31, 1941, 4; S. Kripps, "Dva goda voiny protiv gitlerizma," *Ivzestiia*, September 3, 1941.
82. White, *Report on the Russians*, 55-56. One Russian historian who agrees that this intended effect was achieved is Golubev, "Sovetskoe obshchestvo," 433.
83. Winterton, *Report on Russia*, 21.

Conclusion

1. [Birthe Kundrus,] "Rezeptionen der medialen Meinungs- und Gefühlslenkung," in Jörg Echternkamp, ed., *Das Deutsche Reich und der Zweite Weltkrieg* 9, pt. 2 (Munich, 2005), 145-146.
2. The comparison is mine; on Nazi propaganda, see Aristotle A. Kallis, *Nazi Propaganda and the Second World War* (Houndmills, U.K., 2005), 8-9.
3. Jay W. Baird, *To Die for Germany: Heroes in the Nazi Pantheon* (Bloomington, Ind., 1990), 213; B. V. Sokolov, *Tainy vtoroi mirovoi* (Moscow, 2001), 422.
4. Vanda Vasilevskaia, *Raduga: Povest'*, trans. E. Usievich (Moscow, 1945), 206-207, 213.
5. Siân Nicholas, *The Echo of War: Home Front Propaganda and the Wartime BBC, 1939-45* (Manchester, U.K., 1996), 73-85, 99.
6. For the contrary view that Stalin's call for a war of extermination was "utterly panicked," see Mark Edele and Michael Geyer, "States of Exception: The Nazi-Soviet War as a System of Violence, 1939-1945," in Michael Geyer and Sheila Fitzpatrick, eds., *Beyond Totalitarianism: Stalinism and Nazism Compared* (Cambridge, U.K., 2009), 351.
7. Gustav Herling, *A World Apart*, trans. Joseph Marek (Andrzej Ciolkosz) (Oxford, 1987 [1951]), 233.
8. But it has been observed that during both world wars, civilians in the United Kingdom and the United States displaced the guilt of not fighting themselves onto the enemy. Thus they were more prone than people with combat experience to articulate virulent hatred toward the enemy. In addition survivors of aerial bombing were not more but *less* likely to demand reprisals. Joanna Bourke, *An Intimate History of Killing: Face-to-Face Killing in Twentieth-Century Warfare* (n.p., 1999), 148-149, 153.
9. "Za rodinu, za Stalina!," *Bol'shevik*, nos. 11-12 (June 1941): 12-17, partly translated in Erwin Oberländer, *Sowjetpatriotismus und Geschichte. Dokumentation* (Cologne, 1967), 70-72.
10. Nicholas, *The Echo of War*, 231-232.
11. This, combined with my interpretation of the hate campaign, is why I disagree with the view that "on the Soviet side [of World War II], the

passions were systematically unleashed, coupled with brutal coercion against one's own." Edele and Geyer, "States of Exception," 351.

12. Jamie Arndt et al., "Suppression, Availability of Death-Related Thoughts, and Cultural Worldview Defense: Exploring the Psychodynamics of Terror Management," *Journal of Personality and Social Psychology* 73, no. 1 (1997): 5.

13. Peter Kenez, "Black and White: The War on Film," in Richard Stites, ed., *Culture and Entertainment in Wartime Russia* (Bloomington, Ind., 1995), 173.

14. Victor Yurovsky, "Ein Vergleich des Heldenkultes in der Sowjetunion der dreißiger und sechziger Jahre," *Forum für osteuropäische Ideen- und Zeitgeschichte* 5, no. 1 (2001): 164.

15. Eric Lohr, *Nationalizing the Russian Empire: The Campaign against Enemy Aliens during World War I* (Cambridge, Mass., 2003), 20-21; Richard Stites, "Days and Nights in Wartime Russia: Cultural Life, 1914-1917," in Aviel Roshwald and Richard Stites, eds., *European Culture in the Great War: The Arts, Entertainment, and Propaganda, 1914-1918* (Cambridge, U.K., 1999), 16-19; David Brandenberger, *National Bolshevism: Stalinist Mass Culture and the Formation of Modern Russian National Identity, 1931-1956* (Cambridge, Mass., 2002), 15, 234.

16. N. D. Kozlov, *Obshchestvennoe soznanie v gody Velikoi Otechestvennoi voiny (1941-1945)* (St. Petersburg, 1995), 10; L. N. Pushkarev, "Slovesnye istochniki dlia izucheniia mental'nosti sovetskogo naroda v gody Velikoi Otechestvennoi voiny," *Voprosy istorii*, no. 4 (2001): 128; V. F. Zima, *Mentalitet narodov Rossii v voine 1941-1945 godov* (Moscow, 2000), 118.

17. Elena S. Seniavskaia, "Heroic Symbols: The Reality and Mythology of War," *Russian Studies in History* 37, no. 1 (Summer 1998): 83; I. I. Shirokorad, *Tsentral'naia periodicheskaia pechat' v gody Velikoi Otechestvennoi voiny: 1941-1945* (Moscow, 2001), 328; Iu. A. Poliakov, "O massovom soznanii v gody voiny," in Iu. A. Poliakov, *Istoricheskaia nauka: Liudi i problemy* (Moscow, 1999), 189-190; V. T. Aniskov, *Krest'ianstvo protiv fashizma: 1941-1945. Istoriia i psikhologiia podviga* (Moscow, 2003), 73; V. I. Vasil'ev, "Knigoizdanie v gody Velikoi Otechestvennoi voiny," *Novaia i noveishaia istoriia*, no. 5 (September-October 2004): 34. The foreign researcher quoted is Nina Tumarkin, *The Living and the Dead: The Rise and Fall of the Cult of World War II in Russia* (New York, 1994), 73. See also, specifically about war heroes and war correspondents, Rosalinde Sartorti, "On the Making of Heroes, Heroines, and Saints," in Stites, *Culture and Entertainment in Wartime Russia*, 190; Louise McReynolds, "Dateline Stalingrad: Newspaper Correspondents at the Front," in Stites, *Culture and Entertainment in Wartime Russia*, 41; Jeffrey

Brooks, *Thank You, Comrade Stalin! Soviet Public Culture from Revolution to Civil War* (Princeton, N.J., 2000), 193.

18. Compare John Barber and Mark Harrison, *The Soviet Home Front, 1941–1945: A Social and Economic History of the USSR in World War II* (London, 1991), 55, 72; John Barber, "The Image of Stalin in Soviet Propaganda and Public Opinion during World War 2," in John Garrard and Carol Garrard, eds., *World War 2 and the Soviet People: Selected Papers from the Fourth World Congress for Soviet and East European Studies, Harrogate, 1990* (Houndmills, U.K., 1993), 46, 48; John Barber, "War, Public Opinion and the Struggle for Survival, 1941-45: The Case of Leningrad," in Silvio Pons and Andrea Romano, eds., *Russia in the Age of Wars, 1914–1945* (Milan, 2000), 267–268, 275–276.

19. The expression is attributed to older Russians in Szczepan Wiesław Nalepiński, *Syberyjski szlak*, 3d ed. (Lublin, 2006), 59.

20. The Polish man is Tadeusz Kiersnowski, *Moje spostrzeżenia o Rosji Sowieckiej (1940–1942)* (Warsaw, 1997), 65-66. On talking, see Evgenii Krinko, "Neformal'naia kommunikatsiia v 'zakrytom' obshchestve: Slukhi voennogo vremeni (1941–1945)," *Novoe literaturnoe obozrenie*, no. 100 (2009). On convictions, see M. N. Potemkina, "Evakonaselenie v ural'kom tylu: Opyt vyzhivaniia," *Otechestvennaia istoriia*, no. 2 (March–April 2005): 95; G. V. Kostyrchenko, "Sovetskaia tsenzura v 1941–1952 godakh," *Voprosy istorii*, nos. 11–12 (1996): 88.

21. The Harvard Project on the Soviet Social System Online, at http://hcl.harvard.edu/collections/hpsss/index.html, respectively, A323, 46 and A445, 41; A532, 69 and A643, 32; A308, 35; A477, 58; A191, 32; A470, 9. On trust in rumor, see Niels Bo Poulsen, "The Soviet Extraordinary State Commission on War Crimes: An Analysis of the Commission's Investigative Work in War and post War Stalinist Society" (Ph.D. dissertation, Copenhagen University, 2004), 116.

22. For the editor, see Andrei Artizov and Oleg Naumov, eds., *Vlast' i khudozhestvennaia intelligentsiia: Dokumenty TsK RKP(b)–VKP(b)–VChK–OGPU–NKVD o kul'turnoi politike. 1917–1953 gg.* (Moscow, 1999), 490 (*Poslednie izvestiia* staff member A. E. Kolbanovskii, before July 24, 1943). For the commission, see GARF, 6903/1/70/61: "Vyvod komissii o rabote redaktsii 'Poslednikh Izvestii' za iiul' mesiats," n.p. [not earlier than July 1942]. Listless behavior during broadcasts is also recalled in Kiersnowski, *Moje spostrzeżenia o Rosji Sowieckiej (1940–1942)*, 55. For Aleksandrov, see A. Ia. Livshin and I. B. Orlov, comps., *Sovetskaia propaganda v gody Velikoi Otechestvennoi voiny: "Kommunikatsiia ubezhdeniia" i mobilizatsionnye mekhanizmy*

(Moscow, 2007), 495, 513. For a similar observation on oblast papers from the same year, see 241.
23. N. D. Kozlov, *S volei k pobede: Propaganda i obydennoe soznanie v gody Velikoi Otechestvennoi voiny* (St. Petersburg, 2002), 159.
24. Peter Fritzsche, *Life and Death in the Third Reich* (Cambridge, Mass., 2008); Kallis, *Nazi Propaganda and the Second World War*, 223. For different views, see David Welch, *The Third Reich: Politics and Propaganda* (London, 1993), 125-126; Randall L. Bytwerk, *Bending Spines: The Propagandas of Nazi Germany and the German Democratic Republic* (East Lansing, Mich., 2004), 169; Jeffrey Herf, *The Jewish Enemy: Nazi Propaganda during World War II and the Holocaust* (Cambridge, Mass., 2006), 275-276.
25. A. V. Blium, *Sovetskaia tsenzura v epokhu total'nogo terrora: 1929-1953* (St. Petersburg, 2000), 147 (on censorship); Serhy Yekelchyk, "The Civic Duty to Hate: Stalinist Citizenship as Political Practice and Civic Emotion (Kiev, 1943-53)," *Kritika* 7, no. 3 (Summer 2006): 531-532. On actual sentiments, see E. S. Seniavskaia, *Protivniki Rossii v voinakh XX veka: Evoliutsiia "obraza vraga" v soznanii armii i obshchestva* (Moscow, 2006), 107, 117-118; Lev Gudkov, "The Fetters of Victory: How the War Provides Russia with Its Identity," http://www.eurozine.com, May 3, 2005.
26. G. K. Kumanev, *Podvig i podlog: Stranitsy Velikoi Otechestvennoi voiny, 1941-1945 gg.* (Moscow, 2000), 126-137, 155.
27. O. Ie. Lysenko et al., eds., *Kyïv u dni natsysts'koï navaly: Za dokumentamy radians'kykh spetssluzhb. Do 60-richchia vyzvolennia Ukraïny vid hitlerivs'kykh zaharbnykiv. Naukovo-dokumental'ne vydannia* (Kiev, 2004), 385, 405 (on tribunals and the decree); Pavel Polian, "Stalin und die Opfer des nationalsozialistischen Vernichtungskriegs," in Jürgen Zarusky, ed., *Stalin und die Deutschen: Neue Beiträge der Forschung* (Munich, 2006), 97, 103; M. S. Zinich, *Budni voennogo likholet'ia 1941-1945* (Moscow, 1994), 1:36; Mark Edele, *Soviet Veterans of the Second World War: A Popular Movement in an Authoritarian Society* (Oxford, 2008); Katrin Boeckh, *Stalinismus in der Ukraine: Die Rekonstruktion des sowjetischen Systems nach dem Zweiten Weltkrieg* (Wiesbaden, 2007), 300, 303, 318 (on former *Ostarbeiter*); Elena Kozhina, *Through the Burning Steppe: A Memoir of Wartime Russia, 1942-1943* (New York, [2001]), 38-41 (on a teacher).
28. Sabine Rosemarie Arnold, "Gegängelte Helden: Propaganda in der Sowjetunion nach dem Zweiten Weltkrieg," in Ute Daniel and Wolfram Siemann, eds., *Propaganda: Meinungskampf, Verführung und politische Sinnstiftung (1789-1989)* (Frankfurt am Main, 1994), 157.
29. Zvi Gitelman, "Soviet Reactions to the Holocaust, 1945-1991," in Lucjan Dobroszycki and Jeffrey Gurock, ed., *The Holocaust in the Soviet Union:*

Studies and Sources on the Destruction of the Jews in the Nazi-Occupied Territories of the USSR, 1941–1945 (Armonk, N.Y., 1993), 3.
30. Sartorti, "On the Making of Heroes, Heroines, and Saints," 183; Aleksandr Kovalenko and Gennadii Lebedev, *Sekundy bessmertiia* (Moscow, 2001); K. A. Atrashkevich and N. N. Smirnov, *Samopozhertvovanie na Velikoi Otechestvennoi voine, 1941–1945: Opisanie podvigov voinov, zakryvshikh svoim telom ambrazury vrazheskikh ognevykh tochek* (Volgograd, 2005); Gregory Carleton, "Victory in Death: Annihilation Narratives in Russia Today," *History and Memory* 22, no. 1 (Spring–Summer 2010): 135–168.
31. Gudkov, "The Fetters of Victory."

Sources

Although I recognize the validity of studying the years of the Nazi-Soviet pact, this book focuses on the period beginning with the German invasion of June 1941. Only in this way could the research remain within a workable scope. Moreover the Soviet system's greatest test occurred not at the time of the pact, but during the war with Nazi Germany and its allies.

Monographs and scholarly articles proved helpful, but this book is mostly based on contemporary materials and postwar memoirs. The first category includes policy documents from Moscow and Kiev. The available archival record of the Soviet propaganda outlets and controlling agencies is smaller than one would have liked. Some materials appear in a collection prepared by A. Ia. Livshin and I. B. Orlov, *Sovetskaia propaganda v gody Velikoi Otechestvennoi voiny: "Kommunikatsiia ubezhdeniia" i mobilizatsionnye mekhanizmy* (Moscow, 2007). Only a tiny proportion of readers' letters and reports on conventions of newspaper editors with party ideologues have been preserved. The same applies to the archives of editorial boards—mainly, it seems, because there was no strict rule on archival storage and because the journalists themselves cared little about this. As for the propaganda texts themselves, the biggest loss occurred when the original transcripts of the central radio broadcasts from the first months of the war were deliberately destroyed in October 1941, when it seemed that Moscow might fall.

Various ways to systematize the scrutiny of the papers and the radio texts were considered. In the end I became reconciled to the practical impossibility of selecting sources in a way that was systematic (for instance, a predetermined number of issues from one month of a particular newspaper) and simultaneously did not pass over key articles and broadcasts from important dates. The main newspapers studied, in repositories in Moscow and Kiev and from microfilms, were *Izvestiia, Krasnaia zvezda, Pravda,* and *Trud,* with additions from *Komsomolskaia pravda, Sovetskaia Ukraina, Komunist* (in Ukrainian), *Radianska Ukraïna* (in Ukrainian), and *Zviazda* (in Belarusian). Of some use were Soviet bibliographies of newspaper articles, even though they suffer from politically motivated omissions. They are the State Public Historical Library's *Velikaia Otechestvennaia voina sovetskogo naroda: Annotirovannyi ukazatel' literatury za god voiny* (Moscow, 1942) and the Lenin State Library's ten-part *Velikaia Otechestvennaia voina: Ukazatel' literatury* (Moscow, 1942-1945), covering July 1942 through December 1944. For the first year, the All-Union Book Chamber listed articles on Nazi crimes in *Zverstva fashistskikh varvarov: Ukazatel' faktov, opublikovannykh v pechati* (Moscow, 1943). There also exists an index to the republished Soviet Information Bureau reports, *Spravochnik k 1-8 tomam Soobshchenii Sovetskogo Informbiuro* (Moscow, 1945).

The archives used were the following.

GARF

Gosudarstvennyi arkhiv Rossiiskoi Federatsii (State Archive of the Russian Federation, Moscow)
- f. 4459. TASS
- f. 6903. Radio Committee of the USSR
- f. 7021, op. 148. Extraordinary State Commission to Investigate Crimes Committed by the German-Fascist Invaders and Their Accomplices (cited from a copy at U.S. Holocaust Memorial Museum, Archives, RG-22.014M)
- f. 8114. Jewish Antifascist Committee
- f. 9425. Glavlit

The Harvard Project on the Soviet Social System Online

Summary transcripts of interviews conducted with refugees from the USSR during the early years of the Cold War, at http://hcl.harvard.edu/collections/hpsss/index.html.

Hoover Institution on War, Revolution and Peace, Stanford, California

B. I. Nicolaevsky collection, Series no. 178, box 232, folders 10-11: [Lev Vladimirovich] Dudin, "Velikii Mirazh: Sobytiia 1941-1947 godov v ponimanii sovetskogo cheloveka" (n.p., 1947)

Office of Strategic Services, Research and Analysis Branch

R & A no. 2185, "The Nature of Soviet National Feeling (Since June 1941)," n.p., June 15, 1944. Available on microfilm (OSS/State Department intelligence and research reports, ed. Paul Kesaris, 1977).

RGALI

Rossiiskii gosudarstvennyi arkhiv literatury i iskusstva (Russian State Archive of Literature and Arts, Moscow)
    f. 631. Union of Soviet Writers
    f. 1865. P. A. Lidov

RGASPI

Rossiiskii gosudarstvennyi arkhiv sotsial'no-politicheskoi istorii (Russian State Archive of Sociopolitical History, Moscow)
    f. 14, op. 43. Party Committee of Leningrad
    f. 17, op. 3. Records (*protokoly*) of the Politburo of the Central Committee of the All-Union Communist Party (Bolshevik)
    f. 17, op. 125. Department of Propaganda and Agitation
    f. 69, op. 1. Central Staff of the Partisan Movement (cited from a copy at U.S. Holocaust Memorial Museum, Archives, RG-22.005M)
    f. 88. A. S. Shcherbakov
    f. 558, op. 11. I. V. Stalin
    f. 629. P. N. Pospelov

RKP

Rossiiskaia knizhnaia palata, Otdel statistiki (Russian Book Chamber, Statistics Department, Moscow)
    File "Pechat' SSSR za period Velikoi Otechestvennoi voiny 1941–1946 (gazety)"
    K. I. Propina, ed., *Pechat' SSSR za 25 let: 1918–1942 gody: Statisticheskie materialy* (Moscow, 1942)

TsDAHOU

Tsentral'nyi derzhavnyi arkhiv hromads'kykh ob"iednan' Ukraïny (Central State Archive of Civic Organizations of Ukraine, Kiev)
    f. 1, op. 23. Central Committee of the Communist Party of Ukraine (Osobyi sector—sekretnaia chast')
    f. 1, op. 70. Central Committee of the Communist Party of Ukraine, Viddil propahandy i ahitatsiï

TsDAVOV

Tsentral'nyi derzhavnyi arkhiv vyshchykh orhaniv vlady ta upravlinnia Ukraïny (Central State Archive of the Higher Agencies of Power and Administration of Ukraine, Kiev)

    f. 4188. Radio "Radians'ka Ukraïna"

    f. 4915. Radio Committee of Ukraine

USHMM

U.S. Holocaust Memorial Museum, Archives, Washington, D.C.

    RG-22.009. Selected Records from the Archive of the Ministry of Foreign Affairs, Moscow, 1941–1944, holding selected photocopies from Arkhiv vneshnei politiki RF (Archive of Foreign Policy of the Russian Federation, Moscow)

    RG-22.016. Reports and Investigative Materials Compiled by the Military Commissions of the Red (Soviet) Army Related to the Crimes Committed by the Nazis and Their Collaborators on the Occupied Territories of the Soviet Union and Eastern Europe during WWII, 1942–1945, holding selected photocopies from Tsentral'nyi arkhiv Ministerstva Oborony Rossiiskoi Federatsii (TsAMO RF; Central Archive of the Ministry of Defense of the Russian Federation, Podolsk)

Acknowledgments

The main sponsor of this research has been the Netherlands Organisation for Scientific Research. Additional funding was gratefully received from the Netherlands Institute for War Documentation (NIOD) in Amsterdam, where I was based under the ever-trusting guidance of Hans Blom and Research Director Peter Romijn. When I joined the Center for Holocaust and Genocide Studies (CHGS), also in Amsterdam, its directors, Johannes Houwink ten Cate and Wichert ten Have, encouraged me to spend time on this research, for which I am very grateful. Still part of the Royal Netherlands Academy of Arts and Sciences but now merged into a new organization, the NIOD Institute for War, Holocaust and Genocide Studies, both the original NIOD and the CHGS provided a most congenial working environment. Many thanks to my colleagues there for offering inspiration and support, and to Dikus Waanders for his helping hand with computing and files.

This book was also made possible in part by funds granted to me through a J. B. and Maurice C. Shapiro Senior Scholar-in-Residence Fellowship at the Center for Advanced Holocaust Studies, U.S. Holocaust Memorial Museum. (The statements made and views expressed, however, are solely my responsibility.) Although the book was very close to completion during my tenure as the Shapiro Scholar for 2010–2011, that stay—focusing on another research topic—allowed for useful conversations about this work, among others with Martin Dean, and the incorporation of additional sources and studies from the museum's own collection and from the Library of Congress. Earlier, I had the opportunity to obtain such materials thanks to Stephen Kotkin's invitation to present a lecture at Princeton University (2006) and to the invitation to a conference on the 1933 famine in Ukraine at Harvard University (2008).

Among the librarians and archivists in Russia I wish to thank in particular Tatiana Goriaeva (Russian State Archive of Literature and Arts), Aleksandr Dzhigo (Russian Book Chamber), and B. A. Semenovker (Newspaper Department, Russian State Library). At the Institute of History in Moscow, I was fortunate to have interesting and helpful conversations with Aleksandr Golubev, Georgii Kumanev, Vladimir Nevezhin, Elena Seniavskaia, and Nina Petrova. It was also very good to meet in Moscow Boris Sokolov and to work in the State Public Historical Library. In Kiev my research benefited in particular from conversations with Liudmyla and Vladyslav Hrynevych and from the resources and librarians of the V. I. Vernadsky National Library of Ukraine and the State Archives Research Library.

Those who commented on work in progress were also of great help. Presentations were made at annual conventions of the Association for Slavic, East European, and Eurasian Studies, involving what are now Chapters 3 and 4 (2003); Chapter 6 (2007); and Chapters 7 and 8 (2002). Rather different versions of the chapter on the Holocaust were also presented at the conferences The Destruction of European Jewry: Structures, Motivations, Opportunities (Amsterdam, 2003) and Borderlands: Ethnicity, Identity, and Violence in the Shatter-Zone of Empires since 1848 (Marburg, 2007). In addition, I discussed Chapters 8 and 9 at the Washington Russian History Seminar (Georgetown University, 2011) and Chapter 10 at the Department of History of the University of Texas (2011). Of all those who commented on these occasions, or in email correspondence, I thank in particular, at the risk of overlooking someone, Nanci Adler, Omer Bartov, Hans Blom, Holly Case, Michael David-Fox, Catherine Evtuhov, Donald Filtzer, David Goldfrank, Peter Holquist, Johannes Houwink ten Cate, Christine Kulke, Hiroaki Kuromiya, Tatjana Lichtenstein, Eric Lohr, Christoph Mick, Roman Serbyn, Vladimir Solonari, Eric Weitz, Charters Wynn, and Vladislav Zubok. With regard to the reporting on the Holocaust and other Nazi crimes, I also benefited from contacts with Michael Gelb, Martin Holler, Pavel Ilyin, Niels Bo Poulsen, and David Shneer.

Thanks must go to Hans Blom, Johannes Houwink ten Cate, Bruno Naarden, and Alexander Gogun, who commented on all or part of the manuscript, to the reviewers approached by the journal *Kritika* when I submitted what became an article about the Soviet media and the Holocaust, published in 2009, and to *Kritika* for allowing inclusion of this text here, in Chapters 5 and 9, but mostly in Chapter 6. I was very fortunate with the constructive reports from the anonymous reviewers approached by Harvard University

ACKNOWLEDGMENTS

Press. David Brandenberger was a tremendous colleague in not only sharing a book manuscript of his own, but in quickly reading the entire manuscript of *Motherland in Danger* and offering extremely useful comments. For that I am deeply grateful, as I am to Kathleen McDermott, my editor at Harvard University Press, for believing in the project from the very beginning. Thanks are also due to Andrew Kinney, Michael Haggett, and Judith Hoover, who were, respectively, the editorial assistant at the press, the production editor at Westchester Book Services, and the manuscript editor.

I dedicate this book to Simon and Abel, who have given Anneloes and me so much joy during the final years of work on this project.

Index

Absenteeism, 72, 75-76
Adler, Viktor, 218
Agitation, 3
Agitprop, 3; censorship by, 30-31; on Germans, 172; on Russian patriotism, 205
Agriculture, 73-78, 270-271; censorship and, 93-94; collective farm system in, 73-74, 76-78, 82-84, 89, 96, 312n95; competition in, 88-89; gardens in, 98-102; grain losses in, 77-78; subsidiary farms in, 98-99
Aleksandrov, Georgii, 3, 24, 31, 34, 41, 133, 212; and Allies, 261-262, 264; anti-Semitism of, 163; dissatisfied with censorship, 34, 93; Ehrenburg and, 189-190, 193; on German atrocities, 145, 151, 163; on Germans, 172, 190; Jews and, 218-219; on Russia, 216; on shortcomings of the press, 277; on Stalingrad, 49
Aleksii, Bishop, 208

Allies, 161-162, 180, 214, 244-268; aid from, 254-260, 267, 273; bombing by, 257-260; Cairo item in *Pravda* about, 263; invasion of Europe by, 246, 263-264; leaders, 260-261; portrayal of, 244-268, 273; second front and, 250-254; Stalin and, 252-253; victory by, 264-266
All-Union Book Chamber, 15
All-Union Socialist Competition, 85-87, 92-93
American newspapers, 161. See also *New York Times*
American radio, 58, 167
American soldiers, casualties, 56
Anders, Władysław, 247, 267
Andreev, Andrei, 80, 163, 219
Angelina, Pasha, 88
Anti-Semitism, 112, 134-135, 139, 143-144, 147, 155, 162-166, 249, 372. See also Cosmopolitanism
Armenians, 144, 216
Atrocities. See German atrocities

Auschwitz, 130, 155, 156, 158–160, 162
Azarichi, 129

Babi Yar, 138, 139, 142, 149, 151, 195
Baida, Mariia, 53
Baltic peoples, 216
Baryshnikova, Ekaterina, 87
BBC radio, 21, 146, 161, 167, 251
Belarusians, 210–211, 214, 221
Bełżec, 139, 146, 148, 152, 156
Beria, Lavrentii, 142, 235
Berling, Zygmunt, 248
Białystok, 136, 214
Biological warfare, 129–130
Bohomolets, Oleksandr, 212
Bolshevik (journal), 188
Bosy, Dmitrii, 85–86
Bread rations, 98, 108
British Ministry of Information, 167
British propaganda, 167, 271–272
Broadcast letters, 90–91

Censorship, 8, 30–34, 269, 274; complaints about, 52, 56, 184, 229; on labor issues, 74–75, 91–95; military, 31–32, 35, 51–59, 61, 65–67; of negative information, 35, 54–56, 97, 111; of newspapers, 30–34; of photographs, 52, 56, 229; after WWII, 278
Chapaev (film), 8
Chekhov, Anton, 132, 205
Cheliuskin (steamship), 8
Children: as criminals, 114; forced labor of, 69–71, 113; Fund for Aid to, 113; German, 192–193; orphaned, 114; propaganda on, 113–114; in Red Army, 53–54; treatment of, 113–114, 115; used as shields, 127
Chișinău, 36, 37, 194
Churchill, Winston, 214, 250, 258, 260–261, 263, 265, 275
Civilians, killing of, 122, 125–131. *See also* Holocaust
Coal mining, 80–81

Collective farm system, 73–74, 76–78, 82–84, 89, 96, 312n95
Communists, 2, 70, 165, 238
Competition, 85–94
Concentration camps, 120, 129–130, 154–161, 181; in the U.S., 262
Cosmopolitanism, 218–219
Crash landings, 61–62
Crimea, 46, 64, 218
Crimean Tartars, 217–218
Cultural heritage sites, destruction of, 132

Death: acceptance of, 270; of civilians, 125–131; as deliverance, 224–228; as heroic, 59–67
Death camps, 122, 125, 129–130, 151, 155–159, 161, 181
Defeats, cover-ups of, 36–44
Defense Fund, 105
Deportation: to Germany, 121, 131–132; of non-Slavs, 217–218, 365n60; of Volga Germans, 171
Desertion, 19, 69, 110, 217; labor, 70, 72, 74–81
Directorate on Propaganda and Agitation. *See* Agitprop
Dnieper Hydroelectric Station, 38–39
Dobrobabin, Ivan, 278
Documentaries and newsreels, 53, 100, 126, 130, 150, 197, 277; before June 1941, 10, 168; footage of invasion of Normandy for, 264
Donations, 103–107, 115
Dovzhenko, Oleksandr (Alexander), 48, 60, 66, 150, 165, 212
Dresden, 260

Eden, Anthony, 153, 260, 263
Ehrenburg, Ilia, 45, 66, 219; on anti-Semitism, 162, 163; on families of soldiers, 111; on gas vans, 130; on German allies, 194, 196; on German experiments, 129; on German losses, 58; hate propaganda and, 167, 182–193,

200; "Hold Out!" published by, 42-43; on Italians, 196; on Jewish victims, 138-139, 160; on Kharkiv, 51; on media silence, 41-42, 66, 258; Nazi propaganda on, 193; on Russian people, 203; on Sevastopol, 46; on traitors, 235
Eisenhower, Dwight, 263
Eisenstein, Sergei, 162
Epstein, Shakhno, 137
Erlich, Henryk, 218
Estonia, 145, 151
Ethnic particularism, 209-216
Evacuees, 98, 107-110, 115
Express notices, 15-16
Extermination policy: of Germany, 123-125, 129-131, 169-170; against Jews, 134-166
Extraordinary State Commission, 121-122, 125, 132, 150, 195, 204-205, 215
Eynikayt (newspaper), 136, 137-138, 160-161, 219

Factories: censorship and, 92-94; evacuation of, 108-109
Factory workers, 70, 78-80, 83-84
Fadeev, Aleksandr, 162, 213, 219, 234, 236
Families, of soldiers, 110-112
Famine, 70, 97, 115, 116-117, 123, 128-129
Farmers. *See* Peasants (farmers)
Fascism, 9-10, 169, 170, 196
Fefer, Itsik, 138
Fighting leaflets, 15-16
Filchenkov, Nikolai, 64
Films, 162, 176, 196, 203, 232, 274, 277, 270; before June 1941, 8, 135, 245; Stalin and, 3-4
Financial aid, 96
Finland, 51, 195-196, 245
Food deliveries from Allies, 256
Food rations, 96-98, 108, 114
Food supply, 82, 98, 114
Food theft, 100-103
Forced labor, 68-95, 108, 270-271; under Germans, 131-132, 238-239

Foreign correspondents, 13, 38, 41, 183, 200, 206
Foreign events: censorship of, 32; information about, 245-246; reporting of, 9-10, 20
France, 244
Free Germany, 179-182, 198, 199, 263
Freies Deutschland (newspaper), 161
Front: concept of second, 250-254, 262, 264; maps of, 52; reports from the, 36-44, 45-47
Fund drives, 105-107
Fund for Aid to Children, 113
Fund for the Health of the Defenders of the Motherland, 106
Fund of the Main Command of the Red Army, 106

Gaidar, Arkadii, 113
Gardens, 98-102, 115, 271
Gas chambers, 158-159, 160
Gassings, 129-130, 156
Gastello, Nikolai, 61-62, 67, 209
Generals, coverage of, 54
General Staff, 36, 52, 57
Geneva Conventions, 51, 124
Georgia/Georgians, 216, 217
German atrocities, 116-133; against Jews, 134-166; against POWs, 123-125; propaganda on, 117-133, 271; reports and statements about, 117-122, 132-133
German beast, 180-181, 182
German bombing, 10, 36, 43, 127-128
German emigrés, 172
German invasion, reporting of, 36-44
Germanization, 123, 131, 145, 169
German military losses, 57-59
German nationalism, 169, 182
Germans: collaboration with, 223, 226-228, 239-240; dehumanization of, 175-176, 178, 184; Ehrenburg on, 182-193; forced labor for, 238-239; hatred of, 167-201, 271-272, 278;

Germans *(continued)*
 incitement to kill, 186–189, 192–193; Russian, 275; Soviet, 171, 198; sympathy for, 168, 197–198
German soldiers: capture of, 49–50; casualties among, 49, 301–302n76
Germany: Allied bombing of, 257–260; allies of, 194–197, 199; attack on Soviet Union by, 10–11, 36–44; civilians killed by, 125–131; defeat of, 44–49; deportation to, 121, 131–132; extermination policy of, 123–125, 129–131, 169–170; invasion of Poland by, 10; losses by, 49; nonaggression pact with, 9–10, 168; retribution against, 189; surrender by, 265–266
Glavlit, 31–33, 340. *See also* Censorship
Glinka, Mikhail, 245
Goebbels, Joseph, 4, 50, 269
Golovaty, Ferapont, 105
Gorbatov, Boris, 156, 164. *See also The Unsubdued* (Gorbatov)
Grain losses, 77–78
Great Britain. *See* United Kingdom
Great Patriotic War, 1, 206, 268
Great Terror, 8–9, 202, 217
Grossman, Vasilii, 54–56, 155, 160–161, 191, 227
Gulag prisoners: forced labor of, 72–73; newspapers for, 15, 32
Guliam, Gafur, 114
Gurarii, Samarii, 127
Gypsies, 136, 162

Hague Convention, 124
Halan, Iaroslav, 226
Harriman, Averell, 256
Hate propaganda, 167–201, 271–272; before June 1941, 194, 195–196, 244–245; dehumanization in, 175–176, 178, 184; Ehrenburg and, 182–193, 200; Free Germany and, 179–182; from June 1941, 168–173; shift in, 173–179

Hate speech, 167
Heroes/heroism, 8–9; betrayal of, 235–236; labor, 82; of partisans, 229–234, 273; propaganda about, 275, 278, 279; of Soviet people, 84; of Soviet soldiers, 59–67; of women, 232
Hess, Rudolf, 262
Heydrich, Reinhard, 151
Himmler, Heinrich, 148, 161
Hitler, Adolf, 10, 56, 185, 193; declaration on attack on Soviet Union by, 12; extermination of Jews and, 148
Hitlerites, 43, 145, 170; vs. Germans, 183, 190, 191; hatred of, 184–186; persecution of Jews by, 137, 141, 144, 147, 154, 157–160. *See also* Nazis
Holocaust, 120; concentration camps in, 130, 154–161, 181; foreign coverage of, 147–148, 161; intelligence reports about, 135–136; media coverage of, 125–127, 134–166, 279; in Poland, 153–159; alleged Soviet media silence about, 330–332n3; Soviet victims of, 149–153; Stalin's awareness of, 135–136; statements by prominent Jews about, 136–139
Holy war, 207, 275
Hrechukha, Mykhailo, 121, 214
Hull, Cordell, 159
Human shields, 127, 227
Hungarians, 159, 195

Iaroslavskii, Emelian, 205
Indebtedness, 81, 94, 274–275. *See also* Obligation
Industrial labor reserves, 69
Industrial workers, 86–87
Intelligence reports, 117–122, 135–136, 215. *See also* Surveillance reports
In the Name of the Motherland (film), 203
Invalids, 112–113, 115
Islam, 216–217
Italians/Italy, 196, 264

Izvestiia (newspaper), 16, 17, 107, 163, 276; circulation of, 17–18; distribution of, 28–29

Japan/Japanese, 167, 196–197, 251
Jewish Anti-Fascist Committee, 136, 137–138, 163, 218, 235
Jews, 109; attitude of, toward Germans, 168; European, 146–148, 154; help for, by non-Jews, 224–226; in Red Army, 138, 163, 219, 222; killing of, 116, 118–119, 125–127, 135–136, 141, 142; murder of Polish, 153–159; pogroms against, 135, 136, 141, 203, 226; Soviet suspicion of, 223–224; statements about, 121; statements by prominent, 136–139, 161. *See also* Anti-Semitism; Holocaust; Soviet Jews

Kalinin, Mikhail, 24, 34, 44, 105, 140, 172, 233
Kalmyks, 217
Kaluga, 42, 127
Kamianets-Podilsky, 135, 140
Kantaria, Meliton, 220, 279
Katiusha, 52–53
Katyn, 131, 153–155, 158, 162, 247–248
Kazakhstan, 216
Kerch, 127
Kharkiv, 45–46, 49, 50–51, 117, 128, 130, 150, 168, 197, 223–224
Khavinson, Iakov, 13
Khmelnytsky Order, 212, 267
Khrushchev, Nikita, 151, 168, 233, 249; and Ukraine, 121, 212, 214, 215
Kiev: fall of, 38, 39–42; forced famine in, 117, 128–129; Jewish victims in, 141, 153; Nazi crimes in, 151, 205; recapture of, 149; Soviet mining of, 39. *See also* Babi Yar
"Kill" (Ehrenburg), 186–187
"Kill Him!" (Simonov), 177
Kirsanov, Semen, 179

Klochkov, Vasilii, 63
Klooga camp, 151, 181
Kolas, Iakub, 129
Komsomol, 16, 53, 73, 204, 205, 231, 233–234, 236, 238
Komsomolskaia pravda (newspaper), 17
Kondakov, N. I., 163
Konev, General Ivan, 54
Kopelev, Lev, 200
Korniichuk, Oleksandr, 146, 211
Korniiets, Leonid, 121, 145, 211
Kosmodemianskaia, Zoia (Tania), 230–232, 235–236, 243, 270
Kozhubergenov, Daniil, 64
Krasnaia zvezda (newspaper), 16, 17, 107, 193; letters received by, 111. *See also* Ortenberg, David
Krasnodar, 130, 240
Krasny flot (newspaper), 17, 52, 128, 129–130, 143, 194
Kravchenko, Victor, 36–37
Krieger, Evgenii, 156
Krivitskii, Aleksandr, 63
Kube, Wilhelm, 229
Kubiiovych, Volodymyr, 215
Kuibyshev, 21, 28, 29, 234
Kuznetsov, Vasilii, 152–153

Labor army, 108
Labor duty, 72, 74, 95, 270
Labor laws, 69–75, 95
Labor propaganda, 74–95
Labor shortages, 92
Lācis, Vilis, 145
Latest News (radio program), 22–23, 33, 277
Latvia, 106, 144, 145, 150, 152, 160, 164
Lawrence, John, 245
Leaders: Allied, 260–261; political speeches by, 24
League of Nations, 245
Lebedev-Kumach, Vasilii, 195, 207
Lend-Lease program, 254–256

INDEX

Lenin, Vladimir, 3, 7, 81, 236
Leningrad, 11, 25, 28, 30, 113; anti-Semitism in, 165; blockade of, 116; famine in, 97, 128, 276; hatred in, 197
Leonov, Leonid, 181
Levitan, Iurii, 23, 25, 266
Lidov, Petr, 230–231, 243
Linkou, Mikhas, 210
Liskow, Alfred, 170
Lithuania, 106, 152, 250
Lithuanians, 145, 225, 226, 250
Liubchenko, Arkadii, 215
Local radio, 26–27
London, bombing of, 182, 260
Lottery drawings, 104–105
Loyalty oaths, 89
Lozovskii, Solomon, 13, 38, 41, 164
Lviv, 152, 154, 164, 211, 226, 246
Lysenko, Trofim, 100

Main Directorate on Matters of Literature and Publishing Houses. *See* Glavlit
Majdanek, 139, 151, 155–159, 164, 181
Malenkov, Georgii, 17, 48, 163
Malnutrition, 96–97
Maresiev, Aleksei, 55
Masaryk, Jan, 154
Mass culture, heroes in, 8
Mass killings, 118–119, 121, 122, 129–131, 141, 142
Material privations, 96–115
Matrosov, Aleksandr, 65, 67, 279
Medical experiments, 129–130
Mekhlis, Lev, 33–34
Mickiewicz, Adam, 132
Mikhoels, Solomon, 136–137
Military. *See* Red Army; Soviet soldiers
Military affairs: cover-ups of, 36–44; reporting of, 35–67
Military censorship, 31–32, 35, 51–59, 61, 65–67
Military industry, 15, 32, 70–71

Military police, 47–48
Miners, 80–81
Minsk, 37, 153, 229; Jews in, 130, 139, 143, 152, 225
Mobilization, 4, 8, 11–12, 82, 94, 95, 199, 269
Moldavians, 216
Molotov, Viacheslav, 10–11, 17, 119, 120, 121, 124, 132, 262; on anti-Semitism, 134–135; criticism of British by, 244–245; on Jewish victims, 141–142; note of April 1942 by, 119, 128, 144
Molotov-Ribbentrop pact, 9–10, 168
Morale, 35, 47, 66, 67, 115, 133, 274
Moscow: bombing of, 127–128; German advance on, 38, 42–44; rations in, 96–97
Motherland, 6, 8, 60, 106, 203, 206, 220–221, 272
The Motherland Is Calling (film), 8
Music, 25, 266
Muslims, 13, 216–217
Mussolini, Benito, 9, 196

Nagorny, V. A., 86
Nationalism, 204; German, 169, 182; Russian, 202, 204; Ukrainian, 211–216
National military formations, 209–210
Nazi propaganda, 35, 95, 175, 193, 204, 277, 380n58; on Ehrenburg, 193; on Jews, 155, 164–165, 187; vs. Soviet propaganda, 4, 199, 269, 270
Nazis: atrocities by, 116–133; Holocaust by, 134–166. *See also* Hitlerites
Negative information, 35, 54–56, 97, 111
Newspapers, 14–20; American, 161; central, 17–18, 27–29; circulation of, 17–18; city, 20; classified, 15; distribution of, 27–29; factory, 29, 91, 270; Gulag, 15, 32; krai, 20; languages of, 18; local, 14, 15–16, 18–19, 31, 80; mobilization by, 11–12; number of, 14–15, 16; oblast, 14, 20; occasional, 15; paper

shortages threatening, 16-17; parochialism of, 9-10; raion, 14, 16, 18-20, 32; rationing of, 27-30; republican, 20; role of, during war, 11-12; rules on, 16; Soviet Ukrainian, 213-215; Soviet Yiddish, 219-220; wall, 3; youth, 16
Newsreels. *See* Documentaries and newsreels
New York Times, 146, 159, 161, 249, 259
NKVD, 15, 21, 32, 220, 233, 234-235, 236
Nonaggression pact, 9-10, 168
Non-Russians, Soviet, 202, 209-222, 272-273
Non-Slavs, Soviet, 216-220
North Caucasus, 47, 130, 150-151, 217

Obedience, 60, 270
Obligation, 60, 81, 94, 227. *See also* Indebtedness
Occupied territory: partisan activity in, 228-234; suspicion of citizens in, 118, 223-228, 273, 279
Odessa, 195; Jews in, 126, 141, 194
Operation Frantic, 257
Operation Gomorrah, 259
Organization of Ukrainian Nationalists (OUN), 215
Orlemanski, Stanislaus, 249
Ortenberg, David, 33, 38, 41, 46, 54, 55, 56, 63, 223; dismissal of, 55, 162-163, 164; reproaches against, 43, 52, 55
Orthodox Church, 107, 207-209

Paleckis, Justas, 145
Panfilov, Ivan, 62
Panfilovites, 48, 62-64, 209, 278
Partisans and underground fighters, 228-234, 273
Patriotism, 8, 207; non-Russian, 209-211; Soviet, 12, 84, 173-174, 207, 221, 229, 272
Paulus, Friedrich, 50
Pavlichenko, Liudmila, 53
Pearl Harbor, 246, 251

Peasants (farmers), 71, 73-74, 76-78, 82-83, 84, 88-89, 97; prominent, 86, 105. *See also* Village elders
The People Immortal (Grossman), 55-56
Pereiaslav Agreement, 212, 214
Photographs/pictures: not allowed to be published, 52, 56, 229; published, 10, 34, 44, 50, 53, 170, 220, 252, 256; showing German atrocities, 123, 124, 125, 126, 127, 156, 231, 232
Pius XII, Pope, 181
Plekhanov, Georgii, 3
Pogroms, 119, 135, 136, 140, 141, 203, 226
Poland: as enemy, 245; German atrocities in, 129-131; German invasion of, 10; murder of Jews in, 146, 153-159; Soviet relations with, 246-250; Ukraine and, 211-212, 215
Polevoi, Boris, 55, 159-160, 181-182
Policemen, auxiliary, 226, 240-241
Polikarpov, Dmitrii, 13, 26, 90
Politburo, 16, 17, 21, 25, 210, 241
Poltava, 257
Ponomarenko, Panteleimon, 135, 145
Pospelov, Petr, 156
Posters, 14, 40, 53, 175, 231, 261
POWs. *See* Prisoners of war (POWs)
Pravda (newspaper), 9-10, 17, 19, 31, 34, 107, 178, 197, 210, 276; Cairo item about Allies in, 263; circulation of, 17; correspondents and printers publishing local newspapers, 16, 80; distribution of, 28-29; editorials, 14, 22; letters received by, 111; military censorship and, 31-32, 52
Prisoners of war (POWs): coverage of, 123-124; German, 170, 181-182, 192, 262; killing of, 122; punishment of Soviet, 236, 278-279; Romanian, 194-195; starvation of, 117; as traitors, 236-237, 278-279; treatment of, by Germans, 123-125, 173, 236
Production targets, 85, 87, 92

Professor Mamlock (film), 135
Propagandist (periodical), 178
Public inspectors, 103
Punishment: of thieves, 101, 102, 110; of traitors, 234-235, 241; of workers, 75-77

Racism: against Germans, 176, 178, 183, 191, 275; Nazi, 160
Radianska Ukraïna (newspaper), 50, 179, 233, 238
Radio, 20-27; American, 167; British, 161, 167; censorship of, 33, 269; citizens' letters read on, 90-91; German, 21, 26; receivers confiscated, 21-22; silence of, 30; TASS transmissions via, 14; transmission of, 20-21, 29-30
Radio Committee, 13, 14, 25, 26, 29, 33, 88, 90
The Rainbow (Wasilewska), 176-177, 208, 211, 224, 226-227, 232, 237, 240, 270
Rape, 131, 176; commited by Red Army soldiers, 168, 193, 355n80
Rasulev, Abdurrahman, 216
Rationing, 27-28, 96-98, 114
Red Army: behavior of, 163, 193, 200; children in, 53-54; deserters from, 110-111; gifts for, 103-104; incitement of hatred for Germans in, 173-174; Jews in, 138, 163, 219, 222; losses by, 45-51, 56-57, 59, 302n79; loss of banners in, 55; offensives by, 45, 46, 48-51; retreats by, 47-48; women in, 40, 53. *See also* Soviet soldiers
Red Army Fund, 106
Red Banners, 87, 88
Refugees, 107-110, 115, 145, 164; as sources of information, 117, 130, 144, 170, 276
Reichenau, Walter von, 124, 142-143
Relay centers, 26, 33
Religion, 207-209, 263
Ribbentrop, Joachim von, 184

Rodionov, Mikhail, 92, 94
Rokossovskii, Konstantin, 50, 54, 264
Roman Catholics, 2
Romanians, 194-195
Roosevelt, Franklin D., 214, 253, 261, 263
Rostov, 11, 30, 149, 197; anti-Semitism in, 165; censorship in, 93-94; under Germans, 1, 47, 125-127
Rovinskii, L. Ia., 162
Rumors, 30, 70, 276, 312n95; warnings against, 19, 234
Russian people: elder brother role of, 202, 272; non-Russians and, 209-222; Russocentrism and, 202-209, 220-222
Russian People (Simonov), 77, 203
Russocentrism, 202-209, 216, 220-222, 272-273
Rybak, Natan, 165
Rylsky, Maksym, 212, 246
Rzhev, 48-49

Sadchikov, N. G., 31, 32-33, 51-52, 91, 92, 93
Scarcity: material, 96-115; of media, 27-30
"The Science of Hatred" (Sholokhov), 125, 144, 174-175, 200, 236-237, 343n89
Scorched-earth policy, 38-39, 132
"Scorn of Death" (Simonov), 59-60
Second front, 250-254, 262, 264
Selflessness, 61, 74-85, 94, 270, 274-275, 279
Sergeeva, I., 154
Sergii, Metropolitan, 207-208
Sevastopol, 46-47, 52; five marines from, 64, 66-67
Shalaev, Vasilii, 86
Shcherbakov, Aleksandr, 17, 26, 238, 278; approval sought from, 34, 38, 42, 46, 53, 64, 88, 107; as author, 13, 36, 37, 56, 58; dissatisfaction of, 43, 55, 256; and Jews, 135, 138, 156, 163-164; letters from Ehrenburg to, 41, 138, 258; on Russians,

INDEX

205, 206; speaking on Moscow wire radio, 43; on traitors, 235, 236
She Defends the Motherland (film), 232
Shevchenko, Taras, 132
Shock workers, 85, 87
Sholokhov, Mikhail, 125, 144, 174-175, 200, 219, 236-237
Shostakovich, Dmitrii, 25, 232
Shvernik, Nikolai, 121-122, 151, 255
Sikorski, Władysław, 246-247
Simonov, Konstantin, 56, 59-60, 131, 155-156, 177, 181, 203, 223
Slovakia, 196, 250
Smolensk, 37
Sobibór, 139, 155, 156, 157, 341n70
Socialist competition, 85-94
Soldiers. *See* German soldiers; Soviet soldiers
Sotsialisticheskoe zemledelie (newspaper), 17
Sovetskaia Ukraina (newspaper), 143, 146, 233
Soviet Finns, 195
Soviet Germans, 171, 198
Soviet Information Bureau, 13-14; censorship by, 31-32; reports by, 20, 22, 35
Soviet Jews: blaming of, 223-224; Holocaust and, 134-166; in Red Army, 138, 163, 219, 222; reporting on atrocities against, 140-148; statements by prominent, 136-139, 161; treatment of, 218-220; as victims, 149-153
Soviet losses, cover-ups of, 36-44
Soviet Muslims, 13, 216-217
Soviet patriotism, 12, 84, 173-174, 207, 221, 229, 272
Soviet soldiers: behavior of, 168, 193, 200; capture of, 56, 57; casualties among, 46-48, 56-57, 302n79; families of, 110-112; heroism of, 59-67; injured, 112-113, 115; retreats by, 47-48; sacrifice by, 36; surrender by, 60; treatment of captured, 123-125, 173. *See also* Red Army

Soviet system, 206-207
Stakhanov, Aleksei, 8, 85, 211
Stakhanovite movement, 85, 87, 211
Stalin, Joseph: active interest in propaganda of, 3-4, 13, 34, 35, 43, 54, 256; announcement of German surrender by, 266; announcement of year of final victory by, 44-45; bombing and, 257-258; censorship and, 31; classified information provided to, 12-13, 17, 30, 117-118, 135-136, 145, 255-256; concern about Nazi propaganda of, 54, 55, 56, 74, 95, 193; editing of report on Romanian atrocities in Odessa by, 141; editing of reports on German atrocities by, 127, 142-143; editing of statement on Katyn by, 131; editing of war reports by, 36-37, 42, 43, 45, 49, 50, 52; executions ordered by, 234-235; family members of POWs and, 110, 236; generals and, 54; German atrocities and, 118-119, 121, 127, 133, 149; Germans and, 169-170, 172, 173, 174, 178-179, 180-181, 182, 186, 193, 198-199; hatred and, 172, 181, 199, 271; hinterland and, 69, 72, 80-82, 84, 95, 97; Holovaty and, 105; Jews and, 118-119, 134, 141, 142-143, 147, 155, 162, 165-166, 218; Matrosov and, 65; military police and, 47-48; partisans and underground fighters and, 228, 233; Poland and, 155, 274-250; praise for, 40, 44, 49, 82-83, 129, 208, 213-214, 230, 248; public speeches by, 24; public speech of July 1941 by, 25, 38, 239, 255; reports on diplomatic relations and, 9; ritualized exchanges with, 89, 105, 107; Russians and, 202-203, 206, 220-221; second front and, 251, 253, 264; Soviet patriotism and, 8, 207, 221; Stalingrad and, 50; Ukraine and, 120-121, 212, 213, 214

Stalingrad, 49-51, 165
Starvation, 96-97, 116-117, 128
State anthems, 210
State bonds, 104-106
State Defense Committee, 102, 111
State farmers, 88, 89
Stevens, Edmund, 183
Streicher, Julius, 192
Subsidiary farms, 98-99
Sudoplatov, Pavel, 117-118
Suicide attacks, 64-66
Sunday work, 105
Surkov, Aleksei, 177-178
Surveillance reports, 67, 197, 198, 255-256, 275. *See also* Intelligence reports
Suslov, Mikhail, 209
Suvorov, Aleksandr, 174, 203

Talalikhin, Viktor, 62
Tambovskaia pravda (newspaper), 19
TASS. *See* Telegraph Agency of the Soviet Union (TASS)
TASS Windows, 14
Tehran conference, 90, 180, 214, 262
Telegraph Agency of the Soviet Union (TASS), 12-14; office bulletin of, 12-13; reports by, 19-20, 154, 245
Theft, 97-98; of abandoned property, 110; of food, 100-103; from gardens, 100-102
They Fought for the Motherland (Sholokhov), 219
Tikhonov, Nikolai, 63, 150
Tokhtarov, Tulegen, 209
Tolstoi, Aleksei, 38, 47, 140, 173, 176, 183, 205, 226, 251; on crimes in North Caucasus, 130, 150-151
Tolstoy, Leo, 132, 203
Trade Union Council, 87, 98, 99, 101
Trade unions, 100, 102-103
Traitors, 48, 63, 223, 226-228, 234-242, 278-279
Traveling Red Banners, 87, 88

Treblinka, 136, 139, 154, 157
Trud (newspaper), 17, 75; circulation of, 18; distribution of, 27
Tsibulko, Vasilii, 64
Tukhachevskii, Marshal Mikhail, 8
Tvardovskii, Aleksandr, 24, 204, 245
Tychyna, Pavlo, 212

Ukraine: anti-German hatred in, 197; forced famine in, 128; fund drives in, 105-106; German atrocities in, 120-121; mass killings in, 145; nationalism in, 211-216; Poland and, 211-212
Ukrainian Insurgent Army (UPA), 215-216
Ukrainians, 210, 211-216, 221
Undasynov, Nurtas, 216
Union of German Officers, 180
Union of Polish Patriots, 249-250
United Kingdom, 180, 244, 253-254; aid from, 255, 256-257; bombing missions of, 258-260; military agreement with, 251. *See also* Allies
United States, 180, 195, 244, 253-254; aid from, 255-256; bombing missions of, 257-258; Lend-Lease program and, 254-256; military agreement with, 251; Soviet relations with, 262. *See also* Allies
The Unsubdued (Gorbatov), 113, 204, 208-209, 224-228, 237, 238, 239, 240
U.S. War Bonds, 56
Uzbeks, 216-217, 218

Vares, Johannes, 145
Vasilevskii, Aleksander, 52
"Vasilii Terkin" (Tvardovskii), 204
Vatutin, Nikolai, 54
Vedomosti Verkhovnogo Soveta SSSR (newspaper), 17
Village elders, 239-240
Vinnytsia, 155, 180
Vishnevskii, Vsevolod, 67, 201

Vlasov, Andrei, 43-44, 46, 204
Volga Germans, 171
Vrba, Rudolf, 158

War bonds, 104; U.S., 56
War crimes, 117-133, 262
War invalids, 112-113, 115
War reporting, control of, 31-32, 35, 51-59, 61, 65-67
Warsaw: ghetto in, 154-155, 161; Polish uprising in, 250
Wasilewska, Wanda, 226, 248. See also *The Rainbow* (Wasilewska)
Werth, Alexander, 197-198, 200, 262
Wetzler, Alfred, 158
White, William, 268
Wilkie, Wendell, 252
Winterton, Paul, 254, 268
Wolna Polska (newspaper), 161, 248
Women: affairs with Germans by, 237-238; heroism of, 232; in Red Army, 40, 53; used as shields, 127; workers, 84-85
Worker-peasant correspondents, 4, 19
Workers: censorship and, 91-94; child, 69-71, 113; competition among, 85-94; desertions by, 74-85; factory, 70, 78-80, 83-84; female, 84-85; forced labor of, 68-95, 270-271; industrial, 86-87; mine, 80-81; shock, 85, 87; state farmers as, 88; transport, 82
World War I, 2, 275

Yalta conference, 189, 190
Young Guard, 233-234, 236
Youth brigades, 87

Zaslavskii, David, 223-224
Zhdanov, Andrei, 163, 264
Zhukov, General Georgii, 43, 48, 54, 62, 254, 265
Zhytomyr, 51, 135